Y0-DVO-311

3 2109 00532 8241

The Moving Image

Production Principles and Practices

"The Moving Image

Production Principles and Practices"

Gorham Anders Kindem

University of North Carolina at Chapel Hill

Scott, Foresman and Company

Glenview, Illinois
London, England

For Nancy

Acknowledgments

p. 39 ''Nielsen's National Television Index'' for the week ending January 19, 1986. Reprinted by permission of A. C. Nielsen Company.

p. 77 Edward Jay Epstein, *News from Nowhere*. Random House, 1973, pp. 4–5.

p. 197 ''Typical Running Times of Films'' from *Basic Production Techniques for Motion Pictures*. Copyright © 1971 Eastman Kodak Company. Reprinted with permission, Eastman Kodak Company.

p. 293 From ''Eleanor Rigby'' by John Lennon and Paul McCartney. Copyright © 1966 NORTHERN SONGS, LTD. All Rights for the United States, Canada and Mexico Controlled & Administered by BLACKWOOD MUSIC INC. under license from ATV MUSIC (MACLEN). All Rights Reserved. International Copyright Secured. Used by permission.

p. 401 From ''Big Rental Films of '85 (U.S.-Canada Market Only),'' *Variety*, January 8, 1986. Reprinted by permission.

Library of Congress Cataloging-in-Publication Data

Kindem, Gorham Anders.
    The moving image.

    Includes bibliographies and index.
    1. Moving-pictures—Production and direction.
2. Television—Production and direction.   I. Title.
PN1995.9.P7K54   1987   791.43′0232   86-15482
ISBN 0–673–15574–9

12345678910-RRC-9089888786

Preface

The Moving Image introduces students to the exciting and challenging world of media production. As a basic textbook, it offers a refreshing approach to production, one that emphasizes preplanning and conceptualization skills in addition to practical production techniques and equipment. It also presents students with a range of aesthetic options rather than prescribing a single approach for all types of production.

The Moving Image provides a consistent conceptual framework for approaching a diverse set of production problems and helps future professionals learn to make good decisions and choices. It prepares students for production work in many different fields using several different technologies—helping them learn to make key decisions, such as how to use video or film and how to combine film and video.

Focusing upon similarities and differences between video and film is an efficient and effective way to learn about production. Each chapter in this book begins with a discussion of aesthetic approaches and production practices common to video and film, followed by a discussion of those which are unique to one of these two media. Presenting concepts and information applicable to several media in a single textbook offers an alternative approach to more equipment-oriented production manuals. Students learn to consider a full range of options and in the process become better prepared to function successfully in a dynamic and rapidly changing field. One of the best ways to prepare for future changes in our media environment is to be broadly based in the production of moving images and sounds.

The organization of the book facilitates learning by following a logical progression from preproduction planning through actual production to postproduction. Knowledge is cumulative, but cross-references presented in each chapter help students see the interdependence of various production elements throughout the overall production process. The preproduction section considers producing, production management, and basic fiction and nonfiction scriptwriting concepts and formats. The second section of the book focuses upon directing, camera operation, visual recording, lighting, sound recording, scenic design, graphics, animation, and field production. The third section examines postproduction visual editing, sound editing, distribution, and exhibition. Thus, the organization of the book mirrors the successive stages of actual production.

Students and other readers are encouraged to explore and experience many different production approaches and techniques. Basic principles and practices are applicable to the production of nonfictional information, commercial entertainment, and expressive works of art. Numerous illustrations help students visualize and absorb a wide variety of concepts and techniques. Lists of additional readings at the end of each chapter encourage the exploration of many topics in greater detail than is possible in any introductory textbook, and exercises are designed to develop specific production skills through actual practice using limited production resources and equipment.

Production demands both theory and practice, aesthetics and practical techniques, creativity and organizational/technical skills. *The Moving Image* immerses students in many different aspects of production without allowing them to lose sight of the overall production process, the interdependence of various production areas, and the necessity of making consistent aesthetic choices and sound production decisions.

The people who were helpful to me during the writing of this book are too numerous to mention. Many colleagues in the Department of Radio, Television, and Motion Pictures at the University of North Carolina at Chapel Hill were helpful and encouraging, including Richard Simpson, Richard Settle, David Haynes, William Hardy, John Freeman, and Seth Finn, as well as Richard Elam, John Bittner, and Robert Allen. A Junior Faculty Development Grant from UNC provided me with some time to write during the early stages of manuscript preparation. A year spent teaching and writing overseas at the University of Trondheim in Norway helped me put many ideas into perspective at the same time that it added mailing costs. Many people and organizations provided helpful illustrations for the book. While most of them receive credit elsewhere, I want to thank George Grills and WBTV and Jefferson Productions in Charlotte, NC, for allowing me to photograph their facilities and operations, as well as the UNC Center for Public Television, WTVD in Durham, NC, and several students who helped set up photographs in and around my Department, including Ruth Barlow, Neil Beard, Walter Boyle, and Laurie Schulze.

The reviewers of various portions of the manuscript include Robert Avery and Bob Tiemens of the University of Utah, Ralph Bardgett of Southern Methodist University, David Champoux of Herkimer County Community College, Timothy Lyons of Southern Illinois University, Robert Miller of Northern Illinois University, Craig Ness of the University of Houston, George Rogers of California State University at Chico, Paul Traudt of the University of New Mexico, and Donna Walcovy of Boston University. An extremely able and energetic group of people at Scott, Foresman and Company worked very hard on this book, including Barbara Muller, Louise Howe, Ginny Guerrant, Heidi Fieschko, and Michael Anderson. Last, but certainly not least, I want to thank my wife, Nancy, whose patience, love, encouragement, criticism, and support made the completion of this book possible.

Hap Kindem

Overview

Table of Contents

The Moving Image

Production Principles and Practices

CHAPTER 1

The Production Process

Not long ago I traveled to West Africa, where I directed a film/video production about traditional African dancing. Our intent was to preserve an illusion of reality in our recordings of traditional dancing and village life. Each day's shooting would be discussed in advance with the village drummers and dancers who were to be involved in the actual production. Rather than try to shape and reshape traditional African dance in the villages and towns of Senegal and The Gambia into a formal or highly stylized artistic conception, we sought to record images of dancers that would give a realistic, "you are there" impression of time and space. This choice of what is known as a "realist" aesthetic approach to our subject was an important element in planning the production process.

PUTTING PRODUCTION PRINCIPLES INTO PRACTICE

The planning process began long before we set out for the airport. None of us had been to West Africa before, so we began by doing some investigative research in the library. We tried to learn as much as we could about traditional West African dancing and village life. Illustrations and photographs from books and magazines helped us visualize the people and settings we would find there. Interest in this part of the world had been stimulated by the success of the television miniseries called "Roots," which depicted traditional village life in The Gambia, so we found many helpful publications.

We also tried to anticipate what our production needs would be. Unable to scout actual locations in West Africa in advance, we talked to knowledgeable people who had been in Senegal and tried to find out what conditions would be like. The climate, we learned, would be hot and humid. We were uncertain how our video equipment would hold up in such a climate and we could not afford to take along an engineer to help maintain it. We would have limited access to production equipment, so we would have to bring everything we needed with us. Also, since the U.S. television system differs from the system used in many countries in West Africa, we would be unable to get replacement parts or have repair work done there. We therefore decided to record with film and later transfer from film to videotape.

Field productions are physically demanding and require careful advance planning. We tried to take along backup equipment, so that if a piece of equipment failed, we would have something else we could use. As it turned out, we used several of our pieces of backup equipment. If we had not brought them along, we would have had tremendous difficulty completing the project. One day, for example, our camera failed while we were recording dancers in a village some distance from the city in which we were staying. Fortunately, we had brought along replacement belts for the camera; thus we were able to repair it and continue recording.

Our preliminary choice of a realist aesthetic approach influenced many of our subsequent decisions about production techniques. Dances and movements were recorded so that they seemed to flow continuously without interruption. We let the camera run steadily for relatively long periods of time within a single shot. A wide-angle lens on a shoulder-mounted camera was used to get in close and follow continuous action, while keeping everything in proper focus from the foreground to the background. Sometimes specific dances were repeated so that the same or similar actions could be recorded by a single stationary camera from two or three different angles. During editing, these shots would be combined and intercut so that they all seemed to be recordings of the same dance at the same time. Actual sounds, such as drumming and crowd sounds, were recorded synchronously with the pictures, using microphones that enhanced the realist impression.

Our experiences in West Africa were very positive. We had never been there before, and we were not exactly sure what we would find, but we had made thorough advance preparations. Careful planning gave us the confidence to undertake and successfully complete a new project in unfamiliar territory. We took risks, made minor mistakes, and learned from our mistakes. Advance planning saved our production by helping us avoid unnecessary or disastrous problems. The overall aesthetic approach, a realist one, guided the choice of techniques and equipment and ensured consistency in the final product. Equipment lists and backups helped avoid and overcome problems in the field. Our production experiences were gratifying because we returned with most of the material that we needed to complete the project. We produced an exciting documentary about West African dance that was eventually shown on public television.

Planning for Positive Production Experiences

Everyone wants to have positive production experiences. While there probably is no secret formula for success, a thorough understanding of production principles and a positive attitude toward the overall production process is helpful. Exuding confidence in a project enlists the support of others. This requires knowing what is needed and how to get it. Making good creative choices demands careful advance planning of every logistical and conceptual aspect of production.

This chapter presents an overview of the entire production process and defines some effective approaches to production. Essentially the production process boils down to a series of important choices and decisions that must be made. Decision making requires conceptualization skills as well as familiarity with specific techniques and pieces of equipment. Different aesthetic approaches usually call for different production practices at each stage of the production process.

Many production techniques can be mastered through practice exercises, such as those recommended at the end of each chapter in this book, and through actual production experience. Truly benefiting from these experiences requires taking risks and learning from one's mistakes. Learning to work within present levels of ability, avoiding unnecessary or repeated errors through careful planning, and the development of strong conceptualization skills are also essential.

Avoiding Negative Production Experiences

One of the first laws of production that everyone eventually encounters is called Murphy's Law: ANYTHING THAT CAN GO WRONG, WILL GO WRONG. I have vivid memories of an early encounter with Murphy's Law. When I was employed by a film and video postproduction company in Chicago, a client with over fifteen years of experience as a professional camera operator came in to see me about a problem he had with a film he was making. He had contracted to film a national competition sponsored by a major fast-food chain.

Just before he began this project, he had purchased a new model camera. He believed that it was basically the same as the previous camera he had owned, since it was made by the same company. He had been too proud to let the salesperson explain to him how to load the camera properly with film. He gave the camera manual a cursory reading. Then he went about recording thousands of feet of film just as he had always done, confident that the results would be completely satisfactory. On his way back home he noticed that the film that he had loaded in an extra camera magazine looked as though it was improperly loaded. The emulsion or light-sensitive side, which should have faced towards the lens of the camera, faced the opposite direction. On closer inspection he determined that he had loaded this magazine no differently than any of the others. Had all of the film he had just recorded been exposed inside out? It certainly had!

He came in to see me hoping that I could somehow fix his film before he had to show it to his client. I pointed out to him that by exposing the film inside out he had made it completely out of focus, tremendously underexposed, and basically of two colors. In effect, the projected film looked as though it had been recorded through a dirty beer bottle—hardly what his client expected to see. Unfortunately, the events that he had been hired to record could not be restaged. It was a one-of-a-kind event. The film would have to wait until a similar event occurred the following year, when another camera operator would undoubtedly be asked to take the job.

The extent of the technical problems involved in his project almost obscure the conceptual and methodological mistakes he made, which were even more basic. The camera operator decided to use a realist approach. The film was made "on location" in an actual fast-food restaurant. He used a hand-held camera to follow participants around the restaurant. This gave the recorded images a rough appearance. Lighting sources were not carefully controlled. Camera movements were somewhat unpredictable and rough. The events looked more like an exposé from "60 Minutes" than a pleasing, fast-paced commercial or employee promotion for a fast-food chain. While the images he recorded were certainly more honest than a television commercial-production style might normally produce, a realist aesthetic approach was distinctly at odds with the client's goal—to present his product, work environment, and workers in an extremely positive light. The camera operator's approach would have been more appropriate for a hard-hitting documentary exposé of the problems inherent in fast-food preparation than a company-sponsored celebration of employee efficiency, speed, and cleanliness. The camera operator's planning had been both conceptually and technically inadequate. The inevitable result was a negative production experience.

The second law of production that every successful production person eventually puts into practice is an antidote to Murphy's Law: PROPER PLANNING PREVENTS POOR PRODUCTIONS. Many production problems are preventable. Ignoring conceptual and aesthetic considerations, failing to learn how to load a camera properly, forgetting to bring necessary equipment, and having no backup equipment are preventable mistakes. No one is beyond the point of needing to think carefully about what they are doing or to learn how to use new equipment. Everyone should use detailed equipment check-off lists, specifying every necessary piece of equipment, which are checked and rechecked prior to going into the field. Every production needs to have some backup equipment and contingency plan to turn to when things start to go differently than planned.

Some production problems are not preventable. No one can predict exactly when it is going to rain or when a camera will stop working. But everyone must have an alternative or contingency plan if such a problem occurs. Equipment should be properly maintained, but not everyone can or should try to repair equipment in the field. Certainly, the option to record another day, if major problems should occur, must be available. Good quality productions are rarely made in a panic atmosphere, and careful planning is the best antidote to panic, Murphy's Law, and negative production experiences.

Quality productions are shaped and re-shaped many times on paper before they are recorded and edited. Preproduction planning is extremely important. It is always cheaper and easier to modify a project before actual recording takes place than to do so after production is under way. The organization of this text reflects the importance of preproduction planning and the development of conceptualization skills.

The first section is devoted entirely to preproduction planning. Some degree of advance planning and conceptualization is implicit in later stages of production and postproduction as well. Thus the beginning of each chapter in these two sections focuses on conceptualization skills and making sound aesthetic choices and production decisions.

STAGES OF PRODUCTION

The production process can be organized into three stages: preproduction, production, and postproduction. Everything from a project's inception to setting up for actual recording is referred to as **preproduction**. This includes the writing of a proposal, treatment, and script and the breakdown of the script in terms of production scheduling and budgeting. The second major phase of production is the **production** stage. Everything involved in the set up and recording of visual images and sounds, from performer, camera and microphone placement and movement, to lighting and set design, is part of the production stage. **Postproduction** consists of the editing of the recorded images and sounds and all of the procedures needed to complete a project.

Preproduction

Preproduction consists of the preparation of project proposals, premises, synopses, treatments, scripts, script breakdowns, production schedules, budgets, and storyboards. A proposal is a market summary, which is used to promote or sell a project. A premise is a concise statement that sums up the story or subject matter. For example, the basic premise of Joan Didion's film, *The Panic in Needle Park* (1971) is the following: "it's Romeo and Juliet on drugs in New York's Central Park." A synopsis is a short paragraph that describes the basic story line. Treatments are longer plot or subject-matter summaries in short-story form, while scripts are virtually complete production guides on paper. Scripts can be ''broken down'' by listing all equipment and personnel needs for each scene, so that a production can be scheduled and budgeted. A storyboard provides a graphic visualization of important shots, which will eventually be recorded by a camera.

Production

Production begins with setup and rehearsal. The director stages and plots the action by rehearsing scenes in preparation for actual recording. Charting the movement of talent on the set is known as **performer blocking,** while charting the movements of the cameras is called **camera blocking.** Every camera placement and movement of the talent must be carefully worked out prior to recording. If the action cannot be controlled, as in the live transmission of a sporting event, the director must be able to anticipate exactly where the action is likely to go and place the cameras accordingly.

During actual production the entire project is essentially in the hands of the director. In multiple-camera studio production the television director selects the shots by commanding the technical director (or TD) to press certain buttons on a device called a switcher, which makes instantaneous changes from one camera to another. In single-camera production the director remains on the set and communicates directly with the talent and crew. The **script supervisor** or **continuity person** watches the actual recording session with a sharp eye to ensure that every segment in the script has been recorded. Perfect continuity between shots, in such details as a consistent direction and flow of performer movements from one shot to the next, must be maintained so that these shots can be combined during editing with no breaks in continuity.*

Postproduction

Postproduction begins after the visual images have been recorded. The edit points can be determined during the preview stage, when the recorded images and sounds are initially viewed. Pictures and accompanying sounds are examined and reexamined to find exact edit points before various shots are combined. Separate sound tracks can be added later to the edited images, or the sounds can be edited at the same time as the picture.

The postproduction stage ties together the audio and visual elements of production and smooths out all the rough edges. The visual and audio elements must be properly balanced and controlled. Sophisticated optical, mechanical, and electronic devices help editors and technical specialists mold sounds and images into their final form.

The three stages of production are separate only in a chronological sense. Proficiency in one stage of the production process necessarily requires some knowledge of all other stages. A director or writer cannot visualize the possibilities for recording a particular scene without having some awareness of how images can be combined during production or postproduction editing. In short, while the overall organization of this text into three stages (preproduction, production, and postproduction) follows a logical progression, mastery of any one stage demands some familiarity with other stages as well.

----

*Continuity is discussed more fully in chapter 6.

VISUALIZATION: IMAGES, SOUNDS, AND THE CREATIVE PROCESS

Visualization can be defined as the creative process of translating abstract thoughts, ideas, and feelings into concrete sounds and images. This demands strong conceptualization skills and a thorough understanding of video and film production methods and techniques. Video and film scriptwriters and directors must have something significant to say and the means to say it. Quality production work requires an ability to organize one's creative thoughts and select and control many technical devices that record, edit, and transmit visual images and sounds.

Scriptwriters and directors must acquire a basic understanding of the overall production process before they can fully develop their visualization skills. A knowledge of production principles and practices stimulates the search for innovative ways to translate abstract ideas into concrete sounds and images. It also sets limits on a writer's creative imagination. A scriptwriter must be practical and realistic about production costs and logistics. An imaginative script may be too difficult or expensive to produce. A scriptwriter must also have some knowledge of camera placement and editing, even though his or her work is basically completed during the preproduction stage.

To visualize means to utilize the full potential of video and film for creative expression. Video and film productions often draw on other art forms, such as literature, painting, theater, and music, with which scriptwriters and directors have some familiarity. But video and film are also distinct from these other arts and media. Motion is an important aspect of video

and film. Moving images make video and film distinct from photography and painting. Unlike words used in novels and poetry, actual images are often concrete and specific rather than abstract and general. The spoken word is more central to theater and drama than to video and film, which are far less limited in terms of action, movements, and changes of time and place. Video and film possess the motion and emotion of music, which can be incorporated into any production, but recorded images and sounds often add concrete references to the world of common everyday experience, which is largely absent from more abstract and mathematical musical designs. Video and film constitute a blending of several art forms into a unique medium of artistic expression. Visualization demands some understanding of these unique and shared properties.

Film and television communicators must be constantly open to new ideas, technologies, and techniques, because these media are constantly changing. But they cannot ignore traditional communicative practices and ways of structuring messages. Other media and older forms of communication provide a wealth of information about the communication process. In a sense, the attempt to use visual images and/or sounds to communicate with others is as old as the human species itself.

Early human beings, for example, drew pictures of animals on the walls of caves. Cave drawings may have been created out of a desire to record a successful hunt for posterity, to magically influence the outcome of future hunts by controlling symbolic images, or to express the feelings and thoughts of an artist toward an animal or hunt. These three purposes of communication can be summarized as conveying information, rhetorical presuasion, and artistic expression. To some extent, these

A cave painting of a bison and wild boar from the Cave of Altamira in Altamira, Spain. This painting dates from eleven to seventeen thousand years old.

explanations are also applicable to contemporary uses of television and film.

Conveying Information

Communicating with pictures and sounds may have a single purpose: to convey information. What is communicated, the specific content or meaning of the message, consists of informative signs and symbols, images and sounds, which are transmitted from one person to another. We tend to think of certain types of films and television programs, such as documentaries, educational films and videotapes, and news programs as primarily intended to convey information. Few media messages are exclusively informational, however. Other types of communication are needed to arouse and maintain audience interest and enliven an otherwise dull recitation of facts and information.

Rhetorical Persuasion

Rhetoric is the art of waging a successful argument. Persuasive devices and strategies are designed to shape opinions, change attitudes, or modify behavior. The term rhetoric has been applied to the use of stylistic as well as persuasive devices and techniques in artistic works, such as novels (see Wayne Booth's *The Rhetoric of Fiction*, for example). An artist can select a rhetorical device, such as the point of view of a specific character, to tell or stage a story, so that the reader or audience becomes more emotionally involved. Rhetorical devices often stimulate emotions. They can make a logical argument more persuasive and a work of fiction more engaging and emotionally effective. In television and film we tend to think of editorials, commercials, political documentaries and propaganda as rhetorical forms of communication. Many fictional dramas can also be thought of as rhetorical in structure and intent.

Artistic Expression

Artistic works often communicate an artist's feelings and thoughts toward a person, object, event, or idea. Sometimes artistic expressions are extremely personal, and it is difficult for general audiences to understand them. At other times the artist's thoughts and feelings are widely shared within or even between cultures. An artistically expressive film or television program can convey a culture's ethos and ideology, its shared values and common experiences in unequaled and innovative ways. Works of art communicate an artist's unique insight into his or her own self, culture, and/or medium of expression. Artists often experiment with new expressive techniques and devices, presenting ordinary experiences in new and provocative ways. They can challenge a viewer's prior preconceptions and stimulate a serious and profound reexamination of personal or cultural goals and values. They can also reinforce traditional conceptions and cultural values.

:::::::::::::::::::::
PRODUCTION AESTHETICS
:::::::::::::::::::::

Production is an artistic process: it demands creative thinking and the ability to make sound aesthetic decisions. How should you approach a specific topic? What techniques should you use? Important aesthetic choices have to be made. To make these choices you must be aware of many different possibilities and approaches. Every production choice implic-itly or explicitly involves aesthetics. Some production techniques go unnoticed and enhance an illusion of reality, for example, while others are formative devices that call attention to themselves and the production process.

The aesthetic alternatives from which you must choose at each stage of the production process can be divided into three basic categories: functionalist, realist, and formativist aesthetics.

Functionalist

Functionalist aesthetics stresses a practical goal or function, which is the practical use to which a project will be put. Aesthetically this suggests that form follows function. The set for a news or talk show is often designed to facilitate recording, for example. This is not to say that strong design elements do not enter into the equation, but they are always subservient to the pragmatic purpose or goal of the project.

Realist

A **realist** approach to production involves the use of a set of conventional techniques that help to create or sustain an illusion of reality.* Realist techniques rarely call attention to themselves. Space and time seem continuous and uninterrupted, just like our everyday experience of the world. A news set that gives the appearance of being a newsroom in actual operation with constant activity going on in the background is realist, not just functionalist in

---

*Realist aesthetics can also apply to works of art that reveal underlying social forces, not just a perceptual illusion of reality. See Terry Lovell's *Pictures of Reality*, London: BFI, 1980.

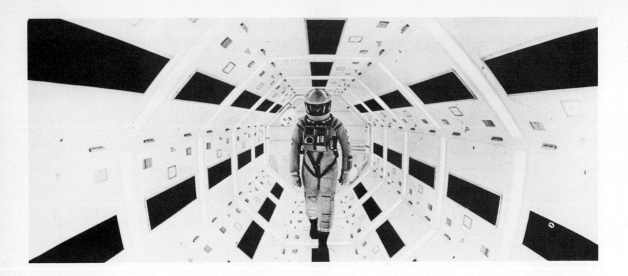

A still from *2001: A Space Odyssey.* A combination of formativist and realist techniques helps to create exciting and interesting films.

design. A standard Hollywood film sustains an illusion of reality which sometimes makes us forget that we are watching a movie, but this illusion is based on realist choices and conventions in terms of camera placements and editing.

Formativist

A **formativist** approach to production, such as that exemplified by many avant garde works of video and film, often calls attention to forms and techniques themselves. A formativist artist is free to explore the possibilities and limitations of the video or film medium itself. Form often exists independently of function.

Obviously these aesthetic choices are not absolute or exhaustive. Many projects combine these aesthetic approaches in various ways. Think of the formativist sequences that you have seen in many realist movies, such as the light show in Stanley Kubrick's *2001: A Space Odyssey* (1968). Consider the abundance of techniques that call attention to themselves as artistic devices in Brian De Palma's films, such as *Scarface II* (1983), *Carrie* (1976), and

Obsession (1976). These are not purely realist films. Formativist devices and techniques are often incorporated into basically functionalist works as well to give them emotion, power, and a strongly aesthetic emphasis. By the same token, few basically formativist works are completely without function or purpose or touches of realism. The choice between these aesthetic approaches is not absolute or irreconcilable. Different approaches can be combined, but this still should be a matter of conscious choice on your part.

Because aesthetic decisions are basic at every stage of the production process, most of the chapters in this text begin with a discussion of functional, realist, and formativist production techniques. This is followed by a discussion of production practices that are common to both video and film production. The chapter concludes with a consideration of practices and equipment that are unique to one or the other of these media. This organization is designed to emphasize aesthetic principles and production practices which are common to video and film rather than the unique attributes and operation of specific pieces of production hardware. Combined with actual hands-on production experience, this text will provide you with the basic information you need to make production decisions with the confidence that you have explored and considered many possible alternatives and have selected the best approach from among them.

PRODUCTION TERMINOLOGY

Acquiring a basic video and film terminology is crucial to understanding the entire production process. The use of production technology and techniques requires a rather specialized vocabulary. As **key words** are introduced throughout this text, they are defined and highlighted in **bold type**. When chapters are read out of sequence, the reader can refer to the glossary and index at the end of the book to find a specific definition or the initial mention of a term.

We almost intuitively understand the meaning of such words, as **television, video,** and **film**, but it is important to be as precise as possible when using these and other terms in a production context. Television refers to the electronic transmission and reception of visual images of moving and stationary objects, usually with accompanying sound. The term television has traditionally referred to images and sounds which are **broadcast** through the air waves. Electronic television signals can be broadcast by impressing them on a **carrier wave** of **electromagnetic energy**, which radiates in all directions from a television tower and is picked up by home receivers. Electrical energy travels in waves, much like ocean waves that crash on the surf at the beach. A carrier wave is usually rated in thousands of watts

of power channeled through a television transmitter. Electromagnetic energy ranges from long radio waves to very short light waves. These waves can travel through the atmosphere and be picked up by home receivers. (See Color Plate II.)

Television signals can also be sent through **closed-circuit television** systems, that is, along electrical wires rather than through the air waves. Prior to the 1930s, television was primarily closed circuit, but the commercial exploitation of this technology as a mass medium and means of distributing television to large numbers of private homes, known as **cable** television, did not occur until much later. Since the 1960s it has been possible to transmit television signals via **satellites** across continents and around the world. Satellites are communications relay sta-

A television tower from which electronic television signals are broadcast.

Satellite dishes pickup television signals that have been transmitted from satellites orbiting the earth.

tions that orbit the globe. Line-of-sight **microwave**, i.e., high-frequency, transmissions of television signals are frequently used for **live**, nondelayed, "real-time," news reports in the field and for sending signals to outlying areas where broadcast signals are not well received.

The terms television and video are sometimes used interchangeably, but it is generally agreed that television is a means of distributing and exhibiting video signals. Video, on the other hand, is a production term. Sometimes the term **video** is used very narrowly to refer to the visual portion of the television signal, as distinguished from the audio or sound. The more general definition of video, as a production term that refers to all forms of electronic production of moving images and sounds, is rapidly gaining acceptability. This is the preferred use in this text. Today, the term "video" also refers to a 3-to-5-minute popular song with accompanying visuals on videotape; this is actually a shortened from of such terms as "music videos" and "rock videos." **Videotape** refers to magnetic tape, which is used to record both the video and the audio portions of the television signal. Videotape allows television signals to be transmitted on a time-delayed basis, rather than live, and when used with various electronic **editing** devices, it allows recorded images and sounds to be changed and rearranged after they have been recorded.

Film has a variety of meanings in production. Defined very narrowly it simply refers to the light-sensitive material that runs through a motion picture camera and records visual images. When film is properly exposed to light, developed chemically, and run through a motion picture projector, moving objects recorded on the film appear to move across a movie screen. In a more general sense, the term film can be used interchangeably with such words as motion picture(s), movie(s), and cinema. The first two words in the singular refer to specific products or works of art that have been recorded on film, while in the plural, they can also refer to the whole process of recording, distributing, and viewing visual images produced by photochemical and mechanical, i.e., nonelectronic, means.

Making clear-cut distinctions between video and film is becoming increasingly difficult. For example, when a feature film, a television series, music video, or a commercial advertisement is initially recorded on film but distributed on videotape via television, is this video or film? Using a single video camera to record a program in segments, rather than using multiple video cameras to transmit it live or record it **live on tape** is often called **film-style** video production. The techniques used in single-camera video production are often closer to traditional film practice than to that of multiple-camera video. Thus, while it is important to be as precise as possible in the use of video and film terms, it is equally important to realize that the meanings of these terms can change over time, reflecting changes in the technology on which these media are based and the ways in which that technology is used.

A SHORT HISTORY OF FILM AND TELEVISION

Film and television have interesting and overlapping histories. Films, or moving pictures as they were first known, were projected on movie screens to audiences as early as 1895. Film developed out of a number of different technological innovations and experiments. Metal and glass plates were being used to record still photographs early in the nineteenth century. Advances in still photography later in the 1800s resulted in the development of a pre-perforated, flexible support base on which light-sensitive materials, such as silver halide, could be suspended and driven through a camera. Motion picture cameras and projectors, capable of exposing and projecting a rapid series of still-frame images, were developed in the 1890s. Above a certain speed, the flickering of still photographs disappeared and objects appeared to move quite naturally on the movie screen. With the introduction of sound in the 1920s, motion picture recording and projection speed was standardized at twenty-four frames per second. Prior to that time, the speed varied between sixteen and twenty-four frames per second.

The perceptual mechanism or illusion on which motion pictures depend was labeled an instance of the **phi phenomenon** by perceptual psychologists well after the introduction of film. Gestalt psychologists were fascinated by perceptual tricks and illusions, because they provided a convenient means of studying the way our brains process sensory information. One such illusion, the phi phenomenon, produces apparent motion out of stationary lights or objects. (See Figure 1.1.) It occurs when two lights, separated by a short distance, are flashed or strobed very rapidly. Above a certain threshold of flashes per second the human eye is deluded into thinking that one light is moving, rather than two stationary lights flashing. This same phenomenon helps to explain the perception of apparent motion from rapidly flashed still photographs. The mind's eye fills in the gaps between frames and produces apparent, not real, motion. During the 1800s, many toys that exploited

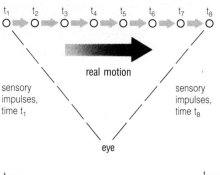
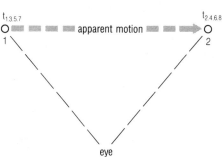

Figure 1.1
The Phi Phenomenon

The Phi Phenomenon illustrates how our eyes and brain create apparent motion from stationary images. The upper figure shows the apparent movement of a light from point a to point b. The lower figure shows that the stimulus consists of two rapidly blinking but stationary lights. Our eyes and brain fill in the gaps in between to create the illusion of movement. This is the basic principle upon which the illusion of movement in film and video is based.

this phenomenon were successfully introduced and marketed. These toys used hand-drawn frames as well as photographed images, and were the forerunners of animated films, such as Disney cartoons.

The first motion pictures combined developments in still photography with those of animated toys based on perceptual illusions. The earliest film projectors appeared in penny arcades, somewhat like today's video game parlors. Thomas A. Edison's Kinestoscope was a coin-operated movie box for individual viewers. As more ingenious devices were developed, allowing film images to be projected on large screens in auditoriums and vaudeville theaters, the potential audience for films grew dramatically. The fact that films could be shown simultaneously to large audiences in theaters throughout the world allowed film to become a major source of mass entertainment and news. Theatrical film became primarily an enter-

An early Kinestoscope parlor in San Francisco, California, in 1894.

Le zootrope.

tainment medium, but other uses of this technology, such as news, documentary, advertising, instructional training, and, of course, home movies, appeared very early and have continued to this day.

A number of changes have taken place in film technology, but the basic mechanisms and principles of film have remained remarkably unchanged since 1900. The introduction of sound transformed the motion picture industry in the late 1920s. Color film developed more gradually than sound. While Kodachrome film was used by amateurs and Technicolor by professionals in the 1930s, the real proliferation of color film did not occur until Eastmancolor film stock was introduced in the early 1950s, and television converted to color broadcasting in the mid-to-late 1960s. Of course, experiments with film sound and color date back to the turn of the century. Film gauges (width formats) have changed very little over the last forty years. While 35mm film continues to be the professional standard for feature films and television commercials, 16mm film, which was an amateur film gauge in

the 1930s, has become a professional medium. Its use was widely expanded during World War II by the military. The amateur film medium today is Super-8mm, although in the home market this format is gradually being replaced by one-half inch videotape recording formats, such as Beta, VHS, and 8mm videotape.

Like film, television began as a black-and-white visual medium, but unlike film, television has had sound accompaniment almost since its inception. Experiments into the transmission of visual images by other than photochemical means were being undertaken around the turn of the century, but the practical realization of a television system required the development during the 1920s of sophisticated electronic tubes, such as the cathode-ray tube. During the 1920s early television signals were transmitted through wires in self-contained, closed-circuit systems. (See Figure 1.2 for a drawing of this early all-electronic television system.) Not until 1939, when the National Broadcasting Company (NBC) began its first regularly scheduled programming for the New York

World's Fair and a home receiver along modern lines was developed and marketed, did television become a true broadcast medium.

Television technology is based on light coming through a camera lens and striking a light-sensitive surface on a camera pickup tube. This surface is bombarded on the opposite side with a steady stream of electrons, which scan the surface of the tube in a regular pattern. As electrons strike the surface of the tube, an electrical current passing through that surface changes its voltage in direct relation to the intensity of the light striking the same point on the opposite side. These fluctuations in electrical current are then fed to a television picture tube, which reverses the process. Bright light striking specific points on the camera pickup tube correspond to bright light emitted by the phosphors of the television receiver's picture tube.

A television screen is scanned completely thirty times every second, thus the images move at a speed of thirty frames per second, rather than the twenty-four frames per second of sound film. Television, like film, depends on the ''phi phenomenon'' to produce apparent motion,

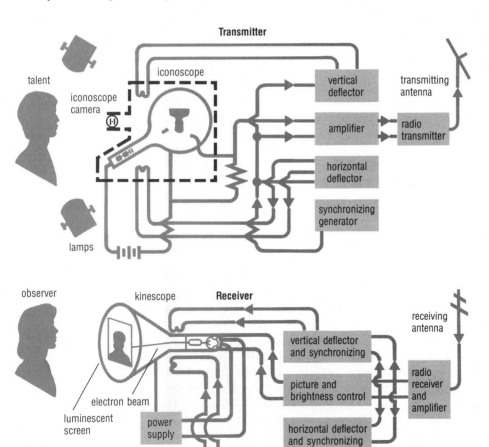

**Figure 1.2
An Early All-
Electronic Television
System**

but it also relies on **persistence of vision** to fuse the continuous scanning of the picture tube into complete frames of picture. Persistence of vision refers to the temporary lag in the eye's retention of an image, which can fuse one image with those that immediately precede or follow. This phenomenon does not explain apparent motion, because the fusion of images in the same position within the frame would result in a confused blur, rather than the coherent motion of objects.

World War II interrupted the commercial development of television, but after the war the medium expanded rapidly. The sales of home television receivers skyrocketed in the late 1940s and early 1950s. During these early years of broadcasting, much more television programming was broadcast live than is the case today. Prerecorded films and film recordings of live programs, known as **kinescopes**, provided the only means of delaying or repeating a broadcast until the advent of videotape. Due to time differences and the absence of a transcontinental cable connection, network programs were sometimes kinescoped, and flown from the east coast to the west coast, where they would be broadcast in the same time slot one week later.

Film was also used quite early as a recording medium for many television series, but in 1956 Ampex Corporation marketed the first **videotape recorder** or **VTR**, which allowed television programs to be recorded on magnetic tape for delayed or repeat broadcast. Videotape recording did not begin to offer the many editing advantages of film until the 1960s, however. While it was always possible to splice videotape mechanically, this crude technique presented a number of technical problems during playback and therefore had to be used very sparingly. During the 1960s electronic editing systems were developed so that videotapes could be shot out of sequence with a single camera or with several cameras and quickly and efficiently edited together in the desired sequence. Editing is also used to remove mistakes and to create greater viewer interest and excitement.

In the late 1960s and 1970s a number of important changes began to take place in the television industry. Color television became the standard broadcast mode. Television production equipment became much smaller and less expensive with the aid of new electronic devices, such as transistors and electronic chips. The greater availability and high quality of smaller format production equipment allowed television to challenge film in areas that had been previously dominated by photographic technology. **ENG** or **electronic news gathering** equipment virtually replaced news film in broadcast journalism, because it offered a tremendous savings in time over film, which had to be chemically processed and physically spliced during editing. Many corporations, government agencies, and educational institutions no longer found television equipment too awkward or expensive to use for their own internal recording purposes.

During this period satellites became widely used to transmit images around the world. Satellite transmission also stimulated the development of cable television. Specialized program channels, such as Home Box Office, ESPN, and Cable News Network, could be transmitted via satellite across the country, where they were picked up by the satellite receiving stations of local cable operators and delivered via cable to private homes. Currently a new type of television transmission is under development, known as **high definition television (HDTV)**. This new technology offers television images that rival 35mm film in terms of image sharpness and resolution. HDTV has almost twice the number of scanning lines per frame of traditional broadcast television.

A number of technical problems must be overcome before HDTV can be used to transmit signals, however. For the time being it simply provides a high quality initial recording system, but it offers great potential for television distribution and exhibition, as well as production.

:::::::::::::::::::::::::

PRODUCTION CATEGORIES AND LEVELS

:::::::::::::::::::::::::

Productions are frequently categorized as fiction or nonfiction, commercial or noncommercial. Fictional works are generally "made up" by writers. Most feature films and television series are works of fiction. Nonfiction works usually present recordings of actual, unstaged events. News programs and documentaries are examples of nonfiction. In some productions, such as docudramas and dramatized documentaries, fiction and nonfiction overlap. Commercial productions are usually designed to make a profit, while noncommercial productions are designed primarily to serve social and artistic functions rather than make a profit.

Within each of these categories there are different production levels and values, relative to cost, sophistication, and potential audience size. For example, feature films, **network** television programs, e.g., those produced by or for ABC, CBS, NBC (commercial networks), and PBS (Public Broadcasting Service, a noncommercial network), generally have high budgets and production values. Works produced by small production studios, avant-garde artists, and nonprofessionals on the other hand, tend to be made on a small budget and have lower production values.

The highest budget level of commercial video and film production includes feature films, network television programs, and network-level commercials. In terms of production budgets, the next levels are cable and local programming and commercials, small studio produced films, videotapes, and videodiscs of a commercial nature, such as sales programming. But it is important to separate production costs and values from artistic merit and overall cultural contribution, since a low-budget film may in fact be artistically superior in virtually every respect to an extremely high-budget Hollywood feature film.

An average Hollywood feature film handled by a major distributor, such as UA/MGM, Paramount, 20th Century-Fox, Universal, and Columbia, costs over $10 million to produce. Production at this level demands an extremely high level of artistic and technical skill. Work is highly specialized and intensely competitive. Independently produced and distributed feature films are often made for less than $1 million, but they rarely attain one-tenth the audience or financial return of a major Hollywood film.

While an average network made-for-TV movie costs far less than an average theatrically released feature film, the most expensive television miniseries, such as "Shogun" or "Roots," costs as much as the most expensive theatrical films. Almost all network television programming, with possible exception of daytime soap operas, requires high production budgets. Networks buy much of their entertainment programming from independent Hollywood production companies, but they produce virtually all of their own news, sports programming, and soap operas. The audience for network television programs, such as the Super Bowl football game, can exceed 100 million people. The networks sell advertising time to major advertising agencies, such as J. Walter Thompson, Leo Burnett, and MacCann-Erickson, who contract with independent production companies for the production of network-level commercials, which are usually made on 35mm film. Television time is sold on a cost-per-minute or cost-per-thousand (viewers) basis, and can be as high as one-half million dollars for one minute of national air time.

Some cable television channels have made a dent in network television's share of the total TV audience. While many of the most lucrative cable television channels, such as HBO, simply sell feature films to cable subscribers, others, such as Cable News Network and ESPN, produce their own specialized programming. The production values of cable programming are not always equivalent to those of network television, but the budgets for cable programs obviously rise as their audience grows. Cable offers the potential to reach many minority audience needs, such as those of the elderly, which are often neglected by the major networks. Commercial networks compete primarily for consumers between the ages of eighteen and thirty-four. Most commercials are aimed at this audience. Pay cable sells programming, not commercials, to audiences. However, some cable channel **superstations**, such as WTBS in Atlanta, are glorified local stations, which attempt to attract and sell a national audience to advertisers by using satellites to send signals to a national cable audience.

Local commercial television stations are either affiliated with major networks or they are independent. Affiliates are paid a fee by the networks to broadcast network programming, but they also produce their own news, public affairs, and some sports

Cable television channels have grown rapidly enough over the past few years to warrent a convention such as this one, held in Dallas, Texas.

programming. The local news is one of the most competitive areas of local broadcasting, since it attracts large numbers of viewers to locally produced programming. Stations can then sell advertising time on the basis of the size of the audience they attract. But local stations are also involved in selling syndicated programming to viewers. Syndicated programs are either produced independently of the networks, such as old movies and some game shows, or they are repeats of old network series, which are broadcast daily, rather than weekly, in the same time slot. Local stations often produce commercials for their own markets, as well as public affairs and children's programming. Almost all local television production work is done with video rather than film. Independent local television stations use more syndicated programming than affiliates.

The term **independent** can have a variety of meanings in production. It is usually applied to any production company that is not affiliated with a major corporation, but it is also used to designate a small studio or an individual producer. Many small film and video production companies produce commercials, documentaries, educational, and industrial films and videotapes to the specifications of clients or sponsors or purely on the speculation that they can be sold. Sometimes these programs are shown on television to general audiences in nonprime-time slots, and they provide a form of indirect advertising for the sponsor. Drawing a sharp line between the small studio and the independent, free-lance production specialist is often difficult. Film and television industries are small enough in even the largest metropolitan areas that highly skilled artists, craftsmen, and technicians are well known, highly paid, and in frequent demand for a variety of projects without the need of a permanent staff position. Small studios and free-lance specialists produce a substantial number of commercial films and television programs.

At the lowest level of commercial production in terms of budgets is often found the local cable operator in a small town. Local cable programming attempts to meet the more parochial interests of a community, such as coverage of high-school sporting events, parades, and even local news and public affairs. These production situations often provide a convenient training ground for production students and offer excellent prospects for initial employment.

Noncommercial television and film production is less hierarchical than the commercial world, because there is considerable diversity of values and budgets within different categories, such as public television and corporate, government, educational, and religious production. Clearly network public television or PBS has much higher production values than community-access cable television channels and home movies and videotapes.

Network public television programming may achieve higher artistic levels than much commercial network programming, but PBS shows that cost more than prime-time commercial network programs of equivalent length are quite rare, unless the cost was shared in production by a foreign broadcaster. Public television stations are frequently supported by state and local governments, private foundations, individual contributions, and federal government grants. They produce programming for local, regional, and even national distribution through PBS, the Public Broadcasting Service. PBS program production is often partially financed by the

Corporation for Public Broadcasting, a federally funded institution, as well as by private foundations, individuals, and corporations. PBS programming is often aimed at a higher intellectual and artistic level than commercial television. Programming produced by and for a local PBS station can range from the most parochial topic, such as quiltmaking or a new water project, to a local controversy that attains national attention. In general, public television attempts to offer an alternative to commercial television.

Corporate television and within-house media production is an expanding area and offers media professionals a wide range of employment opportunities. Both small and large companies produce their own corporate training and public relations videotapes and films. These are frequently used by corporate executives to communicate with groups of employees about new company programs and benefits. Programming is also produced which management believes will stimulate productivity or reduce accidental injury and damage to products and equipment. Some large corporations have production studios which are as well equipped with state-of-the-art technology as an average broadcasting station. Others function quite well with limited staff and equipment by farming out major projects to independent studios and free-lance artists and technicians.

Government media production is still a cottage industry, which generally lacks central control at the federal or state level. Each different government agency tries to control the creation of its own messages, whether the communication consists of public information, in-house training, or simply a record or statement of administrative policy. Government messages often must be created within a highly charged political atmosphere. They must be carefully constructed and controlled by administrators who sometimes limit creativity and freedom of expression for their own protection. With-in house units offer almost unlimited employment possibilities for people who are well trained in media production, however.

Religious, educational, and health-related institutions also offer excellent opportunities for television and film production. Several religious denominations operate their own satellite networks. Religious programmers embrace television as a means of reaching millions of people with a religious message and raising funds.

Video and film production also plays a major role in colleges, universities, and medical schools and hospitals. Some educational and health-related production units have more sophisticated production equipment than local public television stations in their area. They often create instructional programs for classroom use as well as channeling information from one location to another within an institution or building. Many hospitals use television and film to educate patients, train their staff, and develop better public awareness of medical problems and preventive techniques. A growing area in educational production is the creation of interactive videos, which integrate videotapes and computers and allow viewers to respond to questions or control the presentation of images and sounds.

One of the most specialized, challenging, and provocative uses of television and film equipment is the production of personal artistic works for limited audiences. Television and film are not simply industries and communications media. They are also art forms. Video artists, such as Nam

June Paik, and film artists, such as Michael Snow, Stan Brakage, and Jordan Belson, have aroused significant interest within the art world. Their work is often supported by public and private grants and exhibited in art museums. New techniques and conceptual approaches developed by avant-garde artists may later be incorporated into the mainstream of mass communications and industrial practice.

At the lowest end of the noncommercial scale in terms of production costs and values is personal, home film and videotape production. Still photography and 8mm movies have long been dominant forms of domestic production, but the purchase and use of portable, small-format VHS, Beta, and 8mm videotape recorders is rapidly expanding. Many individual consumers use inexpensive production equipment to record weddings, family gatherings, sporting events, vacations, and simply as documentation for a family album on childhood development.

SINGLE-CAMERA AND MULTIPLE-CAMERA PRODUCTION

A film or television producer or director must make two basic decisions before production begins. First, he or she must decide whether just one or more than one camera should be used to record or transmit images. Using one camera is called **single-camera production**, while using more than one camera is referred to as **multiple-camera production**. Second, a decision must be made about whether the images should be recorded inside or outside the studio. Shooting inside the studio is known as **studio production**, while production outside the studio is called **lo-cation production** in film and **remote production** (involving cable/microwave links to the studio) or **field production** in video.

Multiple-camera production techniques are used to record continuous action quickly and efficiently without interruption. Such techniques are the basis for television news programs, entertainment programs involving a studio audience, as well as much corporate, educational, and religious programming. Remote coverage of sporting events almost always requires multiple cameras. Multiple film cameras are frequently used to record dangerous stunts simultaneouly from a variety of angles, as well as to obtain footage for highlight films of events that cannot be repeated, such as football games and automobile races. Multiple film cameras are sometimes used in the production of dramatic feature films, so that the performance can run continuously without interruption, as in stage drama, rather than being broken up to repeat segments of the same actions for filming from different camera positions.

In single-camera production each separate shot is set up and recorded individually. The main artistic advantage of single-camera production is that few compromises have to be made in lighting or microphone placement in order to accommodate the viewing requirements of several different cameras. Logistically, only one camera needs to be set up or carried into the field at a time.

Single-camera production usually begins with the recording of a **master shot**, which covers as much of the action in a scene as possible from a single camera position. Then the same actions are repeated and recorded again with the camera placed closer to the action. The resulting material is combined during postproduciton editing. Single-camera production techniques are used to record feature films, documentaries, and television commercials, as well as in new recording.

Except for live coverage of sports events, single-camera production is the norm for location and remote production situations. In some production situations it is simply impossible to record events inside a studio even though studio production facilities and techniques are usually more efficient and economical. Lighting and sound recording are more easily controlled in a studio than at a remote location. Most production studios are designed to provide ideal recording conditions by insulating the recording space from outside sounds, reducing the echo of interior sounds, and allowing easy overhead or floor positioning of lights and access to power supplies.

Location production can give a film or television production a greater sense of realism or illusion of reality. Exterior locations often create a sense of authenticity and actuality. But location settings rarely provide ideal lighting and acoustical environments. Extraneous sounds can easily disrupt a production. Confined settings often create sound echo and make it difficult to position lights and control the shadows they create. Inclement weather conditions outdoors can delay the completion of a project. Since location production sometimes increases production risks and costs, a producer must have strong justification for recording outside the studio. Of course, the construction of sets inside a studio can also be extremely expensive in addition to creating an inappropriate atmosphere, and location production in this case is easily justified on the basis of both costs and aesthetics.

THE PRODUCTION TEAM

The production team can be organized hierarchically and/or cooperatively. In a hierarchical situation, the commands flow downward from the producer to the director and from them to the rest of the creative staff or production crew. In a cooperatively organized production situation every member of the production team has equal authority and control and decisions are made cooperatively. Most production situations combine aspects of both the hierarchical and the cooperative models although a hierarchical approach is clearly dominant in the commercial world. The producer and/or director makes most of the decisions, but the help, support, and guidance of all the creative staff and some of the technical crew is actively sought and obtained. Production is rarely a purely democratic process, but it is almost always a collective process that requires the support and cooperation of large numbers of people.

The members of any television or film production team can usually be divided into two distinct groups: the creative staff and the technical crew. This basic division is often used for budgeting purposes. Dividing the team and costs into **above-the-line** creative aspects and **below-the-line** technical aspects (as shown in Figure 1.3), allows for a quick financial comparison between investments in the creative and technical sides of a production. The costs of paying the producer, director, scriptwriter, and performers are considered above-the-line while those for equipment and the crew are below-the-line. The two should be roughly equivalent in terms of the allocation of financial support to en-

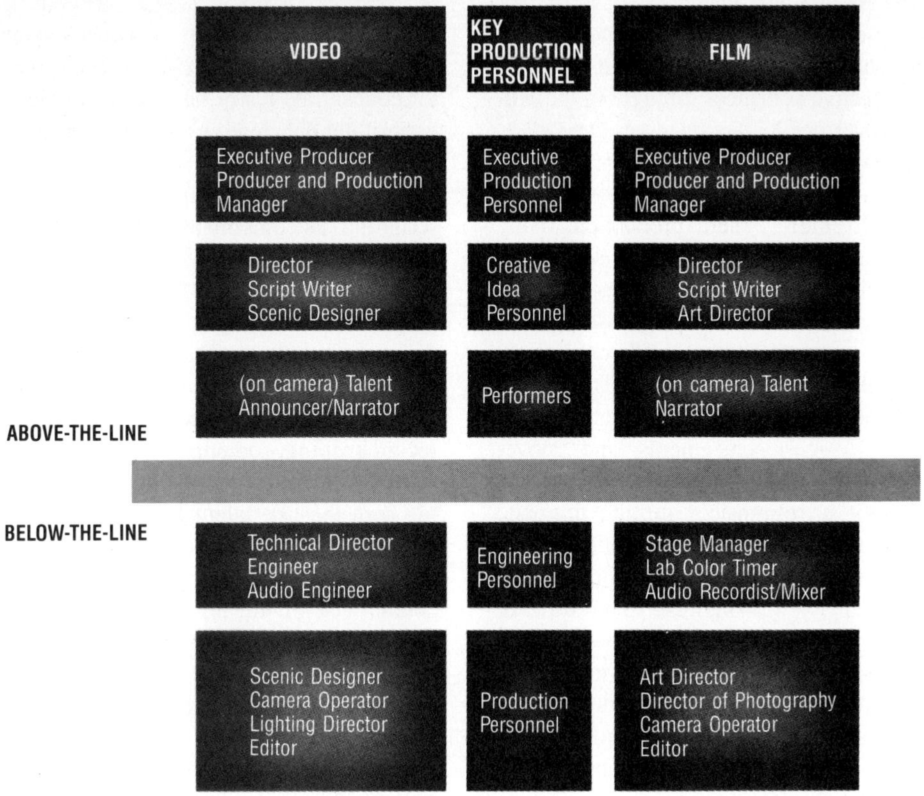

Figure 1.3
Key Production
Personnel

VIDEO	KEY PRODUCTION PERSONNEL	FILM
Executive Producer Producer and Production Manager	Executive Production Personnel	Executive Producer Producer and Production Manager
Director Script Writer Scenic Designer	Creative Idea Personnel	Director Script Writer Art Director
(on camera) Talent Announcer/Narrator	Performers	(on camera) Talent Narrator

ABOVE-THE-LINE

BELOW-THE-LINE

VIDEO	KEY PRODUCTION PERSONNEL	FILM
Technical Director Engineer Audio Engineer	Engineering Personnel	Stage Manager Lab Color Timer Audio Recordist/Mixer
Scenic Designer Camera Operator Lighting Director Editor	Production Personnel	Art Director Director of Photography Camera Operator Editor

sure that neither the creative nor the technical side of the production is being overemphasized.

Creative Staff

The creative staff includes the producer, director, assistant director, scriptwriter, and the talent or performers.

The Producer   There are many different types of television and film producers: excutive producers, independent producers, staff producers, line producers, and producer hyphenates (e.g., producer-writer-directors). The exact responsibilities of the producer vary greatly between different commercial and noncommercial production categories and levels. In general, the producer is responsible for turning creative ideas into practical or marketable concepts. The producer secures financial backing for a television or film production and manages the entire production process, including budgeting and scheduling. Some producers become directly involved in day-to-day production decisions, while others function as executive managers, who largely delegate production responsibilities to others. The producer ensures that the financial support for a production is maintained and usually represents the views of his or her clients, investors, or superiors as well as those of prospective audiences throughout the production process.

The Director   The director creatively translates the written word or script into specific sounds and images. He or she visualizes the script by giving abstract concepts concrete form. The director establishes a point of view on the action that helps to determine the selection of shots, camera placements and movements, and the staging of the action. The director is responsible for the dramatic structure, pace, and directional flow of the sounds and visual images. He or she must maintain viewer interest. The director works with the talent and crew, staging and plotting action, refining the master shooting script, supervising setups and rehearsals, as well as giving commands and suggestions throughout the recording and editing.

The director's role changes with different types of production situations. In live, multiple-camera video, the director usually is separated from the talent and crew during actual production, remaining inside a control room. In the control room the director supervises the operation of the **switcher**, a live television editing device that controls which picture and sound sources are being recorded or transmitted. The director also gives commands to the camera operators from the control room. A **stage manager** or **floor manager (or FM)** acts as the live television director's representative in the studio, cueing the talent, and relaying a director's commands. In single-camera production the director remains in the studio or on the set or location and works closely with the talent and the director of photography.

The Assistant Director   The assistant director helps the television or film director concentrate his or her major function, controlling the creative aspects of production. In feature film production the assistant director (or AD) helps break down the script into its component parts prior to actual production for scheduling and budgeting purposes. The AD then reports to the **production manager**, who supervises the use of studio facilities and personnel. During actual production the AD becomes involved in the day-to-day paperwork and record keeping, sometimes actually taking charge of a shooting unit, but always making sure that the talent and the crew are confident, well informed, and generally happy. In studio video production the AD keeps track of the time, alerts the crew members and performers to upcoming events, and sometimes relays the director's commands to the camera operators.

The Scriptwriter   The scriptwriter is a key member of the production team, particularly during preproduction. A scriptwriter outlines and in large part determines the overall structural form of a production project. He or she writes a preliminary summary of a production project called a treatment. A treatment lays the groundwork for the script and is written in the third person, present tense, much like a short story. The script provides a scene-by-scene description of settings, actions, and dialogue or narration and functions as a blueprint that guides the actual production.

The Production Crew

The production crew includes the director of photography, camera operator, lighting director, art director or scenic designer, editors, and perhaps a number of specialized engineers and technicians, depending on the size and sophistication of the production. Figures 1.4 and 1.5 illustrate a more complete breakdown of the organization of a motion picture company and of a television station.

The Director of Photography The overall control of film lighting and **cinematography**, or the creative use of a movie camera, is usually given to one individual, the director of photography (or DP). A DP supervises the camera crew, who are sometimes called **cameramen** (referred to as **camera operators** in this text), **assistant cameramen**, and **grips**, and the electrical crew, who are sometimes called **engineers** and **gaffers** and actually control the lighting setup. The DP works very closely with the director to create the proper lighting mood and camera coverage for each shot.

The DP is considered an artist who paints with light. He or she is intimately familiar with composition and all technical aspects of camera control and is frequently called on to solve many of the technical and aesthetic problems that arise during film recording. The DP rarely, if ever, actually operates the camera.

The Lighting Director In video production the camera recording and lighting functions are usually kept separate. The lighting director is responsible for arranging and adjusting the lights in the studio or on location, according to the director's wishes or specifications. The lighting director supervises the lighting crew, which hangs and adjusts the various lighting instruments.

The Camera Operator The camera operator controls the operation of the video camera. Many adjustments of the video camera must be made instantaneously in response to movements of the subject or commands from the director, such as changing the positioning of the camera or the focus and field of view of the image. The director's commands come to the camera operator in the studio via an intercom system connected to the camera operator's headset. The camera operator must smoothly, quietly, and efficiently control the movement of the support to which the camera is attached in the studio and avoid any problems with the cable, which connects the camera to the switcher and/or videotape recorder.

The Art Director or Scenic Designer
The art director (film) or scenic designer (video) supervises the overall production design. He or she determines the color and shape of sets, props, and backgrounds. Art directors frequently work very closely with **costume designers** and carpenters to ensure that costumes and sets properly harmonize or contrast with each other. In feature films, the art director delegates the supervision of set construction and carpentry to the **set designer,** while in video the scenic designer often supervises both the abstract design of a set on paper and its actual construction.

The Technical Director The technical director (or TD) operates the switcher, a multiple video camera editing device, in the control room. At the director's command, he or she presses the buttons, which change the television picture from one camera or playback device to another. In some television studios the technical director supervises the entire technical crew, including relaying the director's commands to the camera operators, while also operating the switcher.

Figure 1.4
Organization of a
Motion Picture
Company

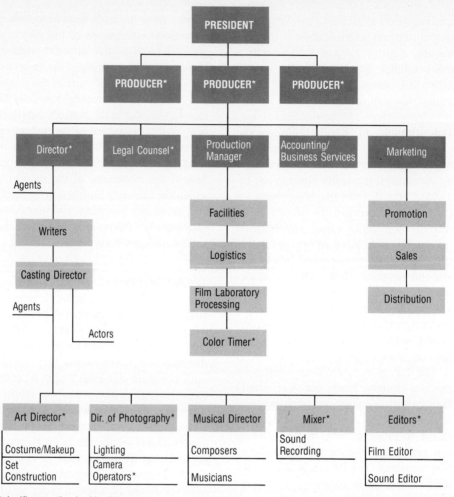

*signifies mention in this chapter

The Editor In video postproduction, the editor operates an editing system that *electronically connects* the individually recorded segments into a sequential order. A film editor *physically cuts* together various pieces of film into a single visual track and an accompanying sound track. The sound editor is a specialist who constructs and organizes all the various sound elements so that they can be properly blended or **mixed** together into a final soundtrack. In film the sound segments are usually physically spliced together, while in video they are edited electronically. Film can also be transferred to videotape for electronic editing.

The Audio Engineer or Mixer In video production the individual responsible for all aspects of initial audio recording is called the audio engineer. In film production this person is referred to as the mixer or audio recordist. In studio video production the audio engineer sits behind a large audio console in the control room, where he or she controls the sound from the mi-

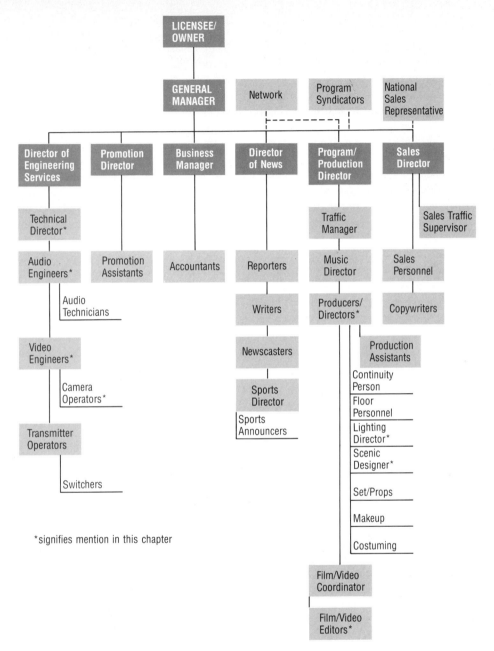

Figure 1.5
Organization of a
Television Station

LICENSEE/
OWNER

GENERAL
MANAGER

Network

Program
Syndicators

National
Sales
Representative

Director of
Engineering
Services

Promotion
Director

Business
Manager

Director
of News

Program/
Production
Director

Sales
Director

Technical
Director*

Traffic
Manager

Sales Traffic
Supervisor

Audio
Engineers*

Promotion
Assistants

Accountants

Reporters

Music
Director

Sales
Personnel

Audio
Technicians

Writers

Producers/
Directors*

Copywriters

Video
Engineers*

Newscasters

Production
Assistants

Camera
Operators*

Continuity
Person

Transmitter
Operators

Sports
Director

Floor
Personnel

Sports
Announcers

Lighting
Director*

Switchers

Scenic
Designer*

Set/Props

Makeup

Costuming

*signifies mention in this chapter

Film/Video
Coordinator

Film/Video
Editors*

crophones and playback units. The audio engineer also supervises the placement of microphones in the studio.

The film mixer or audio recordist, like the audio engineer in video, adjusts and controls the various audio recording de-vices, but unlike the audio engineer, re-mains on the set rather than in the control room. The film mixer usually operates an audio tape recorder that runs synchron-ously with the film camera. The mixer tries to record a consistent, balanced audio signal throughout all the different single-camera setups, so that a smooth, even sound track can be created during subsequent editing and mixing.

The Video Engineer or Laboratory Color Timer

The quality of video and film images depends on the technical specialists who can control image, color, brightness, and contrast levels. In video production the setting and adjustment of camera recording and transmission levels is usually controlled by a video engineer. The engineer is responsible for ensuring that all cameras are functioning properly and that multiple cameras all have comparable image qualities. A video engineer can also make color corrections to individual shots during postproduction. The color timer at a film laboratory performs a similar role, but does so after the film has been edited and before copies are made.

Summary

To have positive production experiences you must have a positive attitude toward the entire production process. You must know what you want and how to get it. You must develop strong conceptualization skills and plan your production carefully.

Careful advance planning during the preproduction stages is the best way of avoiding negative production experiences and circumventing the operation of Murphy's Law "ANYTHING THAT CAN GO WRONG, WILL GO WRONG."

Production is divided into three stages: preproduction, production, and postproduction. Preproduction designates all forms of planning that take place prior to actual recording, including producing, production management, and writing. The producer tries to attract investors and sponsors and tries to organize and solve many financial problems involved in production. Logistical and personnel problems are resolved through effective production management. Scriptwriting occurs in distinct stages, from writing a proposal, which helps to attract sponsors, to treatments and scripts. Production begins with the director's preparations to record sounds and images. It includes all aspects of sound and image recording, from camera operation to lighting, set design, and graphics. Postproduction refers to the last stage of production, when the editing of recorded images and sounds begins and the completed project is distributed and exhibited.

Visualization is the creative process of image and sound construction. Video and film record moving images and sounds. These recordings can be edited. Writers and directors must be skilled at visualization. They must understand the relation between abstract words in a script and the concrete sounds and images which are recorded and edited.

Ever since early humans painted pictures on the walls of caves, the human race has used images and sounds for informational, rhetorical, and aesthetic purposes. Rhetoric is the art of waging a successful argument, but it also refers to the use of persuasive and artistic devices and techniques in fictional as well as expository or nonfictional writing and media production. Aesthetics refers to the use of artistic forms and devices, which can be conventional or inventive and original. Strictly informational programs will be dull and lifeless if they are completely lacking in rhetorical and aesthetic techniques.

There are three basic aesthetic approaches to TV and film production: functionalist, realist, and formativist. A functionalist approach emphasizes message clarity, utilizing techniques that simply and clearly communicate the intended message. Form follows function. A realist approach relies on techniques that enhance an illusion of reality. Time and space are relatively continuous, and images and sounds are recorded so that they do not call attention to the recording process. A formativist approach actively shapes and manipulates the material which is recorded into an abstract or poetic form, often focusing attention on the recording medium itself. The choice of an aesthetic approach guides the selection of specific production techniques.

The histories of film and television are interrelated and overlap. Film is based on photochemical means, discovered in the nineteenth century, of recording light. Television and video technology, which developed somewhat later, reproduces images by electronic means. Both film and television have undergone substantial changes during the twentieth century. From the late 1940s to the present day, the two media have been economically interdependent.

Productions can be differentiated in terms of whether they are fiction or nonfiction, commercial or noncommercial, but there is not a firm separation between either set of categories. Docudramas and dramatic documentaries, for example, are partly fiction and partly nonfiction. Production values vary widely, and production budgets can range from those of feature films and television miniseries, which are often quite expensive to produce, all the way down to home movies, which are relatively inexpensive to produce.

Both video and film recording can be done with multiple cameras or a single camera, depending on the demands of the situation. Production can take place either in a studio or on location, again depending on the nature of the events to be recorded.

The production team is usually organized somewhat hierarchically, in the sense that a producer or director is in charge, and everyone is accountable to a staff head, who specializes in a particular area. But to work together effectively, a production team should also be cooperatively organized, so that individual specialists function collectively as a team.

The production team can be divided into the creative staff and the production crew. The creative staff consists of the producer, director, assistant director, and scriptwriter. The production crew includes all the various technical specialists, from camera operators to audio engineers or mixers and scenic designers.

Additional Readings

Allen, Robert C., and Douglas Gomery. *Film History, Theory and Practice*. New York: Random House Knopf, 1985.

Andrew, Dudley. *The Major Film Theories*. New York: Oxford University Press, 1976.

Arnheim, Rudolf. *Visual Thinking*. London: Faber and Faber, 1969.

Barnouw, Erik. *Tube of Plenty: The Evolution of American Television*. New York: Oxford University Press, 1975.

Becker, Samuel L. *Discovering Mass Communication*. 2nd ed. Glenview, IL: Scott, Foresman and Company, 1987.

Burch, Noel. *Theory of Film Practice*. New York: Praeger, 1973.

D'Agostino, Peter, ed. *Transmission: Theory and Practice for a New Television Aesthetics*. New York: Tanam Press, 1985.

Ellis, Jack C. *A History of Film*. 2nd ed. Englewood Cliffs, NJ: Prentice-Hall, 1985.

Zettl, Herbert. *Sight, Sound, and Motion*. Belmont, CA: Wadsworth, 1970.

PART 1

PREPRODUCTION

CHAPTER 2

Producing and Production Management

A producer is often the only key member of the production team who stays with a project through all phases of production from preproduction planning through postproduction editing and distribution. A producer gets a project off the ground initially by assembling the necessary personnel, finding sources of financial support, and then managing and overseeing the entire production process. He or she also ensures that the completed project reaches its target audience and satisfies the people who have provided financial support. A producer provides necessary continuity between one stage of production and the next and tries to ensure consistency in the final product.

While the producer plays an important part in all three production stages, this chapter focuses on the producer's role during preproduction and production. The producer's role during postproduction is covered in the final chapter of this book, ''Distribution and Exhibition.''

THE PRODUCER

The Role of the Producer

Producers are risk takers, who seize an idea, run with it, and convince others to follow them. Producers are creative administrators who act as links between corporate executives, managers, financial concerns, investors, or distributors who finance video and film productions and the artists who create them. Such productions can require large sums of money, which come in the form of bank loans, outright grants, risk capital, and governmental or within house budget allocations. These productions also require a great deal of logistical planning and administration as creative artists rarely have the time or the desire to deal with many of these administrative tasks, such as financing, budgeting, scheduling, and overall production management.

Producers try to create high quality products as efficiently as possible. They know how to turn unappealing or extravagant ideas into workable material and marketable concepts. They understand the diverse needs of creative people, corporate executives, investors, product buyers, and audiences. Producers tread a fine line between the creative talent's need for artistic expression and the necessity of providing concrete returns on production investments.

Good producers are effective decision makers and people managers. A producer's ability to understand and work with people is constantly tested throughout the entire production process. Ultimately, the production ''buck'' stops with the producer, who assumes responsibility for the successful completion of the project. If the production is running **over schedule** or **over budget**, that is, beyond the initial guidelines in terms of production time or money, it is the producer who must step in and decide what to do. Should production be terminated, a key individual replaced, or additional time and funds allocated to complete the project? These decisions can be extremely trying and difficult. If a problem develops with a particularly unruly and disruptive actor or staff member, the producer or the director must try to resolve the dispute amicably or take disciplinary action.

Types of Producers

Producers often specialize in particular types of programs. High-level specialists who work with television commercials, dramas, sports or news, for example, rarely work outside of their program type because success in one type of production does not guarantee success in another. Producers are further typed into at least four different categories according to the nature and extent of their responsibilities: staff producers, independent producers, executive producers, and "producer hyphenates."

Staff producers are employed on a continuing basis by a production company or organization. Producers are often assigned to specific projects in a small video or film production company. Local television station staff producers often work in several areas simultaneously, sometimes floating from news to sports to public affairs. At the network television level, staff producers are assigned to specific divisions, such as news or sports, and they work exclusively within these domains. Staff producers in film often specialize in the production of feature films, educational films, commercials, documentaries, sports films, or industrial films.

Independent producers put together and sell production ideas to studios, film distributors, network television executives, and syndicators. Independent producers are responsible for the bulk of all theatrically released entertainment films and prime-time television programming. They put together marketable story, staff, and talent packages.

Executive producers function at a higher managerial level and are less involved in day-to-day production decisions than other types of producers. They often delegate many production tasks to others and focus on project development and evaluation instead. They may supervise several productions simultaneously and are constantly developing and promoting new concepts and ideas.

Finally, "producer hyphenates" combine the role of producer with those of writing and/or directing. Writer-producer-directors immerse themselves in preplanning and the day-to-day production process, almost totally controlling the quality of the final product and preserving the integrity of their original idea.

GENERATING MARKETABLE CONCEPTS

Ideas

Where do film and television production ideas come from? Creative minds? Obviously creativity is a necessary asset in production, but it is not sufficient in itself to guarantee success. Producers must also be sensitive to the needs, preferences, and desires of investors, executives, managers, buyers, and audiences. Project ideas can arise from a variety of sources: current events; a pre-sold property, such as a successful book or play that suddenly becomes available; a desire to make a statement or explore a specific issue or social problem; a need expressed by a corporate executive, government administrator, or a consumer or labor group; or a previously successful television program or film. Exactly where an idea comes from is not as important (unless it is copyrighted material that is being used illegally) as what is done with that idea to make it marketable. Successful producers are people who not only develop or recognize good ideas but also know how to package, promote, and execute their ideas.

Packages

Producers put together marketable **packages** featuring components of known or presumed value to reduce the uncertainty that investors feel about whether or not a proposed project will be successful. Many people in the television and film industries believe that the prior success of a similar venture or of the creative staff enhances the chances of success for a new project. According to this view, a producer, writer, director, or star performer who has recently had successful films or television programs is likely to be successful again. Obtaining production financing for proven talent is always easier than for unproven talent. The prior success of a novel or play on which a film or television program is based is also presumed to provide some guarantee of success.

Noncommercial projects initiated by people with previous success and experience are more likely to receive funding than those by beginners. Previous success in noncommercial production is often defined in terms of awards, reviews, and specialized showings, or simply satisfied clients, rather than in terms of profits. But in any case an attractive media package plays on prior success to appease sponsors and partially reduce financial risks inherent in production investments.

Unfortunately, producers rarely have the luxury of waiting for prior success of a property to be amply demonstrated before they initiate a project. Screen rights to novels and plays are often secured prior to

publication or staging. A ''hot'' topic may have lost its popularity before a project is actually completed, due to the long lead time between project initiation and completion. Successful producers anticipate trends almost before they happen, and package new ideas to help a sponsor or investor see how marketable a new concept can be.

Audiences

An accurate estimate of the size, demographic makeup, and needs of a prospective audience is essential for the development of marketable film and television ideas. What media should a producer use to reach a specific audience? How large is the potential audience? What size budget is justified? What needs and expectations does a particular audience have? What film or television format should be used? These questions can only be answered when the prospective audience is clearly defined.

Audiences differ in size and demographics. The age and sex of the members of an audience is often just as important as the overall audience size. Television advertisers, for example, often design television commercials to reach specific demographic groups.

The process of assessing audience preferences for and interest in specific projects has become more scientific in recent years. Detailed audience information can facilitate later stages of the production process by giving the audience an input into production decisions. The nature and preferences of the audience can be used to determine a project's format, subject matter, and structure, as well as its budget. For example, the feature film *The Life and Times of Grizzly Adams* (1975) was targeted specifically for working-class families interested in outdoor-adventure dramas. Everything from the actual locations to specific character types was selected on the basis of audience pretesting. While the artistic merit of using audience-survey research to make production decisions may be questionable, since it can produce a hodgepodge of styles and content rather than a unified work, its success has to some degree validated the technique in the commercial marketplace. It has also proved vital for noncommercial productions, where audience response is a primary measure of program effectiveness.

Research can also be used during postproduction to assess the impact and effectiveness of a project. While audience research is no substitute for professional experience, it can give scientific, statistical validity to production decisions that might otherwise be based solely upon less reliable hunches and guesses.

PRODUCTION STRATEGIES

Audience research is only one part of a producer's overall production strategy. The development of a production strategy involves at least three steps: (1) defining the goals and objectives of the project, (2) assessing the potential audience, and (3) researching the topic. A producer who fails to develop an effective production strategy in each of these areas is unlikely to meet with continued success. While adopting an effective production strategy does not ensure that a project will be artistic, creative, or innovative, it does provide an organizational framework within which creative energies can be effectively channeled.

Project Goals and Objectives

It is important to specify a project's goals and objectives during preproduction to ensure that all members of the production team reach agreement on the project's purpose. A director's or a writer's goals may be exclusively artistic, while those of the producer may represent the investors' concern with profits. Tension between various goals and objectives can enhance the quality of a project in some cases and negatively affect others. In any case, failure to specify any goals at all eventually leads to unresolved conflicts during actual production.

Project goals differ between and within various program types and categories. Commercial films and television programs are created primarily to make money. The main objective may be to sell tickets at a movie theater, to interest more consumers in subscribing to a cable channel, to sell or rent a specific videotape, or to sell television advertising time at a higher rate.

The secondary purposes of commercial production are often the same as the primary concerns of noncommercial productions: information dissemination, rhetorical persuasion, and artistic expression. A commercial television station's public affairs or news documentary may have as a secondary goal informing the public about a specific social problem, such as poverty or alcoholism. A television producer may want to express his or her feelings about love or war. That such goals are often secondary in the case of commercial production may not always be obvious. Successful news programs, for example, while motivated by a social purpose to keep the public well informed, are often important determinants of advertising rates and profits for local television stations. Public affairs programming, while serving a need in the community for the expression of minority interests and concerns, may only be useful to television executives to the extent that it, like news programming, justifies a station's continuation through FCC license revewal of its right to broadcast.

Just as commercial programs often have secondary goals beyond making money, noncommercial programs sometimes have secondary goals that are remarkably economic in origin. For example, large-scale public television productions often justify their private foundation or corporate funding on the basis of the size of the audience they attract to cultural and artistic programs, giving an indirect form of advertising to the corporations that provide funding. PBS programs are often selected for funding on the basis of the potential viewership by affluent, cultured subscribers who will continue or begin a regular pledge of individual contributions (annual memberships). Even in noncommercial production, the production budget and values must be justified to some degree on the basis of the potential size and demographics of the audience.

Audience Assessment Techniques

Estimating the size and **demographics**, e.g., the age, sex, and other characteristics, of the potential audience for a prospective television or film project can be quite complicated. Sometimes a project's potential audience can be estimated from the prior success of similar productions. For example, the A. C. Nielsen and Arbitron ratings for television audiences drawn to previous programming of the same type can be consulted. Television ratings, as shown in Figure 2.1, provide audience in-

formation in the form of program ratings, shares, and demographic breakdowns for national and regional television markets.

Ratings refer to the percent of *all* television households, that is of all households with a television set regardless of whether that set is on or off at a particular time, that are tuned to a specific program. If there are 80 million television households and 20 million of them are tuned to a specific program, then that program has a rating of 25, which represents 25 percent of the total television population. **Shares** indicate the percent of television households with the set *on* at a specific time that are actually watching a specific program. Thus if 20 million households are watching something on television at a particular time and 10 million of those 20 million households are watching the same program, then that program has an audience share of 50, which represents 50 percent of the viewing audience. Demographic breakdowns of the television audience help advertisers and media-time buyers and sellers to target programs for specific audiences. Consulting ratings data about earlier programs of the same general type provides only a rough estimate of the potential drawing power of a future program, since audience interest in that type of programming can increase or decrease with time and repetitive presentations.

Commercial producers and distributors often rely on market research to estimate audience size and the preferences of audiences that might be drawn to a particular project. The title of the project, a list of the key talent, the nature of the subject matter, a synopsis of the story line, for example, might be given to a test audience, and their responses recorded and evaluated. Research has shown that by far the best predictor of feature film success is **advertising penetration**, that is, the number

CURRENT WEEKLY RANKING

RANKING FOR WEEK ENDING JAN 19, 1986

NIELSEN NATIONAL INDEX

RANK	PROGRAM	NOTE	NET	DAY	TIME	DUR	RTG	SHARE	LAST
1	BILL COSBY SHOW		NBC	THU	8:00	30	38.5	55	1
2	FAMILY TIES		NBC	THU	8:30	30	34.8	49	2
3	MURDER, SHE WROTE		CBS	SUN	8:00	60	28.1	41	3
4	60 MINUTES		CBS	SUN	7:00	60	26.6	42	6
5	CHEERS		NBC	THU	9:00	30	25.4	36	6
6	NBC SUNDAY NIGHT MOVIE	1	NBC	SUN	9:00	120	24.4	37	62
7	GOLDEN GIRLS		NBC	SAT	9:00	30	24.2	39	8
8	DALLAS		CBS	FRI	9:00	60	23.2	36	12
9	NIGHT COURT		NBC	THU	9:30	30	22.9	33	14
10	MIAMI VICE		NBC	FRI	10:00	60	22.2	37	8
11	KATE & ALLIE		CBS	MON	9:00	30	21.9	31	15
12	NEWHART		CBS	MON	9:30	30	21.6	31	19
13	227		NBC	SAT	9:30	30	21.4	35	13
14	GRAND OLE OPRY'S 60TH ANV		CBS	TUE	9:00	120	20.9	32	S
15	WHO'S THE BOSS?		ABC	TUE	8:00	30	20.8	30	10
16	KNOTS LANDING		CBS	THU	10.00	60	20.7	33	16
17	DYNASTY		ABC	WED	9:00	60	20.4	30	18
17	GROWING PAINS		ABC	TUE	8:30	30	20.4	29	16
19	HIGHWAY TO HEAVEN		NBC	WED	8:00	60	19.9	29	11
20	A TEAM		NBC	TUE	8:00	60	19.7	29	34
21	FALCON CREST		CBS	FRI	10:00	60	19.1	32	21
22	SCARECROW & MRS. KING		CBS	MON	8:00	60	18.9	27	23
23	HOTEL		ABC	WED	10:00	60	18.6	31	28
24	HUNTER		NBC	SAT	10:00	60	18.4	31	40
25	MOONLIGHTING		ABC	TUE	9:00	60	18.2	26	41
25	SIMON & SIMON		CBS	THU	9:00	60	18.2	26	31
27	CBS SUNDAY NIGHT MOVIE	2	CBS	SUN	9:00	120	18.1	28	4
27	GEORGE BURNS 90TH B/DAY		CBS	FRI	8:00	60	18.1	29	S
29	CAGNEY & LACEY		CBS	MON	10:00	60	18.0	29	27
30	FACTS OF LIFE		NBC	SAT	8:30	30	17.9	29	24
31	BLACKE'S MAGIC		NBC	WED	9:00	60	17.2	25	20
32	HILL STREET BLUES		NBC	THU	10:00	60	16.7	27	34
32	TV BLOOPERS & PRAC. JOKES		NBC	MON	8:00	60	16.7	24	29
34	MACGYVER		ABC	WED	8:00	60	15.9	23	
35	20/20		ABC	THU	10:00	60	15.4	24	32
35	GIMME A BREAK		NBC	SAT	8:00	30	15.4	26	36
37	MAGNUM, P.I.		CBS	THU	8:00	60	15.2	22	39
38	ALFRED HITCHCOCK PRESENTS		NBC	SUN	8:30	30	15.1	21	45
38	ST. ELSEWHERE		NBC	WED	10:00	60	15.1	25	36
40	AMAZING STORIES		NBC	SUN	8:00	30	14.9	22	29

MORE

CURRENT WEEKLY RANKING

RANKING FOR WEEK ENDING JAN 19, 1986

NIELSEN NATIONAL INDEX

RANK	PROGRAM	NOTE	NET	DAY	TIME	DUR	RTG	SHARE	LAST
40	RIPTIDE		NBC	TUE	9:00	60	14.9	21	43
42	ABC SUNDAY NIGHT MOVIE	3	ABC	SUN	9:00	120	14.8	23	42
42	HARDCASTLE & MCCORMICK		ABC	MON	8:00	60	14.8	21	51
44	WEBSTER		ABC	FRI	8:00	30	14.6	24	22
45	ABC MONDAY NIGHT MOVIE	4	ABC	MON	9:00	120	14.5	22	33
46	REDD FOXX SHOW		ABC	SAT	8:00	30	14.2	24	
47	KNIGHT RIDER		NBC	FRI	9:00	60	14.1	22	47
47	NBC MONDAY NIGHT MOVIES	5	NBC	MON	9:00	120	14.1	21	25
49	DYNASTY II: COLBYS		ABC	THU	9:00	60	13.9	20	53
49	REMINGTON STEELE		NBC	TUE	10:00	60	13.9	23	47
51	MARY		CBS	WED	8:00	30	13.8	20	44
52	CRAZY LIKE A FOX		CBS	SUN	8:00	60	13.6	20	
53	AIRWOLF		CBS	SAT	8:00	60	13.3	22	55
54	LOVE BOAT		ABC	SAT	10:00	60	13.1	22	60
55	B BUNNY/LOONEY TUNES 50TH		CBS	TUE	8:00	60	13.0	19	S
56	MR. BELVEDERE		ABC	FRI	8:30	30	12.9	20	25
57	FUNNY		ABC	SUN	8:00	60	12.8	19	S
57	SPENSER: FOR HIRE		ABC	TUE	10:00	60	12.8	21	62
59	FOLEY SQUARE		ABC	WED	8:30	30	12.8	18	55
60	MISFITS OF SCIENCE		NBC	FRI	8:00	60	12.7	20	58
61	EQUALIZER		CBS	WED	10:00	60	12.2	20	P
62	BENSON		ABC	SAT	8:30	30	12.1	20	
63	DIFF'RENT STROKES		ABC	FRI	9:00	30	11.8	18	49
63	SILVER SPOONS		NBC	SUN	7:30	30	11.8	18	51
65	LADY BLUE		ABC	WED	9:00	60	10.9	18	66
65	CBS SATURDAY NIGHT MOVIE	6	CBS	SAT	9:00	120	10.8	18	53
67	HE'S THE MAYOR		NBC	SUN	9:30	30	9.4	15	60
68	PUNKY BREWSTER		NBC	SUN	7:00	30	9.2	15	50
69	RIPLEY'S BELIEVE IT-NOT		ABC	SUN	7:00	60	8.3	13	65
70	FALL GUY		ABC	FRI	10:00	60	6.7	11	68
71	SHADOW CHASERS		ABC	THU	8:00	60	5.0	7	69

1	MAFIA PRINCESS
2	PASSION FLOWER
3	CLUB MED
4	RIGHT OF THE PEOPLE
5	FATAL VISION, PART 2
6	TWILIGHT ZONE-THE MOVIE

S = SPECIAL
P = PRE-EMPTED
1 RUN COMPLETE

of people who have heard about a project, usually through advertising in a variety of media. Other significant predictors of success appear to be the financial success of the director's prior work, the current popularity of specific performers or stars, and interest generated by basic story lines pretested in written form.

Audience research has been used for a variety of purposes in commercial production. Sometimes often prior to production, researchers statistically compare the level of audience interest (''want-to-see'' index) generated by a synopsis, title, or credits of a production to the amount of audience satisfaction resulting from viewing the completed project. A marketing and advertising strategy is often chosen on the basis of this research.

A film that generates a great deal of audience interest prior to production, but little audience satisfaction after viewing a prerelease screening of the completed film might be marketed somewhat differently from a film that generates little interest initially, but is well received in completed form. The former might be marketed with an advertising blitz and released to many theaters before ''word of mouth'' destroys it at the box office, while the latter might be marketed more slowly to allow ''word of mouth'' to build gradually.

Some television programs and commercials will be dropped and others aired solely on the basis of audience pretesting. Story lines, character portrayals, and editing are sometimes changed after audience testing. Advertising agencies often test

Figure 2.1
A Nielsen National Television Index

Charts such as this help in providing basic information about program ratings, shares, and demographic breakdowns.

several versions of a commercial on sample audiences before selecting the version to be aired. A local news program may be continuously subjected to audience survey research in an attempt to discover ways to increase its ratings or share. A sponsor or executive administrator may desire concrete evidence of communication effectiveness and positive viewer reaction after a noncommercial production has been completed.

Audience research has to be recognized as an important element in the production process. While it is no substitute for professional experience and artistic ability, research nonetheless can provide some insurance against undertaking expensive projects that have no likelihood of reaching target audiences or generating profits. Informal assessments of viewer responses to media products, such as viewer letters of praise or interest or having audiences fill out questionnaires after viewing can provide some index of success. Even a film or video project whose main purpose is self-expression and aesthetic pleasure can benefit from audience response in the form of published criticism.

Noncommercial audience research often focuses on assessments of audience needs and program effectiveness. A project that is not designed to make money often justifies production costs on the basis of corporate, governmental, or cultural needs as well as audience preferences and size. Sponsors need to have some assurance that the program will effectively reach the target audience and convey its message. Audience pretesting can help to determine the best format for conveying information and reaching the audience. Successful children's programs are often based on audience research that assures program effectiveness. For example, the fast-paced, humorous instructional style of "Sesame Street," which mirrors television comedies such as "Laugh-In" and television commercials, was based on exhaustive audience research.

Topic Research

Researching a topic is one of the most important steps in the production process. **Topic research*** is an attempt to gather accurate information about a specific film or television topic. Careful research ensures that news and sports as well as entertainment programming and films do not misinform. The quality of the research directly affects the integrity of the entire project. A hastily produced, poorly researched production can generate a great deal of antipathy from its audience. Sometimes pressure groups are aroused and legal actions, such as libel suits, are taken against the producer or production company.

Careful research can make the difference between promoting and exploiting misinformation versus carefully examining the key issues and stimulating a reasonable debate. Clearly, those African segments of the popular dramatic miniseries, "Roots," that were based on careful research, are more valuable than those in which the tribal customs and dances of distinctly different tribes are intermixed. Exciting drama and intense, well-acted performances contribute a great deal to the impact and success of any project, but thorough topic research gives a project significance, depth, and lasting value and promotes the long-term interests of the producer.

---

* Topic research is also discussed from a scriptwriter's standpoint in chapter 3.

Topic research requires imagination and determination. New sources of information are only uncovered with extreme diligence and persistence. Research can involve the collection and inspection of at least three different types of data or material records: written, visual, and oral.

Books, magazines, newspapers, diaries, and private correspondence may have to be uncovered, read, and analyzed. Specific locations may need to be scouted for use in production. Photographs and drawings of relevant settings, props, and costumes may also need to be examined. Interviews may be conducted with actual participants or recognized experts. In some cases these experts may be retained as consultants throughout production. Sometimes consultants are supplied by specific organizations, such as the American Medical Association, which do not want to be slighted by improper or inaccurate treatment, although care must be taken to avoid giving interested parties too great a veto power over program content. Nonetheless, topic research helps a producer make intelligent production decisions. Sacrificing authenticity in a documentary or docudrama for dramatic purposes or due to inadequate research raises many ethical problems for the producer.

Ethics

The "illusion of reality" inherent in nonfiction programming and films, it has been argued, gives television and film producers the power to shape as well as reflect public opinion. Some nonfiction programming, such as network news broadcasts, function as a primary source of public information about current events. Since nonfiction media producers can influence public opinion, they have an ethical responsibility not to intentionally mislead the public.

The fact that many nonfiction film and television producers are concerned with making a profit as well as performing a useful social function often means that individuals will be tempted to compromise their ethical responsibilities. While it is true that nonfiction works must have entertainment or dramatic value to attract audiences and prove cost effective, there is a point at which a shortsighted pursuit of profit forces abandonment of long-term social goals and values.

Self-serving creators of nonfiction programming have the potential to do harm to individuals and our democratic institutions. The Federal Communications Commission (FCC) attempts to ensure that broadcasters operate in the "public interest, convenience, and necessity." The concept of Equal Time, requiring broadcasters to provide equal time for presenting alternative points of view is an attempt to compensate for limited channels of television information. Private citizens are protected from media abuse by the possibility of bringing libel, slander, or invasion of privacy suits. Documentary filmmakers, for example, must obtain written permission (releases) from private citizens before they can publicly exhibit television or film recordings of them. Public figures are less well protected than private citizens, and even private citizens who are involved in bonafide, public news events may legally be filmed or taped without their permission. But beyond the legal and public policy limitations, writers and producers of films and television programs have an ethical responsibility to use the "illusion of reality" inherent in nonfiction formats wisely and to treat their human and nonhuman subjects fairly.

From a production standpoint, documentary and news people must be concerned about the potentially negative effects a publicly exhibited work may have on the people who are photographed or recorded. What is done to a human being, when his or her picture is shown to thousands or millions of viewers, especially when that person is a private citizen rather than a public figure? Lance Loud, the gay son who appeared along with the rest of his family before a national public television audience when "An American Family" (1972) was broadcast, made a public exhibition of coming "out of the closet." Is he still laboring under the impact of this program over ten years later? The same could be asked about Edie Beale, the reclusive cousin of Jacqueline Kennedy Onassis, who was featured along with her mother in the Maysles' *Grey Gardens* (1975). Was she exploited by the filmmakers, or did she try to use the film to further her own career as a would-be performer? She was offered a singing engagement at a New York nightclub as a result of her participation in this film. Who was using whom? Are we talking about exploitation or the pursuit of mutual self-interest?

How are releases or permissions to use the images of private citizens obtained? Are people coerced into signing a release or do they freely choose to be publicly exhibited? Does the unannounced appearance of a news or documentary camera crew at a private citizen's home or office constitute a form of coercion? Does the subject's initial permission allow the producer or editor to use the recordings in any manner that he or she sees fit, or does a writer, editor, director, or producer have some responsibility to show the completed work to the subject before it is publicly

shown, so that a follow-up permission can be obtained? These are ethical questions that should concern documentary and news writers, directors, and producers, who must weigh the public's right to know against the citizen's right to privacy. They frequently arise in many different types of nonfiction programming, not only documentaries and news stories, but also commercials and educational programming.

Project Presentations

A producer who has interested a potential funding source usually tries to make a personal, face-to-face **presentation** to the investor, sponsor, or executive who is considering funding the project. Sometimes the presentation will be made over lunch or dinner. At other times it will be a more formal presentation in an office. At the very least it will consist of a telephone conversation. Regardless of the setting, it is essential that the producer capitalize on any interest generated by a written proposal (discussed in chapter 3) during the presentation. A producer who lacks enthusiasm in presenting his or her project to a prospective sponsor or investor is destined to fail. Sometimes the acceptance of a project hinges on the availability of a well-known creative staff member or star performer. If a producer has some well-known talent under contract before the face-to-face presentation, that presentation is more likely to solidify funding support. The presentation also offers a producer the opportunity to present additional, less fully developed, future project ideas to a funding source, gauge his or her interest, and make adjustments later based on some of the funding source's reactions and recommendations.

PRODUCTION MANAGEMENT

Producers are usually responsible for production management. **Production management** includes the supervision, acquisition, use, and scheduling of the production staff, equipment, and facilities. The producer or another member of the staff under the producer's direction, such as a production manager for a major film studio, breaks a script down according to its component locations and settings. The personnel and facilities needed for each scene are easily specified by an experienced individual who is intimately familiar with essential production equipment needs, budget limitations, personnel contracts, and salary scales.

Script Breakdown

A **script breakdown** helps a producer estimate and follow realistic schedules and budgets by providing a complete record of all equipment, personnel, and facilities needed for every scene or sequence. It also makes it possible to shoot the production efficiently **out of continuity**, that is, by ignoring the chronology of sequences in the script, and shooting all the scenes that take place in one setting at the same time, regardless of where they will appear in the finished product. This procedure is obviously more efficient than returning to the same settings or locations several times in the course of production.

After the script has been broken down according to its settings and locations, **breakdown sheets** (Figure 2.2) are filled out. Each sheet lists the cast members, staff, sets, props, costumes, and equip-

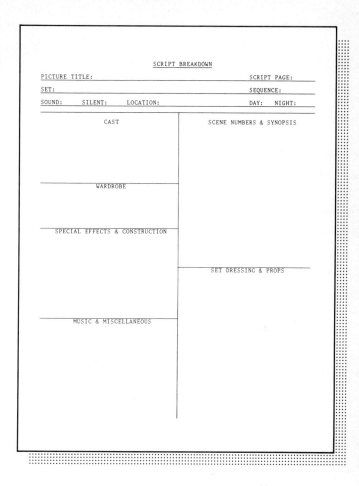

ment needed at one setting or location. An overall shooting schedule and equipment and personnel list can be made and total costs estimated from all the breakdown sheets put together.

Scheduling

A **shooting schedule** (Figure 2.3) indicates the total number of days of recording that will actually be required to complete the project. Shooting schedule information has traditionally been assembled on a production board containing movable

**Figure 2.2
Script Breakdown
Form**

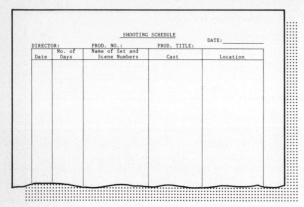

Figure 2.3
Shooting Schedule Form

Above right: A production board with the individual strips that indicate equipment and personnel needs for any given day.

cardboard strips, each of which represents one day's shooting at a specific location or studio. An individual strip indicates all major personnel and equipment needs for one day at one place. The strips can be moved around on the board if the production schedule must be altered. Since shooting is scheduled primarily on the basis of scenes and locations, the strips for all the days of shooting of the same scene or location usually appear sequentially on the schedule board. The expense or lack of availability of key production personnel at a certain period can complicate scheduling, sometimes forcing a producer to return to a location or studio more than once during actual production. Once the shooting schedule is finalized, the production board strips can be fitted into a master production board that is used to schedule a production company's overall use of facilities and personnel for several simultaneous or overlapping projects.

Today, scheduling boards are gradually being replaced by computer software, which can generate as many hard copies as needed and allow instantaneous changes to be made in production scheduling.

Budgeting

Production budgets are usually divided into above-the-line and below-the-line costs. Above-the-line costs include the salaries of the creative staff members, such as the producer, the director, and the scriptwriter, and fees paid to performers or talent, such as actors or narrators. Below-the-line costs cover technical facilities, equipment, and personnel, such as production engineers and crew. When below-the-line costs are approximately equal to above-the-line costs, the production values, or overall level of sophistication of the equipment and crew, are usually appropriate for the investment in creative talent. (The production budget for the film/video of traditional African dancing is shown in Figure 2.4. An example of a budget that resembles one used by a major film studio is also shown here.)

Running Time   **Running time**, the total duration of a completed project or a specific scene, is an important determinant of overall budget. While it is generally true that longer running times require larger budgets, the case of high-budget network-level television commercials suggests that there are some exceptions to this rule (as shown in Figure 2.5). Running times for specific types of programs are often standardized. A public television program might run for about twenty-eight or fifty-six minutes whereas the same program would be only about twenty-three or forty-six minutes long if it were to be commercially broadcast, to allow time for the commercials. **Theatrical films**, those which are shown in commercial theaters, are rarely more than three hours in duration, because it is difficult for a theater owner to show films longer than this more than twice a day: once in the afternoon and once in the evening. Film length can directly affect box-office revenues.

Shooting Ratios

Shooting ratios represent the ratio of footage shot during production to footage actually used in the final edited version. Such ratios vary considerably from format to format. Shooting ratios for a cinema verité documentary in which a single camera is used to record unstaged events, can range anywhere from 20:1 to more than 100:1 of recorded material shot to material used. An efficiently

GRIZZELDA PICTURES INC.	PRODUCTION BUDGET			
TITLE "Flamingo Bay"	PRODUCER Louise Howe			
START DATE May 18, 1987	DIRECTOR J. D. Guerrant			
FINISH DATE September 1, 1987	PRODUCTION DAYS 68 + 6-2nd unit			
PRINCIPAL ACTORS Ann-Marie Buesing, William Poole	4 Post-Prod.			

Acct. No.	Description	Page No.	Budget	Remarks
001	Producer & Staff	1	22,500	
002	Continuity	1	229,500	
003	Story & Rights	2	369,600	
004	Director & Staff	2	780,300	
005	Talent	3	3,837,600	
006	Supplemental Labor	25	147,600	
	TOTAL ABOVE THE LINE		**5,387,100.**	
007	Production Staff	4	368,100	
008	Camera	5	183,300	
009	Set Construction & Striking	6	1,126,800	
010	Dressing	7	361,200	
011	Electrical	8	267,900	
012	Set Operations	9	314,100	
013	Action Props	10	190,500	
014	Special Photographic	12	166,500	
015	Locations	28	573,300	
016	Wardrobe	13	501,900	
017	Makeup & Hairdressing	14	214,500	
-018	Sound Operation	15	80,400	
019	Extras	16	123,900	
020	Transportation	17	239,700	
021	Film	18	214,500	
022	Sundry	19	37,500	
	TOTAL SHOOTING PERIOD		**4,964,100.**	
023	Editing & Projection	20	147,600	
024	Film & Stock Shots	21	46,200	
025	Sound Recording	22	76,200	
026	Music	23	108,900	
027	Titles, Opticals & Inserts	24	35,400	
	TOTAL COMPLETION PERIOD		**830,100.**	
028	Insurance	25	322,500	
029	Supplemental Labor	25	900,900	
030	Unit Publicist & Stillman	26	130,800	
031	Other	27	29,400	
	TOTAL OTHER		**1,383,600.**	
	DIRECT TOTAL		**12,564,900.**	
	STUDIO OVERHEAD		**3,141,225.**	
	GRAND TOTAL		**15,706,125.**	

DATE COMPILED May 25, 1987 APPROVALS Louise Sheldon L. Howe

Figure 2.4
A. Production Budget Form Resembling That of a Major Film Studio
B. Budget for Author's Documentary (excluding in-kind contributions for equipment and personnel)

Transportation, Lodging and Meals: Senegal & The Gambia 4 weeks	5,000.00
Film: 16mm ECN 7291 20, 400 ft. cores @ $69.20/core	1,384.00
Audiotape: ¼-inch tape on 5 inch reels, 40 reels @ $3.58/reel	143.20
Film Processing and Workprinting: 8000 ft. @ 30¢/ft.	2,400.00
Magnetic Film: 12,000 ft. @ $30/1000 ft.	360.00
Edge Numbers: 8000 ft. @ 4¢/ft.	320.00
Titles and Animation	600.00
Editing Supplies	100.00
Shipping and Insurance	400.00
Conforming of A and B rolls	1,200.00
Optical Sound Track: 1100 ft. @ 31¢/ft.	341.00
Answer Print: 1100 ft. @ 84.5¢/ft.	929.50
Inter Positive for Video Transfer: 1100 ft. @ 81¢/ft.	891.00
Film to 1-inch Master Videotape with Sound	450.00
	$14,518.70

Figure 2.5
Range of Production Costs

Project Type	Project Cost Range	Project Length
Feature Film	$500,000 to $50,000,000	90 min. to 180 + min.
TV Miniseries	$5,000,000 to $40,000,000	8 hours to 20 + hours
Made-for-TV-Movie	$300,000 to $5,000,000	80 min. to 105 min.
Series Episode	$100,000 to $1,000,000	24 min. to 48 min.
Network Commercial	$30,000 to $300,000	15 sec. or 30 sec.
Daytime Soap Opera	$30,000 to $100,000	24 min. to 48 min.
Game Show	$20,000 to $80,000	24 min. to 48 min.
Local Commercial	$1,000 to $30,000	15 sec. or 30 sec.
Corporate	$1,000 to $20,000 (average $10,000)	Maximum of about 1 hour (average 20 min.)
Educational	$50 to $10,000	Maximum of about 1 hour
Student Project	$25 to $10,000	Longer than it should be!!

produced sponsored film or videotape, on the other hand, may be produced at a 4:1 or 5:1 shooting ratio of footage shot to footage used. An average feature film or television action drama requires a shooting ratio of 15:1 or more. Television commercials can easily run up shooting ratios as high as 50:1 or more. In some categories, such as certain soft drink commercials, as much as 50,000 feet of 35mm film may be originally exposed in order to produce just 45 feet (thirty seconds) of final product.

Equipment Costs and Other Fees

Producers must determine the exact cost of almost every production item, from equipment rental or purchase to union salary scales, talent **residuals**, and **copyright royalty fees**. Television and film equipment can be rented from businesses that specialize in these services, or it can be purchased by a studio or individual and amortized—that is, depreciated in value for tax purposes—on a yearly basis over the period of time that it is actually used. Residuals are payments made to performers and talent for repeat uses of produc-

tions in which they appear that continue to earn money.

Producers are often involved in legal matters, many of which require the involvement of a qualified entertainment lawyer. Music and written materials are usually protected by copyright. Any use of copyrighted materials is usually secured on the basis of a royalty fee that is paid to the owner of this property. **Legal releases** free the producer from threat of lawsuits from people who appear in a film or television program and must be secured before that work is publicly exhibited. Private citizens can sue for libel, slander, invasion of privacy, or defamation of character, if they believe they have been unfairly portrayed. The law is somewhat different for public figures but they are still protected to some extent and, as noted earlier, producers must exercise great care in the treatment of human subjects to avoid lengthy and expensive legal actions. The large number of legal services that are often required for commercial production has resulted in legal specialists, known as **entertainment lawyers**, who cater to the specific needs of the industry.

Some producers maintain their own **music libraries**, so that they do not have to commission expensive original music for every production need. These music libraries are collections of musical recordings that are available from organizations such as ASCAP, the American Society of Composers, Authors, and Publishers, and BMI, Broadcast Music Incorporated. These music recordings on phonograph records require royalty payments in the form of **needle drop fees**, which simply means that every time the phonograph needle is dropped on one of these records a specific fee must be paid, regardless of how long the record or recording runs. Production music libraries are also available on tape, although the "needle drop fee" still applies.

Unions, Guilds, and Nonunion Working Conditions

Talent and technicians in many states are protected by **union** or **guild contracts**, that have been worked out with major producers and production companies. Union or guild-negotiated contracts specify salary scales, working conditions and policies, and many other factors, such as residual payments. The unions or guilds with which a producer may work or at least honor in terms of salary and working conditions, include AFTRA (American Federation of Radio and Television Artists), SAG (Screen Actors Guild), WGA (Writers' Guild of America), DGA (Directors' Guild of America), AFM (American Federation of Musicians), IATSE (International Alliance of Theatrical and Stage Employees), NABET (National Association of Broadcast Employees and Technicians), and IBEW (International Brotherhood of Electrical Workers).

Some states, of course, have **right-to-work** laws, which prohibit the formation of completely **closed shops**; that is they prevent unions from requiring all workers to join their union, pay dues, and abide by union-negotiated contracts. Production in most metropolitan areas is heavily unionized, especially at the highest levels of production, such as network and broadcast station television, feature films, and 35mm film commercials. In these areas salary levels must meet or exceed certain specified minimum levels. A union member who fails to abide by these conditions and works for less pay is vulnerable to disciplinary fines or expulsion from the union, while the producer or production company may have to renegotiate its union contract, since its violation of the agreement makes the document null and void. In right-to-work states union contracts of this type do not always exist, and salaries and working conditions are often negotiated on an individual basis.

Nonunion productions are often difficult to distribute or air at the highest, most lucrative levels. It is well-known that the major Hollywood feature film distributors cannot purchase or distribute more than one nonunion produced film per year without jeopardizing their union contracts, for example. Most producers of feature films and network television programs must face the added costs of union salary scales during production or accept the added difficulties of finding an effective means of national distribution.

While the highest levels of television and film production are heavily unionized, except in right-to-work states, a great deal of commercial and noncommercial production is accomplished without union talent and crews throughout the country. Much public, cable, local, corporate, government, educational, and religious television and film production takes place in nonunion or partially unionized work environments. It is often easier to obtain initial production experience and employment in these nonunionized production settings.

Contingency Fund

Every final budget should include a contingency fund that represents from 10 percent to 30 percent of the estimated budget. The contingency fund permits some latitude for error, which can arise in a number of areas, for unpredictable circumstances such as inclement weather that delays production, and talent or labor difficulties. A budget that does not include a contingency fund is unlikely to attract any but the most naive sponsors or investors.

Hierarchical and Cooperative Approaches

There are many different ways to organize and structure production personnel and the production process, but most approaches can be placed somewhere along a continuum from a strict hierarchy to a loose cooperative. A hierarchical model is basically a pyramid structure. Authority flows downward from the producer to the director and other members of the production team. In short, everyone has an immediate supervisor who is responsible for making production decisions. These decisions flow downward from the top.

A cooperative model divides production tasks and responsibilities equally among each of the various areas of specialization. A different individual or group is responsible for each aspect of production, and all decisions are made cooperatively and collectively within and between different divisions.

Few actual production situations are exclusively hierarchical or cooperative in approach. Television and film production is necessarily a cooperative, collective process to some extent. In large-scale productions specialization forces producers and directors to delegate responsibility to experts, whose cooperation and creative innovation is essential to the completion of a quality product. But media production is rarely a purely democratic art. Most productions are organized somewhat hierarchically around the funding source or the producer, who represents that source. Responsibility for daily decisions is frequently delegated to the director and by the director to specialists in each area, such as the stage manager, the art director, and the lighting director. The producer and the director must coordinate and supervise the overall production. They must create an effective communication network which ensures that information flows freely from the bottom up as well as the top down.

Production Meetings

One means of ensuring adequate communication among the various staff and crew members is to schedule regular production meetings before, during, and after actual production. Coordinating the overall production minimizes the risk that continuity will be lost, that costumes will clash with sets, that lighting will be inappropriate to the mood of a particular scene, or that staff members will simply misunderstand the overall purpose and design of the production. Involving people in production decision making encourages their support and cooperation. A production meeting may also require some exercise of authority on the part of the producer or director to ensure production efficiency and consistency. In general, the more time allocated to production meetings, provided that these are not simply drink fests or ''bull sessions,'' the less time and money the production team will later need to spend on costly reshooting.

Evaluation

Producers must constantly evaluate the efficacy of procedures being used in production. Short-term evaluations focus on gathering daily information. The producer fills out daily production reports, based on information received from each production area. Accurate records are kept for financial purposes, and some secretarial or clerical skills are essential. The forms to be filled out concerning a feature film production, for example, are almost endless. There are daily call sheets, weekly budget summaries, revised shooting schedules, lab reports, and work orders. An example of a Summary of Production Costs is shown in Figure 2.6. The producer must supervise a staff of assistants and secretaries who are able to organize and maintain production records and quickly respond to daily production needs. Long-term evaluations focus on applications to future projects.

Casting

The producer often works in consort with the director in casting the major talent for a specific production. Many variables must be considered before casting decisions are made. Selections from the available talent pool are sometimes suggested by individual agents, but actors are finally selected and tested at **auditions**, in which they read segments of the script in the presence of the director, the producer, and sometimes the casting director. The actor's appearance, voice quality, talent, and salary have to be carefully considered. Sometimes an inexperienced actor or "real" person from the actual locale will offer a more authentic portrayal than a professional actor. Producers often consider the "box-office appeal" (theatrical film popularity) or "TVQ" (television quotient, an index of popularity based on the star's fame and popularity which is used by television networks) of specific star performers, as a means of justifying the added expense of acquiring proven talent. Directors are often more concerned about aesthetic values, such as whether or not a particular actor or individual is perfectly right or natural for the role, than is the producer, who also worries about salaries and "box-office" appeal. The producer is often the funding source's sole

PRODUCTION #: TITLE:					DATE:
PRODUCER:			DIRECTOR:		
CLASSIFICATION	BUDGET	COST TO DATE	ESTIMATED COST TO COMPLETE	ESTIMATED TOTAL COST	OVER OR UNDER BUDGET
Supervision					
Story,Script,Mimeo					
Music					
Direction					
Cast and Extras					
Production					
Camera					
Sound/Recording					
Grips					
Electrical					
Property Labor					
Special Effects					
Wardrobe					
Make-up					
Video/Film Editor					
Set Construction					
Transportation					
Location Videotape/Film & Laboratory					
Titles					
Projection					

Figure 2.6 Summary of Production Costs Form

representative during production and must therefore consider many financial, as well as aesthetic, factors.

Producers on Small-Scale Productions

Staff producers in small corporate, governmental, educational, and local cable television production units function much the same way as other producers. Their budgets may be smaller and the people they work with are fewer in number, but the same basic skills are required.

To illustrate the fact that all producers perform essentially the same role, let us consider a student production made in an academic setting. A student who is producing an assigned project for a grade must obtain funding for the project, either by earning the money, negotiating with parents, or finding a sponsor who can use the finished product. The student producer must procure the necessary equipment, supplies, and personnel to make the best possible film or video project with limited resources. Scheduling the production and acquiring talent within an academic environment is often extremely difficult, since students have different class schedules and responsibilities. Once the actual shooting is scheduled, the weather may not cooperate and the shoot may have to be rescheduled. Perhaps special costumes or props are needed, and the student must undertake delicate negotiations with the drama department or the head of buildings and grounds on campus. If the work is to be publicly screened or used on a local cable channel, the producer must be sure to pay all copyright fees for prerecorded music or commission original music from a friend in the music department. Release forms should be obtained from people who appear in a work that will be publicly exhibited. Finally, when the project is finished, the student must evaluate feedback from a number of people, including an instructor's unexpectedly high or low grade.

The producer, then, has to be an effective supervisor of people, an administrator, a salesman, a sensitive but objective critic, and above all a good fund-raiser and money manager. These diverse skills, which combine business acumen and organizational ability with creativity and sensitivity to people are not plentiful in the profession, nor are they easily ac-

quired. Good producers should be recognized for their unique value to both the artistic and the business sides of the production process.

Summary

Producers plan, organize, and supervise the production process from the initial idea to its eventual distribution and exhibition. There are four different types of producers: staff producers, independent producers, executive producers, and "producer hyphenates." Producers provide an important link between investors and creative talent.

Producers adopt conscious production strategies to turn creative ideas into marketable concepts. A production strategy involves at least three steps: defining the goals and objectives of the project; assessing the potential audience; and researching the topic. Producers must also estimate the production budget and make a proposal to a potential source of funding, during a face-to-face presentation of the project's ideas and goals.

Production management involves breaking the script down into its component parts so that the project can be shot cost effectively out of continuity. Script breakdown sheets also aid in the preparation of a budget and the scheduling of production facilities and personnel.

Production team interaction can be structured in two different ways: hierarchically or cooperatively. Few actual production situations are organized exclusively according to just one of these models.

Effective producers possess a variety of supervisory skills, from the ability to manage people and resolve disputes, to strong organizational skills, which facilitate the flow and recording of information as well as budgetary decisions. Together with the director, the producer becomes involved in casting decisions. The producer is frequently the sponsor's or investor's sole representative during actual production.

The role of the producer is essentially the same in high-level and low-level production situations. The budgets may be smaller, and fewer numbers of people may have to be supervised and managed, but the requisite skills are essentially the same for both levels of producing and production management.

Additional Readings

Adams, William B. *Handbook of Motion Picture Production*. New York: John Wiley, 1977.

Barnouw, Erik. *The Sponsor*. New York: Oxford University Press, 1978.

Bluem, A. William, and Jason Squire, eds. *The Movie Business*. New York: Hastings House, 1972.

Curran, Trisha. *Financing Your Film: A Guide for Independent Filmmakers and Producers*. New York: Praeger, 1986.

Gayeski, Diane M. *Corporate and Industrial Video*. Englewood Cliffs, NJ: Prentice-Hall, 1983.

Gitlin, Todd. *Inside Prime Time*. New York: Pantheon Books, 1984.

Jowett, Garth, and James M. Lonton. *Movies as Mass Communication*. Beverly Hills: Sage Publications, 1980.

Kindem, Gorham, ed. *The American Movie Industry: The Business of Motion Pictures*. Carbondale, IL: Southern Illinois University Press, 1982.

Klein, Walter J. *The Sponsored Film*. New York: Hastings House, 1976.

Lees, David, and Stan Berkowitz. *The Movie Business*. New York: Vintage, 1978.

Owen, Bruce M., Jack H. Beebe, and Willard G. Manning. *Television Economics*. Lexington, MA: Lexington Books, 1974.

Pryluck, Calvin. "Ultimately We Are All Outsiders: The Ethics of Documentary Filming." *Journal of Film And Video* 28 no.1 (Winter 1976): 21–29.

Shanks, Bob. *The Cool Fire: How to Make it in Television*. New York: Vintage, 1977.

Singleton, Ralph S. *Film Scheduling/Film Budgeting*. Beverly Hills, Calif.: Lone Eagle Publishing, 1986.

Exercises

1. Perform a script breakdown of a segment from a published feature-length film script or a television script. Fill out a script breakdown sheet, and determine the overall production scheduling time and budget that would be required to record this segment. Then figure the most efficient shooting sequence in terms of the utilization of the most expensive personnel and equipment.

2. Compose a cover letter, preliminary project proposal (described in chapter 3), and budget for a short documentary concerned with consumer or interest-group advocacy on one of the following issues: air/water pollution, disposal of nuclear/chemical waste, forest fire prevention, preservation of small family farms, or hunger and poverty. Tailor your proposal to the most likely funding sources, specifying who they are and what benefit the project would be to them. Indicate where, how, and to whom the finished product would be shown.

CHAPTER 3

Basic Scriptwriting: Fiction

Scriptwriting can be divided into two basic categories: fiction and nonfiction. Most feature-length films, television series, miniseries, serials, and made-for-TV movies are works of fiction, and most documentaries, news programs, commercials, educational and corporate productions are basically nonfiction. Fiction scripts generally present stories that are imaginatively invented by the scriptwriter. Nonfiction scripts often convey information about actual events.

The line separating fiction from nonfiction is not always clear and distinct, however. Many projects fall into a gray area between the two. Some works of fiction, such as historical dramas and docudramas, are based on actual historical events. Some works of nonfiction, such as certain ''news'' magazines and talk shows, are presented as entertainment with little information value. Many documentaries are presented as entertaining feature-length movies at theaters.

Every scriptwriter should be familiar with basic elements of fiction *and* nonfiction writing. Principles of dramatic structure are also applicable to the development of entertainment value and audience interest in a documentary or news story. Principles of rhetoric and persuasion used in documentaries and commercials are often helpful in terms of structuring a message about a social problem in a made-for-TV movie.

Distinctions between fiction and nonfiction persist within many media institutions. Newswriters rarely write feature film scripts. The news division of a television station or network is usually administratively separate from the entertainment division. Fiction scripts usually conform to the full-page script format, while nonfiction scriptwriters often use a split-page format. But some institutional overlap exists, such as the production of documentaries about the space program and dramatic miniseries (''Roots'') by a single producer and production company, David L. Wolper.

This chapter provides an introduction to visual thinking and a sequential overview of the scripwriting process. It also examines some of the ways that fictional scripts can be effectively organized. The focus is on elements of dramatic and narrative structure, which are of practical value to scriptwriters working in a variety of areas and formats. The succeeding chapter will focus on the writing of nonfictional scripts.

VISUAL THINKING

A script guides the production of a television program or film and can be compared to an architectural drawing or blueprint. It provides a preliminary sketch or outline for a project that is to be constructed and given concrete form. Just as an architect must be knowledgeable about building construction methods and materials, a scriptwriter must understand the entire production process. Scriptwriting cannot be completely divorced from all the other preproduction, production, and postproduction activities discussed in this book.

A script orients the director and other key members of the creative staff to the story or topic. Economy of expression is one of the hallmarks of scriptwriting. Every setting, prop, or character in a fictional story, for example, can only be briefly described. Their presence in the script indicates that they are essential and integral parts of the story rather than peripheral details.

Unlike a novelist or short story writer, a scriptwriter rarely writes long passages describing the setting or a character's state of mind and feelings. Television and film are temporal and visual media. A scriptwriter often depicts a setting and defines characters in the midst of movements and actions that propel the story forward. Character is usually defined by actions, reactions, and dialogue as well as the characters' thoughts and ideas. The emotional texture of settings, objects, and actions is presented in terms of concrete sounds and visual images, which can only allude to a more abstract or symbolic world of thoughts and ideas. Unlike printed words, recorded sounds and images are not abstract and general. They are concrete and specific. A recorded sound or image does not speak in terms of "people" or "screams" in general, but of this specific person and this specific scream.

Unlike a playwright, a scriptwriter does not need to rely exclusively or even primarily on dialogue and a few settings to tell a story. A scriptwriter can use a variety of settings to reflect different moods, atmospheres, and aspects of a character, as well as different times and places. A stage play, on the other hand, is usually restricted to just a few settings, all of which must be set up quickly between scenes or acts. A film or television program can depict many existing settings around the world or reconstruct them in a studio. Dialogue can be substantial, as in the film *My Dinner With Andre* (1981), or it can be practically nonexistent, as in *Occurrence at Owl Creek Bridge* (1964).

One of the skills that scriptwriters must develop is **visual thinking**. To think visually means to utilize the unique creative potential of recorded moving images and sounds. Images and sounds occur in time as well as space. Film and video are different from other media, such as print, drama, painting, still photography, and music. Print media, such as novels and newspapers, deal primarily with words and still pictures. Words are abstract and general, not concrete and specific. Still pictures lack movement and action. Staged dramas present specific images and sounds, but the sounds and images cannot be manipulated in time and space. Space and time are necessarily continuous in a drama, although there may be significant changes in time and place between scenes or acts. The spectator stays relatively stationary and does not move in relation to the action as a camera does. Paintings and still photographs are certainly visual media, but they lack both temporal dimension and sound. Music is a temporal art, but it does not deal with visual space. Film and video recordings of each of these art forms can be incorporated into a specific production, but film and video constitute a distinctly different art form and medium of expression.

A scriptwriter is not the same as a reporter, a novelist, a playwright, or a composer. A scriptwriter crafts a story specifically for film or video recording. This requires visual thinking. A script facilitates the recording of specific moving images and sounds and is based on a firm understanding of the production process. By reading the production and postproduction sections of this book, especially those chapters which focus on the aesthetics of recording and editing sounds and images, a beginning scriptwriter can acquire some understanding of the creative potential of moving images and sounds, or visual thinking. Quality scriptwriting demands a firm grasp of production aesthetics.

PREPARATION FOR SCRIPTWRITING

The scriptwriting process has several distinct stages, beginning with the writing of a proposal. A script proposal is a short description of basic story lines, themes, topics, and messages; it is used to obtain financial support for a project. Before the actual scriptwriting begins considerable research must be carried out. Research provides insurance against implausible stories and is also a source of inspiration and creative ideas. Several story outlines may be drafted after the research phase before a treatment is prepared. A treatment is a plot synopsis in short-story form, which is much more fully developed than a proposal and serves primarily as a guide or outline for the writing of a complete script. The next stage in the scriptwriting process is the writing of the script itself. A script may go through several drafts and involve the participation of several writers before it is complete and production can begin. The final stage is the preparation of a shooting script, which indicates all camera placements, transition devices, and various types of effects. This is usually done by the director.

Proposals

A **proposal** is necessary in order to obtain financial support for a project. In consists of a short description of plot lines, characters, and situations or documentary subject matter. It graphically communicates the approach to a topic. It implicitly answers a funding source's questions about why he or she should invest in this project rather than another. The proposal must generate interest and excitement. It must force a corporate, executive, or another funding source to sit back and take notice and then request a face-to-face or telephone presentation. The proposal must contain sufficient information to arouse interest, but it must also be concise. A long proposal is unlikely to be read in its entirety. A short, but effective, proposal will stimulate reader interest and is more likely to lead to a personal presentation.

There are two basic types of proposals, commercial and noncommercial. In a proposal for a commercial project, several or all of the following factors should be implicitly or explicitly stated: how the topic fits into popular trends and capitalizes on previously successful films or television programs; the universality and wide appeal of the subject matter or theme; and any special ways in which the project might be advertised and marketed. These statements of marketability are usually interwoven with the plot summary or synopsis.

Packaging the most marketable or serviceable ingredients in the proposal can be as important as actual content. How the information in the proposal is presented—its style—is often just as important as exactly what is said or its content. The proposal must be highly readable, entertaining, and concise. A poorly organized, carelessly written proposal is unlikely to be taken seriously.

If the proposal is for a project that is not a commercial venture, it will be structured somewhat differently. Rather than highlighting its commercial appeal, the proposal will focus on those factors that give the project significance and make it unique. The general topic may be particularly pressing, as in the case of a contemporary social problem, such as race relations or the growing number of homeless in our cities. An artistic work may exhibit unique qualities which are nonetheless of interest to a general audience or to some particular audience for which it is intended. Rather than arguing that the prior success of similar ventures guarantees a measure of success, as might be the case for a commercial project, the noncommercial project proposal will highlight what is unique about a project and what distinguishes it from all other films and television programs that cover the same topic or fit into the same general category.

Writing a proposal that generates interest and outlines the basic subject matter requires imagination, a thorough knowledge of the production process, and an understanding of the funding source's expectations. Do not underestimate the value of personal contact in this process, either your own personal contact with a producer or an agent's. Try to personalize a proposal and tailor any cover letter to the expectations of the person to whom you are applying, but do so in a professional manner. Always follow up with some form of personal contact. The best written proposal may never receive funding if it is not followed up with a personal, face-to-face interview with the funding source.

Research

The second stage of scriptwriting is the research phase. Every aspect of the topic should be carefully and thoroughly researched before the script is written. Whether the project is to be primarily entertaining, informative, or persuasive, its overall quality directly depends on the quality of research that has gone into the development of the script. The more care-

fully documented the information contained in a script is, the more realistic, authentic, accurate, and responsible the finished product will seem to be.

Careful research is both a form of insurance and a source of inspiration. Carefully documenting sources of information can protect a producer from legal prosecution. Newswriters, for example, have an obligation to research their stories carefully. It is often necessary to find hard evidence from reliable sources in order to support a basic statement or argument. For example, when a CBS news documentary about General William Westmoreland suggested that Westmoreland knew much more about North Vietnamese troup strength during the Vietnam War than he reported to the President and the American people, its findings were openly disputed by the General himself, who sued the network and the producer of the program. Westmoreland suggested that the producer had access to and had, in fact, recorded testimony and information which clearly contradicted the central thesis of the program, but it was eliminated from the program. Similar charges concerning other people and issues have been made against CBS News', "60 Minutes" and other programs. Westmoreland's suit suggests that it is important for researchers to obtain reliable information, which is corroborated by a number of sources, in order to back up a story. It also raises a number of ethical questions about evidence gathering, producer bias, and editing discretion.

Thorough investigation of a subject frequently leads to the revelation of information that stimulates the creative process and challenges and excites the viewer. Research is a creative process of uncovering new sources of information. A project researcher begins by acquiring a general background in the area on which the project will focus. He or she collects as many books and articles as possible dealing with the general topic area and reads those that seem most helpful and pertinent to the specific issues at hand. Armed with this general knowledge, the researcher progresses by focusing more narrowly on specific problems and concerns. General understanding of the topic stimulates the creation of insightful questions that can be raised during interviews with an expert or a participant in the events. The more knowledgeable a writer or researcher becomes, the more information he or she will elicit from additional sources of information. Like a good detective, a writer learns that one piece of evidence leads to the discovery of another.

Production research is either journalistic or novelistic in approach. A fiction writer or novelist conducts research in order to find details that stimulate reader interest and authenticate events and settings. A fictional film or television program is often researched in this manner. Strict authenticity is sometimes sacrificed for dramatic interest and action. Consider the tremendous amount of research that went into two different novels, Alex Hailey's *Roots* and James Michener's *Space*. Both were adapted to television as mini-series. In both cases some of the research on which the novels were based got lost during the adaptation process, such as that concerning Kunta Kinta's family and village life in The Gambia or the technical and scientific aspects of space exploration. Both miniseries focused primarily on melodramatic emotions and romantic relationships between characters, which was deemed necessary to attract a wide, diverse audience. Nonetheless, the fact that the novels were originally based on careful research gave them more power and value than they might otherwise have had.

The well-publicized (yet unsuccessful) suit brought about by General William Westmoreland against CBS's "60 Minutes" and its producer, points out the obligation that newswriters have to research topics thoroughly.

Treatments

A **treatment** (Figure 3.1) is an important step in the development of a fictional screenplay. Always written in the third person, present tense, it provides a narrative summary of the basic story lines. A treatment visualizes the story as it will unfold on the screen and gives a play-by-play of all major actions and scenes in reduced form. A writer composes a treatment so that he or she can receive a commission to write the script. When a producer initiates a project, the treatment is sometimes preceded by a proposal. The producer then requests a treatment and a script. A writer often initiates a project with a treatment.

Every good treatment begins with the writing of a simple idea or concept, called a **premise**. A premise is a "what if" statement, which describes the basic story idea. For example, "what if" Romeo and Juliet sang and danced and were caught between rival gangs and ethnic groups in New York? This is the basic premise of *West Side Story* (1961). "What if" Romeo

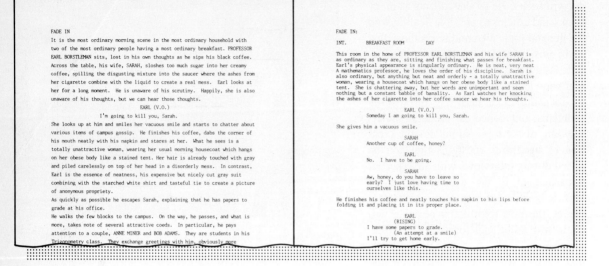

FADE IN

It is the most ordinary morning scene in the most ordinary household with
two of the most ordinary people having a most ordinary breakfast. PROFESSOR
EARL BORSTLEMAN sits, lost in his own thoughts as he sips his black coffee.
Across the table, his wife, SARAH, sloshes too much sugar into her creamy
coffee, spilling the disgusting mixture into the saucer where the ashes from
her cigarette combine with the liquid to create a real mess. Earl looks at
her for a long moment. He is unaware of his scrutiny. Happily, she is also
unaware of his thoughts, but we can hear those thoughts.

          EARL (V.O.)
      I'm going to kill you, Sarah.

She looks up at him and smiles her vacuous smile and starts to chatter about
various items of campus gossip. He finishes his coffee, dabs the corner of
his mouth neatly with his napkin and stares at her. What he sees is a
totally unattractive woman, wearing her usual morning housecoat which hangs
on her obese body like a stained tent. Her hair is already touched with gray
and piled carelessly on top of her head in a disorderly mess. In contrast,
Earl is the essence of neatness, his expensive but nicely cut gray suit
combining with the starched white shirt and tasteful tie to create a picture
of anonymous propriety.

As quickly as possible he escapes Sarah, explaining that he has papers to
grade at his office.

He walks the few blocks to the campus. On the way, he passes, and what is
more, takes note of several attractive coeds. In particular, he pays
attention to a couple, ANNE MINER and BOB ADAMS. They are students in his
Trigonometry class. They exchange greetings with him, obviously more

---

FADE IN:

INT.   BREAKFAST ROOM   DAY

This room in the home of PROFESSOR EARL BORSTLEMAN and his wife SARAH is
as ordinary as they are, sitting and finishing what passes for breakfast.
Earl's physical appearance is singularly ordinary. He is neat, very neat
A mathematics professor, he loves the order of his discipline. Sarah is
also ordinary, but anything but neat and orderly - a totally unattractive
woman, wearing a housecoat which hangs on her obese body like a stained
tent. She is chattering away, but her words are unimportant and seem
nothing but a constant babble of banality. As Earl watches her knocking
the ashes of her cigarette into her coffee saucer we hear his thoughts.

          EARL (V.O.)
      Someday I am going to kill you, Sarah.

She gives him a vacuous smile.

          SARAH
      Another cup of coffee, honey?

          EARL
      No. I have to be going.

          SARAH
      Aw, honey, do you have to leave so
      early? I just love having time to
      ourselves like this.

He finishes his coffee and neatly touches his napkin to his lips before
folding it and placing it in its proper place.

          EARL
        (RISING)
      I have some papers to grade.
        (An attempt at a smile)
      I'll try to get home early.

Figure 3.1
An Example of a
Treatment and the
Accompanying
Script.

and Juliet were involved with drugs in Central Park? *The Panic in Needle Park* (1971) operates on the basis of this simple premise. A good treatment is always based on a simple, but interesting concept.

The next step in the writing of a treatment is to compose a **synopsis**, which is a short paragraph or précis that describes the basic story line: "Tony and Maria fall in love but because they are associated with rival gangs, the Sharks and the Jets, there are many obstacles placed in the path of their love. After Maria's brother is accidently killed by Tony in a fight, their relationship is filled with suffering and frustration." On the basis of this synopsis of *West Side Story* an outline could be written, developing the major plot lines and characters in the story. This outline also defines all major actions and character reactions. Usually several outlines are written and revised before the treatment is created.

The major portion of the treatment is devoted to a highly visual, but concise, narrative presentation of characters and events. Some examples of dialogue spoken by characters are usually included, and the treatment adopts a short story format. A good treatment adopts a lively prose style that dramatizes the basic premise and effectively communicates the tone and flavor of a piece. Camera directions and shot descriptions are used very sparingly. Graphic images are conveyed by highly visual nouns or adjectives and action verbs. A treatment is not a legal document fashioned with dry regularity and precision. It must excite and interest the producer and serve as a thorough and helpful guide for the writing of a script or screenplay. A treatment provides some protection against future writing problems by forcing the writer to resolve many difficulties prior to actual scriptwriting.

How long should a treatment be? A treatment for a feature-length film screenplay, which will run about two hours, usually has about 20 to 70 double-spaced, typewritten pages. The finished screenplay will be close to 120 pages, since each page of a screenplay usually translates into about one minute of actual screen time. A treatment for a work of short fiction should probably be from 5 to 10 pages in length. It is always preferable to err on the side of brevity, since verbose, overwritten treatments are not likely to be read with interest and enthusiasm.

SCRIPTWRITING FORMATS

After the preliminary stages of scriptwriting have been completed, a writer or group of writers begins to write a full script. The script conforms to one of the following formats: split-page, full-page, or a semi-scripted format, such as a script outline. Scriptwriters rely on a basic set of terms as well as these common formats for accurate communication with the creative staff and the director in particular. A discussion of the standard scriptwriting formats is presented below.

Split-Page and Full-Page Script Formats

Two common scriptwriting formats are split page and full page. In a **split-page script**, the visual information appears in one column of a sheet of paper and the audio information in the other column. (See Figure 3.2.) The split-page script is often used for commercials and multiple-camera nonfiction production. The dialogue and narration are written out fully on the audio side of the page. Visual images are indicated on the opposite side of the page. The latter are often described quite sparingly, leaving wide margins, so that the director or assistant director can make copious notes about specific cameras and shots in these blank areas. Each revision of the script is dated, to ensure that all

```
SHORT TV DOCUMENTARY: PERSONALITY
SUBJECT: ENOS SLAUGHTER (BASEBALL PLAYER)
WRITTEN & PRODUCED BY PAMA MITCHELL FOR UNC CENTER FOR PUBLIC TELEVISION: AUGUST,
1982

          VIDEO                          AUDIO
                                               MITCHELL (VOICE OVER NARRATION)
SLAUGHTER ON TRACTOR (:17)   Ever since 1937, when he played in the minors, they've
  (VARIOUS SHOTS)
                              called him "Country."  Born and raised on a farm

                              outside Roxboro, Enos Slaughter returned here after

                              more than 20 years as a major

                              league star.

MORE SHOTS, ENOS                        SLAUGHTER (VOICE OVER NARRATION)
  ON FARM          (:13)     I enjoy getting out on my tractor...

                              breathing that fresh country air before somebody

                              else does.             SLAUGHTER
CU, SLAUGHTER        (:11)    I've just always enjoyed the countryside...

                              ... stay here until I pass on.

B-ROLL: TROPHIES,                       MITCHELL (VOICE OVER NARRATION)
PHOTOS, MEMENTOES
IN HIS LIVING     (:25)      As much as he loves the countryside, Enos Slaughter
ROOM AND DEN
                              loves the game of baseball.  Now divorced from his

                              fifth wife, Slaughter lives alone amid the mementoes

                              of a illustrious career...from the oil painting

                              that hangs prominently in his living room...to

                              the plaques and trophies that fill his den.
MONTAGE: BLACK &                        MITCHELL (VOICE OVER NARRATION)
WHITE FOOTAGE OF
SLAUGHTER AS      (:36)      He rose quickly through the minors, and played on
PLAYER
                              the "Miracle Cardinals" of 1942, a team that captured

                              the pennant with a late season surge and upset the

                              heavily favored Yankees in the World Series, four

                              games to one.  Slaughter's aggressiveness and "hustle"

                              helped the young Cardinals hand the Bronx Bombers

                              their first World Series loss since 1926.
```

Figure 3.2 Example of a Split-Page Script

performers, creative staff, and crew members are using identical copies of the script during production. In scripts for live television news, visual cues and segment durations are written in full uppercase letters in the visual column, and any information in the script that should *not* be read on-air is circled.

The obvious advantage of the split-page format is that visual and audio elements can be directly compared and coordinated. An empty column suggests that one aspect is being focused on to the exclusion of the other. A rough equality in terms of space devoted to these two tracks or creative elements ensures that both will be fully utilized in the completed project.

The **full-page script** format is frequently used in single-camera film and video production and in multiple-camera production of fiction programs, such as television situation comedies. Unlike the split-page format, the full page is devoted to both visuals and audio. (See Figure 3.3 for an example of a full-page script.) The script is organized into scenes, which are numbered in consecutive order. The location and time of day of each scene are specified. Actions and camera movements are described in full paragraphs. Because a full-page script is organized by scenes, it is easy to reorganize it so that all the scenes requiring a single set or location can be shot consecutively. As we have seen, shooting all the scenes at a specific location at one time is usually more efficient and cost effective than recording the scenes in chronological order.

The writer's full-page script can call for specific shots, but it is much more common for the director to select and indicate specific shots during the preparation of the final shooting script immediately prior to production. Shot descriptions usually specify camera-to-subject distance, angle of view, and/or camera movement. Camera shots, angles, movements, transition devices, times of day, interior and exterior settings, specific character names, and sound effects are generally typed in uppercase letters, while actions and events as well as dialogue are usually in lowercase letters. Dialogue to be spoken by a specific character normally has that character's name listed in the middle of the page immediately above his or her lines of dialogue, which are slightly indented from the paragraph descriptions of actions and camera movements. The information highlighted in uppercase letters is emphasized for the convenience of the producer or production manager, who will break down the script into its component parts for scheduling and budgeting.

Semi-Scripted Formats

Many types of nonfiction television programs and films do not need to be fully scripted in advance of production. A news program, talk show, game show, or even a documentary film or videotape may only be partially or **semi-scripted**. A semi-scripted format may consist of a simple **rundown sheet**, which is a basic outline

**Figure 3.3
Example of a Full-
Page Script**

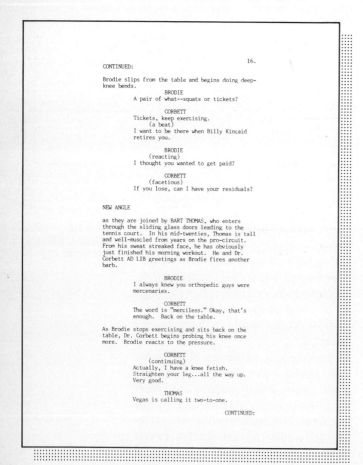

```
CONTINUED:                                    16.

Brodie slips from the table and begins doing deep-
knee bends.
                    BRODIE
          A pair of what--squats or tickets?
                    CORBETT
          Tickets, keep exercising.
               (a beat)
          I want to be there when Billy Kincaid
          retires you.
                    BRODIE
               (reacting)
          I thought you wanted to get paid?
                    CORBETT
               (facetious)
          If you lose, can I have your residuals?

NEW ANGLE

as they are joined by BART THOMAS, who enters
through the sliding glass doors leading to the
tennis court.  In his mid-twenties, Thomas is tall
and well-muscled from years on the pro-circuit.
From his sweat streaked face, he has obviously
just finished his morning workout.  He and Dr.
Corbett AD LIB greetings as Brodie fires another
barb.
                    BRODIE
          I always knew you orthopedic guys were
          mercenaries.
                    CORBETT
          The word is "merciless." Okay, that's
          enough.  Back on the table.

As Brodie stops exercising and sits back on the
table, Dr. Corbett begins probing his knee once
more.  Brodie reacts to the pressure.
                    CORBETT
               (continuing)
          Actually, I have a knee fetish.
          Straighten your leg...all the way up.
          Very good.
                    THOMAS
          Vegas is calling it two-to-one.

                              CONTINUED:
```

of the show from beginning to end, indicating what material or performer is needed at specific times. It is organized on the basis of the running time of each segment and of the entire program. Different electronic sources of material, such as remote feeds and VTR playbacks, are also specified.

A **script outline** is another semiscripted format. Portions of a script outline may be fully scripted, such as the opening or closing segments of a news, talk, or game show, which remain the same from show to show. Other elements are simply outlined in rough form, either because they must be ad-libbed during recording or because the exact information to be read may not in fact be available until just prior to air or recording time. Documentary, news, and sports and talk show directors often use a script outline, as it is difficult to precisely script live or uncontrolled events. The questions to be asked during an interview show can be written down in advance, but the answers cannot, unless the interview is staged. A director or camera operator must be able to respond instantly to unpredictable events as they happen. The actual selection of shots to be used may be delayed to later stages of production, such as postproduction editing. Only the general type of shot or action may be specified in a script outline.

STRUCTURE IN FICTION

A drama is a causally-linked series of actions performed by actors. A narrative is a causally-linked chain of events, which is told or narrated by someone. Fiction scriptwriting has the potential to combine certain elements of drama and narrative structure. While we frequently use the term "drama" when referring to a play performed on the stage and the term "narrative" when we are talking about a novel or a short story, we can also apply these terms to scriptwriting.

Types of Drama

Classical Drama   Classical drama, such as that found in most Hollywood and Western European films and television programs, conforms to many of the philosopher Aristotle's conceptions about drama. He established a basic theory of audience identification with a central character, known as catharsis theory. Classical tragedy, Aristotle said, was characterized by **catharsis**, that is, by an emotional learning process, a sort of purification or cleansing of the emotions. The audience's empathy for the hero causes it to learn a serious lesson about life and have a cathartic experience in sympathy with that hero. In the process we and the hero acquire a new understanding of ourselves and our world.

An emphasis on identification with individual heroes is characteristic of many Hollywood films and much European and American drama. Western art and drama tend to concentrate on individual psychological, as opposed to the broader social and economic, causes of basic events and conflicts. There is usually an emphasis on plot and action and a respect for basic unities of place and time, where time is relatively continuous and events are logically linked through causes and effects. Dramatic structure is unified and problems and conflicts are usually resolved at the end of a film or television program.

The dramatic structure of conventional Hollywood films and television programs is based on realist aesthetics. Art imitates life by following unities of place and time, which are generally continuous, as they are in everyday experience. Hollywood films and television programs follow Aristotle's realist ideas in terms of dramatic structure quite closely. They are designed to promote emotional identification with specific characters and to preserve an illusion of reality through continuity in time and space. Classical Hollywood films and television programs are structured on the basis of character motivations and goals, which propel the drama through a logical cause and effect structure. Individual characters are agents of action, who are motivated to pursue someone or something. Characters come into conflict with one another on the basis of conflicting motivations. These conflicts are usually fully resolved at the end of the drama.

Epic Drama   Another type of drama, **epic drama**, is rooted in twentieth-century critical thought about social and economic conditions. It should not be confused with other uses of the term ''epic,'' including references to extended narrative poems, such as the Greek poet Homer's ''Iliad'' and ''Odyssey,'' or the grandeur and sweep of broad historical events in films such as David Lean's *Lawrence of Arabia* (1962). Epic drama, such as that espoused and practiced earlier in this century by Bertolt Brecht, an East German dramatist, and Sergei Eisenstein, a Soviet filmmaker, substitutes a group or mass hero for an individual hero and examines the social and economic determinants of their problems rather than individual characters' purely psychological motivations.

Reacting against Western individualism and classical Western models of dramatic tragedy since Aristotle, Brecht and other socialist dramatists have attempted to establish an alternative approach to dramatic structure. Instead of consistently encouraging identification with individuals and consequent emotional catharsis, they encourage a distance and emotional separation between the audience and the major characters so that the audience will focus on social, economic, and political issues rather than individual problems. This approach to drama is more evident in Eastern European and Third World films and television programs than in their Western European and American counterparts. Instead of presenting the fictional world as naturally ordered and unified, epic drama opens up a world of contradictions and ambiguities. Collective action is emphasized instead of individual psychological motivations and many conflicts and contradictions remain unresolved at the end.

Realism is one among several approaches to dramatic structure. Epic drama breaks down conventional notions of realism, and calls attention to many of the artificialities inherent in classical drama. Conflicts are rarely fully resolved. Social contradictions persist and ambiguity is maintained throughout.

Many other alternatives to classical Hollywood realism in terms of dramatic structure have been widely practiced. Western European art films generally adopt a much slower pace than Hollywood films and television programs. They place less emphasis on action and focus on character development instead. A story's presentation and resolution in an ''art'' film (sometimes called a ''modernist'' work of art) is often more ambiguous and less complete than that of a Hollywood product. South American and African (Third World) films and television programs offer alternative dramatic structures as well, often borrowing from both Eastern or

Western European (Italian neorealism, for example) dramatic styles, as well as native artistic traditions, such as oral folk tradition in the West African films of Ousmane Sembene.

It is important to keep these alternatives in mind as you read the following discussion of dramatic and narrative structure. While Hollywood conventions of realism in dramatic structure certainly dominate the world's screens, they are not the only ways to tell stories. Their dominant position suggests that classical dramatic structure deserves serious attention as both an extremely influential style and a stimulant of aesthetic alternatives. The following discussion is basically classical in approach, but alternative approaches are also discussed where they seem relevant.

Star Wars (1977) was Part IV of an originally planned nine part series. So far, only this film and Part V, *The Empire Strikes Back* (1980) and Part VI, *Return of the Jedi* (1983) have been completed.

Dramatic Structure

Classical drama is sometimes called, "life with the dull moments taken out," but it is also a highly structured series of actions and conventions. Dramatic actions can be plotted into a structural framework that includes: (1) an *exposition* of characters, their goals, and their basic internal and external conflicts; (2) *complications* that arise as obstacles to the successful completion of a character's goals; (3) conflicts that build into specific *crises*; (4) a final *climax*; and (5) a *resolution* of the conflicting elements which led to the climax. This form of dramatic structure ensures that dramatic action builds in an exciting way toward a major conflict that must be resolved. A drama may have a long or short exposition, few or many complications and crises, but it almost always builds towards a climax, if it is to sustain interest and arouse excitement.

Exposition   Exposition refers to the establishment of a basic situation. The audience must be introduced to the major characters, the setting, and the basic goals and conflicts that will drive the action. An exposition may be quite long and detailed or extremely short. Longer expositions inhibit action and slow down the pace of the drama, but extensive character development may be necessary if the full impact of a conflict, problem, or situation is to be understood. In some cases the exposition of characters and settings may simply be revealed piecemeal during the heat of the action. A drama may begin in the middle of things (*en medias res* is the Greek term for this), as in the film *Star Wars* (1977) or Homer's epic poem, "The Iliad" or it can begin with a long, relatively slow-paced exposition as in the film *Heaven's Gate* (1980).

Conflict, Motivation, and the Point of Attack   A drama must arouse interest immediately. The point of attack for a drama, which is usually presented during the beginning moments, must be exciting and stimulate viewer interest. The point of attack is similar to a football kickoff, a basketball tipoff, or a hockey faceoff. It quickly initiates action and focuses attention on a basic conflict or character goal and motivation. The ability of a drama to excite the audience depends directly on the nature and significance of this dramatic conflict or character motivation. If the conflict or goal is a minor one, it is unlikely to sustain viewer interest for very long. An important conflict or goal can propel the action forward for a considerable period of time.

What kinds of conflicts and motivations arouse audience interest and excitement? Conflicts and goals can be purely external. They may simply involve certain actions among specific characters, such as a fight between two men over a woman. In the film *Citizen Kane* (1941), the story is propelled by a reporter's search for the meaning of ''Rosebud,'' the last words Kane uttered before he died. Conflicts and goals can be internalized in the mind of a character who cannot decide what course of action to pursue, such as whether to get married and have children immediately or to pursue a career. But even an internalized conflict must be externalized and graphically portrayed. It must be translated into concrete sounds and images. Internal thoughts can be presented through voice-over narration, but they should also be alluded to and developed through specific actions, images, and sounds. Some decisions are inconsequential. An internalized conflict concerning whether or not to make a peanut butter or a bologna sandwich is not likely to arouse much interest.

But a character who is trying to decide whether or not to commit suicide or murder is likely to stimulate an immediate emotional response in the audience.

It is not necessary to limit one's repertoire of dramatic conflicts to life-threatening situations, although much popular television drama operates precisely from this premise. There are an infinite number of possibilities for serious and exciting dramatic conflicts. A conflict may arise over a political or ideological issue, problems related to work or family, or a general social problem that affects the well-being of a group of people. The more significant the initial conflict is, the longer it can sustain dramatic tension and viewer interest. Presenting a substantial conflict initially as a point of attack gains immediate audience attention. The conflict must be deeply felt by the characters, if the drama to have a significant and long-lasting impact on viewers.

Complications   Once the basic situation is set and we understand the major characters and their motivations, goals, and conflicts, the dramatic action *builds* along a linear path as various *complications* are encountered. Complications are obstacles and new developments that stand in the way of achieving a goal or resolving a conflict. An actor may be struggling to become a star, but an accident or illness occurs, creating a complication to be overcome. A criminal chase may be complicated when the criminal assumes a different identity or a different mode of transportation. Complications create viewer interest. They add variety to a story. If the goals of a major character were attained without any complications, the drama and action would probably be unimaginative and uninteresting and result in a very short film or television program.

Crisis and Climax   Dramatic action that has progressed through several complications inevitably builds to a *crisis*. A drama may have several crises, in which the conflict that has stimulated the action intensifies to the point that something or someone is threatened. We all encounter crises in our lives, but drama removes most of the dull moments between these crises, so that character actions and emotions and viewer interest and involvement are intensified. The major character or characters may have to make an important decision. Perhaps it is a life and death situation. Should a risky surgical procedure be performed? Can a murderer be identified and sacrificed? Should a character choose between a lover or a spouse?

The dramatic action usually builds through several important crises that finally culminate in a major crisis or *climax*. A climax is the most decisive point of confrontation in a drama. It simply demands some form of resolution. One side must win or a compromise must be reached. The climax brings the major conflicting forces together so that they may be openly confronted and resolved. The climax is usually the highest, most intense emotional peak of the drama.

Resolution   Overcoming the basic conflict or fulfilling the goals and motivations which have stimulated the dramatic action is known as a *resolution*. The defeat of the antagonist, the death of the hero, the marriage of the loving couple, or the attainment of the major goal may each represent the culmination of the action. A resolution, like an exposition, is considered a falling action compared to the rising action of a crisis or climax. The resolution section of the drama considers the implications of the climactic actions and gives the audience time to contemplate what has just transpired before new actions are initiated or the drama ends. Emotionally, the audience may need sufficient time to recuperate from the emotional experience of the climax. A drama which ended immediately after the climax might leave some of the audience's expectations unfulfilled.

The resolution of a drama can be ambiguous or unambiguous. An ending can appear to resolve all major conflicts or allow the hero to achieve his or her major goals. In a mystery story the discovery of a secret can answer all questions. But an ending can also be ambiguous. Conflicts can persist and goals remain unachieved. Some dramatic forms have virtually no resolution at all. Soap operas rarely, if ever, reach any resolution. They consist of a series of crises. Any apparent solution, such as a marriage, is usually the source of another conflict. The absence of any resolution establishes a new convention which is unique to the open-ended, serial dramatic form. A closed dramatic form uses resolution to enforce a kind of **closure** at the end. The drama is essentially self-contained, although the dramatic action may continue in the form of a sequel.

Narrative Structure: Point of View and Time

In addition to having dramatic structure (the structure of action), scripts can also have narrative structure (the structure of time and point of view). A fictional work is usually narrated by someone and consists of a story told from a specific point of view or by a specific person. An omniscient or effaced (hidden) narrator tells the story but does not appear within it, while a dramatized narrator is a specific character who is also telling the story. The camera can assume the spatial position of a character within the film. We, the audience, may only know what that character knows at a specific time. An effaced narrator is a substitute for the scriptwriter and the director. They are the unseen people telling or presenting the story when no character takes responsibility for it. An effaced narrator selects what we will see and know and from what point of view (camera placement, etc.) actions will be seen.

Narrative point of view is an extremely important structural component. How something is presented is just as important as what is presented. If we experience a series of events through the eyes of a character as opposed to omnisciently through an effaced narrator, our experience of these events is quite different. Adopting the point of view of a minority character also makes a difference in terms of how actions, events, and their meanings are preceived. Imagine, for example, the presentation of the Battle of the Little Big Horn through the eyes of a Sioux warrior versus those of a U.S. Cavalryman. Arthur Penn's film, *Little Big Man* (1970), presents a shifting point of view on General Custer through the ambiguous cultural identity and affiliation of its main character/narrator. The adoption of a specific point of view colors and even distorts events in a particular way, and such a perspective must be carefully and thoughtfully selected.

Narrative stories occur in time. Time has two important narrative dimensions: the time or duration of the telling of the story and the historical time the story depicts. A narrative can shift historical time from past to present to future. A scene can be introduced by a narrator as past or future events, or we can surmise that the time has changed on the basis of visual cues, such as the aging of characters. The duration of the telling and the duration of historical time can be identical. This is called a dramatic scene, as in the theater. The time of the telling can also be condensed or expanded with respect to the historical duration of the story through editing. Time can even be distorted and completely illogical. Sometimes such distortion is attributed to a disoriented character.

A well-known short film called *An Occurrence at Owl Creek Bridge* (1964), based on the short story of the same name by Ambrose Bierce illustrates most major aspects of classical narrative structure. It tells the story of a Southerner during the Civil War who is about to be hanged from a bridge by Union soldiers. The story is generally presented from the victim's point of view. The victim dreams about his wife as he is about to be hanged, and the images intercut pleasant memories of the past with the present horror of imminent death as he watches the Union soldiers prepare for his execution. We are shown his memories of his wife as the victim narrates past historical time. Cutting back to his present predicament the camera often assumes his physical position within the setting at the bridge. Just when he seems about to die, the rope snaps and he falls into the river. Writer-director Robert Enrico expands historical time underwater. It takes the victim over three minutes of film time to free himself underwater from the ropes that bind him and swim to the surface. Enrico then condenses the time it takes him to swim away down the river, eluding the gunfire of the soldiers along the shore. But when he gets home and is about to embrace his wife, the scene cuts directly to his hanging at the bridge again. In retrospect, the escape scenes can be interpreted by the audience as a wish fulfillment of the victim's hope of escaping death, which is shattered by the reality of his death. The events of the escape have only occurred in the victim's mind. They

These two stills from *An Occurrence at Owl Creek Bridge* (1964) illustrate writer-director Robert Enrico's ability to shift dramatically and effectively historical time within a classical narrative structure.

have been narrated by the victim and exist as a dream outside of the normal ''present'' time of the dramatic scenes of the hanging.

:::::::::::::::::::::::

OTHER CONSIDERATIONS IN FICTION SCRIPTWRITING

:::::::::::::::::::::::

There are almost as many ways to initiate the writing of an original piece of fiction as there are works of fiction. Some writers begin with specific characters. Once they have these characters firmly in mind, they begin to imagine specific, exciting situations within which these people find themselves. Conflicts arise from interactions among characters who have different goals and values. Certain themes begin to emerge as the characters initiate or become involved in specific actions. This organic approach to fiction writing tries to ensure that actions and themes flow ''naturally'' out of ''real'' characters.

Another approach to writing fiction begins with a basic theme, idea, or message. In some ways it is more difficult to begin with the theme and then find three-dimensional characters who can initiate actions to reinforce the theme. There is a real danger that the theme will become overbearing. The opposite danger faced by the ''character-first'' approach is that the actions undertaken by certain characters will not be thematically significant or interesting.

A third way to initiate a fictional script has already been considered to some extent in this chapter, that is, to begin with the plot or story structure and then work in both directions: toward characters who can carry out those actions and the themes that those actions depict. In using this method, there is a danger that characters will simply become pawns to carry out actions and that themes will be tacked on from the outside.

Where a scriptwriter begins is probably less important than the full development of all three aspects of a story—namely plots, characters, *and* themes. Plot has already been considered in detail in our discussion of dramatic and narrative structure. Characterization and theme need further consideration.

Characterization

Developing strong, believable, and interesting characters is just as important as creating an exciting and complicated story. Complex characters give a story depth and a three-dimensional feeling. A character's values and beliefs lead to conflicts with other characters who hold opposing values. If these values are significant and strongly held, the entire fictional experience is enhanced.

Character can be revealed through two primary vehicles: actions and words. What characters do and say reveals in large part who they are. But actions and behavior are usually more important than dialogue. Characters should show us what they believe through their actions. The important thing for the writer to remember is that communication takes place through concrete sounds and images. A character is largely created through external appearances, actions, and speech. But the external surface of a character must reflect a complex internal value system and a set of abstract thoughts, beliefs, and feelings. An external surface that is not based on a solid psychological foundation lacks depth, understanding, and true artistic potential.

Characters can be roughly divided into three categories: central characters, principal characters, and secondary or incidental characters. The **central character** or characters figure prominently in a story. They are the primary sources of audience satisfaction, interest, and identification. The decisions they make and the actions they initiate propel the drama. Their values, beliefs, feelings, and goals determine to a great extent how meaningful and significant the entire drama will become.

The **principal characters** are usually friends or foils to the central character(s). They can offer support to the actions and thoughts of the central character or they can present significant obstacles to the attainment of his or her goals. In a longer drama there is usually sufficient time to give most or all of the principal characters sufficient depth so that their interactions with the central character become important and convincing.

Secondary and **incidental characters** may help create a situation that provokes a conflict, but they are contributors to rather than initiators of major actions. There is rarely time to fully develop all the minor characters in a drama into complex individuals. They have certain traits and mannerisms that distinguish them in a crowd and add spice to the drama, but these can easily deteriorate into stereotypes or clichés. Stereotyping secondary or incidental characters often runs the risk of stereotyping certain occupational or ethnic groups and minorities. Some reliance on character types (as opposed to stereotypes) ensures immediate audience recognition of the most important aspect of a character and contributes to the drama as a whole. What minor characters say about any major character helps to develop the latter's characterization. A good deal of information about the central character can be communicated to the audience through the words of secondary and incidental characters, sometimes reinforcing and sometimes contradicting the central character's own speech and actions.

Themes

A **theme** is basically a significant statement that a work of fiction makes or an important issue that it raises. Themes generally emanate from the values, beliefs, and goals of the central characters, but a general theme may be much broader and universal than the attitudes of any single character. The film *Citizen Kane* (1941) has several broad themes, for example. The portrayal of Kane's life focuses on such issues as the absence of love in his life and his pursuit of fame, fortune, and power. Symbols such as ''Rosebud'' suggest, perhaps, that the absence of a happy childhood or family or parental love and guidance can lead to an inability to love and a meaningless pursuit of money and power. This film also develops other themes concerning democracy, politics, and the press, including, perhaps, a criticism of American society and capitalism in general. Of course, not all films are so heavily thematic, but the greatness of this film is that it does not sacrifice characterization and dramatic structure in order to make meaningful statements. Important themes coexist with strong characters and a complex plot. The themes are not the sole interest of the story.

Adaptation

An **adaptation** is a relatively faithful translation of a play, history, biography, short story, or novel into a film or television program. The adaptor is usually very familiar with the original form of the work and makes every attempt to translate the work into a different medium with the basic story line virtually intact. A television or film script that is less faithful to the original is frequently said to be **based on** that source, while a work that uses the original written piece as a springboard for essentially new ideas is said to be **freely adapted** or simply **suggested by** the original.

Before an adaptation can commence, the rights to a published and/or copyrighted work must be secured. An original novel, short story, play, history, or biography may be protected by copyright for up to seventy-five years, and any television or film producer who attempts to adapt it, however freely, without paying for the right to do so can be held liable for damages to the value of that property.

The art of adaptation is quite complex. The adaptor must not only be intimately familiar with the original work but must also have a thorough understanding of how film and video differ aesthetically from other media. Adapting a novel to the screen inevitably involves removing or changing certain elements of the original. A lengthly novel may exceed the normal time restrictions of most media productions. The adaptor must decide which elements are crucial to the story, which will be the most dramatic, what scenes or portions of the plot can be eliminated entirely, and how others can be shortened. Sometimes characters can be combined, so that the ideas and values they espouse are not lost but simply condensed. Dialogue or action scenes may have to be added to dramatize information that was presented in the novel as pure description or thoughts. Written lines of dialogue must work well as *spoken* dialogue. They should not simply be dull renditions of descriptive exposition. Dialogue should not become so lengthy and informative that it substitutes for action. Whenever possible, action should be shown rather than described. The adaptor must understand the production problems and costs involved in creating a faithful adaptation of an original piece of writing. He or she must also understand the needs and expectations of the audience so that an effective, exciting, and interesting presentation of characters, actions, and themes will be created on the screen.

Program Length

Short Fiction   The number and types of dramatic narrative fiction are almost endless, but a basic separation can be made according to film or television program length or duration. For example, half-hour episodes in a television situation comedy series present the same set of characters in a slightly different situation each week. The relatively short duration of an individual episode encourages a formulaic approach.

A sit-com episode is usually organized into two acts with three scenes per act and a **tag** or epilogue after the last commercial to keep the audience tuned in and reinforce any message or theme. The opening of an episode must grab the attention of the audience to prevent them from switching channels. A major conflict or problem must be presented in the first five minutes (Act One, Scene One), prior to the first commercial break. The dramatic device that grabs the audience is called a **hook**. It often takes the form of a problem or conflict that excites the viewer and foreshadows events that occur later in the story. A specific object or idea introduced early in a drama, which becomes an important factor during the final resolution, is called a **plant**. Planting and **foreshadowing** are effective devices in terms of hooking the audience. The conflict builds through a series of complications or misunderstandings until the end of Act One, where a new complication is introduced. In Act Two things begin to get sorted out and the main conflict is resolved in Act Two, Scene Three. With the opening credits, closing tag, and commercials between scenes, a series episode writer only has about twenty minutes to quickly develop the basic conflict or situation, add a few complications, and then neatly resolve it. The structure of a situation comedy follows this basic formula, regardless of the exact setting and characters. There is a constant need for imagination and creativity within the format, which programs, such as ''The Cosby Show'' and ''Cheers'' have demonstrated week after week.

Other types of short fiction are not as formulaic as situation comedy, but they nonetheless demand tight dramatic structure. There simply isn't enough time to develop many minor characters or a complicated plot structure. A short drama usually has a short exposition section. New characters and situations must be developed very quickly and efficiently. A few lines of dialogue can establish who new characters are and their basic motivations. The plot must develop several complications to promote interest and variation, but it must also build toward a climax. Loose ends are quickly tied up and resolved.

Long Fiction   Television miniseries, theatrical films, made-for-TV movies, and hour-long episodes of TV series are long fiction. A television miniseries can last as long as twenty hours. A miniseries presents a continuing story in several sequential episodes, often aired during the same week, and provides an opportunity to adapt a relatively long novel, such as *Roots*, with little or no loss of character or

plot development. An average theatrical feature film is about two hours in duration. Only a few features run as long as three hours. Some are made as sequels, such as *Star Wars* (1977) and *The Empire Strikes Back* (1980) which are part of a multi-episode story with the same general characters or *Superman I,* (1978) *II,* (1980) and *III* (1983) and *Rocky 1* (1976), *II* (1979), *III* (1982), and *IV* (1985), which take some of the same characters forward or backward in time. But most movies are almost entirely self-contained products with a definite beginning and ending. Writers of most feature films and made-for-TV movies cannot depend on the audience's previous experience with the characters or basic situations. These must be carefully developed through more extensive dramatic exposition. Hour-long episodes in a television series have the advantage of a continuing set of characters, settings, and situations as well as a longer period of time for developing characters and resolving the major conflicts than is possible in a half-hour television series.

Long fiction introduces a more complicated plot structure, often with subplots or multiple plots. A **subplot** is a sequence of events involving secondary characters. The subplot often parallels the main plot in an hour television series episode. The parents' problems can be paralleled by similar problems involving their children, for example. Subplots and main plots often come together and are mutually resolved at the end of a drama. **Multiple plots** are different stories occurring among different characters at the same time. They may be linked thematically to the same issue or topic, but they do not always bring the different sets of characters together during the resolution. Multiple plots with different sets of characters must be carefully orchestrated and arranged so that they can be intercut with each other. Often some degree of recapitulation or redundancy, such as characters retelling the previous events in one of the plots after it has been interrupted for a time by another plot, is necessary. Foreshadowing and planting are just as important in long as in short fiction, but the slower pace permits more thorough development of characters, themes, plots, and settings.

Regardless of the length of the commercial television program, the basic strategy is the same: grab the audience's attention immediately and hold it for a sufficient period of time to hook the viewers for that episode of a series or miniseries or complete movie. Whether the writing is an original script or an adaptation, the scriptwriter must gain the attention of the television audience immediately and then hold it through the entire length of the program. The former demands a hook of some sort, and the latter requires a series of interesting complications and variations on more basic plot structures.

Summary

Scriptwriting demands visual thinking. Scriptwriters know how to use the full creative potential of moving images and sounds. They understand the differences between film/video and other media, such as literature, drama, painting, and music. Film and video recording and editing provide a unique treatment of time and space. Scriptwriting begins with a thorough understanding of the aesthetics of visual and sound recording and editing.

Scriptwriting occurs in distinct stages, from proposals and treatments to research, the writing and rewriting of a script, and the development of a shooting script. A proposal is designed to attract the interest of a funding source or executive supervisor. There are two basic types of proposals: commercial and noncommercial. A commercial proposal highlights the most marketable feature of a project, while a noncommercial proposal emphasizes what is unique and significant about a project. In a commercial proposal, a description of the most marketable features of a project such as its topicality or the "stars" and creative personnel who are involved in the production, is sometimes interwoven with a synopsis of the story or subject matter, called a treatment.

The quality of a finished screenplay depends directly on the thoroughness with which a writer researches the topic. Accuracy is extremely important for nonfiction projects, but even fictional works require careful research to promote authenticity, realism, and a responsible treatment of historical events.

A treatment provides a summary of the project in short story form. It performs two basic functions: stimulating the interest of the producer and providing an outline of the script which can serve as a guide for future writing.

There are two basic script formats: split page and full page. The split-page script places the visual elements on one side of the page and audio elements on the opposite side. It allows for a direct comparison and coordination of images and sound elements. The full-page script is used more frequently for dramatic production. Much informational and live television programming is semi-scripted. Elements that are standardized or repeated from one show to the next, such as intros, are scripted, while improvised content, such as interview answers, does not appear in the script. While it is the director rather than the scriptwriter who normally determines the precise shot types and camera placements, a scriptwriter's familiarity with actual production stimulates visual thinking.

There are two basic categories of script-writing: fiction and nonfiction. Fiction scripts generally present stories that are invented by the scriptwriter. Nonfiction scripts often convey information about actual events. Fiction and nonfictional structures frequently overlap, and scriptwriters should be familiar with both types of scriptwriting.

Classical dramatic structure unifies a story by using character motivations to link one event with another. Psychological causes and effects that stem from character motivations are emphasized. Empathy and identification with specific heroes is encouraged. Problems raised at the beginning of a story are resolved by the end. Time is generally continuous. Epic drama focuses on social and economic causes and effects. Separation and distance from individual characters is encouraged. Problems are not always neatly resolved. Contradictions and conflicts persist at the conclusion of the drama. Thought rather than emotion is stressed.

A ficitional story has dramatic structure. Dramatic action can be plotted or structured as exposition, complications, crises, climax, and resolution. An exposition establishes the characters, their motivations, and the basic situation. Complications are problems or obstacles that arise as characters attempt to achieve a goal or pursue an action, which create viewer interest by making the action more complex. Complications build to crises which in turn lead to the final climax. The climax is a major crisis which brings the conflicting forces of the drama together for a final confrontation, leading to an eventual resolution of these forces.

Fictional stories are usually told or narrated by someone. Narrative structure has two basic elements: time and point of view. The historical time of a story can be manipulated or changed from present to past or future time. Time can also be compressed and expanded through editing. Point of view refers to the person or perspective from which a story is told. A narrator can be omniscient and effaced or a narrator can be a character in the story, called a dramatized narrator. Point of view can be revealed through actual spoken narration or through what is shown and where a camera is placed.

Fiction scripts are either original creations or adaptations. Original scripts begin with plots, characters, or themes. A writer can begin with any of these aspects, but eventually all three must be fully developed. Characters reveal themselves through actions and words. The writer's job is to externalize these values through speech, mannerisms, and actions which reflect a more complex internal value system and give a character depth and significance. Characters can be divided into three basic categories: central characters, principal characters, who are the friends and foils of the former, and secondary or incidental characters, who are often heavily typed or even stereotyped for immediate audience recognition.

A theme is a significant statement made by a work of fiction or an important issue that is raises. The topicality of a theme generates audience interest, while the significance and universality of a theme in large part determines a work's lasting value.

Adaptation is a complex art, which requires that the writer be thoroughly familiar with the original work. Adaptations that are not entirely true to the original are often referred to as "based on," "freely adapted from," or "suggested by" another work. Published works are copyrighted, and permission must be obtained from their authors or publishers before they can be adapted and recorded as films or television programs. Changes, additions, and deletions inevitably are made in the original piece of fiction to make it more compatible with film or television media. A writer must consider the unique aesthetic characteristics and possibilities of recorded and edited moving images and sounds as a unique art form. The requirements and limitations of institutionalized formats and structures within which films and television programs are produced and consumed must also be considered.

There are a variety of specific formats within which writers of film and television must work, but a basic division can be made between long and short fiction. Long fiction includes miniseries, feature films, made-for-TV movies, and hour-long episodes of series. Short fiction includes half-hour series episodes and a variety of fictional film and video shorts. A writer must consider the lengths and structures that are conventionally practiced within each format. Writers of half-hour television series, for example, must work somewhat more formulaically than writers of feature films, who are freer to develop more complicated plot structures and characters. But creative writers can often turn limitations to artistic advantage.

Additional Readings

Armes, Roy. *The Ambiguous Image: Narrative Style in Modern European Cinema*. London: Secker and Warburg, 1976.

Barry, Jackson G. *Dramatic Structure: The Shaping of Experience*. Berkeley: University of California Press, 1970.

Beckman, Henry. *How to Sell Your Film Project*. Los Angeles: Pinnacle Books, 1979.

Blum, Richard A. *Television Writing, from Concept to Contract*. New York: Hastings House, 1980.

Booth, Wayne. *The Rhetoric of Fiction*. 2nd ed. Chicago: University of Chicago Press, 1983.

Bordwell, David, and Kristin Thompson, *Film Art: An Introduction*. 2nd ed. New York: Random House Knopf, 1985.

Bordwell, David, Janet Staiger, and Kristin Thompson. *The Classical Hollywood Cinema: Film Style and Mode of Production to 1960*. New York: Columbia University Press, 1986.

Branigan, Edward R. *Point of View in the Cinema*. New York: Mouton, 1984.

Coopersmith, Jerome. *Professional Writer's Teleplay/Screenplay Format*. New York: Writers Guild of America, East, 22 West 48th St., 1977.

Gabriel, Teshome H. *Third Cinema in the Third World*. Ann Arbor: UMI Research Press, 1982.

Hilliard, Robert L. *Writing for Television and Radio*. 3rd ed. New York: Hastings House, 1976.

Maloney, Martin, and Paul Max Rubenstein. *Writing for the Media*. Englewood Cliffs, NJ: Prentice-Hall, 1980.

Nash, Constance, and Virginia Oakey. *The Screenwriter's Handbook*. New York: Barnes and Noble, 1978.

Rivers, William L. *Finding Facts: Interviewing, Observing, Using Reference Sources*. Englewood Cliffs, NJ: Prentice-Hall, 1975.

Root, Wells. *Writing the Script*. New York: Holt, Rinehart and Winston, 1980.

Swain, Dwight V. *Film Scriptwriting*. New York: Hastings House, 1976.

Vale, Eugene. *The Technique of Screen & Television Writing*. Englewood Cliffs, NJ: Prentice-Hall, 1982.

Willis, Edgar E., and Camille D'Arienzo. *Writing Scripts For Television, Radio, and Film*. New York: Holt, Rinehart and Winston, 1981.

Exercises

1. Adapt a short story to a full-page script format. Write additional dialogue for the script, where it is needed. Convert feelings, thoughts, and ideas into physical actions and concrete sounds and images. Determine a specific point of view from which the story will be told.

2. Adapt a one-act play to a full-page script format. Replace some dialogue with physical actions and rewrite dialogue that is too stilted or insufficiently intimate. Create additional locations and make more frequent changes of time and place. Tell the story from a specific point of view.

3. Write a proposal, treatment, and script for an original work of short fiction such as a situation comedy with three or four characters or less. Pattern one or two characters after people you actually know. Give them interesting personalities and idiosyncrasies and place one character's values in conflict with another's. Write at least one scene with dialogue that brings these characters and opposing values into direct confrontation with each other.

CHAPTER 4

Nonfiction Scriptwriting

Documentaries
Structuring a Documentary
Pace
Narration
Other Nonfiction Productions
Newswriting
Interviews and Talk Shows
Instructional Material
Commercials
Summary

Many different types of nonfiction programs and films are used as informative or persuasive media devices. Documentaries, news stories, instructional programs, and commercials are examples of nonfiction films and television programming. These types of products seem to share some common characteristics. There is usually an emphasis on actuality or the presentation of "real" people, things, situations, actions, and problems. They are often structured or organized to transmit information or to motivate people to do or to buy something. They make frequent use of logical categories to convey information and rhetorical devices to persuade an audience. In many works of nonfiction a narrator introduces, interprets, and summarizes actions and events. However, when pictures and sounds can speak for themselves, accompanying commentary is generally kept to a minimum.

Broadly defined, nonfiction films and TV programs share certain characteristics with dramatic fiction. A documentary that reenacts historical events is called a "staged" documentary or documentary "reenactment" and is very similar to a docudrama. The primary purpose of the former may be to inform, but it is impossible to separate fiction from nonfiction solely on the basis of any supposed intention to dramatize and entertain rather than inform viewers.

Network news divisions have a responsibility to separate fact from fiction at the same time that they feel the need to use dramatic devices to add interest and intensity to news programs. Traditionally at CBS, for instance, reenactment is not permitted in news coverage without explicit specification that a reenactment is being shown. But no news or documentary scriptwriter can ignore dramatic entertainment

values and still expect to attract a sizable audience. All scriptwriters attempt to stimulate viewer interest through the portrayal of dramatic conflicts. Theorist Kenneth Burke has argued that all media presentations (both fictional and nonfictional) are essentially dramatic social devices. Reuven Frank, as executive producer of the NBC Evening News in the 1960s, sent the following memorandum to his news staff:

> Every news story should, without any sacrifice of probity or responsibility, display the attributes of fiction, of drama. It should have structure and conflict, problem and denouement, rising action and falling action, a beginning, a middle and an end. These are not only the essentials of drama; they are the essentials of narrative.

In short, dramatic entertainment values and narrative structure are important to nonfiction scriptwriters, and the material in the previous chapter is applicable to nonfiction as well as fiction scriptwriting.

DOCUMENTARIES

Nonfiction scriptwriters are often called upon to write narration or commentary as well as treatments and loosely or tightly organized scripts for documentaries. Generally speaking, documentaries can be defined as presentations of (contemporary or historical) political, physical, social, or personal situations and events, which use film or television to record or document these events. Documentaries can range from the poetic film stories of Robert Flaherty (*Nanook of the North* [1921], *Moana* [1928], *Man of Aran* [1934], and *Louisiana Story* [1948]) to programs about sci-

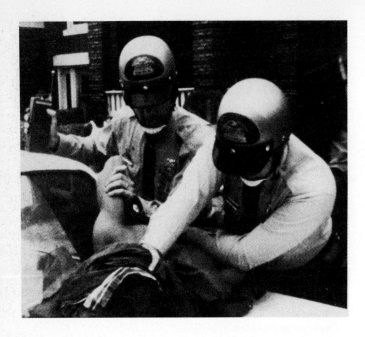

Frederick Wiseman's documentary *Law and Order* is a hard-hitting direct cinema exposé on the maintenance of social order.

ence, such as PBS's "NOVA," National Geographic specials, undersea explorations by Jacques Cousteau, social documentaries on the three major American television networks, and instructional films and videotapes for classroom, governmental, and industrial use.

Public television social and scientific documentaries sometimes place less emphasis on entertainment values than feature film or network television documentaries. Frederick Wiseman, for example, has produced several documentaries broadcast on public television that are serious explorations of social institutions. Films and/or television programs such as *High School* (1968), *Law and Order* (1969), *Hospital* (1970), *Basic Training* (1971), and *Juvenile Court* (1974) probe beneath the surface realities of their subject matter to reveal and expose hypocrisy, bigotry, greed, stupidity, and many other human frailties. The nakedness of laying

bare certain social institutions and people in a "direct cinema" (long, continuously running camera and sound recording takes or shots from an "objective" journalistic viewpoint) style can be provocative. It gives a feeling of "you are there!" spontaneity and realism. This same technique has been used in other public television documentaries, such as *Family,* as well as feature film documentaries, such as the Maysles Brothers' *Grey Gardens* (1975) and *Gimme Shelter* (1974), although the latter are clearly more performance and entertainment oriented than the former.

Network television documentaries often give the appearance of being balanced and objective, and they certainly make some attempt to present different sides on any issue. Producers of social documentaries are concerned about giving a fair presentation of alternative points of view (required by the FCC's Fairness Doctrine) and providing equal air time to political candidates (required by the Equal Time Rule). (See chapter 2, p. 41.) But network documentaries usually adopt a specific point of view. The goal may be to simply arouse public awareness, concern, or indignation about a pressing social problem. It may also be to encourage some type of social action. At the center of the network television documentary is a significant controversy or conflict. A writer must fully exploit this controversy or conflict, if the program is to attract a large audience. A classic television documentary, such as *Harvest of Shame* (1960) places the reporter (Edward R. Murrow) in the role of David who defends the underprivileged migrant worker against Goliath-sized institutions and organizations. This same technique is exploited in a news magazine, such as CBS' "60 Minutes," in which a different Goliath is taken to task in each story. Stories are dramatically structured so that participants themselves reveal more and more evil and corruption. The popularity of this ''news'' magazine is undoubtedly related to its role as a public watchdog.

Less popular network television documentaries often examine specific social problems in greater depth, but they have a similar motivation to arouse as well as inform. Often a network documentary adopts the point of view of specific social victims and the oppressed in general, although sometimes networks adopt the point of view of the haves rather than the have-nots. The selection of a specific point of view may be related to both majority audience expectations and the beliefs and opinions of the news staff or management. The prejudices of producers are only obvious to audiences when they have different attitudes and conflicting points of view on a topic. Producers try for more balance and ''objectivity'' when treating controversial issues, although some degree of controversy and accusations of partiality sometimes help to attract more viewers.

Some documentaries are made by independent artists for smaller, at times nonspecific audiences that appreciate more poetic, cultural explorations of specific issues and people. Filmmakers such as Les Blank, Stan Woodward, and Bryan Elsom make short documentaries of a more personal, exploratory nature. Films such as *Hot Pepper* (1979), *It's Grits* (1980), and *Night in Tunisia* (1981), explore ethnic themes, foods, and music, reflecting their makers' unique artistic styles of filmmaking. Sometimes documentaries on the making of feature films are more interesting than the fictional films, for example Les Blank's documentary *Burden of Dreams* (1981), which focuses on Werner Herzog's feature film *Fitzcarraldo* (1982).

Performance is a subject well suited to the direct cinema approach. Mick Jagger struts his way across the stage, and the Maysles brothers capture the energy generated by his performance in their popular feature-film documentary, *Gimme Shelter*.

Structuring a Documentary

Writing a script for a documentary that will effectively communicate information, and also be compelling and entertaining, requires extensive planning. The writer's work begins with thorough and well-documented research in the topic area. This research phase, discussed in the previous chapter, is an ethical responsibility of both the writer and the producer. A documentary scriptwriter who lacks knowledge about the topic, almost inevitably misleads the public with a distorted picture of a situation or event. Even the most talented director cannot simply react to situations as they come up during actual recording without adequate planning and research and expect to do justice to the topic. Many types of written and visual records must be consulted, before a writer knows the crucial elements and issues that must be recorded and presented in a documentary. It is impossible to know what additional information must be recorded until existing recordings have been examined. A documentarian can gain expertise in a particular area by reading as much relevant published materials as possible and consulting with recognized authorities. Poorly researched documentaries fail to live up to the authoritativeness which audiences so frequently ascribe to documentary films and television programs. Presenting inaccurate information can also result in lawsuits from adversely affected parties.

Documentary scripts cannot be completed until most of the recorded images and sounds have been examined by the scriptwriter. Scriptwriting usually takes the form of developing an overall structure for the documentary in terms of dramatic action, a logical argument, and a logical presentation of information. We have already discussed basic principles of dramatic action. Logical arguments are fashioned on the basis of rhetorical devices. A documentary argument is a form of inartistic or artistic proof. Inartistic proof is dependent on factual material available to the writer, editor, or speaker, such as interviews with various participants, witnesses, observers, and authorities. There are three main types of artistic proof, which are dependent on the speaker or narrator: ethical, emotional, and demonstrative. An ethical proof relies quite heavily on the moral integrity and credibility of the speaker, such as a network news commentator. An emotional proof relies on the speaker's appeal to audience emotions and feelings. A demonstrative proof relies on a series of expositions (showing, not just telling), which have recourse to actual events or oppositional points of view. A specific script might rely on all of these different forms of proof and argument.

A documentary script also organizes information in a logical manner. Some of the most common forms of organization include effects-to-causes, problem/solution, enumeration, classification into logical categories, and theme/countertheme. Many network documentaries begin with scenes that dramatize the effects of a particular social problem. These highly charged, emotional scenes act as a hook to grab the audience's attention. A dispassionate narrator then begins to explore some of the causes that have produced these effects. In a classic documentary, such as *Harvest of Shame* (1960), the program ends with tentative solutions to the problem. Specific goals are cited and specific courses of action are recommended to viewers. The program is structured as an argument for the elimination of a pressing social problem, and the information is logically presented through a problem/solution and effects-to-causes organization. Visual and audio information can be edited to contrast different opinions and points of view. This can take the form of a theme/countertheme structure, where one idea or point of view clashes repeatedly with another, much like a theme and countertheme in a piece of music. Enumeration refers to a listing of various possibilities or realities, while logical categories might consist of different aspects or approaches to a subject. For example, an educational documentary about a Latin American country might examine political, social, economic, cultural, and artistic aspects of that country. These are logical categories by which documentary information can be organized.

Actual documentary scriptwriting consists primarily of writing words that a narrator or commentator can deliver on or off camera, but it also provides a basic outline for image and sound recording and editing. Narration provides links between different segments and a basic commentary that explains or summarizes what will be or has been seen. The narration is usually written after images and sounds have been recorded and edited. A preproduction script or treatment can help an editor to establish visual and audio links between primary arguments and logical categories of information.

Once the general topic has been thoroughly researched and an overall structure has been determined, the actual process of selecting, ordering, and refining basic elements can begin. The scriptwriter of a documentary usually follows four general guidelines. *First,* the opening sequence is selected to gain the audience's attention and establish the audience's expectations for what is to come. This is similar to dramatic hooks, foreshadowing, and planting, as discussed earlier in chapter 3. *Second*, the writer establishes a point of view toward the material. Usually this involves an attempt to humanize and dramatize events by focusing on conflicts, by establishing a particular participant's point of view, or by somehow involving the "objective" reporter or filmmaker in the action. Humanizing and dramatizing the documentary material helps to create emotional appeal. *Third*, the information presented from this point of view must follow a logical or natural order. *Fourth*, once the crucial elements have been selected and ordered, the writer and the documentary producer must critically examine the recorded materials in terms of their contribution to pace and viewer interest. Based on the time constraints of the entire project and the pace of individual segments, the project can gradually be refined down to an effective length.

Opening Sequence   There are many ways to gain audience attention at the beginning of a documentary. One is to begin by simply presenting an important conflict and problem that needs to be resolved. (See Figure 4.1, a documentary on civil defense.) The opening sequence should be powerfully dramatic. A "talking head" discussing the problem in matter-of-fact, objective terms fails to capture the audience's interest and attention and can be intensely boring. Actuality footage—that is, a recording of actual events that graphically depict a problem, whether it be drug

Figure 4.1
Example of a Short
Documentary Script

```
SUBJECT: CIVIL DEFENSE PLANNING IN NORTH CAROLINA
Written and Produced by: Pama Mitchell, UNC Center for Public Television

VIDEO                           AUDIO

H-BOMB EXPLOSION                (Sound of bomb explosion)

ED DEATON CU                             ED DEATON
Tape 194                        "I think if we have..."
14-14-01                        "... is going to save us."
14-20-10

MORE EXPLOSION                  (Explosion)

TOM PUGH CU                             TOM PUGH
Tape 5519                       "The widespread effects of nuclear war..."
04-55-00                        "...probably the whole nation."
05-03-17

MORE EXPLOSION                  (Explosion)

STEVE LEIGHTON CU                       STEVE LEIGHTON
Tape 5257                       "Perhaps the biggest deception..."
08-00-27                        "...fallout shelter system."
08-06-00

WIDE SHOT, THE                      AUDREY KATES (VOICEOVER)
BULLETIN OF THE ATOMIC
SCIENTISTS, COVER               In January of 1981, the Bulletin of the Atomic

CU, CLOCK, THEN                 Scientists moved the hands of its doomsday clock to
   PULL OUT
                                four minutes to midnight.  That means they think we're

                                closer to nuclear holocaust than at any time since 1959.

                                And a recent survey in Newsweek magazine showed the

SHOTS OF PEOPLE ON              American public agrees.
CROWDED STREETS,
WITH NEWSWEEK                   Almost sixty percent of those polled felt there was
FIGURES SUPERED
                                at least a fair chance of all-out nuclear war with the

                                Soviet Union sometime in the next ten years.

                                With the threat of war seemingly growing, what is the

                                government doing to protect the population?

TOM PUGH, CU
Tape 5519                              TOM PUGH
03-40-18                        "The planning for disaster..."
03-51-02                        "... so many things you can do."

(SUPER HIS NAME AND
   TITLE)
```

addiction, child abuse, or the high cost of housing—arouses interest through the portrayal of dramatic actions and conflict. An "on-camera" narrator who is a well-known personality can indicate his or her personal involvement with an issue and in so doing involve the audience on a personal, human level. But on-camera narration by celebrities often becomes boring and seems somewhat ingenuous and should be kept to a minimum. It is always better to show something than to simply talk about it. Presenting a problem or conflict in dramatic, human terms is one of the best ways of gaining immediate audience attention.

Presenting a particularly exciting segment of scenes or vignettes that will be shown in their entirety somewhat later, acts as a teaser that can stimulate interest. Short segments from longer interviews can be edited together to dramatize a conflict or present alternative points of view at the start. The writer's job is to find a way in which the documentary's main idea, theme, point of view, or conflict can be concisely dramatized in human terms that the intended audience will immediately understand.

Establishing a Point of View   Most documentaries establish a particular point of view. Sometimes the basic approach is reduced to simplistic fictional formulas, such as good versus evil. In other instances, however, the point of view is an important angle or perspective from which the problem can be productively approached. Rarely in television and film is equal time fully given to both sides of a conflict or problem, except perhaps in a news show such as PBS's "MacNeil/Lehrer News Hour." Documentaries often adopt a primary perspective or point of attack, such as that of the underdog. Estab-

lishing a specific point of view helps to dramatize and humanize the problem. The audience frequently identifies with the underdog or the injured party, and this can be used to increase the audience's emotional involvement in the problem.

Despite the fact that most television documentaries adopt a specific point of view, it is important to maintain a degree of fairness in the portrayal of a problem, so that actuality is not completely distorted for the sake of entertainment. The norm in commercial television, for example, is to be provocative without offending anyone. In an attempt to attract a large audience, network documentaries often examine controversial issues, but they also make some attempt to be fair in their portrayal of the opposition so that they inhibit hostile audience responses and follow FCC policy, such as the Fairness Doctrine. In news and documentary work there is a constant tension between a professional sense of fairness or sensitivity to the attitudes of any substantial segment of the popular audience and the need to provide a return on production investments. When the latter tendency is unchecked by the former, this can lead to the exploitation of topics, such as pornography or sexual harassment, in shallow terms simply to raise rating points and advertising revenues.

Ordering Information   Once a point of view toward a particular problem has been established and the basic elements of the story to be told have been selected, the writer's task is to give order and coherence to the presentation of those elements. The presentation of documentary elements can follow a chronological order (a behind the scenes look at the sequence of events in a presidential election in *Primary* [1960]), a cause and effect order or a problem and solution order (soil erosion, deforestation, and the Tennessee Valley Authority in *The River* [1939]), a preexisting categorization, such as age, sex, geographic location, a socioeconomic hierarchy (landowners and migrants in *Harvest of Shame* [1960]), or a thematic order, such as a theme/countertheme alternation (anti-Vietnam War versus pro-Vietnam War interviews and statements in *Hearts and Minds* [1975]). Each of these patterns or structures provides a logical sequence for the presentation of documentary elements.

Clarity, simplicity, and logical sequencing are primary virtues in documentary writing. Complex problems must be reduced to simple terms that the audience can easily understand. A logical presentation of elements and ideas is one in which all the information the audience needs to understand about any event or idea has preceded the presentation of that event or idea. Technical terms must be replaced with simple concepts. A commentary or narration track should tranform complex ideas and information into concepts that are clear to the average viewer. The script must also make clear the relationship of supporting points to the main idea.

Pace

A documentary writer must also consider the pace of any segment. Pace is a rather subjective, aesthetic value that refers to the speed and intensity of the action or narration and dialogue. It determines the length of time that a segment or element can play before it proves ineffective or boring. A dynamic interview or dramatic piece of actuality footage can sometimes ''play'' for a considerable period of time before it proves tiresome, but other segments may need to be cut short or interspersed with graphic visuals that create action, speed, and viewer interest. Pacing

is difficult to control during the writing stage, because it depends on so many factors that are evident only when the actual sound and image recordings are available. While the writer must exhibit some concern for pacing during the scriptwriting phase, it is really the documentary director and editor, who finally determine the pace of specific elements and of the documentary film or videotape as a whole. Pacing is affected by the editing together of long- and short-duration camera shots as well as the speed of actions within shots, dialogue, and the narration.

Narration

It is often advisable to keep narration or voice commentary to a minimum when recorded visuals and sounds are self-explanatory. The dramatic value of a documentary is always increased when the sounds and images tell the story without the need for much descriptive or explanatory commentary. A basic rule in documentary writing and recording is always to show some action, not simply talk about it. A narration track can sometimes be used to tie together loose ends or comment on the action as an aid to interpretation, but it should not duplicate or completely dominate the visual presentation of information. Strong sounds and images must be combined with an effective and concise narration track.

A narration track can be used for a variety of purposes in a documentary, including adjusting the pace of the action, creating logical links between diverse segments, verbally emphasizing specific points, clarifying the meaning of a segment, ordering the presentation, and summarizing the main points and major issues that have been explored.

Some types of documentaries, such as American direct cinema or French cinema verité, dispense with narration entirely. Others try to keep the narration to a minimum so that the basic story is told in sounds and images rather than in words. Classic British documentaries of the 1930s and 1940s, such as Basil Wright's *Night Mail* (1936), sometimes used poetry as a form of narration or commentary on the sounds and images, adding to the depth and texture of this art form, rather than serving as a redundancy, duplicating in words what the audience has seen for itself.

Theatrical film newsreels sometimes used ''voice of history'' narrators, who had commanding voices. Today this type of narration seems oppressive and didactic. It insults the intelligence of the audience. Good narration needs to be more subtle than this. It is possible for a narrator to sound authoritative without becoming authoritarian. Involved, personable narrators, such as Dick Cavett in Time, Inc.'s and HBO's ''Remember When'' (1980), offer a radical departure from the more remote and detached forms of narrators and narration used in previous eras, such as that of Westbrook Van Vorhees in the *March of Time* (1930s and 1940s) newsreels. A narrator can appear on the screen, sometimes becoming a participant in the action.

OTHER NONFICTION PRODUCTIONS

Many principles of documentary scriptwriting are applicable to other types of nonfiction productions, such as news stories, interviews and talk shows, instructional programs, and commercials. Each of these additional forms of nonfiction

writing has its own unique principles and practices as well.

Newswriting

A television newswriter writes copy to be read by on-camera or off-camera anchor people and reporters. Most reporters write their own stories. Only in larger markets do anchor people generally read copy written by a newswriting specialist. Network and most local station newscasters are generally involved in writing their own copy. Whether one is working as a news anchor, reporter, producer, or director, some knowledge of basic newswriting is essential.

Unlike print journalism, television newswriting does not begin with a who, what, when, where, and why approach. There is not time to answer all of these questions immediately. Television story leads quickly identify the situation. Key information is usually delayed until the second sentence delivered by the newscaster. The first sentence orients the viewer to the general issue to be discussed. ''Another accusation of voter fraud surfaced today,'' leads into a story about a close senatorial election. ''Candidate Sherlock Holmes accused the committee to reelect Senator Moriarity of foul play in Baskerville County,'' then provides the specific information.

News copy generally plays a subservient role to accompanying sounds and pictures. (See Figure 4.2.) Like good documentary narration, good newswriting doesn't try to compete with visual information, but rather sets a context for its interpretation. Newswriting does not have to describe what happened, when news clips are available. The writer simply sets a context for the viewing experience, establishes links or transitions between different stories, and provides a limited summary or conclusions. When commentary accompanies images and sounds, it should identify key participants. Since the camera cannot jump from one participant to another as quickly as they can be verbally identified, a descriptive phrase about each person allows sufficient time for close-ups to be edited together. The alternative to this practice is to use a less dramatic long shot, which includes all participants at once and allows them to be quickly identified as a group or in any case by no more than three individual identifications.

Newswriting should be simple and conversational, so that a newscaster can clearly and concisely communicate the essential information as though he or she is talking to a friend. Remember that a newscaster is an invited guest in private homes. A writer must use discretion when discussing difficult issues. Shocking or disturbingly violent visuals should be clearly identified in advance, giving children and sensitive adults an opportunity to avoid them. Newswriters, like print reporters, must be careful to attribute information to specific sources and protect themselves from charges of falsehood. All too often, careless TV news reporters present suppositions as ''facts.'' False broadcast news reports can have an immediate and profound effect on viewers. Many listeners to Orson Welles' dramatic radio broadcast of *War of the Worlds* in 1938, which was presented as a series of news bulletins, took to the streets and highways in panic over the ''invasion'' from space. Ten years later in South America irate victims of a similar dramatic hoax burned down the radio station in retaliation.

The first component of a field-recorded news story to be written and recorded is usually the reporter's on-camera commentary. This commentary introduces the subject, provides bridges between various

PAGE: 1 SLUG: plane	Not even air-traffic
TIME:_____ ANCHOR: LS _ ss/landing	controllers could've helped the pilot of a small plane.. who tried to land at Fayetteville this afternoon.
VTR/ANVO/NATSOT S/ Fayetteville This Afternoon	Roy Funderchuk flew into a strong crosswind as he tried to touch down at Grannis Field. His single-engine plane was blown off the runway...pushed over onto the grass...as his landing gear collapsed. Don Wade saw it happened...
VTR SOT: 08 S/ Don Wade Eyewitness	IN: He lost... OUT: good landing.
VTR/ANVO/NS CON'T VTR OUT	Luckily...Funderchuk wasn't injured.

Figure 4.2
Example of a Television News Copy Script

segments, and offers a summary at the end. It is used as voice-over narration to order dramatic visual images and sounds that illustrate what the reporter is talking about. (This process is discussed more fully in chapters 14 and 15.)

A newswriter must be concerned with pace. Numerous stories are presented during a half-hour (actually twenty-three minutes plus commercials) newscast. Each must be cut down to minimal length in a way that retains excitement and interest. While a newscaster often seems calm and in control, the delivery and pace of the entire newscast must be both rapid and smooth. A television newswriter emphasizes active rather than passive verbs to increase pace and viewer interest. The sources of information must be given at the beginning of a sentence rather than at the end of a sentence for better oral communication. The order of words must result in an unambiguous interpretation of events. The purpose of a commercial television newscast is to describe events rather than to interpret them or editorialize about them.

Each story must be typed on separate pages. When the producer determines the best order of the stories, the pages can be arranged in that order. Stories must be accurately timed. A good average reading speed is about 150 words of copy per minute. The combination of written copy and edited visuals and sounds must be precisely timed so that the total program fits into the allotted time slot. The completed script indicates when commercials will be inserted, and functions as a timing and source guide to live production for the entire staff and crew. A copy of the script goes to the producer, the director, and all on-set newscasters, often called talent. The copy to be read should include phonetic spellings, so that pronounciation is understood.

Sources of News Stories   The material a newswriter edits, rewrites, condenses, or originates comes from a variety of sources. Broadcast news often relies on wire services, such as Associated Press and United Press International. Some stories are simply taken off printed teletype copy. However, using these stories verbatim fails to establish a unique news style. Although wire services usually offer different story renditions for print and broadcast news clients, it can be quite risky to present unedited copy written by print-oriented wire-service journalists. Relying on wire-service copy also fails to provide viewers with news of local or regional interest. Assigning print journalists who have no experience with broadcast journalism to write broadcast copy can also be disastrous. Network and the most comprehensive local news usually originates from experienced reporters in the field who are investigating specific events, issues, and topics and who receive tips from interested participants. Local stations also keep a close eye on the print media and competing newscasts to catch up on stories they might otherwise miss. Follow-ups on major stories from preceding days are another important news source.

Organizing the Newscast   The news producer must determine the significance of each story and the viewer interest it is likely to arouse, so that the **lead story**, or most important beginning segment, can be selected and the other stories coherently ordered. Which stories will actually be aired depends on a number of factors, including program length, the availability of accompanying film or videotape, the number of major events that have occurred that day, and the producer's own preferences and priorities. A large number of stories will be written each day; some of those will actually be aired and others either presented later, if they have accompanying visuals of continuing interest, or abandoned entirely. The selected stories are usually presented in blocks that reflect geographical or topical relationships. Innate interest and importance to the audience are equally valid considerations. Many producers try to end a news program with a humorous or human interest story. Many factors, including the quality of the news writing, affect the selection and placement of news stories for a particular broadcast. Ordering stories in a newscast can be somewhat subjective and quite complex.

The trend in commercial television broadcasting is toward many short items rather than a few long reports on selected topics, and a significant use of actuality footage and flashy graphics. While this fast-paced structure and format for a news broadcast raises many questions about the quality of ''in-depth'' understanding available to the American public on any single topic through commercial television, this approach is obviously economically advantageous to commercial broadcasters, since it attracts many viewers.

Interviews and Talk Shows

News and entertainment functions are combined in an overt fashion on many interviews and talk shows. There are basically two types of interviews conducted on these shows: **celebrity interviews** and **authority interviews**. Celebrity interviews are frequently seen on afternoon and evening entertainment programs. Comedy or singing performances often accompany such interviews. Celebrity interviews generally try to explore the human side of guests and coax them into revealing more about themselves than they may have initially intended. The interview can be purely a performance to entertain the audience or an occasion for self-disclosure, depending on the interviewer's success in gaining the confidence of the celebrity. Celebrity interviews almost always have a commercial purpose. The guest is often promoting a recent book, film, or television program. Sometimes he or she simply wants to become better known to the general public.

Authority interviews focus for the most part on issues, information, ideas, and attitudes rather than personalities. The interviewer's purpose is often to play devil's advocate and force the guest to clarify and substantiate a position and possibly to reveal some important detail that has been omitted in previous reports and interviews. It is not the authority's personality that is of primary interest, but his or her knowledge and/or opinion of some significant topic. The authority interview comes perilously close to the celebrity interview, however, when the primary objective is simply to find a political skeleton in the guest's closet.

Writers and researchers must carefully prepare the interviewer for his or her interaction with the guest. A good interviewer is at least as well informed as the audience, and has anticipated what questions audience members would ask if they could. Interviewers often write the questions they plan to ask on note cards. They then go over these cards, paring them down to a reasonable number of questions which they are confident will appeal to their audience. A good interviewer is less con-

In an interview situation, Johnny Carson is always well-prepared and is able to provide his audience with a satisfying interview.

cerned with impressing the audience with brilliant questions than with functioning as an effective representative of the audience during the interview.

Background information on the guest or topic must be thoroughly researched. But the interviewer must also be a glib respondent to unpredictable events, a careful and sensitive listener, at times a cajoler and at other times a provocateur or a catalyst. While a tremendous amount of writing may be compiled prior to the interview, only a small fraction of it will actually be used during the interview. The interview must appear to be unrehearsed and spontaneous. Questions cannot be read from a sheet of paper. They must be presented as though they are spontaneous. A written script provides a general outline of guests to be interviewed and topics to be discussed. Introductions and background material can be written out and dis-

played at the appropriate time on a teleprompter, which projects copy on a see-through mirror in front of the camera lens. Cue cards are also created for the interviewer's use. A script also indicates when commercials will appear and the precise timing of segments of a show.

A talk-show writer or interviewer, like a good documentarian or newswriter, is concerned about ethical issues, such as the potential conflict between the public's right to know and the citizen's right to privacy. When a sensitive topic or personal problem is to be discussed, the interviewer must satisfy the audience's curiosity without embarrassing the guest or placing him or her in an awkward position. A good interviewer knows how to phrase questions in a tactful manner so that the guest is not offended, although the audience's curiosity and expectations are fully satisfied.

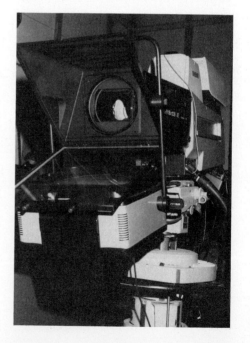

Cue cards (left) are oftentimes written out for a television interviewer to use and are easily read from a teleprompter (right).

Indirect methods of questioning can be quite effective, and they raise fewer ethical dilemmas about pressuring a private citizen into revealing more personal details than they really care to have the public know. Discussing her celebrity-interviewing techniques, Barbara Walters has said that she often uses indirect methods of questioning. For example, she felt that it would be in bad taste to ask Mamie Eisenhower, the former President's widow, any direct question about a supposed problem with alcohol. Instead, she simply asked Mrs. Eisenhower if there was ever a time that she felt concerned about public impressions of her in the White House. Mrs. Eisenhower answered by revealing that she had an inner ear problem that sometimes caused her to lose her balance, and that the press had misinterpreted this as a sign of alcoholism.

Instructional Material

Instructional programs or films often serve three different purposes: to supplement lectures in the classroom; to inform the public and government employees about new government policies; or to inform employees and/or the public about corporate practices, policies, and points of view. These three purposes reflect the institutional needs of producers in educational, governmental, and corporate environments, respectively.

Instructional programs are designed as either supplementary or primary materials. They may accompany an educational, government, or corporate speech or they may have to stand on their own without the help of a person who can set a context for viewing or answer questions. The most important factor in planning instructional programs is to understand the needs, expectations, and level of knowledge of the audience. Different demographic (age, socioeconomic status, and educational level) groups often require entirely different instructional strategies. A four-year-old child requires a different approach than a ten-year-old. While the overall objective of any instructional program is to impart knowledge, effective communication depends on the writer's awareness of the audience's sophistication, age, and educational level. A writer must use terms with which the audience is already familiar or define new terms in words the audience already understands.

The information must be clear and well organized. Each step or concept must follow logically from preceding steps and concepts. Suppose, for example, that a program is designed to instruct beginning photography students about basic concepts of developing film. It is logical to begin with a description and graphic demonstration of a piece of film, showing the various light-sensitive layers and substances. The camera can be described next, along with the process of exposing the film to light. Finally, the stages of developing and printing the film, using different chemicals and pieces of equipment, can each be described sequentially. A short review of the fundamental steps then summarizes the overall process.

An instructional program must be more than clear and logical, however. It must graphically demonstrate concepts and ideas. Otherwise what is the point of making a videotape or film? Cross-sections of a piece of film and the working parts of a camera can be drawn. Actual scenes might be shot in a photographic darkroom under red lights, which give the impression of a darkroom setting, but provide sufficient light for recording purposes. A photographer can actually demonstrate the various stages of developing and printing photographic images, so that students are brought out of the classroom into an actual work environment. Educational films and videotapes present materials that cannot be easily demonstrated through a lecture or the use of other less expensive media, such as slides, audiotapes, or graphic projections. Moving images should move. There is no justification for using film or videotape recording for something that can be done just as well and much less expensively with still pictures. Carl I. Hovland's experiment comparing slides/lecture with movies as teaching devices demonstrated that slides/lecture were better, not just less expensive. Of course, motion is an important component of many educational subjects.

The narration that accompanies this graphic material must be concise, clear, and easily comprehended. A sense of drama, like a sense of humor, can add interest and excitement, but it can also be overdone. The main object is to show rather than tell. The narration should be authoritative, but not condescending. It must impart accurate information, linking various parts of the demonstration, and establish a context within which the accompanying images can be clearly and completely understood.

Commercials

Commercials are brief messages that advertise products, company names, and services. Unlike many other types of nonfiction, commercials aim directly at modifying audience behavior and attitudes. The chief test of a commercial's success is not that people watch and enjoy it. The true test is that people buy a specific product or are positively predisposed toward a particular company. Commercials are primarily persuasive; they are informative only to the extent that audiences become aware of the existence of new products and services or corporate "goodwill."

Commercials vary considerably in terms of their production values and formats. Network commercials and national spot commercials (network level commercials aired on local stations in major markets) are generally written and controlled by major advertising companies, such as Leo Burnett, J. Walter Thompson, and McCann-Erickson, which oversee all aspects of the creation of a commercial from writing, through storyboarding, to actual production by an independent production company. They are often shot on 35mm film, and budgets can run as high as several hundred thousand dollars. On the local level, commercials are usually made on videotape by a television station or by a small production studio. The people who produce local commercials often write them as well.

The Goal   The first step in writing a commercial is to establish the main goal. In most cases the goal is to sell a specific product or service, but some commercials sell corporate goodwill. Public utilities do not always compete directly with other companies supplying the same type of power or service. They nonetheless need to maintain a positive public image, if only to obtain periodic rate increases. Specifying a goal in terms of products, services, or corporate goodwill is helpful in terms of selecting a specific selling strategy.

Selling Strategies   Commercial scriptwriters rely quite heavily on advertising research to determine the best way to sell a product or service. The "look" and selling approach of a television commercial are often dictated by audience testing and "positioning." Positioning refers to the most effective means of reaching prospective buyers for a product or service. Audience testing and positioning determine the overall approach that a writer should take, how a commercial will look, and how it will communicate to a selected target audience. Market research reveals the best selling strategy.

Writers of commercials try to define three things before they begin writing the script: the intended audience, the major selling points of the product, and the best strategy or format with which to sell the product. The audience can be defined quite generally or very specifically in demographic terms of sex, age, race, socioeconomic status, and so on. Air time for the presentation of the commercial can be selected on the basis of this well-defined target audience. The writer must be familiar with the types of expressions and selling techniques that will appeal to the intended audience. Advertising agencies conduct research before actual writing begins, trying to ascertain why a particular group of people likes or uses a product and why others do not. A commercial is usually designed to broaden the appeal of the product without alienating the current users or consumers.

Writing a commercial requires a firm understanding of the specific product or service which is being sold. Listing the major selling points of the product will help the writer select those elements which appeal primarily to the main target audience and to determine the best selling format, whether it is a hard sell or a soft sell, a serious or a humorous tone, a testimonial, and/or a dramatization.

Hard Sell and Soft Sell Approaches

Both hard sell and soft sell commercials are used to promote specific products. They are usually based on a careful study of the nature of the product and its appeal. Consumer testing reveals that a hard sell works well with automobiles and soap products, for example. An aggressive pitch does not turn off potential customers. Many soap-product commercials present "real-life" dramatizations, which end in a hard sell from a typical consumer who is satisfied with the product. Other products rely on a soft sell or a less direct appeal. They create a particular image that entices consumers to seek beauty aids or brand-name clothing in order to have a more satisfying social life. A commercial can create an attractive image, which is associated with the product and which the customer aspires to emulate. This approach often reinforces social stereotypes, such as traditional or emerging trends in male and female roles. Commercials generally reinforce the status quo, because advertisers are afraid of offending potential customers. Testimonials, which are endorsements of a product or service made by celebrities, often rely on hard sell techniques. Dramatizations, except in the case of soap products, usually offer a more indirect approach. The viewer is left to draw his or her own conclusions about why someone is so attractive, successful, or satisfied.

Humorous and Serious Approaches

Generally, humorous treatments work well in certain areas, but not others. Obviously humorous treatments of products or services related to death, personal hygiene, or profound social problems are generally in poor taste and can be offensive to audiences and thus counterproductive. Humor can be used effectively to deflate the sophisticated image of a specialized foreign product, such as Blue Nun wine, or to associate a product with fun and good times, as McDonald's commercials have done. Humor can create amusement and attention, but if poorly handled, it can also distract attention from the product or company name. Appropriate use of humor generally requires talented performers.

Jingles

A variety of means can be used to help the audience remember the product or company name, such as simple name repetition or a song with a catchy phrase or slogan, called a **jingle**. Many commercials begin with the creation of a song to which the visual elements will be edited. The lyrics and music are frequently performed by top-name musicians and performers, and they often set the tone and pace for the entire commercial. The emphasis in jingles is on repeatable phrases that will help the consumer remember the product or company name.

Audience Testing

Network commercials are often extensively tested on audiences and potential consumers prior to purchasing expensive "air" time. The objective of most scientific tests is to determine the effect of the commercial on product recall or name retention. It is assumed that if viewers can recall the product or company name, they are likely to buy the product. Other tests examine actual or simulated purchasing behavior, such as the opportunity to select a soft drink from among several competing products after viewing commercials. Sometimes several versions of a commercial may be tested, only the most effective of which will actually be used.

Advertising Copy

Written or spoken copy must be clear, succinct, concrete, and active. Clarity is of utmost importance. If the message is to be understood, it must be expressed in terms that the average viewer can easily comprehend. Time for commercials is both limited and expensive. The message must be short and direct. There is no time for wasted words that distract attention from the central point. It is usually best to use very concrete nouns and adjectives, as well as active verbs. Passive verbs are too tentative and rarely help sell products. Writers of commercials try to use words that will be popular with the anticipated audience and consumer. Key words or "buzz words," such as "natural" or "no artificial ingredients," can increase the appeal of a product for potential buyers, despite the fact that chemists often consider such words to be imprecisely applied to soft drinks and food, since very few edible substances are actually "artificial."

Storyboards

A **storyboard** is a pre-production tool consisting of a series of drawings and accompanying written information. In some ways a storyboard is similar to a comic strip. The storyboard tells the commercial story or message in still pictures. Narration or dialogue, camera movements, sound effects and music are usually specified under or next to each frame. An advertising agency usually creates a storyboard to show clients and producers what a commercial will look like. The storyboard suggests how images and sounds will be ordered, the placement of the camera, and the design of the set. A photoboard is a series of still-frame photos created after a commercial has been shot. The "Bud Light" photoboard in this text (See Color Plate I.) illustrates the basic concept of using still pictures to represent moving images. Directors sometimes use storyboards along with the script as a guide to actual recording of the finished commercial on film or videotape, and its use is highly recommended for any type of production where step-by-step planning is possible. Many feature film directors compose their shots on storyboards prior to actual production.

A television storyboard consists of four elements: hand-drawn sketches, camera positions and movements, dialogue or narration, and sound effects or music. (See Figure 4.3.) Each hand-drawn sketch is composed within a frame that has the same proportions as a television screen, (4 units wide by three units high, a ratio of 4:3). A frame is drawn for each shot. Camera positions and movements (discussed in chapter 5), lines of dialogue or narration, and sound effects (SFX) and music are specified under or next to each frame.

Public Service Announcements

An often neglected type of announcement, which is produced much like a commercial, is known as the public service announcement or PSA (Figure 4.4). PSA's are usually aired free of charge by commercial broadcasting stations, and most noncommercial stations offer no other form of announcements. PSA's often promote nonprofit organizations. They can attempt to raise public awareness of specific social problems and social service agencies and are usually persuasive in the sense that they have clear behavioral objectives, such as appeals for help or money. In the case of a social need or charity event, the emphasis is usually on developing audience empathy for people in need rather than on appealing to the audience's materialistic needs and drives.

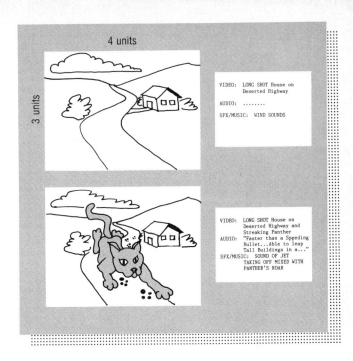

The writing of a PSA is virtually identical to that of a commercial. The same steps and procedures can be followed, including researching the particular organization or cause, specifying the goal, matching the selling or promotional stategy to the intended audience, and creating a storyboard. PSA's offer an opportunity for students and beginning production people to obtain valuable experience in writing and production, because they are usually produced on very low budgets and incur few, if any, expensive "air time" costs.

**Figure 4.3
Storyboard for
Panther Paw Tires**

Summary

Scriptwriting can be divided into two basic categories: fiction and nonfiction. Nonfiction scripts often convey information about actual events. Fiction and nonfictional structures frequently overlap, and

Video	Audio
GRADUAL ZOOM IN TO MAX ROBINSON IN NEWS ROOM	HELLO, I'M MAX ROBINSON REMINDING YOU THAT AS PARENTS WE ARE OUR CHILDREN'S FIRST AND POTENTIALLY MOST IMPORTANT TEACHERS. AS A MATTER OF FACT WE CAN GIVE OUR CHILDREN'S EARLY EDUCATION A BOOST BY TURNING EVERYDAY EXPERIENCES INTO LEARNING EXPERIENCES.
CUT TO CAR INTERIOR CHILD AND PARENT POINTING TO CARS 45 SPEED LIMIT ROAD SIGN CUT BACK TO PARENT AND CHILD TOGETHER IN CAR INTERIOR	IT'S AS SIMPLE AS POINTING OUT AND READING ROAD SIGNS ON THE WAY TO THE STORE OR COUNTING THE CARS YOU SEE ALONG THE WAY
CUT TO CHILD, PARENT IN PARK LOOKING AT BIRD'S NEST CUT TO CLOSE UP MEASURING SPOON	IT'S AS EASY AS STOPPING TO NOTICE AND TALK ABOUT THE TREES AND INSECTS.
CUT TO CHILD, PARENT IN KITCHEN MEASURING FLOUR CUT TO CHILD, PARENT USING TYPEWRITER	IT'S LETTING YOUR CHILD LEARN BY DOING, MEASURING AND MIXING KITCHEN INGREDIENTS OR FIGURING OUT HOW A TOOL WORKS.
ZOOM OUT TO PARENT READING BOOK TO CHILD, AT HOME	OR JUST GIVING THE TV A REST AND READING TO YOUR YOUNGSTER, WHICH IS ESPECIALLY IMPORTANT, AND LETTING THEM READ TO YOU AT HOME OR IN THE LIBRARY.
CUT TO PARENT SHOWING CHILD HOW TO USE A TELEPHONE CUT TO CLOSE UP CHILD USING TELEPHONE	IT'S ASKING AND ANSWERING QUESTIONS THOUGHTFULLY, EXPLAINING THE HOWS AND WHYS OF EVERYDAY LIFE.
CUT TO PARENT AND CHILD LOOKING AT MARINE MAP ON SAILBOAT	IT'S USING YOUR IMAGINATION AND ENCOURAGING YOUR CHILDREN TO LEARN BY SHOWING THEM YOU CARE WHAT THEY LEARN.
CUT TO MAX ROBINSON SUPER TITLE OF MAILING ADDRESS	I'M MAX ROBINSON HOPING YOU'LL FIND OUT MORE ABOUT THIS IMPORTANT SUBJECT BY WRITING "SCIENCE BRIEFS" AT THE UNIVERSITY OF NORTH CAROLINA, CHAPEL HILL, NORTH CAROLINA 27514

**Figure 4.4
Example of a Public
Service
Announcement**

scriptwriters should be familiar with both types of scriptwriting.

Nonfiction scriptwriters work in a variety of formats, including documentary, news, interviews and talk shows, informational and educational programs, and various types of commercials.

Generally speaking, documentaries can be defined as presentations of factual, political, social, or historical situations and events, which use film or television to record or document these events. At one extreme documentaries border on fictional art forms. Dramatic recreations of fact, which have tremendous entertainment as well as information value, have been offered in the form of television docudramas and feature film documentaries. At another extreme, documentaries can be almost purely informational (scientific films) or persuasive (television social documentaries). Some documentaries, called ''direct cinema'' or ''cinema verité,'' films simply record slices of life. Others contain interviews and actuality footage edited into persuasive social appeals. Some documentaries explore scientific topics that are of interest to the general

public. Others place journalists in the role of social or moral watch dogs.

Documentaries must be carefully structured. The opening sequence must immediately gain the audience's attention, and a consistent point of view must be established. The scriptwriter must review the materials to be included and organize them into a coherent presentation. Lastly, an appropriate pace must be established during postproduction editing. Narration in documentaries can serve a variety of purposes: introducing a topic, issue, or personality; creating logical transitions between diverse segments; underscoring points that are being made visually; clarifying or interpreting meaning; and summarizing the main points and issues of a segment or of the documentary as a whole.

A newswriter's job is to organize a story and to describe events straightforwardly, clearly, and succinctly. The building blocks for most news segments are the picture and sound sequences that have been recorded. The newswriter or reporter does some initial research into the topic area and determines what additional material must be recorded. After all the necessary material is recorded and edited, the newswriter composes narration that can be used to link various recorded segments in a concise, logical order. "In-the-field" or "in-the-studio" voice-over narration can be used to provide logical links between separate actions.

There are two types of interviews: celebrity interviews and authority interviews. Celebrity interviews concentrate on the personality of the guest and are often intended to promote his or her latest work. Authority interviews usually focus on a specific topic or issue rather than the personality of the guest. Writers and researchers for interview shows must thoroughly prepare the host with information that can serve as the basis for questions, but the host must be able to alter the predetermined format and respond immediately to situations as they develop.

Instructional programs graphically present educational materials that cannot be as effectively communicated by other means. They must be clear and well-organized. Writers must rely on terms and concepts that will be easily comprehended by the appropriate educational level or demograhic group to which the instructional material is directed.

Commercials are brief messages which are broadcast as persuasive appeals. They provide the primary source of income to commercial broadcasters, who sell television time to advertisers and local companies. The main purpose of commercials is to sell products or services or to promote corporate goodwill.

Writers define their intended audiences, major product selling points, and basic selling strategy prior to writing the script. Writers use a variety of selling strategies, such as hard sells and soft sells, humorous and serious treatments, dramatizations and testimonials. Commercials are frequently tested on specific audiences and consumers prior to purchasing expensive air time. Usually these tests examine name recall or actual purchasing behavior.

Advertising copy must be clear, succinct, concrete, and active. It must be quickly comprehended by an average viewer. The script for a commercial is usually written after a visual storyboard, consisting of sequentially drawn images similar to a comic strip, is constructed. Commercials which are aired free of charge for nonprofit organizations and various causes are called public service announcements or PSA's. They offer beginning production people an opportunity to gain valuable experience in writing and production.

Additional Readings

Arlen, Michael J. *Thirty Seconds*. New York: Penguin Books, 1981.

Barnouw, Erik. *The Sponsor: Notes on a Modern Potentate*. New York: Oxford University Press, 1978.

——————————. *Documentary: A History of the Non-Fiction Film*. New York: Oxford University Press, 1977.

Barsam, Richard Meran. *Nonfiction Film*. New York: E. P. Dutton, 1973.

Bliss, Edward, Jr., and John W. Patterson. *Writing News for Broadcast*. New York: Columbia University Press, 1971.

Bluem, A. William. *Documentary in American Television: Form, Function, Method*. New York: Hastings House, 1964.

Blum, Richard A. *Television Writing: From Concept to Contract*. New York: Hastings House, 1980.

Braddeley, W. Hugh. *The Technique of Documentary Film Production*. New York: Hastings House, 1975.

Bronfeld, Stewart. *Writing for Film and Television*. Englewood Cliffs, NJ: Prentice-Hall, 1980.

Epstein, Edward Jay. *News from Nowhere*. New York: Vintage, 1974.

Fox, Walter. *Writing the News*. New York: Hastings House, 1978.

Gans, Herbert J. *Deciding What's News*. New York: Pantheon Books, 1979.

Garvey, Daniel E., and William L. Rivers. *Broadcast Writing*. New York: Longman, 1982.

Hall, Mark W. *Broadcast Journalism: An Introduction to News Writing*. 3rd ed. New York: Hastings House, 1978.

Heighton, Elizabeth J., and Don R. Cunningham. *Advertising in the Broadcast Media*. Belmont, CA: Wadsworth Press, 1976.

Hilliard, Robert L. *Writing for Television and Radio*. 3rd ed. New York: Hastings House, 1976.

Hovland, Carl I., et al. *Experiments on Mass Communication*. Princeton: Princeton University Press, 1949.

Maloney, Martin, and Paul Max Rubenstein. *Writing for the Media*. Englewood Cliffs, NJ: Prentice-Hall, 1980.

Rivers, William L. *Finding Facts: Interviewing, Observing, Using Reference Sources*. Englewood Cliffs, NJ: Prentice-Hall, 1975.

PART 2

PRODUCTION

CHAPTER 5

Directing: Aesthetic Principles and Production Planning

Video and film directors are artists who can take a completed script and imaginatively transform it into exciting sounds and images. Directors creatively organize many facets of production to produce works of art. They know how and when to use different types of camera shots and have mastered the use of composition, image qualities, transition devices, and relations of time and space. Directors know when and how to use different types of sound and how to control sound and image interaction. By using all of their creative powers, directors are able to produce films and television programs that have lasting value.

Directors prepare a shooting script by specifying specific types of images and sounds to be recorded within each scene. They usually select and organize images and sounds according to one of the three basic aesthetic approaches introduced in chapter one.

PRELIMINARY DECISION MAKING

Aesthetic Theories

A convenient way to organize aesthetics, or approaches to the creative process, is to use three very general categories: functionalism, realism, and formativism. Most artistic approaches reflect one or more of these three aesthetic tendencies, which differ in their emphases on function, form, and content. Function refers to *why* something is expressed; its goal or purpose. Form can be thought of as *how* something is expressed in a work of art. Content refers to *what* is expressed. Function, form, and content are closely connected aspects of any work of art.

Functionalism

Functionalism stresses the idea that form follows function. Expressive forms and techniques are selected on the basis of how well they help the artist achieve practical goals. Works of art might be expected to serve such functions as fulfilling audience expectations or serving the needs of a state, organization, or company. In video and film, directors use whatever forms and techniques best serve the purpose at hand. A commercial might require rapid action and many short-duration shots to stimulate viewer interest and to sell a product. Similar techniques might be used in a children's television program, such as "Sesame Street", for entirely different purposes. An informative program might adopt a much slower, more deliberate pace to increase clarity and viewer comprehension, as opposed to creating dramatic action and excitement. The function of a work of dramatic fiction might be to entertain, of a documentary to inform, and of a commercial to persuade. A director can select forms and techniques that will enhance the performance of these functions and the achievement of these goals.

Realism

Realism stresses content more than form. In realist works, artists use forms and techniques that do not call attention to themselves, a so-called "transparent style." Realist artists depict a world of common experience as "naturally" as possible. Smooth, continuous camera movements and actions, continuity of time and place, and the use of actual locations and "real" people (i.e., nonactors) help to sustain a sense of reality. Realist art relies on conventions which some artists and viewers believe will preserve an illusion of reality. While realist techniques and conventions change, as in the shift from black-and-white to color images for added realism in photography, film, and television during the 1950s and 1960s, the mimetic tradition and the intention to preserve an illusion of reality in Western art has persisted over time. A realist artist is a selector and organizer of common experience, rather than a self-conscious manipulator of abstract forms, principles, and ideas.

Formativism Formativism stresses form more than content. Much modern art is basically formativist in approach. Abstract paintings, for example, often appear to have little or no real content beyond the shapes, patterns, and colors the artist organizes. Formativist works of art call attention to specific expressive forms and techniques. In video and film these forms and techniques might include camera movements, composition, image qualities, and specific ways of combining images and sounds, known as editing techniques. Rarely, if ever, are these forms used to represent common experience or to preserve an illusion of reality. Purely formativist artists are often more concerned with their own self-expression than with social functions of art and pragmatic or practical goals. But formativist art works are extremely valuable because they can sharpen our powers of preception, introduce us to new forms of creative expression, and make us question the validity and objectivity of realist illusions and conventions.

Image and sound selection is guided by a director's aesthetic approach. Functionalism, realism, and formativism are not mutually exclusive nor do they exhaust all aesthetic possibilities, but they offer a convenient means of organizing the field of aesthetics from the standpoint of production. The relation of expressive forms and techniques to program content and purposes often reflects these three general tendencies. They are applicable to all the aspects of production that will be covered in this section, including visualization, lighting and set design, as well as post-production editing.

Preparing the Shooting Script

Directors begin to apply aesthetic principles to concrete production problems when they plan a production. Production planning is usually done on paper. Directors specify shots and sound effects for each scene in the script as they prepare a final shooting script. (See Figure 5.1.) After the shooting script is completed, shot lists are often written up for camera operators. Sometimes a storyboard consisting of still-frame drawings of every shot in the final shooting script is drawn up as a visual guide to production. (See chapter 4, p. 92 and chapter 12, p. 293.)

After carefully analyzing the script, a director begins to prepare a final shooting script by indicating specific types of shots, transition devices, and sound effects. The following description of image and sound possibilities offers an introduction to production planning and aesthetics. Directorial terms for specific types of visual images and sounds must be thoroughly learned before a shooting script can be created. **Shots** are continuous recordings of actions within a scene made by a single camera. Abbreviations are used to specify camera placements and movements, such as ECU (extreme close-up) or MS (medium shot), which specify the desired distance of the camera from the subject. Where the camera is placed can have a considerable impact on what action is viewed or how a subject appears. Camera movements, such as CAMERA PANS

Act III

Fade in camera # 4, O'Brien standing over Winston in the torture area. As the scene progresses...

Boom up T-4 [#2 vt x fingers front So face to O'B, eventually ⑧2-5]

Take 4 (Camera #2 go very tight across fingers in front of Winston's face to O'Brien, eventually dolly back to two-shot)

With action T-2 [#4 vt on O'B]

Take 2 (Camera # 4 very tight on O'Brien)

T-4 [H-2]

Take 4 (Camera #2 hold)

92

WINSTON

How can you control memory? You haven't controlled mine! *(Boom up T-4)*

O'BRIEN

On the contrary, you have not controlled it. That is what has brought you here. You have been lacking in humility, in self-discipline. *(With action T-2)*

..How many fingers am I holding up?

HE HOLDS UP FOUR FINGERS.

WINSTON

Four.

O'BRIEN

And if Big Brother says not four, but five... then how many?

WINSTON

Four.

O'BRIEN TOUCHES THE LEVER AND THE *(T-4)*

NEEDLE SHOOTS UP TO FIFTY. THERE IS A GASP OF PAIN FROM WINSTON, AND O'BRIEN MOVES THE LEVER BACK. CAMERA HOLDS O'BRIEN AND THE MACHINE. WINSTON REMAINS OUT OF FRAME, AND, DURING THE NEXT FEW EXCHANGES, CAMERA DOES NOT RETURN TO HIM. ONLY HIS VOICE, BECOMING HOARSER, MORE GUTTERAL, LESS CONTROLLED, INDICATES THE EFFECT OF THE INCREASING SHOTS OF PAIN ARE HAVING ON HIM.

**Figure 5.1
Example of a Marked Shooting Script**

RIGHT or CAMERA DOLLIES IN, are also specified in a shooting script, as are transitions between one shot and another, such as CUT TO, FADE OUT, FADE IN, and DISSOLVE. Camera movements add motion to the recording of a scene and can also change the perspective or point of view on a subject or action. Various transition devices are used to communicate changes of time and/or place to the audience. Sound effect designations, such as SFX (Sound Effect): PLANE LANDING, specify concrete sounds that should accompany specific images. Preparing a final shooting script allows a director an opportunity to ''shoot'' and reshoot a video or film production on paper at minimal expense before actual recording begins.

To compose a final shooting script, a director must understand a full range of aesthetic possibilities. There are many different ways to record a specific scene in any script. A director interprets the action and decides on the best shots, transition devices, and sound effects for each scene.

Directors select specific recording techniques, such as different types of shots, for each scene on the basis of the aesthetic approach they have chosen. A director's overall aesthetic approach in large part determines the ''meaning'' of images and sounds by setting a context for interpretation. A functionalist approach usually calls for camera positions and movements that clearly and simply communicate essential information. A realist approach often involves the use of tech-

A still illustrating the scene from the marked shooting script of *1984* (Figure 5.1).

niques that help to preserve an illusion of reality through a transparent or unnoticed style. A formativist approach calls attention to techniques and highlights a director's manipulation and control over the recording medium and subject matter.

Some types and combinations of visual images and sounds can be functionalist or realist in one context, but formativist in another. For example, **jump cuts** are discontinuities in human actions or movements from one shot to the next. Since they disrupt the continuous flow of realist time and space, jump cuts are often considered a formativist technique, but they are also used in news and documentary interviews. A jump cut indicates that something has been removed and is often considered more honest than using techniques which disguise the fact that editing has been done. From a formativist perspective, jump cuts such as those in Jean-Luc Godard's *Breathless* (1959), call attention to directional control by breaking down the illusion of temporal continuity or the smooth, continuous flow of time from shot to shot, but from a realist perspective in news and documentary productions they make it clear that the recording of an event has been edited.

PLANNING VISUAL IMAGES

Types of Shots

A director's ability to select and control visual images begins with an understanding of specific types of shots. The camera can be close to or far away from the subject. It can remain stationary or move during a shot. The shots commonly used in video and film production can be described in terms of camera-to-subject distance, camera angle, camera (or lens) movement, and shot duration.

A jump cut consists of a gap or mismatch in time or action from one shot to the next. Jean Luc-Godard makes effective use of the jump cut as a stylistic device in his ground breaking film, *Breathless*. Today jump cuts are quite common in commercials, interviews, and feature films.

Camera-to-Subject Distance

Long shot (LS)   The **long shot** orients the audience to subjects, objects, and settings by viewing them from a distance; this term is sometimes used synonymously with the terms *establishing shot* and *full shot*. An establishing shot (ES) generally locates the camera at a sufficient distance to establish the setting. Place and time are clearly depicted. A full shot (FS) provides a full frame (head-to-toe) view of a human subject or subjects.

An establishing shot introduces the general setting and situates characters or people in relation to the setting.

Medium shot (MS)   A **medium shot** provides approximately a three quarter (knee-to-head) view of the subject. The extremes in terms of camera-to-subject distance within this type of shot are sometimes referred to as a medium long shot (MLS) and a medium close-up (MCU). The terms *two shot* and *three shot* define medium shots in which two or three subjects respectively, appear in the same frame.

Close shot (CS) or Close-up (CU)

The terms close shot and close-up are often used synonymously. A close-up refers to the isolation of elements in the shot, and normally indicates the head and shoulders of a person. When someone is making an important or revealing statement or facial gesture, a close-up will draw the audience's attention to that event. Close-ups focus and direct attention and create dramatic emphasis. When they are overused, however, their dramatic impact is severely reduced. A very close camera position is sometimes called an **extreme close-up** (ECU). See Figure 5.2 for an illustration of a long, medium, and close-up shot.

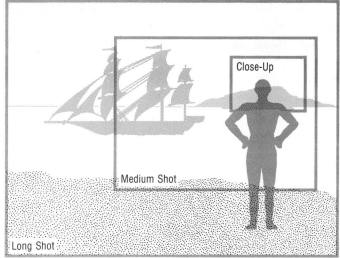

Long Shot

Medium Shot

Close-Up

Close-Up

Medium Shot

Long Shot

Figure 5.2
Long, Medium, and
Close-Up Shot
Illustration

Camera Angle   Camera angle is frequently used to establish a specific viewpoint; such as, to involve the audience in sharing a particular character's perspective on the action. The goal may be to enhance identification with that person's psychological or philosophical point of view.

Point-of-view shot (POV shot)   A point-of-view shot places the camera in the approximate spatial positioning of a specific character. It is often preceded by a shot of a character looking in a particular direction which establishes their spatial point of view within the setting, and followed by a shot of that same character's reaction to what he or she has seen. The latter shot is sometimes called a **reaction shot**. A commonly used point-of-view shot is the over-the-shoulder shot, in which the camera is placed behind and to the side of a subject so that the shoulder of that subject appears in the foreground and the face or body of another in the background.

Subjective shot   A variation on the point-of-view shot is the **subjective shot**, which shows us what the person is looking at or thinking about. Visual distortion or blurring of the image is sometimes used to suggest a person's subjective state of mind. A subjective shot can be something dreamed, imagined, or recollected by a character or person. It brings the audience inside the mind of a character and forces them to experience subjective impressions, imagined worlds, and memories of past events. Like point-of-view shots, subjective shots offer a nonobjective viewpoint on actions and events, and can enhance audience identification with more subjective points of view.

Reverse-angle shot   A reverse-angle shot places the camera in exactly the opposite direction to the previous shot. The camera is moved in a 180-degree arc from the shot immediately preceding it.

Low-angle shot   A low-angle shot places the camera closer to the floor than a

A point-of-view shot places the camera in approximately the same spatial position or point of view as a character or person in the film or videotape. It is usually preceded by a close-up of that person looking or glancing in a specific direction. This establishes both the point in space from which they are looking and the direction in which they are looking. A point-of-view shot is often followed by a close-up of the person's reaction to what they (and we) have just seen.

"normal" camera height, which is usually at eye level. A low angle tends to exaggerate the size and importance of the subject.

High-angle shot   The high-angle shot places the camera high above the subject and tends to reduce its size and importance.

Overhead shot   An overhead shot places the camera directly overhead and creates a unique perspective on the action. This can sometimes be accomplished by a set of periscope mirrors, an overhead track, or by attaching the camera to an airplane, helicopter, or crane.

Stationary Versus Mobile Camera Shots

An objectively recorded scene in a drama establishes a point of view that conforms to the audience's main focus of interest in the unfolding events. This "objective" placement of cameras can still be quite

varied. A director can use a continuously moving camera gliding through the scene to follow the key action. This approach establishes a point of view that is quite different from recording a scene from several stationary camera positions. Both approaches can be objective in the sense that neither attempts to present a specific person's point of view, although a moving camera creates a greater feeling of participation and involvement as the audience moves through the setting with the camera.

A moving camera adds new information to the frame and often alters spatial perspective. A moving camera shot can maintain viewer interest for a longer period of time than a stationary camera shot. But a moving camera shot can also create difficulties. It is often difficult to cut from a moving camera shot to a stationary camera shot. The camera should be held still for a moment at the beginning and end of a moving camera shot so that it can easily be intercut with other shots. One moving camera shot can follow another so long as the direction and speed of movement remain the same. Both moving the camera and cutting from one stationary camera shot to another can give us a spatial impression of the setting from a variety of perspectives, but the former generates feelings of smoothness and relaxation while the latter creates an impression of roughness and tension.

Many types of "mobile" camera shots can be recorded with the camera remaining in a fixed position.

Pan shot   A camera can be panned by simply pivoting it from side to side on a fixed tripod or panning device. This shot is often used to follow action without having to move the camera from its fixed floor position.

Tilt shot   A camera tilt is accomplished by moving the camera up and down on a swivel or tilting device. This shot is also used to follow action, such as a person standing up or sitting down. It can also be used to follow and accentuate the apparent height of a building, object, or person.

Pedestal shot   A camera can be physically moved up and down on a pedestal dolly. A hydraulic lift moves the camera vertically up and down within the shot, such as when a performer gets up from a chair or sits down. A pedestal shot allows the camera to remain consistently at the same height as the performer, unlike a tilt shot, where the camera height usually remains unchanged. Pedestal shots are rare, but a pedestal is often used to adjust the height of the camera between shots.

Zoom shot   A zoom can be effected by changing the focal length of a variable focal length lens in midshot. A zoom shot differs from a dolly shot in that a dolly shot alters spatial perspective by actually changing the spatial positioning of objects within the frame. During a zoom shot the apparent distance between objects appears to change because objects are enlarged or contracted in size at different rates. During a zoom-in objects appear to get closer together, while during a zoom-out they seem to get farther apart.

Other types of mobile camera shots require camera supports that can be physically moved about the studio.

Dolly shot   A dolly shot is a shot in which the camera moves toward or away from the subject while secured to a movable platform on wheels. It is often needed to follow long or complicated movements of performers or to bring us gradually closer to or farther away from a person or object.

Trucking shot   In a trucking shot, the camera is moved laterally (from side to side) on a wheeled dolly. The camera may truck with a moving subject to keep it in frame. If the dolly moves in a semicircular direction, the shot is sometimes referred to as an **arc** or **camera arc**.

Crane or **boom shot**   The camera can be secured to a crane or boom so that it can be raised and lowered or moved from side to side on a pivoting arm. This type of shot can create a dramatic effect when it places the subject in the context of a large interior space or a broad exterior vista.

Shot Duration   One of the director's key jobs, which is shared by the editor during postproduction, is to determine the precise duration of each shot. An exposition section may call for a number of long takes that slow down the action and allow the audience to contemplate character, situation, and setting. A dramatic climax, on the other hand, may call for many different short duration shots, which help intensify the action. The famous three-minute shower scene murder in Alfred Hitchcock's *Psycho* (1960), for example, is made up of well over one hundred separate pieces of film cut together to intensify the action. Formativist aestheticians, such as Sergei Eisenstein, have advocated the use of many short-duration shots, while realist aestheticians, such as Andre Bazin, have often recommended the use of longer duration shots. The functionalists' belief that form follows function suggests that the duration of shots should be suited to the particular situation.

Composition

Composition is a term used by painters, graphic artists, and still photographers to define the way in which images can be effectively structured within a frame. Composition is affected by the frame dimensions or aspect ratio of the specific media format. Two basic principles of composition discussed later are symmetry and closure. Composition is complicated by the fact that video and film images move in time. Therefore composition is constantly changing.

Frame Dimensions   A **frame** limits the outer borders of the image to specific dimensions. The ratio of these dimensions, that is, the ratio of a frame's length to its height, is called the **aspect ratio** of the frame. Composition is obviously slightly different for different aspect ratios. If you were to put identical paintings in frames with different dimensions and aspect ratios, for example, the paintings would look very different. The relations between shapes and objects or composition within the frames would not be the same. Video, Super-8mm, and 16mm film all have the same aspect ratio: 4:3 or 1.33:1. But feature films in super 16mm,

35mm, and 65mm, which are made for wide-screen projection in theaters, have aspect ratios that vary from 1.85:1 to 2.35:1. (See Figure 5.3.) HDTV is designed in the 1.85:1 academy aperture feature film format or aspect ratio. Wide-screen images can enhance an illusion of reality by involving more of our peripheral or edge vision, but they also alter the aesthetics of object placement and composition within the frame. Consider the different impressions created by a wide gulf between two characters on wide screen and a greater proximity of two characters in the same video frame. It is difficult to copy or transfer visuals from one aspect ratio to another intact, such as copying magazine photographs with a video camera or showing a widescreen film on television.

An important factor in terms of frame dimensions is the concept of **essential area**. The full video or film camera frame is rarely, if ever, viewed in its entirety. Part of the border or edge of the full frame is cut off during projection. Essential area refers to the portion of the full frame that will actually be viewed. All key information, actions, and movements must be safely kept within this essential area.

Rule of Thirds   One well-practiced theory of composition involves dividing the frame into thirds, both horizontally and vertically. If you mentally draw two vertical and two horizontal lines which divide the frame into thirds, objects can then be arranged along the lines. Important objects may be placed at the points where these lines intersect for added interest or emphasis. Following the rule of thirds allows a picture to be quickly comprehended in an aesthetically pleasing way. Placing subjects in this manner is more interesting than simply bisecting the frame. Other slightly more complicated forms of visual

**Figure 5.3
Aspect Ratios**

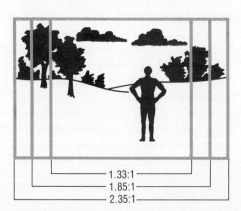

1.33:1
1.85:1
2.35:1

The photo on the left illustrates poor lookspace in terms of frame composition. Insufficient empty space is presented into which the person can look within the frame. The photo on the right illustrates good lookspace with a sufficient amount of empty space into which the person can look in the frame.

composition can also be used with success, but they are not always comprehended so quickly and easily.

Symmetry   **Symmetry** is an important aesthetic principle of composition in any two-dimensional, framed visual medium. A director can create a symmetrical or balanced spatial pattern by using objects in the frame. A symmetrical frame appears stable and solid, but eventually uninteresting and boring as well. An asymmetrically or unbalanced frame is more volatile and interesting but can also be extremely distracting. When properly used, both symmetrically and asymmetrically organized frames can be pleasing and effective. The key is to know when it is appropriate to use one form of composition rather than the other.

Framing the head of one person talking directly into the camera in an asymmetrical pattern can be distracting. The audience's attention is supposed to focus on the spokesperson, but it is distracted by the lack of balance in the frame. An asymmetrical image of one or more people in the frame can suggest that someone or

something is missing. The entrance of another person or character then balances the frame. An asymmetrical frame can suggest that something is wrong or that "the world" is out of balance.

The concept of symmetry must be integrated with the rule of thirds and other concepts such as lookspace, walkspace, and headroom. **Lookspace** refers to the additional space left in the frame in the direction of a performer's look or glance at something or someone outside the frame. **Walkspace** is the additional space in the frame left in front of a moving performer. Following the rule of thirds, the performer's face in the case of a look or glance and the performer's body in the case of a walk or run is placed on one of the trisecting vertical lines, leaving two thirds of the remaining space in the direction of the glance or movement. This asymmetrical composition is much better than having the performer in the exact center of the frame. **Headroom** refers to the space left in the frame above the subject's head, which is most pleasing visually when there is a slight gap between the top of the head and the top of the frame.

The photo on the left illustrates poor walkspace in terms of frame composition. Insufficient empty space is presented into which the person can walk within the frame. The photo on the right illustrates good walkspace with a sufficient amount of empty space into which the person can walk in the frame.

Closure   The concept of lookspace is related to another aspect of visual composition, called **closure**. On-screen space, that is, space within the frame, often suggests continuity with off-screen space. An open frame suggests that on-screen space and objects continue into off-screen space. A completely closed frame, on the other hand, gives the illusion of being self-contained and complete in itself.

The way in which an image is framed and objects are arranged can create a sense of closure or a sense of openness. Symmetrically framing a performer's head in the center of the frame creates a sense of closure. The composition does not allude to parts of the body which are missing off-screen. An asymmetrically framed portion of a hand, arm, leg, or face, on the other hand, suggests continuity in off-screen space. Something appears to be cut off, although our memories readily fill in the missing parts.

Formativist and realist aestheticians, such as Rudolph Arnheim and Andre Bazin respectively, have suggested that closed and open compositions have differ-

ent aesthetic effects. Bazin suggested that there is an analogy between a window and a camera frame in that there is a constant interaction between on-screen and off-screen space. He advocated the use of an open frame as a realist technique which suggests a continuity between on-screen and off-screen space. This continuity reminds us that the camera is giving us but a small part of the real world. Arnheim, on the other hand, advocated the use of a closed frame. The camera formatively isolates objects within the frame, separating them from surrounding off-screen objects in the real world. The film or video artist is then free to establish a more abstract world within the frame, which has lost its connection to the real world. Functionalist aestheticians, of course, suggest that open and closed compositions should be used in different situations to help achieve the desired purpose of a specific sequence.

Depth and Perspective   Screen composition can enhance an illusion of **depth** and three-dimensionality. Lighting can add depth to the image by helping to separate foreground objects from their backgrounds. Placing the camera at an angle so that two sides of an object are visible at the same time creates three-dimensionality. Including foreground objects in a frame can enhance the illusion of depth by setting a "yardstick" by which the distance, size, and scale of the background can be determined. A person, tree branch, or object of known scale in the foreground can set a context for depth. Diagonal or parallel lines, such as those of a railroad track, can guide the eye to important objects in the frame and create a greater illusion of depth. Placing objects or people at several different planes of action within the frame and frames within frames, such as a person

standing inside a doorway, increase the perception of depth within the frame. Of course, a certain degree of care must be exercised when using multiple planes of action so that two planes do not unintentionally connect to create one confused plane, as when a plant in the background appears to be growing out of a person's head.

Image perspective refers to the apparent depth of the image and the spatial positioning of objects in different planes. Perspective can be affected by the type of lens that is used. Telephoto or long focal-length lenses often seem to reduce apparent depth, while wide-angle or short focal-length lenses seem to expand space and

Framing the same subject differently can create a sense of closure or a sense of openness. A closed frame such as the one on the right seems self-contained. The oval shape of the head positioned in the center of the frame seems symmetrical and self-contained. The tight closeup on the eyes and mouth of the same person in the photo on the left creates a sense of openness. The cropping of the head thrusts us outside the frame to fill in missing parts, just as the subject's eyes make us wonder exactly what is he looking at outside the frame.

apparent depth. Lenses help an image look deep or shallow. A moving camera, as in a dolly shot, can also affect the apparent depth and perspective by changing the relationship between objects in the frame. Cutting from one camera angle to another can help create an illusion of three-dimensionality out of two-dimensional video and film images.

Frame Movement   A moving frame changes visual composition. In video and film, composition is constantly in flux due to camera or subject movement. In this respect film and video are quite unlike photography and painting, which present motionless images. One type of composition can quickly change to its opposite. A symmetrical frame can quickly become asymmetrical or an open frame closed.

The illusion of depth can be enhanced by the movement of a camera or of objects within the frame. Objects that move toward or away from the camera naturally create a greater sense of depth than those that move laterally with respect to the camera. Diagonal lines of movement, like diagonal lines within a static frame, add dynamism and force to the composition. A canted frame can also add a sense of dynamic strength to an image, such as an exciting shot within a car chase, but a canted frame used in less intense action sequences often looks out of place.

Image Qualities

Tone   A director must be conscious of subtle differences in image tonality, especially when editing or combining images. **Image tonality** refers to the overall appearance of the image in terms of contrast (gradations of brightness from white to black) and color. Image contrast can be affected by lighting and recording materials. Combining two shots that have very different contrast levels can be disconcerting to the viewer, but it can also arouse attention. A high-contrast scene, that is, one which has a limited range of gray tones with mostly dark black and bright whites, will look quite different from a low-contrast scene, which has a wide range of intermediate tones. Matching image tonalities in terms of contrast and color can help effect smooth transitions from shot to shot and scene to scene. Combining mismatched tones can have a shock or attention-getting value. Excessive contrast is a common problem in video production, especially field production, where outdoor lighting is difficult to control. High contrast is sometimes more of a problem in video than in film, due to the wider range of contrasting shades or tonalities the latter can record, but it is an important consideration in both media.

Scale and Shape   Scale refers to the apparent size of objects within the frame. Camera-to-subject distance, camera angle, and the type of lens used can affect the apparent size of objects. Lower camera positions and angles sometimes increase the apparent size of an object in the frame. The apparent size of an object can increase or decrease its importance.

Directors can create a balanced/symmetrical frame by arranging objects of equivalent size or similar shape in different parts of the same frame. Graphic similarities, such as similarities in the shape or color of objects, can create smooth transitions between shots. Graphic differences can be used to create an asymmetrical frame or emphasize transitions from one shot to another.

A human figure, such as the child standing on a rock overlooking a lake in this picture, can help establish size, scale, and distance.

Speed of Motion   Images can have different speeds of motion. **Speed of motion** refers to the speed at which objects appear to move within the frame. This speed can be changed by altering the film recording speed or the video playback speed to produce **fast motion** or **slow motion**. Editing many short-duration shots together can enhance the speed of motion, while using fewer shots of longer duration can help slow down actions and the speed of motion. The pace of editing is called **editing tempo**. The apparent motion of objects is also affected by camera placement, lenses, and the actual motion of the photographed objects. A long focal-length lens often slows down apparent motion by "squashing" space, while a wide-angle lens can speed up motion by expanding the apparent distance traveled in a given period of time.

Combining Shots

A good director is usually a good editor; that is, directors know how and when to combine specific images. Editing begins with an understanding of composition, image qualities, and different types of shots. Shots can be combined using a variety of transition devices, including straight cuts, fades, and dissolves.

Straight cut or take   A straight cut or take is a direct, instantaneous change from one camera shot to another, say from a long shot of a scene to a close-up of a performer's face. Time is assumed to be continuous over a straight cut, except in the case of **jump cuts**, where actions are discontinuous and do not match from one shot to the next, suggesting a gap of time. If a cut is made from a shot of a person talking to someone on one side of a room to a second shot showing the same person talking to someone else on the opposite side, the result is a jump cut. Jump cuts are widely used in commercials, in which stories are condensed to thirty seconds by using rapid editing tempos, and in documentary and news interviews where this procedure is sometimes considered more honest than using cutaways to mask deletions. It is becoming more and more common to use jump cuts to compress time in fiction as well.

Fade   The picture of a video program or film can **fade in** from blackness to image or **fade out** from image to blackness. A fade-out followed by a fade-in usually indicates a significant passage of time. A fade, like a curtain on the stage, can be used to mark the beginning and the end of a performance and to separate acts or scenes.

Dissolve   A dissolve is actually a simultaneous fade out and fade in. One scene or shot fades out at the same time that another shot fades in to replace it. For a very short duration the two shots are superimposed on one another. Dissolves are frequently used to conceal or smooth over gaps in time rather than emphasizing them as in a fade-out and fade-in. A very rapid dissolve is sometimes called a **soft cut**.

Defocus   Placing one image out of focus and gradually bringing a replacement image into focus is a defocus transition.

Swish pan   A rapid movement of the camera on the tripod swivel or panning head causes a blurring of the image, which can be used as a swish pan transition from one scene to another. This transition is frequently accompanied by up-tempo music which accelerates the sense of action and movement rather than creating a pause.

Wipe   A wipe is a transition device created on a switcher, special effects generator, or an optical film bench whereby one image or shot is gradually replaced on the screen by another. A wipe may begin on one side of the screen and move across to engulf the opposite side. It can also begin in the middle of the frame and move outward. Ending one shot by dollying or zooming in to a black object which fills the frame and beginning the next shot by dollying or zooming out from a black object is sometimes called a **natural wipe**.

Special Effects

Split screen or shared screen   Having one image occupy a portion of the same frame with another image is called shared screen. When the frame is split into two equal parts by the two images, it is called split screen. Sometimes these techniques make it possible to show two different but simultaneous actions on the same screen.

Superimposition   Having two different shots occupy the same complete frame simultaneously is called a superimposition. One shot is usually dominant over the other to avoid visual confusion. The superimposed images should not be excessively detailed or busy. In effect, a superimposition looks like a dissolve that has been stopped while in progress. Combining a long shot and close-up of the same person from different angles sometimes creates an effective superimposition.

Keying and chroma key   A specific portion of a video image can be completely replaced with a second image using keying or chroma key techniques. Titles and graphics can be inserted into a portion of another image. A scene from a still photograph or slide can be inserted into a blue or green colored area (a green or blue screen on the set, for example) in another shot, using video chroma key. The monochrome blue or green portion of the latter shot is replaced with the former shot.

Matte and blue screen   A matte is used in film to black out an area in one image which will then be filled in with a second image. Matting is to film what keying is to video. Blue screening in film is equivalent to chroma key in video, since the blue screen area in one image is replaced by a second image.

Negative image   A normal visual image is positive. A negative image reverses the brightnesses and darknesses of the original image. Blacks become whites and whites become blacks. Colors turn into their complements. In television this can be done by simply reversing the polarity of the electrical picture signal. In a film a negative print can be made from a positive image.

Freeze frame   A freeze frame is a continuing still image from one frame of a video or film shot created during postproduction. Usually the action stops by freezing the last frame of a shot, such as at the conclusion of a film or video program.

Scene Construction   A **scene** is a series of shots of action occurring in continuous time at one place. It is important to ensure that significant changes in camera angle and/or camera-to-subject distance occur between two successive shots within a scene. The camera angle should change at least forty-five degrees with respect to the subject from one shot to the next, unless there is a significant change in camera-to-subject distance. A few aesthetic reasons for making a cut that involves a change of camera-to-subject distance are (1) to depict an action that was omitted in the previous shot; (2) to provide a closer look at an event or object; (3) to emphasize an object or action; and (4) to draw back and establish the setting. A cut from a medium shot to a close-up provides a closer look at an object or event, while a cut from a long shot to a close-up emphasizes an object or action. Cutting from a medium shot to a long shot helps to reestablish the setting and place the action in context or in broader spatial perspective.

A conventionally constructed scene might begin with a long shot or establishing shot to place the subjects within a specific setting. Then the camera gets progressively closer to the subject as the action intensifies, and finally the camera pulls back to reestablish the setting at the conclusion of the scene. An alternative approach is to begin a scene with a close-up and gradually pull back from shot to shot to reveal more and more of the setting as the action progresses. The latter approach is initially somewhat confusing and spatially disorienting, but it also arouses viewer curiosity.

Certain types of cuts involve quite severe changes in camera-to-subject distance, such as those from long shot to close-up or vice versa. In functionalist and realist situations these dramatic changes of scale should be used sparingly and primarily for emphasis, because they often have a distracting effect on the audience. More gradual changes of scale are less disruptive, and provide a smoother transition.

A new shot or image should serve a purpose different from that of the previous shot. It can anticipate the audience's next point of interest, that is, it can be psychologically motivated on the basis of viewer expectations. It can present additional or contrasting information by revealing actions that were hidden from a previous angle. In general, every shot should be cut as short as it can be without inhibiting its function. A good director separates essential from nonessential information to determine how long a specific shot will maintain viewer interest.

Continuity Editing

Continuity editing usually means creating a smooth flow from one shot to the next. Actions that begin in one shot are completed in the following shot with no apparent gaps in time. There is continuity in the spatial placement and the screen direction of moving and stationary objects from shot to shot.

Conventional continuity can, of course, be disrupted in time and space. Gaps or jump cuts in the action can be consciously edited into a scene. Actions can be repeated over and over again, slowed down and speeded up. But it is important to learn the basics of continuity editing before attempting to disrupt it. Beginning video and film directors need to first acquire some appreciation of the difficulty inherent in trying to maintain continuity and in meeting conventional viewer expectations.

Pace and Rhythm

The selection of long- and short-duration shots affects the pace or rhythm of a scene. A director must be very sensitive to changes in pace and rhythm. To build a scene out of different shots, a director must match the tempo or rhythm of the editing to the subject matter and the audience's expectations. Rapidly cutting together many short-duration shots for a "how-to" film about woodworking, for example, distracts the audience's attention from the primary subject matter. Slow-paced editing for a soft drink commercial may be extremely boring and an ineffective persuasion technique. A fast-paced exposition and a slow-paced climax in a dramatic production usually fail to achieve the desired emotional effect and dramatic structure.

Compression and Expansion of Time

Directors can compress and expand time through editing, even while preserving the illusion of temporal continuity. For example, suppose that you wish to record the action of someone getting dressed and ready for work in the morning. A single shot of this activity that preserved exact temporal continuity might last ten minutes or more in actual duration. But by recording different segments of action and editing them together, the essential elements of the activity can be preserved without creating any readily apparent gaps in time. How can this be done? Simply by cutting from a long shot of the action to a close-up of a hand or an object in the room and then cutting back to a long shot in which the person is more completely dressed than could actually have occurred in the duration of the close-up. A director can speed up an action by eliminating unimportant or repetitious actions between cuts. The action and time are condensed and compressed. The same technique can be used for someone crossing a street. Perhaps we begin with a full shot or long shot of the person starting to step off one curb, then cut to a medium shot and then a close-up of his or her feet or face. Finally, we present a long shot of the person reaching the other side of the street. This edited version of the street crossing might last just five seconds, while actually walking across the street takes more than twenty seconds. Condensing or compressing action can increase the pace and interest of actions.

Actions can also be expanded through editing. For example, recall Robert Enrico's classic short film *Occurrence at Owl Creek Bridge* (1966), discussed in chapter 3. The protagonist, a Confederate plantation owner, is being hanged from a bridge by Union soldiers. He appears to escape his captors when the noose around his neck breaks and he falls into the water beneath the bridge. But his long escape down river turns out to be an expanded dream sequence in the instant before he dies. Underwater images of him struggling to free his tightly bound hands and feet are edited together in such a way that time is expanded. It takes the protagonist about three minutes of actual film time to finally reach the surface of the water and gasp for air. This would be a marvelous feat for even an experienced diver, not to mention someone who has been choked by a noose just before unexpectedly entering the water. The expansion of time through editing in this scene increases the tension and suspense of his supposed escape.

Screen Directionality   Depicting a three-dimensional world in a two-dimensional medium presents the director with special problems of screen directionality. **Screen directionality** refers to the consistent direction of movements and object placement from one shot to the next. Inconsistent screen direction causes spatial confusion. What viewers actually see seems to contradict their expectations. This type of confusion can be effective in music videos and formative works of art. But in general, maintaining directional consistency of looks and glances, object placements, and subject movements within the frame reduces viewer confusion by increasing spatial clarity in realist and functionalist works.

Directional Glances   It is important to record a consistent pattern of performers' spatial looks and glances within the frame to preserve an illusion of reality. The improper placement of a camera can result in confusing inconsistencies (which again can be useful in a formative approach). A close-up of one character looking screen left at a second character is usually followed by a shot of the other character looking screen right to suggest that he is looking back at the first character. When one person looks down at another person, the other should look up within the frame of the second shot, and so on. The camera must be placed and the image framed so that there is directional consistency from one shot to the next.

The 180-Degree Axis of Action Rule
The **180-degree rule** of camera placement ensures directional consistency from shot to shot. An imaginary line can be drawn to connect stationary subjects. Once the camera is placed on one side or the other of this **axis of action**, all subsequent camera placement must occur on the same side of the line to prevent a reversal in the placement of objects in the frame. (See Figure 5.4.) A moving subject establishes a vector line and all camera placements are made on one side of this line or the other to maintain consistent screen direction of movement. If the camera crossed this line, a subject going from left to right in one shot would appear to be going in the opposite direction in the next shot.

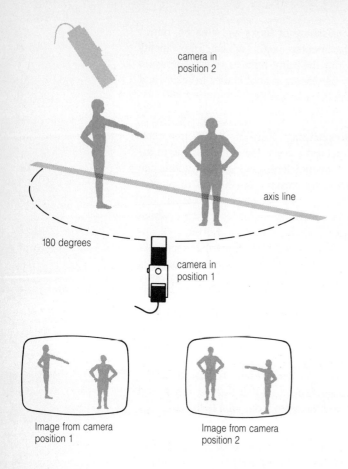

camera in
position 2

axis line

180 degrees

camera in
position 1

Image from camera
position 1

Image from camera
position 2

Figure 5.4
The 180-Degree
Action Axis
Crossing the 180-
degree action axis
line with the camera
from one shot to the
next can create
directional confusion
for viewers. A person
moving left to right in
one shot will appear
to have reversed
direction if they are
moving right to left in
the next shot. Keeping
the camera on one side
of the action axis
maintains directional
clarity and consistency.

There are ways to break the 180-degree rule without creating spatial confusion or disrupting an illusion of reality. First, the camera can move across the line during a single shot, establishing a new rule on the opposite side of the line to which all subsequent shots must conform. A director can also cut directly to the line itself by placing the camera along the line and then cross over the line in the next shot to establish a new rule. Finally, the subject can change direction with respect to the camera during a shot and thus establish a new line.

An overvaluation of visual images can lead directors to neglect accompanying sounds, but sound is an extremely important aspect of video and film production. Sound can complement and fill out the image. It can also conflict with corresponding images or produce an independent experience. Sound can shape the way in which images are interpreted. It can direct our attention to a specific part of the image or to things not included in the image. Some sounds and music have the ability to stimulate feelings directly. Sounds can create a realistic background or a unique, abstract, impressionistic world.

It is important to recognize the ways in which sounds relate to other sounds before examining the ways in which sounds and images interact with one another. By initially focusing on visuals and sounds as separate elements, a more logical and coherent understanding of the complexities of sound and image interaction can be acquired. Three general areas of sound aesthetics are: types of sound, sound qualities, and relationships between sounds.

Types of Sounds

Sounds can be divided into four basic categories: speech, music, sound effects, and background sounds.

Speech   Two common uses of speech are narration and spoken dialogue. Narration provides an oral commentary on visual images. It can interpret images, prepare the audience for future images, provide additional information, and summarize what has just been shown. Narration is frequently recorded separately from the visuals it accompanies. In a documentary, a narration can consist of a series of interviews that are edited to provide a commentary on the visual action. **Voice-over narration** refers to spoken commentary by a speaker who does not appear on screen.

Spoken dialogue is usually recorded so that it will synchronize with the on-screen speakers' lip movements. A director must be sensitive to subtleties of acting and performance, such as the intonation, intensity, and appropriateness of a line of dialogue. A director who cannot judge the quality of a performance has no basis for selecting and editing spoken dialogue. To direct or edit a sequence of spoken dialogue a director must be equally sensitive to visual and audio qualities.

Music   While it is rarely necessary for a director to have as much knowledge of music as a composer or music theorist, some knowledge of music is essential. A director should be familiar with different types of music and musical structures, so that the best music can be selected and combined with visual images.

The basic elements of music are rhythm, melody, harmony, counterpoint, and tonality or timbre. Rhythm refers to the **beat** or **tempo** of music. The rhythm of a piece of music affects the perception of **pace** or speed in actions and editing. Marches, waltzes, disco, folk, and rock music have a distinctive, recognizable rhythm, such as the 3/4 time of a waltz.

A **melody** is a series of notes or tones. When we whistle a familiar tune or song, we are generally recalling the melody. In symphonies and large musical compositions melodies are often called **themes**. In Wagnerian opera, themes are often repeatedly associated with specific characters. These are called **leitmotifs** and are often used in television and film as well. For example, when the character Amanda first entered the Carrington household in "Dynasty," her entrance was accompanied by an eighteenth century European musical variation of the "Dynasty" theme, reinforcing the idea of aristocracy and tradition. Most melodies are written in one of the two basic musical keys, major or minor. In general it can be said that **major key** music is bright, happy, and strong, while **minor key** music is dark, sad, and uncertain.

Harmony refers to the combined effect of playing several notes simultaneously that are consonant with one another. That is, they harmonize in a pleasing manner when they are played together. When notes of music do not harmonize, they are called dissonant.

Counterpoint is the simultaneous presentation of two distinct melodies that exist separately and equally in their own right. The two melodies, one principal and the other secondary, do not fuse together to create one harmonic melody, but remain separately distinguishable instead, although one melody's rhythm is usually congruent and synchronous with respect to the other's. Musical forms such as the canon and the fugue rely on counterpoint.

Tonality or **timbre** indicates the particular quality or unique characteristics of a sound source, such as a musical instrument or voice. The way in which a sound resonates within an instrument affects its tonality or timbre; thus the same note sounds different when it is produced by a different instrument or voice.

There are several ways of categorizing music. Musical form refers to the overall structure of a piece of music. Folk songs, minuets, rondos, suites, sonatas, concertos, symphonies, and overtures represent different musical forms. Each has its own characteristic rhythms, harmonies, and tones. While music from any of these forms could be adapted to a video or film production, such selection and adaptation requires great care. Music composed specifically for video and film usually takes an attenuated or shortened form, with rapid development of themes and their variations. The form of the music should match the specific needs of the visual sequence.

Music can be divided into broader categories on the basis of both its form or structure and the audience it attracts. Popular, folk, jazz, rock, and classical music are relatively broad categories. The type of music selected for a specific sequence involves a consideration of its geographical and historical source and its audience, as well as its structure and form.

Music for film and television is commonly divided into two basic categories: scoring and source music. **Scoring** is usually written by a composer for a specific production. It is added to the visuals and is rarely performed or played within the picture. **Source music**, on the other hand, comes from a source within the actual scene portrayed on the video or film screen, as when a character is playing the piano.

Sound Effects

Sound effects are generally "realistic" sounds not originally recorded with their corresponding visuals. Sounds effects can also be impressionistic sounds which add color, depth, and dimension to a sound track. Prerecorded sound-effects libraries are readily available on audiotapes or phonograph records and are usually organized into basic categories such as animal sounds, vehicle sounds, human sounds, bells and chimes, and so on, as well as alphabetically on the basis of specific sounds and sound sources. Selecting the precise prerecorded sound effect that will enhance a specific scene can involve considerable research and listening or auditioning time.

Sometimes it is impossible to find the best sound effect for a scene in a prerecorded sound-effects library. Recording original sound effects requires considerable imagination and ingenuity. Often the best sound impression comes from a source that is quite different from the supposed on-screen sound source. The production of original sound effects for video and film has borrowed techniques from "live" radio broadcasting. To create the sound of a Martian space ship opening its door in Orson Welles' famous "War of the Worlds" radio broadcast in 1938, a jar lid was slowly unscrewed inside a toilet bowl. In George Lukas' film *The Empire Strikes Back* (1980), the footsteps of giant robot soldiers were actually produced by striking a telephone guy wire in a rural location. Original sound effects, particularly those for which an audience has little experience on which to base a "realistic" comparison, often use everyday objects to create an imaginative audio impression. Sound effects can often stir an audience's unconscious emotions as effectively as music.

Background Sound

Whether we are conscious of it or not, every different location has its own background sounds. Background sound is sometimes called **ambient sound**. It is considered a type of sound effect. Background sound may be caused by ventilators, lights, electrical equipment, and people in a room. If we completely eliminated these sounds in film and video our sound track would seem flat, lifeless, and unrealistic. In everyday life we are able to ignore much of this noise through selective perception. We can concentrate on the sounds that we are interested in and ignore the rest. But in film and video our perception of sound is heightened, and we cannot tolerate extreme fluctuations in background sound or its total absence.

It is sometimes an advantage to record foreground and background sounds separately. Primary spoken dialogue can be recorded in a studio without background sounds. This technique avoids the problems of occasionally having background sounds disrupt the dialogue. A continuous, constant level of background sounds can be recorded separately and added later. In this way the dialogue can be edited and changed while the background sounds remain uninterrupted, helping to maintain an illusion of reality and continuous time.

Sound Designations Directors often use the following terms and abbreviations in a shooting script to specify the types of sounds they need at various points in a program.

Sound effects (SFX) Special sound effects that are necessary to the action are often designated in the script. These are rarely described in great detail; either the specific sound or its supposed source is identified. For example, (SFX: EERIE METALLIC SCREECHING) or (SFX: CREAKY DOOR).

Voice-over (VO) Voiceovers are speech sounds that are not synchronized to visual images. A character can narrate actions, tying them together in a drama, documentary, or news segment. The speech alternative to a voice-over is called **lip-sync** or **direct voice (DV)**, where speech sounds are synchronized to images of speakers.

Music Music can be indicated in a very general, unspecific way by simply writing (MUSIC). A specific character's musical theme or leitmotif might be indicated by writing (MUSIC: CHARACTER'S THEME). Period music or specific selections can be indicated as follows: (MUSIC: RENAISSANCE) or (MUSIC: PROKOFIEV'S "PETER AND THE WOLF").

Sound Qualities

Loudness and Pitch Loudness and pitch are sound qualities that can be controlled during initial recording, although this is finalized during a postproduction audio mix. In some instances it is desirable to alter the sound level or loudness for different types of shots. For example, a speaker who appears in a long shot may eventually be recorded or mixed at a slightly lower sound level than when he or she appears in close-up. Varying sound levels or loudness with camera-to-subject distance creates **sound perspective**. Audio distance perception can parallel or reinforce visual distance perception. Another technique for establishing sound perspective is placing a subject off-mike, that is, at a distance away from the microphone, as opposed to on-mike or well within the best mike pickup position. A performer's ability to "work" a microphone in terms of on-mike and off-mike positioning is called **presence**.

Loudness can be an effective means of manipulating audience attention. An unexpectedly loud sound can jolt an audience out of its complacency and add emphasis.

Soft sounds and silence can be equally effective. The E. F. Hutton commercials that used a silent pause after the line, "My broker is E. F. Hutton and E. F. Hutton says . . . "silence" . . . (narrator) When E. F. Hutton talks, everybody listens," gained attention without resorting to loud sounds.

The pitch or frequency of a sound can also have some effect on emotional response. A squeaky, high-pitched voice can be grating or irritating. A deep voice can have a soothing effect. Some changes in pitch help to sustain an illusion of reality. The well-known **Doppler effect** is a change in the pitch of a passing car or train sound. The sound gets louder as the vehicle approaches and softer as it departs and at the same time the pitch rises and drops.

Tone and Reverberation   Every human voice, musical instrument, and sound source has its own characteristic tone or tonality, which refers to the precise mixture of pure tones and overtones it emits. The size of one's throat can affect tone, just as the length and tautness of one's vocal chords affect pitch. The exact tone that a sound source emits can be important in terms of identifying a specific sound source or judging its accuracy or authenticity. Tone can be altered and adjusted through audio equalization, to be discussed in chapter 10.

Reverberation is caused by sound waves bouncing or reflecting off of various walls or surfaces in an enclosed space. Some reverberation is present in every room. A large open hall will cause a longer delay in reflected sounds, because they must travel a greater distance than reflected sounds in a small room. The degree to which materials in a room absorb or reflect sounds can also affect reverberation. Reverberation is an important means of creating a sense of space and enhancing visual depth. It can be controlled in postproduction with the use of signal processors, such as a reverberation unit, discussed in chapter 10.

Fidelity and Distortion   Sound fidelity refers to the accuracy of a sound recording. Our ears are very sensitive to sound qualities and can easily detect discrepancies between sounds and their supposed sources. Sound effects that fail to create the type of fidelity audiences expect often lead to unintended humor or groans of discontent.

Sometimes it is desirable to distort sounds intentionally and subvert sound fidelity. Distorted sounds can simulate the subjective perception of a person, such as the dazed reaction of a battered fighter. Conscious distortion can be used to create abstract sound impressions that elicit the desired emotional response without attempting to reproduce sounds accurately.

Combining Sounds

Transition Devices

Segue   An instantaneous change from one sound track or sound source to another is called a segue (seg′wā). When several separate sound tracks are being combined or mixed, the sound editor can instantly switch from one to the other. A musical segue can be made smoother by establishing continuity between the final note of the first piece of music and the beginning note of the second. One melody blends smoothly into the next.

Fade   A gradual elimination or introduction of a sound track or sound source is called a fade. The gradual elimination of sounds is called a **fade-out**, and the gradual introduction of sounds is called a **fade-in**. Fades are used to mark major breaks in terms of time, space, and subject matter.

Cross-fade The audio equivalent of a visual dissolve is called a cross-fade. One sound track or sound source fades in while another fades out. This kind of transition device is usually smoother than a segue. It is used to mark minor breaks of time, space, and subject matter or to try to hide or conceal such breaks.

Lightning mix Continuing the same speech or line of dialogue or music across major changes or cuts in time and place is called a lightning mix. For example, a politician can give the same speech in several different locations. Instead of presenting repetitions of the same speech, it can be presented once with each line of text spoken in a different setting. This technique is often used with jingles in commercials. Different people sing consecutive lines of the same song.

Audio punctuation A change in time or place can be emphasized by beginning the new scene with a very loud or shrill sound. This is a form of audio punctuation. It produces the opposite effect to a cross-fade. Rather than concealing or smoothing over a transition, it jolts the audience and emphasizes the fact that a transition has been made.

Pace and Rhythm Pace is a subjective response to the speed of sounds, lines of dialogue, and the musical beat or tempo. Obviously pace is inherent in any piece of recorded sound. Lines of dialogue can be delivered slowly or very quickly. The rhythm of a piece of music can be changed by the composer or the performers. But the director also has means of controlling the pace or rhythm of sounds, dialogue, and music. Sounds can be selected and ordered to speed up or slow down the action. The delivery of dialogue can also be speeded up or slowed down by increasing or decreasing the gaps between different lines during editing. A director's ability to alter the audio pace can have a tremendous effect on the dramatic action. An exposition section of a drama may call for a slow pace, while a climactic action may demand a fast pace. Music, lines of dialogue, and sound effects can be selected and edited to enhance the overall pace.

Continuity Versus Discontinuity A story told in temporal continuity follows a chronological or sequential course from beginning to end. Any apparent gaps or jumps backward or forward in time disrupt temporal continuity. By leaving out a word in midsentence or a key sound in a sequence a director can create an audio jump cut. Temporal discontinuity disrupts the illusion of reality, while preserving temporal continuity can help maintain this illusion. By varying the ways in which sounds are combined or cut together, a director can affect the audience's perception of time.

Repetition of Motifs Motifs are symbolic sounds that develop specific themes, concepts, and ideas. Like a poet who repeatedly uses certain words as provocative imagery, such as Shakespeare's use of astronomical symbols in his play *Romeo and Juliet* (e.g., stars and "star-crossed" lovers), a director can use specific sounds as imagery that carries symbolic meaning and value. A particular sound effect, such as the sound of an animal, or a specific musical theme or melody can be repeatedly presented in conjunction with a character or setting. Through temporal repetition the audio motif acquires symbolic value. Each occurrence of the motif seems to enrich the drama. The theme not only helps to identify a specific character, it can also symbolize and add depth to a personality.

Spatial Relationships Between Sounds

The way in which sounds are recorded and edited can affect the audience's perception of space as well as time. Sound reverberation conveys a spatial impression, as mentioned earlier. A sense of space can also be effected by using audio editing to limit and direct the attention of the audience. For example, it is possible to present a variety of sounds coming from both the foreground and the background at equal intensities. The listener/viewer must then decide which of the competing sounds to listen to. This ''open'' recording technique is analogous to open visual composition, deep focus, and long duration shots advocated by realist aestheticians. It can be contrasted with ''closed'' recording and editing, which directs the attention in a formative way by simplifying audience choices and limiting information to prominent foreground or background sounds that rarely overlap. Audio can be edited in a more abstract way to stimulate subjective impressions rather than depict a realistic world of common experience.

Another way in which sounds can create a spatial impression is through stereo or multichannel recording and playback. By using stereo recording techniques, the spatial placement of sound sources can be controlled and manipulated. A plane passing overhead, a car moving from left to right, or a dialogue between two characters on opposite sides of the frame can be enhanced by using stereo sound.

IMAGE AND SOUND INTERACTION

Sound and image relations can be divided into four oppositional categories: (1) on-screen versus off-screen sounds; (2) commentative versus actual sounds; (3) synchronous versus asynchronous sounds; and (4) parallel versus contrapuntal sounds. Understanding each of these categories opens up a broad range of aesthetic possibilities. This section concludes with a separate consideration of combining music and visual images from two different standpoints: editing images to prerecorded music and composing original music for video and film.

On-Screen Versus Off-Screen Sound

A sound coming from a source that is visible within the frame is called an **on-screen sound**. **Off-screen sounds** come from sources assumed to be just outside the frame. The use of off-screen sounds can enhance spatial depth. Noel Burch, a media theorist, has pointed out that an off-screen sound can seem to come from six possible positions outside the frame: from the left, from the right, from above, from below, from behind the wall at the back of the frame, and from behind the camera. The precise spatial placement of an off-screen sound is not always discernible. Stereophonic or multichannel sound obviously helps us to determine the position of an off-screen sound, but the effect is the same. Our attention is directed off-screen to the source of the sound, particularly if on-screen performers are looking in the appropriate direction. By arousing our curiosity, off-screen sound can set up an expectation of the visual presentation of its source. It can also break down some of the limitations of a visual frame, opening it up as a realistic window on the world, as opposed to a more abstract, self-contained, formativist aesthetic world.

Commentative Versus Actual Sound

Sound and image relations can also be classified on the basis of the supposed actuality or artificiality of their sound sources. **Commentative sound** has no known source, while **actual sound** is presumed to come from some actual or real sound source either inside or just outside the frame. Spoken dialogue is usually actual sound. Narration is commentative sound, unless the narrator appears on-screen. Music can be either commentative or actual sound. Scoring is commentative sound, and source music is actual sound.

Commentative sound effects, such as shrill metallic sounds that have no readily apparent apparent source, can help to create a impressionistic emotionally charged atmosphere. Commentative music, narration, and sound effects can be effectively used to reinforce specific feelings. Lush, romantic music, for example, might complement a romantic scene, such as the reunion of long-separated lovers, although such conventions easily become musical clichés.

Synchronous Versus Asynchronous Sound

Synchronous sounds match their on-screen sources. Lip-sync sounds synchronize with the lip movements of the on-screen speaker. Sound effects match their on-screen sound sources. For example, the sounds of a runner's feet striking the pave-

ment should be synchronized with the corresponding visual images. Music can also be said to be synchronous with visual actions or cuts that precisely follow the beat or rhythm.

Asynchronous sound does not match its sound source. Poor quality lip-sync is asynchronous sound, such as a film dubbed into a foreign language that fails to match the lip movements of the speaker. But asynchronous sound is not always poor quality sound. In fact, asynchronous sound offers many exciting aesthetic possibilities, such as providing a basis for contrapuntal sound. Commentative sound effects can be used asynchronously to contrast with their corresponding visuals. One example is the substitution of a train whistle for a woman's scream in Alfred Hitchcock's *The Thirty-Nine Steps* (1935). Commentative, asynchronous sound effects can produce emotional effects or meanings that counterpoint rather than parallel their accompanying visual images.

Parallel Versus Contrapuntal Sound

The emotional effect or conceptual meaning of sounds and images can be virtually the same or completely different. Speech, sound effects, and music can parallel the meaning or emotions of the visuals or they can counterpoint them. The term ''counterpoint'' in music refers to two separate and distinguishable melodies that are played simultaneously, as discussed earlier. The same term has been applied to image and sound interaction in video and film. **Contrapuntal sound** has an emotional effect or conceptual meaning that is separate from its corresponding visuals. Sounds and images are aesthetically separate and often contrast with one another.

Parallel sound, like musical harmony, blends together with its corresponding visuals. Like musical notes played simultaneously and in harmony, sounds and images can have parallel meanings or emotions that are mutually supportive.

Suppose that the visually depicted events are sad or tragic but the accompanying music is upbeat and in a major key, so that it communicates a bright, happy, strong feeling. In this case the music counterpoints the corresponding visuals. The same thing happens when sad music accompanies a happy event. But when sad, minor key music accompanies a tragic scene, the sounds and images parallel one another in emotional tone.

Speech sounds and sound effects can parallel or counterpoint their corresponding images. For example, the film musical *Singin' in the Rain* (1952), begins with the main character, Don Lockwood, describing his path to Hollywood stardom. Lockwood gives a short autobiography to his fans in which he claims to have received his training and background at elite, high-class schools and cultural institutions. But what we see contradicts his voice-over narration. We see that he actually began his performance career in pool halls and bars and gradually worked his way into the movies as a stuntman. His elitest posturing provides a pseudosophisticated, tongue-in-cheek commentary on Hollywood. The meaning of what we see contradicts the meaning of what we hear, producing a powerfully humorous effect.

Composing Images for Prerecorded Music

The use of music in video and film is a rather complex art. It is important for directors to understand some of the basic aesthetic possibilities inherent in two approaches to combining images and music: (1) editing visual images to prese-

lected, prerecorded music and (2) composing original music for video and film, even if the responsibility for music is in the hands of a specialist, such as a music director, composer, or performer.

Visual images can be selected and ordered into a pattern which is prescribed by prerecorded music. For example, fast-paced music might be accompanied by rapid cutting of visual images and rapid action within the frame, while slow-paced music might call for less frequent cutting and slower movements. The visual action might reach its climax at the same time as a musical crescendo or swelling in the volume and intensity of the music. The timing of the visuals can be made to coincide with the timing of the music so that both begin and end at the same points and achieve a parallel structure throughout.

Dancing and singing sequences require a high degree of synchronization and parallelism between the music and visuals. The music can be recorded in advance and used as a basis for the choreography. Prerecorded music establishes a basic structure and timing to which the performance and editing of visual images must conform, unless conscious asynchronization or contrapuntal relations between the sounds and images is desired.

Composing Music for Prerecorded Images

Another approach to music and image interaction is to compose original music for specific film or video sequences. Music composed for video or film usually serves one or more of the following functions: (1) intensifying the action or dramatic tension; (2) establishing the period or place; (3) setting the atmosphere or mood; (4) stimulating a specific emotion in conjunction with a character or theme; and (5) avoiding screen silence.

Music rhythm can intensify action and

create dramatic tension. The pace of music can increase with the speed of the action, such as a crescendo that accompanies a dramatic climax or crisis. Music can communicate time and place by virtue of its source, period, and style. Selecting a specific mode of music affects the overall mood or atmosphere. A specific melody can develop an emotion in conjunction with an important character or theme. Leitmotifs can intensify audience identification with specific people or characters and stimulate emotions. Finally, music can be used simply as a filler to cover silence or attempt to create viewer interest during slow-paced visual action sequences. Background music is all too frequently used to fill a void rather than to create a specific effect in conjunction with visual images. Careful selection and design of music is a much better approach to the problem.

Original music for television and film can consist of sounds from a single instrument, such as a solo guitar or flute, or a fully orchestrated symphonic score. The number of musicians required and the complexity of the music can vary considerably depending on the specific needs and requirements of the project and the available budget. Sometimes a scarcity of materials and resources can be an advantage. Simple music and solo performers can be easier for beginning producers to obtain and control. New computer music programs and synthesizers make it easier to have original music composed, played, and recorded by one person. Regardless of the sophistication of the music, video and film directors should make every attempt to collaborate with composers and musicians so that the music can be designed and performed for their specific needs. Original music can be tailored to a video or film production much better than prerecorded library music.

Jan Hammer, the composer for "Miami Vice." He receives a copy of each week's show at his home and views the tape in his private studio while simultaneously creating the original music on a synthesizer.

Summary

Video and film directors are artists who can turn a completed script into a shooting script and produce works of art from recorded visual images and sounds. They understand basic functionalist, realist, and formativist aesthetics. Functionalist aesthetics suggests that form follows function. The function of a work can be defined in terms of audience needs, preferences, expectations, and responses, as well as in terms of the presentation of specific subject matter. Realist aesthetics stresses content more than form, and formativist aesthetics stresses form over content. These aesthetic approaches can be applied to the use of specific visuals and sounds.

To prepare a shooting script, a director must know when to use different types of shots. Shots can be categorized by camera-to-subject distance, camera angle, camera (or lens) movement, and shot duration. By placing the camera in the same spatial position as one of the characters, a technique known as a point-of-view shot, the audience's involvement in the action and identification with that character can be enhanced. This subjective point of view allows us to participate in the action through a character's eyes and mind, whereas an independently placed camera establishes a more objective point of view.

Directors know how to control various aspects of visual composition, such as frame dimensions, symmetry, closure, perspective, and frame movement. They must also understand image qualities, such as tone, scale and shape, depth, and speed of motion, and the use of various transition devices and special effects. A director can create smoother transitions between different spaces through graphic similarities of shape and color between shots, or create more emphatic or shocking transitions through dramatic differences in shapes, sizes, and colors.

In scene construction, shots of varying camera-to-subject distance may be combined for one of the following aesthetic reasons: to include an action that could not be shown in a prior shot; to render a closer look at an action or subject; or to draw back and establish the setting. Conventional continuity often begins with a long shot and gradually moves closer to the subject as the action intensifies. Often the shot length is shorter during crises and climaxes. Continuity suggests an uninterrupted flow of time, with no apparent gaps or mismatched actions from shot to shot. Shot changes may be psychologically motivated to anticipate the audience's next point of interest or based on a specific point of view or approach adopted by the director.

Video and film are temporal and spatial arts. The perception of time can be controlled. Time can be condensed or expanded through editing. The editor of a dramatic production can manipulate historical or story time as well as actual film or video time. Actions presented within and between scenes can be continuous or discontinuous in time, depending on the program design and objectives. The perception of space can also be manipulated. Classical continuity implies respect for "rules" of screen direction, such as the 180-degree action axis rule, and the maintenance of spatial clarity. Spatial disorientation can dissipate an audience's emotional involvement in realistic action.

The aesthetic use of sound is an extremely important, if often neglected, aspect of film and television production. While sound can be used simply to accompany and complement the visuals, it can also be treated as an independent aesthetic element.

There are four basic categories of sound: speech, music, sound effects, and ambient noise. Speech usually consists of dialogue or narration. A director must be sensitive to speech intonation and levels of performance to be able to select and order different recordings of dialogue or narration. Music will either be selected from prerecorded tapes and records or composed and recorded for a specific project. A director must be familiar with the basic elements of music, such as rhythm, melody, harmony, counterpoint, and tonality or timbre as well as different types of music. Sound effects are sometimes used to enhance an illusion or reality or to create imaginative sound impressions. Background sounds are present in any location. Background sounds can be used to preserve temporal continuity and create an illusion of spatial depth.

A director should be familiar with different sound qualities, such as loudness and pitch, reverberation and tone, pace and rhythm, and fidelity and distortion, and the various means of controlling these qualities.

Temporal relations between sounds include continuity versus discontinuity, repetition of specific motifs, and audio transition devices. A director can affect the preception of temporal continuity through the selection and ordering of sounds. Mismatched levels and gaps in the presentation of sounds can create discontinuity, thus disrupting the flow of time. It is possible to condense and expand time without disrupting the illusion of continuity, however. Certain sounds, such as musical themes, can also be presented repeatedly in conjunction with specific characters or settings. Through repetition these sounds can acquire symbolic value and meaning.

Sound can also be used to create or enhance spatial impressions. Reverberation obviously affects the preception of space. Depth can be partially affected by the relation between foreground and background sounds. Sound levels and other qualities can be used and controlled to focus the audience's attention on an object, action, or event.

Spatial directionality can be effected by using stereo or multichannel sound. All of these relations and qualities of sound can be used to complement or fill out the image. They can also be used independently of the image to create a unique aesthetic experience.

Sound and image interaction can be divided into four basic oppositional categories: (1) on-screen versus off-screen sounds; (2) commentative versus actual sounds; (3) synchronous versus asynchronous sounds; and (4) parallel versus contrapuntal sounds.

Visual images can be edited to prerecorded music or music can be originally composed for video and film. A piece of prerecorded music must be carefully analyzed so that connections between the music and specific visual images can be made, such as cuts that occur on the beat. Music composed for television or film often performs one of the following functions: intensifying the drama; establishing the period or place; setting the mood or atmosphere; stimulating a specific emotion in conjunction with a character or theme; or simply filling in and avoiding silence. Leitmotifs are specific melodies which are repeatedly associated with a character or theme. The director and the composer should collaborate with one another, fully and creatively exploring the artistic potential of visual image and music interaction.

Additional Readings

Andrew, J. Dudley. *Major Film Theories*. New York: Oxford University Press, 1976.

Barrett, Gerald R., and Thomas L. Erskine (compilers). *From Fiction to Film: Ambrose Bierce's An Occurrence at Owl Creek Bridge*. Encino, CA: Dickenson Publishing Company, 1973.

Bordwell David, and Kristin Thompson. *Film Art: An Introduction*. 2nd ed. New York: Alfred A. Knopf, 1986.

Burch, Noel. *Theory of Film Practice*. trans, Helen R. Lane. New York: Praeger, 1973.

D'Agostino, Peter, ed. *Transmission: Theory and Practice for a New Television Aesthetics*. New York: Tanam Press, 1985.

Mantell, Harold, ed. *The Complete Guide to the Creation and Use of Sound Effects for Films, T.V. and Dramatic Productions*. Princeton: Films for the Humanities, Inc., 1978.

Roberts, Kenneth H., and Win Sharples, Jr. *A Primer for Film-Making*. New York: Bobbs-Merrill, 1971.

Weis, Elisabeth. *The Silent Scream, Alfred Hitchcock's Sound Track*. Rutherford, NJ: Farleigh Dickinson University Press, 1982.

_____ and John Belton. *Film Sound: Theory and Practice*. New York: Columbia University Press, 1985.

Zettl, Herbert. *Sight, Sound, and Motion: Applied Media Aesthetics*. Belmont, CA: Wadsworth Publishing Co., 1973.

Exercises

1. Repeatedly view a scene or sequence from a completed production and write a (postproduction) shooting script or shot analysis for it based on actual shots in the finished product. Compare your shooting script or shot analysis for this segment to a published version to determine if you have made proper use of shooting script terms and concepts.

2. Take a segment from a completed script and attempt to transform it into a shooting script by adding specific shots, sound effects, and so on. Use techniques that are consistent with a functionalist, realist, or formativist approach when creating your shooting script.

CHAPTER 6

Directing: Methods and Practices

Armed with a final shooting script, a director is ready to organize production. A shooting script provides a detailed production guide for the recording of specific images and sounds. In order to record the different scenes and sequences described in the script, the director must organize the activities of many different people who are involved in production. Problems affecting various areas and aspects of production are discussed and ironed out during production meetings. The director, often together with the producer, selects specific performers during casting sessions. Logistical problems of performance and production are worked out during rehearsals and blocking sessions in which performer or camera positions are finalized on the set. The rehearsal process allows a director time to make changes and refine his or her conception of a project before actual recording occurs. The role of the director is quite different in multiple-camera and single-camera recording, and these two production situations are considered separately in this chapter.

PRODUCTION COORDINATION

Video and film directors are personnel managers as well as artists with moving images and sounds. Directors coordinate production by working with their staff, crew, and performers. Frequent production meetings facilitate coordination. A cooperative, collective effort has to be carefully orchestrated and managed by the director if a quality product is to be achieved. The director must be a good judge of character. The success of a video or film production often hinges on selecting the right people for the right roles, es-

pecially during the casting of performers. Directors must be effective communicators to ensure that their intentions are fully and precisely carried out. They must be familiar with a specific terminology to effectively communicate with their staff, crew, and talent.

Production Meetings

Frequent production meetings provide the director and the production staff with an opportunity to work out important details and problems collectively. Prior to actual production the director usually meets with key staff members, such as the producer, the art director or scenic designer, and the lighting director. The overall goals and objectives of the film or video project are clarified during these meetings. Each staff member is apprised of his or her responsibilities and at the same time informs the director about any problems or questions that pertain to a specific area. Each key staff member is considered a specialist in at least one area, and it is expected that all problems relevant to that area will be raised and resolved during these meetings, Everyone must understand the overall purpose and design of the production to prevent members of the production team from working at cross purposes.

Everything must be worked out and all problems solved prior to actual "live" video production, since "live" production means that there is no postproduction and therefore little or no room for production mistakes. During prerecorded production, meetings between key personnel help work out unforeseen problems that have arisen. The director must be able to communicate effectively with the staff, if these problems are to be quickly and efficiently resolved. The more talented, independent, and opinionated the staff, crew, and performers are, the more likely it is that problems and disputes will arise, unless a common purpose has been collectively determined or hierarchically imposed at the beginning. Directors must be able to combat, suppress, caress, and cajole strong egos. A disruptive prima donna performer may need to be carefully controlled by the director to obtain the best possible performance. The director's authority may be questioned and his or her status with the staff, crew, and other performers jeopardized if an unruly participant is allowed to dominate the proceedings. The director must be explicit and authoritative about commands. Other members of the staff, crew, and talent are constantly depending on the director to make many different types of decisions. But the director must also listen to the needs, desires, and problems of the staff, crew, and talent. Production meetings provide the director with an opportunity to exercise authority and give commands, but also to listen to the ideas, needs, and problems of others. Effective managers are often good listeners. The more frequently production meetings take place, the less likely it is that a problem will escalate to the point that costly, irrevocable mistakes are made or production is unnecessarily slowed down or curtailed.

Casting

To cast a specific performance effectively, the director must have a firmly established interpretation of each character or role. Each role, however small, is important in terms of the quality of the final product, and a video or film program is often only as good as its worst performer. It is often said that almost any director can evoke an excellent performance from an experienced, talented performer but that good

direction is most evident in the quality of smaller roles and bit parts.

Good casting depends on a director's understanding of at least three factors: the audience, the character or role, and the physical appearance of specific performers. Audience expectations must be carefully considered in casting. The personality projected by the actor must match audience expectations for the role. It is important to select people who look the part and who can act naturally. The natural look and feel of a performer is probably the most important factor in terms of his or her appropriateness for a specific role, although skilled actors can drastically change their appearance and still appear ''naturally'' suited to a role; e.g., Dustin Hoffman in *Tootsie* (1982).

Directors often have to deal with performers who have different levels and types of acting experience. Experienced stage actors need to be cautioned not to

Dustin Hoffman on the set of *Tootsie* (1982). There was concern that he might break fingernails while playing football on the set.

project as emphatically or loudly as they might on the stage, since video and film cameras can reveal subtle details and expressions in close-up. Inexperienced actors need to be explicitly told what is wanted. Most fail to understand or prepare themselves for the rigors of video and film acting. Inexperienced performers have difficulty relating to an awkward, unfeeling camera. Constant feedback and praise from a director can greatly improve the quality of a performance. Helping them relax, being explicit in terms of adjustments needed in their performance, and encouraging them to be natural can be of benefit to nonprofessionals. Experienced professionals, on the other hand, may require more freedom in some situations and a firmer hand in others. Some directors prefer to wait for the performer to discover and refine his or her own interpretation of a role and only offer advice as a last resort, concentrating instead on providing a positive environment. Other directors prefer a more authoritative approach, which assures a consistent interpretation but can also lead to power struggles between the director and the performer. Most directors fall somewhere in between these two extremes.

Rehearsals

Once the performers have been selected, a director can begin a preliminary run-through of the production by helping the actors to develop their specific characters. Preliminary practices of a performance are called **rehearsals**. Many rehearsals may be necessary before the performers are fully prepared to perform unerringly before the camera(s). All the bugs have to be worked out before a performance can proceed without problems or disruptions. The final rehearsal, which usually takes place with the sets fully dressed and the performers in costume is called a **dress rehearsal**. It simulates the actual recording session in virtually every respect.

Multi-camera and "live" productions usually demand more rehearsal time than single-camera productions, because entire scenes or programs are recorded at one time rather than broken up into segments for a single camera. The entire performance must be worked out to perfection so that even minor mistakes are avoided during actual recording. Actors in single-camera productions do not always know how one shot relates to another. Single shots are often recorded in isolation, and performers cannot build a performance in perfect continuity as they would on the stage or for multiple-camera production. Close-ups are often recorded out of sequence, for example. The director must be able to provide the performer with a context that will achieve a proper performance level so that shots can be combined during postproduction editing. One of the director's primary responsibilities during rehearsal and production is to ensure that the actors maintain continuity in the dramatic levels of their performances from one shot to the next. Some directors use a "start-stop" production method that combines meetings and rehearsals with actual production. Production is halted until a problem is solved and then continues until another problem is encountered. A "start-stop" method can lead to added problems, when decisions made early on make it difficult to change the position of a camera, light, or performer later. Thus many directors prefer to have a complete rehearsal in advance. Obviously a "stop-start" method cannot be used in "live" production.

Performer and Camera Blocking

The director usually stages and plots the action in two distinct stages, performer blocking and camera blocking. Prior to selecting final camera placements, angles, lenses, and so on, the director will frequently run through the basic actions to be performed by the talent. This is called **performer blocking**. A director must carefully preplan the entire performance in advance. Only rarely are the performer's movements precisely set during performer blocking alone. Instead a general sense of the action is determined which facilitates camera blocking and prepares the performers for actual recording.

    Camera blocking refers to the placement of cameras so that they can follow the movements of the talent. (Figure 6.1 shows camera blocking for the marked shooting script of *The Crocodile*, seen later in this chapter.) Whether several cameras or a single camera will actually record the action, the director must be able to anticipate the types of shots which will provide adequate coverage, dramatic emphasis, and directional continuity from shot to shot. **Shot lists** can be drawn up and supplied to the camera operator(s). Shot lists are a helpful guide to camera operation during blocking sessions and actual production. Every consecutive shot in each scene for each camera is written on a piece of paper that the camera operator can tape to the back of the camera for easy reference. Shot lists indicate types of shots and camera movements called for in the final shooting script. In some recording situations there is minimal time to block the cameras and the performers separately, and the two stages are combined. During camera blocking the performers, the director, and the camera operator(s) exchange

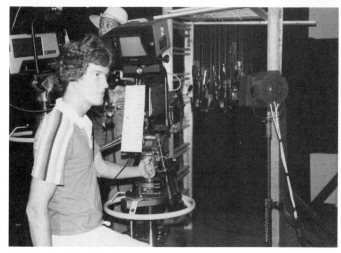

ideas and discuss problems as the action is blocked or charted on the floor. The director refines his or her conception and interpretation of the script, making notations of any deviations form previous shot selections. Performers not only learn and remember their lines. They must also remember their marks, that is, the precise points where they must position themselves during actual recordings.

Above: A director works with the actors during performer blocking and rehearsals. Below: The shot list is attached to the camera and enables the camera operator to follow the correct sequence of camera positions and movements.

**Figure 6.1
A Camera Blocking
Diagram**

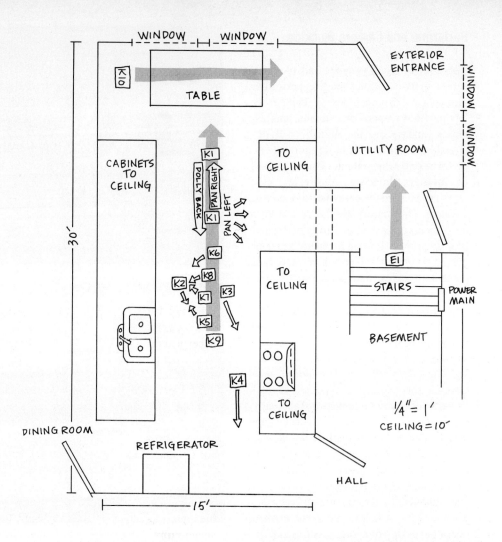

MULTIPLE-CAMERA DIRECTING

Directing several cameras simultaneously requires a different approach from that of single-camera recording. The preproduction planning stages are always very extensive, because major changes are more difficult to make once recording has begun. Performers must learn the lines of dialogue for several scenes since more script material will be recorded in a single session. Camera operators must anticipate what camera positions, lens types and positions, and framing they are to adopt for upcoming segments. Ample time and space must be provided for the cameras to be moved during recording. Every detail must be worked out in advance, and a detailed shooting script or camera shot sequence must be provided to each key member of the production team. While the director can sometimes make instantaneous changes during actual production, communicating them to camera operators and so on via an intercom or talk-back system, the risk of making major mistakes increases with each major change that is made during production.

Tremendous economies in the time and expense can be accomplished by using multiple-camera recording, when the recording session has been properly planned and practiced. But a multiple-camera situation can also be extremely frustrating if a key individual is improperly prepared or the director has failed to anticipate all the problems that can arise. Murphy's law that "IF ANYTHING CAN GO WRONG, IT WILL," is an optimistic expectation in multiple-camera and live television recording situations where directors, crews, and talents are insufficiently prepared.

For multiple-camera recordings of uncontrolled events, such as sporting events, cameras are often placed in fixed positions which keep them on the same side of the action axis, preferably with the sun behind them, if outdoors, for best lighting. Each camera operator is responsible for covering a specific part of the action from one position. The director of a "live" production may have to watch and control as many as ten cameras, some of which are connected to slow-motion recorders. The director must be able to respond instantaneously to any action that occurs, rapidly cutting from one camera to another. The director selects from among the images displayed on a bank of television screens. Since only minimal scripting is possible, the action and atmosphere within the director's control room itself often becomes very intense during a sporting event or similar production. Accurate decisions must be made very quickly. To anticipate actions and cuts directors must be intimately familiar with the particular sport.

An intercom system often used by directors to communicate with the floor manager (depicted here) who relays commands to the performers as well as the camera operators.

Timing

An important function performed by the director is timing. The control of program pace in terms of the speed of dialogue, actions, and editing is one form of timing. As discussed in chapter 5, dramatic pacing is a subjective impression of time in video and film. Through effective editing, a sequence of action can be made to seem longer or shorter in duration to the audience. Other types of timing are equally important in the production process.

Running Time   A director is responsible for ensuring that the program length or actual **running time** of a completed program conforms to the required length. In video production, running time should be distinguished from **clock time**. The latter refers to the actual time of day on the studio clock. A schedule of programs to be broadcast, for example, indicates the clock time at which they will begin and end. This is the time at which viewers can actually watch specific programs on television. Each program or program segment has its own running time, which is the exact duration of the program, regardless of what time of day it is actually shown. The

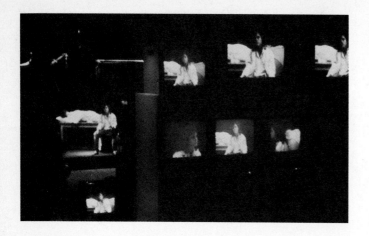

Multiple camera shots of the same scene. The director must select the best shots sometimes quickly and often under tense conditions.

collective running times of various programs and program segments must match the actual clock time allotted for them in the overall daily program schedule. During live productions, a stopwatch is used to calculate the running time of each program segment, so that the total running time will conform to the actual clock times listed in the schedule.

Timing During Production   Television commercials, public service announcements, and broadcast or cablecast programming must be accurately timed during production. When recording a commercial, for example, a director tries to obtain shots that will add up to exactly thirty or sixty seconds. Often the running times of individual segments or shots, such as different scenes or vignettes, are specified in the script. The screen time of the various shots and vignettes must add up to the exact screen time of the commercial format that has been chosen. Live video production demands precise screen timing with a stopwatch as well as a studio clock, since the show cannot be reedited, lengthened, or shortened.

Backtiming is the process of figuring the amount of time remaining in a program or program segment by subtracting the present time from the predetermined end time. Music is sometimes backtimed so that it will end at the conclusion of a live production. This means that if the music should last three minutes, you backtime in three minutes from its end and start playing it three minutes before the end of the program—gradually fading it up. In other words, if you want it to end at 6:59, you backtime it three minutes and start it at 6:56.

In multiple-camera video production, the talent is often told how much time remains by means of hand signals. Five fingers, followed by four, three, two, and one, indicate how many minutes of running time remain for that segment. Rotating the index finger in a circle indicates that it is time to wind up a performance, since the time is almost up. A cut-off signal (the hand cuts across the neck, as though the stage or floor manager's own head is coming off) indicates the actual end of a segment or show.

"On-the-Air" Timing   Prerecorded videotapes and films, such as commercials, which will be inserted into a program as it is being broadcast or cablecast must be accurately backtimed and set up on a projector or playback machine. A **countdown leader** displaying consecutive numbers from 10 down to 0 is placed just ahead of the prerecorded pictures and sound. The numbers indicate how many seconds are left before the start of the prerecorded material. The playback can then be **prerolled**; that is, begun the appropriate number of seconds before the commercial is due to start.

Production Switching

In multiple-camera video production the director supervises virtually all of the editing in the control room during actual production. Production editing is done by means of a switcher, a device that allows shots to be selected from among several different cameras instantaneously. The director usually commands the technical director (or TD) to change the transmitted image from one camera to another. (In many local stations, the director actually operates the switcher.) The TD then pushes the correct buttons on the switcher. Each button on the switcher is connected to a different camera or image source. When the TD pushes a button, the switcher automatically substitutes one picture for another. The TD and the director view these changes on television monitors (closed-circuit TV screens) as they are taking place. The images sent out of the switcher can either be directly transmitted and broadcast during live production or recorded on videotape. A videotape recording can be used for subsequent post-production editing and/or delayed broadcast, cablecast, or closed-circuit showing.

A switcher is both an electronic editing device and a special effects machine. The TD can not only cut from one image or camera to another, but also fade in, fade out, dissolve, wipe, key, chroma key, and superimpose images. Various transition

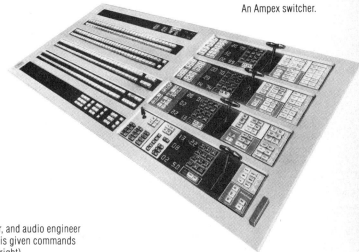

An Ampex switcher.

While in the control room (left), the director, technical director, and audio engineer view the monitors during a production. The technical director is given commands from the director as well as directions on the shooting script (right).

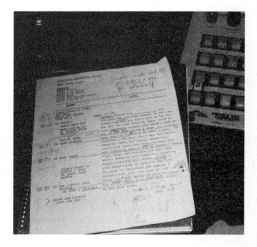

devices can be used in changing from one image or camera to another.

A switcher consists of a series of buttons organized into units called **buses**. (Figure 6.2) There are three types of buses: preview, program, and special effects or mix. Individual buttons within each bus are linked to specific sources, such as camera 1, camera 2, camera 3, the telecine camera (a camera into which a film is projected), a videotape player, a remote (field camera), and a constant black image. Each bus has one button assigned to each of these image sources. Thus a bus allocated to previewing images prior to sending them out of the board, called a **"preview" bus**, would have at least five individual buttons connected to the five image sources listed above. When one of these buttons is pressed, the image from that source appears on the preview monitor. A second bus having the same number of buttons is assigned to the actual **"program"** feed; on a simple switcher, this is the signal that will actually be transmitted or recorded. A switcher having just two buses would only allow the TD to preview images and to cut directly from one image to another. If any special effects are to be created, the switcher must have **special effects** or mix buses. These two **effects** or **mix** buses are usually designated **"A"** and **"B."**

In order to send any visual signal on the effects buses out of the switcher, a button designating the effects buses must be acti-

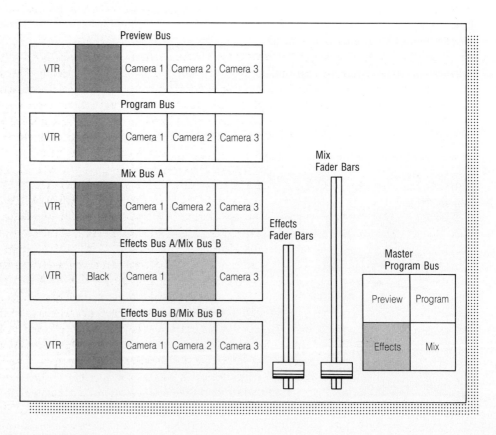

vated on a secondary program bus called the master program bus. The **master program bus** acts as a final selection switch, determining what will be transmitted by the switcher. The TD can select the program bus (which contains one of the five visual sources) or the effects bus, by depressing one of these two buttons on the master program bus. A **master preview bus** is also available on more sophisticated switchers, so that an effect, such as a superimposition, can be previewed prior to recording or transmission via the master program bus.

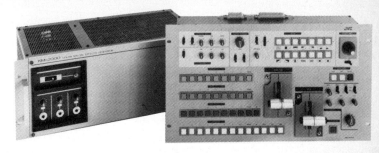

This video special effects generator allows the operator to create many startling and exciting special effects as well as to perform basic switching functions, such as wiping and fading from one image to another.

Creating Transitions with Fader Bars

Two effects or two mix buses can be interconnected by a device known as a **fader bar**. (See Figure 6.2.) A visual fader bar is analogous to an audio volume control. The visual signal or image becomes stronger or weaker as the bar is moved up or down. Two fader bars, each connected to a different effects bus (A or B), are locked together, so that when they move in tandem, one signal fades in at exactly the same rate or intensity that the other fades out. That is, as the two fader bars are moved from effects ''A'' to ''B'' positions, the image designated on bus ''A'' fades out as the image on bus ''B'' fades in. Thus moving the fader from ''A'' to ''B'' creates a dissolve. To accomplish a fade-out or a fade-in from black, one of the two effects buses must be linked to a constant black signal. As the fader is moved, blackness either takes the place of an image or is itself replaced by an image on another bus. The former is called a fade-out and the latter a fade-in.

One special effect that can be created on the switcher by using fader bars is a superimposition. Placing the fader bars assigned to ''A'' and ''B'' effects buses halfway between the two buses creates a combined image or superimposition. Separating the two bars and individually adjusting the intensity of each image allows the brightness of each of the two superimposed images to be controlled. This also runs the risk of a video signal overload and should therefore be approached with extreme caution if attempted at all.

Wipes and Split Screens   In addition to the common effects described above, such as fades, superimpositions, and dissolves, many switchers can create various types of wipes and shared screens. A wipe refers to the gradual replacement of one image by another without reliance on any form of superimposition. The new image begins on one part of the screen and gradually spreads across the screen to replace the old image. A shared screen is actually a wipe which is never fully completed. Two separate images, from different buses, occupy separate portions of the same frame. Wipes and shared screens can assume many different shapes, such as circles, stars, diamonds, squares, and rectangles. With proper camera and fader bar positioning a wipe or shared screen can be used to provide new information, such as a box score of a sporting event, or multiple perspectives, such as a second view of the same action from a different camera position.

A wipe is created on most switchers by turning a switch that converts the effects bus faders to wipe controls. The speed at which the fader bars are moved determines the speed at which the image from effects bus "A" replaces or wipes off the image from effects bus "B." Selectors near the top of the switcher allow the TD to select a specific type or shape of wipe. A lever called a **"joy stick"** next to the wipe selector allows the TD to manipulate the screen position of the replacement image. By not completing the fader bar movement, a split or shared screen effect can be obtained. Some switchers create a **soft wipe** by creating a slight superimposition of the two images at the points where they intersect during a wipe. Some sophisticated switchers provide for multiple-source shared screens, allowing three or more images to be presented simultaneously in different parts of the same frame.

Keying   Other types of commonly used special effects on a production switcher are insert keying, chroma keying, and a whole range of digital video effects. A keying process removes selected portions of one image and replaces them with a second image. Titles are frequently inserted into a background scene by the use of **keying** or **insert keying**. Instead of superimposing titles or letters over the background image, insert keying removes only the portion of the background scene which the titles or letters will occupy. This prevents the kind of bleeding or double image which would occur with a superimposition. Letters or titles which are to be keyed are normally white on a black card placed in front of the camera selected on one of the effects buses on the switcher. The insert-key mode is then selected on the key select switch and the intensity is turned up to its proper level.

A commonly used production effects technique, which is rapidly being replaced by digital technology, is called **chroma key**. In chroma keying a specific color or wavelength of light is used to determine those portions of the background that will be replaced. Wherever this color appears on the set or the primary image, the second image is inserted and seen. Chroma key is sometimes used in news broadcasts (Figure 6.3) as a means of combining graphics or action scenes with the central image of the newscaster. On the set, a solid green or blue board is positioned next to or behind the newscaster. Using chroma key, a second image such as a slide, film, or vi-

Figure 6.3
A Simulated Chroma Key Window

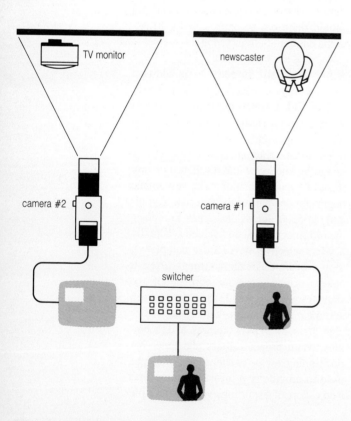

deotape can be inserted in the designated area of the screen. Care must be exercised in selecting the color of the newscaster's clothing and other items in the set so that they are not also replaced by the second image. The color board must be evenly lit, and the camera carefully adjusted. Many chroma key-type images are easier to create today with digital effects.

Still-frame storage and image squeezing are two other commonly used digital effects. Titles, graphics, and still images can be stored as still frames in digital form and recalled at the touch of a button. Digitized still or moving images can be squeezed, expanded, and manipulated in numerous ways to create multiple images and other special visual effects.

The Switcher in Operation Operating the switcher during production requires careful preparation. The technical director must know in advance exactly what buses will be used for specific types of shots. It is very easy to become confused and push the wrong button or get locked into a corner from which there is no smooth, undetected escape. The director must convey clear and distinct commands to the TD and provide him or her with adequate time between the preparation of a cut or effect and its actual execution.

The best way to conceptualize the operation of the switcher is to consider a specific situation. Imagine that you are in the control room for a local news program. Everything is being broadcast live, so there is no room for error. The tension and pressure have become intense. The program begins with the videotape playback of the opening title and credit sequence. Prior to the start of the program the director has asked that the opening videotape be prerolled and prepared. The tape must be prerolled for five seconds prior to the be-

The technical director operating the switcher.

ginning of the program. The TD has punched up the VTR or videotape recorder on the preview bus and black on the program bus at the request of the director. The master preview bus is set on preview, and the master program bus is set on program. Five seconds prior to the start of the show the director commands, "roll opening credits on VTR" and the engineer begins to roll the tape. As they count down the seconds on the preview monitor, the TD punches up VTR on the program bus. The credit sequence now appears on both the program and the preview monitors. As they watch the credits, the director commands, "preview camera 1." The TD punches the button for camera 1 on the preview bus. They now see the newscaster in the studio on the preview monitor and the credits on the program monitor. Just as the credit sequence is ending the director commands, "take (camera) 1," and the TD punches the button for camera 1 on the program bus. The director then commands "preview (camera) 2" (unless there is a separate monitor assigned to each camera) and when the TD presses the camera 2 button on the preview bus, a close-up of the newscaster comes up on the preview monitor. The director says, "take (camera) 2," and the TD presses the camera 2 button on the program bus.

The word "camera" is placed in parentheses in the above example because a director uses the word "camera" only when directly addressing a specific camera operator, such as "Camera 2, zoom in" or "Camera 3, tilt up a little." This avoids giving a false signal to the TD, who will push the appropriate camera button when he or she hears, "Take 2." Directors sometimes combine camera and switcher set-up or "ready" commands, however, by saying for example, "Ready Camera 1. It will be a Take." This prepares two people for the next take, the camera operator and the TD, without sending any false cues. Scripted shows often employ an assistant director who gives these "ready" commands and frees the director to concentrate on calling takes, fades, dissolves, and so on, at the precise time indicated in the script.

Director's Commands

A director can only coordinate the production team effectively if he or she can communicate with every member of that team. Video and film directors have developed a relatively precise terminology with which to communicate with their staff and crew. A director can use the following terms to communicate with the technical director and camera operators during multiple-camera recording.

I. To the Camera Operator
   A. Always begin each command with the specific number of the camera to which the command is directed. If three cameras are being used, for example, they can simply be called Cameras 1, 2, and 3.
   B. Before actually giving a command, prepare the camera operator for the fact that a command is about to be given. The term "Ready, Camera 2," prepares Camera 2's operator for an upcoming command.
   C. Be specific and brief in your commands. Say, "Camera 3, zoom in to a close-up" not "Camera 3, I think that you need to get closer on the subject." In the latter case the camera operator doesn't know whether to zoom or dolly. Preferably, the command should also indicate how far to zoom in or out, such as "Camera 3, zoom out to a two shot," or "Camera 3, zoom in to an extreme close-up."
   D. Use the terms specified in our discussion of composition and camera movements to indicate precise camera commands.
II. To the Switcher Operator and Playback Operators
   A. Again, if possible, give the switcher operator and playback operators a "ready" signal before actually giving a command.
   B. Give a specific number to each playback unit or telecine device, such as VTR1 or VTR2.
   C. Use the precise terms provided in the section on transition devices to tell the switcher operator the exact type of transition you desire. For example, "Take 1" indicates a direct (straight-cut) transition from whatever is presently on the screen to camera 1, while "fade" or "dissolve" or "wipe" indicates a slower type of transition, the speed of which will also need to be specified. To indicate the speed of a transition you can simply specify

the time, such as "three-second dissolve to (camera) 3."

D. Any switcher operator (TD) requires substantial advance warning when several effects will be required in succession or a complicated effect is needed. "Chroma key," "super," "wipe," and "insert" frequently indicate complicated effects that require advance notice and "ready" commands.

E. The TD is the last member of the production team to be given a command that affects the camera operators, talent, and TD. For example, if the TD is eventually going to dissolve from camera 1 to camera 3, the director should first prepare the camera 3 operator for the transition and "ready" that station, then tell the stage manager to prepare to cue the talent for a camera change, and finally tell the TD to prepare for and make the proper transition.

Live-On-Tape Recording

A live-on-tape (multiple-camera) director can use the techniques of live multiple-camera video to record events quickly and efficiently but also has the option to change the shot sequence during postproduction. This is accomplished by recording the images from several cameras simultaneously while at the same time making some editing decisions on the switcher. Editing decisions made during production can then be changed during postproduction by inserting different camera shots. This method gives the director maximum flexibility to produce a program economically in the shortest possible time without jeopardizing the quality of the final prod-

uct, since changes can always be made later. In this way multiple-camera recording techniques can be combined with the techniques discussed next, allowing the director to benefit from the advantages of both methods.

SINGLE-CAMERA DIRECTING

Basic Setups

Single-camera recording uses three different types of setups for one camera: (1) master shots, (2) inserts, and (3) cutaways. Single-camera recording normally begins with a shot of the entire action in a scene, or as much of the complete scene as it is possible to record in a single shot. This is often called a **master shot**. Master shots are usually, but not always, long shots. Master shots are rarely designated as such in a shooting script. Instead, an opening long shot is extended throughout the scene, implicitly serving as a master shot.

Specific actions occurring within the master shot are then repeated after the camera has been placed closer to the subject for shots known as **inserts.** Inserts are usually the medium shots and close-ups indicated in a script. Master shots and inserts may be re-recorded several times before an acceptable recording has been made. Specific recordings are called different **takes** of the same shot. The shooting script is then marked (as shown in Figure 6.4) by a script continuity person with the number of the exact shot specified in the script and each take circled at the beginning point of actual recording. A line is drawn vertically through the script to the point where actual recording of that take ends. Inserts are normally extended before

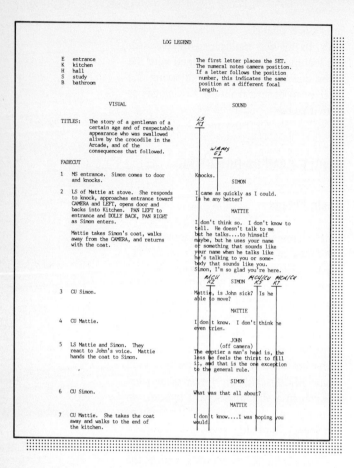

Figure 6.4
A Marked Shooting Script

Master Shots   Master shots provide relatively complete coverage of the entire action in a scene. They also allow the talent to focus on building a performance. The entire scene can be played at one time. In single-camera recording the actions performed during a master shot also establish the types of gestures, movements, and vocal intonations that must be duplicated during the recording of matching close-ups and medium shots. A **script continuity** person usually makes careful notes on the shooting script concerning specific actions, clothing that is put on or taken off during a master shot, specific gestures, such as extending a right or left hand, and any other information that will be of value when attempting to duplicate the same actions and movements for matching medium shots and close-ups. Instant photographs are sometimes taken of the scene. If the talent fails to repeat actions precisely during subsequent recordings, it will be difficult for the editor to find matched-action edit points between shots. The master shot or long shot can act as a safety net in the event that matching medium shots or close-ups specified in the script do not prove satisfactory. A continuously running long shot or master shot can be quite boring in comparison to using several different long shots, medium shots, and close-ups for emphasis and variety. But the knowledge that the master shot covers the entire action and can be used at any point can be of some comfort to the editor.

Inserts   Shots which record some of the same actions as the master shot, but from a closer camera position or a different angle of view are called **inserts** or cut-ins, since they will be cut into the master shot. Recording with a single camera usually

and after the exact edit points in the script to allow for overlapping action and a range of editing choices. A marked shooting script provides a complete record of actual recording in terms of master shots and inserts.

Cutaways are additional close-ups and medium shots of objects or events that are not central parts of the action and are often not specified in the script. They can be inserted into a scene to bridge mismatched actions or to hide mistakes within or between a master shot and an insert.

takes longer than multiple-camera recording. The lighting, the camera, and the set are sometimes moved and readjusted for each shot. Better quality images are often obtained using this method, since fewer compromises have to be made in terms of recording logistics. Each shot is composed and the action repeated so that an optimal recording is made. But potential problems can arise in terms of discontinuity or mismatched action from one shot to the next. The director and the script continuity person must observe and duplicate every detail recorded in the master shot during the recording of the inserts. The actors must perform the same gestures, wear the same clothing, and repeat the same actions and lines of dialogue, if actions are to overlap and match from one shot to the next. In extremely low-budget situations, where it is impossible to record several takes of each insert, a director is well advised to record a few cutaways for use in bridging mismatched actions between shots that are discovered during postproduction editing. It is the director's responsibility to provide adequate coverage of events and actions so that a program can be edited with minimal difficulty. Good coverage provides insurance against costly reshooting.

Cutaways   Cutaways are shots of secondary objects and actions that can be used to hide mismatched action and to preserve continuity or simply to add depth and interest to the primary action of a film or television program. Cut-ins depict actions that appear within the frame of master shots, while cutaways depict actions and objects outside the master shot frame. A **reaction shot**, for example, is a shot of one character's or participant's response to something he or she has just seen, as in a POV shot (see chapter 5, p. 107) or heard, such as dialogue of another person. A reaction shot usually consists of a person's facial expression in a close-up. It can be inserted into the shot of the primary action or dialogue as a cutaway, when the master shot fails to reveal that person's facial expression. In single-camera news recording a reaction shot of the reporter or interviewer is sometimes used to bridge gaps or avoid jump cuts in a condensed version of an interview or simply to use facial expressions to comment on what is being said.

Close-ups of hands gesturing and relevant props can be also used as cutaways. They can be inserted at almost any point to bridge mismatched action in master shots and inserts or simply to add more detail to the spatial environment. Cutaways provide an editor with something to "cut away to" when editing problems are discovered.

Shooting Ratios

While every single-camera director tries to get an acceptable shot in as few takes as possible, nonetheless there can be considerable variation in shooting ratios from one production to another. Shooting ratios, which refer to the ratio of visual material shot to visual material actually used, can range from about 5:1 to 100:1 in different types of production situations. Obviously, more takes of each shot translate into higher shooting ratios. Network commercials often have the highest shooting ratios. At the other end of the spectrum, student productions often have shooting ratios as low as 5:1 or even 3:1, due to limited production funds. Low budget situations call for highly efficient production methods.

Director's Terminology

Since a single-camera director is normally present on the set with the camera operator rather than isolated in a control room as in multiple-camera production, he or she can communicate directly with the crew and talent. Directorial terminology for camera placements and movements is generally the same as that for multiple-camera recording, but a few commands are quite different. When the crew and the talent are ready to record a single shot, the director says "roll tape" to the videotape or audiotape (in film) recordist and "roll film" to the film camera operator. When the tape or film is up to speed the operator says "speed" or "camera rolling." The director then calls, "slate," and a grip or camera assistant slates the shot by calling out the scene, shot, and take numbers, which are also written on a board called a slate. In film the slate has clapsticks which are brought together so that separate sounds and pictures can be synchronized later. The scene, shot, and take numbers displayed on the slate are used as a reference during postproduction editing. They are usually written down on a **camera report** sheet, which is sent to the film laboratory. (See Figure 6.5.)

When the talent is ready and the slate has been removed from the shot, the director says "action," and the performance begins. When a shot is over or a problem develops in midshot, the director says "cut." If the director wants a scene printed for later viewing, the command "print" will be given. This type of command is noted on the camera report. Since editing can be done during postproduction, there is no need for the director to communicate with a technical director (switcher operator) during actual production. Editing decisions will be made later.

Figure 6.5
A Camera Report Form

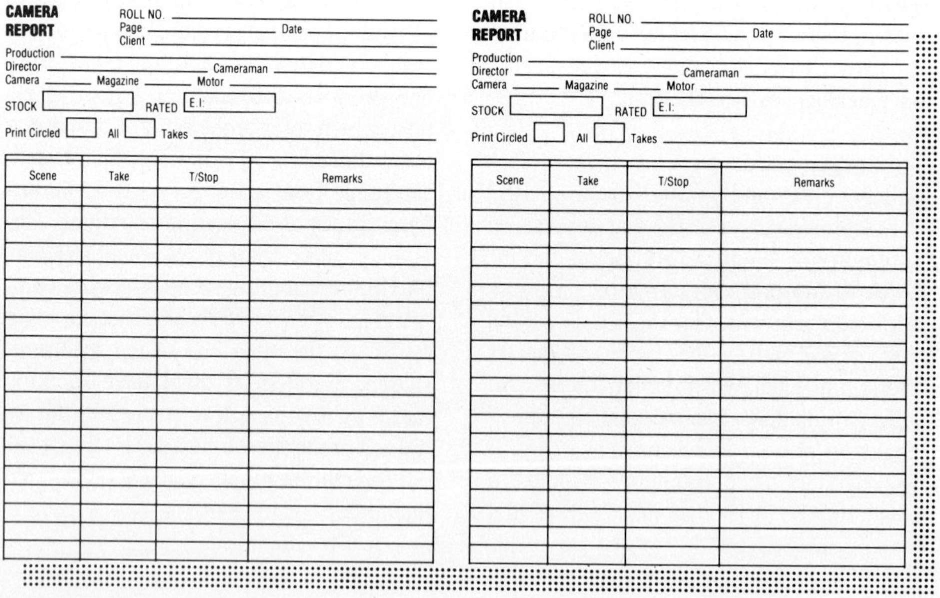

CAMERA REPORT

ROLL NO.
Page Date
Client
Production
Director Cameraman
Camera Magazine Motor
STOCK RATED E.I:
Print Circled All Takes

Scene	Take	T/Stop	Remarks

CAMERA REPORT

ROLL NO.
Page Date
Client
Production
Director Cameraman
Camera Magazine Motor
STOCK RATED E.I:
Print Circled All Takes

Scene	Take	T/Stop	Remarks

Summary

The director supervises the creative aspects of television and film production by coordinating the production team, initiating and chairing preproduction and production meetings, casting the film or television program with the producer and casting director, and organizing production rehearsals. Working with the talent is one of the director's most important responsibilities. Excellent performances must be obtained with extreme efficiency, but a director must also be sensitive to the emotional needs of performers. Working with the talent and crew during rehearsal is so essential to the quality of the final product that it is sometimes considered a separate stage of production.

The director plots and stages the action by determining the positioning and movement of talent and camera, plans the composition of the images within the camera frame, and establishes and maintains continuity of action and screen direction. In live and multiple-camera production, directors are usually directly involved in the selection of specific types of shots, and the creation of transition devices and special effects. In live, multiple-camera, and live-on-tape productions directors employ a technical director (TD) to operate a video switcher and take (straight-cut) or dissolve from one camera or shot to another.

The director also controls the timing of a television program or film. Timing can refer to the subjective pace of the action or objective running time and clock time. The running times of individual segments must add up to the total running time of a television program or film. In live television production, the total running time must fall within the designated studio clock time allocated to a specific program or program segment. Back-timing is frequently used in live television production to cue the talent or preset closing music or a videotape or film segment.

A video switcher consists of several sets of switches, called buses, such as preview, program, and effects or mix buses. The switches on each bus allow an operator (usually the technical director) to select a specific visual input, such as one of several different camera inputs, VTR playbacks, remote feeds, and visual black. The specific visual source selected on the preview bus is simply displayed on a preview monitor, while that on the program bus is both viewed on a program monitor and passed out of the switcher to a transmitter or a VTR. The effects and mix buses allow special effects, such as dissolves, wipes, fades, and various keys to be created as transitions between or combinations of two or more different visual inputs. Most transitions and effects are controlled by fader bars, which vary the intensity of electronic visual images, much the same way that audio faders allow the intensity of sounds to be controlled. Operating a switcher requires careful preparation. The director must give the TD explicit commands and sufficient warning prior to complicated effects to ensure effective production editing.

The director's function can vary considerably between multiple-camera and single-camera recording situations. The multiple-camera video director frequently sits in a control room isolated from the talent and crew during actual recording. The single-camera director, on the other hand, is usually present on the set during the shooting. The multiple-camera director supervises the movement of several cameras, using an intercom, and controls the editing by having the TD punch buttons on the switcher, changing the main signal from one camera or source to another. The single-camera director often works directly with the talent and crew during the period of time between shots, when the camera is being moved and the lighting and sound recording devices reset. The editing of single-camera production is usually left to a specialist who cuts the film or electronically edits together videotape during postproduction.

Additional Readings

Armer, Alan A. *Directing Television and Film*. Belmont, CA: Wadsworth, 1986.

Bare, Richard L. *The Film Director, A Practical Guide to Motion Picture and Television Techniques*. New York: Collier Books, 1971.

Kingson, Walter K., and Cowgill, Rome. *Television Acting and Directing*. New York: Holt, Rinehart and Winston, 1965.

Lewis, Colby. *The TV Director/Interpreter*. New York: Hastings House, 1968.

Lukas, Christopher. *Directing for Film and Television*. New York: Anchor Press/Doubleday, 1985.

Millerson, Gerald. *Basic TV Staging*. New York: Hastings House, 1974.

Zettl, Herbert. *Sight-Sound-Motion: Applied Media Aesthetics*. Belmont, CA: Wadsworth Publishing Co., 1973.

Exercises

1. Chart out the camera and performer blocking for a dramatic scene in a shooting script designed for multiple-camera production. Determine the best location for each camera to efficiently record all of the shots specified in the shooting script. Be sure to allow ample time and space for camera movements, which will take place within or between specific shots.

2. Chart the camera and performer blocking for a short scene or sequence in single-camera production. Designate a long shot or medium long shot as the master shot, which will be used to provide continuous coverage within the scene. Select the best camera positions for the recording of matching close-ups and medium shots, which can be inserted into the master shot at the appropriate points designated in the shooting script.

3. Design a segment for a news program in terms of camera and performer blocking. Use multiple-camera directing techniques for the in-studio, broadcaster segments and single-camera directing techniques for the news stories by reporters in the field, that will be inserted into the program at appropriate points.

CHAPTER 7

Camera Control

Camera operators try to provide directors with the best possible pictures that will enhance a particular aesthetic approach. To accomplish this they must know how to use basic framing, composition, and camera movements and how to control numerous technical camera and lens devices. To record clear, functionalist images, for example, camera operators must understand how lenses work and then place key information in sharp focus. Significant image depth, that is, having a wide range of distances from the camera in sharp focus, can be an effective realist approach to camera operation. Limiting or restricting image depth can help to create a new formativist perspective on everyday objects.

Some aesthetic aspects of camera use, such as composition and camera movement, were considered in terms of directing in chapter 5, but they bear repeating here from the standpoint of camera placement and control. After reading this chapter and before attempting to use any camera, you should read the instruction manual carefully for the specific camera you wish to operate. Continual practice with the camera is necessary to make it an extension of your eyes and body. Basic camera exercises, such as those recommended at the end of this chapter, can significantly improve your skills as a camera operator.

CAMERA PLACEMENT

Placing a camera in the best position for recording functionalist, realist, or formativist images consists of three camera operations: framing, positioning, and movement. Framing refers to the arrangement of actions and objects within the camera frame. Positioning includes the selection of camera-to-

subject distance and angle, while movement of the camera is accomplished by means of various camera mounting devices.

Framing

Four key concepts help camera operators frame visual images: essential area, lookspace, walkspace, and headroom. **Essential area** refers to the safe recording area within the camera frame. All key information should be placed within the essential area of the frame so that it is not cut off by mistake. Objects and actions can be placed within the essential area by moving the camera closer to or farther away from the subject or altering the focal length of a zoom lens. Lookspace is the frame area in front of an on-screen performer who is looking at an off-screen object or person. Leaving some space in the frame for the performer's look or glance creates the best spatial composition. Lookspace can be increased by panning the camera. Walkspace refers to the additional space left in the frame into which a performer can walk or run. When following a performer with a camera, as during a panning or trucking shot, walkspace should be placed in front of the subject within the frame. Otherwise the edge of the frame acts as a restrictive border and the visual composition seems awkward. Another important aspect of composition is providing an appropriate amount of headroom, i.e., space above the performer's head within the frame. Too little headroom creates a sense of confinement, while too much gives an impression of limitless space that sometimes dwarfs the performer. Of course, tight close-ups often have little or no headroom. Changes in headroom result from tilting the camera, moving the camera closer or farther away, or zooming the lens. (See Figure 7.1.)

Camera operators also need to be familiar with the basic rules of camera placement and composition. For example, the 180-degree action-axis rule should be followed in camera placement, if the directional relationship of objects in the frame and subject movements is to remain spatially consistent from shot to shot. Crossing the line with the camera can reverse screen direction. In terms of composition, the rule of thirds—that is, dividing the frame into three parts both vertically and horizontally—allows the camera operator to place objects along the lines and at the intersection points to help achieve a satisfying frame composition. Additional compositional factors from the standpoint of aesthetics, such as symmetry or balance and closure, should also be considered. (See chapter 5.)

Positioning   Camera operators and directors control the placement and movement of cameras and put aesthetic principles into actual practice. A specific terminology is often used to refer to common types of camera placements and movements. Terms such as "medium shot," "dolly," "pan," "pedestal," and "crane shot," have specific meanings when they appear in a final shooting script and/or shot lists supplied to camera operators by the director.

A close-up is basically a head and shoulders shot of a person. An extreme close-up fills the frame of the camera with a character's face, a part of the face, or some specific object. Close-ups are used for emphasis, to achieve a degree of intimacy or involvement, or to focus the audience's attention on a particular detail. Used sparingly, close-ups can be an effective way of achieving dramatic emphasis. Close-ups are created by moving the camera closer to the subject or by zooming in.

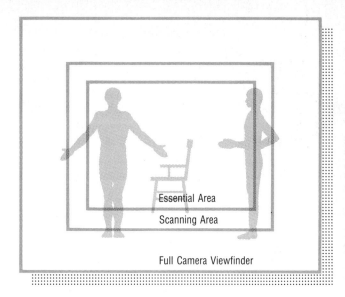

Essential Area

Scanning Area

Full Camera Viewfinder

Figure 7.1
Essential Area

A medium shot includes one half to three quarters of a character's body. The camera is placed farther away from the subject or the lens is zoomed out from a close-up. This type of shot is a compromise between the long shot and the close-up. Some details and facial gestures are readily apparent, but many broad actions of several characters can sometimes be included within the frame as well. A **two shot** is generally a medium shot that presents two people or characters within the same frame. Television and film directors frequently frame the image as a two shot so that the audience can see the actions and reactions of two characters simultaneously.

A long shot gives a full-body image of a character or characters. An **extreme long shot** might include a broad exterior vista. Long shots allow audiences to see broad action, but do not provide emphasis or subtle details. The long shot is often called an **establishing shot** when it sets the character(s) in the context of the setting or location. Many standard scenes begin with an establishing shot to set the context or physical location and then cut to combinations of closer shots of specific actions and characters.

A camera is normally placed at about shoulder height in television and film production, but some shots call for a higher camera angle, while others call for a much lower camera position. These **high- and low-camera angles** can be used to simulate the spatial positioning and points of view of specific characters or simply to provide perspectives which will exaggerate or reduce the apparent size of the object(s) in the frame.

Movement   Camera movements in midshot should be made only when they significantly improve our understanding of what is being presented. When overused, they can be visually distracting. Moving camera shots usually begin and end with the camera stationary so that they can be intercut or combined with stationary camera shots. (See Figure 7.2 for a more complete guide to camera movements.)

When a camera is placed on a moving tripod or dolly, it can be moved toward or away from the subject. These camera movements are called **dolly shots**. They differ from **zoom shots**, which result from changing the focal length of a zoom lens. Dolly shots alter perspective, that is, they change the apparent spatial positioning of objects in a scene. They give the audience the feeling that they are actually moving through the scene, as well as shifting their perspective and focus of attention.

Physically moving the camera horizontally or laterally with respect to the subject is called a **trucking shot**. Trucking shots can be used to keep a moving subject in frame. A lateral movement of the camera in a semicircular path is called an **arc**. To perform a trucking shot or arc the camera must be mounted on a wheeled dolly. Sometimes tracks are laid on the floor or ground so that the wheels of the dolly will

Figure 7.2
Camera Movements

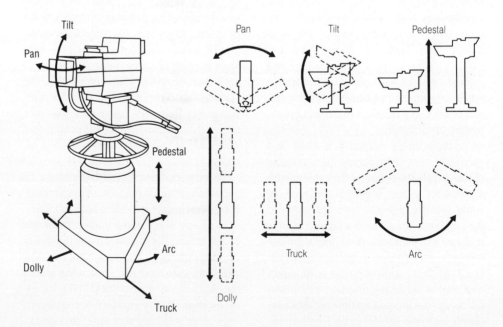

follow a prearranged path. If the tracks are laid properly, minimal bounce of the camera will occur, even over rough terrain. During trucking and dolly shots it is often advisable to use a wide angle lens to minimize the bouncing of the image. Telephoto lenses accentuate camera bounce.

A stationary tripod usually has a panning and a tilting device. A **pan** action slowly and smoothly rotates the camera from side to side on a tripod pivot, while a **tilt** action moves it up and down. These movements can be used to change the angle of view or to follow action. Panning too quickly can cause vertical lines or objects to strobe or flicker. Pans and tilts can also be used to follow performer movements. Tilts are often used to follow a performer sitting down or standing up. Like all camera movements, they usually begin and end with a well-composed stationary frame.

A camera can be physically moved up and down on a pedestal dolly. A hydraulic lift pushes the camera straight up or brings it straight down. This technique is called a **pedestal movement** and is used to adjust the camera for a high- or low-angle shot rather than to move the camera in midshot. A **crane shot** uses a long pivoting arm to move the camera up and down or from side to side in the studio or on location. It is usually reserved for wide establishing shots and is often used to move the camera in midshot.

Mounting Devices

Camera placements and movements usually require the use of specific camera mounting devices in order to record steady images. Mounting devices for television cameras range from pistol grips to cranes. A **pistol grip** is used to hand hold a lightweight portable small-format camera.

This device is rarely used for professional recording. The **crane** is a relatively large mounting device, which consists of a long counterweighted arm on a four-wheeled dolly or truck. It allows a camera to be raised to extreme heights in a studio or field situation and usually requires several technicians to assist the camera operator in actually moving the camera. In between these two extremes we find the shoulder harness, tripod dolly, and pedestal dolly.

Body Braces A **shoulder harness** can be anything from a built-in camera mold or special body brace that fits perfectly over the operator's shoulder to a more elaborate servostabilizer, such as a **Steadicam**®, which minimizes vibration of the camera and allows the camera operator to move around freely. A Steadicam uses a complex system of springs and

A basic shoulder mount for a film camera.

A Steadicam® mount, a more elaborate and sophisticated device for body mounting a video or film camera.

ever, a Steadicam positions the camera in such a way that the normal film camera viewfinder cannot be used. The camera is usually at the operator's waist and is detached from his or her body. A video pickup tube is fitted into the camera viewfinder, and a video signal is fed to a small black-and-white picture tube on the top of the camera, where it can be viewed by the operator. The video signal can also be fed to a recorder, so that immediately viewable television images are recorded at the same time as the film. Film, of course, cannot be screened until it is developed.

Tripods A **tripod** is a three-legged device upon which a stationary camera can be secured. The legs of the tripod can be extended to raise or lower the camera. Tripods arc one of the most frequently used single-camera supports. They usually consist of three extendable legs, with pointed **spurs** on the tripod shoes, a **cradle** and

counterweights to smooth out the jerky movements of the operator and simulate dolly or crane movements of the camera. The Steadicam can be used with a film camera as well as a video camera. How-

Left: A tripod on a spreader. Right: A tripod on a hitchhiker.

ball joint for leveling, a fluid head or other form of panning and tilting device, and a camera locking bolt. A fluid head allows the camera to be smoothly panned or tilted on the tripod. When used outdoors, the spurs of the tripod can frequently be secured in soft ground, but on hard surfaces and indoors the spur must be secured in a spider (sometimes called a triangle or spreader), which provides a device for locking down the shoes of a tripod to prevent them from slipping. Tripods for small-format video cameras often have flat rubber shoes rather than pointed spurs and are intended for both indoor and outdoor use without a spider.

The head of a tripod frequently has a bubble device for proper leveling of the tripod. Leveling a tripod refers to making the camera horizontally level, so that the horizontal frames of the image are parallel with the horizon outdoors or the lines formed by the floor and the back wall or the ceiling and back wall in an interior setting. The nut that secures the head to the tripod cradle can frequently be removed to allow the tripod head to be secured to another support device, such as a high hat. The high hat places a camera just a few feet above the ground, but well below the lowest tripod height. When it is equipped with suction cups a high hat can be secured to almost any flat surface, such as the hood of an automobile or the top of a boat. A tripod can also be secured to a hitchhiker, which is a spider with wheels on it. The hitchhiker allows a tripod and attached camera to move around the studio and transforms a stationary tripod into a moveable dolly.

Dollies   A dolly is a camera platform or support device on wheels, which allows the camera to move smoothly about a studio. A pedestal dolly can be vertically

A high hat. Note that it is positioned on a film can and that everything is balanced on an equipment box!

moved up and down to raise or lower the camera in midshot. A tripod can be attached to a hitchhiker to create a dolly. The wheels of a hitchhiker, like those of a pedestal dolly, can usually be locked to prevent movement of the camera. Three wheels give the hitchhiker or pedestal dolly ample stability and ease of movement, although care must be taken to plan the movement of a camera so that the bulky coaxial cables connecting the camera to the camera control unit do not get in the way. A dolly should never roll over audio or video cables on the studio floor.

Various types of dollies and other mobile mounts can be used with film and video cameras. A crab dolly allows up-and-down pedestal movements. Some dollies, like the Elemac spider dolly, are collapsible yet extremely versatile and stable. Sometimes a wheelchair or moving

A pedestal dolly.

vehicle, such as a car or van, can serve as an excellent dolly. A special mount, such as the **Tyler mount**, can be used to record vibrationless images from a helicopter or an airplane in combination with a special fluid-filled lens called a **dyna lens**. Finally, a crane can be used in studio or field productions to raise even the heaviest film camera to tremendous heights.

LENS CONTROL

Another way in which camera operators control the presentation of visual images is by using various camera lenses. A camera lens consists of one or more pieces of glass that focus and frame an image within the camera. Lens control begins with an understanding of basic optics.

Basic Optics

A lens is a curved piece of glass that causes light rays to bend. Because glass is denser than air, light slows down at the point where it enters the lens. Lenses bend light so that it can be controlled and projected in proper focus and size at a specific point behind the lens, where a light-sensitive material can record or transmit the image. The curvature of the lens as well as the type of glass from which it is made affects how much the light bends and, to a certain extent, determines the classification and function of a specific lens.

Simple, single lenses fall into two basic categories: concave and convex. (Figure 7.3) **Concave** lenses, which are thinner at the center than at the edges, bend light rays away from the center of the lens, causing them to diverge from each other. **Convex** lenses, on the other hand, are thickest at the center and bend light towards the center so that the light rays converge or intersect at a specific point behind the lens, known as the **focal point**. The distance from the optical center of a lens to its focal point is known as a lens's **focal length**. The curvature of a lens affects its focal length.

Lenses can be classified according to their focal lengths. For example, film and television lenses with short focal lengths are sometimes called **wide-angle** lenses. Beyond the focal point the light rays diverge from each other and at some point behind the lens, known as the **focal plane**, they form an inverted, reversed image of the objects reflecting light in front of the lens. Images at the focal plane are in **acceptable focus**, that is, the objects are clear and sharp. A piece of light-sensitive material, such as the front surface of a film or an electronic pickup tube, placed at the focal plane will record an inverted and reversed image of the original scene.

Modern film and television lenses are composed of more than one piece of glass and are called **compound lenses**. Compound lenses combine several concave and convex lenses in various configurations to cut down on disruptions of or imperfections in light transmission, which are called **aberrations**. A simple convex lens, such as a magnifying glass, creates several types of aberration, including field curvature, distortion, and chromatic aberration. **Field curvature** refers to the fact that the image projected by a simple convex lens falls into best overall focus on a curved, rather than a flat plane or image surface. Motion picture film and front surfaces of television pickup tubes are flat, not curved. **Distortion** is caused by changes in magnification that occur in different parts of the image projected by a simple, convex lens. **Chromatic aberration** refers to the fact that various color wavelengths bend at different angles when they enter a piece of glass, such as a prism or a simple lens.

A modern lens combines several concave and convex lenses to reduce these types of aberration. Modern lenses are also coated with substances such as magnesium fluoride that reduce the reflection of light entering the lens and therefore increase light transmission. The **lens coating** is usually placed on the outside element of a lens. Never touch the front surface of a lens with your finger. Body oils can etch the lens coating, if they are not removed immediately with lens cleaning paper and proper cleaning solutions. Clean the lens with fluids infrequently since repeated

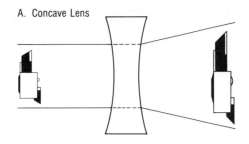
A. Concave Lens

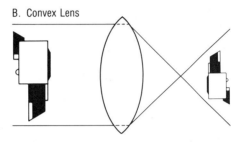
B. Convex Lens

Figure 7.3
A. Concave Lens
B. Convex Lens

cleanings can wear down the lens coating. An air blower or camel-hair brush usually does a good job of cleaning loose dirt off a lens. Lenses must be handled carefully, and cleanliness is essential.

Lens Perspective

Focal Length and Angle of Acceptance

Lens perspective, or the way in which a lens presents the spatial relations between the objects it records or transmits, varies with a lens's focal length and angle of light acceptance. The **angle of acceptance**, or the angle at which a lens gathers light in front of a camera, is determined by the focal length of the lens and the format (size) of the recording medium. Shorter focal-length lenses generally have wider angles of acceptance than long focal-length lenses. Focal lengths usually range from 10mm (about 1/2-inch) or less to 200mm (about 8 inches) or more. Short focal-length lenses are usually called wide-angle lenses, while long focal-length lenses are frequently referred to as telephoto lenses. Normal lenses are so called because they present an image perspective which seems to approximate that of normal monocular (single-eye) human vision.

Zoom Lenses   A zoom lens (as illustrated in Figure 7.4) allows a camera operator to change the focal length of a lens from wide angle through normal to telephoto and vice versa by manually turning the zoom barrel (or by pushing the button for an electric zoom motor). Zoom-ins and zoom-outs in midshot are easily misused and overused by beginning students. A zoom-in should direct our attention to something within the frame, while a zoom-out presents new information, often clarifying the setting. A zoom-in or zoom-out during a shot should be made smoothly and precisely. A zoom lens also makes it easier to change focal length between shots, since one lens does not have to be physically replaced by another on the camera. Changing the focal length magnifies and demagnifies the image. At a long focal length the objects in the frame seem to be closer together, and at a short focal length they seem to be farther apart. A zoom lens should first be focused at its maximum focal length (telephoto). This ensures proper focus at all other focal lengths, including the end point of a zoom-in. Zoom lenses are available in a variety of focal length ranges, with minimum focal lengths as short as 10mm and maximum focal lengths as long as 200mm.

Field of View   **Field of view** refers to the exact dimensions of the image framed by the camera. (See Figure 7.5.) The field of view of an image captured by a specific film or video camera is largely determined by the focal length of the lens and the video or film format. Shorter focal-length lenses present a wider field of view than longer focal-length lenses, when used in the same film or video format. But the field of view provided by any lens changes when the format of the recording medium changes. A 25mm or 1-inch lens provides a narrower field of view in 16mm film or 2/3-inch video camera pickup tubes than it does in 35mm film or large pickup tubes. In short, lens classifications, such as wide-angle, normal, or telephoto, and fields of view for specific focal length lenses vary from one format to another. Whether a specific lens is wide-angle, normal, or telephoto, whether it has a wide or a narrow angle acceptance and field of view, depends on both its focal length *and* the dimensions of the film or video format.

Image Depth

Image depth is a general term describing the overall range of distances and objects which appear to be in sharp focus within the frame. It can be affected by a variety of specific factors, including the type of lens used, various lens adjustments, the

**Figure 7.4
Zoom Lens**

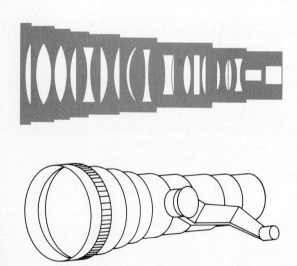

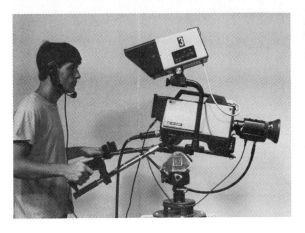

placement of the objects within the set, and the lighting; the latter two are discussed more fully in subsequent chapters. In this chapter, depth is considered from the standpoint of specific lens factors that affect one aspect of image depth, called depth of field. The primary factors creating depth of field are focus distance, lens aperture, and focal length. It is easier to understand the concept of depth of field by first explaining the primary factors which can be used to control it on a lens.

Focus Distance
Focus distance refers to the distance of the subject from the focal plane of a camera. On film cameras the focal plane is indicated on the outside of the camera by a line drawn through the center of a circle. Focus distance can be accurately measured with a tape measure stretched from the focal plane to the subject. The **focus ring** on the lens barrel is adjusted according to the exact distance in feet or meters. On a reflex camera, focus distances can be set by simply turning the focus ring, while viewing the subject through a properly adjusted viewfinder. The **viewfinder diopter** on the reflex film camera is a device which adjusts the focus of a lens to the eyesight of a particular camera operator. This can be done by

setting the lens focus ring on infinity and then looking through the viewfinder at an object that is at least fifty feet away. Turn the diopter focus ring until the object appears in proper focus and then lock down the diopter. Now the focus ring on the lens can be turned to set the focus on any subject regardless of its distance from the camera. A video camera does not have a viewfinder diopter or focus adjustment, since the viewfinder is usually a black-and-white TV screen.

Zoom lens controls on a TV camera and close-up of same.

Figure 7.5
Field of View

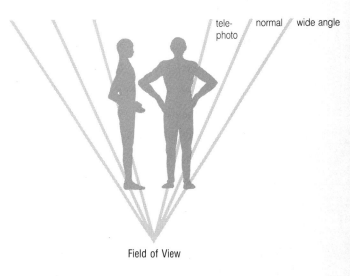

Field of View

Lens Aperture   An **aperture** is an opening through which light is allowed to pass. A camera has a fixed rectangular aperture or frame with a specific aspect ratio, where the film or pickup tube is actually exposed to light. A lens has a variable, circular-shaped aperture or **iris**, which allows the amount of the light passing through the lens to be increased or decreased. The amount of light a lens transmits to a recording device can be controlled by varying the diameter of the lens aperture.

Lens aperture settings are calibrated in sequential f-stops or T-stops. **F-stops**, which are the most commonly used measure of light transmission, have been mathematically calculated from a lens's physical characteristics. Some lenses have both T-stops and f-stops. **T-stops** provide an accurate index of actual light transmission by a specific lens. They are often used with zoom lenses, because the complex elements within the lens and the many air-to-glass surfaces can absorb a great deal of the light before it finally reaches the film or pickup tube. The most commonly labeled f- and T-stops on an aperture setting ring are 1, 1.4, 2, 2.8, 4, 5.6, 8, 11, 16, and 22. The higher the number, the narrower the opening in the lens and thus less light is actually transmitted through the lens. It is sometimes helpful to conceive of the increasing numbers as reciprocals or fractions, i.e., 1.4 = 1/1.4 and 16 = 1/16. Each higher f-stop represents a 50 percent decrease in light transmission from the f-stop immediately below it in numerical scale and two times the f-stop above it. Thus, an f-stop of 2 transmits half as much light through a given lens as an f-stop of 1.4 and twice as much as an f-stop of 2.8. Deciding exactly which f-stop to use is complicated by the many other variables which can affect exposure, such as the sensitivity of film stocks and pickup tubes, as well as the amount of available light.

In the 1930s many Hollywood cameramen always tried to light a scene for an f-stop of 5.6. There were several reasons for this beyond mere habit. First, and most important in terms of image quality, every lens has an optimum aperture, which is usually two to three full stops down from wide open. At an optimum aperture, such as a mid-range f-stop of 5.6, the objects in focus are at their maximum sharpness. When the iris is closed down to a tiny hole, **diffraction** occurs around the blades of the iris, causing the sharpness of the image to be reduced. Such diffraction is more severe with wide-angle than with telephoto lenses. Studio cameramen selected 5.6 because even with poorer quality lenses it consistently produced sharp images.

A lens iris consists of a concentric series of overlapping leaves that cut down on the light passing through the lens as the iris closes and the size of the light hole shrinks. The iris control ring settings on the barrel of the lens are marked as f/stops and t/stops of light transmission.

Second, certain studios simply wanted to preserve a theoretical "normal" depth of field. A great deal of studio video recording today follows the same practice of using an f-stop of 5.6 for similar reasons.

Depth of Field

Depth of field refers to the range of distances in front of the lens which are in acceptable focus at the focal plane. (See Figure 7.6.) Depth of field depends on the lens factors described above: (1) focus distance (which is usually the same as camera-to-subject distance), (2) lens focal length, and (3) the lens aperture or f-stop number. It also varies with the size of the recording format. Depth of field increases as the camera-to-subject distance increases, the focal length of the lens decreases, and the lens aperture narrows *within a single format*. Moving to a larger recording format increases the depth of field of a particular lens. For example, a 25mm lens offers a greater depth of field when used with 1-inch diameter video camera pickup tubes than when used with 2/3-inch pickup tubes.

Depth of field charts for different focal-length lenses and film or video formats indicate the range of distances in front of a lens where objects will appear to be in focus at different lens settings. The range of distances are mathematically calculated from f-stop settings, focal lengths, and camera-to-subject distances. Obviously focus does not immediately drop off beyond the nearest and farthest distances listed for each combination of focal length, camera-to-subject distance, and lens aperture setting. But the chart recommendations provide a relative standard for gauging depth of field and acceptable focus range.

Changing the focal length, either by rotating a lens turret to change lenses or by zooming out or in, obviously changes the depth of field. So does moving the camera

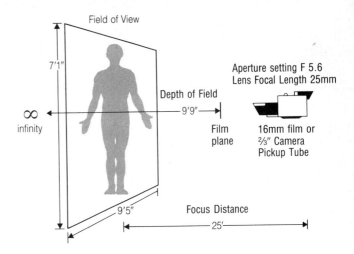

closer to or farther away from the subject and changing the focus distance setting of the lens. The same holds true if the subject moves and the focus setting is changed. If a subject begins to exceed the depth of field range, the camera operator may have to adjust the focus distance setting, which is known as "pulling focus."

Sometimes a camera operator may intentionally try to limit the depth of field either to isolate the subject from the background by putting the background out of focus or to shift the viewer's focus of attention by pulling focus from an object or face in the background to another in the foreground or vice versa. Depth of field limitations are extremely important in terms of the placement and movements of the talent, who must be accurately informed about the range of distances within which they can safely walk and still hit their marks during a shot. Controlling depth of field affects the perception and aesthetics of image depth within the frame, which was discussed more fully in chapter 6. A camera operator who learns the basic principles of depth of field can fully exploit the creative and aesthetic potential of film and television images.

**Figure 7.6
Depth of Field**

The range of objects in focus is very narrow when the depth of field is shallow as in the photo on the left. The photo on the right shows that the range of objects is in focus and apparent depth within the shot increases with the depth of field. A shallow depth of field tends to isolate the objects at the plane of focus from the surrounding space.

VIDEO CAMERAS

Video and film cameras are sophisticated pieces of electronic and mechanical equipment. There are many different types of video and film cameras, which must be fully understood before they can be artistically controlled. This section considers basic camera design, function, operation and artistic control.

**Figure 7.7
A Basic Video
Camera**

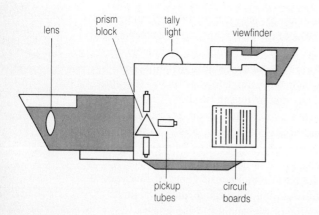

Basic Video Camera

A basic video camera (as shown in Figure 7.7) consists of pickup tube(s), a black-and-white viewfinder, a tally light, a lens, and all the electronic and mechanical controls needed to operate each of these devices. Color cameras have one or more light-sensitive pickup tubes, while black-and-white cameras have only one pickup tube. Even on color cameras, most **viewfinders** present black-and-white images, which show the camera operator what is being recorded by the camera. The **lens** focuses light rays on the television camera pickup tube. Most modern cameras have a single zoom lens, which allows for power or manual control of the image size. Older cameras have a three-lens turret, which allows the operator to select one of three lenses: telephoto, normal, or wide-angle. Telephoto lenses magnify the image, while wide-angle lenses present a wide field of view and demagnify the image. The **tally light** is usually positioned on the top of the camera. It lights up to inform the talent and crew which of several cameras in multiple-camera production is actually being used for recording or transmission.

The Camera Chain

A basic video camera chain consists of five separate parts: (1) a camera; (2) a power supply; (3) a sync generator; (4) a camera control unit; and (5) an encoder, which combines the luminance (brightness or amount of light) and chrominance (saturation or amount of color and hue or shade of color) channels of visual information into a single video signal. The power supply for American television systems consists of either 120-volt AC current for a studio camera or a 12-volt DC battery (usually) for a field camera. A separate sync generator (which is housed inside a field camera) supplies the signal that ensures proper synchronization between the scanning of the camera pickup tube and the scanning of a videotape or a monitor or receiving picture tube, such as a video camera viewfinder. A **camera-control unit** for a studio camera allows the video engineer to ''**shade**'' the camera; that is, to control the brightness and color values in the video camera signal. This is done by adjusting the pickup tube's brightness, contrast, and color. Multiple cameras must be shaded and balanced so that all shots will be comparable in brightness and color. Field cameras have built-in controls, which also allow the color signal to be properly set for color balance and brightness.

Video Camera Filters   There are two types of filter controls used on video cameras: a filter wheel or a filter switch. A filter wheel consists of several different filters arranged around the perimeter of the wheel so that each filter can be positioned between the lens and the camera pickup

A camera control unit allows the video engineer to shade the cameras by adjusting the brightness, contrast, and color settings of the television signals coming from each camera. Multiple cameras are usually shaded so that they reproduce virtually identical images.

tube(s). One of the wheel settings has no filter for normal studio operation. A ''cap'' filter on the wheel is opaque. It is used to protect the pickup tube when the camera is not actually recording. Color correction filters on the wheel alter the color temperature of sunlight so that it corresponds with the preset color sensitivity of the video camera. Neutral density filters reduce the intensity of excessively bright light. The amount of light or brightness in a signal can also be controlled by adjusting the lens aperture and/or the brightness control on a field camera. A filter switch is commonly used on a portable video camera in place of a filter wheel. This switch allows a color correction filter to be positioned between the lens and the pickup tube(s) when recording under sunlight.

White Balance   Some video cameras have an automatic **white balance** device. White balance refers to the adjustment to equal intensities of the red, green, and blue components of the video signal coming from a camera. This assures that a white object placed in front of the camera lens will appear white on a properly adjusted TV monitor. White balance is normally accomplished by placing a white card or a **reference white** in front of the lens so that it virtually fills the camera frame. The white balance button is then depressed to equalize the color components and reproduce a white image (a color correction filter must be positioned behind the lens outdoors under sunlight since white balance corrects for minor fluctuations in color temperature). White balance operations can be supplemented by camera shading in the studio. A video engineer shades multiple cameras by adjusting the color levels of each camera signal after placing a gray scale in front of each camera. Each camera should reproduce the same color and brightness levels. Shading of digitally (microprocessor) controlled video cameras can be done on location by using a remote control unit (RCU), which serves the same function as a camera control unit for digitally controlled cameras.

Types of Video Cameras

The most basic distinction between video cameras is that of color versus black and white, but the standardization of color for most broadcast and nonbroadcast situations suggests that the most important distinctions today are those of field cameras, studio cameras, and convertible cameras, which can be converted for either field or studio use. Within each of these categories there is considerable variation in terms of image quality, and a distinction is often made between broadcast versus nonbroadcast quality cameras. Recorded images must be of high quality to be broadcast, and this usually requires more sophisticated and expensive equipment. The image quality of a video camera should be matched with the format and quality of the videotape recorder being used (to be discussed in chapter 8). It is as pointless to use an expensive, three-tube, studio camera to make a 1/2-inch VHS or Beta original videotape recording as it is to use 1-inch helical, 2-inch quad, or 1/2-inch Recam or Betacam VTR with an inexpensive single-tube portable video camera. The charac-

White balance device as shown on a Zenith VM6000 camera.

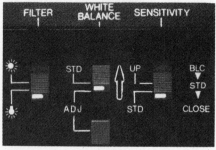

teristics and image quality of both the video camera and recorder must be compatible with the production expectations and standards of the specific task at hand.

Field Cameras   Field cameras vary from lightweight, 8mm or 1/2-inch VHS and Beta home movie cameras that can be hand held with a hand or pistol grip to expensive Recam* and Betacam machines. Many of the least expensive, consumer model cameras are primarily intended for personal home video use and come with a 1/2-inch Beta and VHS videocassette recorder, or with a built-in camcorder. These field cameras are sometimes used in educational, corporate, and government television production situations as well. Recam and Betacam machines employ more sophisticated electronics, such as three pickup tubes instead of one, and have built-in high speed video recorders. They produce images of broadcast quality and are often used for professional recording. It is rarely possible to record images and sounds of sufficient quality for television broadcasting, using low-end video movie cameras. These cameras allow insufficient control over the quality of recorded images and sounds. Some field cameras designed for use with

---

*A high-speed VHS format. A major limitation of Recam and Betacam is the twenty minute recording capacity of the videocassettes.

3/4-inch U-matic videotape recorders are still used in documentary and news situations, where an image quality slightly less than Recam or Betacam will suffice for television broadcast.

Field Camera/Recorder Setups   There are three basic field camera/recorder setups. A camcorder is a self-contained video camera and VCR. Separate cameras and portable VCRs are often connected by a short cable. The portable VCR is then carried by the camera operator or an assistant. A third setup uses a long cable connection or microwave link between the camera and a stationary VTR which records high quality images. Digitally controlled cameras are fed through an RCU before they are recorded on videotape so that image quality can be carefully controlled.

Three field cameras. Far left: Sony Betacam, top left: JVC compact video camera, bottom left: RCA Camcorder.

Left: A Sharp convertible camera in a field setup. Right: A Sharp convertible camera in a studio setup.

Convertible Video Cameras

Many video cameras offer a compromise in size (portability) and electronic hardware (control) between studio and field cameras. So-called **convertible** cameras can be used both in the studio and in the field. They are relatively expensive because they are nearly equivalent (in terms of the attachments which control electronic image quality) to the best studio cameras, and yet they quickly convert to more portable field operation. Several convertible video cam-

An RCA studio camera. Notice that an intercom headset is worn by the camera operator for ease in communicating with the director.

eras have been developed for electronic field production (EFP) in the 1-inch Helical videotape recording format. They often weigh less than twenty pounds and use multiple, high quality pickup tubes. Expensive cameras, such as the EC-35 (EC stands for electronic cinematography), use sophisticated electronics to record "film-style" images. At the top end of the convertible cameras in terms of price are "portable studio" cameras that use sophisticated camera pickup tubes to record high quality images, but they are much more bulky and unwieldy in the field than film-style video cameras. Recordings from convertible cameras are usually made on 1-inch or in some cases ¾-inch helical scan tape recorders.

Studio Cameras

Studio cameras must be mounted in a relatively fixed position, as they are usually too large to be shoulder mounted or hand held. Such cameras frequently feature a large viewfinder, high quality lenses, and sophisticated camera pickup tubes. The quality of the optics, the number of attachments, the size and configuration of the pickup tubes, and the sophistication of the electronics can vary considerably among studio cameras. The highest level studio cameras, such as those used in network broadcasting situations,

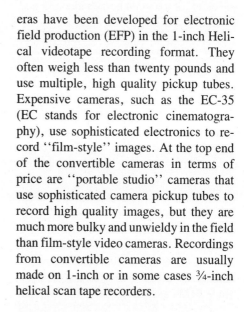

are capable of reproducing high-quality images under a full range of lighting situations. The older top-quality color cameras are extremely bulky and heavy, since they incorporate much circuitry that has recently been replaced by small electronic chips, consolidating many electronic functions. Many newer studio cameras are digitally controlled by microprocessors or electronic chips. Recordings from studio cameras are usually made on 1-inch helical scan, 2-inch quad VTRs, or in some cases, ¾-inch VCRs.

A spring-wound camera.

FILM CAMERAS

Film cameras can be categorized in terms of their film formats (the width of the film in 8 millimeters), viewing systems, and sound recording capabilities. The most basic distinction between film cameras is that of film format. Film format is a major determinant of image quality. As the width of the film increases, so does the quality of the recorded image. Small-format cameras, such as Super-8mm cameras, are much smaller and more portable than 16mm, 35mm, or 65mm cameras. The latter are manufactured primarily for professional use, while the former are made primarily as consumer (home movie) products.

Film cameras have one of two types of operator viewing systems. **Reflex** viewing is a system whereby the operator's eye sees exactly what is coming through the camera's eye, or **objective lens**. Older cameras sometimes have **nonreflex** viewfinders. When the camera operator looks into the viewfinder, he or she does not look directly through the objective camera lens, but sees an entirely separate image of the

same scene. The discrepancy between what the viewfinder sees and what the objective lens sees is called **parallax**. Parallax can usually be corrected by changing the angle of the viewfinder so that its image or **field of view** is the same as that which the camera actually records.

Film cameras can also be differentiated on the basis of sound-recording capabilities. Mechanical or spring-wound cameras cannot run the film at a consistent speed and therefore cannot record synchronous or matching sounds. There are two basic systems by which electronic film cameras can record synchronous sounds: single system and double system. **Single-system** or sound-on-film (SOF) recording refers to the recording of synchronous sounds on the edge of the film as it runs through the camera. The camera records images and sounds at the same time. The sounds are recorded by a magnetic sound head, which is 18 (Super-8mm) or 26 (16mm) film frames ahead of the picture aperture, on magnetic tape striping on the edge of the film. During **double-system**

recording, a separate high quality audio-tape recorder records sounds, which can be played back in perfect synchronization with the recorded film images. The camera and sound recording motors for double-system recording are usually crystal controlled for extremely accurate and precise recording and playback.

Types of Film Cameras

8mm Cameras

Most Super-8mm cameras have reflex viewfinders, and are used for recording home movies, but a few pro-

A Canon 1014XL-S Super-8mm film camera.

fessionals prefer to work in this small format as well. The Super-8mm home movie format is being rapidly replaced by 8mm, VHS, and Beta videotape recordings. While most Super-8mm cameras are battery powered and manual, as opposed to **automatic**, cameras usually have mainspring drive mechanisms, which are spring wound like a clock, and no exposure meter or sound-recording capability. Super-8mm cameras can usually be run at sixteen frames per second (fast motion) in silent (nonsynchronous sound) mode. Synchronous sound on some Super-8mm cameras can only be recorded at twenty-four fps, while others use a speed of eighteen fps. Some sophisticated Super-8mm cameras can be used with separate synchronous sound tape recorders. Super-8mm cameras use single and double Super-8mm film cassettes, which contain 50 to 100 feet of unexposed film.

16mm Cameras

There are many different types of 16mm cameras. Some lack the ability to record synchronous sound, such as spring-wound mainspring-driven cameras which create considerable camera noise and run at imprecise speeds. Cameras that have quiet running, battery powered electric motors and film advance mechanisms are called **self-blimped** film cameras. Single-system sound-on-film cameras were once widely used for recording news footage; they are now being replaced by ENG video equipment. A few film cameras are capable of both single-system and double-system film recording. Many self-blimped, double-system cameras are driven by crystal-sync electric motors that allow the camera to be used without any cable connection between it and a separate synchronous sound recorder. The absence of a cable connection allows for more freedom of movement and is particularly helpful in documentary situations. The camera operator can move about independently of the sound recordist.

Unlike videocameras, whose viewing systems can be electronically controlled, the viewing system of a reflex film camera is often quite dim during actual recording. Film cameras are often focused with the aperture wide open (lowest f-stop) prior to actual recording; when the aperture is closed down to the proper f-stop for recording, less light is transmitted to the viewfinder. Some viewing systems reflect only 18 percent of the light to the viewfinder and a camera operator must become used to recording under difficult conditions. Sometimes a videocamera is attached to a film camera to monitor the image and provide immediately viewable results.

35mm Cameras   It is important to note that 35mm motion picture cameras differ quite dramatically from 35mm still cameras. The latter run 35mm width film horizontally through the camera, while 35mm motion picture cameras run the film vertically through the camera, recording film frames that are not as wide as still-frame

An Arriflex 16SR-2 film camera.

slides. The aspect ratio and image size of a 35mm motion picture frame are thus quite different from a still-camera frame. A 35mm still-camera frame has a much higher aspect ratio (2.35:1) than video (1.33:1 or 4:3); thus it is difficult to record complete slides on a motion picture or video camera.

Some smaller 35mm motion picture cameras, such as the Arriflex II-C, are used exclusively for MOS (''mitt out'' or without sound) nonsynchronous sound recording. Other, very bulky cameras, such as the Mitchell BNC and Panavision, are used almost exclusively for studio synchronous sound recording situations. A Panavision camera is frequently used for widescreen feature film recording in the studio. The latter has an extremely lightweight and portable stepchild, called the Panaflex camera, which is frequently used for feature film work on location. Only extremely high budget feature films use 65mm cameras for original recording. Most 70mm feature film prints are not made from 65mm camera originals but rather from 35mm original recordings that have been blown up to this larger format.

This 35mm self-blimped film camera might be used to record a television action drama or a commercial. Precision engineering and optics facilitate high quality recording. A 1000 foot roll of 35mm film is loaded into the circular film magazine on the back of the camera. The viewfinder eyepiece is on the top left side of the camera, and a large lens focusing nob is on the bottom left. A lens hood or matte box covers the front of the lens where it allows filters to be inserted.

Professional motion picture camera recording in 16mm, 35mm, and 65mm sets a very high standard in image quality which is gradually being rivaled by Beta-cam, EC-35, and HDTV (high definition television).

Film Camera Accessories

Many cameras have attachable **matte boxes** or **lens hoods** which shade the lens from direct sunlight and allow filters to be attached to the lens for color correction or special effects. A frequently used film camera accessory is the **cable release**, which minimizes the vibration to the camera when single frame images are exposed individually. Another important camera accessory is a **changing bag**, which is a black, lighttight bag that can serve as a portable darkroom for loading and unloading longer rolls of film wound on open cores.

Cameras are extremely delicate instruments. They must be handled with great care because they can be damaged very easily. Cameras should be kept clean and dry. Never leave a camera unprotected and exposed to elements, such as rain, sleet, snow, or sand. Never leave a camera unattended or in a hazardous position, where it is likely to fall. Always make sure that you have sufficient battery power by charging batteries well before actual recording begins. Nothing is more frustrating than having a group of people waiting around for the batteries—especially slow-charge batteries—to be recharged.

Video cameras can be permanently damaged by exposing the camera pickup tubes to direct sunlight or allowing the camera to focus on a bright light or reflecting surface for an extended period of time. *Never, never, never* point a video camera directly at the sun; a permanent spot on the pickup tube may result! If the video camera has a built-in recorder, use the same operating procedures you would for a separate VCR (discussed in the next chapter) to avoid having the tape jam within the recorder. Video cameras are even more sensitive to high heat and humidity than film cameras and therefore require shading under intense sunlight, insulation from the cold, and careful use of videotape in high humidity.

Operating a film camera requires extreme care and sensitivity to every possible malfunction of the equipment. Since film is quite expensive to record, minor mistakes can translate into significant financial losses as well as reshooting time.

A power pack for recharging batteries.

Videotape, on the other hand, is immediately viewable and can be reused.

It is important to develop a checklist of camera operating procedures and to make sure that every item on the list is checked off before recording. First, make sure that the lens is clean and that there are no hairs or pieces of film stuck in the film gate of the camera where it is exposed to light. On professional film shoots for commercials the camera lens is usually removed from the camera periodically to check the film gate for hairs or debris, since the image must be perfectly clean. If a filter must be placed in the camera or on the lens, make sure that it is completely clean so that there will be no spots or marks on the film and no loss of light. Carefully load the film into the camera and its magazine and then run the film with the camera and magazine cover open to make sure that it is running properly and not tugging at the film gate, which will cause jittery images. (If you are shooting 8mm film in a cartridge there is no way to check this, since loading is automatic.) Finally, close the camera and the magazine where the film is exposed and stored and listen to a properly running and loaded camera. It has a characteristic sound. If this sound changes during actual recording, stop shooting immediately! Something is wrong. The camera should be opened and the aperture area inspected for problems. The film will probably need to be reloaded.

Summary

Camera operators must be thoroughly familiar with camera techniques and equipment to provide directors with the best possible visual images from the standpoint of a particular aesthetic approach.

A camera operator controls image composition and camera placement by employing four key concepts: essential area, lookspace, walkspace, and headroom. Key information must be placed within the essential area of the screen. Some space must be left within the frame in the direction a person is looking or walking and above a person's head. Camera operators also employ the rule of thirds and realist conceptions, such as the 180-degree action-axis rule.

Camera operators understand the best position and angle at which to place the camera. Long shots, medium shots, and close-ups describe camera placement in terms of camera-to-subject distance. High-angle and low-angle camera positions alter the perception of people and actions.

Camera movements alter spatial perspective and are often used to follow performer movements. Pans, tilts, and pedestals and crane movements can be made with a stationary tripod or camera mounting device. Dollies, trucking shots, and arcs are accomplished using movable camera mounting devices. Moving camera shots are used primarily to keep moving subjects within the camera frame or to reveal new information by altering spatial perspective.

Camera operators must understand how lenses function in order to control them. Lenses are curved pieces of glass that bend light in a predictable manner. Lenses help a camera operator control an image's field of view, brightness, focus, perspective, and depth of field. Lenses can be categorized by their focal lengths within a specific video or film format into wide-angle, normal, and telephoto lenses. Wide-angle lenses have a wide field of view, while telephoto lenses have a narrow field of view and magnify an image. Zoom lenses allow an operator to manipulate field of view by varying the focal length of the lens. A zoom lens should usually be focused at its longest focal length (telephoto).

Varying the aperture, or iris, of a lens changes the amount of light transmitted through the lens. Adjusting the focus setting of a lens puts some objects into focus and others out of focus. The depth of field of an image, that is, the range of distances in front of the lens which remain in focus, will vary with changes in focal length, aperture, and camera-to-subject distance or focus distance within a specific film or video format. Changing the format changes the depth of field as well. Depth of field is an important determinant of image depth along with the placement of objects or scenic design and lighting.

A video camera contains one or more light-sensitive pickup tubes. The camera chain consists of a camera, power supply, sync generator, and a camera control unit. Power can be supplied by line current or a battery. A sync generator and control of image brightness and color can be built into a camera or housed in a separate camera control unit. A color video camera must be white balanced for a proper balance of red, green, and blue colors in the video signal.

Video cameras can be divided into three basic categories: field cameras, convertible cameras, and studio cameras. Field cameras are lightweight and portable. They can range from home video cameras to sophisticated and expensive Recam and Betacam high-speed 1/2-inch videotape recording equipment, which records broadcast quality images. Convertible cameras can be used in the studio with more cumbersome studio attachments or they can be stripped down for use in the field. Convertible cameras often use a 1-inch or ¾-inch helical videotape recording format. Studio cameras are usually much heavier and more cumbersome then portable units. They afford a camera operator maximum control of high quality images, usually recorded in 1-inch or ¾-inch helical or 2-inch quad videotape formats.

Film cameras can be divided into different levels of image quality on the basis of film formats, such as Super-8mm, 16mm, 35mm, and 65mm, which refer to the width of the film in millimeters. Super-8mm film cameras are often used for home movies, although they are rapidly being replaced by home video cameras. Some film cameras have quiet and precise (often crystal controlled) electric motors which allow synchronous sounds to be recorded, either single system (sound-on-film) or double system with a separate high quality sound recorder. Single-system film cameras were once used to record news footage, but they have been virtually replaced by field video cameras. Professional film camera recording still sets a high standard of image quality, which is gradually being rivaled by video technology.

Additional Readings

Lipton, Lenny. *Independent Filmmaking*. New York: Fireside, 1972.

Malkiewicz, J. Kris. *Cinematography*. New York: Van Nostrand Reinhold, 1973.

Mathias, Harry, and Richard Patterson. *Electronic Cinematography*. Belmont, CA: Wadsworth, 1985.

Millerson, Gerald. *The Technique of Television Production*. 10th ed. Woburn, MA: Focal Press, 1981.

Pincus, Edward, and Steven Ascher. *The Filmmaker's Handbook*. New York: Plume, 1984.

Spottiswood, Raymond. *The Focal Encyclopedia of Film and Television Techniques*. New York: Focal Press, 1969.

Wilson, Anton. *Cinema Workshop*. Hollywood: American Society of Cinematographers Holding Corporation, 1983.

Wurtzel, Alan. *Television Production*. 2nd ed. New York: McGraw-Hill, 1983.

Zettl, Herbert. *Television Production Handbook*. 4th ed. Belmont, CA: Wadsworth, 1984.

Exercises

1. Use a hand-held or shoulder-mounted video camera to follow a person moving around in a random fashion outdoors. Maintain good framing and focus while following this unpredictable action. Move your body and the camera as slowly, smoothly, and deliberately as you can without missing any key action. View the recorded videotape to determine why problems occurred at certain points.

2. Use a dolly-mounted video camera to follow a person moving around in a random fashion within a studio. Maintain good framing and focus while following this unpredictable action. Move the dolly as slowly, smoothly, and deliberately as you can without missing any key action. View the recorded videotape to determine why problems occurred at certain points.

3. Select the best lens settings for each shot designated in a shooting script scene by determining the depth of field that will be necessary to keep the performers safely in focus throughout each shot. Remember that depth of field depends on the camera-to-subject distance, the focal length of the lens, and the aperture of f-stop opening of the lens.

CHAPTER 8

Visual Recording

Acquiring a basic understanding of media technology increases our ability to control many aesthetic variables. If we understand the means by which images are recorded, we can consistently obtain high quality images that enhance a functionalist, realist, or formativist approach. Visual media are based on optical, electronic, and photochemical recording processes. This chapter provides an introduction to visible light as electromagnetic energy, video electronics, and film photochemistry.

LIGHT AND COLOR

Visible Light

Light is electromagentic energy which stimulates receptors in our eyes. Our eyes have receptors, called rods and cones, that are responsive to different levels and wavelengths of light. Rods respond to different brightnesses in low light levels and cones respond to different colors or wavelengths in high light levels. Light, like all electromagnetic energy, travels in waves at a speed of 186,000 miles per second. Visible light occupies a small range of wavelengths near the middle of the electromagnetic spectrum. The term **wavelength** refers to the distance between the crests or valleys of each successive wave of energy. The portion of radiant energy to which our eyes are sensitive extends from about 760 nanometers (a nanometer is one billionth of a meter) to 400 nanometers. The entire electromagnetic spectrum extends from radio waves, which are over 100,000 meters in wavelength, to extremely short wavelength gamma and cosmic rays, which are less than one nanometer long. (See Color Plate II.)

Types of Light

Direct light, such as direct sunlight, is called **incident light**. White incident light is actually made up of many different wavelengths or color hues. A color filter placed in front of a direct white light source, such as sunlight, transmits certain wavelengths and absorbs others. For example, a yellow filter allows yellow light to pass through it while it absorbs blue light.

Reflected light is light that has been reflected from objects as shown in Figure 8.1. Reflected light takes on the color of the reflecting surface. A colored object reflects some wavelengths and absorbs others, just like a color filter placed in front of incident light. A green chair or wall reflects green light, for example.

**Figure 8.1
Incident Versus
Reflected Light**

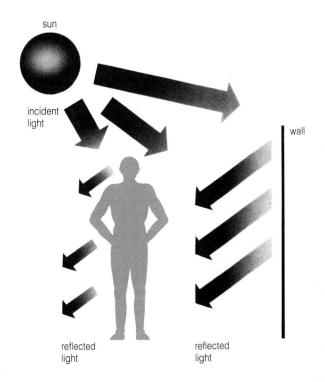

sun

incident
light

wall

reflected
light

reflected
light

Aspects of Color

Hue refers to a specific wavelength band, such as red, green, or blue. Different wavelengths of light are perceived as different colors, or color hues, such as red, green, and blue. Our eyes have three different types of cones, which are responsive to red, green, or blue light. Our perception of different bands of color wavelengths is described in Figure 8.2.

Video and film color systems are capable of recording and projecting a wide range of color hues. Like our eyes, these systems depend on three basic hues: red, green, and blue.

Light can be described in terms of its color saturation and brightness as well as its hue. The **saturation** of a specific hue indicates its color purity, that is, the amount of grayness the color contains. A vibrant but pure color of red, such as on a stop sign, is heavily saturated. In video, saturation is often referred to as **chroma** or chrominance.

Brightness refers to a light's intensity, its lightness or darkness. Bright lights have strong intensities. In video brightness this is often called **luminance**. **Black-and-white** television and film recording devices are only sensitive to the brightness or luminance of a light, not its hue or saturation. Two distinctly different colors may contrast with each other to the naked eye, but if they are equal in brightness, a black-and-white recording depicts them as virtually identical. When recording in black and white, hue and saturation can generally be ignored, since brightness values are paramount. Hue, saturation, and brightness play key roles in video and film color recording processes.

Color Processes

Additive Color   The basic principles of colored light, which provided the foundation for color video and film, were discovered by Isaac Newton more than three centuries ago. Newton found that different wavelengths of visible light refract or bend at slightly different angles as they pass from air into and through a glass prism. Glass is a denser medium than air—its molecules are closer together—and light rays bend as they enter a denser medium and slow down. A prism fans out a white light into a rainbow of colors. Newton discovered that white sunlight is actually composed of many different color wavelengths. Three of these wavelengths, or hues, namely red, green, and blue, can be combined in different amounts to produce almost every visible color, including the color white. By varying the relative brightness of each of these primary colors, intermediate colors can be reproduced. For example, blue light and red light can be combined in equal brightnesses to produce magenta. The process of adding together red, green, and blue lights to reproduce other colors in the visible spectrum is known as **additive color**. A color video screen, for example, uses small red, green, and blue light-emitting phosphors

Figure 8.2
Colors and Their Respective Wavelength Bands

Color Sensation	Wavelength Band (in nanometers)
Red	630–700
Orange	590–630
Yellow	560–590
Green	490–560
Blue	430–490
Violet	380–430

in combination with each other to reproduce many different colors. (See Color Plate III.)

Subtractive Color

Subtractive Color   Another method of color reproduction uses the principle of color-filter absorption or subtraction of specific wavelengths of light to re-create the various colors of the visible spectrum. This process is called **subtractive color**. Color filters, as mentioned earlier, absorb certain wavelengths of light and transmit others. When three specific color filters, namely cyan (blue), magenta, and yellow, are placed in front of a white light source, various colors of the visible spectrum can be reproduced. These three filters subtract the three primary additive colors: red, green, and blue. A cyan filter, for example, subtracts red light and transmits the remaining green and blue components of white light. A yellow filter subtracts blue light. Cyan is called the **complement** of red, and yellow is the complement of blue. When a cyan filter is combined with a yellow filter, red and blue light are both removed from white light and only green remains. A magenta filter, which subtracts green light, combined with a yellow filter, which subtracts blue, transmits only red light. By placing a piece of film with various combinations of cyan, magenta, and yellow filters in front of a white light source, virtually all colors of the visible spectrum can be reproduced. (See Color Plate III.) This subtractive method of color reproduction is the basis of color film recording. **Color film** consists of three layers of filtering material (cyan, magenta, and yellow) attached to a flexible support base. These filters subtract specific wavelengths of light from a projector's white light source, and transmit others to the movie screen.

Basic Video Transmission

Video cameras record and transmit visual images by converting light energy into electrical energy. A video recording of a visual image can be transmitted along an electrical conduit or wire in a closed-circuit system to a video monitor or a videotape recorder. It can also be encoded and broadcast over the airwaves by being combined with a carrier wave, and then decoded and presented as visual images by a television receiver.

The device that actually converts light entering a video camera through a lens into electrical signals is known as a camera **pickup tube**. (See Figure 8.3.) The front surface of a pickup tube is coated with a light-sensitive material (an optoelectronic semiconductor) that increases its electrical conductance, that is, becomes less resistant to the free flow of electrons, when it is struck by light. This surface is regularly bombarded with electrons by an electron gun at the rear of the pickup tube. The

Figure 8.3
A Camera Pickup Tube

A camera pickup tube converts the light energy striking its light sensitive front surface to electrical impulses. The strength of the signal corresponds to the brightness of the light striking the pickup tube. To convert light to electricity the front surface of the pickup tube is bombarded with electrons in a regular scanning pattern.

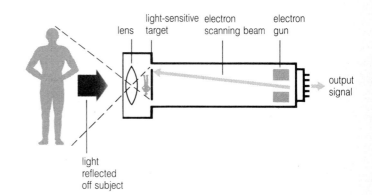

light reflected off subject / lens / light-sensitive target / electron scanning beam / electron gun / output signal electrons are guided by a magnetic field inside the tube which directs them to different parts of the screen. The electrons move across the horizontal lines of the pickup tube in a sweeping motion that starts at the top. The electrons sweep or **scan** every odd-numbered horizontal line, which is called a **scan line**, from left to right. (See Figure 8.4.) Between lines, they are turned off and start up again on the left side, which is called **horizontal blanking**. Gradually the electrons are guided line by line down to the bottom of the tube surface by the magnetic field. Then they rapidly pop back up to the top left hand corner during **vertical blanking** and scan the even-numbered lines on the screen horizontally, until they reach the bottom again. Vertical blanking is important in terms of synchronization between video equipment, such as video

cameras, monitors, and recorders. On a monitor or receiver the two sets of scan lines are woven together or interlaced to produce a complete picture or frame at regular intervals; this pattern of electron bombardment is called **interlaced scanning**.

In the American standard video system, known as NTSC (National Television Standards Committee), each passage from top to bottom covers 262 1/2 (odd or even) lines sixty times every second. There are a total of 525 lines that are electronically scanned by the electron beam in this manner thirty times every second. Each scan of all even or odd lines is known as a **field**. Together, two fields complete an entire 525 line **frame** of the visual image. The European PAL and SECAM systems have more lines and different frame rates and are based on different forms of electrical current than American video. Both PAL

**Figure 8.4
A Scanning Beam
Illustration**

Interlaced scanning of the camera pickup tube and the television receiver picture combines two separate movements. The odd lines are scanned alternately with the even lines. The combination of odd and even lines occurs thirty times every second and is called a video frame. The scanning of all odd or even lines occurs sixty times every second and is called a video field.

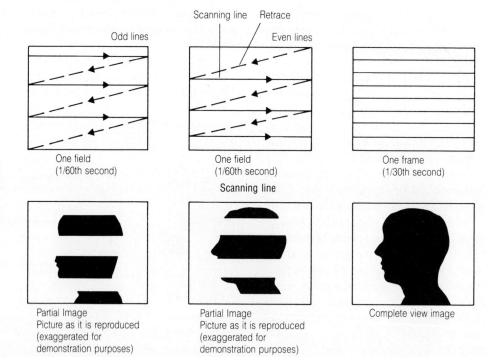

182   Visual Recording

and SECAM have 625 lines and frame rates of twenty-five frames, or fifty fields, per second.

As electrons strike the back side of the pickup tube surface, the strength of the electron flow varies directly with the intensity of the light striking the front side. When the light is very bright at a specific point on the tube, the resistance to the flow of electrons decreases, and more electrons flow out of the tube. The fluctuations in the electrical current flowing out of the pickup tube directly correspond to the variations in brightness across the scan lines of the camera pickup tube. The electrical signal produced by this process is then **amplified** or increased in electrical intensity and carried along a wire to either a closed-circuit television set, called a **monitor**, or combined with a carrier wave that is broadcast over the airwaves to a video **receiver**, which is capable of decoding a broadcast video signal.

A video monitor or receiver changes the electrical energy created by the camera pickup tube back into light energy inside a video picture tube or **cathode ray tube (CRT)**. It does this by bombarding light-*emitting* optoelectronic semiconductors, known as **phosphors**, with a beam of electrons whose intensity is determined by the electrical signal coming from the camera. The phosphors emit light in direct proportion to the intensity of their electron bombardment. (See Figure 8.5 for a diagram of a cathode ray tube.)

The scanning of the video picture tube must be synchronized with the scanning of the camera pickup tube, if corresponding images are to be reproduced. In order for a video monitor or receiver to use the electrical signal transmitted from a camera pickup tube, it must have some referent for determining the scanning rate. A **synchronization signal** or **sync signal**,

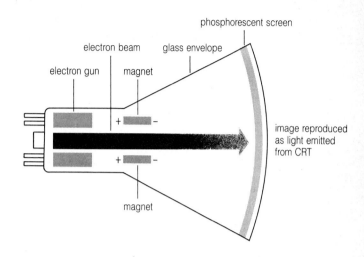

which functions like electronic sprocket holes, is fed to the camera during recording. The sync signal controls the magnetic field in the electron gun and directs the scanning of the front surface of the video receiver tube. There are actually two sync signals: **horizontal sync** and **vertical sync**. The horizontal sync signal controls horizontal scanning and blanking, while the vertical sync signal controls the rate of vertical scanning and blanking. These sync signals are passed along to the television set, where the CRT then scans the image at the same rate and direction as the camera pickup tube. The sync signal directs the scanning rates of both the camera pickup tube and the video picture tube, locking them into synchronization with each other.

Color Video

Thus far our description of the television process has only described the transmission of black-and-white images. A black-and-white system transmits only the brightness values of light, not hue or saturation. There are several different camera pickup tube sytems for creating color

Figure 8.5 Diagram of a Cathode Ray Tube

A basic television picture tube is often called a cathode ray tube or CRT. Electrons bombard light emitting phosphors in an interlaced scanning pattern to transform electrical energy back into light and reproduce visual images.

video images. Some use only one pickup tube, while others use two or three. While the image quality of these systems can vary considerably, the principles of color reproduction they employ are essentially the same.

Light entering video cameras can be divided into its red, green, and blue components by using color filters. Sometimes the separation of light into these three different color components is accomplished by a **prism block** that bends or refracts each color component somewhat differently and directs each separate color wavelength band to a different pickup tube. (See Color Plate IV.) Other systems use a set of **dichroic** mirrors which reflect and filters which transmit different bands of color light to different pickup tubes. A three-tube system records each of the three color bands on separate tubes. A two-tube color system mathematically derives the third color component from the two colors it actually picks up, comparing them to the overall brightness. In a single-tube color system a mosaic of tiny red, green, and blue filters is attached to the front surface of the pickup tube. (See Color Plate IV.) The red, green, and blue components occupy different points of the same image rather than providing separate but complete color renditions of the entire visual image.

The three-color information picked up by color tubes is then encoded as two **chrominance** or color signals, which are called the **I** and **Q signals**, and one **luminance** or brightness signal, which is called **Y signal**. (See Figure 8.6.) This chrominance and luminance information is then transmitted to the television monitor or receiver, where it is decoded. The video screen or CRT usually has three separate electron guns, although some picture tubes have only one gun, which combines

several functions. The three guns are directed through a series of windows called **shadow masks** or aperture deflectors that prevent electrons from one color gun striking any phosphors except those assigned specifically to it. Each gun is assigned to phosphors that emit light of a specific color: red, green, or blue. The electron guns of a CRT are placed either **in line**, that is, on top of one another so that they are directed at parallel red, green, and blue emitting phosphor *lines* or in a triangular configuration so that they are directed at triangularly arranged red, green, and blue emitting phosphor dots or circles.

Pickup Tubes

Most black-and-white video cameras have a single **vidicon** pickup tube. Vidicon tubes are the least expensive type of pickup tube and yet are capable of transmitting high resolution images. Vidicon tubes require a relatively short warm-up time and have a fairly extensive **contrast range**, or range of gray tones from white to black. Unfortunately vidicon tubes are quite sensitive to **smearing** or **comet-tailing**, which refers to the lingering image of a bright object as it moves in front of the camera. They are also susceptible to **blooming** or **halo effects**, which appear as an added brightness or halo around bright objects and lights.

Color camera pickup tubes come in three basic types of modified vidicon tubes: **Saticon** (a trademark of Hitachi), **Plumbicon** (a registered trademark of N.V. Phillips), and **Newvicon**. Saticon tubes are interchangeable, that is, the same tube is used for all three colors. Plumbicon tubes are designed for specific colors of light: red, green, or blue. Plumbicon tubes are relatively expensive; they have a special lead-oxide coating on the front surface

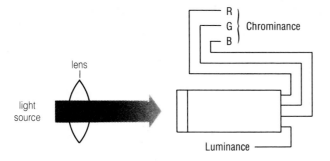

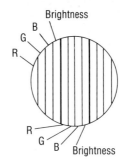

Brightness
B
G
R

R
G
B Brightness

Figure 8.6
Chrominance and
Luminance Signals
The video portion of a
television signal
consists of two basic
channels of
information, called
chrominance and
luminance.
Chrominance refers to
the color information
which is determined by
the phase of the
electrical television
signal, while
brightness is a function
of the signal's
intensity. A black-and-
white television set
uses only the
luminance information.

which results in less blooming around bright objects. Both the Plumbicon and Saticon are susceptible to comet-tailing around moving objects recorded at low light levels. Newvicon tubes are much less susceptible to comet-tailing, and function well at low light levels. Some Plumbicon tubes have extended red sensitivity which attempts to compensate for deficiencies in reproducing highly saturated reds, since most pickup tubes are slightly less sensitive to red than green light.

Both black-and-white and color pickup tubes are available in a variety of sizes. Common color pickup tube diameters are 1/2 inch, 2/3 inch, and 1 inch. There are also different "grades" and lines of resolution that can be reproduced for different types and qualities of tubes. Overall, pickup tubes with larger surface areas reproduce better quality, sharper, more detailed pictures than smaller pickup tubes within specific types and grades. Yet different sensitivities and recording characteristics of various light-sensitive surfaces are a complicating factor. Recent technological advances have concentrated for the most part on improving television image resolution, response, and sensitivity while decreasing the size of the tube. For example, the Ikegami EC-35 camera, which was designed to produce "film-style" images of high quality, has 2/3-inch Plumbi-

con pickup tubes. Pickup tube size is not always synonymous with image quality, but as a general rule it is.

Generally, color cameras with large, separate tubes for each color will produce better quality color images than single-tube cameras with smaller tubes. Using multiple tubes can introduce additional problems, such as registration problems caused by misaligned tubes, which show up as a color outline around objects. Solving registration problems is a task for a qualified video engineer. Budgetary restrictions and shooting conditions may make it difficult to use expensive, high quality recording equipment, but image quality must ultimately meet the broadcast or nonbroadcast standards for the specific presentational situation. Image quality standards for network and local broadcasting are sometimes higher than those for local cable television or corporate communications. The image quality of any video recording must meet the standards and expectations of the sponsor and the audience.

A relatively recent development in video cameras is the charge-coupled device (CCD). The front surface of a CCD (Figure 8.7) contains minute silicon particles that are light-sensitive. Light that hits a silicon device stimulates an image charge called a **pixel**. Each line of a video

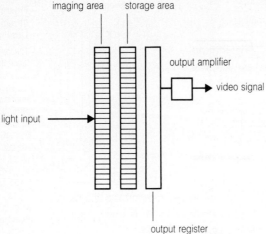

imaging area   storage area

output amplifier

video signal

light input

output register

Figure 8.7
A Charge-Coupled
Device

Some small format
video cameras use a
charge coupled device
or CCD to transform
light into electricity.
CCDs are very compact
and do not use the
same form of electron
bombardment as
conventional camera
pickup tubes and CRTs.

image consists of numerous pixels. The
pixel information is transferred line by line
and is amplified into a recordable video
signal. CCDs are used in some small format video cameras and a few professional
models; the process holds great potential
in terms of improving image quality while
reducing camera size.

Videotape Recording

Videotape* contains iron oxide or other
metallic particles that store electrical information in magnetic form. These micro-
scopic particles are attached to a flexible
support base, such as cellulose acetate or
polyester (mylar). **Videotape recorders**
or **VTRs** are capable of both recording
and playing back video information on

---

* It is extremely important to record a slate or shot
identification of five seconds duration at the beginning of
each recording of a single-camera take for postproduction
editing. (See chapter 10 p. 249 and chapter 14 p. 337.)

reels of videotape. A VTR records a sync
signal, which is needed to synchronize the
scanning of the camera pickup tube with
the scanning of a television picture tube.
A sync signal which is recorded on a videotape is called a **control track**. The control track synchronizes the scanning of the
television picture tube with the scanning
of the videotape during playback. An erase
head erases previous information stored on
the videotape prior to recording new images. A **servo capstan**, that is, a rotating
tape drive cylinder with an accurate motor
that varies the speed of the playback so that
proper synchronization is maintained,
moves the videotape through the recorder
at the correct speed.

The actual recording of video and audio
signals is done by video and audio record
heads, which also function as playback
heads. The audio and video heads are usually separated from one another because
the recording of a video signal requires a
complex movement of the head with respect to the videotape while an audio head
remains stationary. **Hi-fi** recording in 1/2-
inch VHS and Beta formats and digital recording in 8mm videotape recording are
important exceptions. They both record
audio signals using rotating audio heads
parallel to the video heads. There are two
basic methods of recording the video signal; these further distinguish the two general categories of videotape recorders:
helical scan and quadruplex.

Helical Scan Recording   Helical scan
recorders (Figure 8.8) use two or more
video heads, which continuously record
electrical video signals. As magnetic tape
travels from left to right across the recording heads, the heads rotate in a clockwise
direction, opposite to the movement of the
tape. On a two-head recorder, each time a
single head passes over the tape it records

a complete field of 262½ lines of video. At the exact instant that the first rotating head disengages from the tape, the second head engages it, so that a continuous recording of the television signal is made along the tape by consecutive heads. The passage from one head to the next corresponds to the vertical blanking period and is a crucial part of maintaining synchronization. The combined passage of the two heads records a complete frame of 525 lines. The videotape is wrapped around semicircular drum, and the heads maintain continuous contact with a semicircular wrap of tape around the drum, moving in a downward diagonal direction as they rotate past the tape. Because the recording is made in a slanting movement of the head across the tape, a helical scan recorder is sometimes called a **slant-track** recorder. A 3/4-inch tape runs through a helical machine at about 3¾ inches per second, and the heads rotate counterclockwise at slightly less than 200 inches per second, producing a combined tape-to-head speed of about 700 inches per second (3¾ × 200 = 700 +). While the speed of initial recording cannot be varied, a helical scan recorder can be slowed down or speeded up in playback to create **slow** or **fast motion** action. During slow motion, scan lines are repeated, while during fast motion, some are skipped. The image can also be stopped and action frozen by repeating one recording line or complete field of the video image, called a **freeze frame**, which is often designated as the ''pause'' mode during playback.

Quadruplex Recording Quadruplex or simply ''**quad**'' videotape recorders scan the tape vertically in a transverse direction, and are sometimes called **transverse** recorders. The term ''quad,'' meaning four, describes the four vertically

A. 1-inch Type C Helical Videotape Recording Format

direction of tape travel

audio 1
audio 2

direction of head travel

video

control track
sync signal
audio 3

B. 1-inch Type B Helical Videotape Recording Format

direction of tape travel

audio 1
control track
audio 2

video

direction of head travel

audio 3

rotating heads on these machines. The four heads rotate at about 100 inches per second while the tape is driven through the recorder at a speed of about 15 inches per second, producing a combined videotape-to-head speed of about 1500 inches per second and reproducing high quality images. The passage of one head across the tape in a quad machine records several scan lines of actual television pickup tube information. Since the quad machine divides up complete television fields among several tape scanning lines and does not record a single field for each transverse pass of a record head, the speed of playback cannot be varied to produce fast/slow motion or freeze frames. High quality 1-inch *helical scan* recorders and playback dubbers allow for special effects creation without sacrificing image quality.

Figure 8.8
A. 1-inch Type C Helical Videotape Recording Format
B. 1-inch Type B Helical Videotape Recording Format

There are two different types of 1-inch helical scan recording: Type C and Type B. These systems are not compatible. The tape recording configurations of each are depicted above. Type C is used more widely than Type B.

A video engineer operates a traditional workhorse at many television stations, a 2-inch quad VTR. Images from a 2-inch quad VTR are generally of high quality, although they are subject to banding and therefore require constant monitoring and maintenance. The portable 1-inch Type C VTR on the right is quite compact compared to the 2-inch quad VTR on the left, but it is nonetheless capable of recording extremely high quality sounds and images in the field. Both types of VTRs are of professional broadcast quality.

Videotape Formats

The **format**, or width, of videotape ranges from 8mm to 2 inches. Quad recorders use 2-inch-wide videotape. Helical scan recorders (as shown in Figure 8.9) use one of the following formats: 8mm, 1/2-inch, 3/4-inch, 1-inch, or 2-inch-wide videotape. **Small-format** helical scan recorders use 8mm, 1/2-inch and 3/4-inch videotape, while 1-inch or 2-inch videotape is used in state-of-the-art or highest quality **large-format** helical scan recorders. The latter are sometimes called **high-band** (as opposed to low-band) recorders, because they can record higher frequencies of video information.

Video recorders that use self-contained cassettes of videotape as opposed to open reels are called videocassette recorders or VCRs. Eight millimeter videocassettes and VCRs are capable of recording images which have approximately the same quality as some 1/2-inch VHS and Beta videotapes and VCRs. Eight millimeter cassettes are extremely compact. Recent availability of digital audio recording in 8mm has significantly improved audio recording capability in this format as well. Many people predict that 8mm will become the dominant format for home videotapes and audiotapes. There are four different helical scan systems for recording on 1/2-inch video cassettes: **VHS**, **Beta**, **Recam**, **Betacam**. These systems all use 1/2-inch videotape in closed cassettes and helical or slant tracking techniques, but the actual scanning of the videotape is sufficiently different so that they are noncompatible systems. A VHS recording, which uses a slightly larger videocassette and a different loading mechanism, cannot be played on a Beta machine and vice versa. Recam and Betacam are both high speed, high quality recording systems, but they are also incompatible with each other and with VHS or Beta. Most 1/2-inch wide videocassette recording systems have only sufficient track space for the recording of a control track,

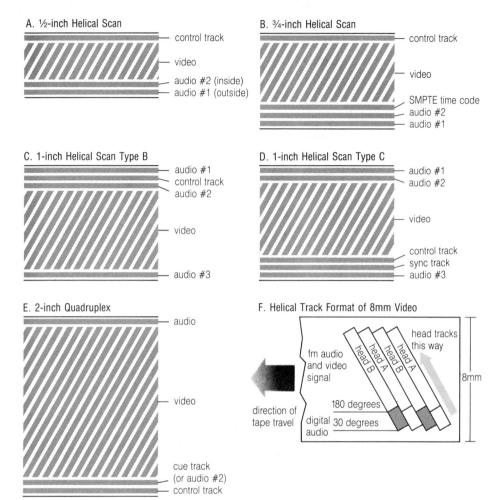

A. ½-inch Helical Scan
- control track
- video
- audio #2 (inside)
- audio #1 (outside)

B. ¾-inch Helical Scan
- control track
- video
- SMPTE time code
- audio #2
- audio #1

C. 1-inch Helical Scan Type B
- audio #1
- control track
- audio #2
- video
- audio #3

D. 1-inch Helical Scan Type C
- audio #1
- audio #2
- video
- control track
- sync track
- audio #3

E. 2-inch Quadruplex
- audio
- video
- cue track (or audio #2)
- control track

F. Helical Track Format of 8mm Video
- head tracks this way
- head B
- head A
- head B
- head A
- 8mm
- fm audio and video signal
- 180 degrees
- direction of tape travel
- digital audio
- 30 degrees

**Figure 8.9
Helical Scan
Videotape in ½-inch,
¾-inch, 1-inch,
(Types B and C), 2-inch Quadruplex, and
8mm Formats**

two audio tracks, and the video scanning line track. Some 1/2-inch videocassette recorders are capable of running at a variety of speeds, so that anywhere from one to six hours of recording can be made on the same videocassette.

Three-quarter inch tapes and recorders are called **U-matic** videocassettes and VCRs. The added width of 3/4-inch tape allows sufficient space for recording more tracks than on 1/2-inch tape. The video signal takes up about 80 percent of any videotape tracking space. The rest of the videotape is divided among the control track and audio track(s). A 3/4-inch tape has space for two audio tracks. One of the audio tracks—usually Track #1—can be used as a **cue track**, which records the director's commands or cues during recording, or a special frame reference code for editing known as a **time code**, which is discussed later in connection with electronic editing. (Time code can also be used in 1/2-inch videotape formats.) Some vid-

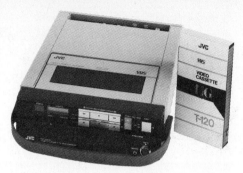

A JVC portable ½-inch VHS recorder.

Different videotape formats. Clockwise from right: ¾-inch U-matic, VHS ½-inch, Beta ½-inch, 1-inch, and 2-inch.

eocassette recorders in 1/2-inch or 3/4-inch U-matic formats are capable of recording and playing back several different types of television signals, such as NTSC, PAL, and SECAM, using different types of electrical current.

The 1-inch and 2-inch tapes used for professional recordings allow sufficient space for a control track, three sound tracks, and one (Type C) or two (Type B)

A Sony ¾-inch U-matic videocassette recorder.

video tracks. Such tape comes on an open reel, rather than a cassette, and it must be manually loaded into a *VTR*. One inch Type C standard recording tape records an additional sync track. The video track is nonsegmented, which means that each video track represents a whole video field—this allows more speed control, viewing with better images during rapid and slow advance, and freeze frames. One inch Type B is less popular than Type C and records a segmented video track which inhibits viewing during faster and slower speeds, but reproduces a more stable image and can be used with portable, lightweight equipment.

Larger format videotapes generally reproduce images which are superior in quality to smaller formats. Quad recordings are less useful for special effects and high or slow speed viewing than 1-inch helical. They are also subject to "banding" (the appearance of horizontal color bands) during playback. Professional broadcast standards of image quality usually demand 1-inch helical or 2-inch quad recordings. Smaller format videotapes can sometimes be broadcast, when they have been channeled through an image stabilizer, known as a digital **time base corrector** or **TBC**, which accurately synchronizes

1. (MUSIC):

2. COACH: No second shots, Wallace. No second shots.

3. WALLACE: I'm used to him yelling.

4. COACH: Wallace, you've got to keep him out of there.

5. WALLACE: But not at me.

6. COACH: Box him out. Box him out.

7. ANNCR: The best never comes easy.

8. That's why there's nothing else like it. Budweiser Light.

9. SINGERS: BRING OUT YOUR BEST.

10. BRING OUT YOUR BEST. BUDWEISER LIGHT.

11. BRING OUT YOUR BEST. BUDWEISER LIGHT.

12. ANNCR: The best. COACH: Nice game.

13. ANNCR: You've found it in yourself.

14. And now you've found it in the beer you drink.

15. SINGERS: BUDWEISER BUDWEISER LIGHT.

Color Plate I
Budweiser Photoboard

A photoboard is a series of still-frame images from a completed television commercial. It is similar to a storyboard, which is a series of images drawn during preproduction. Each frame represents a different shot. In this sixty-second spot a potential conflict between a basketball player and his coach is resolved when the player reaches inside himself and displays excellent defensive skills. The intercutting of the coach and the player in separate shots highlights their potential conflict in shots two through seven, while their simultaneous appearance in shots twelve and thirteen resolves the conflict. In shot fourteen, the player celebrates the victory. Notice that almost every shot in the photoboard is a medium shot or a close-up shot. Also note that the product is presented and its name is repeated at the beginning, middle, and end of the commercial. The commercial appeals to beer drinkers by associating athletic prowess and light beer consumption with inner strength and the pursuit of excellence.

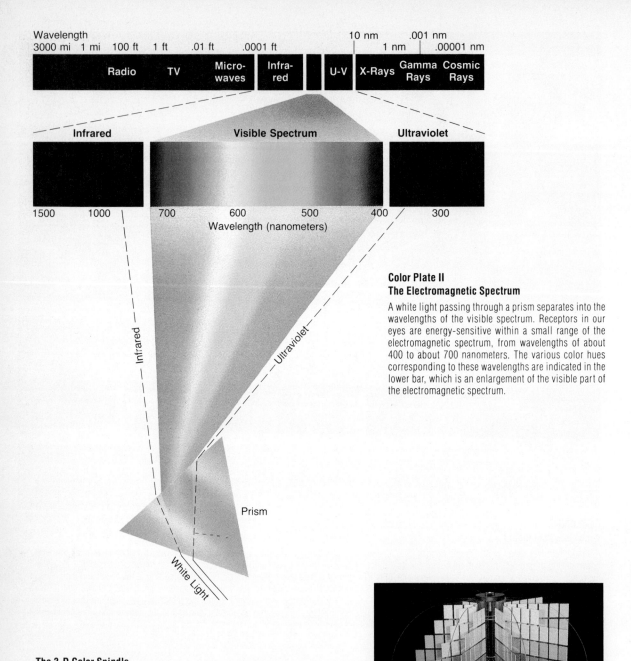

Wavelength

3000 mi	1 mi	100 ft	1 ft	.01 ft	.0001 ft		10 nm		.001 nm	

| Radio | TV | Micro-waves | Infra-red | | U-V | X-Rays | Gamma Rays | Cosmic Rays |

1 nm   .00001 nm

Infrared   **Visible Spectrum**   **Ultraviolet**

1500   1000   700   600   500   400   300

Wavelength (nanometers)

Infrared

Ultraviolet

Prism

White Light

Color Plate II
The Electromagnetic Spectrum

A white light passing through a prism separates into the wavelengths of the visible spectrum. Receptors in our eyes are energy-sensitive within a small range of the electromagnetic spectrum, from wavelengths of about 400 to about 700 nanometers. The various color hues corresponding to these wavelengths are indicated in the lower bar, which is an enlargement of the visible part of the electromagnetic spectrum.

The 3-D Color Spindle

The color spindle (or 3-D color wheel) locates specific colors on the basis of hue, saturation, and brightness. Colors increase in brightness from bottom to top, and each spoke of the wheel depicts a specific hue, which increases in saturation or color purity as it moves outward from the central brightness axis. A 3-D color wheel is a useful means of selecting and matching specific colors for sets and costumes and determining their relative brightness.

Color Plate III
Additive Color Mixing

A television screen reproduces color through additive color mixing. If we examined a TV screen with a magnifying glass, we would see that it is composed of tiny red, green, and blue dots or lines (as shown in Color Plate IV). These dots or lines are phosphors that emit colored light. Red, green, and blue lights mix together to create the different colors of the visible spectrum. The same process is demonstrated here with three slide projectors, one equipped with a blue filter, one with a green filter, and one with a red filter. Since two or more colors add up to create a specific wavelength or color hue, the mixing process is an additive one.

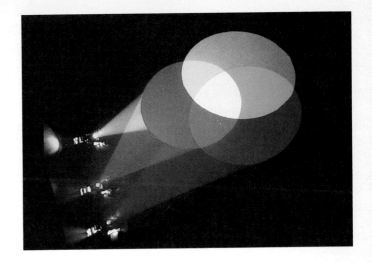

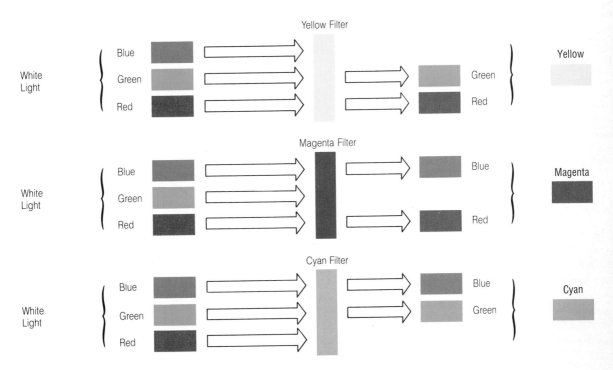

Subtractive Color Process

Yellow Filter

White Light — Blue / Green / Red → Yellow Filter → Green / Red → Yellow

Magenta Filter

White Light — Blue / Green / Red → Magenta Filter → Blue / Red → Magenta

Cyan Filter

White Light — Blue / Green / Red → Cyan Filter → Blue / Green → Cyan

Subtractive Color Mixing

Motion picture film reproduces color through subtractive color mixing. If we carefully examined a piece of film, we would see that it is composed of yellow, magenta, and cyan layers, which act as color filters. When a white light from a projector lamp passes through each filter, specific color wavelengths or hues are absorbed or reflected by each filter layer, while others are allowed to pass through. Different colors of the visible spectrum result from various thicknesses of each color filter layer. Since specific wavelengths are created by subtracting colors from white light, the mixing process is a subtractive one.

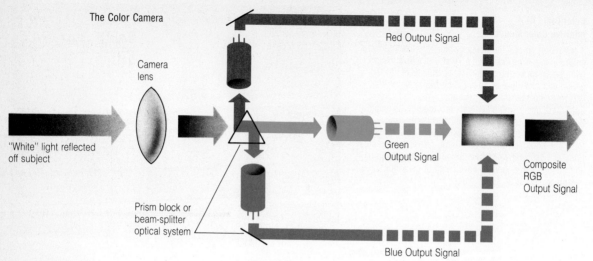

The Color Camera

Camera lens

"White" light reflected off subject

Prism block or beam-splitter optical system

Red Output Signal

Green Output Signal

Blue Output Signal

Composite RGB Output Signal

Color Plate IV
Color Video Camera

A color video camera uses a prism block (or beam-splitter optical system and color filters) to split the light coming through the camera lens into red, green, and blue components, which are sent to separate pickup tubes (some small format video cameras place a mosaic of tiny red, green, and blue filters in front of a single pickup tube or a CCD). The separate color information is encoded into a television signal so that it can be sent to a television receiver where it will be decoded.

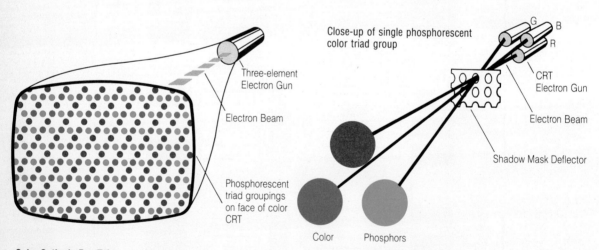

Close-up of single phosphorescent color triad group

Three-element Electron Gun

Electron Beam

Phosphorescent triad groupings on face of color CRT

G B R

CRT Electron Gun

Electron Beam

Shadow Mask Deflector

Color   Phosphors

Color Cathode Ray Tube

A color cathode ray tube in a television receiver uses a decoded television signal to bombard light-emitting color phosphors with electrons and produce color images through additive mixing. A conventional dot matrix picture tube uses three electron guns in a triangular configuration to bombard separate color phosphor *dots*. An in-line picture tube uses electron guns on top of each other or in-line to stimulate color phosphor *lines*. It is easy to distinguish between these two different types of tubes by looking at the screen with a magnifying glass and determining whether there are color dots or color lines. Each cluster of red, green, and blue dots or lines forms a triad group. Color dots or lines added together create a specific hue or wavelength.

the scanning process by changing a conventional analog signal into a more easily controlled digital one and provides a high quality video signal. (See chapter 10, pg. 248.) Minor variations in synchronization which cause a picture to jitter are eliminated. Using a TBC, smaller format recordings, such as ENG news or documentary recordings on 3/4-inch U-matic cassettes, can be conventionally broadcast or dubbed up to larger 1-inch or 2-inch videotape formats.

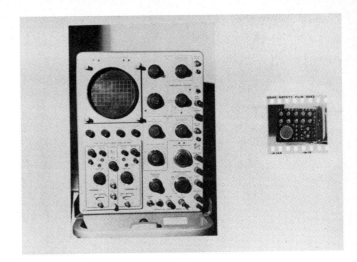

FILM RECORDING

Basic Photochemistry

Photography uses light energy to transform the chemical properties of light-sensitive substances. **Photographic film** consists of light-sensitive materials, such as silver halide crystals or grains, attached to a flexible support base, such as cellulose acetate. Silver halide forms an invisible latent image when it is exposed to light in a camera. Light stimulates a chemical change in silver halide crystals, which can only be made visible and permanent by **developing** the image in certain chemical solutions. During development, the light-stimulated silver halide crystals are converted into metallic silver so that they become opaque to light. Metallic silver either reflects or absorbs all light attempting to pass through it. The film is then **fixed** in a fixing solution where the unstimulated silver halide crystals are chemically washed from the film. After fixing, the film is no longer sensitive to light. Film development and fixing take place in complete darkness. The film image now appears dark or opaque where it was struck by light and clear where the

light energy was not strong enough to stimulate the silver halide crystals. The resulting image is called a **negative** image. It inverts the whites and the blacks of the original scene. A white wall appears black and a black curtain appears white.

In order to get a **positive** image, which reproduces the whites and blacks of the original scene, the negative film must be **printed** or copied on to another piece of film on a device called a **contact printer**. The contact printer puts the developed negative in contact with an unexposed piece of negative film and passes both of them together over a strong light. When the copy is chemically developed in the same manner as the negative film from which it was printed, it reproduces the correct whites and blacks. The bright areas in the original scene are now white and the black areas are black. This method, in which a negative is copied to produce a positive image, is called the **negative/positive process**.

An alternative approach to this two-stage, negative/positive process is known as the **reversal process**. The difference between negative/positive and reversal

Negative and positive photographic film.

film is similar to the difference between snapshots and slides in still photography. Reversal recording is a single-stage process which produces a positive image after one development of the originally exposed film. The negative image resulting from initial exposure is converted to a positive image during several stages of development. The stimulated silver halide crystals are removed and the remaining, unexposed crystals are changed to metallic silver. Now the film is opaque where there was too little light striking the film, but clear where there was too much light. Reversal film produces a positive image immediately. It does not have to be printed to view the original scene, as does negative film.

The size and composition of the silver halide crystals in large part determine the overall light **sensitivity** and **graininess** of the **film stock**, of a particular variety or brand of film, such as Kodak's Eastman Color Negative. Light sensitivity or film speed is rated in **EI**, which stands for **exposure index**. The American standard rating, called **ASA**, (or **EI**), or a German standard, called **DIN**, is often printed on the film package. These indices of a film's overall sensitivity to light provide a relative indication of how much light will be required to properly expose a specific film. Slower films, with lower numbers, require more light than those with higher numbers. The term graininess refers to the size and visibility of particles in the film. A **grainy** image is one in which these particles are readily visible, and a **fine-grain** image is one in which they are not. Faster film stocks, which are more sensitive to light and therefore have higher EI numbers, generally have a greater proportion of large as opposed to small silver halide crystals or other light-sensitive particles than slower films. As a result, faster film

stocks also have more visible grain structures than slower films. They produce grainy images. The size of the grain in the image can affect its **resolution** and **sharpness**, which refer to image clarity. Slower film tends to have higher resolution and sharpness than faster film.

The type and size of photosensitive material used in a specific film stock can also affect the **contrast range** that the film is capable of recording. Contrast range refers to the range of gray tones from white to black to which a film is capable of responding. The term **exposure latitude** also refers to the range of white to black tones that can be recorded. In general, negative film stocks have a much wider exposure latitude and contrast range than reversal stocks. Some negative film stocks have a contrast range or ratio of 100:1, that is, they can record and differentiate light-reflecting objects that are 100 times as bright as very dark objects in the same scene. Compare this to a standard video camera pickup tube, which has an effective contrast ratio of 20:1 or at most 30:1. If there is a wide range of dark to light reflecting objects in a scene, a video camera will not record them all. Many neutral tones will be recorded as completely black or completely white rather than some shade between them. In film a full range of tones may be recorded. The effect of contrast ratio on lighting and scene design is discussed more fully in chapters 9 and 11 and the difference between film and video is an extremely important one.

Color Film

We have so far considered only the recording of different brightnesses of light on black-and-white film. Color film responds to different hues and saturations of light, as well as different levels of brightness. A

Left: An exposure latitude chart. Center: Checking lighting on the set in the studio using the chart. Right: Checking the lighting over the television monitors using the chart.

color-film emulsion consists of a multilayered suspension of light-sensitive particles and color dyes attached to a flexible support base, such as cellulose acetate. When light enters a camera, it strikes three different layers of color dyes and light-sensitive particles. These layers are sensitive to blue, green, and red light, respectively. Light first strikes the blue-sensitive layer, where only the blue light affects the particles and dyes. The other colors of light then pass through this layer and a yellow filter, which removes excess blue light, before striking the green- and red-sensitive layers. These layers are sensitive to blue light, as well as their own wavelength bands. The blue-sensitive layer thus records the blue component, the green-sensitive layer the green component, and the red-sensitive layer the red component of white light.

During image development and fixing, the light-sensitive silver particles are completely removed and all that remains are the color dyes that were attached to the stimulated particles in their emulsion layer. These dyes create yellow, magenta, and cyan filters in the three emulsion layers. As was previously explained, these three filters can subtractively reproduce all the colors of the original scene, when white light is passed through them and projected onto a movie screen. Like black-and-white film, color-film stocks come in negative or reversal processes and a variety of light sensitivities and contrast ranges.

Film Exposure

Film is exposed inside a lightproof mechanism called a **camera**. (See Figure 8.10.) A basic film camera consists of a **lens**, which focuses an image on the film, a **viewfinder**, which allows the camera operator to see the image that is being recorded, a film **feed** and **takeup** mechanism which supplies film to the exposure area and rolls it up after it has been exposed, a **motor** that drives the film through the camera, a rotating opaque **shutter**, which rapidly opens and closes to expose each

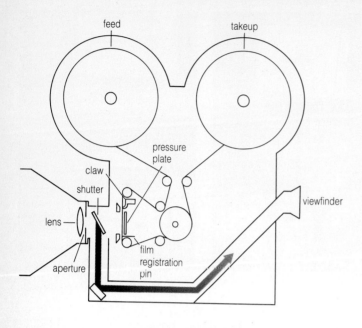

feed takeup

pressure
plate

claw

shutter

lens —

viewfinder

aperture

film
registration
pin

**Figure 8.10
The Basic Film
Camera**

frame of film, an **aperture**, which determines the dimensions of the frame which is exposed, a **pressure plate**, which holds the film flat against the aperture to ensure good focus, a **pulldown claw**, which intermittently grabs film **sprocket holes** or perforations to advance the film for each single frame or still photograph at the aperture, a **speed control**, which determines how many individual frames will be exposed each second, and a **run/stop** button, which turns the camera on and off.

Motion-picture film is perforated at regular intervals so that it can be driven intermittently by a camera and a projector. This intermittent movement allows a single frame of film to be held stationary while a rotating shutter opens up and allows light passing through the lens to expose the film. A projector uses the same mechanism to project recorded images through the lens onto a screen. The feed and takeup mechanisms push the film continually through the camera, while the

claw pulls the film at the aperture. Film is constantly pushed and pulled through a 16mm camera at a rate of thirty-six feet per minute or ninety feet per minute in 35mm. Normal sound speed exposes twenty-four frames per second (fps) in 35mm and 16mm and either eighteen or twenty-four fps (depending on the system) in 8mm. The projected images fuse together into an illusion of continuous motion on the basis of flicker fusion and the phi phenomenon, two properties of human visual perception. The human eye fills in the gaps between successive still frames, when they are rapidly flashed on the screen. The eye and mind perceive apparent motion from the rapid flickering or strobing of still frame images.

The camera shutter and claw must be synchronized so that the shutter stays open when the claw disengages the film and retracts behind the aperture plate. At this point the film is stationary in the aperture. Sometimes it is held stationary by a device known as a **registration pin**, which holds the film in firm **registration**, that is, it holds it very steady when it is not being pulled by the claw. The shutter must be closed when the registration pin retracts and the claw engages the film to advance it, or the film images will blur as they pass the light in the aperture. The speed control allows the camera operator to alter the frames-per-second speed of the camera. Film recorded at speeds above twenty-four frames per second will reproduce images in slow motion when it is **projected** or played back at normal sound speed (twenty-four frames per second). Camera images recorded at fewer than twenty-four frames per second will produce fast motion. Thus slow and fast motion are produced during actual recording in film, unlike video recording, which always occurs at thirty frames per second. Increasing the film recording speed also changes the synchronized shutter speed and affects the amount of light exposing the film. Faster recording speeds produce more rapid shutter speeds and less light reaches each frame during exposure, since the duration of each exposure is reduced. To compensate for these changes in exposure, the lens must be adjusted so that more light passes through it and strikes the film when the camera speed is increased.

Motion Picture Formats

Motion picture film, which is exposed to light inside a camera, is available in a variety of formats or film widths, including 8mm, 16mm, 35mm, and 65mm. These distinctions between various formats refer to the width of the film in millimeters. The width of the film affects image size and quality, as well as the cost of supplies and equipment.

There are two 8mm formats: *standard* 8mm and *Super*-8mm. Super-8mm cameras record images which are 50 percent larger than those of standard 8mm cameras. 8mm cameras are designed to record either standard 8mm or Super-8mm, not both. Standard 8mm is now virtually obsolete. All subsequent references in this book are to Super-8mm, which is sometimes used for home movies, as well as for some independently produced, low-budget films.

Film formats. From left: 70mm color positive print with six magnetic sound tracks, Standard 35mm positive optical sound track, Standard 35mm print with optical-magnetic sound (sprocket holes arranged with optical on left side, magnetic on right side), 35mm full coat magnetic stock, Regular 8mm guage, Super-8mm guage, 16mm single perf guage (color stock), 16mm double perf guage (black-and-white stock), 16mm optical sound track projection print, 16mm magnetic sound striped stock (color), Super-8mm optical sound print, Regular 8mm camera original Kd II with magnetic stripe, 16mm magnetic recording stock with ¼-inch magnetic recording tape for original sound, 16mm optical sound color print, 16mm optical sound black-and-white print, and 16mm camera original ECO #7252.

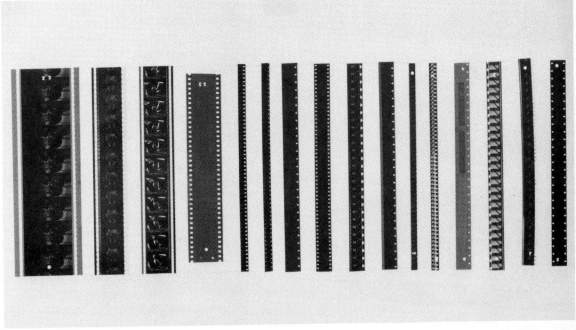

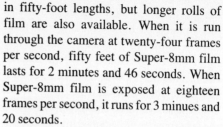

The 16mm format is widely used for professional recording of industrial, educational, governmental, and documentary films, as well as some commercials and low-budget feature films. Network-level commercials and television programs are recorded in 35mm, as are most feature films. Some feature films are recorded on 65mm film, which is then printed onto 70mm film, the added 5mm's being the width of the sound track area, for projection in large, specially outfitted theaters. Other 70mm film prints for projection are enlargements or **blowups** from original 35mm recordings.

Film stocks are available in different film lengths and loading arrangements or configurations. Super-8mm film usually comes in a lightproof cartridge and is exactly 8mm wide. It is normally packaged in fifty-foot lengths, but longer rolls of film are also available. When it is run through the camera at twenty-four frames per second, fifty feet of Super-8mm film lasts for 2 minutes and 46 seconds. When Super-8mm film is exposed at eighteen frames per second, it runs for 3 minues and 20 seconds.

Sixteen millimeter film is available on daylight spools, which contain 100, 200, or 360 feet of film. It is also available on plastic **cores**, which simply provide a firm center on which the film is wound and do not protect the edges of the film from light. Film which comes on a core must be loaded in complete darkness. The standard length of 16mm film cores is 400 or 1200 feet. A 100-foot daylight spool of 16mm film, when exposed at twenty-four frames per second, runs for 2 minutes and 46 seconds. Thirty-five millimeter film comes on cores in standard lengths of 100, 200, 400, and 1100 feet. Ninety feet of 35mm film runs for 1 minute at 24 frames per second. (See Figure 8.11.)

Film stocks differ in terms of their **perforation** or sprocket hole sizes and placements. Super-8mm film has sprocket holes on only one side of the film, while 16mm films are available with single-sided or double-sided perforations, which are called **single perf** and **double perf** film, respectively. Magnetically striped 16mm film has audiotrack in place of one row of sprocket holes. Thirty-five millimeter film is always double perf.

Film Aspect Ratios

Aspect ratio (Figure 8.12) refers to the relation of frame width to frame height. Super-8mm film and 16mm film are recorded at an aspect ratio of 4:3, which means that the frame is 4 units wide by 3 units high, the same as television. This

Sixteen millimeter film spools. From top: 100 foot spool, 200 foot spool, and 400 foot spool.

Figure 8.11
Typical Running Times of Films

Film Format	Super 8		16mm		35mm	
Projection Speed in Frames per Second	18	24	18	24	24	25
Inches per Second	3.0	4.0	5.4	7.2	18	18.6
Film Length and Screen Time	Minutes / Seconds	Minutes / Seconds	Minutes / Seconds	Minutes / Seconds	Minutes / Seconds	Minutes / Seconds
Feet 50	3 / 20	2 / 30	1 / 51	1 / 23	/ 33	/ 32
100	6 / 40	5 / 0	3 / 42	2 / 47	1 / 7	1 / 4
150	10 / 0	7 / 30	5 / 33	4 / 10	/	/
200	13 / 20	10 / 0	7 / 24	5 / 33	2 / 13	2 / 8
300	20 / 0	15 / 0	11 / 7	8 / 20	3 / 20	3 / 12
400	26 / 40	20 / 0	14 / 49	11 / 7	4 / 27	4 / 16
500	33 / 20	25 / 0	18 / 31	13 / 53	5 / 33	5 / 20
600	40 / 0	30 / 0	22 / 13	16 / 40	6 / 40	6 / 24
700	46 / 40	35 / 0	25 / 56	19 / 27	7 / 47	7 / 28
800	53 / 20	40 / 0	29 / 38	22 / 13	8 / 53	8 / 32
900	60 / 0	45 / 0	33 / 20	25 / 0	10 / 0	9 / 36
1000	66 / 40	50 / 0	37 / 2	27 / 47	11 / 7	10 / 40
1100	73 / 20	55 / 0	40 / 44	30 / 33	/	/
1200	80 / 0	60 / 0	44 / 27	33 / 20	/	/

ratio is more commonly expressed in film production as 1.33:1. The standard aspect ratio of 35mm used for recording television programs and commercials is also 1.33:1. Theatrically released 35mm feature films, however, use a slightly wider screen to stimulate the audience's peripheral vision: 1.85:1, which is known as **Academy aperture**. The aperture in the feature film camera and projector have been altered to make the image proportionately shorter and wider by simply not exposing or projecting the entire 35mm frame area. **Anamorphic** or optically "squeezed" wide-screen images, such as CinemaScope or Panavision, can be about 2.35:1. These processes require special lenses, called anamorphic lenses, to squeeze and unsqueeze the image during recording and projection. The aspect ratio of a film is

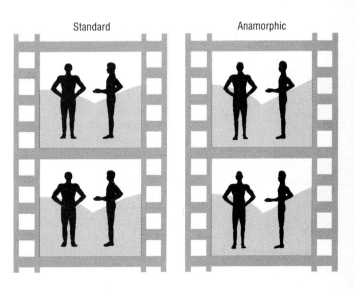

Figure 8.12
Film Aspect Ratios

Standard

Anamorphic

determined by the dimensions of the aperture, as well as any special lenses on the camera and projector. The significant effects of aspect ratio differences on film composition are discussed in chapters 5 and 7.

Summary

Understanding the technology that makes video and film recording possible helps us to obtain better quality images. Visual media are based on optical, electronic, and photochemical recording processes.

Visible light represents only a small portion of the entire electromagnetic energy spectrum, which ranges from radio waves to gamma rays. Colored light can be described in terms of hue, saturation, and brightness. Virtually all colors of the visible spectrum can be reproduced by mixing three colors of light. In the additive process used in television red, green, and blue light-emitting phosphors combine to reproduce many different colors. Film uses a subtractive mixing process, where cyan, magenta, and yellow filters embedded in different layers of the film subtract different color wavelengths from a white light source to produce a variety of colors on a screen.

A video camera records and transmits visual images electronically. Camera pickup tubes convert light energy into electrical energy. Color video cameras divide the light entering the camera lens into red, green, and blue components, which are converted to electrical impulses and sent to a television monitor or receiver, where the electrical impulses stimulate red, green, and blue light-emitting phosphors to reproduce the original colors before the camera.

Videotape contains iron oxide particles that can store electrical information. Helical scan and quadruplex are two different types of videotape recording, which differ primarily in terms of the way the images are recorded. There are many different helical scan formats as well, including 8mm, 1/2-inch VHS, Recam, Beta, Betacam, 3/4-inch U-matic, and 1-inch highband recording.

Film records visual images photochemically. Film contains silver halide crystals, which form a latent image when they are exposed to light. These latent images become visible through chemical processing. There are two basic film development processes, negative and reversal, which are analogous to color prints and slides in still photography.

Color film uses a subtractive process to reproduce the colors of objects in a recorded scene. Different layers of the film emulsion, which contain light-sensitive particles and color dyes, are responsive to red, green, or blue light. These layers form complementary-colored filters of cyan, magenta, and yellow, which subtract red, green, and blue light from a white light source in direct proportion to the intensity of the color light reflected by objects in the recorded scene. The white light source in this case is a light bulb in a projector.

Film generally has a wider contrast ratio than video. Some film stocks, such as Eastman Color Negative, can record and differentiate brightness levels that are 100 times as bright as the darkest object in a scene, yielding a contrast ratio of 100:1. The maximum contrast ratio in video is usually 20:1 or 30:1.

Videotape and film recording materials are available in a variety of formats. Quadruplex recorders generally use 2-inch-wide videotape, while helical scan recorders use 1-inch, 3/4-inch, 1/2-inch, or 1/4-inch (8mm) videotape. Super-8mm,

16mm, 35mm, and 65mm film require different cameras and recording equipment. Wider or large-format recording materials generally reproduce higher quality images than smaller formats. However, some smaller formats, such as Recam and Betacam, reproduce extremely high quality images.

Additional Readings

Happe, Bernard. *Basic Motion Picture Technology*. New York: Focal Press, 1974.

Lipton, Lenny. *Independent Filmmaking*. New York: Fireside/Simon & Schuster, 1972.

Mathias, Harry, and Richard Patterson. *Electronic Cinematography*. Belmont, CA: Wadsworth, 1985.

Millerson, Gerald. *The Technique of Television Production*. 10th ed. Woburn, MA: Focal Press, 1981.

Pincus, Edward, and Steven Ascher. *The Filmmaker's Handbook*. New York: Plume, 1984.

Wilson, Anton. *Cinema Workshop*. Hollywood: American Society of Cinematographers Holding Corporation, 1983.

Wurtzel, Alan. *Television Production*. 2nd ed. New York: McGraw-Hill, 1983.

Zettl, Herbert. *Television Production Handbook*. 4th ed. Belmont, CA: Wadsworth, 1984.

Exercises

1. Record the same scene on two or three different videotape or film formats, such as 8mm, 1/2-inch, and 3/4-inch videotape or 16mm and Super-8mm film. Compare these formats for quality in terms of image contrast and resolution. Is there a noticeable difference in the image quality of long shots between smaller and larger formats?

2. Record the same scene on videotape and film. Then transfer the film to a videotape that has the same format as the originally recorded videotape. Compare the two videotape images in terms of image contrast, hardness and softness, and resolution. Then record and view several network television commercials. Try to determine which ones were originally recorded on videotape and which ones were recorded on film and then transferred to videotape. Do some commercials use the apparent contrast and hardness or softness of videotape and film to good effect? When might you prefer to use videotape or film for original recording?

CHAPTER 9

Lighting

One of the most creative and visually exciting tasks in video and film production is lighting. Visual artists refer to lighting as "painting with light." A lighting director or director of photography can use lights just as effectively and expressively as any painter uses color pigments to evoke a specific mood or visual impression. Lighting can be used to emphasize and dramatize a subject by bringing objects into sharp relief or contrast, or it can be used to soften and to harmonize. Lighting directly affects the overall impressions and feelings generated by recorded visual images. It is a complex art, but basic video and film lighting can be reduced to a limited number of concepts and techniques. This chapter provides an introduction to the basic aesthetic approaches, techniques, and equipment needed to design and control the lighting of moving images.

BASIC LIGHTING AESTHETICS

Aesthetic Approaches

The expressive design and effect of a lighting setup can be described as functionalist, realist, or formativist. **Functionalist lighting** conforms to the specific needs of the program, the requirements of the set, and the movements of performers. The normal aesthetic effect is one of image clarity through balanced or even lighting. A primary function of lighting is simply to provide a sufficient **exposure** or **base light level** so that clear and coherent images can be recorded. **Realist lighting** appears to come from actual light sources in a setting or location. It enhances an illusion of reality. **Formativist lighting** tries to achieve a specific emotional effect or abstract design through nonnaturalistic patterns of light. The actual sources of light are often of little interest.

Functionalist lighting is designed to create even or balanced brightness, so that every space on the set is clearly and brightly lit. The lights are placed so that the talent and the set are not only clearly visible but attractively presented. Only in rare instances is the lighting intentionally uneven or unbalanced in terms of brightness, perhaps to direct the viewer's attention to a specific part of the framed image. Functionalist lighting is designed to facilitate movements of the talent and the camera(s) on the set. The talent must be able to move around freely without creating noticeable or objectionable shadows. The brightness of the lighting falling on them should remain unchanged as they move.

Functionalist lighting provides sufficient overall illumination to record clear images that are easily comprehended. Functionalist lighting for this interview consists of cross key and fill lights that separate foreground subjects from the background and brightly illuminates their faces.

Realist lighting preserves an illusion of reality and rarely calls attention to itself. A grip for this commercial holds up a diffusion screen to prevent the light falling on the pillar from becoming too bright and distracting attention away from the main character, the newsboy. Lighting is usually subservient to the character and the story in realist productions.

Realist lighting conforms to the audience's expectations of how a scene should normally or naturalistically appear in "real life." In conventional popular dramas the lighting is usually realistic. The major problem for the lighting director is to determine the actual light source in the scene. The brightest lights are positioned according to the direction and intensity of the central or main source of light. Directional lighting continuity is maintained from one shot to the next in the same scene. If the main source of light is a window, the direction of the lights basically preserves the spatial positioning of the window on the set. The same holds true for firelight or candlelight. The lighting director tries to match the natural scene under normal vision using artificial lights. Multiple shadows should be minimized, if not eliminated, so that the lighting rarely calls attention to itself. There is a logical consistency to the direction and intensity

of the lighting, which has a presumed cause or real source.

Few productions are completely realist. Some degree of formativist stylization is often needed to stimulate dramatic interest. Lighting directors use lighting to bring out and emphasize specific aspects of a personality or setting. They highlight details that add depth to performers and actions. Strict authenticity often fails to stimulate emotions and viewer interest, and a purely realist lighting setup often seems flat and boring.

Formativist lighting has no "real-life" referent. The lighting director is much freer to design a lighting setup according to purely abstract or subjective emotional criteria, that is, to stylize the use of light. The lighting director literally paints with light to create emphasis and spatial impressions. Formativist lighting stimulates emotions and creates a dynamic visual impression. For example, the lighting setup for a musical variety program may light an empty stage with pools of colored light, creating abstract patterns. The mood or atmosphere can coincide with the central theme or emotion expressed by a song or dance.

Even in a "realist" drama, a dream sequence might call for highly stylized lighting that mirrors the internal state of mind of the central character. These are often highly abstract and unrealistic visual sequences, but they effectively convey the character's feelings, emotions, and state of mind. Excessive or inappropriate stylization calls attention to the lighting and distracts viewer attention from the central message or information of a nonfiction program. It can also destroy the "illusion of reality" in a realistic drama, but the absence of any stylization at all leads to viewer disinterest.

Formativist lighting often draws attention to itself as a stylistic element. This scene from Paul Nickell's live television adaptation of George Orwell's *1984* projects an ominous figure of Big Brother looming over the actors' shoulders.

Three- and Four-Point Lighting

Three-point and four-point lighting are functionalist and realist techniques that help create an illusion of three-dimensionality and depth in two-dimensional media such as video and film. (See Figure 9.1.) Three-point and four-point lighting setups use three specific types of light, which have different directional placements, degrees of softness and hardness, and intensities. The three major light sources are called key light, fill light, and separation light. The **key light** is the brightest, hardest light. It provides modeling or texture. **Modeling** refers to the appearance of a textured surface that has shadows where there are indentations in the surface. A surface with good modeling looks three-dimensional. **Fill light** is soft-

ened, lower-intensity light which helps to fill in some of the shadows created by the key light and reduce the contrast between light and shadow areas. **Separation light** comes from behind the subject. It creates a halo effect which outlines the subject and helps to separate it from the background.

Key Light   The key lights are the brightest and in some ways the most important lights on the set. The key light determines the overall recording or exposure level. The placement of a key light suggests the direction of the primary source of light within a scene, such as a window, an overhead light, the sun or moon, or even a candle or fireplace. When the key light strikes a subject directly from the front or camera side of the subject, few shadows or variations in surface texture are created

Figure 9.1
Three- and Four-
Point Lighting Setups

A. Three-Point Lighting Setup

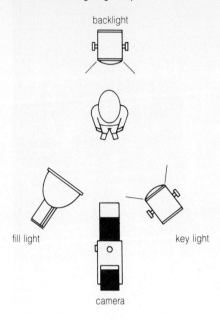

B. Four-Point Lighting Setup

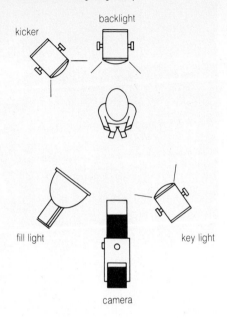

and the result is a flat, uninteresting image. For optimal modeling and aesthetic effect, the key light should be thirty to forty degrees away from the camera-subject axis, and it should light the short or narrow side of a face, that is, the side of the face that is least exposed to the camera. Moving the key light up and down and from side to side affects the direction and length of facial shadows and increases or decreases facial modeling.

Key light usually has a hard quality. The beam of light is narrowly focused and rarely if ever diffused or softened, except perhaps in a situation where softness is needed to create a romantic or light mood. The height of the key light affects the length of shadows falling on the set. Key lights should be placed high enough that long shadows do not spill onto the background from foreground subjects. The key

light is usually placed much higher than the camera, unless a special effect is desired, such as the presentation of a flat, untextured image (in which case the key light is at camera height) or a mysterious and horrifying face (in which case the key light is placed lower than camera height).

In multiple-subject setups, the same light that functions as a key light for one subject can also function as the separation or back light for another (Figure 9.2). The term key light simply refers to the brightest light source striking a subject from the camera's viewpoint. The specific instrument designated as the key light can change as the camera or subject moves.

Fill Light   Fill light is used to provide general illumination on the set and to fill in the shadows created by the key lights. Fill light is usually softer than key light. It

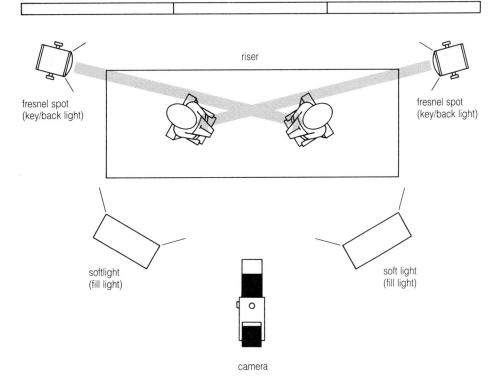

Figure 9.2
Key Light Diagram

is frequently diffused by reflectors or translucent materials placed in front of the lighting instrument.

The fill light is often placed at approximately camera height or just slightly above so that shadows created by overhead key lights can be properly filled in. It is usually on the opposite side of the camera from the key light. The intensities and physical placement of the key and fill lights will determine to a significant extent the emotional mood and lighting atmosphere within the scene.

Separation Light One or two **separation lights** complete the three-point lighting triangle or four-point rectangle. A **back light** is usually placed above and

behind the subject to create a halo effect that outlines the subject, separating it from the background. The back light completes the three-point lighting setup, but it is not the only light that can be used to separate the subject from the background. In a four-point lighting setup another separation light, called a **kicker**, may be placed exactly opposite the key light on the set. A kicker functions similarly to a back light, but it is directed from the back and the side of the subject (usually opposite or facing the key light) rather than from directly behind and above the subject's back and head.

Separation of subject and background through back lights and kickers is extremely important in black-and-white re-

Backlighting isolates the foreground subject, separating her from the background in this frame from Rainer Werner Fassbinder's film *Effie Briest* (1974).

cording. The height of the back light or kicker and its intensity in comparison to the key light affect the amount of separation that takes place. The use of different colors for the subject and background can effect much the same separation in color production, but separation lights have not been entirely abandoned in color production because they add so much texture, dimension, and depth to the visual image.

In an optimal three-point lighting setup, the key, fill, and back lights form the points of a triangle or a "Y." When a kicker and a backlight are used together, the four lighting points form a rectangle or an "X." Such "ideal" placements are rarely, if ever, consistently maintained. Only static artificial, intensely boring still scenes with subjects and cameras that never move would allow for a permanent, perfectly triangular three-point or rectangular four-point lighting setup. A more typical situation is characterized by constant movement of the subject(s) and cameras, and a complex, constantly varying relationship between keys, fills, and backlights or kickers. The three-point and four-point lighting procedures outlined above

simply provide a starting point and an idealized model that is necessarily and continually manipulated in complex recording situations.

Background Light

Background light illuminates the background or set. It affects every lighting setup and is extremely important in the overall aesthetic appearance of a scene. While fill lights and key lights frequently spill over onto the background and partially illuminate it, it is important to light the background separately so that its appearance can be more carefully controlled. The amount of light cast on the background obviously affects subject/background separation. It can also affect visual emphasis within a scene. If the background is brighter than the subject, the viewer's attention will be distracted from the primary focus of interest. If the background is too dark, the set may look unnatural or the scene too contrasty. To add interest and texture to an otherwise flat, monochromatic background, patterns can be cast on the background to break it up and give it some modeling and texture. While too much patterning can be distracting, a flat, monochrome, evenly lit background looks dull and unimaginative.

Controlling Shadows

Background light should not be used to try to burn out shadows from foreground performers that fall on the background. The most effective means of eliminating bad shadows is proper placement of the key lights. Key lights should be placed high enough above the performers that prominent shadows are not cast on background walls as they move around the set. Performers should also be kept at a safe distance from the back wall whenever possible.

Another complicating factor in three- and four-point television and film lighting is the creation of objectional shadows by microphone booms. Since the key light creates the most noticeable shadows, microphone-boom placement and movement must be arranged to minimize interference with the key lights. Sometimes this can be accomplished by adjusting the barn doors of the key lights so that light does not spill into the microphone-boom area. In other cases the key lights may have to be placed higher overhead than normal, so that boom shadows fall on the floor, rather than on more noticeable parts of the set. A microphone-boom shadow can often be hidden in a part of the set that is already riddled with a shadow pattern. Obviously, the planning of the lighting setup must include consideration of the placement and movement of the microphone boom, before the key and fill lights are firmly positioned.

Lighting Moving Subjects   The discussion of lighting to this point has assumed that the subject to be recorded is relatively stationary. A moving subject significantly complicates a lighting setup. The major problem inherent in lighting a moving subject is how to maintain relatively consistent light levels as the subject moves about the set.

A moving subject in the studio must be lit by multiple key lights (Figure 9.3). If a subject were to walk too close or too far away from a single key light, he or she would become too light or too dark, and functionalist or realist continuity in lighting would be lost.

Multiple key lights are hung at constant distances from the moving subject so that the subject can move from one key light to another without a noticeable change in lighting. Problems arise when key light beams overlap or when there are gaps of darkness between key lights. To prevent these problems, the barn doors or shutters on the key lights are adjusted so that key light beams are exactly adjacent to each

Top: This illustrates the combined effect of cross-key lights and fill lights. Center: Here, the fill lights illuminate the broad side of the faces and the rest of the bodies to reduce contrast within the scene and to fill in shadow areas. Bottom: The cross-key lights provide good facial definition and modeling by illuminating the short sides of the subjects' faces with strong key light, while also backlighting their shoulders and the backs of their heads. Cross-key lighting provides an effective way to light a two person interview with only four lights: two key and fill lights.

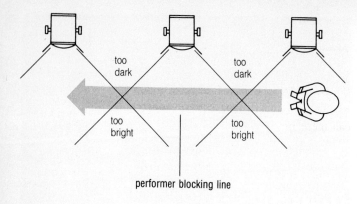

too dark

too dark

too bright

too bright

performer blocking line

Figure 9.3
Multiple Key Lighting

other along the performer blocking line (where a subject will move on the set). As long as the talent follows this prearranged line of action and hits his or her marks, no gaps or overlaps of lighting will occur.

Low-Key Versus High-Key Lighting

The terms low-key and high-key lighting originated in the studio eras of feature film production in Hollywood. They seem counterintuitive, that is, the terms mean the opposite of what we think they should mean. **Low-key lighting** refers to the minimal use of fill light, that is, to a relatively high key-to-fill ratio. This kind of lighting creates pools of light and rather harsh shadows. Many Warner Bros. gangster films and detective films produced in the 1930s and 1940s used low-key lighting for aesthetic effect. It has sometimes been suggested that Warner Bros. used this form of lighting simply to hide the frayed edges of its sets. However, a whole genre of Hollywood films, called *film noir* (literally French for "black film"), relied on low-key lighting in the 1940s. European emigré technicians from the German cinema in particular influenced Hollywood practice with respect to low-key lighting in the 1930s and 1940s. Low-key lighting evokes a rather heavy

and serious mood or feeling that enhances the emotional atmosphere of certain types of films.

Low-key lighting is similar to an effect in painting known as *chiaroscuro*. This technique is evident in the paintings of Rembrandt, for example, where shafts of light illuminate central figures in the painting, while the remaining parts of the scene are dimly lit and heavily shadowed. Low-key lighting can have a similar effect in video and film, although contrast ratio differences between video and film (see chapter 8) call for different lighting techniques to create the same effect in the two media.

High-key lighting presents a brightly lit scene with few shadow areas. It has been suggested that during the 1930s and 1940s MGM (Metro Goldwyn Mayer) studios used high-key lighting for its lavish musicals so that no detail in its elaborate and expensive sets would be hidden in shadows. MGM was also influenced by Broadway theatrical practice, glamour/fashion still photography, and studio head Louis B. Mayer's emphasis on sunshine and wholesomeness. In any case the use of high-key lighting in musical comedies is another example of form following function. The light, happy atmosphere stimulated by high-key lighting contrasts with the somber, mysterious, or threatening atmosphere of low-key lighting. Thus, an important consideration in selecting either high- or low-key lighting styles is attempting to match the form of the lighting to the specific function it is intended to serve.

Lighting Plots

A specific lighting setup can be outlined or diagrammed on a gridded piece of paper that represents an overhead scale diagram of the studio. This outline is called a **lighting plot**. The overhead lighting grid to which specific instruments can be attached is drawn onto the studio diagram. The basic elements of the set are added to this overhead view. The placements and movements of the talent and camera(s) can be added to the diagram after preliminary performer and camera blocking, so that the lights can be positioned accordingly. Several key lights may have to be arranged so that they maintain an even or balanced brightness on the moving performer throughout the set. Only when the exact blocking line of the talent is known can these lights be properly placed. The

A completed lighting plot diagram. Notice the legend which explains the various lights that were used.

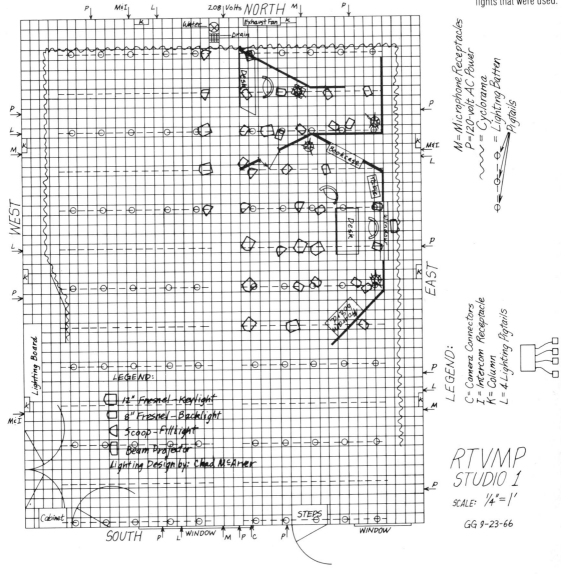

M = Microphone Receptacles
P = 120-volt AC Power
~~~ = Cyclorama
= Lighting Batten
= Pigtails

LEGEND:
C = Camera Connectors
I = Intercom Receptacle
K = Column
L = 4 Lighting Pigtails

RTVMP
STUDIO 1
SCALE: 1/4" = 1'
GG 9-23-66

LEGEND:
12" Fresnel - Keylight
8" Fresnel - Backlight
Scoop - Filllight
Beam Projector
Lighting Design by: Chad McArter

distance of the key lights from the talent can be determined by relying on the **inverse square law** (light intensity changes according to the square of the distance of the light source from the object) and the scale dimensions of the gridded paper. One-quarter inch on paper may equal one foot of actual studio floor space, for example.

Composing a lighting plot allows the lighting director to consider all relevant factors that can affect the selection and placement of lighting instruments prior to actual production. He or she must consider placement and movement of the talent, cameras, and microphone booms, as well as the electrical and spatial capabilities and limitations of the studio or location environment. The lighting plot must also incorporate many aesthetic or stylistic variables. It can be low key or high key; functionalist, realist, or formativist. The lighting director must develop a lighting setup that is both aesthetically satisfying and practical from an engineering standpoint.

Single-Camera Versus Multiple-Camera Situations

In single-camera recording situations the lighting is sometimes changed for each shot or each major change in camera position. Of course, changing the lighting slightly for each separate shot can be extremely laborious and time-consuming. Subtle changes in lighting are made in realist productions, not drastic changes that call attention to the lighting. Lighting continuity from shot to shot and scene to scene will break down with too much shifting of lighting instruments. Feature films and network television commercials, which have big budgets, long shooting schedules, and large production crews,

can better afford the luxury of lighting each separate shot perfectly than can lower-level productions. The aesthetic expectations of audiences and the demands of clients make lighting a high priority in some single-camera productions. Still, the lighting for any single-camera production can benefit from the added time and care this production method affords.

Since recording is continuous in multiple-camera production, the lights cannot be reset for different shots. Lighting decisions and compromises must be fully worked out prior to actual recording. The same lighting setup is used for long shots, medium shots, and close-ups. The lighting director must be able to anticipate every camera angle and placement that will be needed before arranging and setting up the lights on the set.

LIGHT SOURCES

There are a variety of light sources which can be used for television and film recording. Each of these can be distinguished in terms of the color temperature of the light it emits. **Color temperature** is usually defined in technical terms of degrees Kelvin. **Degrees Kelvin** is a unit of measurement that refers to the type of light that would theoretically be given off by a perfect light radiator (what physicists call a **black-box radiator**) when it is heated to a specific temperature. White light, as noted in chapter 8, is actually composed of relatively equal amounts of all the colors in the visible spectrum, but light sources with different color temperatures emit slightly different amounts of the various color wavelengths (red, green, blue light) which together make up white light and the visible spectrum.

Sunlight has a relatively high color temperature, about 5400 or 5600 degrees Kelvin, while tungsten or incandescent light, such as that given off by many living room lamps and much professional lighting equipment has a much lower color temperature, about 3200 degrees Kelvin. Sunlight has somewhat more blue light (short wavelengths) than does tungsten light, which has slightly more red light (long wavelengths.) As a result, a film stock or television camera designed or preset for tungsten light will record bluish images when it is exposed under sunlight, and a film stock or television camera rated or adjusted for daylight (sunlight) will record reddish images under tungsten light. Because television and film recording devices are often more sensitive to these differences in color temperature than our eyes, specific light sources must be carefully selected and controlled.

Sunlight

Sunlight is a natural light source. Burning gases on the sun's surface emit light which has a relatively high color temperature when it reaches the earth's surface, 5400°K. Sunlight contains approximately equal proportions of all color wavelengths in the visible spectrum. Unless it is broken up and diffused by clouds, direct sunlight produces intense, harsh, contrasty light. This kind of light quality is called **hard**, as opposed to **soft**, **light**. It creates harsh shadows. Diffusion screens and reflectors can be used on location to reduce the intensity and contrast of direct sunlight and create soft light. Indirect sunlight, often called **skylight**, has a higher color temperature than direct sunlight: from 6000°K to 20,000°K. Indirectly lit shadow areas also contain a higher proportion of ultraviolet light than

areas lit by direct sunlight. To reduce the bluish cast that is often produced by this ultraviolet light, an ultraviolet (UV) or skylight filter can be placed over the camera lens.

Tungsten Light

One of the earliest sources of electrical lighting was Thomas Edison's incandescent bulb. An **incandescent bulb** consists of a **tungsten filament** in a glass-enclosed vacuum. A strong electrical current encounters considerable resistance at the filament, generating both heat and light. In general, a tungsten light source produces somewhat more light of longer wavelengths, such as red and orange, than of shorter wavelengths, such as blue and violet. Tungsten light has a color temperature of 3200°K. Tungsten-halogen-quartz bulbs (usually called **quartz lights**) have become an important source of 3200°K indoor lighting. Caution needs to be exercised in the handling of quartz bulbs, however. They should never be touched, since the oil in your skin breaks down the quartz-like glass and reduces the life of a bulb. Quartz lights are usually rated in terms of the watts of electrical energy they consume: the most common sizes are 650 and 1000 watts.

Carbon Arc Light

Carbon arc lights produce intense light, which has very high color temperature. Light is produced by passing a spark between two carbon poles. Carbon arcs generally require vast amounts of DC electrical current and produce intense heat and noxious vapors and exhaust, which must be ventilated. The high intensity and high color temperature of arc lights make them useful for location production in combination with sunlight. However, they are extremely bulky and require special electrical generators on location.

HMI Light

A relatively recent development in location lighting is the **HMI lamp**. HMI lamps give almost four times the amount of light for the same electrical input as tungsten-quartz-halogen lamps. This light source produces high intensity, high color-temperature light (similar to daylight) with great efficiency. It generates little heat and operates on standard 120-volt, 60Hz AC current (although a few use 220 volt current). HMI lights are frequently used to raise the lighting level at outdoor locations, which may be partially lit by indirect sunlight. HMI lights are fully glass enclosed arc lamps which require separate start and ballast mechanisms to control electrical current. One potential problem with HMI lamps is that they can cause strobing or flickering when a film camera is run at speeds other than twenty-four frames per second (standard sound speed). A video camera operating on NTSC (American) standards, like a film camera running at twenty-four fps, records no flickering effect. HMI lights can also be filtered so that they duplicate 3200°K tungsten light sources.

Fluorescent Light

Unlike all the other types of light sources discussed thus far, **fluorescent light** is discontinuous throughout the visible spectrum. Certain bands of colored light, such as bands of red, yellow, green, or blue light, are strong while others are almost nonexistent in a fluorescent light source. Light is produced through phosphores-cence rather than incandescence, and different phosphors produce different wavelengths of light. In film recording, color filters placed over the light source or camera lens can compensate for some of this spectral discontinuity, but there are so many differences between most fluorescent bulb types and brands that no simple filter or combination of filters wil properly remedy every situation. Video recording devices can be at least partially adjusted for fluorescent light sources by white balancing the camera under fluorescent lighting. Some professional fluorescent lighting instruments have been developed which produce highly intense but diffuse light of 3200°K color temperature using minimal electricity. While these instruments are expensive, they are also highly efficient sources of fill light.

Conventional fluorescent lighting often produces humming and flickering. The alternating current mechanisms used to create fluorescent light can cause flicker in a recorded image and produce an audio hum, which is easily picked up by even distant microphones and affects the recorded sound track. Because of these negative audio and visual effects, it is often advisable to shut off conventional fluorescent lights if possible, and use tungsten or HMI lighting instead. In some situations, such as certain industrial locations, it is virtually impossible to replace all the preexisting fluorescent lights with other artificial lighting. In this case, one type of light source is selected as primary and all other light sources are reduced as much as possible in intensity. Light sources having different color temperatures should not be used simultaneously unless filters can be placed in front of light sources, including windows, to change and equalize different color temperatures.

LIGHTING EQUIPMENT

Lighting Instruments

The housing within which a light source or lamp is encased is called a **lighting instrument** or **luminaire**. Lighting instruments can be generally classified according to the directness or indirectness and hardness or softness of the light they emit. Sharply focused and concentrated light produces harsh shadows and high contrast. Diffused or softened light minimizes shadows and reduces contrast. Lighting instruments with lenses that sharply focus light are referred to as **spotlights**. Lighting instruments without lenses that have reflectors that spread and soften light are called **floodlights**.

Spotlights   Fresnel and ellipsoidal lighting instruments are two different types of spotlights. **Fresnel** refers to a specific type of lens, which bends the light so that it travels in a relatively narrow path. The term **ellipsoidal** refers to the shape of a mirror or reflector at the back of the instrument that concentrates the light rays focused by a lens. Both types of spotlights concentrate the light emitted by a lamp or bulb into a narrow, intense band of light.

Floodlights   The most commonly used types of floodlights are scoops, broads, soft lights, and strip lights. These open lights lack lenses and mirrors that focus light into a narrow beam. Instead, they diffuse or spread light, decreasing both its intensity and its harshness. Scoops, broads, and soft lights usually consist of one, two, or three lamps, and have somewhat larger, and more diffuse reflectors

Top: Fresnel lights. Bottom: A Colortran light.

than spotlights. Strip lights have several bulbs, each with its own built-in reflector, placed in close proximity to one another so that they diffuse and soften the light in combination. Floodlights are frequently

Left: A "broad" light. Center: A "scoop" light. Right: A Lowel softlight 2.

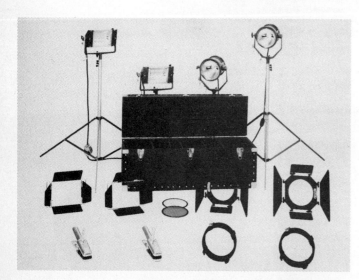

Top: A portable lighting kit. Note the alligator clips, barn doors, and screens. Right: A Lowel light.

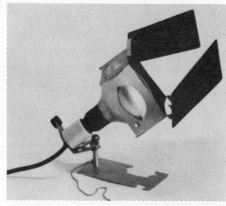

used to light wide areas. They are also used to fill in the shadows created by spotlights and thereby reduce contrast within a scene.

Portable Lights   There are a wide variety of lighting kits available for use on location. **Portable lighting kits** usually have open, nonlensed, lighting instruments and quartz lamps rated from 650 to 2000 watts. These instruments lack some of the controls of studio spotlights. Lighting kits contain several open reflector quartz lights and collapsible light mounting equipment, power cords, and other lighting accessories. **Photofloods**, such as lowel-light units, are highly portable lamps with self-contained reflectors inside the bulb.

Some lightweight lighting instruments have their own portable power supply or rechargeable battery pack. Battery-powered lights, such as the Sylvania Sun Gun, can be used in moving vehicles or on remote locations, where a standard power supply is not available. The batteries should be fully charged, since the color temperature gradually decreases as the battery weakens and the voltage drops.

Left: A Cine portable battery-powered lighting kit. Top right: A pipe grid used to hang lights. Bottom right: A C-clamp used to hang lights. The clamp provides some flexibility in positioning each lamp.

Mounting Devices

Studio lighting is done with overhead lighting instruments, which are attached to a grid. This makes it easier for cameras and performers to move about the studio floor without running into lights. The **pipe grid**, which consists of a series of pipes suspended in parallel rows above the studio floor to which instruments are attached with **C-clamps**, is probably the most common type of grid. Safety chains or heavy gauge wire loops ensure that no accident will occur if the C-clamp slips on the pipe. Another type of grid has a sliding **track** to which instruments can be attached and along which they can be moved.

A **collapsible floor stand** is one of the most frequently used light mounting devices on location. The seven- or eight-foot stand telescopes for portability. Sandbags can be placed over the three legs of the stand for added stability. Lights can also be mounted on special clips and clamps, such as a spring-tension **alligator clip**, or simply taped to a wall with a strong adhesive **gaffer's tape**. The latter must be used with care as it sometimes damages paint or wallpaper on removal.

A view of an overhead light track. Notice the mixture of the various types of lights shown throughout this chapter.

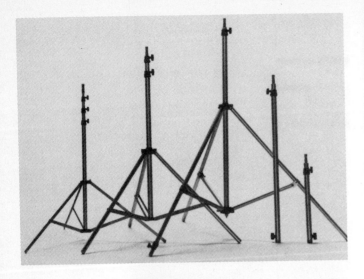

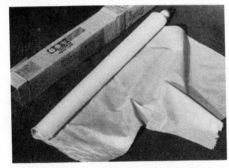

Top left: Lowel light stands. Center: Spun glass diffusion material. Bottom: A gel holder for a scoop light.

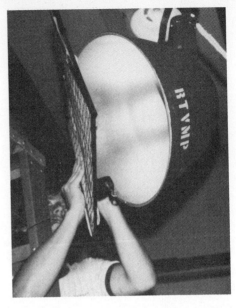

A diffusion screen is added to a scoop light.

Shaping Devices

Light can be shaped, manipulated, and controlled by a variety of devices such as barn doors, scrims, diffusers, flags, gels, cookies, and reflectors. These are often attached to a lighting instrument. **Barn doors** are black metal flaps, which can be attached to the top, bottom, and sides of a lighting instrument. When properly positioned, they prevent light from spilling into areas of the set where it is not wanted. **Screens** are pieces of wire mesh that can be placed over the front of a lighting instrument to cut down the amount of light transmitted. **Scrims** and **diffusers** are pieces of translucent material, such as spun glass, that break up direct light and spread it out in all directions. **Flags** are opaque pieces of metal, plastic, or cardboard that prevent light from spilling into an undesired area. **Gels** are flexible sheets of transparent colored plastic, which can act as color filters when they are placed in front of light sources, such as windows or lamps. A gel can be used to convert 5400°K light coming through a window to 3200°K light, which is the same color temperature as interior room lighting. A **cookie** or **cucaloris** is a piece of opaque material with holes in it, which patterns the light into shadowed and brightly lit areas. **Reflectors** provide indirect, reflected light, which is usually less harsh than the primary direct light. Sunlight, for example, can be reflected to function as fill light outdoors, while direct, unreflected sunlight functions as a key light.

Control Devices

Lighting Control in the Studio   Electrical lighting in a studio can be controlled by means of patch panels and dimmer boards. A **patch panel** or electrical distribution center consists of a series of plugs for specific electrical circuits to which

Top: A ''cookie pattern'' on the backdrop of a set. Bottom: Various types of Lowel reflectors.

Left: A lighting board patch panel. Bottom: A close-up of the many patch wires.

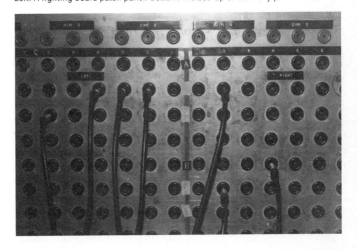

A studio lighting board.

tached to each circuit without blowing a fuse or tripping a circuit breaker. For example, six 1000-watt, 120-volt lamps can be safely plugged into a 50-amp circuit, since each lamp will draw slightly more than 8 amps (watts/volts = amps; 1000/120 = 8.3 amps per lamp 6 × 8.33 = 49 total amps).

The dimmer board is a useful means of reducing or adjusting light intensity for black-and-white production, but it is not very useful in this respect for color recording. A dimmer board reduces the light intensity by dropping the voltage, and dropping the voltage below 120 volts causes a consequent drop in color temperature, which is not acceptable in color production. In color production, lighting intensity is reduced by moving a lighting instrument or using a screen.

Lighting Control on Location   Securing adequate electrical current for lighting on location presents more problems and hazards than does studio production. The most pressing problem is how and where

lighting instruments can be connected. The voltage carried by each circuit can be controlled by a **dimmer board**. Each circuit has a limited electrical capacity, varying from about twenty to over fifty amperes. Using the formula **watts = amps × volts**, you can determine the maximum number of lamps that can be safely at-

Bottom left: A lighting dimmer board in operation. Bottom right: A computerized dimmer board.

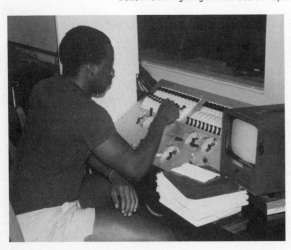

to secure adequate power. If sufficient electricity is not available, portable gasoline generators are sometimes brought in.

When using a private home or office, a lighting director and electrician may decide to tap the main power supply or use the existing circuits. If the former course is taken, a qualified electrician must perform the operation of tapping into the 100 amp (or more) main supply, which can then be channeled to a portable circuit board for distribution to individual instruments. If you decide to use existing circuits in the home or office, you can determine which outlets are on the same circuits and how many amps each circuit can carry by simply checking and closing a circuit at the main circuit box or fuse box and then testing outlets in the rooms where filming is to take place. Load demands should never exceed those specified at the circuit or fuse box, because excess power traveling along a line can melt the wires and start a fire. Any situation in which an extensive amount of lighting and electrical energy is required demands the expertise of a qualified electrician.

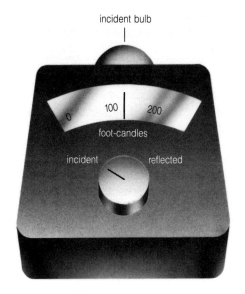

Figure 9.4
Basic Light Meter

LIGHT MEASUREMENT

The basic unit of light intensity measure is the **footcandle**. One footcandle is an agreed upon standard which represents the approximate light intensity produced by a candle one foot away. The normal measurement range of a light meter is from 1 to about 250 footcandles. A **light meter** (Figure 9.4) is extremely useful in both video and film production for determining lighting levels and contrast within a scene as well as for properly positioning and setting individual lights. In film recording a light meter must be adjusted to the proper

Front and back views of
a Spectra light meter.

sensitivity scale or EI number (DIN in Europe) so that it provides the correct f-stop readings for the specific sensitivity of the film stock.

Types of Light-Meter Readings

There are four basic types of meter readings: incident, reflected, spot, and TTL (through the lens). Some light meters are capable of producing only one type of reading. Others can be used for several different types of readings. Each reading has a specific purpose in terms of lighting control.

On some light meters a white hemisphere or flat circle is placed over the photoelectric cell so that the meter can measure the intensity of the light *falling on* the subject. This white surface gathers and diffuses light falling on the meter from several directions. For a reading of direct light falling on the subject, the meter is pointed at the camera from the position of the subject. (See Figure 9.5.) A reading of incident or direct light is called an **incident reading**. Because such a reading measures the light falling on the subject, it is not affected by the reflectance of the objects to be recorded.

A measurement of indirect light, that is, light *reflected by* the subject is called a **reflected reading**. (See Figure 9.5.) The white covering is removed from the photocell for a reflected reading. A reflected reading of the subject or whole scene averages the amount of light reflected by objects in the scene to determine the best overall exposure or base light level. A **spot reading** is a *reflected* light reading done with a light meter that isolates a small area within the frame and then averages the intensity of the light reflected within that area. Spot meter readings are often used to take light readings of objects that are too far away to make an incident reading practical. A **TTL** or **through the lens reading** provides a reflected reading of the exact image framed within the camera and can be used to adjust the lens automatically. Some TTL systems do not respond instantaneously to light changes, and the proper exposure lags slightly behind actual changes in light intensity.

Figure 9.5
Incident and Reflected Light Readings

A. Incident Light Reading

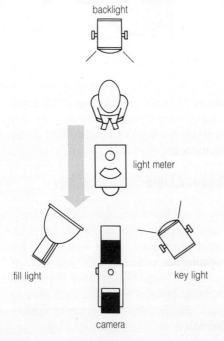

B. Reflected Light Reading

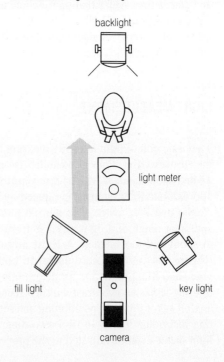

Determining Contrast Ratios

A light meter can be used in both video and film production to determine contrast within a scene. Apparent contrast within the image can affect image clarity as well as the overall emotional mood. There are three important **contrast ratios** in a three-point lighting setup: key-to-fill light ratio, key-to-back light ratio, and reflectance contrast ratio. The mathematical relationship between light intensity in footcandles or between f-stops on a light meter can be used to determine these specific contrast ratios. (Footcandles can be directly compared, whereas each higher f-stop number indicates a doubling and each lower f-stop a halving of the light intensity.) (See p. 164 in chapter 7 concerning lens f-stops.)

Key-to-Fill Ratio **Key-to-fill ratio** (as shown in Figure 9.6) indicates the proportion of key light to fill light in any lighting setup. This is sometimes called **lighting contrast ratio**, but should not be confused with the inherent contrast ratio of a video camera or film stock, discussed in chapter 8. Lighting contrast is caused exclusively by lights. It is actually a comparison of key plus fill light to fill light alone. Some fill light always spills over into the key light area and increases its intensity. An incident reading is taken of the key and fill lights together. Then the key light is shut off and a fill light reading is taken. A comparison of the two readings in terms of footcandles or recommended f-stop readings indicates the key-to-fill light ratio. A key plus fill light reading of 250 foot candles compared to a fill light reading of 125 foot candles equals a 2:1 lighting contrast ratio. One f-stop difference between the two indicates a 2:1 ratio, two f-stops a 4:1 ratio, and three f-stops an 8:1

back light
200 foot-candles

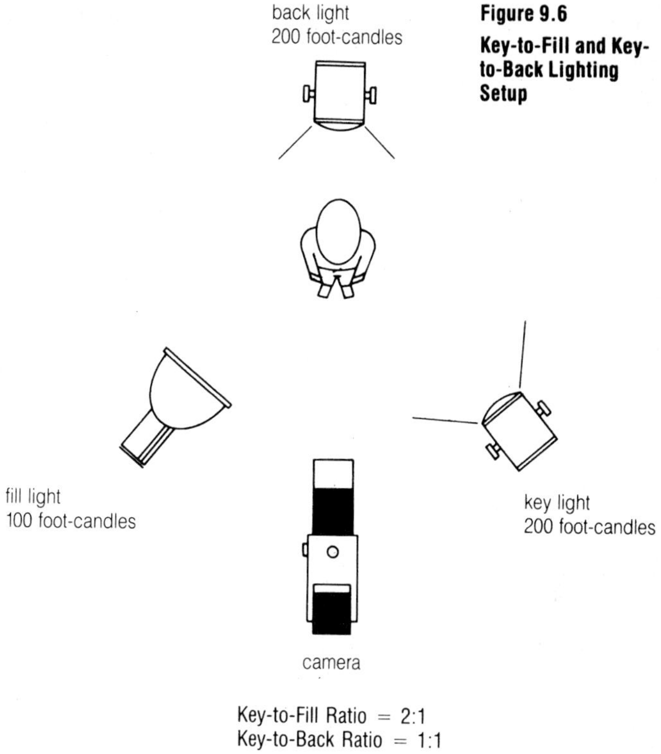

Figure 9.6

Key-to-Fill and Key-to-Back Lighting Setup

fill light
100 foot-candles

key light
200 foot-candles

camera

Key-to-Fill Ratio = 2:1
Key-to-Back Ratio = 1:1

ratio, and so on. In most situations, video and film recording is done under a key-to-fill light ratio of 4:1 or less, unless a highly dramatic effect with high contrast is desired. Since video has less tolerance for contrast than film, it generally is advisable to use a 2:1 or lower key-to-fill light ratio in video recordings or film recordings that will be transferred to video.

The key-to-fill ratio determines whether a high-key or low-key aesthetic of lighting is in effect. Low-key lighting has a high key-to-fill ratio while high-key lighting has a low key-to-fill light ratio.

Key-to-Back Ratio The relative proportion of key light to back light is called the **key-to-back ratio**. (See Figure 9.6.)

A key-to-fill ratio is calculated by comparing an incident light meter reading of the key plus fill light falling on the subject to that of the fill light alone. A key-to-back ratio is calculated by comparing an incident light meter reading of the key light falling on the subject to that of the back light. The key and back lights have equal intensities of 200 foot candles, yielding a ratio of 1:1, while the key plus fill light is twice as intense (200 foot candles as the fill light alone, yielding a ratio of 2:1).

In most instances back lights and key lights should have approximately the same intensity. This ratio is usually kept at about 1:1 or 1:1.5. A weak back light does little to separate the subject from the background or create a halo effect. An extremely strong back light, on the other hand, can cause an excessively bright halo to form around the subject's head and back.

Reflectance Contrast Ratio

Reflectance contrast ratios can be determined by taking reflected light meter readings of the brightest and darkest reflecting objects in the scene. A spot meter is a great help in isolating a specific object, although moving a standard reflected-light meter closer to an object without interrupting the light falling on it accomplishes the same goal. Again a comparison of light meter footcandle or f-stop readings indicates the contrast ratio between the brightest and darkest reflecting areas in the scene. Video cameras cannot record a reflectance contrast ratio greater than 20:1 or at most 30:1 (four or five f-stops). Some standard film stocks, such as color negative, can often record reflectance contrast ranges as high as 100:1 (six or seven f-stops).

Adjusting Contrast

There are several ways of altering a scene's contrast to make it more acceptable for visual recording. Specific lights that are too strong or too weak can be moved farther from or closer to the subject. Scrims and diffusion materials can be used to cut down on the light intensity. Additional instruments can be focused on the subject, although care must be taken to keep these multiple keys and fills close together so that objectionable multiple shadows are not created. Altering the lighting contrast ratio can affect the reflectance contrast ratio since the two are interdependent: objects reflect key and fill light. In some cases, a change in the color or brightness of props, sets, or costumes may be required to increase or decrease light reflectance.

Summary

Aesthetic lighting setups can be divided into three categories: functionalist, realist, and formativist lighting. Functionalist lighting aims at an equal lighting distribution within the scene so that all actions and subjects are clearly visible and pleasingly presented. Realist lighting attempts to re-create the presumed natural sources of lighting within a specific location. Key lights are used to maintain the consistent directional placement of the presumed central light source in a room, while fill lights reduce contrast to a "normal" or acceptable level. Lighting can also be used in a formativist or stylized manner to achieve a particular atmospheric effect, psychological mood, or abstract design.

Three-point and four-point lighting consist of a triangular or rectangular arrangement of three types of light: key light, fill light, and separation light. The key light is the brightest, most direct light source on the set. It is usually produced by a spotlight. Fill light fills in the shadows created by the key light, reducing the contrast and providing general illumination. Back lights and kickers create a halo that outlines the subject and helps to separate it from the background. A background light is often used to illuminate the set separately.

Basic three- or four-point lighting in television and film production is complicated by movement of subjects and cameras, which give a dynamic, constantly changing character to a lighting situation. Multiple key lights can be used to maintain consistent light levels as a subject moves through a scene. A lighting set up should be carefully planned to avoid problems on the set, such as blocking difficulties, unbalanced light intensities, and microphone-boom shadows. A lighting plot, which presents an overhead view of the studio floor or actual location drawn to scale, can help a lighting director to organize and plan a lighting set up. Lighting instruments can be positioned and repositioned on paper, so that logistical problems are solved and aesthetic decisions are made prior to actual production.

Low-key lighting refers to a relatively high key-to-fill light ratio that creates pools of bright light surrounded by dark shadow areas. It is frequently used to effect an atmosphere suitable for horror and gangster films and television programs, although it might be an effective dramatic device in many productions. High-key lighting, which has a low key-to-fill light ratio, presents few shadows and is frequently used in comedies and musicals.

Light sources, such as the sun and incandescent, carbon arc, HMI, and fluorescent lamps, emit light of a specific color temperature. Color temperature ratings in degrees Kelvin indicate the proportion of short wavelength (blue violet) and long wavelength (red) light and so on, emitted by a specific "white" light source. Daylight, carbon arc, and HMI light have higher color temperatures and a greater proportion of blue in comparison to red light than incandescent or tungsten light. Fluorescent light is discontinuous throughout the visible spectrum. Color film stocks must be selected and video cameras balanced for the color temperature of the primary light source, if a "normal" color rendition is to be recorded.

Spotlights and floodlights are two different types of lighting instruments. Spotlights produce bright, narrow beams of light, while floodlights provide softer, more diffused lighting for wider areas. A fresnel lens on the front of a spotlight focuses the light rays into a narrow beam. An ellipsoidal instrument uses an ellipsoidal mirror and a lens to focus the light rays. Scoops, broads, soft lights, strip lights, and clusters provide general floodlight illumination by spreading the rays of light in many directions. Portable lights are somewhat smaller, open lighting instruments, which can sometimes be flooded or spotted without lenses, and a portable lighting kit usually contains portable light stands and various light shaping devices.

Lighting instruments can be secured to a variety of mounting devices, including overhead studio grids and lightweight portable light stands. Light shaping devices, such as barn doors, scrims, flags, and cookies, help direct and control lighting and create shadow patterns.

Artificial lighting consumes significant amounts of electricity. Load limits for specific electrical circuits must be carefully observed to avoid dangerous overloading, and the help of a qualified electrician should be obtained if the electrical requirements for a specific production situation are at all unusual. A patch panel and a dimmer board help to route and control electrical supply and light intensities by varying the voltage of the current. However, in color production the drop in color temperature that results from a drop in voltage affects the color quality of the recorded image. In color production light intensity can be reduced by moving lighting instruments or using screens.

Light meters measure light intensity. An incident light meter reading measures the intensity of the light falling on a scene, while a reflected reading measures the intensity of the light reflected by objects in the scene. These readings help to determine image contrast, as well as the proper exposure level. Key-to-fill and key-to-back light contrast ratios can be determined by using incident light meter readings to compare specific lights in terms of their intensity. Reflectance contrast is indicated by comparing the intensity of light reflected off the darkest object in a scene to that of the brightest reflecting object. Reflectance contrast in video is usually restricted to 30:1 or 20:1, while it can be as high as 100:1 for certain film stocks. Key-to-fill contrast ratios rarely exceed 2:1 in video, while key-to-back light ratios are normally 1:1 or 1:1.5. Contrast ratios in a scene affect visual aesthetics and techniques such as low-key and high-key lighting.

Additional Readings

Clark, Charles G. *American Cinematographer Manual*. 5th ed. Hollywood: American Society of Cinematographers, 1980.

GTE/Sylvania Lighting Handbook, 5th ed. GTE/Sylvania.

Malkiewicz, J. Kris. *Cinematography*. New York: Van Nostrand Reinhold, 1973.

Mathias, Harry, and Richard Patterson. *Electronic Cinematography*. Belmont, CA: Wadsworth, 1985.

Millerson, Gerald. *The Techniques of Lighting for Television and Motion Pictures*. New York: Hastings House, 1972.

Wilson, Anton. *Cinema Workshop*. Hollywood: American Society of Cinematographers Holding Corp., 1983.

Exercises

1. Design two sets of lighting plots for a specific dramatic scene; one for single-camera recording and another for multiple-camera recording. Make subtle changes of light placements for close-ups in the single-camera production that will enhance the view of the subject without disrupting the overall appearance of the lighting, when the camera is moved to another perspective. Find the best (compromise) position for lights used in multiple-camera production so that the subject looks reasonably good from many different camera perspectives at the same time.

2. Light a stationary, two-person interview, using cross-key lights and fill lights, such as the setup described and illustrated on p. 205 creating a 2:1 key-to-fill ratio and a 1:1.5 key-to-back light ratio.

3. Set up multiple key, fill, and separation lights, which will keep a moving subject lit be relatively constant light intensity, while maintaining a 2:1 key-to-fill ratio and a 1:1 key-to-back light (or kicker) ratio.

CHAPTER 10

Sound Recording

Recording good quality sound is extremely important as poor quality sound can destroy the impact of high quality visuals. Some directors feel that sounds and visual images should be almost completely independent of one another so that each component could stand entirely on its own, while others feel that sounds should reinforce accompanying visual images. The former approach is consistent with formativist aesthetics, while the latter reflects a realist approach to production. Some directors combine these approaches and suggest that high quality sound should function well on its own as well as in combination with visual images. These basic aesthetic approaches to sound recording are explored in this chapter, along with commonly used production techniques and the equipment used to control sound recording.

AESTHETICS OF SOUND RECORDING

Sound recording can be approached from the three aesthetic perspectives of functionalism, realism, and formativism. A functionalist approach emphasizes message clarity. From this perspective anything that stands in the way of the primary purpose or message of a production should be minimized or eliminated. A realist approach uses sound to stimulate an illusion of reality, reinforcing the temporal and spatial continuity of visual images. Formativist recording develops sound independently of accompanying visual images, breaking down realist conventions and stimulating more abstract impressions and visceral feelings.

Functionalist Sound Recording

Functionalist recording keeps primary sounds clear and distinct so that they can be easily understood. Background sounds and surrounding noise are not allowed to impede the presentation of key audio information. One of the best ways to maintain the clarity of primary sounds is to keep the **microphone** or ''**mike**'' relatively close to the sound source. If the mike gets too close to a speaker, the recorded sounds will be distorted and unintelligible. But if the mike is too far away, the quality of the speaker's voice will deteriorate and background sounds and surrounding noise may drown it out completely.

A constant distance should be maintained between the mike and the sound source to prevent undesired fluctuations in loudness. Changes in loudness levels of a speaker can be extremely distracting. If an off-camera mike is used, the operator can move the mike as the speaker moves to maintain a constant subject-to-mike distance.

News reporters often hand hold a mike so that it stays six to nine inches from their mouth for best quality voice recording on-camera. Mikes can be placed on a stand in a studio or hung around the speaker's neck to maintain a relatively close subject-to-mike distance. The performer should not walk away from a stationary mike or turn his or her head from side to side when speaking into a microphone, or the loudness of the recorded sounds will vary and distract the listener's attention.

Realist Sound Recording

Realist sound recording is designed to maintain an illusion of reality in time and space. Realist sound recording differs from purely functionalist recording in three ways. First, realist recording normally requires that mikes remain off-screen or be hidden on the set or in the performer's clothing.

Second, realist sound recording differs from functionalist recording in terms of **sound perspective**, or the perception of spatial depth it creates. This can be achieved by varying the mike-to-subject distance between different shots, placing the mike slightly closer to the subject for close-ups than for long shots. Thus sounds that appear to come from sources close to the viewer also *sound* as though they are closer. While a realist spatial impression can be achieved during actual recording, it is often created during postproduction mixing, when many different sounds within each scene are combined. (See chapter 15.)

Realist recording also differs from functionalist recording in terms of the relative importance of background sounds and surrounding noise within a scene. Functionalist recording stresses the clarity of primary sounds. Secondary background sounds are relatively unimportant. But in realist recording background sounds can be extremely important. They can help to establish the audio details that create a realistic impression. The continuous, unbroken flow of background sounds helps establish the illusion of continuous time across a variety of visual cuts. Background sounds are sometimes recorded separately from the visuals so that they can be used as continuous background within a scene which has many cuts from one shot with accompanying dialogue or primary sounds to another. Background sounds can also be recorded with primary sounds by using a mike that has a wide pickup pattern and which is sensitive to sounds throughout the setting, or by using two mikes during production: one for primary sounds and another for background sounds.

Off-screen sounds (Figure 10.1) are another form of realist background sound. They call attention to spatial continuity; that is, they create an illusion of continuous space from what is seen on-screen to what is heard off-screen. Just as deep focus or image perspective and a moving camera create spatial and temporal realism, so can background sounds and off-screen sounds enhance a realist impression through audio recording.

Formativist Sound Recording

Formativist sound recording often highlights rather than disguises the sound recording process. The appearance of sound recording equipment within the visual im-

Figure 10.1
Off-Screen Sound

Sound coming from a source which is visible within the camera frame is called on-screen sound, while sound coming from a source outside the frame is called off-screen sound.

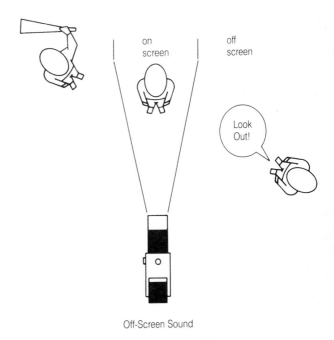

Off-Screen Sound

age in a formativist recording is not simply a matter of functional utility. Formativist techniques call attention to themselves and break down realist illusions. The use of musical instruments and natural sounds that could not possibly be created by what we see on the screen also calls attention to sound mediation and control. It stimulates our emotions and creates vivid sound impressions.

In a formativist approach to sound recording, sound is often developed independently of visual images. Audio impressions conflict with accompanying visuals rather than simply reinforcing them and serving a subservient or secondary role. A formativist sound recording is likely to be made separately from the recording of accompanying visual images. For example, a shot of someone performing a futile task might be accompanied by a "laughing" clarinet rather than actual synchronous sounds. The abstract musical sound comments on the visuals and develops a related, but independent idea.

Functionalism, realism, and formativism are not mutually exclusive aesthetic categories. They can be and often are combined. Formativist approaches to sound are often used within essentially functionalist or realist projects. Commercials and Hollywood feature films may use formativist approaches to sound recording to gain attention and spark viewer interest in a specific product, service, or character. Unexpected silence has been used to good effect in both E. F. Hutton commercials and films by Alfred Hitchcock. Hitchcock was noted for using sound in provocative and unexpected ways that put us inside the "mind" of specific characters. (See Elisabeth Weis' book, *The Silent Scream.*) Formativist approaches to sound can be combined with realist or functionalist approaches in highly effective ways.

SOUND RECORDING SITUATIONS

Single-Camera Recording

A high degree of control over the quality of sound recording for each separate shot is achievable during single-camera production. The mike can be precisely positioned to obtain the best loudness level and sound perspective for each shot. Different shots and accompanying synchronous sounds are intercut and combined during postproduction editing.

In order to ensure that synchronous sounds for each shot can be effectively combined during postproduction editing, great care must be exercised during initial recording. The loudness level and audio quality of the sound recorded with the master shot (discussed in chapter 6) usually set the standard for other recording levels. The single-camera sound recordist must maintain consistent loudness levels from one shot to the next so that sound takes recorded at different times can be combined without distracting changes in loudness and other audio qualities. For example, if the mike is brought too close to a speaker during the recording of a close-up shot, it may be difficult to combine this sound with that recorded from more distant mike and camera positions. To avoid complicated audio problems, it is often best to try to record everything at approximately the same loudness level and make desired adjustments during postproduction, using techniques discussed in chapter 15.

It is usually advisable to make a separate recording of **ambient noise** or background sounds at every location. Relative silence can be an effective attention-getting device, but ambient noise should normally accompany visual recordings. Ambient noise can also be used during editing of single-camera recordings to replace unwanted sounds, such as the director's cues to the talent or crew, or prop and equipment noises.

Multiple-Camera Recording

In multiple-camera recording the director must cut instantaneously between long shots, medium shots, and close-ups, while the same mike is generally used for sound recording. This involves compromises in mike placement. It is virtually impossible to move the mike instantaneously to retain realistic sound perspective. An off-camera mike is usually placed as close as possible to the talent without entering the frame of the longest camera shot. Moving an off-camera mike and keeping it out of the screen area can create tremendous difficulties for the audio engineer or boom operator. To avoid this, the sound recordist views an underscanned television monitor which shows the edges of the full camera frame on the screen so that the mike can be seen before it enters the viewing area of a standard (overscanned) television receiver. On-camera mikes, which appear within the frame, are much easier to place and use in multiple-camera production. Sometimes multiple-camera videotape recordings are mixed and edited during post-production. In such situations, multiple-camera and single-camera audio recording techniques can be combined during production.

TYPES OF MICROPHONES

Functionalist, realist, and formativist uses of sound in single-camera and multiple-camera situations depend on careful mike selection and placement. This means choosing a mike designed for the specific purpose at hand and positioning it properly.

A microphone is a type of transducer. **Transducers** are devices that change one form of energy to another form of energy. Mikes convert sound wave action into fluctuations in electrical voltage.

Sound is created by the very rapid vibration of objects, and **sound waves** consist of rapidly contracting and expanding particles of air. A tuning fork, for example, causes air molecules to compress and expand as it vibrates, creating a **sound pressure wave**. As one arm moves forward, it pushes the air molecules, and as it moves backward, the air molecules, which are elastic or resistant to being pushed, expand again to fill the partial vacuum or void. Rapid vibration creates a pressure wave of alternately compressed and expanded air molecules. (See Figure 10.2.) This pressure or sound wave moves in a relatively straight line and strikes other objects, such as the human ear or a microphone element. The eardrum vibrates in response to the sound wave and produces an auditory impression in the mind. A mike has an element that is sensitive to these air waves and converts the wave action into corresponding fluctuations in electrical current. The electrical signal thus becomes an analog, or copy, of the sound wave. Mikes can be classified on the basis of the type of transducer element

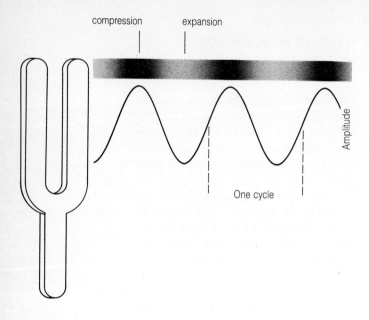

compression   expansion

One cycle

Amplitude

**Figure 10.2
Sound Waves**

they use into three basic categories: dynamic, ribbon, and condenser. One type of mike element may be better suited to a specific recording situation than another.

Transducer Elements

A **dynamic mike** consists of a moving coil attached to a vibrating **diaphragm** or disc suspended between two magnetic poles. As the diaphragm vibrates with the sound wave, the coil moves up and down within a magnetic field and changes the voltage of the electrical current flowing through the coil. In general, dynamic mikes are very durable and not extremely susceptible to wind noise.

A **ribbon mike** contains a narrow strip of corrugated foil suspended in a magnetic field. This ribbon vibrates in response to the difference in air pressure in front and in back of it and produces an alternating current along the length of a coil. The ribbon itself is quite fragile and can easily be damaged by simply blowing into the mike.

A ribbon mike usually produces a smooth, bass-accentuated sound and is preferred by many radio and television announcers for that reason.

Condenser mikes are relatively complex in comparison to dynamic or ribbon mikes. They have a **capacitor** between two charged plates: a diaphragm and a fixed backplate. As the diaphragm vibrates, the space between it and the fixed plate changes in capacitance; that is, in its ability to pass an electrical current or signal. The strength of the electrical sound signal increases or decreases accordingly. The signal is very weak, however, and a **preamplifier** is required to boost the signal to a usable level. Additional current is often supplied to the preamplifier by a battery in the mike handle. Condenser mikes are often quite expensive though some inexpensive cameras and cassette recorders have built-in condenser mikes of lesser quality. Condenser mikes generally reproduce high-quality sound but may be quite sensitive to handling noises.

Pickup Patterns

Mikes can be classified according to their directional sensitivity or **pickup patterns**, as well as their transducer elements. Different recording situations require the use of mikes that pick up sounds from a very narrow or very wide area. Some mikes pick up sounds coming from every direction, while others are sensitive to a very restricted area. The three basic categories of pickup patterns are: omnidirectional, bidirectional, and unidirectional or cardioid.

An **omnidirectional** mike (as shown in the polar diagram, Figure 10.3) is equally sensitive to sounds from all directions; that is, from the entire 360-degree area surrounding it. A **bidirectional** mike (Figure 10.4) is sensitive to sounds coming from two opposite directions. Its sensitivity drops off rapidly at sixty degrees on either side of these two opposite directional points. At ninety degrees (perpendicular to the two optimal sound source directions), it is almost totally insensitive to sound.

Unidirectional mikes are sensitive to sounds from one direction only. A **cardioid** mike is a type of unidirectional mike so named because its pickup pattern is heart-shaped. A cardioid mike (Figure 10.5) is quite insensitive to sound emanating from directly behind it, but it is very sensitive to sound coming from directly in front of it.

A **supercardioid** mike is somewhat more sensitive to sound coming from the rear of the mike, but has an even narrower optimal response area (about 60 degrees as opposed to 120 degrees for a cardioid mike). **Shot-gun** mikes are long narrow tubes; they frequently have a supercardioid pickup pattern.

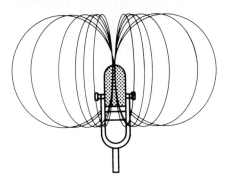

Figure 10.4
Bi-Directional Pickup Pattern

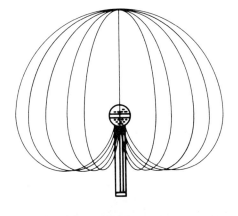

Figure 10.5
Cardioid Pickup Pattern

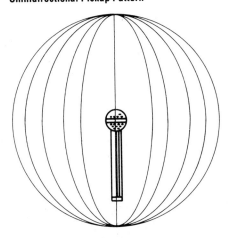

Figure 10.3
Omnidirectional Pickup Pattern

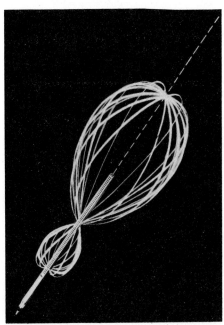

A Sennheiser condenser microphone such as this one with an untracardioid (or supercardioid) pickup pattern is often called a shotgun mike.

:::::::::::::::::::::::

MIKE PLACEMENT AND SELECTION

:::::::::::::::::::::

Mike placement during recording can be either on camera or off camera. **On-Camera** mikes, such as a reporter's hand-held mike, are visible to the viewer. **Off-camera** mikes are not visible to the viewer. An off-camera mike can be hidden somewhere on the set or under a speaker's clothing, or it can be situated just outside the camera frame.

On-Camera Mikes

Hand mikes are the most common on-camera mikes. Mikes that are to be hand-held should be shock mounted; that is, they should be well insulated so that noise is not created as the performer moves the mike. Since a hand mike can be moved and controlled by the performer it does not always stay in a fixed position, and it generally has a relatively wide pickup pattern, such as omnidirectional or cardioid. It is wise to use a mike with a durable element, such as a dynamic mike, in a hand-held situation. An inexperienced performer should be instructed in how to keep the hand mike at a relatively constant distance from his or her mouth in order to keep the loudness relatively constant. A problem that frequently arises with the use of a hand mike is controlling the mike cable. Performers must learn to move the mike around without stretching the cable or tangling it.

Desk mikes often have less durable elements than hand mikes. If a desk mike is placed in a relatively permanent position, it does not have to be shock mounted. If a desk mike is to be removed from its

A cardioid desk microphone which can be easily removed from its desk stand.

mount and also function as a hand mike, as frequently occurs, it must have some of the same qualities as a hand mike. Most desk mikes have cardioid pickup patterns and are placed one to two feet from the speaker. Sometimes a single bidirectional or omnidirectional desk mike can be used for two speakers to limit the number of mikes needed.

A **stand mike** is supported on an adjustable pole in front of the performer; thus it offers a distinct advantage to a person who has his or her hands occupied with a musical instrument. The stand mike can usually be tilted and adjusted to a comfortable height for different performers. In general, more sensitive ribbon and condenser mikes are used on a stand to record relatively soft sound sources such as stringed instruments, while dynamic mikes with omnidirectional or cardioid reception patterns are often used for singers and amplified instruments. Sometimes more than one mike may be attached to a single stand, perhaps a condenser mike positioned from below to pick up the sounds of a guitar and a dynamic mike above to pick up the singer's voice.

A ribbon stand microphone.

Lavalier mikes also leave a performer's hands free and do not require a stand that restricts his or her mobility. This type of mike, which is either hung around the performer's neck with a strap or clipped to a tie or outer garment (as shown in Figure 10.6), is relatively unobtrusive compared to a desk mike or a stand mike. Care should be taken in the placement of a lavalier mike to ensure that it will not create noise by rubbing against rough clothing or jewelry. Lavalier mikes are often susceptible to cable problems because their cables are relatively thin and fragile. To guard against this on live broadcasts, performers such as newscasters often wear two lavaliers clipped together to create a **dual-redundancy** system, where one mike serves as a backup for another. Only one mike at a time is live to prevent phasing problems, which are discussed later in this chapter. A lavalier microphone can be hidden or concealed behind clothing, although this can lead to added rubbing noise.

Some hand-held and lavalier mikes have battery powered FM transmitters, which allow the speaker using the mike to move around quite freely without a restrictive mike cable. Wireless lavalier mikes can also be used as hidden mikes by concealing the mike and its transmitter under clothing. An FM receiver at the audio input of the recording machine receives the

**Figure 10.6
The Lavalier Mike**

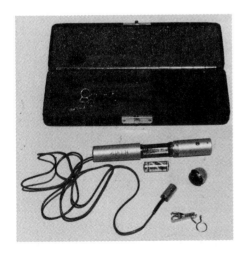

Left: A Sony ECM-50 Condenser Lavalier microphone kit. Right: A Condenser microphone in use. The small ball-shaped object on top of the microphone is the windscreen.

Figure 10.7
Wireless Mike and
Receiver

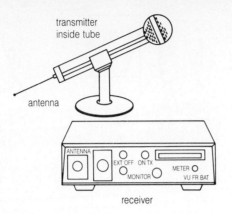

transmitter
inside tube

antenna

receiver

dle of a recording, especially when performers forget to turn them off. Finally, wireless mikes are relatively expensive to rent or purchase.

Off-Camera Mikes

Off-camera mikes may be attached to a **mike boom**. A mike boom is a long pole that can be placed (usually above the heads of the talent) just outside the camera frame. It can also be hidden on the set. There are three different types of mike boom: fishpole, giraffe, and perambulator booms.

A **fishpole** boom is an aluminum pole with a mike mounting device at one end. Some fishpoles can be telescoped to allow for maximum extension during recording and contraction for compact storage. The fishpole's greatest asset is its portability. A fishpole and the attached mike are usually lightweight enough to be hand-held for a relatively long period of time without

transmitted signal. (See Figure 10.7.) While wireless mikes can be extremely helpful in many difficult recording situations, they also have a number of pitfalls. Like any FM radio, the wireless receiver can pick up interfering signals, such as noise from CB radios. They can also be affected by electrical interference from equipment and steel structures in any building. Batteries can expire in the mid-

Bottom left: A wireless microphone in use. The lack of any type of wire enables the person using this type of microphone to move about freely without fear of getting the wire entangled. Bottom right: A fishpole microphone boom.

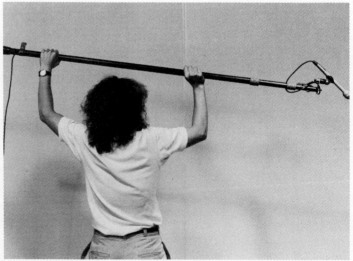

excessively tiring the operator. One disadvantage of the fishpole boom is that the length generally cannot be changed during recording. The boom operator must move as the talent moves. Also, the entire pole must be twisted to change the positioning of the microphone, making it somewhat difficult to alternate the placement of a directional mike between two different performers.

A **giraffe** boom is somewhat more bulky and less portable than the fishpole, but it allows for greater mobility and flexibility during recording. The giraffe is basically a fishpole attached to a three-wheeled dolly. It can be quickly and easily moved around the studio. It also has the advantage of allowing the operator to rotate the mike on a swivel to which the pole is attached. It requires only one operator and can be extended to different lengths during camera setups.

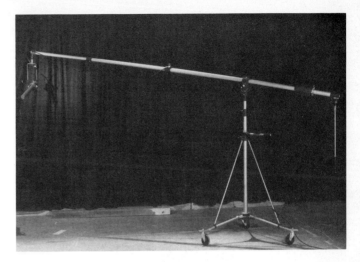
A giraffe microphone boom.

A peramubulator boom with a swivel for the microphone.

The **perambulator** boom is the heaviest type of boom. It has a large pole which can be telescoped during a camera take, a swivel mechanism for rotating the mike, an operator platform which can be raised and lowered, heavy-duty rubber tires, a guide pole, which requires the presence of a second operator to push or pull the boom around the studio, and a boom pan and tilt control. The perambulator boom is designed primarily for studio use. It is not very portable. It is counterweighted so that it can support a heavy microphone and a mounting device. Some perambulator booms allow an attached microphone to be panned or moved a full 180 degrees, so that a highly directional mike can be used to pick up a moving performer or to switch from one speaker to another.

Boom Operation   Operating a boom demands great care and manual dexterity. Movements of the mike and the boom must be smooth, precise, and carefully planned. Excessively rapid movements of the boom or mike will create objectionable

Left: A perambulator microphone boom. Right: The perambulator boom in operation.

noise. The movement of the talent must be fully anticipated by the boom operator. If the boom operator has not preplanned the movements of the boom so that it can follow the talent, it will be difficult to maintain a constant sound level or avoid crashing into other equipment on the set. The boom operator's job is to keep a moving sound source within the mike's primary pickup pattern. The operator listens to the sounds on headphones, which serve the same function as a viewfinder for a camera operator. Omnidirectional mikes are rarely used on a boom; even though they might make it easier to follow the movements of the talent, they simply pick up too much unwanted additional noise. Unidirectional mikes seem to work best on a boom. They cut down on unwanted sounds by focusing on the sound source, and they provide good reception at a greater distance from the subject than mikes with wider pickup patterns. This

can be especially helpful when recording long camera shots with an off-camera mike.

Boom Placement   The optimum placement of a cardioid mike on a boom is one to four feet in front of and one to three feet ab9ve the speaking subject. In general, the boom operator should keep a uniform distance between the subject and the mike. Sometimes it may be necessary to vary this distance, however. To achieve proper sound perspective in single-camera recording, the mike may have to be slightly closer to the subject for close-ups and father away for long shots.

An overhead boom can create harsh shadows that disrupt the image. The placement and movement of a boom must be carefully preplanned to prevent objectionable shadows on the set. Sometimes, it is simply impossible to place the microphone directly overhead on a boom without noticeably affecting the lighting or camera and performer movements. In these situations a fishpole boom may be placed at the bottom or side of the frame, or a hidden mike may be used. Boom operators who are attempting to record the best quality sound often place the mike as close to the subject as possible without entering the camera frame. In multiple-camera production, the audio engineer informs the boom operator when the mike has entered an underscanned TV monitor. In single-camera productions, the camera operator carefully monitors the frame area. One strategy boom operators sometimes use to obtain good quality sound is to place the mike within the camera frame during a rehearsal or blocking session. This forces the director, audio engineer, or camera operator to ask for the mike to be raised out of the frame. This strategy ensures that the mike will always be as close as possible to the subject and forces the director to consider whether the camera placement is compromising the quality of the sound. While directors usually are well aware of these limitations, a periodic reminder can go a long way toward preventing subsequent objections to the quality of the sound recording.

Hidden Mikes   There are three different types of hidden or concealed mikes: the hanging mike; the prop mike; and the concealed lavalier mike. Hanging and prop mikes are stationary, while the concealed lavalier moves with the talent to whom it is attached.

A stationary **hanging mike** can be attached to an overhead grid. It is usually an omnidirectional mike capable of covering a wide area of action. Its chief advantage is that it does not require a boom operator. Its obvious disadvantages are that it cannot be moved to vary or improve the audio during visual recording, and it often picks up ambient noises below it, such as footsteps and equipment being moved.

Prop mikes are microphones that are concealed on the set. A telephone at the center of a table around which several performers are seated can conceal a mike. Since a prop mike is stationary, it often has a relatively wide pickup pattern so that the talent does not have to stand immediately in front of the prop, calling attention to the presence of the mike or making it the focal point of a scene. A prop mike can be extremely useful in situations in which it is difficult to use a boom, such as when the camera is recording an extreme long shot or when the space is so confining that a boom necessarily affects the lighting.

A **concealed lavalier mike** is frequently used as a hidden mike for extreme long shots and complicated movements of the camera or talent. The concealed lavalier mike is usually wrapped in foam rubber and taped to the subject underneath his or her clothing. It should not be free to rub against garments or jewelry and create noise, and care must be taken to ensure that the sound reaching it is not muffled by heavy clothing.

Selecting the Best Mike

Selecting the best mike for a specific recording situation depends on an understanding of sound aesthetics and different mike characteristics. One of the more versatile and widely used mikes is the dynamic cardioid. It has an extremely durable element and a pickup pattern about halfway between a full-range omnidirectional and a narrow unidirectional mike. As an on-camera mike it can be hand held (in this case it must be "shock mounted") or mounted on a floor or desk stand. As an off-camera mike it can be suspended overhead on a mike boom just outside the frame.

A dynamic cardioid works best when it is relatively close to the speaker or sound source; thus it is not always the best mike to use. Suppose an off-camera mike at some distance from the speaker must be used during the recording of an extreme long shot. A unidirectional condenser mike, such as a supercardioid shot-gun mike, may be the best choice. The narrow pickup pattern isolates the primary signal from the surrounding space. The condenser element provides a stronger signal because of its built-in preamplifier. Care must be exercised when using a shot-gun mike, however, so that noise coming from directly behind the speaker is not amplified along with the primary voice signal.

A second concern with the dynamic cardioid mike is that it is difficult to make inconspicuous on camera. A lavalier condenser mike can be the size of a tie tack. It can be placed very close to the speaker without dominating the frame. It can also be completely hidden in a person's clothing. When connected to a tiny transmitter, it can even allow for freedom of movement without mike cables or extremely long-range camera shots with extremely high quality voice sounds. This can be an advantage when recording functional sound, but realistic sound perspective is better achieved by using a shot-gun mike.

The ribbon mike is best left to completely stationary functionalist recording situations, such as talk shows or interviews. The ribbon mike can be quite versatile in such a situation since it is capable of producing a very resonant sound. It can be set for an omnidirectional, bidirectional, or unidirectional pickup pattern so that it can be used by several speakers, a single speaker, or two performers facing each other. An omnidirectional dynamic or condenser mike is often used to record several speakers simultaneously. It can be suspended overhead in a fixed position or permanently positioned at a central location on the set.

Using Multiple Mikes

Using a single omnidirectional mike is not necessarily the best way to record several different sound sources, such as several talk show performers. For one thing, even if the mike is centrally located it will probably pick up a good deal of unwanted background sound along with the primary signals or voices. Using a different mike for each sound source provides better control and higher quality sound recording, provided each mike can be placed close to its sound source. One advantage is that each mike can be selected for the particular characteristics of its sound source.

For example, suppose that you are recording a singer on camera, while a band is playing off camera. If the singer moves with a hand-held mike the loudness of the band music will vary with the mike direction, unless one or more stationary mikes are set up specifically for the band. These two sound sources should be separately controlled and combined (or "mixed") together, using two mike inputs on a recorder or a device called a mixer. The music now maintains a constant loudness. The singer can use a dynamic cardioid, while an omnidirectional dynamic or ribbon mike is set up for the band. Better yet, several different mikes can be set up for different instruments in the band.

Separate mikes can be set up for several different speakers at a table. Each mike must be carefully placed, however, so that different mikes do not pick up the same signals. This can lead to **multiple-microphone interference**, in which some of the sounds picked up simultaneously by two different mikes cancel each other out. Such cancellation is a phasing problem that occurs when similar sound waves passing through the same medium are 180 degrees out of phase with respect to each other. Phasing is sometimes used deliberately, to create special audio effects such as the noise of a robot, or to disguise a speaker's identity.

The best way to find out if multiple-microphone interference exists is to set one mike at its proper level and then turn on the other mike. If the volume goes down rather than up when both mikes are "on," there is interference which must be corrected by changing the distance between the two mikes and/or their directional placement. Some sophisticated audio consoles allow the audio engineer to eliminate phasing problems electronically.

Multiple-microphone interference can be prevented by keeping "live" mikes well separated, using directional mikes, and having them directed at different sound sources. If two subjects are seated quite close together, a single mike should be used for both, either by swiveling an overhead mike or a boom or placing a stand mike or a desk mike with a relatively wide pickup pattern between them. When more than two people are involved, two or more mikes should be set up so that they are at least three times as far apart as their subject-to-mike distances. This **three-to-one rule** ensures that there will be no phasing problems with multiple mikes. Another solution is multi-channel record-ing, where each mike is fed to a separate recording channel on an audiotape recorder.

Using multiple mikes can also cause problems with excessive ambient noise. Each mike picks up the same ambient noise, and when more than one mike is used the ambient noise adds up and can become disturbingly loud. Placing mikes as close as possible to their sound sources so that loudness levels can be turned down helps reduce ambient noise in some instances. At other times different speakers can simply share the same mike.

Stereo Mike Placement

Stereo provides an additional spatial dimension by giving sound a directional placement from left to right. This is accomplished by recording sounds with at least two mikes. Two cardioid mikes can be arranged, as shown in Figure 10.8, so that they crisscross one another forming a forty-five to ninety degree angle. Each mike picks up sounds from a different direction. This setup works quite well for speech. Using two parallel cardioid mikes separated by ten to fifteen feet and well in front of an orchestra or band works well for music. The sounds picked up by each mike are kept separate and recorded on

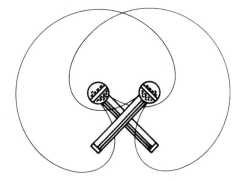

**Figure 10.8
Stereo Pickup
Pattern**

different audio channels, which can then be played back through speakers that are spatially separated from one another. (See Figure 10.9.) For proper balance, the mikes must be adjusted so that a sound coming from a source directly between them creates a signal which is equally strong on both channels. Cardioid mikes are well adapted to stereophonic use because they are slightly more receptive to sounds directly in front of them than to sounds coming from the right or left.

Stereophonic sound can be used to bring added realism or simply more spectacular audio effects to a film or television program. But stereo can also bring added production problems. In terms of production logistics, it is often difficult to record stereophonic sound on location. Handling additional mikes and audio equipment inevitably leads to greater risks and problems. Stereophonic recording also complicates the postproduction process, since many additional sound elements must be smoothly combined and balanced during final mixing. Finally, the producer often has little control over the conditions under which the final product is actually viewed. The improper adjustment of audio levels for separate sound channels can totally destroy the added spatial dimension the producer sought to provide. An added problem with stereophonic sound is that there is normally only one location ideally suited to listening to two or more speakers. Anyone who occupies a seat outside of this area is unlikely to hear a well-balanced stereo reproduction.

SOUND-SIGNAL CONTROL

Audio Problems: Distortion and Noise

One of the most common problems encountered in audio recording is **distortion**. The most common type of distortion encountered by beginning media production students is **loudness distortion**,

**Figure 10.9
Stereo Recording
and Playback**

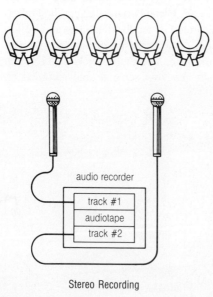

Stereo Recording

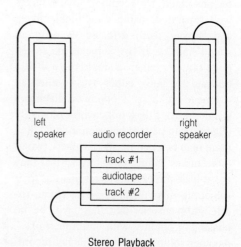

Stereo Playback

which occurs when a sound is recorded at a level that exceeds the limitations of the electronic system. The peaks or high points of the sound wave are flattened, and new, unwanted frequencies of sound are produced. The end result is a reproduction that sounds like there is some kind of variable interference or garble on the line. Loudness distortion is controlled by setting the volume so that it does not exceed the limits of the system. A volume unit or VU meter allows the recordist to set the volume controls as high as needed for a good quality recording without distorting the sound.

There are basically two types of noise, ambient noise, discussed earlier, and system noise. Ambient noise comes from "open" mikes (e.g., those being fed into an audio console or tape recorder) which pick up the sound of air ventilators, lights, cameras, or other devices. (Fluorescent lights frequently cause a hum or buzzing sound, for example.) A second type of noise is called **system noise**, which can come from the electrical recording system and equipment. Microphone lines placed too close to lights and electrical cables often create system noise. So do worn volume controls or bad circuit boards and cable connections. Most ambient noise and some system noise can be controlled, but most system noise is simply inherent in the recording equipment.

An important determinant of sound quality is a system's **signal-to-noise ratio**. This is the ratio of desired sounds to unwanted system noise. Many professional audio systems have signal-to-noise ratios of 55:1 or above; that is, the main signal is fifty-five times as loud as the system noise level. Quality audio production requires the maintenance of high signal-to-noise ratios throughout all stages of the process.

Sound Intensity Measurement

There are many different devices for indicating the volume intensity or loudness of a sound signal. Less expensive tape recorders often have a red light which flickers with volume peaks. **Overmodulation** or loudness distortion is indicated when the light stays brightly lit for a continuous period rather than flickering intermittently. Other recorders employ a needle device that indicates loudness distortion when the needle enters a red zone. These less expensive meters are quite small and do not have precise volume scales. More expensive meters are calibrated in specific units of sound intensity, such as **volume units** or **percentages of modulation**.

There are basically two types of professional sound intensity meters: **volume unit (VU) meters** and **peak program meters (PPMs)**. The VU meter (Figure 10.10) is the American standard. It is a special type of electrical voltmeter, which reads voltage shifts in electrical current as changes in sound intensity. Needle readings are calibrated in both percentages of modulation and volume units or decibels (dBs). Approximately every three dB increase indicates a doubling of sound inten-

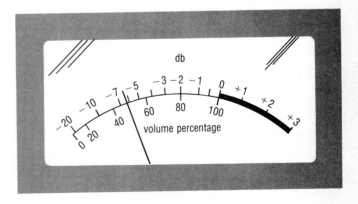

**Figure 10.10
Volume Unit (VU)
Meter**

sity. (A decibel is a logarithmic unit of sound intensity.) The modulation percentages are usually indicated on the lower scale of a VU meter. They range from 9 percent to 100 percent, the thresholds of *signal detection* and *distortion*, respectively. The upper scale indicates volume units or dB. A reading of 0 dB usually corresponds to 100 percent modulation or peak loudness before distortion occurs, and the scale reads down on the left side and up on the right side ($+1$, $+2$, $+3$, and so on) of 0 dB.

A VU meter provides an electrical analog to human hearing. It does not show instantaneous peaks and immediate distortion, but indicates the average sound intensity over a very short period of time. This average reading closely approximates the response of the human ear to peak sound intensities.

In general, signals on a VU meter should register between 50 percent and 100 percent modulation or between -6 dB and 0 dB. Below 50 percent modulation or -6 dB the signal-to-noise ratio becomes relatively low. Above 100 percent modulation or 0 dB loudness distor-

tion occurs. Sounds that intermittently peak above 100 percent modulation, or 0 dB, for very short periods of time rarely cause noticeable distortion, but sounds that continuously "pin" the needle to its maximum above 100 percent modulation or 0 dB not only cause distortion but frequently cause meter damage as well. The sound recordist continually watches the VU meter and makes minor adjustments in the sound level throughout a recording, using a volume control mechanism such as a **potentiometer (pot)** or a sliding **fader bar**. Volume level adjustments should be made smoothly and slowly. Major shifts in volume level affect the noise levels and background sounds as well as the primary signal and change the sound perspective and dynamics of the recorded sounds.

The PPM (sometimes called a **modulometer**) is another type of loudness or voltmeter and is the European standard. Rather than averaging sound intensities, a PPM responds immediately to peak sounds. The human ear cannot perceive extremely rapid loudness distortion, but many PPM users believe that such distortion nonetheless affects a sound recording.

Volume Unit meters (VU) on an audio console.

Fader bars on the Volume Unit Meter (VU) console.

Obviously a recordist using a PPM or modulometer must respond to needle readings on the devices somewhat differently, probably more reservedly and slowly, than one would respond to a VU meter reading. Both types of meters facilitate sound signal control, however.

Some recorders have **automatic gain controls (AGC)** or automatic level controls for a mike input. An AGC prevents loudness distortion automatically. However, it also boosts the ambient noise level when primary sounds are at low levels, as at pauses in dialogue. To avoid this problem, levels should be set manually using a VU meter and the AGC turned off, if possible. **Peak limiters** are sometimes more useful than AGCs, as these simply limit the upper level of loudness without automatically setting the basic recording level and running the risk of increasing ambient noise levels. But most professionals prefer to control recording levels manually.

Cables and Connectors

Professional **mike cables** have two conductor wire lines and a ground. These **balanced** lines are less susceptible to cable noise than **unbalanced** lines, which have a single conductor wire. The two conductor lines are usually well insulated from each other, the ground wire, and the cable exterior in balanced lines. Poorly insulated cables are much more susceptible to interference from other electrical cables and devices. Mike cables should never be placed near lighting instruments or electrical power cables, which can cause interference. Nor should they be wound tightly together or twisted in any manner that will reduce their life expectancy and damage the wire conductors. Less expensive recorders sometimes have mikes attached by an unbalanced line cable with a single-prong miniplug at one end which is inserted into the front or side of the recorder.

Balanced line cables are attached to three-prong **SLR connectors** which can be plugged into mikes, audio consoles, or tape recorders. These connectors have separate prongs for the two conductors and the ground. Male and female connector ends lock into each other so that they do not easily become disconnected.

It is probably a good idea to wrap two cables together in a loose knot around the connectors, so that any pulling on the cables will pull the connectors together, rather than apart. Even though this procedure may place considerable stress on the cables in the case of an accident, such as someone tripping over a cable, it would undoubtedly be more expensive to reshoot the entire sequence in the event of a complete disconnection. Care should be taken, of course, to minimize the amount of twisting and stress that occurs at the juncture of the cable and connector, since this part of the cable is extremely vulnerable to damage and wear.

Mixing

An audio console or **mixer** is designed to combine sounds from several different sound sources such as mikes, tape recorders, and playback units. These devices can vary from an elaborate studio audio console to a simple multiple-input mixer, which allows for separate volume control over each input. Basically the au-

A Shure microphone mixer.

An Otari 24 channel multi-track audio recorder.

dub can be made, for example. It can combine or mix together several sound sources into one (monophonic) or onto two or more (stereophonic) sound tracks or channels, which are recorded as a final or **master** audiotape. (See Figure 10.11.)

An audio console consists of a series of faders, each of which controls the volume level of a single input. The inputs can come from microphones, record players or turntables, audiotape recorders, compact (laser) disc players, or audio playbacks from videotape recorders. The output is controlled by a single (or dual) master pot(s). Each pot or fader often has its own equalization controls for increasing or decreasing bass and treble (low frequencies and high frequencies) directly above or below it. Most television studio audio consoles also have a **talk-back** system that allows a director or assistant director to communicate with the crew and thus does not affect the program signal.

Most audio consoles and mixers have two types of audio inputs: **high imped-**

dio console routes signals from sound sources or playback units to a control device or recording unit. It can send a signal from a particular mike or a playback unit to a recorder, so that a duplicate copy or

**Figure 10.11
Full-, Half-, and
Quarter-Track Audio
Recording**

Monaural Full-Track Audio Recording

Monaural Half-Track Audio Recording

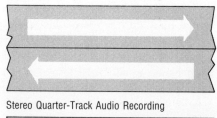

Stereo Half-Track Audio Recording

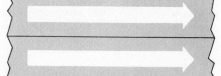

Stereo Quarter-Track Audio Recording

There are many different audio tape recording configurations, such as stereo and monaural, as well as full-track, half-track, quarter-track, and multi-track. A stereo recording separates sound recorded on the left side from that recorded on the right side to create a spatial separation of sound. Monaural sound does not record separate sounds coming from left and right. A full-track monaural machine records only one sound signal on an audio tape, while a half-track machine records two separate signals on the same tape either as accompanying stereo signals in the same direction or two monaural signals in opposite directions. A stereo quarter-track machine records four separate signals on the same audio tape; two accompanying signals in each direction. A multi-track recorder records four or more accompanying signals in the same direction. (See also Figure 10.12.)

ance and **low impedance**. Impedance cuts down on the flow of alternating current; it is analogous to resistance in devices operated on direct current (batteries). Impedance and resistance are measured in **ohms**. High-impedance signals come from some nonprofessional mikes, from playback machines, and from some signal-processing equipment. Low-impedance signals usually come from professional quality microphones and other equipment. Professional mikes usually have an impedance of about 50 ohms, while playback units and other high-impedance sources are about 600 ohms. An impedance imbalance or mismatch between the sound source and the mixer or console input will result in a signal that is either too loud and distorted or too soft and weak to be useful for recording purposes.

Different sound sources can have different **levels** of sound intensity or signal strength (volts), as well as different impedances (ohms). These also require separate inputs on an audio console. *Mike levels* are usually lower than *line levels* from playback units. Preamplifiers in the audio console can boost a low-level signal to a higher level so that it equals that of other sound sources. When a high-level signal enters the console through a low-level input, distortion occurs.

Console Operation   Once the impedance and line levels of source and input match, the console operator can set the proper loudness levels for recording each sound source. To accomplish this on an audio console or mixer with only a single VU meter, all of the faders should be closed, except the one being set. If each input has its own VU meter, then it can be set independently of the others. The level for each input should be set between 80 percent and 100 percent modulation for an optimal signal-to-noise ratio. In some in-

Top: An audio console for a TV studio production. Bottom: A basic audio recording and production studio.

stances, such as background music and sounds, the level may be set somewhat lower for a proper overall balance between sounds. **Balance** is an aesthetic concept which refers to the best proportion of sound intensities from different elements, such as speech and music. Generally speaking, music must be toned or faded down to achieve a proper balance with accompanying dialogue or narration. In addition to balancing sounds, a sound recordist should check for multiple-microphone interference by determining if the volume levels of specific sources increase as others are shut off. It is generally a good idea to label each fader with the number or name of the mike or sound source it carries, and to mark the best volume setting for each sound source and fader to eliminate any confusion when adjustments have to be made during actual recording.

Recording and Mixing Commands

To perform well at the audio console or mixer, the audio recordist should be familiar with each of the following audio terms, cues, and commands:

Fade in Audio: The sound intensity is gradually raised to an audible level and its proper volume setting.

Fade out Audio: The sound intensity is gradually lowered to an inaudible level.

Segue: (seg'wā) One sound source is immediately replaced with another.

Cross-Fade: One sound source is faded out while another is faded in over it.

Open Mike: The fader or pot for a specific mike is raised immediately to its proper level or is simply switched on.

Cut Sound or Kill Sound: The fader or pot is abruptly closed.

Sound Up and Under: The sound cuts in at its proper level and then is faded down to a lower level, where it is still audible but less prominent.

Back-Time: Prepare a prerecorded sound or music track so that it will end at a specified time. This requires some preparation or set-up time before actual recording. The playback machine must begin running before the pot or fader assigned to it is turned up, so that the sounds or music can be gradually faded in at the appropriate point.

TAPE RECORDING

Tape Formats

Electrical sound signals can be magnetically recorded on **audiotape**. Audiotape is made up of particles of iron oxide or other metallic substances attached to a flexible support base.

Tape formats can be categorized on the basis of two factors: the size of the tape and the form in which it is packaged. Audiotape sizes differ in terms of thickness and width. Audio quality generally increases with increasing thickness and width. The thickness of audiotape is measured in mils (thousandths of an inch). The most common tape thicknesses are 1½, 1, ½-, and ¼- mil. The most durable tape is 1½ mil; it is less likely to "print through" (see pg. 248) from one layer to the next. This has become the professional standard. Audiotape also comes in a variety of widths such as ¼-inch, ½-inch, 1 inch, and 2 inches. **Multitrack** tape recorders (each track is a separate tape path) require wider audiotape. As many as sixty-four separate tracks can be recorded on some multitrack machines, using 2-inch-wide

Audiotape formats. Left: 16mm magnetic film. Center top: An audio cartridge. Center bottom: An audio cassette. Right top: A 7-inch reel of ¼-inch width audiotape. Right bottom: A 5-inch reel of ¼-inch width audiotape.

audiotape. (See Figure 10.12.) Audio signals in video recording are usually recorded directly on videotape in a variety of formats which were discussed in chapter 8. Film audio may be recorded on a separate ¼-inch audiotape or directly onto the film itself. In the latter case, the edge of Super-8mm or 16mm film is coated with magnetic material; this is called magnetically-striped film. One-quarter inch film audio and magnetically-striped film recordings are normally dubbed or copied onto a separate roll of magnetic film which has the same format as the film images for editing.

The enclosures in which tape is packaged provide another means of differentiating recording formats. Tape can be obtained in the form of cartridges and cassettes as well as on open reels. **Cartridges** consist of continous loops of 1½-mil, ¼-inch audiotape ranging from a few feet to several hundred feet in length and from a few seconds to several minutes in duration. **Cassettes** are pairs of small reels encased in a plastic housing. Thirty to sixty minute cassette tapes are usually

**Figure 10.12
Multi-Track Audio
Recording**

½-mil thick, while longer playing ones are only ¼-mil thick and are decidedly inferior in terms of their potential recording quality. The standard width of cassette tape is ⅛-inch, and the normal cassette

Right: A cartridge tape recorder. Bottom: Portable cassette audio recorders.

tape recorder speed is relatively slow: 1⅞-inches per second. As a result, the potential quality of a cassette recording cannot equal that of many other formats. Open reel tape has the advantage that it can be edited (see chapter 15), runs at higher speeds, and is available in a variety of tape sizes. Cartridges are quicker and easier to set up and recue; that is, find a particular starting point. Cassettes are inexpensive, but are difficult to cue and are only available in smaller tape sizes and slower recording speeds, which limit recording quality. To partially compensate for these deficiencies, many cassette tape recorders use a tape noise reduction system, such as the Dolby systems discussed in connection with other signal processors in chapter 15.

Basic Tape Recording

The most common form of audiotape recording, called analog recording, produces a magnetic copy, or analog, of the electrical fluctuations stimulated by the original sound waves. Magnetic tape passes over a magnetic **sound record head**, consisting of a magnet with a coil wrapped around it which carries the electrical sound signal. As the voltage in the electric sound signal fluctuates, the magnetic field through which the tape is passing changes, and the sound signal is recorded on tape. A **bias signal** (30,000 Hz or above, which is outside the range of human hearing) produced by an **erase head** erases the tape by aligning the magnetic particles prior to the recording of the sound signal. In the playback mode, the tape is passed over a **playback head** (in some recorders the same head is used for both record and playback), which picks up the prerecorded tape's magnetic variations and causes a weak electrical current pass-

ing through the magnetic head to fluctuate accordingly. This signal is them **amplified**; that is, it is increased in strength and intensity, so that it can be sent to a loudspeaker, headphones, or another tape recorder.

Digital Recording

A digital audio recorder samples or evaluates the electrical sound wave thousands of times every second and gives an exact numerical value to the electrical sound signal for each specific instant of time. The numerical values are coded into a series of ''on'' and ''off'' electrical pulses, known as binary code. These electrical pulses are not an electrical copy or analog of the sound wave. The only signal that is recorded is electricity that is either *entirely on or entirely off,* rather than different gradations of electrical current as is the case in analog recording. Digital recording extends the recordable range of intensities and frequencies and virtually eliminates many other problems inherent in analog recording, such as tape noise, **crosstalk** (two recorded tracks on the same tape interfering with each other), and **print through** (one layer of recorded tape ''bleeding'' through and interfering with another). **Flutter** (an unwanted fluctuation in pitch) is another common recording problem, but it is caused by the transport system and can occur in both analog and digital recording. Digital recording produces a much more permanent record than analog recording. Fine gradations of analog signals can completely fade away and be lost forever, while a magnetic signal that is completely ''on'' or ''off'' can easily be restored to its original state as the ''on's'' begin to fade. For these reasons, digital recording is gradually replacing analog recording as the professional audio standard.

Tape Speed

The speed at which an audio tape is driven directly affects the amount of tape that is used and, more importantly, the quality of the tape recording. In general, faster recording speeds produce better quality recordings. Some tape recorders have a speed control setting that can be adjusted to two or more of the following standard tape speeds: $15/16$, $1\frac{7}{8}$, $3\frac{3}{4}$, $7\frac{1}{2}$, 15, and 30 inches per second (ips). Professional recordings of live music are usually made at tape speeds of 15 ips or above. Most multitrack sound recording is done at a speed of 30 ips. Simple voice recordings are frequently made at $7\frac{1}{2}$ ips or even $3\frac{3}{4}$ ips for reasons of economy, but only rarely is a tape-to-head speed of $3\frac{3}{4}$ ips or $1\frac{7}{8}$ ips used in professional recording situations, except perhaps with a high quality cassette recorder. LP (long play) audio cassette machines have a tape speed of $15/16$ ips.

SYNCHRONOUS SOUND RECORDING

Synchronous sounds match their visual sound sources, and are usually recorded at the same time as the corresponding visual images.

Many different systems have been developed to synchronize recorded visual images with recorded sounds. Some portable ¼-inch reel-to-reel tape recorders have the capacity to record a **sync signal** that allows them to be used in conjunction with a motion picture camera. This allows the separate recording of sounds that are synchronous with their corresponding pic-

tures. These tape recorders have a fourth head for recording the sync signal and then monitoring it during playback. This signal provides a reference for precise recording and playback speeds on the tape recorder so that the sound can be replayed at the identical speed at which it and the visual images were initially recorded. In videotape recording a **control track**, which is a recording of the original sync signal, serves the same function as the sync signal in film. This signal is needed to synchronize the scanning of a TV receiver or monitor with the scanning of a camera pickup tube, as seen in chapter 8. When the videotape is played back the control track controls both the speed of the capstan (tape drive) motor and the scanning of the TV monitor, keeping the latter in sync with the videotape playback.

Videotape Synchronization

Synchronization between sounds and images is very simple to maintain in videotape recording. A single videotape recording machine is usually used to record picture and sound elements simultaneously on the same tape. In ¾-inch videotape recording, **on-set** or synchronous sounds are recorded on track #2 for best quality reproduction. There is a slight distance separating the points at which the sounds and the picture are recorded on the videotape, due to the fact that on most types of videotape recorders the video record and playback heads rotate while sound heads remain stationary. During electronic editing, then, the corresponding sound and images must be picked up from slightly different points on the tape. However, since videotape is always played back on a machine which has the same gap between images and sounds, this distance

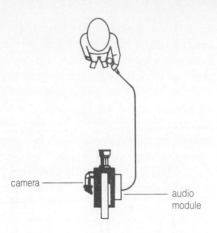

**Figure 10.13
Single-System Film
Recording**

Single-system sound-on-film (SOF) is recorded by a film camera at the same time the visual images are recorded. A microphone is connected directly to the camera, and the sound signal is recorded on the edge of the film.

camera ——

—— audio module

**Figure 10.14
16mm Optical and
Magnetic Sound
Tracks**

Sound-on-film (SOF) is recorded either optically by exposing the edge of the film to a light that fluctuates according to the sound signal or magnetically when audiotape is coated along one edge of the film.

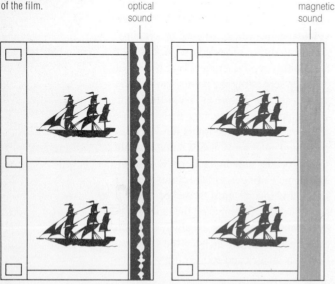

16 mm optical sound

16 mm magnetic sound

creates no real problem in terms of synchronizing sounds and images. Control track recording is an important reference for postproduction editing, although some machines provide another type of reference, called SMPTE time code, which is discussed in chapter 14.

Single-System Film Recording

There are basically two different systems of synchronous sound film recording in common use today: single system and double system. **Single-system recording**, as shown in Figure 10.13, puts sounds and images on the same piece of film; usually, the sound is recorded on the edge of original motion picture film. This technique is called **sound-on-film (SOF)**. As a general rule, 35mm film is not used for sound-on-film or single-system original recording. 16mm magnetic sound-on-film is recorded 28 frames ahead of the picture gate or film aperture. (16mm optical sound-on-film is 26 frames ahead of the picture. Optical sound is created by exposing the edge of the film to light.) Super-8mm sound-on-film is recorded 18 frames ahead of its corresponding pictures. These standard spacings allow the film driven through a camera to change from an intermittent movement at the film aperture, where a rapid series of still frames are recorded, to a continuous movement over the sound recording head. The same 28, 26, or 18 frame advance of sound ahead of the picture is standard in most 16mm or Super-8mm film sound projectors. Single-system sound is commonly used for exhibition purposes. The final film prints marry an optical or magnetic sound track with their corresponding pictures on the same piece of film. (See Figure 10.14.)

Single-system recording is extensively used in small formats, such as Super-8mm film recording. Editing problems arise from the fact that the sounds are always a specific number of frames ahead of the corresponding pictures.

Sound-on-film yields an initial sound recording that is decidedly inferior in audio quality to a double-system film sound recording. It is difficult to design a film camera so that it can record good quality pictures and good quality sounds at the same time. Combining separate movements of the film inside a camera, one intermittent and the other continuous, inevitably leads to a reduction in audio quality. Still, for certain situations, such as news work where ENG (electronic news gathering) equipment is either not available or impractical, a single-system film recording provides a recording of sufficient quality to be conventionally broadcast as news footage.

If SOF is to be edited, either it must be shot with pauses in the voice track, so that edits can be made without losing portions of the sound, or the sound track must be dubbed to a separate piece of film for double-system editing. A third alternative, which was commonly used for broadcasting news film, is to create two separate picture rolls, known as **A** and **B rolls**, with alternating shots on different rolls. They can then be simultaneously projected by two projectors on a **telecine** or **film chain**, which converts film images to video pictures. These editing problems and their solutions are discussed more fully in chapter 14.

Double-System Film Recording

In **double-system** synchronous sound recording (Figure 10.15), the sounds and images are recorded on separate materials. (This approach is normally used for production and editing but not for final projection.) Rather than recording sounds directly on the edge of the film during production, an independent tape recorder is used, which can record and play back sound in exact synchronization with the corresponding images. There are two basic systems for synchronizing the re-

A telecine (or film chain) operator arranges slides in two slide projectors so that they can be recorded by a video camera. A film projector in the center of the telecine allows film recordings to be transferred to videotape using the video camera on the right.

cording of the separate sounds and pictures: cable sync and crystal sync.

Cable sync refers to the use of an electrical cable, which connects the camera to the tape recorder like an umbilical cord. The cable carries a 60 cycle per second sync signal, called **Pilotone**, which is generated by the camera. The Pilotone is recorded on the audiotape by a special

Figure 10.15
Double-System Film Recording

Double-system film recording uses a separate audio recorder to record synchronous film sound. Either a cable connects the camera and audio recorder or an extremely accurate crystal oscillator is placed in each completely separate machine to ensure proper synchronization between them.

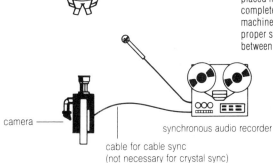

camera —

synchronous audio recorder

cable for cable sync
(not necessary for crystal sync)

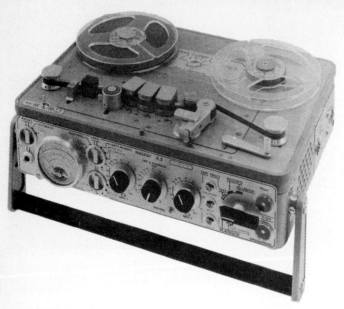

A Nagra 4.2, a high quality portable audiotape recorder that is often used to record double-system film sound.

sync head on the audiotape recorder. If the camera runs at twenty-four frames per second and the recorder runs at 7½ inches per second, for example, then 60 cycles of Pilotone are recorded along 7½ inches of tape. During playback, the audiotape recorder monitors Pilotone through the sync head, comparing the recorded signal to a standard 60 cycles per second, such as that provided by standard line current in a 120 volt AC line. This also compensates for fluctuations or discrepancies in the recorded signal by changing the playback speed. The audio signal is transferred to magnetic film with the same film format as the corresponding pictures so that it can be edited frame for frame with the visuals. The sync signal or Pilotone is no longer needed, since the magnetic film now corresponds frame for frame with the synchronized picture. The magnetic film

recorder that records the sound on this film format runs at precisely twenty-four frames per second.

Crystal sync allows the camera and the tape recorder to be physically separated. This can be a distinct advantage because it increases the flexibility, mobility, and independence of sound and picture recording machines and operators, who are otherwise linked by an umbilical cable. For crystal sync, the speed of the camera is controlled by a crystal oscillator so that the film is driven at a precise speed of twenty-four frames per second. The audiotape recorder uses a separate crystal oscillator to place a sync signal on the audiotape, so that its original recording speed can be duplicated during playback. **Crystal oscillators** are small bits of quartz which oscillate and can be amplified to control the camera speed precisely or to generate precise Pilotone *within* the tape recorder. There is less than one frame of deviation between sounds and pictures in a 400 foot film run. If the sounds and pictures are played back at the same speeds with which they were originally recorded on a common format (8mm, 16mm, or 35mm film) they will match perfectly frame-for-frame when started at a common point.

Slating

Creating a common point where separately recorded elements of sound and picture match is called **slating**. Normally a **slate**, sometimes called a **clapstick** or **clapboard**, is used for this purpose in motion picture production. The clapboard consists of a piece of wood with a hinged arm that makes a clapping sound when it strikes the bottom portion of the clapboard. This device produces a loud recorded sound that can be matched to the corresponding visual image of the closing arm. In the absence of a clapboard, a person can call out ''slate!'' followed by a sharp handclap. If the separate sound and picture tracks are perfectly matched at the beginning of a shot, the editor can be reasonably sure that the entire cable or crystal sync recorded shot will maintain synchronization.

Slating is also used to identify the project title, director, and shot and take numbers during single-camera film or videotape recording. This information is written on the chalkboard surface of the slate or clapstick and read aloud at the beginning of each camera shot; thus each take is fully identified on both film and audiotape. Some film cameras are designed for documentary shooting in situations where the use of a clapboard is impractical. They have an electronic means of providing a reference synchronization point for editing called an **automatic slate**. At the beginning of each camera take, the first few frames (usually the first eight) of picture are flashed or fogged with a small light inside the camera and a signal which is separate from the Pilotone is sent to the tape recorder either by cable, if cable sync is being used, or by radio transmitter, if crystal sync is being used. This signal triggers a **clap alarm** which creates an audible tone, known as the **bloop**. The proper flash frame of picture can then be matched to the bloop at the beginning of the shot for editing synchronization.

Summary

Sound recording can be approached from three aesthetic perspectives: functionalism, realism, and formativism. A func-

A slate or clapsticks. Note that it is marked off with different sections to identify the production's title, director, scene number, take number, and other important information.

tionalist approach to sound emphasizes message clarity above any realistic impression or formative effect. Realist sound appears to be transmitted naturally, as though there were no recording device mediating between the speaker and the listener. Formativist sounds fail to meet our realist expectations and can be effective devices for attracting attention, arousing emotions, and stimulating innovative ideas. Single-camera recording allows for great control over sound recording. Mikes can be set up specifically for each shot to obtain the best quality sound. Multiple-camera recording inevitably involves compromises in the placement of mikes, since they cannot be set up for each different shot.

The aesthetic use of recorded sounds demands an understanding of recording devices and their selection, placement, and control. A mike or microphone is a transducer that converts sound wave energy into electrical energy. Mikes can be classified into three different categories on the basis of their transducer elements: dynamic, ribbon, and condenser. Dynamic mikes are very durable and not extremely susceptible to wind noise. They make good hand-held mikes and are frequently used outdoors. A ribbon mike is quite fragile and susceptible to wind noise. But it is also quite versatile and is frequently used as a stationary mike in a studio. Condenser mikes do an excellent job of boosting weaker sounds but can be quite sensitive to handling noise. They are often used for distant mike placements and wireless (FM radio) mikes.

Mikes can also be classified on the basis of pickup patterns. Omnidirectional mikes are sensitive to sounds coming from all directions and are used when these sounds are equally important. Bidirectional mikes are sensitive to sounds coming from two directions, such as from two speakers on opposite sides of the mike. Unidirectional mikes, such as the cardioid mike, are sensitive to sounds from one direction. Highly directional mikes, such as a supercardioid or shot-gun mike, can be used to exclude all sounds except those from a distant speaker, although they also pick up sounds from directly behind the speaker.

Mikes can be placed in on-camera and off-camera positions. Hand mikes, desk mikes, stand mikes, and lavalier mikes are examples of on-camera mike positions. Mikes on booms, such as fishpole, giraffe, and perambulator booms, as well as various hidden mikes, such as the hanging mike, prop mike, and concealed lavalier mike, are off-camera mikes. Selecting the best mike and mike position depends on an understanding of what mike characteristics and placements are best suited to a specific situation.

When there are several sound sources or speakers, it is often advisable to use several mikes, each positioned to isolate specific sounds. When two mikes pick up the same sounds and some are cancelled out, multiple-microphone interference occurs. Multiple-microphone interference can be controlled through proper mike placement or multi-track recording. Multiple mikes are also used to record stereophonic sounds on separate sound tracks. These separate but simultaneously recorded sounds are then played back through speakers separated by some distance to allow for a perception of the directional placement of sounds.

Sound signal control helps a sound recordist achieve the best quality recorded sound by eliminating specific audio problems. Loudness distortion can be eliminated by setting volume controls so that the volume never exceeds the limits of the electronic system. Ambient noise and system noise can be reduced with respect to the primary signal, such as a speaker's voice, by moving a mike closer to the subject thus making the primary signal stronger. A sound measuring device, such as a VU (volume unit) meter, can be used to set the sound level as high as possible for optimal signal-to-noise ratio, while avoiding loudness distortion. Signals on a VU meter should register between 50 percent and 100 percent modulation. Balanced mike cables should be used to minimize noise and electrical interference.

Audio mixing is done on an audio console or mixer. Mixing refers to combining several different inputs, such as different mikes or playback machines, into a single (monophonic) or dual (stereophonic) output, which is directed to a tape recorder. Faders on the audio console or mixer are used to adjust the volume very gradually. They should be clearly marked for the sound source and audio level designated to them. Audio recordists using a console or mixer must be familiar with basic audio terms, cues, and commands, so that they can effectively communicate with the rest of the staff and crew.

Audiotape is available in a variety of formats in terms of tape sizes (widths and thicknesses) and tape enclosures, such as cassettes and cartridges. An audio signal is usually recorded directly on videotape. An analog audiotape recorder converts the electrical audio signal to magnetic pulses stored on magnetic recording material. Digital recordings consist of a series of ''on'' and ''off'' pulses and are less susceptible to recording problems, such as crosstalk, print through, and fading, than are analog signals, which record the entire electrical signal. Tape speed directly affects the amount of tape consumed, and higher speeds generally produce higher quality recordings. In general, the larger the tape size and faster the speed, the better the quality of the recorded sound.

There are several ways to obtain sounds and images that synchronize with each other. In videotape recording, sounds and images are recorded on the same piece of videotape. A control track, which is a recording of the sync signal, allows the videotape to be played back at the same speed at which it was recorded and synchronizes the scanning of a monitor with the playback of the videotape. Film sound and images can be recorded on the same piece of film, which is called single-system sound-on-film (SOF) recording or they can be recorded on separate sound and picture mechanisms, which is called double-system film sound recording. In the latter case a Pilotone signal is recorded on tape and serves as a reference to ensure synchronization between sounds and images. Double-system recording allows for more editing flexibility than single system. Slating refers to the placement of a common starting point on the picture and sound recordings. It is also used to identify the project title, director, and shot and take numbers during single-camera recording.

Additional Readings

Alten, Stanley. *Audio in Media*. Belmont, CA: Wadsworth, 1981.

Borwick, John. *Sound Recording Practice*. New York: Oxford University Press, 1976.

Frater, Charles. *Sound Recording for Motion Pictures*. New York: A. S. Barnes, 1979.

Nisbett, Alex. *The Technique of the Sound Studio*. New York: Hastings House, 1981.

——————————— . *The Use of Microphones*. New York: Hastings House, 1974.

Weis, Elisabeth. *The Silent Scream, Alfred Hitchcock's Sound Track*. Rutherford, NJ: Farleigh Dickinson University Press, 1982.

——————————— , and John Belton. *Film Sound: Theory and Practice*. New York: Columbia University Press, 1985.

Yale French Studies. Special issue on ''Sound in Film.'' 60 (1980).

Exercises

1. Practice following a moving speaker with a cardioid mike on a mike boom as he or she walks around a studio on a precise, preplanned route. Try to keep the mike one to four feet in front of and one to three feet above the speaker. Record the sounds on audiotape or videotape without changing the pot or fader setting on the recorder so that the initial volume setting is used constantly. Change the mike to a supercardioid or shot-gun mike and perform the same exercise. Did you keep a constant distance between the mike and the speaker? Was the mike always in the best position to pick up the speaker's voice? Listen to your recording critically for fluctuations in the loudness of the speaker's voice. Discuss what you could have done to improve recording consistency. Did the shot-gun mike increase overall sound quality while making it more difficult to maintain a constant recording level?

2. Set up an on-camera narration videotape recording outdoors. Select a location that is relatively quiet. Bring along three mikes: a cardioid hand mike, a small lavalier mike, and a supercardioid or shot-gun mike. Record the same on-camera narration with the speaker looking directly into the camera three times, once with each type of mike. Make sure that each mike has a windscreen and position the speaker with his or her back to the wind, if possible. When using the shot-gun mike make sure that there are no loud sounds coming from directly behind the speaker. Position the shot-gun mike as close to the edge of the camera frame as you can without entering the frame. Have the speaker hold the cardioid mike about six to nine inches from his or her mouth. Attach the lavalier so that no clothing or jewelry rubs against it and the mike cable is well hidden. Compare the three recordings. Which mike gave the best quality recording with the least amount of noise?

CHAPTER 11

Scenic Design

Almost every object that human beings create is the product of a conscious design that organizes spatial forms. **Scenic design** involves the creation and coordination of many different production elements, including sets, costumes, and performer makeup. Scenic designers rely on basic design principles, such as unity, balance, emphasis, proportion, and movement. Designers put these principles into practice when they approach specific production problems from the following aesthetic perspectives: functionalism, realism, or formativism. This chapter examines aesthetic approaches to design, design elements, principles, and commonly used practices in the design and construction of sets, costumes, and makeup. The chapter concludes with a consideration of the overall integration of scenic design with other production components, such as lighting, performance, and visual and sound recording.

A functionalist news set.

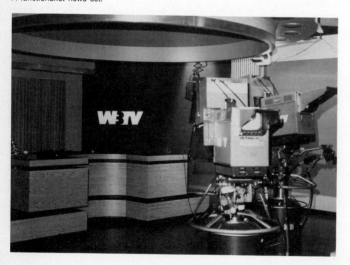

DESIGN: THE AESTHETIC APPROACHES

Functionalist Design

Functionalist sets and costumes are utilitarian in design. They serve specific practical purposes, such as creating the background or setting for a news or talk show. Functionalist designs facilitate the placement and movement of performers and recording equipment. They are efficient without being sterile; simple but not plain or clichéd. There is consistency to the choice of colors and shapes, which harmonize with each other and achieve a degree of balance.

A good functionalist design has some kind of unifying concept or theme. A talk show set, for example, can communicate informality and comfort by employing domestic elements and motifs borrowed from a home living room setting. A news show may appear to take place in a bustling newsroom, giving the impression of being at the center of the action. The lines and colors of the set for an instructional program may be designed to promote a smooth, relaxed rapport between the performer and the audience, rather than an intense air of action and excitement. In each case, form follows function, as the design conforms to specific program needs.

Realist Design

A realist design simulates an existing setting, location, or graphic format. While a realistic set, for example, can be filled with objects and furnishings that one would expect to find in such a place, emphasis is placed on the illusion of reality, not necessarily the depiction of reality itself. Maintaining basic principles of spatial perspective and proportional size are extremely important in realist design, since they help to sustain an illusion of reality. Because sets are often expensive, it is important to efficiently create an illusion of reality. Realistic sets are often constructed out of lightweight materials that give the impression of being real and are much easier to construct and move around than actual objects.

Realist designs are rarely defined by their supposed fidelity to nature or reality alone. Almost every realist design that has emotional impact has some degree of subjective stylization. A realistic setting, title, or illustration should convey a psychological impression that reinforces the central theme of a drama or the central message of an informational program. It can reflect warmth or coldness, tension or relaxation, simply by virtue of the colors, lines, and shapes it presents. It is even possible for a realistic setting to reveal a specific character's emotional state through the feelings that the design conveys.

Formativist Design

Formativist designs are much more abstract than realist or functionalist designs. The subjective feelings they arouse and the subjective impressions they convey are rarely tied to actual experience or production efficiency alone. Formative artists usually have much freer rein to explore specific design elements or subjective impressions for their own sake. A designer may decide to call attention to textures, shapes, lines, and colors themselves. Vis-

A realist set.

ual innovations often stem from such formative experiments, which can be incorporated into more conventional narrative, documentary, or instructional programs. Innovative television programs and films by many experimental artists have shown how a formative approach to scenic design can break down conventional illusions of reality by ignoring spatial perspective and using highly artificial, stylized sets, backdrops, and lighting.

Elements of Design

A designer works with four basic elements: line, shape, texture, and color. The ways in which these elements are selected and combined determines the nature of a setting or illustration. The selection of design elements must support the themes, plots, and characterizations of a drama or the central message of a nonfiction production. Their use conforms to one of the three aesthetic approaches discussed above as well as the basic principles of design to be discussed next.

Line

Line defines the form of a design. An independent line can be straight, curved, or spiral. Edges are lines formed by shapes or objects which overlap each other, such as a foreground door and background wall. Lines can be repeated to create parallel lines or concentric circles. They create a path or direction of movement for the eye. Converging parallel lines create an illusion of depth or spatial perspective, for example.

Straight lines are more dynamic than curved lines and circles. They create a strong sense of directional movement. Smooth curves and circles communicate a smoother, softer feeling of more gradual movement. Sergei Eisenstein's famous ''Odessa Steps'' sequence in *Potemkin* (1925), for example, associates straight-line diagonals with the merciless, advancing Cossack soldiers, and curved lines or circles with defenseless women, children, and students, who are attacked on the steps.

Shape

Shapes are composed of combinations of lines. There are an infinite number of different shapes reflected by specific objects, but some common, recurring shapes with which all designers work are circles, squares, rectangles, triangles, ellipses, trapezoids, octagons, and hexagons.

Shapes can carry symbolic meaning. They can be repeatedly used in conjunction with specific people or settings to evoke specific themes. In the film *Ivan the Terrible* (1942–48), Eisenstein used circular shapes surrounding Ivan to connect the circular shape of the sun to the symbolic meaning of Ivan as the Russian ''sun king.'' Basic design elements often reinforce specific themes.

Texture

Texture provides a tactile impression of form. Texture can be real or represented. Real textures are revealed by directional light, which creates shadows and modeling on a nonsmooth surface.

Cossack soldiers are associated with straight and diagonal lines as they slaughter the Russian people of Odessa in Sergei Eisenstein's famous "Odessa Steps" sequence from *Potemkin* (1925).

Represented textures such as granite, marble, or wood grains have smooth surfaces that create a tactile impression. The texture of a surface affects our perception of depth. A rough texture with heavy shadows provides a greater sensation of depth than a smooth, flat surface. A heavily textured material used in drapes or costumes can create a richness that relates to a theme of opulence, splendor, or decadence, for example. Texture, like shapes, can create a sense of space that affects our emotions and relates symbolically to the major themes of a story.

Color   Three aspects of color are of primary importance to a designer: color harmony, color contrast, and the emotional or symbolic effect of color. Various relationships between color pigments on a two-dimensional color wheel in large part determine the degree to which specific colors will harmonize with each other. A **two-dimensional color wheel** is a series of different colored chips or samples arranged in a circle from cool (short wavelengths of light) colors, such as violet, blue, and green, to warm (long wavelengths of light) colors, such as yellow, red, and orange (see also chapter 8). Colors distant from each other on the wheel harmonize better than close colors, which tend to clash with each other. Several harmonious colors for sets and costumes can be selected by laying an equilateral triangle or square on top of a color wheel and using the colors at the points. As the triangle or square is rotated the group of harmonious colors changes.

Different colors help separate objects in a scene through their mutual contrast. In fact, lines and curves in any setting are normally perceived through color or brightness contrast. If two objects or shapes did not contrast with one another,

The represented (stone-like) texture of this floor stimulates a tactile impression and adds spatial dimension and impact to the ominous shadow that is cast upon it.

they would appear as one object or shape. Contrast can help us perceive spatial depth. If specific colors of foreground and background are different, we will perceive their separation and hence spatial depth.

Adjacent colors tend to interact. If you place a gray object against different colored backgrounds it will appear darker or lighter depending on the color and brightness of the background. A particular hue takes on a completely different feeling depending on the hues adjacent to it. Complementary colors of the same intensity should not be placed next to each other, because they tend to vibrate and distract the viewer. Color harmony and color contrast are basic design principles that help a designer select adjacent colors within the same scene.

Most designers believe that a general distinction can be made between warm colors and cool colors in terms of their emotional effect on an audience. Colors such as reds, oranges, and yellows create a sense of warmth in a scene. A romantic scene lit by firelight and surrounded by red, orange, and yellow objects on the set uses these warm colors to enhance a romantic mood. Caution most sometimes be used with reds and yellows in video recording, because "banding" (the appearance of lighter and darker bands) and video noise can occur in these colors on a videotape. Colors such as blue and green, on the other hand, are often considered to be cool colors. They are sometimes used to enhance a sense of loneliness or aloofness in a character, or a general mood that is related to a lack of human as well as physical warmth. Some video recording systems have problems with mixtures of blue and green. Blues tend to dominate greens, and some blue greens or aquamarines come out blue.

Cool colors tend to recede, while warm colors tend to advance. For example, pure hues of greenish yellow, yellow, yellowish orange, orange, orangish red tend to advance and call attention to themselves, while pure hues of violet, red violet, blue, and blue green tend to recede. Warm colors can convey a mood of passion or action, while cool colors tend to reinforce a sense of passivity and tranquility. The colors of sets, costumes, and graphic images must be selected with an eye toward their visual prominence—whether they recede or advance—as well as the degree to which they contrast with other colors.

Colors that are repeatedly associated with specific objects, people, and settings can take on symbolic or thematic meaning. The red dress of a character in a drama can be used to signify sensuous passion. This color might contrast with the cool green or blue colors associated with a competitor for the affections of a male character. The fact that one of these colors harmonizes better with those worn by the male can suggest a natural affinity between these two characters. These types of symbolic color associations are commonly used in family melodramas and soap operas, for example.

Principles of Design

A designer organizes basic design elements by using principles of unity, balance, emphasis, proportion, and movement. These principles can be applied to any visual design problem, including the arrangement and selection of sets, props, furniture, and costumes. They are concepts employed by designers in many other fields as well.

Unity   In a unified design all of the elements blend together and seem to belong with each other. Unity implies the fitting together of different facets of a design and maintaining order. At least three different strategies promote unity: repetition, simplicity, and the use of a common theme.

The repetition of a similar shape, color, or texture can enhance the perception of unity. Sequential repetition suggests continuity. But excessive repetition can be monotonous. If the same shape or color is repeated endlessly, unity comes at the expense of viewer interest. Changes or variations in a design promote interest and relieve monotony. Variations can be repeated at regular intervals themselves to create a pattern composition, such as for a border.

It is easier to perceive unity in a simple design. Other things being equal, a simple design is usually preferable to a complex one. Simplicity results from efficient, uncluttered designs. Everything that is extraneous must be removed. In complex designs various elements seem to compete for dominance, causing chaos and confusion rather than order and unity.

When all of the elements seem to reflect the same theme or idea, a high degree of unity is inherent in a design. The design functions like an amusement park or "theme" park, where every exhibit, building, and setting in one area reflects the same general theme, concept, or idea. This allows for considerable diversity in the basic elements, since different elements indicate alternative ways of expressing the same thing or different facets of the same idea. Shapes, colors, and textures reflect common themes and feelings in a unified design. Circular shapes, soft pastel blue colors, and soft gentle fabrics and materials can all be related to a common theme of gentleness and tranquility, for example.

Balance   A design is balanced when there is an equal distribution of visual weight on each side of an imaginary center line bisecting the image. Balance or equilibrium enhances unity and order. There are at least four different types of balance: symmetrical, asymmetrical, radial, and occult. Symmetrical balance consists of a mirror image of one half of a design in the other half. Identical but reversed elements are arranged on either side of the axis line, which seems to cut the design in two. Asymmetrical balance does not have completely identical elements or mirror reflections on either side of the axis line, but the

Swedish director Ingmar Bergman and his cameraman Sven Nykvist achieve a high degree of asymmetrical balance within this frame from *The Seventh Seal* (1957).

weight or size of the elements on both sides is nonetheless equivalent. Asymmetrical balance permits a higher degree of variation and viewer interest than symmetrical balance. In radial balance two or more similar elements are placed like the spokes of a wheel about a central point. This creates a strong sense of motion or movement around this point, while preserving balance. Occult balance is a sense of equilibrium achieved through the placement of unlike elements. Balance is intuited without reliance on conventions or rules. There is usually a strong sense of movement and a dynamic quality to the design.

Emphasis   Emphasis refers to the use of various elements to draw attention to the most important aspect of the image, which is called the **focal center**. A common focal center is the performer, but more abstract aspects of a frame can also function

Frames within the camera frame can be used to add emphasis. To emphasize the soldiers' isolation and subordinate position at their court-martial, Stanley Kubrick captures them through the legs of a table from below in his film *Paths of Glory* (1957).

as a focal center. Brightness and contrast, size and placement, and directionality are devices that help create emphasis.

Generally, a bright object attracts attention more readily than a dark object. Our eyes are drawn immediately to the brightest part of a design. However, if the image is almost completely white, emphasis can be achieved by using contrasting image darkness for an object. Objects in contrasting colors can create emphasis. Since warm colors advance and cool colors recede, emphasis can be created by using contrasting reds, oranges, or yellows for important objects. In a sense, any shade of gray from white to black and any color can acquire emphasis through contrast to a single-brightness scene or monochromatic background.

The size or dimension of an object and its placement within the frame can also create emphasis. In general large objects attract more attention than small objects. However, if most of the objects in an image are large, then a single small object is emphasized by virtue of its deviation from the norm. The placement of objects in a frame can also create emphasis. Closer objects are usually more prominent than distant objects. If several objects are grouped together, the one that is set apart acquires emphasis through variation and contrast. An isolated, individual object can be singled out from a group and thus be emphasized. If the single object outside the group is also different in size, brightness, or color from the members of the group, emphasis is reinforced.

One of the most common forms of directional emphasis is created by the use of converging parallel lines that direct the eye to a specific object. These lines enhance the illusion of perspective and depth at the same time that they add emphasis. The lines can be formed by natural objects, such as a row of trees or a road leading to a house, for example. Many different lines and shapes can direct the eye to various parts of the image, focusing attention in the desired direction. A radially balanced image, for example, naturally draws the eye to the center of the design, which then becomes the focal point.

Proportion   Proportion refers to the relative scale of one element or object with respect to another. When an object is disproportionate, its scale is simply too large or too small with respect to other objects. Scale within an image is usually determined by human performers. We can easily judge the degree to which the scale of any object is proportionate to a human being. But proportional relationships also exist between abstract shapes or masses and the intervals or spaces between them. A rhythm or sense of movement is created by repetition or variation of the size and scale of this interval. The space between objects has an effect on their apparent size and the proportional relationship of one object to another.

Movement   Movement can be real or imaginary. The movement of performers on a set is real movement, while the illusion of movement stimulated by a series of still drawings or stationary backgrounds is imaginary. In design, imaginary movement is just as important as real movement. The illusion of movement can be enhanced by the use of parallel diagonals in a design, for example. It can also be

limited or reduced by the use of verticals and horizontals. Specific shapes and lines, such as spirals, concentric circles, and radial designs, can generate significant movement in a static frame. Transference can take place between real or imagined movement and otherwise stationary objects. A simple figure placed against a pulsating background will appear to dance or vibrate itself. A moving background can transfer the illusion of movement to a sta-

A bold sense of proportion guides the composition of this frame from Sergei Eisenstein's *Ivan the Terrible* (1942–46). Ivan is huge and oppressive in the foreground as he surveys from above a carefully choreographed and arranged line of marchers who trail off into the distant background. The intricacy and complexity of Eisenstein's design is reflected by the way in which he arranged the line of marchers so that it mirrors the shape of Ivan's body and staff and by his use of frames within frames.

The illusion of movement is enhanced in this frame from Robert Wiene's *The Cabinet of Dr. Caligari* (1919) by the series of jagged, intersecting lines and swirls which cover the walls and the floor.

tionary figure placed in front of it. Movement throughout a stationary image is carefully controlled through changes in color, shape, space, and direction that guide the eye through a design.

DESIGN PRACTICES

Scenic design can be divided into at least three categories: set design, costume design, and makeup. Set design includes the creation of scenery, props, and backgrounds. Costume design focuses on the creation of costumes for performers, while makeup enhances or changes the facial features and physical appearances of performers. All three of these aspects of scenic design must be coordinated with one another to effect a consistent and unified approach to all elements that appear within the frame.

Functions of Scenic Design

Scenic design has three basic functions in a dramatic production: to establish the time, place, and mood, to reflect character, and to reinforce specific themes. A historical time period and setting must be easily identifiable. Costumes, sets, and props denote a specific time and place at the same time that they reflect a specific style or mood. The mood or atmosphere results primarily from the abstract, emotional aspects of design elements and principles. Specific colors and shapes create an emotional mood that can reveal character and reinforce themes.

The idea that you can tell a great deal about people from where they live and what they wear can be applied to scenic design. A cold, formal setting or costume reveals a great deal about a character, as does as a warm, relaxed setting or costume. Different types of personalities are reflected by different spatial environments and clothes. Specific themes can also be reinforced through settings and costumes. A theme such as the struggle for financial and social success, for example, can be reinforced by a transition from poverty to wealth in settings and costumes. Scenic design is an important contributor to overall characterization and thematic meaning.

Script Analysis and Research

The first stage of scenic design is analyzing the script to determine what kinds of sets, costumes, and makeup will be required. A script usually provides a clear indication of general time and place, even if it does not describe settings and costumes in detail. Judgments concerning time, place, mood, character, and theme can only be made after the script has been carefully and thoroughly analyzed. The script itself can be broken down into a list of specific times and places, in much the same way as a breakdown is done for production scheduling and budgeting. A designer can then note the specific psychological mood of the action and characters for each time and place. Finally, more abstract concepts, ideas, and themes which result from in-depth analysis can be integrated into and reinforced by the selection of specific settings, costumes, and makeup.

Like the research phase of writing, the research phase of design is crucial to the quality of the finished product. Whether settings and costumes are functional, realistic, or purely stylized and abstract, a designer usually does careful research into different design possibilities.

Scenic design research is often conducted in a public library. Published drawings and photographs can be consulted to try to uncover characteristic styles and designs for both settings and costumes. Book illustrations frequently provide a wide assortment of design possibilities, especially for historical subjects. A scenic artist might also refer to paintings, other art objects, and previous films and television programs using a similar design style, as a source of inspiration and ideas. Another method of scenic design research involves photographing specific contemporary locations which are later reconstructed in the studio.

Set Design

The design of specific sets can be conveniently divided into two stages: layouts/floor plans and actual set construction. Design research, layouts, floor plans, and costume sketches are considered ''above-

the-line'' expenses. (See chapter 2.) They are created prior to actual production and before a commitment is made to actual construction, so that changes can be made before more sizable ''below-the-line'' construction expenses have been incurred. Each stage of design from planning to execution results in a specific two-dimensional or three-dimensional product. By following these stages, a designer refines rough ideas into workable sets that can be efficiently and economically constructed, significantly contributing to overall program effectiveness.

Cycloramas   Before undertaking the work and expense of set design and construction, many designers consider the use of a neutral background, called a **cyclorama** or **cyc**. A cyc is a heavy, monochrome curtain that provides a neutral set backdrop. It is convenient to set up in a studio and can be used for many production settings. A cyc will often suffice in many functionalist and formativist situations.

Layouts and Floor Plans   During preproduction a designer first draws an unscaled layout and rough sketch for each set. These preliminary drawings give an approximation of the type of settings which will eventually be constructed. An **unscaled layout** provides a bird's eye view of the studio and set. It is not drawn precisely to scale; that is, the dimensions are not necessarily proportional to those of the actual set. The unscaled layout indicates how objects are to be arranged, so that talent and camera movements can be determined for each setting. A **rough sketch** of the set usually provides a frontal view of the set. It is neither very detailed nor drawn precisely to scale but gives a

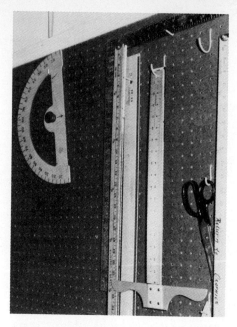

Tools used in the designing of a set. Various sizes of "T-squares" and other tools are needed to complete an accurate and "to scale" floor plan.

general picture of the set as it will be captured by the camera. These preliminary drawings are extremely important preproduction elements. They provide a focus for discussions at preproduction meetings, facilitate the estimation of set construction costs, and serve as a preliminary guide for the actual construction sets.

The **fully scaled floor plan** translates actual set dimensions into a proportional quarter-inch scale on a piece of gridded paper. The designer creates a bird's eye view of the proposed set in reduced dimensions that are proportional to the actual size of objects on the set. If a wall is to be eight feet long, it will be two inches long on the scaled floor plan (eight quarter-inches). Using a fully scaled floor plan, a director can determine if there is sufficient room to move the cameras or talent from one position to another in the set. A fully scaled floor plan can also be used by the

Bottom left: A close-up of a scaled layout over its backdrop. The layout is done to aid the director in the positioning of cameras and talent on the set. Right: The finished "to scale" backdrop for a production.

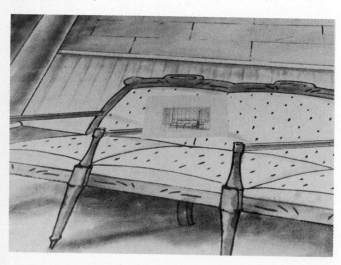

lighting director to prepare the studio lighting. The final floor plan layout will include such things as scenery, set pieces such as furniture and props, and set dressings such as curtains.

There are two types of elevations that are used to guide the actual construction and painting of the set: carpenters' elevations and painters' elevations. The **carpenters' elevation** depicts a frontal rather than an overhead view of the actual dimensions of the set. A draftsman translates the overhead floor plan into an accurate frontal view of the set elements, indicating forms of support and specific construction techniques. **Painters' elevations** depict the color values and painted designs of all set elements in a fully scaled frontal view. The designer frequently uses watercolors to illustrate the colors of the set elements. Skilled carpenters and painters translate the drawings into set materials that conform in every possible respect to the designer's original intentions.

Set Construction   Sets can be constructed out of new materials, which are generally discarded at the end of production, or they can be constructed out of reusable flats and risers. The choice between new and reusable materials is usually made on the basis of budget size and available resources. Obviously a high-budget production can better afford to create and discard new materials than a low-budget production. However, reusable set materials must be stored and maintained. Film and video studios, television stations, and networks often store and maintain such materials. Flats and risers can be simply redecorated or repainted to depict new locations.

Top: A typical scene-making shop complete with saws and other construction tools. Bottom: How flats are stored in a scene shop. This makes reuse and retrieval much easier for the floor crew.

Flats are relatively lightweight rectangular boards, which are braced and supported by $2'' \times 2'''$s or $2'' \times 4'''$s on the back so that they are quite sturdy and durable. Flats can be conveniently stored in a scene shop and then fastened together in a studio to create a temporary wall. A va-

A flat with braces, C-clamps, and sand bags for added sturdiness while on the studio floor.

riety of devices are used to connect flats together: rope tied over pegs, or fastened with metal hinges, or secured with C-clamps. To keep them upright, flats are usually supported by angle braces. The gap between connected flats can be covered with tape so that a series of flats gives the appearance of a continuous wall. Flats can be decorated with wallpaper, fabric, latticework, or paint to alter their appearance for different settings. Normally the materials secured to a flat are removable. **Risers** are hollow rectangular boxes which can be placed on the floor to raise a portion of a set. Risers might be used in a news set, for example, to raise the news desk and seated performers to camera height. Risers can be used on a talk or interview show to raise seated guests above the stage floor that will be used for performances.

Permanent sets are sometimes constructed out of more durable materials. A set that is going to be used day after day, such as for an evening news program, may be permanently secured to the studio floor for added stability. Carpenters construct a set by following the specifications outlined in the carpenters' elevations. Even permanent sets are rarely finished as thoroughly as permanent home fixtures. Since set materials are rarely viewed from behind, carpenters can cut costs by finishing only one side of a set piece and using inexpensive support materials. Set carpenters are highly skilled at creating the appearance or illusion of strength, stability, and permanence.

The designer of a more realistic set must also select the necessary furniture and dressings, which fill in the set with objects and materials that add interest, realism, or atmosphere. Considerable searching may be required to locate unusual items, such as period furniture, drapes, or antiques that are needed to authentically re-create a specific setting or atmosphere. **Props** or **properties** are functional furnishings that are integrated into the program. **Hand props** are actually handled by performers, while **stage props** are simply interesting, perhaps symbolic details on the set. Hand props are often used for bits of stage "business" or action, such as a gun kept hidden from the view of other characters. During camera and performer blocking, the set crew often helps arrange and rearrange the props on the set, so that they work well compositionally, are readily accessible to specific performers, and do not obstruct the movement or placement of cameras and other talent.

Costume Design

Most television and film productions require special costumes and clothing that are selected and designed specifically for that show. For the majority of such productions, the wardrobe person procures costumes from rental houses that specialize in supplying costumes to theater, film, and television productions. In some cases, the clothing will be supplied by clothing manufacturers who want to advertise their products. Higher budgeted productions employ costume designers who create original costumes. Regardless of whether the costumes and clothing will be originally designed, rented, or supplied by a manufacturer, the person in charge of their selection must understand the basic principles of costume design. The garments worn by performers must be consistent with the overall production design.

Stages of Costume Design

A designer of original costumes for a television or film drama usually conducts extensive research into the customs and clothing of the people and period that are to be portrayed. The costume designer may explore actual clothing, photographs, and drawings of authentic apparel as well as examples of costumes designed for previous productions. He or she then sketches various costumes based on this research. Some of these rough sketches are later transformed into full color drawings, depicting every important aspect of the clothing for a costume maker or seamstress. The costume designer and costume maker usually work together to select fabrics and accessories that will provide the intended shape, texture, color, and contrast without exceeding the proposed budget.

An example of a costume sketch.

Harmony and Contrast Between Costumes and Sets

Costume designers must carefully consider color harmony and contrast between costumes and sets. Purple sets and chartreuse costumes, for example, are disturbing when they appear together. A *two-dimensional* color wheel, discussed earlier, helps a designer select colors for costumes and sets which will both harmonize and contrast with each other. (See Color Plate II.) Using a *three-dimensional* color wheel, such as a Munsell 3-D color spindle, costume and set designers can select costume colors that will contrast with sets in terms of both color (different hues) and brightness (different light reflectances). Different colors that also differ in brightness will contrast with each other when projected as black-and-white as well as color television or film images.

Designers of costumes and sets should avoid specific problems that can occur in television and film recording. Contrast extremes between costumes and/or sets should be avoided. The limited contrast range of video in particular recommends that designers avoid pure blacks and whites. Off-white and dark gray will give the appearance of black and white on a video recording much more pleasingly than actual black and white.

In terms of texture, designers know that shiny, highly reflectant materials appear much brighter than thickly or coarsely textured materials. Bold plaids and stripes call too much attention to themselves. Certain fabric shapes and designs should be consciously avoided by the designer of television costumes and sets because they cause problems during recording. For example, parallel lines that are quite close together, as in herringbone cloth, can cause a moiré effect on a television screen. A **moiré effect** is a distracting vibration of visual images caused by the interaction of close-set lines in the materials being recorded and the television scanning lines. In television, the color blue, when it is used for chroma key, is usually avoided in costumes and sets. Both television and film costume designers often avoid horizontal lines and baggy costumes, which further accentuate the performer's size, since people appear about ten pounds heavier than normal in film and video.

Makeup

Types of Makeup   Television and film performer makeup can be divided into two types: cosmetic and prosthetic. **Cosmetic makeup** enhances the appearance of performers by hiding imperfections, adding needed color, and accentuating their better features, while **prosthetic makeup** transforms the appearance of a performer's face through temporary ''plastic surgery'' and other corrective means. Prosthetic makeup can add years to a performer's appearance or entirely transform his or her physical appearance. Cosmetic makeup enhances the beauty of a performer. It compensates for the heightened awareness of imperfections caused by film and video recording equipment and weak features in a performer's face. It also brings out the best features of a performer's face.

Cosmetic makeup hides reddish cheeks and noses, beard lines, freckles, and blemishes. Eyes and lips are the most important aspects of a female performer's face. Makeup can hide or compensate for defects in these facial structures. If a female performer's eyes are too close together, for example, eyeliner can be placed on the outside edges of her lids to make them look farther apart. Male performers often require makeup to cover beard lines, although many newscasters shave just before they appear on the evening news to avoid whisker stubble. Bright shades of cheek and lip color are generally avoided with males to prevent the appearance of a heavily madeup look. A weak chin can be made more prominent with a subtle accentuation of jaw lines and cheek color. Women performers are usually less concerned or embarrassed about applying makeup than men, but properly explaining the technical need for makeup can help to assuage the timidity of inexperienced performers. Men who are unaccustomed to wearing makeup often need to be convinced of its utility. Makeup should always be applied to novice performers in front of a mirror so that they can see its positive effects first-hand. Every makeup action should be explained to novice performers. It is well to assure the person that he or she looks attractive to begin with, but a touch of makeup will simply help to bring this out on camera.

Television makeup is essential, when a performer must make a good impression. Makeup and lighting can improve or eliminate such facial defects as the baggy eyes and pasty complexions often displayed by political candidates at the end of an exhausting campaign. Makeup on a bald head makes a person look better and cuts down on lighting problems, such as back lights reflecting off the top of a head.

It is possible to hide blemishes and create a consistent overall facial color and texture by simply applying a **base** or **foundation makeup** to a performer's face. There are basically two types of television and film base makeup: water-base cake, sometimes called pancake makeup, and grease-base, sometimes called stick,

makeup. Performers who are allergic to these conventional types of makeup can substitute hypoallergenic consumer products that reproduce well on television and film. Choosing between pancake and stick makeup is generally a matter of the makeup artist's personal preference. Some artists find one type easier to apply and remove than the other. Most makeup artists today seem to prefer stick makeup, because of its ease of application and quality of coverage. Some gentle rubbing with cold cream (and numerous tissues) will remove it. The performer's skin should then be washed with soap.

In order to draw attention to a bald actor's facial features, shiny spots on the top and sides of the head must be covered. In this case as well, the brows were darkened and to eliminate stubble, a light base was applied to the beard area.

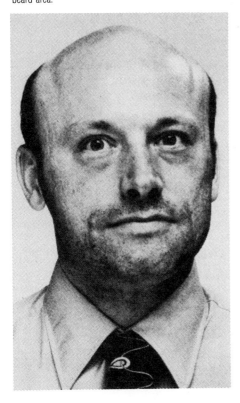 

Makeup Application   To apply makeup, first wash the performer's face. A dry (for stick) or damp (for pancake) sponge can be used to apply the base makeup evenly over the exposed areas of the face. It should be applied to extremities, such as hands and feet, only when absolutely necessary. A balding or completely bald head also requires base makeup, which should be applied up to the hairline. The color of base makeup should be selected on the basis of the closest match to the performer's natural facial color; two base makeups can be mixed to achieve a perfect match. The base will then hide blemishes and eliminate splotches that frequently appear on performers who have blood vessels close to the surface of the skin, giving them an excessively red color on camera. Rouge may be applied above (male) or below (female) cheekbones with a soft hair brush to add to facial contour and highlight the cheekbones, as well as to the chin and forehead, once a thin, but consistent, layer of base makeup has been applied. Translucent face powder can be applied with a puff to inhibit reflectance and shine, especially over stick makeup. The eyes can be accentuated by using mascara and pencil on lashes and eyebrows, as well as eyeliner and eye shadow (which can be removed with oil and tissues). Lipstick may also be applied to make the performer's lips more prominent or simply to help shape and color the face.

Remember that the purpose of cosmetic makeup is usually to enhance the appearance of a performer, not to call attention to itself—unless, or course, a formativist approach is employed. The best way to check a performer's makeup is to test it with a live video camera or an instant film camera. If it does not hide blemishes and improve the appearance of the talent, it should be removed and redone. The performer should look "natural," except, of course, in formative, avant-garde works.

Prosthetic makeup gives mobility to the expressive features of an actor and allows him or her some facial versatility in terms of playing many different roles. Prosthetic appliances can be used to make changes in the apparent age, race, nationality, and even sex of an actor.

Prosthetic appliances are usually made of foam latex, which can be applied to the performer's face and hands. For example, a life mask can be made from an older person by directly applying Prosthetic Grade Cream (P.G.C.), known as alginate, to his or her face. Petroleum jelly is usually applied first to make it easier to remove the alginate. The negative mask is then filled with foam latex to create a positive mask, which can be applied to the performer's face. Openings for the performer's eyes, nose, and mouth are cut into the mask before it is attached to his or her face, using easily removable, nonirritating glue. The mask is then covered with cosmetic makeup so that it has the proper coloration and detail.

Prosthetic appliances can also be used to create specific facial effects, such as sagging folds and a double chin or heavy bags under the eyes. Sometimes an orange peel is rolled over latex to give the impression of porous skin. Prosthetic appliances can entirely restructure a performer's face so that a white performer can portray an oriental or black character or vice versa. Foam latex can be used by makeup artists to create purely imaginary facial structures, such as that of a prehistoric or futuristic creature, as well as life masks of living persons.

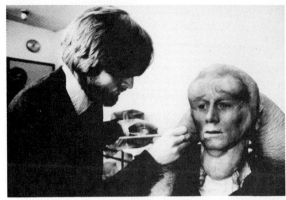

The application of prosthetic makeup is an exacting job. Many hours are put into creating the right "look" for each character. Shown here, from the film *Return of the Jedi* (1983), are but two of the many steps taken in applying this type of makeup and the final result.

Overall Design Integration

Sets, set furnishings, props, costumes, and performer makeup are not completely independent elements in the production process. Elements of scenic design interact with each other and many other areas of production to create an overall visual impression. The most important interactions are those between scenic design and each of the following: lighting, performer movement, and camera and microphone placement.

Lighting Important set elements, such as key props, can be emphasized by lighting them more brightly than other elements. The texture of a rough suface can be accentuated with side lighting, which creates textural shadows in the surface indentations. The color of set elements can be drastically altered by using colored lighting. A colored surface can only reflect wavelengths of light that are present in the light which illuminates it.

Different lighting contrast ratios and lighting styles can enhance a specific mood or atmosphere inherent in the setting. A high key-to-fill ratio and low-key lighting combined with a dark, cool colored set creates a somber, cool, and dark atmosphere. A low key-to-fill ratio and high-key lighting can be combined with a bright, warm colored set to effect a light, happy, or comic mood. The important point is full coordination of the scenic design and the lighting, so that both aspects of production are consistent with the project's overall purposes and goals.

Set materials often complicate a lighting setup. A tall set or flat can obstruct the placement of lights. A low ceiling can make it extremely difficult to hide a back light behind a tall flat and still light the back of a performer's head. Low ceilings are common at location interiors. It is difficult to position the lights in confined settings so that the directional consistency of the main realistic source of light, such as light coming through a window, is maintained. Colored walls tend to reflect some colors of light more than others and can affect the overall mood. Using specific set or background lights and preventing the key lights from falling on the set by using barn doors are techniques that allow the lighting director to enhance and control the spatial impression of a specific interior.

Performer Movement   The placement of sets and props obviously affects the movements of the talent. Hand props must be conveniently placed so that they can be readily picked up by the talent. They may have to be replaced in the identical spot on the set for retakes of the same action. Performer movements can also be controlled by set design. The common problems of performers failing to hit their marks and stay in the lights can be helped by situating furniture and props so that an actor has only one way to get from point A to point B and stay in the lights. When the ceiling is low and the lights cannot be hung very high, the performers' movements can

create objectionable shadows on nearby walls, unless they maintain a considerable distance from various parts of the set. Set pieces can obstruct the light falling on the talent and the lighting may have to be reset so that it remains consistent as the talent moves about the set.

Costuming and makeup can facilitate or restrict performer movement and expression. Certain types of makeup inhibit facial expressions or make it difficult to talk. Some costumes restrict movement, while others create so much noise when the talent moves that they disrupt the audio recording. Costuming and makeup must be believable, but they should also facilitate rather than restrict the movements and expressions of the talent.

Camera and Mike Placement   Sets are usually designed to facilitate the placement and movement of the cameras and microphones, as well as the talent. One of the main advantages of constructing sets in the studio is that there is always an open wall on the set, where the cameras can be placed. A location interior always has four walls. When shooting with a single camera in the studio, the fourth wall can be put up or taken down between shots or camera takes. Single-camera productions can create the illusion of a fourth wall in the final edited product, but during production they maintain the flexibility of the open wall. The elimination of the fourth wall makes it much easier to move a camera around the set to cover the action. During multiple-camera studio production, using only two walls provides a great deal of space within which the cameras are free to move.

Tall flats and sets make it difficult, if not impossible, to position a microphone boom so that the mike extends over the top of a flat. It is usually preferable to place the microphone boom in the open wall of the set, so that it does not obstruct lights or get in the way of set materials. Even when a mike boom is successfully kept off-camera, it can cause objectionable shadows to fall on the set, if it should pass between the lights and the set while following the movements of the performers. The barn doors on a lighting instrument can be used to prevent light from falling on a mike boom.

In a confined setting, transmitter microphones are invaluable. They may also present the best way to obtain a good audio recording in extremely large interiors, where it is impossible to place a mike boom close to the talent without entering the shot. Sometimes a mike can be hidden on the set, but a hidden mike usually restricts the movement of the talent, unless it is a transmitter mike, hidden in or underneath the talent's clothing.

The texture and sound absorption reflection characteristics of set materials can affect sound tone and reverberation. A microphone placed in a corner of a set often picks up a great deal of reverberation, which negatively affects the recording quality. Set materials and sound recording equipment placements interact with one another, affecting the overall quality of the recorded sounds.

Summary

Scenic design can be approached from three aesthetic perspectives: functionalism, realism, and formativism. Functional sets, for example, those used for news and talk shows, are designed for special purposes, rather than to represent a real setting with which the audience is already familiar or to create an imaginary, abstract world. Functional sets are created for the convenience of the performers and crew, using a simple, contemporary design that helps create the intended mood. Realist sets and design formats depict an actual or general type of place or format with which the audience is already familiar. A realist setting can provide an atmosphere that reflects the subjective state of mind or perceptions of a specific character. Formativist designs are relatively abstract. They reflect an artist's abstract conception of space, a subjective feeling, or a state of mind.

Scenic design involves four basic design elements: line, shape, color, and texture. Lines can be straight or curved. Common shapes are circles, squares, trapezoids, and so on. Intersecting or parallel lines create different spatial impressions than curved or circular shapes. A designer can create spatial perspective and control image size by manipulating various shapes. Shapes can also be symbolically linked to specific themes when they are repeatedly used in conjunction with specific characters and settings. The texture of a surface can be defined in terms of its tactile roughness or smoothness. The texture of a design can create a tactile impression that accentuates more purely visual impressions, such as shape and color. It can also affect the lighting and apparent depth or richness of a setting or costume. Color and contrast are interrelated aspects of design, as are color and shape. Contrasting colors can be used to separate foregrounds and backgrounds and to create various shapes. Using different colors in costumes and sets will prevent characters from blending into sets. Colors can be selected in harmony or disharmony with one another or for their coolness or warmth to affect the emotional impact of a scene. Colors can also affect brightness contrast for black-and-white recordings. Finally, colors, like shapes, can be used symbolically, or they can be used repeatedly in conjunction with specific characters, settings, and themes.

Unity, balance, emphasis, proportion, and movement are basic design principles. Unity implies the blending together of design elements through repetition, simplicity, and common themes. There are four different types of graphic balance: symmetrical, asymmetrical, radial, and occult. Proportion refers to the scale of one element with respect to another, and movement in a design can be real or imaginary.

Scenic design includes set design, costume design, and makeup. It begins with a careful analysis of the script and research into appropriate sets and costumes. Set design occurs in distinct stages, from the drawing of layouts and floor plans to the actual construction of sets.

Temporary sets are frequently constructed out of flats and risers. Flats are relatively lightweight sections of temporary walls that can be fastened together using C-clamps or other devices to give the appearance of an interior or exterior wall. Risers are sections of an elevated floor that can be fastened together. Flats and risers can be easily stored in a studio scene shop. More permanent sets may be constructed out of larger set materials that cannot be reused. An economical and convenient alternative to set design and construction is the use of a cyclorama.

Costumes and clothing are either designed specifically for a production or procured from a rental house or studio wardrobe. Costumes should be consistent with the period or mood and be fully coordinated with sets.

There are two types of performer makeup: cosmetic and prosthetic. Cosmetic makeup enhances a performer's beauty, hiding imperfections and blemishes. Prosthetic makeup dramatically transforms the appearance of a performer, giving great facial versatility to the type of roles he or she can play.

Scenic design interacts with other aspects of production, such as lighting, performer movement, and camera and mike placement. Scenic design is an important and integral part of the overall production process.

Additional Readings

Barsacq, Leon. *Caligari's Cabinet and Other Grand Illusions: A History of Film Design*. New York: The New American Library, 1978.

Baygan, Lee. *Techniques of Three-Dimensional Makeup*. New York: Watson-Guptill, 1982.

Kehoe, Vincent J. R. *The Technique of Film and Television Make-Up for Color and Black and White*. New York: Hastings House, 1969.

Millerson, Gerald. *Basic TV Staging*. New York: Hastings House, 1974.

Wade, Robert J. *Designing for TV: The Arts and Crafts in Television Production*. New York: Pelligrini and Cudahy, 1952.

Whyte, Ron, et.al. *Designing for Television: News Sets*. Lincoln, Nebraska: Boomer's Printing Co./Broadcast Designers Assoc., 1980.

Exercises

1. Design and construct a functionalist setting, such as the set for a news or talk show. The placement of stationary set objects should facilitate recording. They should not obstruct camera or performer movements. Colors, lines, and shapes should be pleasant to look at but somewhat muted so that they do not distract attention away from the

speaking talent. Make sure that the set is unified and pleasing to the eye when recorded from many different camera angles and distances.

2. Design a realistic room interior on the basis of the description of this setting in a script, short story, or novel. Carefully select and coordinate furniture, props, sets, and costumes so that all of these elements create a realistic impression of time and place. Color and brightness levels of foreground and background elements, sets, and costumes should contrast but not clash with each other. Provide detailed layouts drawn to scale so that the set can be efficiently and accurately constructed. Incorporate elements into the set that are economical to obtain or already on hand, such as specific flats, props, set dressings and pieces of furniture.

3. Use a cyclorama to create a setting which has no borders where walls and/or ceilings meet so that space appears infinite. Use lighting techniques discussed in chapter 9 to create abstract shapes, colors, and patterns which create a dramatic and unusual sense of space. Discover ways of manipulating the viewer's sense of spatial perspective by simply altering the lighting.

4. Using the description of a specific setting in a dramatic script, short story, or novel, find an existing building which meets the essential criteria needed to represent this place. Assess the difficulties inherent in using this facility from the standpoint of recording and determine what elements will have to be removed or added to make this an ideal setting.

CHAPTER 12

Graphics and Animation

Graphic design, like scenic design, is concerned with structuring pictorial content. Graphic images should be closely tied to overall scenic design, including sets and costumes. For example, the red titles and sepia toned still photographs (black and white pictures with an overall reddish-brown colortone) at the beginning of *Bonnie and Clyde* (1967) foreshadow the violence and bloodshed to come and establish the 1930s setting of the film through costuming and props in each photograph. The ''fence board'' lettering design used for ''Hee Haw'' titles maintains the rural, country atmosphere projected by sets and costumes on this musical comedy television show. A good graphic design organizes visual information so that it can be efficiently communicated to viewers. Graphic designs organize many different types of information, including lettering and illustrations. Titles are often the first images presented on a videotape or film, and they must set a context for what is to follow. Graphic titles and illustrations answer questions about who, what, when, where, why, and how or how much.

Graphic images often convey information more directly than speech and live-action images. They can boil down complex ideas into simple concepts, which are represented by shapes, words, or numbers. Titles and illustrations can clarify the ideas inherent in more complex, live-action images and speech, by removing nonessential information and focusing the viewer's attention on a few simple elements.

Graphic designs provide a basis for one of the most creative areas of video and film production, called animation. Animation, which introduces motion to graphic images, is frequently used to depict actions and events that either cannot be recorded in live action or that would fail to have the same charm or afford an artist the same degree of control and freedom, if conventional recording techniques were used.

This chapter examines basic principles of graphic design, common practices concerning the production of titles and illustrations, and principles and practices of animation.

PRINCIPLES OF GRAPHIC DESIGN

The best graphics often have very simple designs. Trying to convey too much information at one time produces ineffective or unintelligible messages. Each image should convey one general thought or idea. Everything presented within that image must contribute to a central theme. A complex array of statistics can often be boiled down to a simple graph or chart. An arithmetic line or curve chart, a bar or column chart, a pie chart, or simply an array of appropriate symbols can graphically portray information much more effectively than an oral presentation alone.

Titles and subtitles that clarify visual information or give credit to contributors must be clear and concise. Good titles and subtitles do not crowd the image, yet title size is often used to convey their relative importance.

Illustrations should not be filled with complex, busy images. It is much more effective to present a simplified outline, a caricature or a symbolic illustration, than a highly detailed drawing or photograph to illustrate a particular idea. Everything extraneous should be removed. Simple images are generally more intelligible images. They eliminate confusion and frequently have great aesthetic and emotional impact.

Perceptual Organization

Graphic designers rely on a number of basic principles of perception, such as proximity, similarity, figure/ground, equilibrium, closure, and correspondence. All of these principles are based on the common ways in which our eyes and minds attempt to organize visual images. Graphic artists build these perceptual principles into their designs as visual guides to quick identification and rapid comprehension.

Proximity   Objects placed in close proximity to each other form common groupings. Conventional wisdom has it that graphic information should be grouped into common topics within the frame for greater intelligibility. A promotional graphic for a new television program, for example, groups separately information concerning names and titles, time of presentation, and illustrations depicting program content into different parts of the frame. Logical groupings help viewers sort out different kinds of information contained within a single frame. It is unwise to try to pack too much information into a single graphic image. A second graphic frame is usually required, when another topic is introduced or there is a great deal of information to convey about a single topic.

Similarity   The perception of similarity between shapes and objects in a frame provides another means by which graphic images can be organized. Objects with similar shapes, sizes, colors, and directions of movement are united into common groups. Any deviation from this similarity, such as a runner moving in the oppo-

site direction from the pack or a black object in the midst of white objects, draws immediate attention on the basis of its lack of similarity.

Figure/Ground   Figure/ground refers to the relationship between backgrounds and foregrounds. Our eyes try to organize visual images into background fields and foreground objects. Some visual illusions are ambiguous, and we can alternate the foreground and background to create different shapes and objects from the same picture. A corporate logo or graphic marks which consist of letters and words, such as Eaton Corporation or Playmakers Repertory Company, combines white and black letters which reverse figure and ground. The reversal in the Playmakers' logo suggests a rising curtain that is consistent with its theatrical subject matter. Symbols and signs which use figure/ground relationships can be effective means of gaining audience attention and communicating ideas.

Equilibrium   Another way in which our eyes try to organize graphic images is through a principle of equilibrium. An image in equilibrium is logically balanced and ordered. Equilibrium can be based on natural scientific laws, such as gravity or magnetic attraction, as well as a balancing of object weights and sizes on either side of a center line in a frame. This organizing principle reflects a well-ordered, logical universe. When images defy a sense of balance or accepted physical or scientific laws, they are in disequilibrium, which can arouse interest, but also cause distracting confusion. Graphic images that are in equilibrium are quickly and efficiently apprehended and comprehended.

Figure/ground designs and logos often add viewer interest by creating ambiguous images. The Playmaker's Repertory Company logo suggests a rising curtain and links the title of the theater company with its function.

Closure   Viewers have a natural tendency to try to complete an unfinished form, a principle which is called closure. An open form is ambiguous and leaves some questions unanswered. A partially hidden form can still be identified because we expect good continuation of a form off screen or behind another object, but this is a projection onto the image of our need for closure. A designer can frustrate or fulfill our desire for closure by completing graphic forms or leaving them partially incomplete. The former seem stable and resolved, while the latter seem unstable, although they sometimes stimulate creative and imaginative impressions.

Correspondence or Iconic Analogy

Correspondence or iconic analogy is a principle by which viewers extend graphic images into analogous human experiences. The ability of a graphic image of food to stimulate hunger, a smoking gun to arouse fear, or an attractive figure to arouse desire is based on their correspondence with socially learned or acquired experiences. Viewers often organize and comprehend images by projecting them into a world of common human experience.

Readability

Image Size   The size and amount of detail in an image affects readability, which refers to the ease of deciphering and comprehending graphic images. (See Figure 12.1.) The size of a typeface or style of lettering, for example, is an important determinant of how easy it is to read a graphic image. Type of extremely small point size is usually avoided in video production because small titles are difficult to read on a film or television screen. Point

Figure 12.1

Image Size and Readability

Graphic images are much easier to read if the lettering style and size of the typeface used are in proportion to the image area.

size refers to the height of letters; the higher the point size, the larger the letter. (The text you are reading is in 10 point type.) Lettering sizes smaller than $\frac{1}{10}$ to $\frac{1}{20}$ of the full picture height should be avoided in television graphics. Graphic artists also avoid finely drawn lettering and serifs, which are delicate decorative lines that are often difficult to reproduce. Because of the limited size, resolution, and sharpness of television images, boldface type is recommended for titles and subtitles.

Plain backgrounds give prominence to foreground titles and lettering. A highly detailed or multi-toned background is distracting. Good contrast between foreground and background tones and colors is essential for legibility. When titles are superimposed over live-action images, bright lettering should be used, preferably with some kind of border, drop shadow, or edge outline, which gives greater legibility and three-dimensionality.

Image Area   An important determinant of composition in television and film graphics is the aspect ratio or frame dimensions of the recorded and displayed image. As noted earlier, frame dimensions vary in television and film. The aspect ratio, or proportion of height to width, of television images is 4:3 or 1.33:1, while projected film images vary somewhat in terms of their aspect ratios. (See chapter 5.)

A standard 35mm still camera film frame, which is often used for projecting graphic illustrations in a telecine, has an

Figure 12.2   35mm Slide Versus TV Frame
A video camera cannot capture the full frame image of a 35mm slide. The edges of the slide must be cut off when the photographic image is transferred to video and displayed as a TV frame on a television monitor. A slide must be carefully composed when it is originally photographed to prevent essential information from falling outside the TV frame.

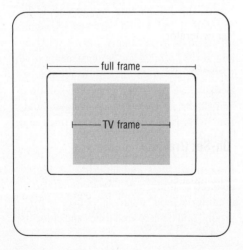

aspect ratio of 5:3 or 1.66:1. Graphic images must be composed for specific formats and aspects ratios. When a still photographic slide, as shown in Figure 12.2, is placed in the telecine, for example, some of the information recorded on the sides of the frame will be cut off by the narrower aspect ratio of the television camera.

Scanning or Full-Aperture Area   The **scanning area** (Figure 12.3) is the full field of view picked up by the television camera pickup tube. The **full-aperture area** is the equivalent in film of this area. It refers to the entire field of view recorded on an individual frame. Any graphic illustration or title card must be framed in the camera so that it is slightly larger than the actual scanning or full-aperture area so that the edges of the card in do not appear in the frame. The scanning area should be about 1½″ inside the outer edge of a 14″ × 11″ or 11″ × 8½″ illustration or title card.

Essential Area   The essential area of the frame is the safe recording portion of the frame. (See Figure 12.3.) Graphic information is placed within the essential area, so that it will not be cut off by somewhat overscanned TV receivers (home TV's usually reproduce less than the full camera frame because the horizontal scanning is expanded) or film projector apertures. The essential area of the video camera should be at least 2″ within the scanning area on a 14″ × 11″ or 11″ × 8½″ card, so that there is no possibility of eliminating essential information. If a graphic image falls within the essential area, an artist can be confident that all key information will be safely recorded and projected.

Brightness Contrast Maintaining brightness contrast between different lines, shapes, and masses is extremely important when designing graphic images for television and film. A television graphic designer cannot rely exclusively on *color contrast,* since a television program may be received in *either* color *or* black-and-white. Adjacent colors should have gray value brightness contrast of at least 30 percent, that is, each object or shape should be 30 percent brighter or darker than the one next to it. Brightness contrast between different shapes and objects can be determined by using a gray scale. A **gray scale** consists of a sequential series of gray tones from white to mid-gray to black. Pure white has virtually 100 percent reflectance, while pure black has 0 percent. The midpoint on the gray scale is about 18 percent reflectance, that is, about 18 percent of the light falling on this shade of gray is actually reflected back to the eye. In order to maintain adequate brightness contrast, dark letters and shapes should be placed on light backgrounds and vice versa.

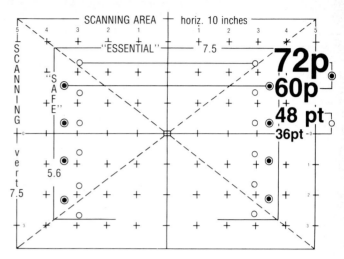

Figure 12.3 TV/Film Graphics Planning Guide
A TV/film graphics planning guide helps a graphic artist to select and compose type within the camera frame. All key information must fall within the essential area of the frame. The scanning area is the full frame captured by a video camera, some of which may be cut off by a television receiver when the videotape is actually viewed. Various point sizes of type are indicated on the right side of the planning guide.

TYPES OF GRAPHICS

Graphics can be divided into two different categories on the basis of the placement and use of graphic images during production. **On-set** graphics are recorded by cameras as part of the set during actual production. **Off-set** graphics are not in the immediate view of the cameras recording the set during production. They may come from a title card, a slide in the telecine, or a computer-generated image fed directly into the switcher. Graphic images can be divided into two additional categories, namely titles and illustrations, on the basis of the nature of the images themselves. **Titles** are various forms of lettering, which either accompany illustrations and live-action images or are presented as written text. The lettering for titles can be drawn by hand, produced mechanically, reproduced photographically, or created electronically on a device called a character generator. **Illustrations** are visual images, such as charts, graphs, and pictures, which are less detailed than live-action images. They can be hand drawn, photographed, or produced with the aid of computer graphics equipment.

On-Set Graphics

The most commonly used types of on-set graphics are hand-held cards, photographic blowups, and three-dimensional graphic set pieces.

Hand-Held Cards

Hand-held cards are images that a performer holds up to the camera during a scene. The talent controls the timing and placement of this type of graphic illustration. It is frequently used for informational or educational programs. The card must be held very steady, while a camera zooms or dollies in on graphic image.

Photographic Enlargements

Still photographs can be blown up or enlarged so that they provide a convenient background or backdrop on the set. The photographs are usually poster size or larger and are often mounted on stiff cardboard or plywood. These **photographic enlargements** can add depth and dimension to a scene or simply place an on-screen narrator in the proper context. Such photographs should have a matte, rather than a shiny or glossy surface, so that they do not reflect a great deal of light, and they should be positioned so that no glare or reflection is directed to the camera lens.

Graphic Set Pieces

Three-dimensional structures placed on the set for illustration purposes are called **graphic set pieces**. A weather board is a commonly used graphic set piece in television news production. The weather board allows various weather symbols and temperature figures to be positioned on a local, state, national, or international map. A chalkboard on which the talent can write or draw with chalk is also a graphic set piece. During elections, tally boards are sometimes used to present updated voting returns. Some tally boards change figures manually or mechanically, while others are entirely electronic in operation.

Off-Set Graphics

The most commonly used off-set graphics devices are camera cards, slides, the character generator, and computer graphics systems. Camera cards and slides are considered in this section, while the character generator and computer graphics systems are discussed more fully later under titles and illustrations.

Camera Cards

Camera cards are titles and illustrations that are placed on an easel so that they can be efficiently recorded by an off-set camera. The cards usually consist of 14″ × 11″ pieces of cardboard on which letters, drawings, or tables and charts have been mounted. Four 14″ × 11″ studio cards for titles, credits, and illustrations can be cut out of one standard 28″ × 22″ poster board. The dimensions of the card must be compatible with the aspect ratio or dimensions of the television or film frame. The surface of the card is usually flat and dull to minimize glare. Camera cards can be accessed during multiple-camera television production by pressing the designated camera button on the switcher.

Camera cards are usually placed on an **easel**, which is an adjustable display platform or graphic support. The lights on the easel, which illuminate the card, are normally placed at a 45 degree angle from the card surface to minimize light reflection in the camera lens. When the cards are attached to the easel by rings, they can easily be flipped, while maintaining perfect registration for the camera. It is also possible to zoom in to different elements in a card or photograph. This adds dynamic movement to static images. Dissolving from one card illustration to another is another common technique. The camera should record a card or illustration directly head-on to avoid keystone distortion. Keystone distortion exaggerates the size of the top, bottom, left or right side of a card, when the camera positioning is slightly off dead center.

Photographic Slides   **Slides** are photographic transparencies in plastic or cardboard frames, which can be fed into a slide projector. A slide projector projects a positive visual image into a telecine or film chain, where it is recorded by a television camera and sent to the switcher. The slide can then be used as a separate television image or combined with other images, using various techniques and special effects on the switcher.

LETTERING AND TITLES

Lettering and titles are used for a variety of purposes in video and film production. One of their most common uses is to introduce the name of a film and television program and to list the **credits** or names of people who have contributed in some way to the production. The opening titles of a program are called a **title** or **credit sequence**. Another common use of titles is to clarify live-action images. **Subtitles** or **name keys** are titles placed in the bottom third of the video or film frame, indicating the person or place being shown. Lettering and titles can also be used to accompany and clarify graphic illustrations, indicating the basic factors depicted in a chart or table, for example. Finally, lettering and titles can be presented as **pure text**, that is, without any other visual accompaniment. Textual materials are used to convey written information in the form of electronic newspapers, advertising, or financial statements.

Types of Lettering

It is important to understand some basic methods and principles of lettering before trying to apply specific techniques to different title uses, purposes, and situations. Experienced artists and calligraphers sometimes draw letters for film and television titles by hand, but a more common technique is to produce them mechanically, photographically, or electronically.

Mechanical Lettering   Mechanical lettering can be created for television and film by using one of two common methods: rub-on lettering and punch-out lettering.

Rub-on lettering consists of multiple copies of each letter in the alphabet attached to a clear plastic sheet. The letters can be applied to virtually any surface, such as a paper title card, by simply rubbing the back of the plastic over the letter to be transferred. Rub-on lettering will adhere to almost any surface, including clear acetate, paper, cardboard, and photographs. To give the appearance of uniform spacing between letters, parallel strokes should be spaced farther apart and round letters closer together. Spacing between words and lines should be uniform, with no more than the width of one small ''n'' between words or the height of one letter between lines.

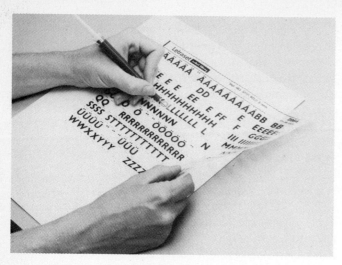

Rub-on lettering or press type. The letters can be applied to almost any surface and help in the creation of credits or titles for a production.

Lettering can also be produced on a punch-out machine, which simply punches the letters out of a continuous roll of plastic. A punch-out machine functions much the same as a household plastic tape label maker. It produces a continuous strip of letters containing a specific word or line, which can then be positioned on a card. The spacing between letters is controlled by the machine's advance mechanism. The Kroy lettering process combines punch-out and rub-on lettering techniques. A specific sequence of letters with uniform spacing can be prepared on the machine and then rubbed onto the title card.

Photographic Lettering   Lettering can be produced photographically by machines such as a VariTyper Headliner. This machine allows an operator to select different letters by turning a wheel. Each letter is then photographed on internally processed 35mm film. Different typefaces and sizes can be obtained by replacing one wheel with another. White letters can be produced on a black background or black letters on a white background. More sophisticated photographic lettering machines allow the operator to use a terminal to select from several typefaces and select position letters on a CRT television screen before a photographic reproduction is made.

Electronic Lettering   The easiest and most efficient way to produce lettering for television is to use an electronic character generator. A **character generator** or **CG** functions like a computer word processor in that it produces words directly on a television screen. It consists of a typewriter keyboard, a small computer, and a television monitor. Letters are positioned on the screen by means of a cursor, a blinking light on the TV screen that is manipulated from the keyboard. Different typefaces or fonts, such as roman and italic letters, different type sizes, and letter borders, edge outlines, and drop shadows can be selected at the touch of a button. A CG is more than a word processor. **Logos** or special graphic identifiers, such as product logos in advertising, and symbols can also be stored. Some CGs can use computer graphics and provide multicolored lettering. A full frame of information can be recorded in **disc frame storage** and accessed later by referring to its designated page or frame number. Several frames of written material can be stored and immediately retrieved during a news, weather, or sports broadcast, for example. The output of a CG or disc storage can be keyed into any video switcher. Electronic keying and matting allows the lettering from a CG to be combined with different backgrounds and live-action images.

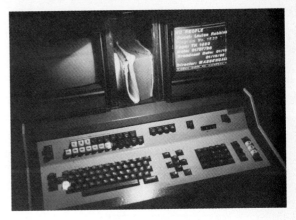

Top left and right: A chyron character generator with still frame storage and retrieval control. Left: A still frame storage unit, which allow electronic lettering to be added to video images and digitally stored as still frames of information.

Subtitles

Titles and subtitles are frequently superimposed on or combined with illustrations in both film and video. Superimposed lettering must contrast sharply with its background, if it is to be legible. Bright letters can be superimposed on a dark back-

ground. White backgrounds are, of course, consciously avoided in video. A light gray or off-white background is often used instead with dark lettering. It is usually best to minimize the detail and design complexity of the background on which lettering will be superimposed. When titles or subtitles have to be superimposed on a detailed photograph or a live-action film or video sequence, a consistently light or dark area of the image is often selected for the placement of lettering. Borders are also used for greater legibility. Video titles can be superimposed by recording them from a telecine or on an illustration card with a studio camera and then mixing them in the switcher, as discussed in chapter 6. With some film cameras, titles can be superimposed during production by winding the film back in the camera after live-action images have been recorded and re-exposing it to white letters on a black background. Superimposition of film titles is normally done in postproduction, however.

Credit or Title Sequences

Credit and title sequences present an opportunity for creative, abstract expression on the part of a graphic artist. They are carefully designed to communicate the central message and feelings of a film or television program. The opening credits or title sequence offers the audience an introduction to the basic subject matter of the program. It must arouse the audience's interest, excitement, and curiosity. Titles should integrate well with overall scenic design.

Graphic design and lettering styles should be appropriate to the overall subject matter. Sloppy lettering and graphic design provide a poor introduction and arouse a low level of expectation. Uneven, poorly spaced or off-centered mechanical lettering looks amateurish. If no one with good mechanical lettering skills is available, electronic lettering machines such as a character generator or even a good quality electric typewriter can be effectively used. Hand-drawn lettering offers another possibility, but normally requires considerable skill. Lettering styles can be related to the program subject matter or topic. Opening and closing credits should be well integrated with other sequences. Above all, imagination and creativity should be exercised.

ILLUSTRATIONS

Illustrations are drawings, photographs, graphs, charts, diagrams, and maps that provide visualizations of abstract concepts. Illustrations are usually intended to simplify information and make it more accessible and understandable. Charts, graphs, diagrams, and maps are often used to display trends or unravel complicated ideas or relationships inherent in statistical data. Illustrations can be used redundantly as an accompaniment to verbal descriptions or independently to add additional information that cannot be as effectively presented through the written or spoken word. Illustrations can be drawn by hand, photographically recorded, or produced electronically.

Hand-Drawn Illustrations

A graphic illustration usually begins with a rough pencil sketch. This sketch simply outlines the basic design; its shape and composition. One of the best ways for an inexperienced designer to achieve a basic outline is to trace the outline of a previously constructed illustration, such as a map, on tracing paper. Conventional maps and illustrations contain too much detail to be used as film or television illustrations, but their outlines often provide a useful starting point. Colors are usually added to the image after the basic outline of shapes has been constructed. It is important to maintain both brightness and color contrast between various shapes and borders on the image, by selecting contrasting color hues and brightnesses. Sometimes specific colors are dictated by product association or convention. A map may require the color blue for the ocean and green or brown for land. Familiar color and shape associations should be used whenever possible to facilitate communication and minimize confusion. Clarity and simplicity are the hallmarks of a good hand-drawn illustration.

Photographic Illustrations

Still photographic illustrations, such as slides and prints, should be clear and unambiguous. They should be in sharp focus, have a good range of tones from white to black, low contrast, immediately recognizable subjects, no extraneous details, and known objects for scale and size comparison. Busy photographs distract attention from the main point they are supposed to communicate. Although "real world" photographs obviously have more detailed complexity than drawn illustrations, they should be carefully composed to eliminate distracting or extraneous information.

A copy stand can be used to photograph art work or other photographic and printed illustrations. A **copy stand** consists of a 35mm camera secured to a movable platform so that it can be raised and lowered to frame the art work. Copy stand lights are normally placed at a 45 degree angle to the art work to minimize glare. Polarizer filters, which function like the Polaroid lenses used for sunglasses, can also be placed over the camera lens or the lights to reduced unwanted reflections from shiny surfaces, such as clear acetate cels. A flat, nonglossy photographic surface reduces glare as does a nonglare coating that can be sprayed onto the surface of a glossy photograph or a highly reflectant piece of art work.

Photographic prints can be mounted so that they can be recorded by a film or television camera. Positive prints made from 35mm negative film are normally used. Photographic prints can be blown up to 8″ × 10″ or 11″ × 14″ from 35mm negatives. The prints can then be mounted on a rigid piece of cardboard in one of two ways: 1) rubber cement can be applied to

A mounting press used to mount titles and graphics.

the back of the photograph, which is then pressed onto the mounting board with a book or heavy object until the cement dries and the excess is wiped off; or 2) a dry mounting press can be used. A **mounting press** consists of a heated set of pressure plates. Mounting tissue is placed between the back of the photograph and the mounting board; this sandwiched material is then secured inside the mounting press, where heat and pressure are applied. A piece of plain paper is often placed over the face of the photograph to protect it during the twenty or thirty seconds that it remains within the heated press. A dry mounting press usually provides a more permanent mount than rubber cement, but it requires additional materials and expense.

Computer Graphics

One of the most promising applications of computer technology to film and television production is **computer graphics**. The advantage of computer graphics systems, like that of the character generator, is that the images do not have to be recorded by a camera and individual frames can be digitally stored.

A variety of hardware and software systems are currently available for use in video and film production. Most systems allow the operator or artist to control the three basic elements of graphic design: line, shape, and color. Images can be created directly on the screen, using a light pencil or stylus. The artist can select and control various lines and shapes, as well as image size, color, and placement on the screen. It is also possible to use a stylus to trace a hand-drawn sketch or outline so that it can be computer manipulated and stored in disc form. Some computers have frame-grabbers, which allow a single video frame from a camera or VCR to be manipulated by the computer. Some computer software allows graphics programs to be integrated with animation programs to create apparent motion. Images can be placed in disc storage and accessed at any time. A graphics computer that has a standard NTSC video signal output can be fed directly to a VCR or a switcher.

The primary advantages of computer graphics systems are savings in time and convenience. In preproduction use, storyboards can be quickly and efficiently generated and then modified immediately prior to actual production to mirror changes. Hard copies can then be printed for camera operators and other members of the production team. During production, illustrations such as charts, graphs, and drawings can be generated quickly and used immediately. Computer-generated graphics are often used and quickly updated for weather forecasts. Titles and lettering can be corrected immediately and then added to images to clarify the information they contain. All of this information can then be conveniently stored and accessed during production without using a camera. Images can also be modified efficiently and easily during production. While sophisticated computer graphics systems are still very expensive, low-cost systems, such as those available with many home computer systems, can be inexpensively purchased and integrated into a television production facility.

ANIMATION

Animation creates apparent movement and motion from still-frame images. A series of single film or video frames in which recorded objects or materials gradually change their spatial position within the frame are recorded individually and sequentially. When they are played back at normal speed (twenty-four frames per second in film or thirty frames per second in video) they produce apparent motion.

Animation is based on an animator's knowledge of time and motion. An animator must be able to break down real or actual motion into its component parts so that motion can be artificially constructed out of static images. One of the best means of analyzing motion is to examine the individual frames of a live-action film. A motion picture camera records twenty-four frames every second. Each frame represents $\frac{1}{24}$th of the change in the subject's spatial positioning that takes place during that second. By looking at the amount of change that occurs between the successive frames of a live-action sequence, an animator can begin to determine how much change there should normally be in the position and movement of objects between successive animated frames.

It is not always necessary to create a different image for each film frame, however. A smooth illusion of continuous motion can often be obtained by recording two identical frames of each change in position. Thus only twelve different images may be required for each second's duration of the final sequence, although single-frame versus double-frame animation is always a trade-off between smoothness and cost. The animator's job is to create the desired illusion of movement. Slower movements will require the preparation of more individual frames and smaller changes of position between each frame than faster movements. Time and distance are interrelated. An object that moves a distance of two feet in twenty-four frames obviously moves more quickly in the final sequence than an object that moves only one foot in twenty-four frames.

CAMERA: Eleanor is a maid. We see her moving her way down the aisles toward the doors. Zoom in from LS to MCU as she moves toward the doors.

AUDIO: Eleanor Rigby picks up the rice in a church where a wedding has been.

CAMERA: MCU of Eleanor. She opens the church doors and we see her dream.

AUDIO: Lives in a dream

A storyboard helps in the visualization of an idea and acts as a guide to the actual creation of animated images. Here the camera tracks right along the church pews in this visualization of lyrics from John Lennon and Paul McCartney's song "Eleanor Rigby," in a storyboard for an animated music video.

Animation Preproduction

Storyboards   An animated sequence often begins with the construction of a storyboard. In this case, the **storyboard** is a series of sequential sketches which depict the composition and content of each shot or key action in an animated sequence. A storyboard is very similar to a newspaper comic strip. It helps a graphic artist or animator visualize the entire sequence on paper prior to preparing the final images. The storyboard can be used to communicate the animator's basic idea and strategy to a producer. It can also serve as a blueprint or guide to the actual creation and recording of images. Storyboard images are not as detailed as the actual film or television images will be. They usually consist of simple sketches, line drawings, or photographs. A storyboard communicates simply and clearly the basic idea of a sequence.

Sound Analysis   Many animators design their storyboards in conjunction with prerecorded music, sound effects, and/or voice tracks. Because timing or synchronization between sound and images is often crucial to the success of an animated sequence, music and sound are initially re-corded and analyzed. In film animation, the music and sound are transferred to magnetic film and the base side of the magnetic film is marked with a china marker or grease pencil to indicate specific synchronization points between sounds and images. A log is kept of the frame numbers of images where specific sounds occur so that the corresponding images can be perfectly synchronized. Synchroniza-tion can be achieved in video animation by dubbing the music and sounds to videotape with a control track or SMPTE time code reference. A **sound log** or breakdown of information produced by sound track anal-ysis can be combined with the frames of a storyboard. A designer can then tell ex-actly how many seconds, and therefore how many film or video frames, are re-quired for each storyboard frame. Frames for each point of synchronization between sounds and images can be included in the storyboard so that there is no confusion about precisely where a specific action is to occur. Once the storyboard has been constructed in conjunction with the re-corded music and sounds, the actual pro-duction phase of animation begins.

Types of Animation

Many different types of images and ob-jects can be animated, including hand-drawn illustrations, paper cutouts, pup-pets, clay figures, still photographs of live actions, and computer graphic images. All of these different forms of animation are based on single-frame recording tech-niques. It is often helpful to distinguish between flat and plastic animation, as well as between film and electronic animation. **Flat animation** includes such techniques as **cel animation** in which individual il-lustrations are drawn for almost every frame of picture. **Plastic animation** en-compasses the use of three-dimensional figures, such as puppets or clay figures. Single-frame recording of people and three-dimensional objects is sometimes called **pixillation**. In a sense, all of these techniques or types of animation elevate the graphic artist or animator to the status of director, editor, and scenic designer.

Bottom left: An example of cel animation. Note the three-dimensional effect that is created when the foreground cel is lifted up from the basic background cel.
Bottom right: An animation rostrum or table used for exact framing and registration of the cels.

Flat Animation   Flat animation refers to the recording of two-dimensional images using single-frame recording techniques. One of the most common forms of flat animation is cel animation. **Cels** are individual sheets of clear acetate on which images can be drawn or painted, usually with ink and opaque watercolors. An ink outline is traced onto each cel from an **outline sketch**. An outline sketch is made on paper for each cel and a film of these sketches, known as a **pencil test**, is often made so that corrections can be made prior to the creation of actual acetate cels. The cel is painted on the opposite side so that the ink lines do not run and so that the rough surface texture of the paint is not apparent. Cels are preperforated with holes at one end so they can be inserted over the pegs of a movable table called an animation **rostrum** for precise registration and framing. An **animation stand** consists of a rostrum, lights, and a movable camera platform.

Basic Cel Animation Techniques   Cel animation gives the animator or graphic artist complete control over the design of the image. However, drawing each frame individually on a cel can be quite time consuming and expensive, so many shortcuts are used to conserve time. Because cels are transparent, they can be sandwiched together to combine images drawn on different cels. A background cel can be used over and over again while changes are made in the placement of foreground objects, eliminating the need to redraw the background for each frame. Individual movements of characters' feet, hands, and mouths can be repeated or **recycled** with different bodies and backgrounds. A series of lip movements synchronized to various consonant or vowel sounds can be used

repeatedly rather than drawn individually for each occurrence. To cut costs more drastically, some animators draw only every fourth or fifth frame of recorded film or videotape. This can, of course, lead to rougher and therefore less pleasing animation.

Rotoscoping   Another commonly used technique for cutting costs and increasing cel-animation efficiency is called rotoscoping. In **rotoscoping** (Figure 12.4) a sequence is first filmed in live action; the individual frames of the motion picture are

Top: These mouth actions are frequently used in animating cartoon dialogues. Bottom: The same mouth action in use for heads of different shapes and sizes.

Figure 12.4
Rotoscoping

projector
(frame-by-frame)

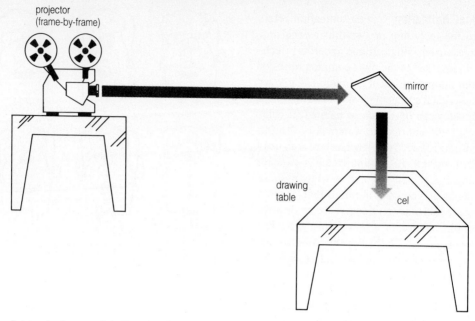

mirror

drawing
table

cel

Rotoscoping is accomplished by using a still-frame film projector to project individual frames of pre-recorded live action onto a copy stand so that key figures and actions can be drawn by hand. Representational images can be made more abstract, and the motion necessary for animation is inherent in the changes from one frame of live action to the next. Rotoscoping sometimes saves money and time, but it produces images that lack the vitality of original animation.

then projected on a cel and an outline of the objects in the frame is drawn and hand colored. Subjects are normally photographed against a contrasting background so that outlines are clearly visible. The drawn outlines are then colored like standard hand-drawn animation cels. While rotoscoping makes the production of cels more efficient, it often produces images that are less aesthetically pleasing than hand-drawn animation.

The difference between rotoscoped and hand-drawn animation is similar to the difference between naturalistic painting and caricature. A caricature of a person emphasizes or exaggerates characteristic

features. In a like manner, hand-drawn cel animation often uses nonrepresentational figures and techniques such as image **squashing** and **stretching** to exaggerate motion. An animator can sometimes create a more vivid impression of motion by exaggerating the compression of objects as gravity pulls them to the ground and then stretching or expanding their shape as they jump or run, temporarily escaping the pull of gravity. Animated motion is not always a direct copy of live action. These subtle differences in apparent motion become obvious when rotoscoped images are compared to original hand-drawn images.

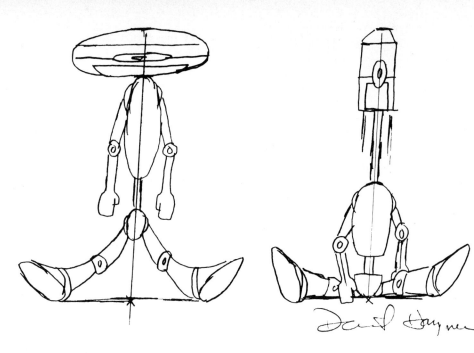

Cel Movement   The illusion of movement in cel animation can be achieved in one of two ways: by drawing a different cel for each change of position of objects within the frame or by moving the cel itself on the rostrum of the animation stand between recordings. If movement is to be achieved through differences between cels, each cel in the sequence must be placed in exactly the same position within the camera frame by using the registration pegs. On the other hand, if motion is to be achieved by moving the cel, this can be done by using the horizontal and vertical controls of the rostrum. One problem that sometimes stands in the way of physically moving a cel is that the background movement within the two-dimensional image may seem unnatural when it moves at the same rate as the foreground. In live-action photography, the background and foreground seem to move at different rates, providing an illusion of depth and three-dimensionality. This problem is sometimes solved by placing the background cels on a separate **peg bar**, or set of registration pegs, on the same rostrum or table so that they can be moved at a slower speed than the foreground. Virtually all animation stands are equipped with double peg bars so that backgrounds and foregrounds can be moved independently of one another.

Paper Cutouts   Hand-drawn illustrations are not the only flat images that can be animated. Paper or fabric cutouts and still photographs can also be set into motion. A paper cutout of a person or animal can be constructed so that it has moving body parts. It can then be placed over a variety of backgrounds so that it seems to

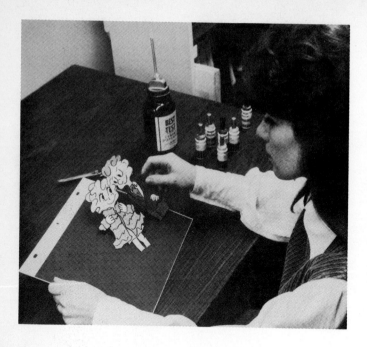

Cutouts such as these can be moved around by hand from one position to another.

come alive and move on the screen. A flicker effect can also be achieved by recording frames of colored paper in between frames of specific photographs or illustrations. The change in photographs can be timed to the beat of music. In this way what might otherwise be a boring presentation of static images acquires kinetic energy. Still photographs and printed illustrations, such as magazine images, can be animated through single frame techniques as those used by Frank Mouris in his famous *Frank Film*. Mouris' film is as much as a feat of optical printing, discussed later in chapter 14, as of animation.

Plastic Animation Many different types of three-dimensional figures and objects can be animated by using single-frame recording techniques. Puppets, clay figures, miniature vehicles, and even still

frames of live action can be animated. While hand puppets and marionettes are usually recorded in live action so that the mouth and body movements can be synchronized to speech or music, it is possible to animate more rigid puppets and figures by moving them slightly between frames.

Unlike the animator of flat, two-dimensional characters, however, the plastic animator must create a miniature three-dimensional world of sets and props within which puppets and figures will move. Careful attention must be paid to minute details. Backgrounds must be painted to scale, and everything must be proportional to the size of the figures. The camera is usually placed in a horizontal position with respect to the scene rather than above it as with an animation stand. Miniature vehicles, such as cars and trucks, can also be animated through single-frame techniques. Sometimes these animated miniatures are used as a substitute for more costly and dangerous stunts and special effects in live-action films. An animated three-dimensional figure sequence is shot much like a live-action scene, except that the pictures are recorded frame by frame. More than one camera is frequently used so that action does not have to be repeated for different shots, as it is for single-camera live action recording. The animation of three-dimensional objects sacrifices the artist's ability to simulate the blurring effect of photographing live-action figures in rapid movement and mechanical, non-life-like movement sometimes results.

Metamorphosis Clay or malleable plastic material is often animated so that unique shapes and actions can be recorded. A technique known as **metamorphosis**, in which one figure gradually changes into a totally different form, can be accomplished with clay as well as with images drawn on cels. A famous animated film, called *Clay*, shows the evolution of one life form from another using clay metamorphosis. Virtually any shape and type of movement can be constructed using clay or malleable plastic materials.

Pixillation   Human figures can also be animated by a technique known as **pixillation**. Images of human beings can be pixillated by recording one frame, moving the image and then recording another frame. Pixillation has been used in many films to animate images of human beings so that they seem to perform extraordinary feats. In Norman McLaren's famous film *Neighbors* (1955), two neighbors fight over their adjoining territory. This clever film offers a symbolic treatment of war by presenting a unique abstract image of human behavior and actions. In one scene the human figures hover across the ground with no apparent movement of their limbs. McLaren achieved this image by photographing single frames of his subjects leaping into the air. Only the apex of each jump was recorded, making the people seem to hover over the ground.

Film Animation

Film animation requires the use of a camera that records motion-picture frames individually. Some film cameras can record both single-frame animation and live-action motion. A frame counter on the camera indicates precisely which frame is being exposed. The camera is normally suspended above the art work by mounting it on an animation stand.

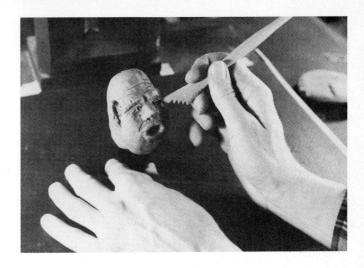

Animation Stands   An **animation stand** consists of a camera platform attached to vertical poles or columns, so that it can be raised and lowered over the art work. The camera platform is suspended above a large horizontal table, called a rostrum, which can be moved east, west, north, and south. The artwork is secured to this horizontal table by placing the hole perforations in proper registration over peg bars on the table.

The vertical columns and horizontal table allow for a variety of camera movements, such as dollies, zooms, pans, and tilts. During a dolly shot the camera is gradually moved toward or away from the art work between exposures. For a zoom shot, the focal length of the lens is changed between one exposure and the next. Pan and tilt shots are made by simply moving the rostrum from side to side or from top to bottom between successive frames. A pantograph is often attached to one side of the stand so that precise movements can be charted on special graph paper by the pantograph pointer.

Clay is an excellent medium for animation. Here a unique character is taking shape for an animated sequence.

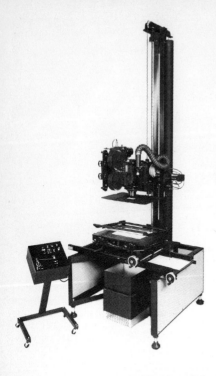
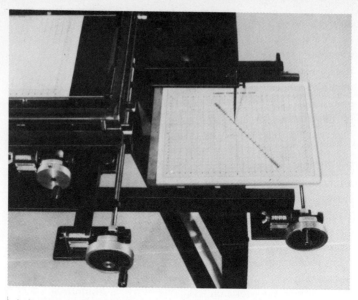

Left: An animation stand and camera. Right: Close-up of an animation stand, showing the pantograph, field guide, platen, registration pegs, and controls for the pegbar tracks.

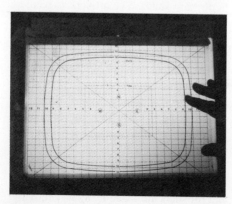

A field guide helps position the rostrum, platen, and animation figures so that they are properly composed and fall within the essential area of the camera frame. Different animation stands and cameras are capable of recording specific fields, usually ranging from a minimum field of ten, which is approximately the size of an 8″ x 10″ still photograph, for smaller, less sophisticated stands to a maximum field of forty, which is more than six feet wide, for the most sophisticated animation stands. Notice that the field guide consists of a cellulose acetate cel which is back lit as it sits in pin registration upon the platen of the animation stand rostrum.

A **field guide**, which is a transparent sheet that has spacing and framing information etched on it, can be placed over the art work to adjust the camera frame. The field guide is proportional to the aspect ratio of the film format, such as 1.33:1 or 4:3 for standard 16mm and Super-8mm filming. It provides spacing and framing information for different field sizes. A field size of 11, for example, indicates a field 11″ wide by 8¼″ high, while a field size of 4 is 4″ wide by 3″ high. A reflex viewfinder is usually required to frame the image precisely for the camera lens.

Lighting The art work can be evenly lit from above with little glare reflected into the camera by using two lights that are suspended at 45 degree angles to the horizontal table. Back lighting can be provided by a diffused lighting source, such as a light box, placed underneath the art work on the table. A glass platen is often used over the art work to keep it flat and in sharp focus. There are often exposure differences between live-action recording and single-frame animation with a film camera. The equivalent shutter speed for single-frame exposure is often different than it is when exposing frames at twenty-four frames per second, for example. (See chapters 8 and 9.)

Animation Cameras   A film animation camera is normally equipped with special controls for specific animation effects. A variable shutter, for example, can be used to fade out from or fade in to a specific piece of art work. By rewinding the film to the beginning of a fade-out as indicated by the frame counter on the camera and then fading in on another piece of artwork, a dissolve can be created. Superimpositions can be made by backwinding and double exposing individual frames.

Aerial Image Photography   Aerial image photography combines a film projector with an animation stand. (See Figure 12.5.) Live action images can be projected from beneath predrawn cels, so that color titles or animated figures can be combined with live action. The opaque portions of the cel block out the background scene which is projected underneath it so that the titles are superimposed over the background scene. The combined image is recorded by the film camera suspended overhead. Aerial image photography elim-

Figure 12.5 Aerial Image
Aerial image cinematography combines live action images with hand-drawn cels of animation. Individual frames of pre-recorded live action are projected from beneath an animation stand so that they are in proper focus at the platen where hand-drawn cels are placed. Each time a cel is removed and replaced by another, the film is advanced on frame in the projector. The result is a blend of live action and animation. Aerial image techniques are often used to combine animated color titles with live action scenes for feature film title sequences.

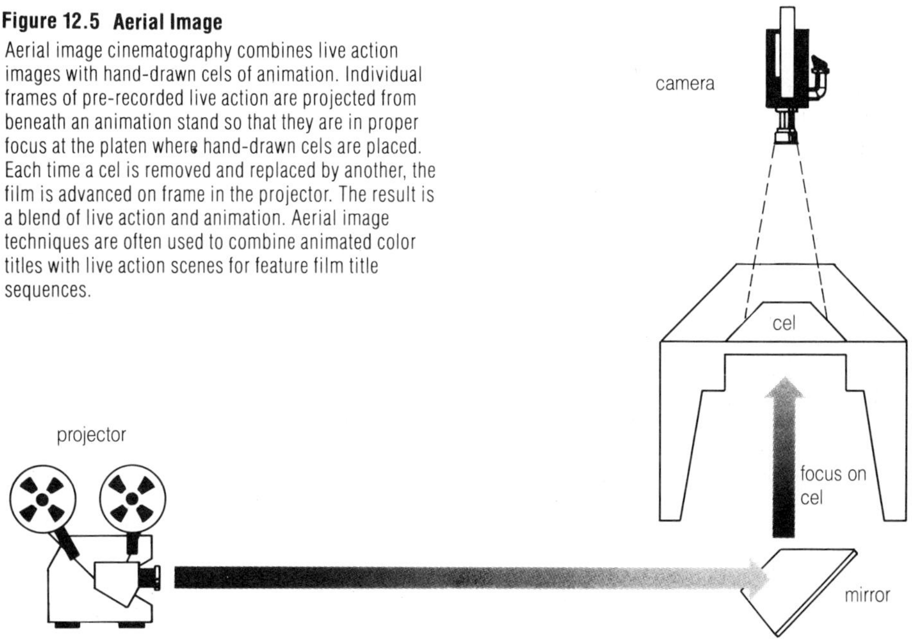

inates the need for special intermediate mattes, such as those which are used during film printing to block out or blacken areas of the frame into which titles and other images are to be inserted. However, aerial imaging requires bright projection illumination.

Computer-Assisted Film Animation

The efficiency and accuracy of film animation has been greatly increased by the development of computer controlled animation stands. All of the complex camera movements such as dollies, fades, focus changes, and movements of the table such as east/west and north/south pans, can be preprogrammed and computer controlled. As many as fifty different pieces of art work can be automatically placed in proper registration in sequential order on some computer film animation stands.

A Sony BVH-2500 animator, which is used for recording animation on videotape.

Computer graphics and animation are often accomplished using a computer keyboard, light pencil, and graphics tablet. Images can be drawn by hand using the light pencil on the tablet so that they can be viewed on a television screen. The keyboard is used to manipulate images and shapes that have been generated by the computer or hand drawn by a graphic artist. Animation programs allow a series of still-frame images to be combined to create an illusion of continuous motion. Individual images and animation sequences can be recorded in videotape or digital disc form.

Computer control dramatically decreases the setup time. Each repetition of a specific piece of art work is recorded at different points on the film. The shutter is simply closed while the frames between them are passed. Thus frames 1, 9, 17, and 25 of an eight frame cycle or repeated action are recorded consecutively before the artwork for frames 2, 10, 18, and 26 is recorded, until all the frames and artwork have been used. Setup time and operator errors are substantially reduced by having the computer control these operations automatically.

Video Animation

Real-Time Animation Images can be electronically animated in a variety of ways. One method does not involve single-frame recording techniques, but relies instead on perceptual illusions in "real-time" recording. A multilayered slotted card can be used to create apparent movement by relying on electronic techniques such as chroma key and black crush. In chroma key the monochrome background surrounding the slot can be replaced by a background scene. When the artwork behind the slot is slid to one side, it appears to move against the background. **Black crush** performs a similar function when the slot is surrounded with black. Through a manipulation of the video signal, ''black crush'' makes the slot movement invisible. Hidden letters, lines, or figures seem to appear magically on the screen.

A disc frame storage unit, which is used for computer graphics and animation. Some of the more powerful units have considerable memory or storage capacity and are capable of storing hundreds of individual frames for animation sequences.

Single-Frame Video Animation

Slo-Mo Recorders and Disc Frame Storage   Another way in which images can be electronically animated is to place a video camera on an animation stand and record single video frames of the artwork on the table using the same techniques as film animation. An important difference between video and film animation is that the video camera records thirty frames per second, instead of twenty-four. Single-frame video animation requires the use of a slo-mo (slow motion) recorder or a disc frame storage unit, rather than a conventional VCR. A slo-mo recorder or video animator can be used to record individual frames for a thirty-second animation sequence. The sequence can then be transferred to conventional videotape. A disc frame storage or memory unit, such as that which is used to store ''pages'' of text composed on a character generator, can also be used to record individual animation frames. Such units often have a limited storage capacity, however. Some units store only sixteen pages of text or frames

of animation, although others are capable of storing and immediately accessing hundreds of figures or pages. A recorded disc can usually be transferred to conventional video tape.

Video Pencil Tests   One advantage of recording animation electronically is that the results can be viewed immediately. Film animators frequently have to wait several days or longer to see the results of their work. Video animation and film animation can be combined by recording a pencil test with a video camera using disc storage of single frames and instantly viewing the results on a monitor so that problems can immediately be uncovered and corrections made. The final cels are recorded with a film camera for optimum quality and maximum storage capacity.

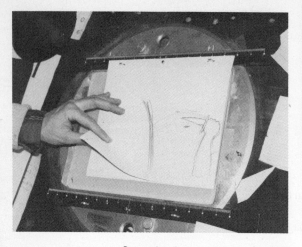

Preparations for a pencil test. In a "before" and "after" sequence, animators can make corrections to the outline sketches before the final cels are drawn and/or painted.

Video Synthesizers

The most primitive computer controlled images for an animation-type special effects sequence consist of live-action images manipulated by a video synthesizer. A **video synthesizer** is analogous to a musical synthesizer in many ways. The synthesizer receives images from a VCR and then manipulates the electrical signal before the images are sent to the switcher. While a video synthesizer allows prerecorded images to be made more abstract and aesthetically pleasing, it does not provide the same degree of control that is possible with computer-generated graphics and single-frame computer animation techniques.

Computer-Assisted Video Animation

Animation programs for some home and office computers can be used for video production. Some animation programs fully integrate with graphics programs so that still-frame graphic images can be used to create apparent motion. Graphic images can be originally designed on a television monitor by using various computer com-

mands and devices such as a **light pencil** or **stylus** to draw on a television screen or electronic tablet. They can then be colored and manipulated by computer. Live-action frames can also be "grabbed" by some computers for further graphic manipulation and/or combined with computer graphic images. Single-frame graphic images can be stored on disc. These images can be expanded in size for detailed work and then shrunk to a smaller size for actual presentation. The animator can manipulate the colors, lines, shapes, and size of the image. Motion can be created by cycling different movements and using the computer to interpolate intermediate frames of motion between two static frames. An NTSC standard video output can then be fed to a switcher or VCR.

Programs are available for **interpolation**, in which the animator composes the first and last frames of a sequence and the computer then creates and interpolates the in-between frames. Even some of the least expensive computers can interpolate as many as fourteen frames. Computer animation allows an almost infinite number of repetitions of the same image. Image cycling is facilitated by simply drawing the first and last frame of a sequence, interpolating the rest, and then recycling this sequence wherever it is needed. It is also possible to make many duplicates of the same image within a single frame.

The greatest advantages of computer graphics and computer animation are speed and accuracy. Results are immediately viewable. An animator need not wait a day or a week for the film animation to be processed and printed at a laboratory. Images and frames can be quickly designed and accurately copied. They can be stored on disc for long periods of time and used again or redesigned for another animation sequence. One of the disadvantages of computer graphics and animation is that it is difficult to create and record all of the fine lines and details that an artist can hand draw or to duplicate the high resolution of film. It is simply not possible to create the look of the original Disney-type multiplane (plates of glass suspended at different levels) animation, such as that which was used for *Fantasia* (1940), using computer-generated images. But even the Disney studio has innovatively used computer graphics to animate objects and backgrounds in films such as *Tron* (1983). A sophisticated computer can interpolate the three dimensions of a design from a two-dimensional image much the same way that an automobile design computer does, so that a completely computer-controlled illusion of three-dimensionality can be obtained in films that combine live-action characters with computer-generated objects and backgrounds. The live-action subject is recorded against a blue screen or a monochromatic background, so that it can be keyed or matted into a computer-generated scene. The availability of these "space-age" techniques has allowed graphic artists to save time and experiment creatively with abstract visual images for film and video.

Summary

Graphic design, like scenic design, is concerned with pictorial content. One purpose of graphic design is to organize and simplify visual material and information so that it can be efficiently recorded and communicated to viewers. Graphic artists design images that convey information. They use basic principles of design, such as simplicity, proximity, similarity, figure/ground, correspondence, equilibrium, and closure, to stimulate viewer interest.

Graphic artists work within the constraints and limitations of visual media. They select lettering that is highly readable and clearly visible. They compose images designed for different aspect ratios and film and video formats which are pleasing to the eye. They avoid designs and colors that are difficult to record or are visually distracting. Titles and illustrations are designed and selected on the basis of their appropriateness for specific topics.

Graphics can be divided into two categories on the basis of use or placement: on-set and off-set. The most commonly used on-set graphics are hand-held cards, photographic enlargements, and graphic set pieces. The most commonly used off-set graphics are camera cards and photographic slides, as well as graphics created on character generators or computers.

Graphic images can be divided into two additional categories on the basis of their nature as images: titles and illustrations. Titles are forms of graphic lettering. Letters for titles can be created mechanically, photographically, or electronically. Mechanical lettering can be accomplished through run-on and/or punch-out letter-ing techniques. A person with minimal design and lettering skills can operate an electronic character generator, or CG, and immediately produce viewable and re-cordable results. A CG allows letters to be created, arranged, and manipulated at the touch of a button. Bold-face, relatively large-size type is normally used for televi-sion. Lettering should contrast with back-ground illustrations in order to be clearly legible.

Subtitles and credit sequences usually combine lettering with live-action images or illustrations. A credit or title sequence names the production contributors. It is usually designed to communicate the fla-vor of a film or television program and to generate audience interest and excitement.

Illustrations are drawings, photo-graphs, graphs, charts, diagrams, and maps which visualize abstract concepts and ideas. They can be produced by a variety of techniques; drawn by hand, photo-graphed, or produced electronically with the help of a computer graphics system.

Animation uses single-frame recording techniques to make static images and ob-jects move. By breaking the motion of an object down into its component parts, an animator can control the movements of otherwise lifeless figures and images. Single-frame recordings of static images can create apparent motion when small changes in the positioning of objects occur between successive frames. Animation begins with the construction of a story-board. A sound chart or "breakdown" of the music and/or lip sync voice is com-bined with the storyboard so that the ani-mator can calculate the precise order and number of frames which will be needed.

Flat animation is accomplished with two-dimensional drawings and illustra-tions. One of the most common flat ani-mation techniques is cel animation, in which an individual clear acetate cel is used for each frame. Techniques that can be used to make cel animation more effi-cient, include recycling recurring lip and body movements, drawing a new image for only every third or fourth frame, and tracing the outlines of live-action filmed images, a technique known as rotoscop-ing. There is a noticeable difference in an-imation style and effectiveness between rotoscoped animation and hand-drawn cel animation, however.

Plastic animation refers to the single-frame recording of three-dimensional fig-ures and objects. Puppets, clay figures, miniature objects and vehicles, and even still frames of live action (a technique known as pixillation) can be animated. Three-dimensional figures are recorded using techniques that combine animation and live-action recording. The camera is usually placed horizontally rather than vertically with respect to the subject, and a three-dimensional miniature world of sets, props, and backgrounds must be con-structed. Single-frame recording allows these inanimate objects to simulate motion and to accomplish seemingly impossible feats.

Film animation requries a single-frame camera and an animation stand. The ani-mation stand consists of a camera platform which can be raised and lowered and an artwork table or rostrum, which can be moved east and west, north and south. A dolly shot can be created by raising or lowering the camera, and a pan can be achieved by moving the table. A variable shutter on the camera allows fades, dissolves, and other special effects to be accomplished. On the most sophisticated animation stands, a computer controls a complex set of camera and table movements, as well as changes of art. A technique known as aerial-image photography combines a projector with the animation stand and camera, so that artwork titles or illustrations on cels can be combined with live-action film images projected from below without requiring more laborious matte printing techniques.

Electronic or video animation can be accomplished with black slotted cards in ''real time.'' A video camera can also be attached to an animation stand, and single frames can be recorded on a slo-mo disc recorder or a disc frame storage unit. The most dramatic development in electronic animation has been the use of a computer graphics system to generate images which can be recorded and stored as single frames on disc. The greatest advantage of computer graphics or computer animation is that images can be immediately viewed as well as accurately recorded and rerecorded. Some computers interpolate the in-between frames, if the animator simply composes the first and last frames of a sequence. A computer can also be used to interpolate the changes in a two-dimensional object which occur when it moves with respect to the camera so that it can be viewed differently from different angles, approximating the three-dimensional world. These three-dimensional illusions can be combined with live-action photography, as was done in the Disney studio's film *Tron*. Computers have opened up a whole new world of illusion and abstract art to film and television audiences.

Additional Readings

Halas, John. *Film Animation: a simplified approach*. Paris: Unesco, 1976.

Hoffer, Thomas, W. *Animation: A Reference Guide*. Westport, CT: Greenwood Press, 1981.

Hurrell, Ron. *Television Graphics*. New York: Van Nostrand Reinhold, 1977.

Laybourne, Kit. *The Animation Book*. New York: Crown Publishers, 1979.

Levitan, Eli L. *Electronic Imaging Techniques*. New York: Van Nostrand Reinhold, 1977.

MacGregor, A.J. *Graphics Simplified*. Toronto: University of Toronto Press, 1979.

Madsen, Roy. *Animated Film: Concepts, Methods, Uses*. New York: Pitman, 1969.

Perisic, Zoran. *The Animation Stand*. New York: Hastings House, 1976.

Exercises

1. Design a credit or title sequence for a specific production project. Determine how you can best use abstract graphic images and titles to introduce a production or select live action images on which titles can be superimposed. Select a letter style or font that is consistent with the overall theme, message, and style of your project. If your project will eventually be shown on a television screen, be sure to use type sizes that are large enough for titles to be clearly legible. Allow sufficient time for each title to be read twice before another title appears on the screen, unless there are too many credits which must be presented within a relatively short period of time. Remember that a title sequence must effectively introduce viewers to the topic.

2. Construct a storyboard for an animation project. Create frames for each shot that will appear in the completed sequence. Either draw each frame by hand or use a computer graphics program to compose them. Make sure that all camera and figure movements are relatively simple to reproduce using an animation stand or a computer animation program. Determine how many individual frames or changes of figure position will have to be drawn or constructed to actually record the sequence on film or videotape at a rate of twenty-four or thirty frames per second.

3. Do a preliminary test for an animation sequence. Compose pencil drawings for each frame needed to complete a short sequence of actions. Draw the figures and backgrounds on white cards which have an aspect ratio of 4:3. Hold the cards together at the bottom using two fingers of your left hand while rapidly flipping them with your right thumb to simulate the effect of animation and to test the speed of actions you are trying to create. Then, record these cards as single frames of film or video on an animation stand and assess the results.

4. Project individual frames of live action film onto a copy stand or a computer drawing tablet in precise registration. Trace the outlines of the figures within the frame. Record these outlines as individual film or video frames. Use this rotoscoping technique to acquire a feeling for how much movement should take place between each animation frame in a purely imaginary animation sequence.

5. Animate cutout paper figures by placing them on an animation stand and moving them slightly between recordings of individual film or video frames. Vary the speed of movement and evaluate the results.

CHAPTER 13

Field Production

Production that takes place outside the studio is called **field production**. The principles and techniques of most field productions are sufficiently different from those of studio production to demand separate treatment. Most field productions use single-camera techniques. Multiple-camera field production, such as live coverage of news and sporting events, is quite similar to studio production, which has been fully discussed in earlier chapters. With careful preproduction planning, many studio production techniques can be used in the field for live, multiple-camera coverage of uncontrolled events.

This chapter will focus on single-camera field production. There are, in fact, distinct advantages to using single-camera techniques for recording in the field and multiple-camera techniques in the studio. The logistics of trying to set up multiple cameras on location are laborious and the results rarely compensate in terms of either the speed of actual production or aesthetic values for the added setup time, technical problems, and aggravation. Live sporting events and political events often require multiple cameras, but in these cases a single camera would not provide adequate coverage and recording in a studio is not an option. In most other field situations, single-camera production is both efficient and aesthetically satisfying, especially when preproduction planning has taken careful account of all equipment needs and major logistical problems. Careful preproduction planning is essential in field production. One of the biggest problems with leaving the studio is that a specific piece of equipment is not "next door." A forgotten item can and often does spell disaster. Equipment checklists that include every piece of equipment are always necessary in field production.

There are three different types of field production: electronic news gathering, electronic field production, and location film production. Each type relies on careful preproduction planning and specific field production setups in terms of the use of cameras, lighting, and sound equipment. Field production units, such as ENG and EFP units, remote vans, and Cinemobiles®, are often used in field or location production.

AESTHETICS OF FIELD PRODUCTION

This chapter examines the aesthetics of field production in terms of rationales for recording outside the studio.

An important question to consider before undertaking a field production is why record in the field rather than in the studio? Functionalist, realist, and formativist arguments can be made for using field production techniques and answering this question inevitably involves aesthetic considerations.

Functionalism

A functionalist response to the question of why record in the field might simply be that it is easier or less expensive to do so than to record in the studio. Trying to reconstruct a specific location interior or exterior in the studio can be very costly compared to using an existing location that is readily available. Suppose that you want to interview a physician in an office or record a dramatic scene in a living room or den. If you have a low budget for set materials but access to someone's private office or home, recording in the field might be the most pragmatic, utilitarian course to follow. On the other hand, recording in the field can involve more logistical problems and time-consuming delays than recording an interview or drama on a simple, functional set in the studio.

Realism

A strong argument for recording in the field is that the demands for realism exceed the available studio resources. It is often much more convincing to use an existing location that has all the necessary realistic details than to try to reconstruct this setting in the studio. A studio reconstruction may fail to sustain the illusion of reality which is crucial to the emotional impact of a dramatic scene, for example. Using a real place, such as the actual site of a scientific discovery, can offer an informative and interesting backdrop for a documentary narrator who is discussing this discovery or invention. Television news magazines, such as the semi-national/semi-local "PM Magazine," often place their local narrator/hosts in community locations analogous to the setting of the national stories that they introduce to their local or regional audience. This technique not only provides realism, it adds community interest and involvement as well.

Formativism

Formativist arguments for field production are many and varied. Abstract shapes and objects, for example, can be isolated from the real world and manipulated by the artist just as effectively as they can be constructed in the studio or on a design or animation table. Using existing objects and settings has the added value of allowing an artist to use familiar things in unfamiliar ways. Fascinating graphic relationships can be developed by combining close-ups of a human body with those of textured object surfaces and existing landscapes, for example. These kinds of relationships can also be incorporated as transition devices in more conventional dramatic and informational programs. Existing places and objects are amenable to formativist manipulations that excite interest, develop abstract ideas and relationships, and evoke subjective impressions.

TYPES OF FIELD PRODUCTION

There are three major categories of field production: **electronic news gathering (ENG), electronic field production (EFP),** and **location film production**. ENG recording techniques and equipment are designed to produce quick, immediate coverage of news events in the field, whether these events are recorded and edited on videotape or transmitted live via microwave. EFP basically grew out of ENG recording and includes all forms of video field production other than news reporting that use film-style, single-camera recording techniques. ENG stresses immediacy and actuality, while EFP emphasizes production quality. Location film production has been around for many years and is similar to EFP production but requires techniques that are tailored to the use of photographic recording equipment.

Electronic News Gathering

ENG essentially replaced newsfilm recording during the 1970s. Prior to that time most news stories and documentaries were recorded on film. The development of high quality portable video cameras and electronic editing equipment stimulated a

An RCA ENG portable camera. Note the microphone on the front right of the camera.

rapid conversion to video technology. Single-camera recording and editing techniques were borrowed from film, although video offered several distinct advantages. First, recordings could be viewed immediately and edited very efficiently to meet news show deadlines. Second, signals could be transmitted live via microwave to the station during a news broadcast. Finally, portable video equipment could also be used in areas other than news, which led to the development of EFP.

ENG recording techniques are basic to single-camera recordings of uncontrolled events. A news camera operator and reporter must select from a variety of events, none of which can be repeated. Continuous coverage of important events (the equivalent of master shots) must be maintained while they happen. Various inserts and cutaways are recorded before or after

the fact, so that edits can be made in the continuously recorded shot without any apparent jumpcuts in the action. Inserts and cutaways must be cleverly selected so that they do not reveal the fact that they were actually recorded before or after the main action, although there is a growing tendency in ENG recording to ignore jumps in interview segments which suggest that the original recordings have been edited. Some editors find gratuitous cutaways to the reporter nodding his or her head disruptive and boring, while others often try to maintain an illusion of continuous time and action while editing together single-camera recordings of slightly discontinuous events.

Live single-camera coverage of news events demands special camera operating techniques. ENG camera operators learn to follow actions and events continuously as they happen. The camera operator must change the focus and focal length of a zoom lens so that the actions are properly focused and framed. Camera or lens movements must be smooth and gradual, not rapid or jerky. This requires considerable practice. A good exercise is to follow someone moving about a room in a random manner, trying to keep the person within the camera frame and in proper focus. This exercise can be practiced for ten to fifteen minutes at a time as a preparation for actual ENG production. (See chapter 7.) Since live sounds and images are sent directly from a single camera to the station and are broadcast immediately, no postproduction editing is possible. The camera operator ''edits'' in the camera by simply moving the camera during the shot or zooming the lens. Changes in camera position alter the viewer's focus of attention and stimulate interest. All too often live news transmissions simply focus upon the reporter's talking head as he or she summarizes the day's events, using the live scene as a mere background. Live news transmissions can also be used to ''frame'' the playback of previously edited footage taken earlier at the same location.

ENG shots must be recorded and edited extremely efficiently so that the completed project can actually be shown within hours, or sometimes just minutes, of the time it was recorded. There is little time to record shots that are not likely to be used. A camera operator and reporter must be decisively selective. They must know what they are looking for and grab it as soon as it comes along. There is no time for a camera operator to contemplate the aesthetic beauty of each shot or to mull over lighting and compositional factors. Efficiency, immediacy, and clarity are the watchwords of ENG production.

Electronic Field Production

EFP developed from ENG. Many stations, in order to recoup their start-up costs for ENG cameras and editors, looked for other ways to produce income from news equipment. Videotape was quickly adapted for use in the field in place of film because ENG cameras were compatible with existing remote truck equipment, recordings could be viewed and edited immediately, and some production costs could be cut. Original purchases of video equipment for news purposes found additional justification in nonnews areas, and video became the standard production medium for television stations. Simultaneously video equipment was adopted for film-style, single-camera production uses by corporate, educational, religious, and governmental institutions. EFP embraces a wide range of nonnews uses of single-camera video recording techniques and equipment.

One of the key features of single-camera production, which was discussed from the standpoint of directing in chapter 6, is the attempt to obtain sufficient coverage of events so that different shots can be efficiently and effectively combined during postproduction editing. This is accomplished by recording controlled events in master shots or long-duration takes, providing a full view of major actions. Actions are then repeated and the camera is moved closer to the action for matching close-ups and medium shots, to be used as inserts. Cutaways, or shots of related but secondary or extraneous actions at the same location, ensure adequate coverage of the action and provide an editor with something to ''cut away to'' if there is a mismatch between master shots and inserts. They also allow for a shortening of character speeches or movements without creating disconcerting breaks in the action. All of the shots recorded by a single camera are eventually assembled into their proper order by an editor.

EFP projects vary considerably in terms of budget levels and the sophistication of cameras and other recording equipment. Television commercials, documentaries, instructional and corporate videotapes, and network entertainment programs often require EFP. But the techniques of EFP are basically the same regardless of the production level. Unlike ENG, EFP stresses production quality, not immediacy or actuality. There is often a rough quality to ENG that is absent in EFP. More time is required to produce a quality product. Considerable time must be spent in preproduction planning to make sure that all aspects of production are fully coordinated. Scouting locations is crucial. Most news recording is done at familiar locations, and production decisions concerning previously unused locations often have to be made on the spot. Such is not the case with EFP. Every detail must be carefully considered in advance and every essential piece of equipment must be checked off on a list prior to departing for a field location.

Actual production in the field is done very systematically. All the shots that are to be recorded at a specific location are done at the same time, regardless of where they will appear in the final product. A slate is used during single-camera recording to identify each shot and take number and accurate notations on the script and shot lists are made to make sure that every shot called for in the script is actually recorded. The shots will be organized into the order or continuity designated by the script during postproduction editing.

Location Film Production

Location film production is basically the same as EFP, which is often called *film*-style video production. Recording with film is more expensive than video recording in some areas, such as film processing and printing, although the use of high quality production and postproduction equipment in EFP can also be extremely expensive. High-budget commercials, feature films, and music videos are often shot on film; thus location film production has an aura of high aesthetic quality about it. Some commercials and music videos, intended solely for video distribution, use cameras that record at thirty frames per second rather than the standard twenty-four frames per second so that a better transfer to video can be made. Using a faster recording speed produces a smoother reproduction of movement.

Photographic and electronic recording equipment is sufficiently different to affect some production techniques. For one thing, film cameras are somewhat more durable than video cameras. During outdoor EFP production a camera operator must be constantly concerned about sunlight directly entering the camera and causing damage to the camera pickup tube. A film camera can be operated more freely without fear of damage from bright lights.

The use of a separate film camera and synchronous sound recorder can also affect production techniques on location. Additional crew members are often needed to handle sound recording equipment. A clapstick must be used to provide a common synchronization point for separate film and audiotape recordings. Film crews use a slightly different terminology during production than EFP crews, as was explained in chapter 6. Effective communication between the creative staff and the crew demands the use of precise commands.

Film has a softer, more glamourous appearance or look than video. Long-distance panorama shots have a clarity on the big screen that is totally lost on a small television monitor. The wider contrast range of film allows a film recording to capture subtle details, shadow areas, and viewable images under harsh lighting and weather conditions. Finally, film production is often more time consuming than EFP production, since the latter produces immediately viewable images that can be efficiently edited electronically. Film postproduction is still a relatively laborious process. These differences between film and video can be important when you have to decide which medium to use, but you should also keep in mind that it is possible to combine film and video by transferring film images to videotape during postproduction.

:::::::::::::::::::::::::
PREPRODUCTION PLANNING
:::::::::::::::::::::::::

Shooting outside the studio requires extensive preproduction planning. A producer and a director will often scout the specific location at which staged or unstaged events will take place. Of course, in some production situations, such as news coverage of unstaged events, there is no opportunity to scout the location in advance of production. Instead, the location is scouted quickly immediately prior to recording.

A film crew on location. In a situation such as this, care must be taken in using each component separately and communications between the crew and the creative staff need to be specific and precise.

Securing permission to record at a specific location sometimes requires considerable persuasive powers. The persons providing the space may need to be convinced that the production crew will not damage the property or disrupt normal day-to-day activities to any significant extent. A contract can be drawn up specifying the period of time any property will be used and the amount of reimbursement required, if any. ENG situations rarely need this protection. ENG enjoys certain ''news story'' protections, such as the fact that no releases are necessary to record actual news events. Shooting a commercial or theatrical film on location is usually done for financial gain and profit and entails certain legal and financial obligations. A gift, offer of production credit, or personal involvement in the production sometimes provides a recalcitrant owner or manager with sufficient incentive to allow a production to proceed.

**Figure 13.1
Example of a Remote
Survey Form**

```
┌─────────────────────────────────────────────────────────┐
│              Remote Survey Form—Mobile Unit                │
│  Title _____    Date _____        │
│  Description _____    Prod. _____        │
│            _____    Dir. _____        │
│  Location Address _____    Contact _____       │
│            _____    Phone # _____        │
│            _____                              │
│                                                            │
│  Building Personnel                                        │
│  Building Manager _____    Phone # _____        │
│  House Electrician _____    Phone # _____        │
│  Security Officer _____    Phone # _____        │
│  Other _____    Phone # _____        │
│  Other _____    Phone # _____        │
│  Location #1                                               │
│  Mobile Unit Power (Requires 220 Single Phase, 60 AMP)    │
│  Location of box _____    Type _____       │
│  Distance from available parking _____ Any Free Breakers? (#) ___ │
│  Circuit Breaker location _____        │
│  Production location _____         │
│  Distance from mobile unit _____  Cameras (#) _____     │
│  Lighting power available _____        │
│  No. of circuits and location _____         │
│  Breaker box location _____         │
│  Nearest available telephone _____         │
│  Remarks _____         │
│            _____         │
└─────────────────────────────────────────────────────────┘
```

The location should be scouted at the time of day when shooting will actually take place. This will facilitate the positioning of cameras and the assessment of lighting needs. Additional lighting may be needed to fill in shadow areas, or the cameras may need to be placed so that the sun is behind them, if an exterior location is being used. The cameras should be positioned so that the basic rules of screen direction will not be violated. Microphones must be selected and placed for different sounds and sound sources. For small productions that do not require substantial artificial lighting, power for portable cameras, lighting, and sound equipment may simply be provided by batteries. Securing more extensive power requires the services of a qualified electrician, who can tie into existing power supplies or provide power from a portable gasoline-driven generator. Figure 13.2, for example, illustrates multiple-camera setups for a basketball and a football game using a remote van—all of the above information must be summarized in the survey report.

Scouting Report or Remote Survey

Once a production site or location has been selected and secured, a **scouting report** or **remote survey** is normally filled out. (See Figure 13.1.) This report indicates the exact location; the contact people who are intimately familiar with this site; the best positioning of cameras, microphones, and lighting; existing power supplies and additional power needs; and additional structures that will have to be built on location. Well in advance of the beginning of the production, easy access to and from the site must be provided and city or private permits and permissions must be secured.

Equipment Lists

It is absolutely essential that every piece of equipment needed in the field be written down on an **equipment list** so that all pieces will actually be transported to the production site. Every equipment item called for in the scouting report or remote survey must be carefully evaluated to ensure that it represents an accurate estimate of actual production needs before the equipment list is finalized. While carrying an excess of equipment into the field can add to the workload of the crew or inflate a production budget, discovering a shortage of equipment on location can be disastrous, if it forces production to be

A. Basketball setup

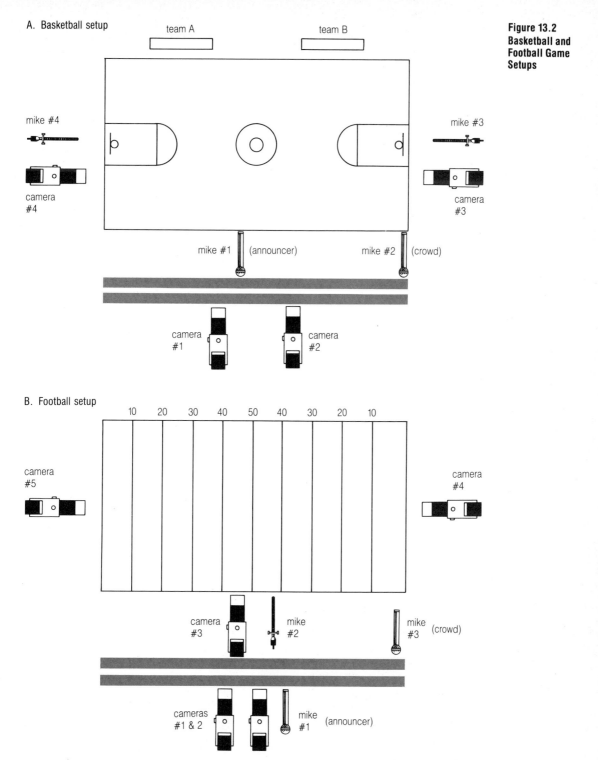

Figure 13.2
**Basketball and
Football Game
Setups**

team A

team B

mike #4

mike #3

camera
#4

camera
#3

mike #1 (announcer)

mike #2 (crowd)

camera
#1

camera
#2

B. Football setup

10 20 30 40 50 40 30 20 10

camera
#5

camera
#4

camera
#3

mike
#2

mike
#3 (crowd)

cameras
#1 & 2

mike
#1 (announcer)

compromised or curtailed. Before traveling to the field site, production equipment lists should be checked and rechecked against the actual pieces of recording and production equipment that have been packed. It is important to pack duplicate items whenever possible, such as several sets of batteries, and to make sure that every power pack is fully charged, especially in cold weather.

FIELD PRODUCTION SETUP

Setting up a location or remote production often requires considerable time. A producer and director should be realistic about how much time it will take to set up the cameras, sound equipment, and lights, so that the talent and other members of the crew do not stand around the set for half a day, waiting for production to commence. Usually a field production is set up the morning before actual shooting begins. The crew should follow a production diagram, so that the setting up of one type of equipment will not get in the way of setting up of another. At the same time that cameras are being set up, the mikes and other sound recording equipment can be positioned, and the lights or reflectors can be arranged and adjusted.

An Ampex camera with built-in recorder.

Visual Recording

Video cameras should be properly warmed up before production begins. Added time may be needed to plan and lay tracks or set up a dolly, such as a car, truck, wheelchair, or golf cart, for a camera movement that is going to be made over rough terrain. It is not uncommon for a camera operator to rehearse camera operations prior to actual production, especially when the events that are going to be recorded cannot be controlled. The camera operator should become familiar with different camera positions and the type of coverage that is possible from each position.

It is difficult to make a sharp distinction between field cameras and studio cameras. Video cameras are often categorized as studio, convertible, or portable cameras and in many different formats are used for both location/remote and studio production. Nonetheless certain camera features are helpful when shooting outside the studio.

While even the largest studio cameras are sometimes taken into the field, most EFP and ENG situations require less bulky and expensive equipment. The development of convertible cameras that can be used in the studio but also carried into the field has greatly improved the portability and mobility of field production without significantly reducing image quality. Many convertible cameras have three two-thirds-inch camera pickup tubes, just like many studio cameras. Single pickup tube cameras are obviously lighter weight and are much more portable in the field than cameras with three pickup tubes, but they cannot record the same quality image. When selecting a field camera, portability must be weighed against image quality.

A Sony BTA-27 Betacam with wireless attachment kit.

Field cameras, unlike studio cameras, rarely have large viewing monitors at the back of the camera. Portable or convertible cameras generally have small monitors or viewfinders located on one side of the camera. Field cameras normally have a zoom lens that can be easily controlled from the front of the camera. Lens controls for studio cameras are usually located on the hand grips of a pedestal dolly.

A video camera should never be pointed at the sun, as this can cause a permanent burn-in to occur in the camera pickup tube. Highly reflectant surfaces lit by bright sunlight can cause similar problems with a stationary camera. Television cameras sometimes malfunction under intense heat. They should be shaded from long periods of direct exposure to the sun. They should also be protected from snow and rain. Intense cold can also cause problems in some situations, and cameras may require insulation, such as a **barney**, a heated camera cover usually used as a sound insulator. High humidity can also affect videotape recording. It increases the friction between the recording heads and the tape, which can cause the tape to shed oxide and clog the heads. In extreme humidity the tape will actually scallop or wrinkle.

An RCA portable camcorder in use.

CINE 60 power belt providing batteries for a portable light called a sun gun.

Extreme weather conditions generally have less effect on film than video cameras, and the drive mechanism of a film camera can in fact be lubricated with graphite, rather than oil, so that it can still function well mechanically at temperatures below 0° Fahrenheit. In extreme cold, however, film becomes brittle and is subject to marking by static electricity generated by its own movement through the camera. Furthermore, the light sensitivity of the film in terms of ASA or EI can change from its normal rating, since film recording is a photochemical process, and all chemical processes are temperature sensitive. Camera and tape recorder batteries, like car batteries, are affected by cold weather; battery life falls off rapidly below 40° Fahrenheit. Batteries, film, and cameras may need to be insulated or heated in cold weather.

Almost any type of film camera can be used for location or remote production. Still, some cameras are lighter weight, more compact and more portable than other cameras with the same format. In 35mm feature film work, for example, a Panaflex camera is much smaller and more portable than a Panavision camera. In 16mm an Arriflex SR is more compact than an Arriflex BL and a Bolex is smaller and lighter weight than a CP 16. In general, cameras designed exclusively for wild or nonsynchronous sound recording are smaller, lighter in weight, and more portable than those designed to record synchronous sound. Obviously, 8mm cameras are the smallest and most portable recording devices available for location production. Many Super-8mm cameras have built-in sound recording capability, but their use is limited by the image and sound quality of 8mm film.

It is extremely important to provide ample camera support in the field. All too often camera operators rely on hand-held cameras, causing the image to waver and jitter in an unsteady manner. This can call attention to the camera and leave an unprofessional impression. Camera supports for field production are usually less bulky than their studio counterparts. Large pedestal or crab dollies are replaced in the field by somewhat smaller collapsible camera dollies and tripods. Some television and film cameras have a built-in shoulder mount which allows the camera to be secured to the camera operator's body. A shoulder harness or Steadicam can be used with other cameras. A Steadicam uses a complex system of springs and counterweights to smooth out the jerky body movements of the operator and thereby simulate the fluid movements of a dolly or crane. Collapsible tripods can be used for camera support on location when no camera movement is required. The points of the tripod can be pressed into soft ground for added stability. A spider or triangle (sometimes also called a spreader) will secure the legs of a tripod when it is used on a hard, flat surface.

Lighting

Studio lighting equipment is both conveniently accessible and relatively easy to set up and control, but field or location lighting can present many problems. It is often difficult to balance the color temperatures of light coming from different light sources. A location interior may be naturally lit by a combination of fluorescent, incandescent, and natural light, for example. An exterior scene, such as a sports stadium, may be lit by both late afternoon sunlight and artificial stadium lighting.

It is always advisable to use light sources that have the same color temperature. Outdoors under sunlight, additional fill light can be provided by arc lights or HMI lighting with a color temperature equivalent to that of daylight (5400° Kelvin). The sun itself can be used to provide additional fill light, by simply using a reflector board to cast indirect sunlight into the shadow areas of the location setting. Always remember that the color temperature of sunlight changes throughout the day, requiring white balancing of the video camera to be redone frequently during late afternoon recording sessions. (See chapter 7.) Indoors, if existing lighting comes from tungsten lights, the key, fill, and back light should also be provided by additional tungsten lights. Whenever possible fluorescent lighting should be turned off, since it is difficult, if not impossible, to obtain high quality color recordings under fluorescent lighting. If this cannot be done, the video camera can be properly white balanced for the best color or the film can be altered during processing or printing.

The absence of a convenient power supply and overhead lighting grid cause lighting problems in the field. It is important to determine the availability of electrical power. For a limited production, batteries or normal electrical outlets and circuits in a home or building may provide sufficient power for a few lights. If more power is needed, a qualified electrician can either tap the nearest main power supply, which in a private home may provide more than 100 amperes of electrical power, or bring in a portable gasoline generator. Hanging and positioning lights in

Top: A portable gasoline generator of electricity. Bottom: A light clamp for use in hanging and positioning lights on location.

the field provides additional problems. A variety of light stands, poles, and temporary clips are available to facilitate hanging instruments on location. Lighting people often use generous amounts of gaffer's tape, which has strong adhesive capacities—so strong in fact that some instruments can actually be taped with it to a wall or ceiling. Care must be exercised in the use and removal of gaffer's tape, however, since paint and other finishes remain stuck to the tape when it is removed.

Significant improvements in field or remote lighting have been made possible by the development of HMI light. This type of portable lighting can produce four or five times as much light as conventional tungsten lights. HMI lights run off conventional 120-volt 20-amp circuits. They can also be powered by a portable generator in the field. The color temperature of HMI lights can be selected for either daylight or indoor tungsten situations as a supplement to existing lighting for filling in shadow areas or raising the overall light level. By using HMI lighting, it is possible to obtain levels and varieties of lighting that otherwise would be possible only with bulky carbon arc lights.

Using a shot gun microphone on location. Proper microphone selection is crucial in order to be assured of the best sound possible.

Sound Recording

Eliminating unwanted sound is one of the biggest problems that a sound recordist must solve in the field. Objectionable wind noise, which can often be minimized or eliminated by using a mike windscreen and positioning performers with their backs to the wind with lavalier mikes, is just one type of unwanted sound. Lacking the sound insulation that is provided by studio walls, the sound recordist must be more effective at isolating desired sounds from their backgrounds. Surf crashing on the beach behind a speaker can severely interrupt the primary signal, as can any nearby traffic noise or construction work. While the sound recordist should voice concerns about potential problems during preproduction meetings, once a site is selected, unwanted noise can only be reduced or eliminated by proper microphone selection and placement or signal processing. A microphone with a narrow pickup pattern can help isolate the wanted signal from unwanted noise. Placing the microphone so that it is close to the desired sound source and pointed away from the source of the unwanted noise can also help. (See Figure 13.3.) Finally, if the noise is restricted to a narrow range of frequencies, unwanted sound can sometimes be eliminated through selective sound equalization or filtration using sophisticated sound recorders. Production may simply have to be stopped when strong, unwanted sounds having the same frequencies as the desired sounds totally disrupt the recording. However, synchronous sounds and dialogue can also be rerecorded and "dubbed" or "looped" during postproduction to replace unusable or poor quality sounds recorded in the field. These techniques are discussed more fully in chapter 15.

Another problem that the sound recordist must be concerned about on location or field productions is reverberation or echo. Reverberation can be a problem at certain indoor locations. Insulating the walls and floors with blankets and carpeting can help, as can placing the microphone as close as possible to the talent. Corners of a room should be avoided, because sound delay and reverberation can cause a cancellation of certain frequencies similar to that which occurs with the phasing problems of multiple microphones. Finally, the sound recordist at a field interior must be careful to avoid placing microphones near cameras, ventilators, fluorescent lights, and electrical wires and equipment, all of which have the potential to create unwanted noise or hum.

It is very important to record some background sounds or ambient noise at every field location. Such sounds can later be used to provide a continuous background sound track. When this uncut track accompanies edited images, it suggests an uninterrupted continuity of action and enhances the illusion of reality. Maintaining audio continuity over the spatially discontinuous visual actions can improve the flow of the action.

The sound equipment used for location or remote recording differs from that which is used in the studio primarily in terms of its portability. Lightweight equipment, such as fishpole mike booms rather than perambulator booms, is frequently used in the field. Supercardioid, cardioid, shotgun and FM transmitter mikes are frequently used on location because they isolate sounds at great distances from their sources.

One of the most difficult but important jobs of the sound recordist is to lay cables so that they will not get in the way of the crew or performers and become disconnected during actual production. Cables should be secured to the floor or to immovable objects so that they will not be inadvertently disconnected. Whenever possible cables should be taped together so that they are easily seen but not easily dislodged. Cable connections can be reinforced with tape and the cables themselves can be tied together in a loose knot at the connection point so that cable tension will bring connectors together rather than pull them apart. Cables can be wrapped around stands, pipes, poles, and table legs. This way, if someone trips over a cable, the tension that is exerted pulls against an immovable object, rather than dislodging a microphone or pulling a tape recorder onto the floor. Cables and cable connectors should be carefully examined prior to recording so that wiring shorts or poor contacts that require soldering are discovered *before* production begins.

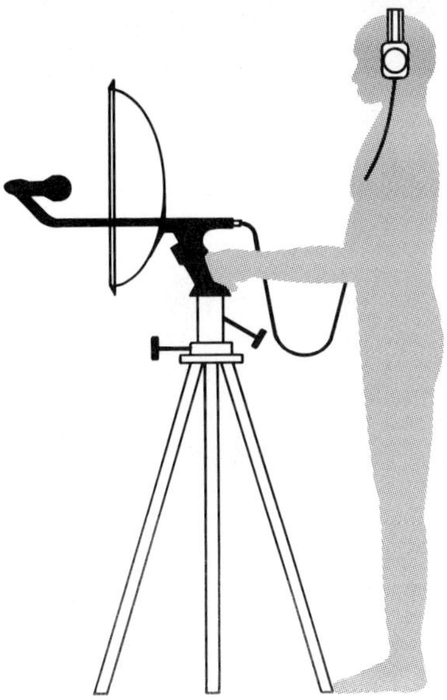

**Figure 13.3
A Parabolic Mike**

Above: An ENG van with a microwave dish and TV antenna on top. Below: An Ikegami portable microwave link on an HL-79E camera.

FIELD PRODUCTION UNITS

There are four basic types of field production units: the ENG (electronic news gathering) mobile units, the EFP (electronic field production) unit, and the remote van and the cinemobile for large scale productions. Field production units often store cameras and microphones, lighting, and videotape or film recording equipment and transport it to the field. More sophisticated and expensive units also supply electrical power and communication links, such as two-way radios and microwave transmissions of video and audio information.

ENG Mobile Units

The ENG mobile unit is used by television stations to record news information on videotape and to provide live transmissions during regularly scheduled or special news broadcasts. Some ENG mobile units are nothing more than a glorified station wagon, which has been slightly modified to contain television recording equipment. Most ENG mobile units, however, are vans designed expressly for transporting recording transmission equipment and news personnel. A local television station's ENG mobile unit is easily identified by the microwave dish that appears on the top of the van.

The ENG mobile unit provides several different communication links: one between the unit and the television studio, and another between the unit and the television crew. Video and audio picked up in the field can be transmitted to the station live via point-to-point microwave. A microwave dish atop the mobile unit sends a signal to a relay station which transmits the signal to another microwave dish at the station. The relay is usually placed on top of the highest building in the area. A microwave signal requires a direct, uninterrupted, line-of-sight connection between the mobile unit and the relay as well as between the relay and the station. When the camera and sound recording equipment must travel a considerable distance from the mobile unit and cable connections are impractical, a second portable microwave is often set up to send signals from the camera to the van. This second microwave unit can be battery powered.

The ¾-inch videotape format has traditionally been standard for ENG recording, but the latest generation of ENG gear, separately developed and marketed by Sony and RCA, called Betacam and VHS-C, consists of a one piece camera/recorder system which records pictures and sounds on ½-inch videotape. Some elaborate ENG mobile units have ¾-inch U-matic or ½-inch videotape recorders and an editing module, so that preliminary editing can be done on a late-breaking story while the unit is returning to the station. The editing unit is powered by a generator driven by the engine of the vehicle as it travels back to the station. Stories edited in the field can then be fed back to the station by microwave before the van returns to its home base.

EFP Units

An EFP unit is often used in the field for the production of television commercials, local programs, and educational and instructional videotapes. This unit or vehicle normally contains fairly high quality recording equipment. All camera, sound, and lighting equipment can be stored so that they are easily accessible for field work. Image and sound quality is usually stressed in EFP. The unit provides ample space for all equipment needs, including high quality monitors that allow the image and sound quality of a production to be immediately assessed. It may contain a portable generator that can power several HMI lights and a portable sound mixer that can record several microphones and sound sources simultaneously. A single or dual mike input(s) on a VCR can be quite limiting when quality sound must be recorded

from several speakers simultaneously. Portable mixers having four or five inputs can provide a convenient solution to this problem. A portable mixer with a VU meter frequently allows for better audio control than does a VCR alone. The most common videotape formats used with an EFP unit is professional 1-inch helical scan rather than ¾-inch or ½-inch helical, although the latter are frequently used for making educational and instructional videotapes. One-half-inch VHS-C and BetaCam formats also provide excellent quality recordings. Larger EFP units also contain electronic editing equipment.

Electronic field productions range from the most elaborate national network level commercials to in-house instructional videotapes. EFP units are designed for single-camera rather than multiple-camera production. If multiple cameras are used for a coverage of news or sports events, for example, the production usually calls for a remote van rather than standard EFP production equipment.

AN EFP Remote van. Used primarily in the field for such events as local programs and educational videotapes, this unit provides good quality recording equipment.

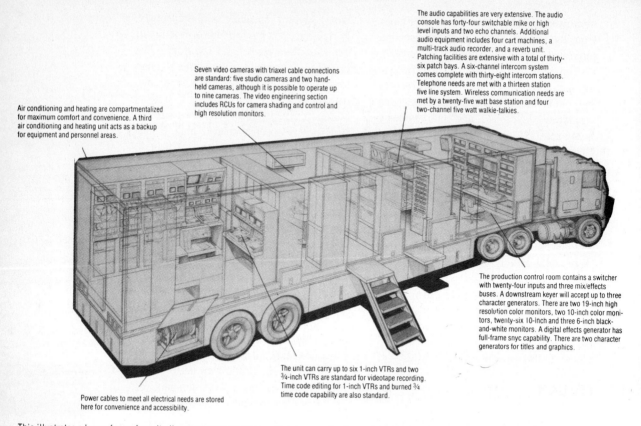

The audio capabilities are very extensive. The audio console has forty-four switchable mike or high level inputs and two echo channels. Additional audio equipment includes four cart machines, a multi-track audio recorder, and a reverb unit. Patching facilities are extensive with a total of thirty-six patch bays. A six-channel intercom system comes complete with thirty-eight intercom stations. Telephone needs are met with a thirteen station five line system. Wireless communication needs are met by a twenty-five watt base station and four two-channel five watt walkie-talkies.

Seven video cameras with triaxel cable connections are standard: five studio cameras and two hand-held cameras, although it is possible to operate up to nine cameras. The video engineering section includes RCUs for camera shading and control and high resolution monitors.

Air conditioning and heating are compartmentalized for maximum comfort and convenience. A third air conditioning and heating unit acts as a backup for equipment and personnel areas.

The production control room contains a switcher with twenty-four inputs and three mix/effects buses. A downstream keyer will accept up to three character generators. There are two 19-inch high resolution color monitors, two 10-inch color monitors, twenty-six 10-inch and three 6-inch black-and-white monitors. A digital effects generator has full-frame snyc capability. There are two character generators for titles and graphics.

The unit can carry up to six 1-inch VTRs and two ¾-inch VTRs are standard for videotape recording. Time code editing for 1-inch VTRs and burned ¾ time code capability are also standard.

Power cables to meet all electrical needs are stored here for convenience and accessibility.

This illustrates a larger form of semitrailer remote van used for multiple-camera live transmissions of sporting events and other similar large-scale events.

Remote Vans

A third type of field production unit and by far the largest and most sophisticated, is the remote van. The remote van (Figure 13.4) is used primarily for multiple-camera live transmissions of sporting and news events such as football games and inaugurations. It consists of a semitrailer that provides a virtually complete studio control room on wheels: an audio console; a switcher; several 1-inch helical scan or 2-inch quadruplex videotape recorders; a slo-mo disc recorder; a character generator; several reel-to-reel and cartridge audiotape recorders; camera control units for several cameras; a bank of monitors; and space for all the major production technicians and creative artists who would normally be present in a studio control room.

A mass of cables connects the remote van to the actual interior or exterior production site. For live transmissions the van will utilize a microwave relay to the studio or a satellite link to the network. One or more mobile cameras can also be connected to the van by microwave. Stationary cameras, however, are usually connected to the unit by cable, as are the audio feeds. An elaborate intercom system must be set up to allow for communication between the van and all key production personnel, such as the camera operators. Multiple-camera recording takes place in a manner similar to that which can be done in the studio. More tension is present on a television remote, however, since it is often done live and runs a greater risk of technical problems.

Cinemobiles

In film production one of the most commonly used location production vehicles for large-scale productions such as feature films and major commercials, is the Cinemobile®. This traveling mobile unit which looks like a mobile home van will often be used to transport the talent and crew, as well as some equipment. It can be used as a temporary wardrobe and makeup facility on location. Some production companies use an actual mobile home van modified for film production in place of a Cinemobile®. A built-in generator supplies power for lighting and recording needs. Cinemobiles seem relatively luxurious when com-

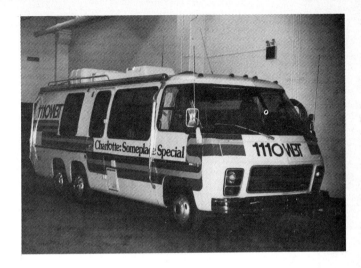

pared to television remote vehicles, but they are more frequently used by performers and key staff members than by technicians. Large scale productions also use large trucks to transport equipment into the field.

A mobile van, which is similar to a Cinemobile®, is used for remote productions.

An RCA studio camera put to use in the "field."

Summary

Production that takes place outside the studio is called field production. Most field productions use single-camera recording techniques. The decision to record outside the studio involves aesthetic considerations, such as those of functionalism, realism, and formativism. Ease of production, cost effectiveness, the need for added realism, and an attempt to use familiar objects in unfamiliar or abstract ways are common reasons for recording in the field.

There are three different types of field production: electronic news gathering, electronic field production, and location film production. ENG provides single-camera coverage of news events. EFP uses single-camera, film-style recording techniques in the field. Location film production is basically similar to EFP, except for certain media-specific differences.

Location or remote production usually requires substantial preproduction planning. Locations must be carefully researched and scouted. Permission to use them must be obtained. Equipment and personnel must be transported to the location. A scouting report or remote survey provides a plan for location utilization which includes everything from equipment and personnel needs to specific location contact people. The scouting report or remote survey helps coordinate all aspects of production. Equipment lists based on the scouting report must identify every piece of equipment that will be needed in the field and must be cross-checked prior to departure for the field. Setup and rehearsal generally require more time in the field than in the studio.

Field production demands special recording techniques. Camera, lighting, and sound equipment is generally lighter weight and more portable than its studio counterpart. Special equipment may be needed to improve the quality of the sounds and images to be recorded, since recording conditions outside the studio cannot be easily controlled. Field cameras are designed somewhat differently from studio cameras. Convertible cameras provide high quality images in the field. Smaller format cameras are more portable but reduce image quality. Film cameras are somewhat more durable then video cameras in the field. Providing adequate camera support in the field is important for recording steady, professional images.

Field lighting is generally more compact and portable than studio lighting. HMI lighting has greatly increased the light output of relatively small instruments, and can be used to supplement sunlight or existing indoor lighting. Sunlight reflectors can be used to create fill light on location. An electrician must provide sufficient power on location to operate artificial lights, either by tapping existing power supplies or by using a portable gasoline generator.

Eliminating unwanted noise is a constant problem confronting sound recording in the field. Microphone wind screens may be necessary to eliminate wind noise, and properly placed directional microphones can help isolate desired sounds on location. Another problem is controlling sound reverberation or echo. It is important to make recordings of background sounds or ambient noise at every field location, which can be used to maintain continuity during postproduction editing. Sound cables should be taped to the floor or firmly secured to stationary objects so that they do not become dislodged during production.

There are four different kinds of field production units: electronic news gathering (ENG) mobile units, electronic field production (EFP) units, remote vans, and Cinemobiles. ENG units tranport transmission and recording equipment into the field. These units are easily identified by a microwave dish on the top of the van which can be used to provide a direct connection to the station. EFP mobile units are used for field recording and sometimes contain editing equipment. The equipment transported by an EFP unit is usually of high quality. Production quality rather than immediacy and actuality generally characterizes EFP production in contrast to ENG production.

A remote television van is normally used for large scale television remotes, whether they are to be transmitted live or prerecorded. The largest vans are virtual studio control rooms on wheels, and they house all the equipment and personnel needed for a studio level, multiple-camera transmission or recording in the field. The film equivalent of the television remote van is the Cinemobile®, a relatively luxurious transport vehicle similar in appearance to a large motor home, that can be used to transport both equipment and talent. It can also provide its own electrical power through a portable generator.

Additional Readings

Adams, William B. *Handbook of Motion Picture Production*. New York: John Wiley and Sons, 1977.
Braddeley, W. Hugh. *The Technique of Documentary Film Production*. New York: Focal Press, 1963.
Shook, Frederick. *The Process of Electronic News Gathering*. Englewood, Colorado: Morton Publishing, 1982.
Wurtzel, Alan, *Television Production*. 2nd ed. New York: McGraw-Hill Book Company, 1983.
Yoakam, Richard D., and Charles F. Cremer. *ENG: Television News and the New Technology,* New York: Random House, 1985.
Zettl, Herbert. *Television Production Handbook*. 4th ed. Belmont, CA: Wadsworth Publishing Company, 1984.

Exercises

1. Scout a specific site outside the studio for a location film or electronic field production. Thoroughly investigate every potential production problem from the availability of electricity indoors to the availability and direction of sunlight outdoors. Determine the best time of day for recording and every piece of equipment that will be needed in the field. Draw up detailed equipment check-off lists and prepare diagrams showing the placement of cameras, lights or reflectors, microphones, and performers.

2. Record an ENG story about a specific problem or issue on your campus. Begin with a reporter's on-camera introduction to the problem. Then record interviews with people who are directly involved in the problem at a location where they actually work or one that is relevant to the issue at hand. Show them performing a relevant task while they talk, if possible. Then record scenes of action or illustration which will depict what the reporter and interviewees are talking about. Finally, record the reporter's closing remarks and summation on camera. This exercise can be combined with subsequent exercises in postproduction editing.

PART 3

POSTPRODUCTION

CHAPTER 14

Visual Editing

This chapter explores one of the most creative stages of the production process: the editing of prerecorded visual images. Single-camera recordings are combined and edited during postproduction. Multiple-camera visual images are often edited during actual production by routing them through a video switcher as discussed in chapter 6. While many of the aesthetic principles presented in chapters 5 and 6 apply to both production and postproduction editing, this chapter develops additional principles and techniques that are applicable to postproduction editing.

EDITING AESTHETICS

The director's aesthetic intentions regarding combinations of images are fully realized during editing. A good editor is both a practical problem solver who comes to grips with the limitations of the visual material which the director has provided and a creative artist who sometimes reshapes and improves this material through the use of imaginative editing techniques.

Visual images can be combined using principles of editing derived from each of the three aesthetic orientations: functionalism, realism, and formativism. Few editing situations are guided by one perspective alone. It is often more effective to combine different approaches.

Functionalism

A functionalist approach to editing emphasizes message clarity and efficiency. In actual practice the editor usually tries to fulfill the director's intentions as specified in the final shooting script as faithfully as possible, but the editor also deviates from the script when necessary.

Editing choices are limited by the quality of the material that has been recorded. In functionalist editing, the editor's primary concerns are eliminating mistakes and clarifying and simplifying the message content. Flubbed lines of dialogue or narration are removed and replaced. Gaps and omissions in coverage are concealed whenever possible. Some mistakes simply cannot be corrected with the material provided. A functionalist editor is an expert at salvaging an acceptable combination of images out of bad material, but sometimes bad material simply has to be reshot by the director or eliminated entirely from the final edited version.

Functionalist editing often follows basic rules of scene construction. A scene or sequence usually begins with an establishing long shot and gradually moves closer to the subject as the action intensifies to reveal more intimate details of character and setting. The overall scene and setting can be reestablished with another long shot at the end of the sequence. A variation on this approach is to begin in close-up to arouse interest and attention and then gradually use more distant shots to establish the setting and orient the viewer. Initial viewer disorientation is gradually overcome and message clarity is eventually reestablished, while interest is added to the scene.

An effective means of enhancing message clarity is to follow a logical cause and effect structure when combining images. In a documentary, an editor can begin with the effect or result of certain actions and then present the causes of this event. For example, an instructional sports program about how to perform a specific gymnastic routine can begin with a presentation of the completed routine and then show the type of preparation and practice that goes into perfecting it. Such a sequence can then conclude with a second version of the completed routine, highlighting the various components.

Realism

Realist editing preserves spatial and temporal continuity from shot to shot. A smooth, unbroken flow of actions and events from one shot to the next maintains an illusion of continuity in time and space. A movement begun in one shot is completed in the next. The editor can cut on the action, such as picking up the same stride of a runner in the subsequent shot, or cut from one shot to the next during a lull or stasis in the action. The first approach adds dynamic energy to the editing, while the second approach slows down the overall pace of the scene.

A realist editor tries to maintain a consistent directional placement of objects and movements in the scene by following basic rules of directionality. The 180-degree axis rule, discussed in chapter 6, is designed to maintain directional clarity. Person A and person B stay on the same side of the screen with respect to each other from shot to shot. If their placement is reversed from left to right, the viewer can become spatially disoriented. By the same token, anything moving from left to right in the first shot should maintain the same direction in the second or the viewer will assume that it has changed direction. Directional glances must be consistent from one shot to the next. If one person is looking up at another person in a close-up, then a close-up of the latter should show him or her looking down. All of this assumes, of course, that the director has followed these basic rules of screen direction during initial recording.

Point-of-view shots can be an effective means of enhancing realism and intensifying viewer involvement and identification with specific participants in a scene. A shot of a character glancing in a specific direction is followed by a shot showing what he or she is looking at from the appropriate perspective. This can be followed by a reaction shot, depicting in close-up the character's emotional reaction to what has been seen. Even in a documentary, point-of-view shots create a ''you are there!'' feeling which adds to the illusion of reality.

Formativism

A formativist approach to visual editing often deliberately disrupts spatial and temporal continuity between shots and calls attention to the editing process. Jump cuts, radical shifts in time and place, a rejection of conventional rules of scene construction, directionality, and continuity all focus the viewer's attention on the manipulative powers of the artist and his or her control of the visual medium. A formativist artist is free to experiment with unusual combinations of shots without the constraints of functionalist clarity or realism. But an artist is not totally free of all constraints and structure. Both aesthetic unity and patterned disruptions of unity are achieved through a conscious and precise manipulation of aesthetic forms.

Formativist approaches to editing often focus on abstract qualities and elements of design within and between shots, such as similarities and differences in shape, color, movement, and texture. Sharp diagonal lines can be juxtaposed to smooth curves and circular shapes. Visual rhythms can be established between shots that are related to audio rhythms in music and sound effects, for example.

Formativist approaches to editing are often incorporated into specific sequences within more conventionally functionalist or realist programming. A dream sequence in a realist drama and a poetic sequence of natural beauty in a documentary about the environment incorporate formative techniques into a more conventional format. Transition devices, such as a dissolve from one scene to the next, can rely on similarities in shape and color between the last shot of one scene and the first shot of the next. Deliberate breaks in temporal and spatial continuity can generate visual interest through temporary viewer disorientation in a more conventional work of fiction or nonfiction.

Common Problems in Functionalist and Realist Editing

Inadequate Coverage
One of the most common problems editors face is poor or inadequate coverage of actions and events in the initial recordings. Some directors operate under the misconception that the editor can solve all problems. At the very best, a good editor can conceal problems resulting from inadequate coverage. At worst, the director will simply have to re-record a few shots or the entire scene. Actions that do not match from one shot to the next, a failure to record every shot called for in the script, or an obvious mistake in every take of a crucial shot are rarely entirely correctable through editing.

Editors rely on specific techniques in an attempt to conceal mistakes in visual coverage. The absence of a crucial shot can sometimes be overcome by using an overlapping shot showing the same action from farther away or closer to the action than originally desired. Cutaways are very useful in terms of hiding mismatched action and movements from one shot to the next, provided the director has supplied them. To be useful, however, cutaways cannot be gratuitous. They must be directly related to the content of the scene. In a documentary, for example, a close-up of a painting that just happens to be in the office of the interviewee can be used as a cutaway only if the content of the picture reveals something important about the individual or relates to the subject matter in some way. Reaction shots, such as one person actively listening to another, are often used to hide mistakes or jumps in the action. In extreme cases the editor may have to entirely restructure a scene and deviate from the script in order to avoid using a problem shot or having the director reshoot a missing shot.

Breaks in Screen Direction
A break in screen direction between shots of the same action or people is difficult for an editor to correct or conceal. Sometimes a cutaway can be used between a shot of someone standing or sitting on another person's right and a shot of the same people with reverse screen direction. The cutaway reduces the impact of this break in continuity by putting additional visual information between these shots and thus helps the viewer forget about the precise directional placement. When a person is moving from right to left in shot A, but from left to right in shot B, a shot directly along the action axis can be used to make a more gradual shift in screen direction. In the absence of cutaways or action axis shots, dramatic changes in screen direction can only be solved by eliminating the deviant shot or by reshooting it.

Combining Moving and Stationary Camera Shots

If the camera is simply tracking along with a moving subject, cutting directly from a moving camera shot to a stationary one rarely causes problems for the viewer. Cutting from one moving camera shot to another or from one zoom shot to another moving in the same direction is not a problem either. But cutting from camera movements that are independent of subject movements to stationary camera shots often causes problems. The editor should wait until the camera movement has stopped within the shot before cutting to a stationary camera shot. The use of moving camera shots tends to slow down the action in comparison to stationary camera cuts, such as from a stationary long shot to a medium shot to a close-up. Using stationary camera shots gives the editor more flexibility in terms of editing possibilities. However, moving camera shots can enhance spatial and temporal realism and provide a somewhat smoother, slower, and more deliberate pace.

VIDEOTAPE EDITING

Postproduction editing can be divided into two stages: preliminary editing and final editing. The difference between these two stages is most clear in large-scale productions, where final editing is eventually performed on large format (1-inch helical) original videotape recordings. These original recordings are often dubbed or transferred to a smaller format for preliminary editing. This preserves the quality of original recordings while allowing an editor some flexibility to edit and re-edit materials without jeopardizing the quality of the final product. The editing decisions made using a smaller videotape format are then used to guide the final editing of the larger format videotape. Some production situations, such as broadcast news, often pass from preliminary to final editing without any clear distinction between the two stages, since a final edited version must be produced quickly and the same small format videotape is used for both recording and editing. Although in this case a firm distinction between preliminary and final editing is more difficult to maintain, preliminary editing generally includes everything that must be done to prepare for the last stages of producing a videotape that can be viewed using the intended means of distribution and exibition. Throughout these preliminary and final editing stages the editor usually follows a script but works creatively, discovering new and unique ways to order, shape, and combine visual images.

Preliminary Editing

Viewing Single-Camera Recordings

One of the editor's first tasks is to organize and catalogue all the material the director has provided. The original recorded images are usually dubbed or copied before they are viewed by the editor. Little if any material that has been rejected during actual production will be copied for viewing purposes. Using a copy protects the original recording, which can be safely stored away. Video copies or dubs made for viewing purposes are often made on a small format, such as 3/4-inch or 1/2-inch videotape. The recorded images are then played back on a VCR and viewed on a monitor. The individual shot and take numbers recorded from the slate at the beginning of each camera take are catalogued on paper. Time code or control track numbers, discussed later in this chapter, are often catalogued at this time as well.

Viewing a copy or dub of the originally recorded shots and selecting and ordering shots is often called **off-line editing.** During preliminary editing a small-format videotape incorporating these editing decisions may be produced through assemble or insert editing, as discussed next, but for simpler editing jobs the editor may jump ahead to final editing.

Assemble Editing   After cataloguing shots that have been recorded, the editor organizes them roughly into the sequence specified in the final shooting script. The editor basically follows the script and selects the best takes of each shot, leaving a five second preroll at the beginning of each camera take. Editing decisions can be gradually refined and tightened up as this stage of editing progresses. Each duplication of a videotape diminishes the quality of the recorded images and sounds. This is why preliminary editing is often done in a smaller format, and preliminary editing decisions are later performed on an originally recorded larger format videotape. An editor should not limit choices too early in the editing process, but rather try out various alternatives before deciding on the final form.

Assemble editing is *only* used to place the shots in rough sequential order, since it does not provide sufficient editing control to edit exactly from one shot to the next. During assemble editing both the control track and the visual images from the original recording are transferred to the new assemble-edited version. Any discontinuities in the control track from one shot to the next cause problems in synchronization and tracking during the playback of the edited videotape. High quality, instantaneous cuts from one shot to the next are simply not possible. Inconsistencies in the control track may cause the picture to roll or jump at edit points. Assemble-edited

Figure 14.1
Assemble and Insert Edited Videotape

A. Assemble Edited

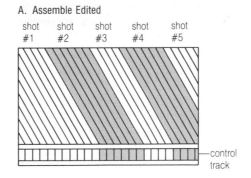

shot #1   shot #2   shot #3   shot #4   shot #5

—control track

B. Insert Edited

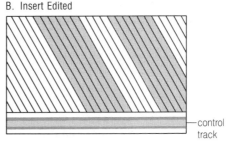

—control track

A. Assemble editing can be a useful way to put complete video shots into proper sequence or order. The main problem with assemble editing is that the control track of the source videotape is transferred to the record videotape. This makes it difficult, if not impossible, to edit smoothly one shot to another at a precise edit point without seeing a roll or glitch on the screen. If assemble editing is used to order shots prior to more precise insert editing, remember to leave at least five seconds of preroll ahead of the eventual beginning point of each shot. Remember also that each successive generation or dub of a videotape degrades or diminishes the quality of the recorded images and sounds.
B. Insert editing allows smooth and precise edits to be made from one shot to the next. A black signal or control track is placed on the record videotape prior to editing (this is also a good time to monitor a new videotape for possible imperfections which can cause noticeable recording and tracking problems during editing and playback). Video images can then be inserted using this prerecorded control track as a guide so that there is no visible glitch or rolling between successive shots. Three modes of insert editing are possible: audio only, video only, and audio plus video, providing considerable editing precision and flexibility.

rough cuts cannot be tightened up later in spots without possibly going through the entire editing process a second time. The main advantage of assemble editing is that it is quite fast, since no tape preparation is necessary. (See Figure 14.1.) *When assembling shots into sequential order be sure to leave at least five seconds preroll space prior to a first cut point for every shot.*

Insert Editing   Insert editing (Figure 14.1) allows for precise, instantaneous cutting from one shot to the next. During insert editing the control track from the original recording is not transferred to the edited videotape. Instead, the entire edited videotape is prerecorded with a continuous black signal and constant control track. Specific shots and visual images can then be inserted into the black signal and playback is governed by this constant control track. Thus there will be no gap or mismatch in control tracks from one shot to the next during insert editing. In addition to the prerecorded black signal and control track, insert editing usually begins with the prerecording of such information as the tape title, **color bars**, which are reference bands of colors, including black and white, and a **timing** or **countdown leader**, which is a sequential series of numbers of time in seconds used for pre-rolling the videotape. (See Figure 14.2.) The first shot is inserted after two seconds of black following the number two on the timing leader. (See Figure 14.3.)

Insert editing allows for considerable editing flexibility. A major advantage of this insert technique is that a portion of one shot can be replaced by another shot. For example, a complete master shot can be recorded first, and then matching close-ups and cutaways can be inserted within it later. A talking head, for example, can be replaced with images showing what that person is talking about.

During insert editing, video-only and audio-only edits can be made, as well as video-plus-audio edits. A portion of the video image can be removed and replaced, while leaving the accompanying audio intact. In the example cited above, the speaker's voice continues and the picture is simply replaced with visuals depicting what is being described. If replacement images require additional sound, a separate track will have to be used on the edited videotape. Audio-only inserts, such as specific sound effects, music, or narration, can be inserted where they are needed to accompany the visuals (on track #1 during 3/4-inch editing, since track #2 is usually reserved for on-set sound, as we will see in chapter 15).

**Figure 14.2
Videotape Head
Leader**

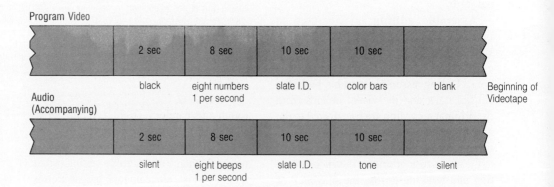

A and B Roll Editing   The term **A and B roll editing** is used for two different processes, one of which usually occurs during preliminary editing and the other during final editing. During final editing, discussed more fully later in this chapter, A and B roll editing refers to an editing system that has two source/playback VCRs wired through individual time base correctors to an editing control unit (Figure 14.4) and a special effects generator (SEG) with the output of the SEG connected to an editing/record VCR. A and B roll video final editing allows many different types of transitions to be made from one shot to another in the final edited version.

The explanation of the preliminary editing process to this point has described A-roll only editing, that is, the process of editing from a single roll of videotape as the source to another roll of videotape. Since A-roll only or "cuts-only" videotape editing systems have just two VCRs and a controller, it is possible to make only direct or straight-cut transitions. To make dissolves, fades, and superimpositions the

**Figure 14.3
Insert Editing**

insert shot #1   insert shot #2

use of a multi-source A and B roll editing system is needed during final editing.

During preliminary editing the term A and B roll editing refers to a specific approach to video editing that is often used in news and documentary postproduction. (See Figure 14.5.) As a preliminary edit-

A. Single-Source Sound Editing

edit control unit

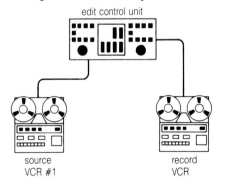

source
VCR #1

record
VCR

B. Multiple-Source Sound Editing

edit control unit

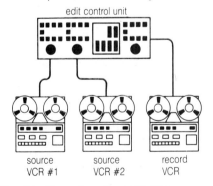

source
VCR #1

source
VCR #2

record
VCR

**Figure 14.4
Single- and Multiple-
Source Editing**

Single-source editing uses one videotape playback or source machine. This allows only one type of transition between shots to be made, namely a straight cut or take. Multiple-source editing uses more than one playback or source machine and allows many different types of transitions to be made, such as dissolves and wipes and special effects, such as superimpositions, when the multiple-source signals are fed through time-base correctors and a switcher or special effects generator.

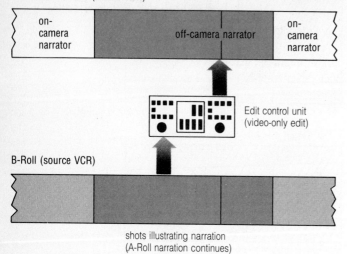

A-Roll and Master (record VCR)

on-camera narrator | off-camera narrator | on-camera narrator

Edit control unit
(video-only edit)

B-Roll (source VCR)

shots illustrating narration
(A-Roll narration continues)

Figure 14.5 Single-Source A and B Roll Editing

Single-source A and B roll editing refers to a convenient editing strategy or approach. Using insert editing on a single-source editing unit, shots are edited together in two sequences. First an A roll of shots and/or key sound bites (dialogue or narration) are edited to determine the overall length of the piece. Then a B roll of secondary illustration material, such as shots depicting the objects or events discussed by an interviewee, or sound effects and music are added. Separate A and B roll videotapes are sometimes assemble edited into rough order prior to insert editing of the A roll and then the B roll onto a single record videotape.

ing method, A and B rolling refers to the preparation of two rolls of videotape that can eventually be edited using an A-roll or cuts-only editing system in two successive stages.

Preparing A and B rolls provides a convenient means of organizing the overall editing process. In nonfiction situations an editor uses the primary on-set images and sounds (those that were originally recorded together on the set) as primary editing reference points. An A roll is created from shots that are given primary value, such as the essential master shots and inserts with accompanying dialogue that make up a conventional scene. The B roll is then composed of shots of secondary importance, such as cutaways and inserts that will be used to add interest to a scene or cover mistakes in the main action.

The editor first combines the various shots from the A roll. The shots from the B roll are then added later. This means that the overall length and duration of the scene is determined by the editing of the A roll only. The B roll shots simply replace portions of shots in the edited A roll. The virtue of A and B roll editing is that the addition of secondary shots does not change the overall length of the videotape. This avoids one of the main problems confronting a videotape editor. When the overall videotape must be shortened or lengthened, the entire tape has to be re-edited from that point on. Separating primary and secondary material helps to prevent this problem and makes the editing process more efficient. The primary shots set the context and limits within which secondary information is inserted.

As an example, suppose you are editing a sequence in a documentary about health care. The primary information consists of an interview with two key professional staff members at a health care facility. The interview was first recorded in two-shot. Then close-ups of the two people were recorded as they repeated important points made during the two-shot. This material is used to create the A roll, since it is of primary importance. Later reaction shots of one person listening to the other and cutaways, such as close-ups of hands and objects used for demonstration purposes, were recorded. Later in the day, shots of the facility itself were recorded to illustrate points made during the interview. All of this material is used to create the B roll.

Following the A and B roll approach, the A roll material is edited first. The edited A roll determines the order of presentation and overall duration of the sequence. Then the B roll material is inserted into the edited A roll wherever it is needed to add interest or cover mistakes and problems. Using video-only editing, shots of the facility can be inserted to accompany the audio interview. A close-up reaction shot, showing one person nodding in agreement with what the other is saying, can be inserted to cover a jump in the action resulting from the editor's attempt to condense the interview and stress the most important points. The result is an interesting sequence that uses the A roll editing of the interview to determine the overall structure and the B roll material to add interest, provide illustrations, and cover mistakes.

Preliminary Editing Systems   An editing system designed for rough cutting or preliminary editing usually allows an editor to perform both assemble and insert edits, video-only and audio-only edits, and video-and-audio edits. Preliminary editing systems generally do not provide for special effects and transitions other than straight cuts from shot to shot, since there is no special effects apparatus. A preliminary editing system is used for final editing in broadcast news and other types of production where the same small-format videotape is used for recording, preliminary editing, and final editing.

A preliminary editing system has three basic components: two VCRs and an edit control unit. One VCR, called a **source**, is used to play a prerecorded videotape; the second, called a **record**, is used to record an edited version of the prerecorded material. The edit control unit is an electronic device that allows the operator to select edit points and transfer images and sounds from the Source VCR to the Record VCR. The edit control unit locks the two VCRs together relying on the videotape control tracks and the servomechanisms in each machine to synchronize the playback and record movements of the two videotapes.

If the two videotapes are not synchronized, there will be a gap or mismatch in the video tracking of the recording between two successive shots. One shot might begin somewhere in mid-frame, such as halfway down the scanning of the image, and the next might begin somewhere else in the scanning of the screen. If two successive shots are not in phase with one another, the image will temporarily flip or break up on the screen when the recording is played back. This problem is similar to that encountered in assemble editing when there is a discontinuity in the control track from shot to shot.

The edit control unit has separate manual drive knobs linked to the Source and Record VCRs. Using these manual drive controls, the editor locates and still-frames the edit points on the two videotapes. The edit point on the Source videotape is the first frame of the shot following the cut, while the edit point on the Record videotape is the last frame in the shot preceding the cut. The edit controller precisely prerolls the two videotapes the same number of frames in front of the two edit points, so that they will reach the two edit points simultaneously when they are rolled at the same time. Most edit controllers allow the editor to preview the cut before it is actually made so that material on the Record videotape is not erased and replaced by the material on the Source videotape. Once the cut has been previewed, it is a simple matter to actually record the new shot by prerolling both machines again and depressing the edit button. The recording from the Source videotape shot is then stopped at a safe distance beyond the next edit point on the Record videotape.

When making a videotape edit and recording it is usually wise to examine the audio and video meters on the record machine during the edit preview to make sure

out boosting background sounds. In addition to the audio and video signal meters and controls, the VCR's **tracking meter** should also be monitored and adjusted for peak reading for every dub to ensure that proper synchronization and speed is being maintained throughout the dubbing process.

Final Editing

Once all the editing decisions have been finalized, the original videotape is edited in conformity to the preliminary edit version and the edit notations made after repeated viewings of the preliminary edited videotape. Final editing is performed using the originally recorded videotape, usually in 2-inch quad, 1-inch helical, or professional high-speed 1/2-inch helical formats such as Recam and Betacam. Sometimes final editing is done using original 3/4-inch U-matic, 8mm, or 1/2-inch Beta and VHS videotape recordings. Final editing often involves special editing devices such as time-base correctors, time codes, and computer controls.

The Time-Base Corrector   The **time-base corrector (TBC)** is a device that stabilizes pictures from a videotape recorder. Extremely accurate digital TBCs modify the video signal so that is can be significantly corrected and stabilized. A TBC improves and stabilizes the tracking of a videotape with mediocre sync, replacing it with entirely new and improved sync when the composite video signal (sync plus picture information) passes through it, but it cannot improve a videotape that refuses to track properly on a playback VCR. A TBC is often used to prepare a small-format videotape for broadcast and

that maximum video and audio levels and signal-to-noise ratios have been achieved during the video or audio dubbing. Weak video or audio signals will produce poor quality recordings. Some VCRs have an **automatic gain control (AGC)** which keeps the audio signal at a constant level although it often boosts background sounds. A **peak limiter** prevents extremely loud sounds from distorting with-then later for use in a larger format. It is also a useful device for allowing several different VCRs to run simultaneously when creating transitions and special effects during A and B roll final editing. Each playback signal must run through a separate TBC.

Time Codes   A **time code** is a series of digits that provides an exact reference for each frame. There are two different types of time code editing that can be used: SMPTE time code editing and control track or frame count editing.

One of the most widely used time codes has been standardized as the **SMPTE (Society of Motion Pictures and Television Engineers) time code**. It is sometimes added to one of the tracks of the originally recorded videotape or it is recorded during the vertical intervals between video fields. It consists of an eight-digit series of numbers beginning with either zero (called **zero start**) or with actual **clock time** in hours, minutes, seconds, and fields (sixty per second). Thus, 01:00:00:01 indicates a point one hour and one field into the recording. Separate cassettes or reels of videotape can be differentiated by hours: 01, 02, and so on. The SMPTE time-code system requires a special generator and reader. The time code can actually be viewed in the video image, which can be helpful during preliminary editing to make editing notations, because the code is actually recorded on videotape.

Another type of editing reference, called **control track** or **frame count**, designates each frame by simply counting the sync pulses in the control track of the original videotape. The frame count is not recorded on the videotape but is calculated by the editing control unit from a specific point where the counter is zeroed. Control

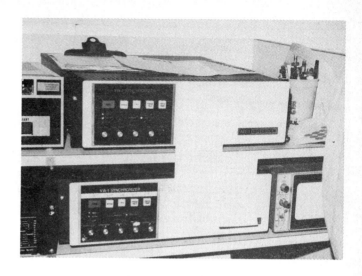

track numbers are not as useful in terms of translating preliminary editing to final editing as SMPTE time code because they are not recorded on the videotape. Both types of time code can be addressed for electronic editing purposes, but SMPTE time code is generally considered more reliable and accurate because it does not depend on monitoring control track pulses, which can themselves be somewhat irregular.

Computer-Assisted Time Code Editing

Recent advances in technology have made it possible to edit videotape automatically by finding and recording the SMPTE time code reference numbers for each edit or effect. **Computer-assisted editing** is often done first in smaller format videotape. A smaller format copy or dub protects the original videotape during the preliminary editing stage. Time code reference capability makes computer-assisted preliminary editing far more accurate and efficient, and the results are directly transferable to final editing.

Time Base Correctors for a multiple-source editing unit.

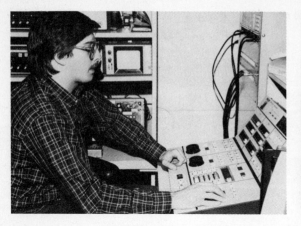

A computerized multiple-source time code editing control unit in operation.

The SMPTE time code numbers can be displayed in the picture so that an editor can make notes during the initial viewing. The editor can then sit down and transfer these numbers into a complete rough cut or preliminary edit of the videotape. The computer will assemble the entire video-

A computerized on-line editing and special effects facility for state-of-the-art 1-inch videotape editing.

tape, when it is properly programmed with the time code reference numbers for the ending and beginning points of each shot in its proper sequence. During final editing, sometimes called **on-line editing**, several playback machines are connected to the **computer control unit** so that they can be fed to the master Record tape. The computer can efficiently record each shot in its proper sequence in the videotape in two ways: either by assembling shots from each different recorder in sequence, or by dubbing shots in their originally recorded sequence on each tape reel to their designated spots on the master Record tape. A multitrack audio tape recorder with a control track is frequently connected to the computer and videotape recorders so that more complex sound tracks can be added to the system. The **edit log** (as shown in Figure 14.6) which was created by preliminary or ''off-line'' editing, can be used on-line to guide the editing process. While minor adjustments may be needed during on-line editing, the creative part of the editing process is usually accomplished off-

Figure 14.6
Example of an Edit
Log

60 Second PSA (Science Briefs) #1

Bars   (30 seconds)
Countdown and slate:

RTVMP Dept. UNC-CH
Science Briefs PSA #1
"Child Development"
6/2/83   60 sec.

10 frame fade in at	01:00:01:10 to 01:00:14:26	Max
cut to	01:03:55:02 to 01:03:57:00	Car
" "	01:14:35:15 to 01:14:36:26	Sign
" "	01:03:07:13 to 01:03:10:07	Car
" "	01:35:58:11 to 01:36:03:01	Pine Cone
" "	01:27:49:06 to 01:27:50:26	Kitchen (CU)
" "	01:27:24:12 to 01:27:26:08	Kitchen (MS)
" "	01:22:45:24 to 01:22:48:18	Typewriter
" "	01:21:25:19 to 01:21:32:17	TV
" "	01:31:18:20 to 01:31:21:18	Phone (MS)
" "	01:32:01:02 to 01:32:03:15	Phone (CU)
" "	01:46:45:05 to 01:46:51:14	Boat
" "	01:00:50:19 to 01:01:00:12	*(10 frame fade out)* Max

ALSO . . . . starting at 01:00:54:22 to fade out, a super at bottom of screen on Max's closing shot:

Science Briefs
The University of North Carolina
at Chapel Hill
Chapel Hill, N.C. 27514

line, since on-line editing time is so expensive.*

Computerized Videotape Editing System

The **computerized videotape editing system** itself consists of a CRT (Cathode Ray Tube) with keyboard and a monitor. The operator programs all the editing manipulations and time-code numbers into the computer. The computer then controls the set up and prerolling of the tapes, the search for subsequent shots, the playback and recording of recorders, and all switcher operations. It is a relatively simple matter to reprogram the computer and make changes. The savings in time can be enormous compared to manually controlled videotape editing or film editing. The CRT terminal displays all the editing information, which can be printed out in hard copy or recorded on a **punch tape**, which is simply a narrow paper roll with coded holes punched in it, as a future editing guide.

There are basically two types of computerized editing systems, the CMX (Consolidated Film Industries and Memorex) system and the EPIC system. Both systems use SMPTE time code numbers for reference and allow all of the edit points to be programmed into a computer, which automatically drives several VTRs.

---

*A fully outfitted, large format, computerized videotape editing and special effects facility, which can cost over $1 million, is too expensive for many producers to purchase for their own exclusive use. Many producers rent a computerized editing facility by the hour, often paying more than $500 per hour for equipment and personnel time. Obviously these cost levels usually prohibit the use of such facilities for creative experimentation.

A and B Roll Final Editing When creating a series of special effects, such as a succession of dissolves, using a computerized editing facility, it is not necessary to make separate A and B rolls prior to editing. The series of effects is not done in "real time." Instead the editor dubs each individual shot in sequential order, regardless of where it occurs in the original recordings. An edit control unit can be used to start the two tapes simultaneously, so that they are synchronized as they enter the special effects generator or switcher. Ex-

tended overlap of the two shots should be included on both tapes to allow some latitude for error when using fader bars to create a dissolve or a wipe. Time code can be used as a reference for creating the precise alternation from A to B roll on the two tapes. A minimum of three VCRs or VTRs are required, since two Source machines and one Record machine are involved, although more Source machines can be added. (See Figure 14.7.)

Electronic Special Effects A switcher, or special effects generator (SEG), is often used in postproduction editing to generate special effects, such as dissolves, wipes, fades, split screens, and graphics and titles from a character generator or computer animation machine (the latter two can be added with a "downstream" keyer, a keying device that changes the video signal after it has left the switcher). In order to produce dissolves, wipes, and split screens, two videotapes must be played back simultaneously using an editing control unit and fed to the switcher through separate inputs. The two VCRs must be connected to TBCs for accurate synchronization. All of these special effects can then be produced on the effects buses in the same manner that they are created during production switching. The output of the switcher is then fed to a master videotape recorder. Fade-outs and fade-ins require that constant black be fed to the switcher, as is the case in a live or live-on-tape production. Graphics can be keyed into the image using various types of keys or a downstream keyer into which a character-generated or computer-animated image can be fed.

The presence of the switcher, a video synthesizer, an SEG, and/or digital video signal-processing devices in a computerized editing system allows many different

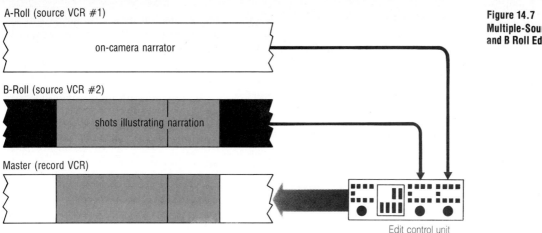

A-Roll (source VCR #1)

on-camera narrator

B-Roll (source VCR #2)

shots illustrating narration

Master (record VCR)

Edit control unit

Figure 14.7
Multiple-Source A
and B Roll Editing

special effects to be created. A variety of wipes, fades, dissolves, and key effects can be accomplished automatically on a postproduction switcher. A **video synthesizer** manipulates the analog video. That is, it can convert the component parts of a video signal, such as each color, into separate electrical signals that can be modified by a computer programmer. The height, width, depth, shape, clarity, or position of an image can be changed by turning a dial or flipping a switch. **Solarization** is a technique which relies on a separation between luminance and chrominance information in a video signal. The color can be drained out of the image to produce a high contrast black-and-white image which can then be synthetically colored by assigning different colors to different shades of gray.

Digital video signal processing devices convert the analog video signal into a digital one by using a numerical code and rapid sampling techniques. The digitally coded signal is easier to store and manipulate than an analog one, and image quality is not lost in dubbing. It is possible to create a wide variety of special effects using digital devices, such as a **digital**

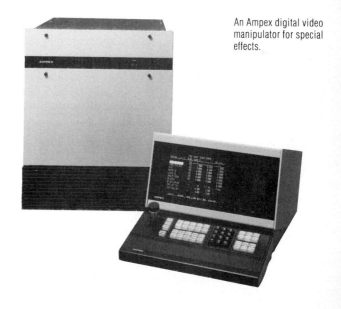

An Ampex digital video manipulator for special effects.

video manipulator (DVM). An image or full frame can be continuously compressed to a point of light. It can be expanded, stretched, freeze-framed, pushed-off or on, made into an abstract ''painterly'' image, and replicated as multiple images on a screen. The DVM can also be connected to the video switcher to create **automatic chroma key tracking** in which the size of the chroma key window can be automatically shaped and positioned. The inserted picture can be proportionately compressed and expanded to fill the window more efficiently and realistically than can conventional chroma key, especially when the main signal camera is tracking or moving and thereby changing chroma key perspective.

::::::::::::::::::::::

FILM EDITING
::::::::::::::::::::::

Postproduction film editing follows a series of stages similar to videotape editing, from preliminary editing that includes viewing a copy of the originally recorded images, called the **workprint**, **rushes**, or **dailies** and selecting and ordering specific shots and scenes, called **rough cutting**, to final editing, called **conforming**. Unlike videotape editing, film is spliced mechanically. Film images can, however, also be transferred to videotape so that they can be edited electronically.

Electronic Versus Mechanical Editing

The choice between electronic and mechanical editing techniques is a simple decision in some areas and is more complex in others. In areas such as broadcast news, electronic (ENG) recording and editing has virtually replaced film and mechanical splicing, but in many other areas, such as television commercials and theatrical films, film mechanical splicing techniques still are widely practiced. It is important for producers who want to be broadly based to acquire electronic *and* mechanical editing skills, since both technologies are widely used in production. Each technology has inherent advantages and disadvantages, which must be recognized before an intelligent choice between them or a decision to combine them can be made.

In comparison to electronic videotape editing, film editing can seem quite laborious and time-consuming, but this is not always the case. For example, it is much simpler to shorten or lengthen an entire film by a few frames during preliminary editing than it is a videotape. An edited videotape cannot be shortened or lengthened without reediting the entire recording from that point on. A film editor has a great deal of freedom to experiment with a variety of different takes and shot sequences and durations at all stages of the editing process.

Preliminary Editing

Screening the Workprint   A copy made from the originally recorded film is called a workprint. The film director usually specifies which camera takes should be printed during production. This information is recorded on a **camera** or **lab report** sheet. Because workprinting is expensive, only takes that are likely to be used during editing will actually be workprinted. The editor, director, and producer view each day's workprint in order to evaluate how well things are going. After viewing and approving the footage, the editor catalogues it before beginning a rough cut. An editor will often view the dailies over and over again to get a feel for the production and to stimulate ideas about how images can and should be combined. Sometimes the original film is immediately transferred to videotape for viewing and editing purposes.

Assemble Editing   The next stage of preliminary editing is to assemble the individual shots into sequential order. Since films are often shot out of continuity, that is, all shots to be made at one location are recorded at the same time, regardless of when they occur in the script, the editor must assemble the shots into the order specified by the script. During the assemble stage of editing, the entire shot is left intact.

As the rough cut progresses and each shot is placed in its proper sequential order, the editor gradually refines the cuts, cutting out all extraneous or unnecessary material. Unused shots are called **outtakes**. They are often left on the original camera rolls. The pieces removed from the shots that are actually used are called **trims**. They are frequently stored on the pegs of a **trim bin**, which is placed near the editing bench. Trims are sometimes spliced back into the film after an editor has tried a specific cut, usually because the cut does not work quite as well as was anticipated. It is therefore unwise to dispose of trims too soon.

Single-System Film Editing   Film images and synchronized sounds can be recorded single system, that is, on the edge of the original film within the camera, or double system on a separate tape recorder. Single-system recording is used chiefly for SOF (sound-on-film) in the 16mm and Super-8mm film recording formats.

In the case of SOF material, such as Super-8mm sound-on-film, sounds and pictures are recorded on film in perfect synchronization. The **magnetically striped film** needs only to be processed after the images and sounds have been recorded before screening and editing can begin. While SOF footage is immediately

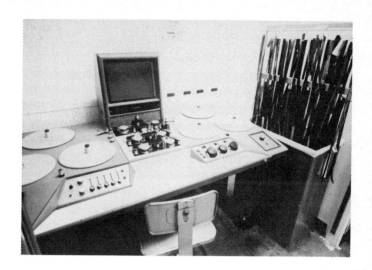

A trim bin next to a six-plate 16mm Moviola flatbed editor.

viewable, it presents certain problems in terms of editing. The magnetic sound that accompanies an image is recorded twenty-eight frames (eighteen frames in Super-8mm) ahead of the corresponding image on the film. If you physically cut the SOF recorded film at a specific point, you have separated the image from its corresponding audio, which is twenty-eight (or eighteen) frames ahead of it. There are three possible solutions to this problem: (1) immediately transfer the film to videotape for electronic editing; (2) make a transfer of the sound track to magnetic film for double-system film editing; and (3) erase or **bloop** (cover over) the sound track where it does not correspond to the visuals and simply present silent visuals where there are no corresponding sounds. It should be noted that the quality of SOF sound is inferior to that of double-system recorded sound. As a result of the editing problems inherent in SOF, double-system recording has become the professional norm. The remainder of this section will consider only double-system film editing.

Double-System Film Editing   In double-system recording, the sound recording is physically separate from the visual, film recording. Film sound is normally recorded on ¼-inch audiotape which can be synchronized with the film recorded in a camera, as was desribed earlier in chapter 6. The ¼-inch tape is transferred to magnetic film so that it can be edited in synchronization with the accompanying pictures. One of the first tasks of film editing is to sync up the film visuals with their corresponding sounds so that the workprint can be screened. This is accomplished by finding a common starting point, such as the visual and audio marker at the beginning of each shot provided by a clapstick. Once the visual image of the closing clapstick or slate is linked up with the "clap" sound, the entire shot will be in proper synchronization. The editor cuts together all of the shots in this manner so that they can be screened by the director, producer, and cinematographer while production is still in progress. The editor screens and carefully catalogues this material while preparing for the rough cut.

Maintaining Sync   The editor must be careful to remove equivalent amounts of picture and sound when trimming a shot, or the film and sound will no longer be in perfect synchronization. If four frames of picture are removed, four frames of sound must be removed. However, an editor can also manipulate the sound track to advantage without completely losing sync. For example, the sound from one shot can be overlapped with the picture of a subsequent shot. The sound accompanying the subsequent shot is spliced into the sound track in midshot after trimming off a portion of its beginning equivalent in length to the overlap from the previous shot. Synchronous sound effects can be spliced into an existing synchronous sound track or added to a second sound track and later mixed with the primary synchronous sound track. When additional sound tracks have been added, the editor must then cut out or add in equivalent amounts on all the tracks wherever a general change is made. Synchronous sounds can also be added to MOS (mitt out sound) footage during editing by simply splicing sounds together so that they match corresponding pictures. (See Figure 14.8.)

Tape Splicing   A **tape splicer** allows the editor to cut photographic and magnetic film and splice the pieces together with tape. The teeth in the splicer hold the film in precise registration so that accurate, frame-line cuts can be made. The tape is placed on both sides of motion picture film, but only on one side (the base or shiny side) of magnetic film, so that it does not affect the sound track. If film is taped on both sides, it will form a proper loop as it goes through the projector gate and thus avoids jamming or breaking. There are a variety of tape splicers and types of splicing tape available. Some are called **guillotine splicers**, because they cut the tape and punch out the sprocket holes, when the editor depresses the handle. Other tape splicers use **preperforated splicing tape**, which must be carefully aligned with the sprocket holes. Regardless of which type of splicer is used, it is important to make sure that all of the sprocket holes are clear of tape, so that the film can be driven properly by the **sprocket teeth** in a projector. Straight frame-line cuts are usually made on the picture film, while a diagonal splice or cut line is often used with magnetic film to suppress popping sounds when the magnetic film passes over a head and to reduce head wear.

Head Leaders Film editing begins with the construction of picture and sound **head leaders**, which are needed to thread up the film on a projector (as shown in Figure 14.9). The leaders identify the film by title and provide a common **start (X) mark** for picture and sound. A timing countdown, such as a standard **academy leader**, normally begins with the number 10 at ten seconds prior to the film's beginning and ends on the number 2 with an accompanying beep on the sound track, indicating 2 seconds to the start of the film. **Opaque black leader** appears after the last number of the academy leader, and the film screen is then black for two seconds until the actual film begins. Having estab-

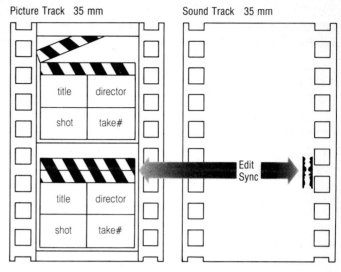

Figure 14.8 Edit/Sync Diagram

Film editing of pictures and sound begins by establishing a common edit sync point. Edit sync refers to exact synchronization between visual images and accompanying sounds. Here an "X" mark on the picture or film leader corresponds to the "X" mark on the sound or magnetic film leader. As editing progresses, every frame of picture will maintain precise frame-for-frame synchronization with its matching frame of sound. If a frame of picture is removed, a corresponding frame of sound must also be removed to maintain edit sync.

Left: A guillotine film tape splicer for splicing pictures and sound during rough editing. Top: The placement of tape over a splice during film editing. Care must be taken to keep the film sprocket holes clear of the tape.

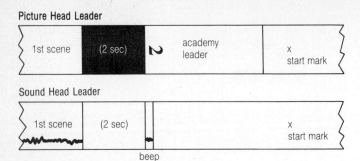

Picture Head Leader

Sound Head Leader

beep

Figure 14.9 Picture and Sound Head Leaders

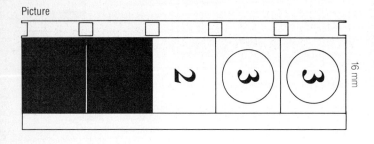

Picture

16 mm

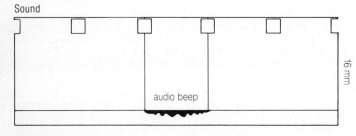

Sound

audio beep

16 mm

Figure 14.10 Head Leader Synchronization Point

Head leaders are placed at the beginning of separate rolls of sound and pictures for a variety of reasons. First, the head leaders identify each roll of film or magnetic film. Second, they establish corresponding edit sync points, such as the corresponding "X's" on the two leaders. The corresponding "X's" can be placed side-by-side on a gang synchronizer at the beginning of each roll to maintain edit sync throughout the editing process. Third, a visual and audio cue can be placed on each roll so that edit sync can be confirmed during projection of sounds and images, such as when viewing the dailies or rushes. If an audio beep is heard at the same time the last number (usually #2) is seen on the film leader projected on a screen, the director and editor know that the sounds and images are in proper synchronization. To check synchronization during actual editing, the editor can rewind the film and magnetic film backwards to the head and check to see if the "X's" still match. If not, at least one shot has placed the sounds and images out of sync, and it must be found and corrected.

lished a common synchronization point at the beginning of the film, the editor assembles shots in the order called for in the script. (Figure 14.10 illustrates the head leader synchronization point.)

Film Editing Systems

Manual Edit Benches A basic **film editing bench** consists of a variety of mechanical and electronic devices which make it possible to view the film and listen to the sound track simultaneously. They also allow an editor to maintain perfect synchronization between the visual and audio tracks, move the film and sound backward and forward, and physically cut and splice the film images and accompanying sound tracks. A **film viewer** projects film frames passing through it on a small screen so that they can be inspected by the editor. The sound tracks run over **sound heads** and are made audible by accompanying amplifiers and speakers. A **gang synchronizer** locks the film and sound tracks in synchronization with each other. The gang synchronizer consists of several sprocketed wheels or hubs on a common drive shaft. A **footage and frame counter** on the drive shaft keeps an accurate record of the footage and frames of the picture and sound tracks.

A set of **rewinds** are hand rotated to move the film and sound tracks through the gang synchronizer, movie viewer, and over the sound heads. The **take-up reels** placed on the rewinds should be equal in diameter so that the picture and sound tracks are driven at the same rate. **Spacers** are needed to separate both the take-up and the feed reels in conformity with the distance between hubs on the gang synchronizer. **Clamps** are needed to secure the reels to each other so that they can be driven by the common drive or rewind shaft, which is hand operated.

Bench editing is a mechanical process. While mechanical editing puts everything under the editor's direct manual control, it also suffers from a number of disadvantages, such as the difficulty in maintaining a constant speed when driving the film and sound by hand. Manually driven edit benches do not reproduce high quality pictures and sounds, making evaluation difficult. To overcome some of these problems, a variety of film editing machines have been developed, such as the Moviola Jr., which uses an electric motor to drive the film on an edit bench.

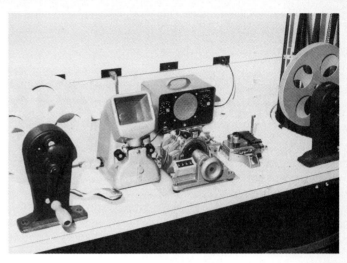

The film bench editing unit includes the following from left to right: rewind, movie viewer, gang synchronizer with sound head and amplifier (in back), a guillotine splicer light box under the synchronizer, and another rewind.

For a clear picture and better quality sound during bench editing, many film editors use the Moviola Jr. film editing machine.

Editing Machines   The **Moviola Jr.** is a relatively inexpensive editing machine, which can be added to an edit bench to provide brighter, clearer pictures and better quality sounds. A motor drives the gang synchronizer, and a viewer and sound playback system are incorporated into the synchronizer. Instead of driving the film and sound tracks by turning the rewinds, an electric motor drives the hubs itself at a constant speed. The bench rewinds simply feed and take up the film and sound tracks as they are moved by the gang synchronizer hubs.

An **upright film editing machine** such as a Moviola Sr. interconnects the sound and picture **drive mechanism** through a common **drive shaft**. They can also be disconnected so that the sound and film tracks can be driven independently by separate motors. The built-in take-up

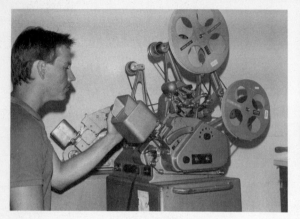

Left: An upright or Moviola Sr. film editing machine. Several sound track or picture elements can be added to this machine. Right: A six-plate Moviola flatbed editor (four of six plates are shown) in operation. There are two sound tracks and one picture track on this editing unit. Sound volume controls are on the front left and picture and sound advance controls are on the front right.

An eight-plate flatbed editor with two picture tracks. Having two picture tracks makes it easier to find transition points and to plan special effects.

mechanism is directly above the feed mechanism thus the name "upright" editor. The picture and sound playback quality are excellent. There is a **variable-speed motor** on the picture side and a **constant-speed motor** on the sound side, used for driving both tracks simulta-

neously. Additional sound track or picture elements can often be added to an upright machine.

Undoubtedly the most convenient film editing machine that has been developed is the **flatbed editor**, which moves the film horizontally on a table. There are many different types and models of flatbed editors. Some advance the picture and sound tracks by a **mechanical interlock** between sprocket drive mechanisms connected to a common motor, while others rely on **electronic synchronization** of separate motors connected to a common electrical distributor. Some flatbed editors can drive only one picture and one sound track at a time. They are called **four-plate flatbed editors**, because they have four take-up and feed dishes or **plates**. More sophisticated flatbeds have six or eight plates, and can run one or two picture tracks and several sound tracks simultaneously in perfect synchronization.

The flatbed offers an editor convenient access to all sound and picture tracks, because of its horizontal configuration. It often provides a **digital readout** of time or footage, a large viewing screen, and a good quality sound playback and amplification system. Some models allow the sound tracks to be **advanced** and **retarded** in relation to the picture, providing added flexibility in finding or manipulating sound/image sync. A flatbed editor can save a great deal of time in comparison to conventional bench editing. It also allows for more accurate editing by virtue of providing higher quality picture and sound playback and better means of manipulating the sound and pictures independently or together. Splices can be made on a flatbed editor by simply turning off one of the feed motors and pulling the marked film out to a splicer at the front of the machine. The open projection gate and sound heads on the flatbed allow the splice points to be easily seen and marked with a grease pencil.

When a splice point is reached on the film, the editor turns off one of the feed motors and pulls the marked film out. Using a grease pencil, as shown above, allows the editor to mark, see, and remove these splice points easily.

Electronic Film Editing   If the final distribution medium for a film project is exclusively videotape, original film recordings are often immediately transferred to videotape for electronic postproduction editing. When both film and videotape final copies are needed for different distribution and exhibition outlets, there are several options in terms of postproduction editing. One option is simply to transfer a final edited videotape back to film. However, recent developments in electronic videotape editing have made it possible to edit film electronically in videotape form and then use the video time code numbers of the edited videotape for final film editing or conforming purposes. A project can be shot as film, edited as videotape, and then conformed as film for film and/or video distribution. This allows a producer to combine the image qualities and char-

acteristics of film with the editing speed and convenience of electronic videotape editing.

While it has been possible for over a decade to transfer a film to videotape for editing purposes, the ability to translate this edited videotape information back to film for final film editing, using SMPTE time code reference, is relatively new. SMPTE time code numbers can be recorded on the edge of original film. These numbers are then transferred to the videotape along with the recorded pictures. After preliminary videotape editing, the original film can be final edited based on the same SMPTE time code numbers produced by preliminary videotape editing.

It is also possible, of course, to follow all of the stages from preliminary to final

A telecine or film chain allows photographic recordings to be transferred to video. The film loaded into the projector on the right is projected into the lens of a video camera through a series of mirrors, called a multiplexer, in the center of the telecine. The multiplexer allows other photographic materials, such as slides, to also be transferred to video.

film editing and then make a film-to-videotape transfer from the final edited film. The choice among these options often hinges on budgetary considerations, completion deadlines, and decisions concerning which medium is most important in terms of distribution markets. If editing speed is critical and videotape is the primary distribution medium, electronic editing will usually be selected. If film is the primary distribution medium, mechanical film editing will often be used.

Final Editing

In film editing, preliminary editing takes the form of rough cutting and tape splicing the workprint. Once the film editing deci-

sions have been finalized, the original film is **conformed** to the edited workprint. Conforming is a professional skill that is often performed by a person called a **conformer**, particularly when a negative original must be cut together without error or getting the film dirty. All of the shots from the originally recorded film are permanently spliced into two or more rolls, called **A and B** (and C, and so on) **rolls**, using a cement splicer which physically welds two overlapping pieces of film together. In 16mm conforming, the individual shots must be divided into two rolls of alternating shots. One difference between 16mm and 35mm conforming is that there is sufficient space between frames in 35mm to be able to make overlapping cement splices on a single roll, although a B roll is required for dissolves, fades, and superimpositions. Individual shots on a roll of 16mm film must alternate with a black leader so that overlap splices always overlap into the black leader and are thus invisible when the film is printed. Film **conforming** is analogous to A and B rolling during final or on-line videotape editing, although considerable preparation time is essential. The completed A and B rolls are printed to a single piece of film, called an **answer print**, at a film laboratory, before a final viewable image is obtained. A film on which picture and sound tracks are ''married'' together is called a **composite print**.

Marking the Workprint   Because the edited workprint serves as a guide for subsequent editing stages, it must be properly marked with appropriate symbols and designations. A grease pencil should be used to mark the film, since these markings can easily be rubbed off the film.

The most commonly used symbols indicate the location of fades, dissolves, superimpositions, extended scenes, and unintended splices. To mark a **fade-in**, simply separate two lines from a point where the shot is to begin fading. The lines reach the outer edges of the frame where the shot is fully lit. The number of frames covered by the lines should equal the length or duration of the effect. A **fade-out** is marked by connecting two lines from the outer edges of the frame, where the fade-out begins to the precise point where the scene is supposed to be completely faded out. Again, the number of marked frames corresponds to the length of the effect. At twenty-four frames per second, a twenty-four frame fade-out will, of course, last exactly one second. A **dissolve** is indicated by placing a fade-out marking on top of a fade-in mark. In this case one shot fades out, while another fades in. For a **superimposition** or **double exposure**, the basic shot or dominant scene is spliced into the workprint at the beginning and ending points of the effect, but the recessive, superimposed shot is cut into the middle section. A wavy line drawn through the entire sequence indicates a double exposure or superimposition. An **extended scene** is one that continues despite the fact that the actual footage for this scene is missing in the workprint. A straight horizontal line shaped like an arrow indicates how far the prior shot extends. Finally, **unintended splices** in the workprint are clearly marked with two short horizontal lines drawn through the splice so that there is no confusion about shot changes at this point in later editig stages. (Figure 14.11 illustrates how workprints are usually marked.)

Edge Numbers   **Edge numbers** are consecutive reference numbers printed onto the edge of original film either by the manufacturer of the film or by the film

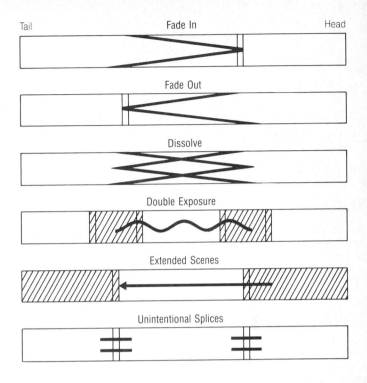

laboratory after processing. The latter are called **yellow ink edge numbers**. Edge numbers corresponding to those of the camera original film from which the workprint has been copied can be printed onto the edges of the workprint. After the workprint has been edited, the edge numbers are used to select the correct shots from the original film for conforming to the edited workprint. The beginning and ending edge numbers of each shot in the edited workprint are written down so that the corresponding shots in the original film can be "pulled" and spliced together in their correct order.

Conforming the A and B Rolls   Once the workprint has been edited and marked, the original film from which the workprint was copied must be **conformed** to the workprint. Instead of editing shots to-

**Figure 14.11
How Work Prints Are
Marked for Effects**

gether into a single roll as in workprint rough cutting, the camera original is conformed into two rolls, an A roll and a B roll. (See Figure 14.12.) This is done to make the splices between different shots invisible in 16mm and Super-8mm formats and to allow for special effects, such as fades, dissolves, and superimpositions. The splices are made invisible by using black leader between successive shots on a single roll of film. Thus, where there is a shot on the A roll, there is black leader on the B roll. The only exception to this rule occurs in conforming fades for negative film, which require clear leader opposite a

fade-out. In negative film, black is created by fading light in, not fading it out. In any case, the two rolls of film are edited in a checkerboard fashion, except for dissolves and superimpositions, where shots are completely or partially overlapped. The individual shots are cement spliced to the black leader. Splices require a slight overlap, so that the two pieces of film can be welded together. To make the splices invisible, the overlap always occurs in the leader area. The emulsion must be scraped off the picture film where it will be bonded to the black leader, so that the two bases come into contact. Film emulsion inhibits

**Figure 14.12
A and B Roll
Preliminary and
Final Editing**

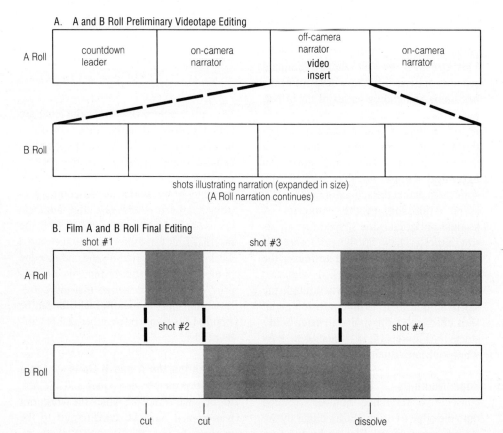

A. A and B Roll Preliminary Videotape Editing

A Roll: countdown leader | on-camera narrator | off-camera narrator / video insert | on-camera narrator

B Roll:

shots illustrating narration (expanded in size)
(A Roll narration continues)

B. Film A and B Roll Final Editing

shot #1 ... shot #3

A Roll

shot #2 ... shot #4

B Roll

cut   cut   dissolve

the action of the cement. The cement splice provides a permanent bond, and it leaves no unsightly marks.

A conformer prepares the original for splicing by pulling all the shots from the camera original and placing them on individual **plastic cores** which are labeled and arranged in sequential order. An alternative approach is to simply pull each shot from its respective camera original roll as it is needed. The conformer makes a complete list of the edge number markings of the edited workprint, and the original camera shots are pulled on the basis of the edge numbers. The film is usually cut with a frame and a half extra at both the head and tail ends of an individual shot, so that there is ample room for overlap. Conformers usually adopt a standard set of procedures with no variations to avoid mistakes while cutting and splicing original film. Cleanliness is extremely important, because dirt and scratches will show up in the final prints. This problem is aggravated when using negative film, because the scratches and dirt then show up as white marks on the final prints. When all the shots have been prepared for splicing, the conformer places the A and B rolls and the workprint in the gang synchronizer on the editing bench, and proceeds to splice the shots alternately into one of the two rolls, leaving overlaps of specified lengths for dissolves and superimpositions.

Cement Splicing
Cement splicing requires the use of a properly adjusted cement splicer. The proper adjustment and alignment of the cutting blade and arms is crucial to the quality of the splice. They should only be adjusted by a trained professional. Cement splicers can be either hot or cold: **hot splicers** have a heating element that was once needed to speed the

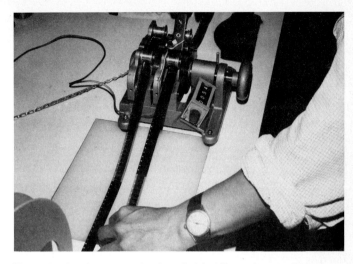

Film conforming places successive shots of original film on alternate rolls so that invisible cuts, other transitions, such as dissolves, and special effects, such as superimpositions, can be made by printing these two separate rolls onto a single piece of unexposed film.

drying process; **cold splicers** do not have any heating element. Today, cement has very little water which must evaporate, so heating is rarely necessary. It is important to use fresh cement, however, since the welding capacity of cement deteriorates with exposure to air.

To make a 16mm splice, the black leader is positioned with the emulsion side up in the right-hand side of the splicer, by placing the teeth of the splicer in the correct sprocket holes of the leader and then locking down the top portion of the arm. Generally this should leave about 1½ frames of excess leader beyond the cutting edge or blade of the splicer. Raising the blade and then bringing it down over the left-hand arm severs the leader at the proper point. Now the adjacent shot is positioned in the left-hand arm so that the frame line where the splice will occur is placed close to the end of the blade or on

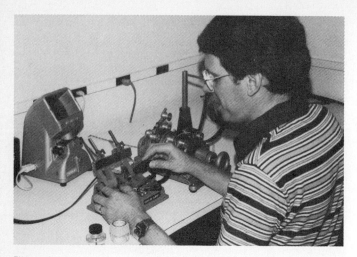

Film conforming normally involves permanent cement splicing. Precision and cleanliness are essential, since no mistakes can be made without damaging the film and dots and lines will be clearly visible on the prints made from conformer originals that are dirty or scratched. The experienced conformer in this picture has made a crucial mistake. Can you catch it? He is not wearing clean white gloves that will keep his oily fingerprints off the film.

Combining the A and B Rolls　Once the A and B rolls are conformed to the workprint, they are sent to the laboratory, so that they can each be printed in succession to a single roll of film, called an **answer print**. The answer print is a test printing of the A and B rolls, after they have been properly **timed**, that is, the color and density of each shot is adjusted by a laboratory professional, called a **color timer**. A composite print marries the A and B rolls together with a sound track so that it can be run in a conventional projector. The composite print usually has an optical soundtrack, which is advanced twenty-six frames in 16 mm or twenty frames in 35mm ahead of the corresponding pictures. A magnetic (sound-on-film) soundtrack, as previously noted, is advanced twenty-eight frames ahead of the corresponding pictures in the 16mm format and eighteen frames in Super 8mm.

Special Effects

An **optical printer** is needed to create most special effects on film, although many effects such as dissolves, fades, and superimpositions can be made more easily and less expensively on a conventional **contact printer** which brings the original film and the copy into physical contact (emulsion to emulsion) as they pass over a light. A and B roll printing is conventionally done on a contact printer. A basic optical printer consists of a camera and a projector. The two machines face each other, and the lens of the camera is focused on the image from the projector. The camera and projector can be moved toward or away from each other to increase the size of the image. An optical blowup can be created by using a larger format and a

the cut line. The emulsion is firmly and evenly scraped off the overlapping portion of the excess 1½ frame of the film so that only the clear base remains. Cement is applied to the scraped portion of the left-hand piece of film and the right-hand arm is brought down quickly and locked it into its welding position. This both cuts off the excess portion of the shot and brings it into contact with the black leader. In five to ten seconds the cement will have completely dried and the spliced film can be removed and inspected. A splice should be able to withstand considerable gentle pulling and twisting. This will ensure that it will not break on the printer.

Black leader is never scraped in the cement splicer, unless you are splicing black leader to black leader, as this will cause the splice line to be visible in a frame of picture.

smaller format projector. Using a smaller format c4mera and a larger format projector creates an optical reduction. The camera and the projector must be precisely positioned so that the full frame of picture in the projector fills the full frame of picture in the camera.

More sophisticated optical effects require the use of additional techniques and equipment. Optical fades can be made by gradually covering or uncovering the lamp in the projector with a fader bar. Optical fades are usually made with a **taper**; that is, with a logarithmic increase or decrease in light intensity. A taper assures that the light changes intensity gradually during a fade-out or fade-in. A strictly linear curve as opposed to a taper is used for dissolves, so that scene ''A'' fades out at exactly the same rate as scene ''B'' fades in. Optical **flips** can be achieved by simply rotating elements within special optical printer lenses. **Freeze frames** are made by exposing many frames in the camera, while holding the same frame in the projector. **Stretch printing** slows down or retards the perceived action by printing each frame more than once. **Skip printing** is often used to speed up a slow-moving sequence by recording every other frame of the original film. Wipes, split screens, and optical combinations of animation and live action involves the creation of special **traveling mattes. Mattes** consist of special high contrast, black-and-white images that are made from normal film images or from artwork.

For example, suppose a color title must be inserted into a background scene. The two images cannot simply be superimposed on one another, since the colors will bleed together rather than producing ''solid'' lettering. A black-and-white high contrast copy of the titles can be made, so that the black letters will block out the portion of the background image where the colored letters are to be inserted. The optical printer must have three projectors to do this: one for the background scene, one for the matte (unless the matte and the background scene are bi-packed or run physically in contact with each other in one projector), and one for the color titles. The combination of the three images is then recorded by the camera.

Wipes and **split screens** can be made from similar traveling mattes, which block out a portion of the screen into which a second image is then inserted. It is possible to combine live action and animation by using traveling mattes in this manner. One sequence can also be recorded against a blue or black screen so that another sequence can be inserted into the blue screen area. Many special effects in science fiction and horror films are achieved by using a **blue-screen process**. Spaceships are often recorded as they move in front of a blue screen. This blue screen portion of the frame is then used to create a matte which blocks out the area of the frame where the spaceship should appear in a highly detailed background scene with stars in outer space. The spaceship is then inserted as a foreground object into this area.

The choice between doing special effects on film versus videotape is often a difficult one to make unless it has already been decided to use film or videotape for an entire production. The obvious advantage of video is the savings in overall production time. Effects can be set up and be viewed immediately, without waiting for laboratory processing. Electronic effects facilities normally have sophisticated computerized editing and switching equipment, so that several images can be run simultaneously. Keys and mattes can be created instantaneously.

The purchase or rental cost of these facilities can be staggering, however. Careful preplanning must go into the creation of a special electronic effect prior to entering the studio. While digital video-signal processing devices have greatly improved the quality of electronic images, it is sometimes difficult to control images with the same accuracy and precision in video as in film. Optical film effects are time consuming to produce, but a very high degree of control and precision can be achieved through multiple passes of the same art work, with film. It is also possible to make sophisticated special effects in film with very low cost equipment. A basic optical printer consisting of a simple projector and camera on adjustable platforms can be purchased for a modest sum, allowing freeze-frames, step printing, superimpositions, dissolves, and many other optical effects to be created.

Summary

Editing aesthetics can be approached from the perspectives of functionalism, realism, and formativism. Functionalist editing stresses message clarity and editing efficiency. Realist editing preserves the continuity of actions and events in space and time. Formativist editing stresses the abstract or formal qualities of the images which are combined, often breaking some basic rules of functionalist and realist editing. Common problems an editor encounters in functionalist and realist editing are inadequate coverage in the original recordings, breaks in screen direction, and difficulties in terms of combining moving and stationary camera shots.

Postproduction editing is done electronically with videotape and mechanically with film. Videotape editing can be divided into two sequential stages: preliminary and final. Preliminary editing begins with the viewing of the originally recorded videotapes, usually using smaller format videotape.

There are two basic types of electronic editing procedures: assemble editing and insert editing. Assemble edits are made sequentially on a blank videotape. The control track of the original recording is transferred to the master tape along with each shot in sequential order. Insert editing can only be done to a prerecorded master tape, since it requires a prelaid sync or control track. A Record tape can be edited in the insert mode by recording visual black and a sync pulse on the Record tape and then replacing the black image with the prerecorded images. Insert editing generally produces a steadier, more consistent image than assemble editing, because there is a constant, prerecorded control track on the master tape, rather than different control tracks for each visual segment. It also allows for video-only, audio-only, and audio-plus-video edits to be inserted in prerecorded material.

A basic videotape editor unit allows an operator to find the precise edit point where a cut or transition from one shot to another is to be made. This edit point must be the beginning or ending of a complete video frame. The basic editor unit consists of two VCRs with accompanying monitors and an edit control unit, which controls the playback, recording and combining of visual images. One of the VCRs acts as a Record machine, while the other is used exclusively as a Source of prerecorded images, portions of which are dubbed to the Record videotape.

Final videotape editing uses the original recordings, often made on larger formats, to complete the editing process. Special editing devices are often required. A time-base corrector (TBC) is usually needed to stabilize control tracks, allowing several playback machines to be synchronized with each other. Specific time codes, such as the SMPTE time code, are needed for exact videotape frame reference, when electronic videotape editing is to be done with computer assistance.

A computer-assisted videotape editing unit usually consists of a CRT terminal monitor and keyboard, several VTR playback machines and monitors, and a VTR recorder. When special effects are needed a video switcher or special effects generator is added to the system and is also computer controlled. An operator enters the edit decisions into the computer on the keyboard and CRT screen or uses a punch tape produced by preliminary editing. Computer editing equipment is extremely expensive to purchase or rent, generally limiting its use to high-budget productions. When a video switcher is connected to the system, a variety of special effects, such as dissolves, fades, wipes, and key effects, can be computer controlled. A video synthesizer and a digital video manipulator (DVM) add additional electronic special effects capability.

Film editing follows a series of stages which are similar to those of videotape editing, from preliminary editing that includes screening the dailies, rushes, or workprint and rough cutting to final editing and conforming. The workprint or dailies are copied from the originally recorded images so that they can be viewed and rough cut without harming the originals. This workprint or dub can be viewed repeatedly in an effort to determine the best way in which images can be combined.

During the rough cutting stage the various shots are first assembled into the basic order specified in the script. The workprint is physically spliced together with tape. Each shot is spliced into its proper sequence, and the rough cutting gradually refines the combinations of shots. Rejected shots are called out-takes, and rejected portions of shots are called trims. Trims are usually saved in the event that editing changes must be made and edit points redone. Double-system synchronous sound recording allows the sound and images to be completely separate during the editing process, avoiding many of the problems inherent in single-system film editing.

A variety of film editing systems have been developed. A conventional mechanical edit bench consists of a set of rewinds, a viewer, sound reader, tape splicer, and gang synchonizer. Various machines can facilitate film editing, such as the Moviola Jr., upright editors, and flatbed editors. Film can also be transferred to videotape and edited electronically.

Film is conformed by cement splicing rolls of original film, which usually "checkerboard" or alternate consecutive shots between an A roll to a B roll. These A and B rolls conform to the edited and marked workprint. Cleanliness and accuracy are essential during conforming, since any damage to the film will affect the quality of the final prints. The A and B rolls allow special effects, such as dissolves, fades, and superimpositions to be created in film. A single film copy or answer print is made by combining the two rolls onto a single piece of film in the lab. A composite print marries the pictures together with an optical or magnetic sound track.

Special film effects are made on an optical printer. A basic optical printer consists of a camera focused on the image from a projector. By manipulating the speed and/or distance of the projector with respect to the camera, a variety of effects, such as freeze frames, skip printing and slow motion, blowups and reductions, can be obtained. Fades and lap dissolves can be accomplished with great precision on an optical printer.

Additional Readings

Burder, John. *The Technique of Editing 16mm Films*. New York: Hastings House, 1970.

Fielding, Raymond. *The Technique of Special Effects Cinematography*. 2nd ed. New York: Focal Press, 1985.

Happe, L. Bernard. *Your Film & the Lab*. New York: Focal Press, 1974.

Levitan, Eli L. *Electronic Imaging Techniques*. New York: Van Nostrand Reinhold, 1977.

Roberts, Kenneth H., and Win Sharples. *A Primer for Film-making*. New York: Bobbs-Merrill, 1971.

Yoakam, Richard D., and Cremer, Charles R. *ENG: Television News and the New Technology*. New York: Random House, 1985.

Zettl, Herbert. *Handbook of Television Production,* 4th ed. Belmont, CA: Wadsworth, 1984.

Exercises

1. Edit together the ENG recordings from exercise #2 in chapter 13. Use A and B roll preliminary editing techniques. Assign the on-camera reporter introduction and closing remarks, as well as the interview recordings, to the A roll. The B roll should be composed of shots that illustrate what the reporter and interviewees are talking about. Try to edit the story to a specific length, such as four minutes, and carefully control the pace and dramatic structure of the sequence, as discussed in chapters 4 and 14.

2. Edit your own version of a professionally recorded scene or sequence. Obtain a copy of the original, unedited recordings of a professional quality production. One example is the film entitled *Film Editing: Interpretation and Values,* which is available from the American Cinema Editors (ACE). This film consists of original camera takes of a sequence from the TV program ''Gunsmoke'' and several different versions edited by professional Hollywood film and television editors. The ACE's annual student editing contest is another potential source of professional recordings or rushes. After you have edited these shots in film or videotape form, compare your version to the version actually produced by a professional editor and determine what you could do to improve your own editing.

CHAPTER 15

Sound Editing

Sound editing is an extremely important stage of postproduction. Sounds can breathe life, realism, emotion, and power into visual images. Sounds can also develop their own form of expression apart from visual images. Sounds can be edited at the same time that visual editing takes place and/or at a later or earlier time during postproduction.

The fact that sounds and images can be edited in tandem or independently of each other allows for considerable flexibility in terms of editing different types of sound and different combinations of sounds and visual images. Each different type of sound, such as speech, sound effects, and music, can be edited in conjunction with visual images. As noted in chapter 5, sounds can be synchronous or asynchronous, on-screen or off-screen, and parallel or contrapuntal in meaning with respect to accompanying visual images. Separately edited speech, sound effects, and music tracks can be blended or mixed together to form one sound track.

This chapter examines sound editing aesthetics, editing and mixing various types of sound such as speech, sound effects, and music, using videotape, film, and audiotape. A complete understanding of sound editing is contingent on familiarity with the material on visual editing, directing aesthetics, and sound recording in previous chapters.

SOUND EDITING AESTHETICS

Sound editing is a complex process. It involves combining many different types of sound using various forms and stages of both editing and mixing. From the standpoint of aesthetics, the complexities of sound editing can be approached from three different perspectives: functionalism, realism, and formativism.

Functionalism

Functionalist sound editing, like functionalist visual editing, emphasizes message clarity. The editor removes mistakes, such as flubbed lines of dialogue or disruptive background sounds, and tries to achieve a proper balance between speech, sound effects, and music. Primacy is usually given to one of these elements at a time, so that the main message is clear and distinct. By simplifying and ordering sounds an editor avoids listener disorientation and confusion. The space between lines of dialogue or narration is made long enough to allow for a smooth, clear, and natural delivery, but short enough to maintain interest and excitement. News stories and prerecorded interviews are examples of situations that often call for a functionalist approach to editing. A reporter's voice-over narration or the responses of an interviewee are often edited to maintain better message clarity and flow.

Realism

Realist sound *recording*, discussed in chapters 5 and 9, preserves a feeling of authenticity and accuracy of specific sounds; realist sound *editing* preserves a continuity of sounds in time and space. Generally speaking, time flows continuously and sequentially from one sound to the next. There are no apparent gaps or breaks in the audio action.

Realist sound editing often reinforces realist visual editing. Sounds can follow the lead set by visual images, enhancing, filling out, and reinforcing the images they accompany. Realist sounds are usually synchronous, on-screen, and parallel in meaning with the accompanying images. They rarely develop an independent meaning and value that can compete with visual images. Sound editing normally is done at the same time as visual editing. Synchronized speech, sound effects, and music are basically conformed to the requirements of specific visuals throughout the editing process. In some situations, such as news and documentary editing, a sound track composed of voice-over narration and interviews is edited prior to the selection and editing of illustrative images. Nevertheless, sounds and images remain parallel in meaning and complement one another.

Formativism

Formativist sound editing, on the other hand, develops sound as an independent aesthetic element. Continuity of time and space is often disrupted. Sounds are frequently asynchronous, off-screen, and contrapuntal with respect to accompanying visual images. Sound effects, for example, create imaginative impressions rather than an illusion of reality or authenticity. Music and accompanying visuals reflect both similarities and differences in pace and meaning. The editor freely develops abstract audio relations and qualities.

Experimental filmmaker Michael Snow's film *Wavelength* plays on various conceptions of audio (sound) and visual (light) wavelength. A specific sound frequency or tone accompanies on-set sounds and a continuously advancing zoom shot ending on a photograph of an ocean wave hanging on the wall of an urban apartment. Sounds and accompanying images are not always on the same wavelength. Nor are the people who are trying to communicate

with each other on-screen and off-screen as the zoom shot advances. Snow's formativist uses of sound run the gamut of aesthetic possibilities from on-screen and off-screen sounds to those that are parallel or contrapuntal with respect to their accompanying images. Formativist sound editing techniques can be incorporated into conventional sequences to add a degree of unpredictability, generating viewer interest and emotional excitement. The films of Alfred Hitchcock made since the coming of sound are good examples of formativist sound editing within realist films.

Visual Versus Sound Primacy

Which element is more important in terms of editing, sounds or images? Editors implicitly or explicitly answer this question when they begin to edit. In some cases sound editing occurs first and sets the context for visual editing. In other cases the reverse is true. There is also a third possibility: visual and sound editing can occur simultaneously, and they can be of equal importance. Even when specific sounds and images are clearly designated in the script, an editor must make decisions about which component is more important when a scene simply cannot be edited as written.

Editing a sequence in a news story or a documentary usually begins with an analysis of the essential verbal information and sound bites that will guide and punctuate editing. The crucial verbal information consists of interviews and narration. A **sound bite** is a specific statement made by someone in the news. The editor usually has dramatic shots and sounds that illustrate the main point and add interest and excitement to the story. In this case the primary information is contained in the recorded sound, not the pictures. Editing decisions are based primarily on sound rather than visual information. Sounds and their accompanying images are edited first. Other visual information is of secondary importance and is edited later. The concept of A and B roll preliminary videotape editing, discussed in chapter 14, is consistent with this approach.

Editing an action sequence in a drama usually begins with an analysis of the primary visual shots that will guide the action. Visual pacing, continuity in space and time, and point of view are primarily visual considerations. Editing decisions focus on visual information, with sound of secondary importance. Illustrative, realistic sound effects and appropriate music can be added and edited later. Some synchronous sounds are, of course, edited in conjunction with the visuals they accompany.

Editing a typical dialogue sequence in a drama or an isolated interview in a news story or documentary often calls for equal stress on visual and audio information. Editing decisions must take both factors into consideration. A specific shot may have good visual material but problems in the sound track, for example. The reverse also occurs and at some point a compromise has to be made. The audio from one shot can be used to accompany the visual from another or the audio can be rerecorded during postproduction. Visuals sometimes have to be reshot as well.

It is not always possible to select the best visual and the best sound recordings, when the two were originally recorded at the same time and are of equal importance. The editor's choices are restricted by the script, which indicates what lines of dialogue must be used as well as which visual shots must be used at a specific time. But the editor must deviate from the script slightly when problems arise in the original recordings and neither the sounds nor the images can be rerecorded.

EDITING AND MIXING SOUND

Mixing Techniques

Sound mixing combines several different sounds or sound tracks which are running simultaneously. Editing, on the other hand, pieces sounds together in sequence, usually on one sound track at a time.

Mixing is a process by which various sound tracks are blended together or combined with each other. Individual sound tracks for speech, sound effects, and music, for example, are first edited into sequential order, often in conjunction with visual images, prior to mixing them together to form one sound track. The volume of each different audio element is separately controlled using a fader on an audio console or mixer.

It is extremely important to maintain a high signal-to-noise ratio in each separate sound track prior to the mix. During the mix, the audio level of one sound track can always be reduced. But speech, sound effects, or music that were initially recorded or dubbed at a low sound level cannot be increased in volume during the mix without simultaneously increasing the accompanying noise level, and thereby reducing the quality of the audio. Whenever possible, sounds should be kept at their maximal level until the mix and then adjusted to accommodate other sounds.

AGCs (automatic gain controls) are sometimes used to maintain consistent audio levels during audio recording and dubbing. This method too often boosts background noise to unpleasant levels during nonspeaking passages. A peak limiter reduces excessively loud sounds without boosting background sounds. Both of these devices can affect the setting of maximal mixing levels.

Transitions   During a mix, the sound editor adjusts the volume of one sound element with respect to another. Sounds can be superimposed on one another, and transitions between sounds such as fades, crossfades, and segues, can be created. During an audio **fade**, the pot or fader for a sound is gradually turned up or down. A **cross-fade** combines a **fade-out** on one track with a simultaneous **fade-in** on another track. A **segue** (seg'-wā) is an instantaneous change from one track to another. Sound mixes usually involve several playback units channeled through an audio console to a single = (monophonic) or dual = (stereophonic) track master tape. The editor or mixer operator must set the proper volume for each playback source and control all special effects and transitions. A mix is carefully preplanned on a mix log or audio cue sheet.

Preparing a Mix Log   A **mix log** or **audio cue sheet** indicates all the volume changes and transitions for every sound source the sound mixer must control. It is organized sequentially according to the overall time of the program. Changes in any sound source or the fader assigned to it are then listed under the column devoted to that source indicating the precise time the change is to occur.

The mixer operator consults the log sheet as a guide to the adjustment of each individual sound source. For example, the opening music may have to be faded in at the beginning of the program and a narrator's voice may then be faded in over the music a few seconds later. The music may

have to be decreased in volume at this point, so that it does not drown out the narration. Forty seconds later the music may segue to another composition, which conveys a different mood or pace. Sound effects may have to be combined with this music, and at certain points, speech, sound effects, and music will probably occur simultaneously. Without a mix log sheet, the editor or mixer could easily become confused during a sound mix.

Editing Speech

Synchronous Dialogue   Synchronous dialogue is generally recorded simultaneously with accompanying visual images. The sounds and images are then edited at the same time in the same format. When editing synchronous dialogue, an editor must be sensitive to the performance level, intonation, and accuracy of the speaker. Speech sounds that are radically different in intensity or intonation should not be edited together, even though their visual images match. Mistakes in the delivery of lines of dialogue should be removed.

Compromises in editing synchronous speech sounds are inevitable, since editing together the best quality images does not always result in the best quality synchronous sounds. The editor is sometimes forced to compromise between image quality and sound quality. An editor must be flexible and creative. For example, it may be necessary to use cutaways, such as a character's reaction to the speech of another character, to cover over mistakes in synchronous dialogue. Two or more portions of the same on-camera speech can be combined to remove missed lines or poor inflection, but unless there are cutaways, visual jump cuts will result. An editor must constantly make decisions on the basis of what is least objectionable, poor quality sounds or poor quality images, when editing synchronous dialogue and visuals.

Looping   **Looping** synchronous sound refers to the creation and replacement of lip-sync dialogue in the sound studio during postproduction. The visual images are repeatedly projected on a sound studio screen, while the talent attempts to repeat the lines of dialogue exactly in sync with the lip movements of the on-screen speaker. These newly recorded speech sounds can be used to replace poor quality original recordings. Looping is often done with the performer trying to speak in unison with the playback (via headphones) of the original, on-set speech which is used as an audio reference. It is usually less expensive to replace defective dialogue than to reshoot the whole sequence. However, sound studio speech often seems dead and lifeless in comparison to the original recordings with which it must be intercut, unless the sound signal is properly processed. An editor must pay particular attention to the pace, intonation, and vocal quality of the specific lines of dialogue that are to be inserted within an originally recorded scene.

Narration   Nonsynchronous or voice-over narration is frequently used to provide a commentary on visual actions. Voice-over narration can be edited together from audio interviews conducted in the field or it can be recorded after visual editing in real time with the narrator watching a preliminary edit of the film or videotape and pacing his or her speech to the changing shots and speed of the action. In the former case the visuals are edited to the narration. In the latter case, the editor's job is to touch up various narration segments so that they coincide with specific

visuals and mistakes are removed. The pace of the narration may need to be speeded up or slowed down during recording or editing to accommodate specific visual sequences. Errors in delivery can sometimes be removed through judicious editing.

Editing Sound Effects

There are basically three kinds of sound effects: prerecorded library effects, spot recorded effects, and actuality recorded effects. **Library effects** are catalogued and maintained on phonograph records, audiotapes, or audio discs for storage convenience and accessibility. **Spot effects** are created in a sound studio to duplicate the supposed off-screen or on-screen source. **Actuality effects** are recorded outside the sound studio. They either accurately reproduce a particular sound or create a vivid sound impression.

Synchronous   Sound   Effects   Synchronous sound effects are immediately dubbed to the videotape or film format of the visuals so that they can be edited in synchronization with corresponding visual images. Library, spot, and actuality sound effects can all be placed in synchronization with visual images. Once the sound effect is dubbed to the proper format it is edited into the videotape or film sound track accompanying the visual image. The sound of a door closing or a fist striking a face can be synchronized with the visual image of the action.

In videotape editing, the sound effect is usually dubbed to a separate videotape along with a control track so that it can be inserted into the proper videotape frame. In film editing the sound effect is dubbed to magnetic film, which will correspond frame for frame with the accompanying visual images. In both cases the sound effect is precisely synchronized with its on-screen sound source.

Computerized Sound Effects Editing

Recent developments in technology have made it possible to use a computer to help edit a complex sound effects track for either videotape or film. Computer control over the loudness, pitch, and duration of a sound effect allows a single sound effect to be used in a variety of ways. For example, a single sound of an airplane can be manipulated to create the complete illusion of an airplane circling an airport. Using this technique, a collection of basic sound effects can be used to provide an infinite variety of sounds. Each basic sound effect is catalogued and described on a computer for easy selection and retrieval. It can be stored digitally on a disc so that dubbing and signal processing does not result in any degradation of quality. Using the SMPTE time code of an edited videotape for reference, a sound effects editor can select, order, and manipulate all the sound effects that will be needed. Once the computer program is created, the sound effects are automatically dubbed, ordered, and processed to the editor's precise specifications.

Mixing Sound Effects with Other Types of Sound

Sound effects may be used either as background sounds that add depth or realism, or as startling effects that stimulate vivid sound impressions. Sound effects can simply "fill out" and accompany the image or they can function somewhat independently of visual images. The way in which sound effects are mixed with other sounds in large part determines their aesthetic function. When sound effects are used as background sounds, they are usually kept well below the volume of the dia-

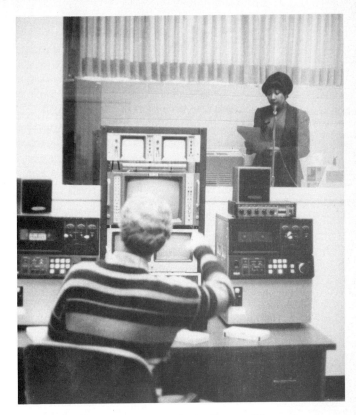

Narration recording during video postproduction. The pace of the narration may have to be slowed down or speeded up to match specific visual sequences.

logue or narration so that they do not disrupt the flow of primary information. Raising or peaking the volume of background sound effects can serve as an effective transition from one scene to another.

Editing Music

Dubbing Music Music is usually recorded and dubbed at a rapid tape-to-head speed to ensure high quality reproduction. Music for a film or television program can come from a variety of sources. Library music, which has been prerecorded on a phonograph record or tape, is often used to accompany visual images and other sounds. For public exhibition, the rights to prerecorded music must be secured as discussed in chapter 2 on producing and production management. Original music can be recorded in a sound studio for a specific project. It can either be recorded in advance of editing, so that visuals can be edited to the music, or it can be recorded after the visual editing has been completed, so that the performance of the music can be matched to the visuals.

Synchronous Music   After dubbing prerecorded music to the proper visual format, the editor carefully analyzes it by finding the precise frames where specific musical effects, such as rhythmic beats, crescendos, and changes in pace or tonality, occur. Visual images can then be added to the videotape or film and edited so that shot changes and changes in the intensity of the visual action and pace correspond with the music. Visual images can also be edited in counterpoint to the music, through the use of shot changes and visual tonalities and pacing that contradicts rather than complements the music.

Synchronizing music to preedited visuals can be quite complicated. Music is usually composed with specific visuals in mind. The tempo of the music may need to be adjusted so that specific effects coincide with the visuals they are intended to accompany. The edited visuals are normally played back while the music is being recorded, and used as visual cues to guide the pace and tempo at which the music is performed.

Mixing Music with Other Types of Sound
There are two basic approaches to the problem of mixing music and speech

sounds. One approach is to lower the level of the music immediately prior to the delivery of a line of dialogue or narration, and then return the music to a normal level after the speech has concluded. A second approach is to keep the music at a consistently low level. If music is mixed at its full value, the speech sounds that accompany it will be difficult to understand. Even when the music is kept at a lower than normal level, it is important to have clear and distinct dialogue and narration. An underlying assumption of both of these approaches to mixing music and speech is that the speech must be clearly understood. But it is sometimes necessary to hear the music at its full value, particularly when its pace, intensity, and mood is essential to the establishment of a particular feeling.

Mixing music requires the smooth operation of faders on an audio console. The music must be relatively stable and consistent in terms of its volume level at points where it is to be effectively faded in or out or cross-faded with other music, speech, and sound effects. Music that varies in intensity or seems erratic is difficult to fade in and fade out smoothly. Faders should normally be moved very slowly so that one piece of music gradually blends into another piece of music or another type of sound. Sometimes "popping on" a sudden burst of music can be an effective transition device, a sort of musical punctuation. **Stingers** are short phrases of music usually characterized by a rapidly descending scale or series of notes, which can also act as punctuation devices. In functionalist and realist situations music is usually mixed smoothly and gradually with other types of sounds.

VIDEOTAPE EDITING AND MIXING

Videotape sound is edited electronically. Audio editing on videotape can be very complex or quite simple, depending on the nature of the audio recordings and the sophistication of videotape equipment. Most electronic videotape editor units allow for video-only, audio-only, and audio-plus-video editing in the insert mode, as discussed in chapter 14. To insert edit sound onto prerecorded images without erasing those images, the sound must first be dubbed to a separate videocassette along with a control track. Sound can then be dubbed onto one of the audio tracks or channels of a prerecorded videotape without disturbing the picture or separate audio information on another sound channel or track. Video can be added to a videotape without disturbing the prerecorded audio signal. Using synchronized sounds and images originally recorded on videotape, an editor can edit the audio simultaneously with the video, maintaining precise synchronization. Audio editing on videotape can involve a single synchronous sound track on the original videotape or the building of complex dialogue, narration, sound effects, and music tracks.

Synchronous Sound Editing

In conventional videotape editing, the sound track from the Source VCR is dubbed to the Record VCR along with the picture. Synchronization between sounds and images from the Source VCR is maintained during assemble editing and insert editing by keeping both the video and audio recording functions operational on the Record VCR. Video-only and audio-only edits are made by turning off either the audio or the video recording function on the Record VCR. This requires that the edit be made in the insert mode.

Sound Inserts

A **videotape editing unit** allows sounds to be inserted at any point in a videotape. To insert audio into a prerecorded video segment, the audio can be dubbed from any sound source to a blank videotape by using the assemble mode on the Source VCR. A sync signal or control track must be recorded on the videotape at the same time so that the sound will play back at a constant speed. The Source videotape, which now contains recorded sound effects, speech, or music, is then played back in conjunction with a Record videotape containing prerecorded images so that the source sound can be inserted into the Record images. A common insert edit point is found and, using the **insert mode** of electronic editing, the sound on the Source videotape is inserted into an audio track on the Record videotape so that it accompanies corresponding images.

If the on-set sound already occupies track #2 on the Record videotape, additional sound effects, narration, or music from the Source videotape can be insert edited onto track #1 of the Record videotape without erasing the on-set sounds. In ¾-inch editing it is common practice to edit on-set sound on audio track #2 of the Record videotape, which generally has better reproduction quality than audio track #1. Postproduction sound is edited onto audio track #1.

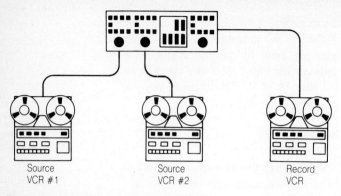

Figure 15.1 Multiple-Source Video Sound Mixing

Several different types of sound can be mixed together during postproduction by using a multiple-source videotape editing unit. Music, synchronous speech sounds, narration, and sound effects can be placed on separate videotapes, which are then played back simultaneously and fed through an audio console so that levels can be properly set.

reference for precise playback can be used to make a synchronous sound mix independently of the videotape. For example, the dialogue that is originally recorded and edited on videotape in synchronization with the video images can be dubbed to an audiotape along with the control track. Other sound elements, such as several music and sound effects tracks can then be combined with the dialogue and mixed back onto an audio channel of the original videotape in perfect synchronization with the images. A potential problem with this multigeneration dubbing and mixing technique, however, is that the music or sound effects may be severely degraded in quality by virtue of having been dubbed several times before a final sound mix is achieved.

Mixing Videotape Audio

Simple videotape mixing is done by combining two separate audio tracks on a single prerecorded videotape. The two tracks are recorded separately and then played back on a Source VCR through a mixer or audio console so that they can be combined onto one track on the Record videotape. (See Figure 15.1.) Mixing videotape audio is limited only by the number of audio tracks and playback machines available. If only one audio track is available, a separate Source VCR or an audio playback machine must be used. When synchronization is not crucial an audiotape recorder can be connected to the Record VCR through a mixer.

Synchronization between multiple audio tracks and video images can also be maintained by using a common control track, usually that which was initially recorded with the video images. (See Figure 15.2.) Any multi-track recorder capable of recording and using this control track as a

Sound equipment in a computerized ¾-inch U-matic editing unit. Included here from bottom left are a ¼-inch reel-to-reel recorder and a turntable, and from top left, cart machines and graphic equalizers.

Mixing Videotape Audio with Computer Assistance

A more expensive alternative to using the control track of a videotape as a synchronization guide or a single Source VCR with just two audio channels is using a computerized videotape editor with addressable SMPTE time code. The computerized editor can control several Source VCRs or VTRs simultaneously. Sound editing and mixing decisions can be programmed into the computer, which will control the playback and adjust the volume of each different sound source. Any audio or video machine capable of reading the SMPTE time code can be used for computerized editing and mixing. With computer assistance, a complex sound track can be designed, programmed, and mixed automatically on the basis of a mix log that is programmed into the computer along with all editing decisions.

FILM EDITING AND MIXING

Synchronous Sound Dubbing

In this section we will be concerned solely with editing double-system film and sound recordings. The problems inherent in editing single-system synchronous sound recordings were discussed in chapter 14. Synchronous film sound is normally recorded on audiotape, using a separate synchronous sound recorder. The originally recorded sounds are accompanied by Pilotone. This sync signal or Pilotone track, which is recorded on the audiotape along with the primary sync sounds, is used to maintain precise synchronization with the separately recorded visuals. It determines

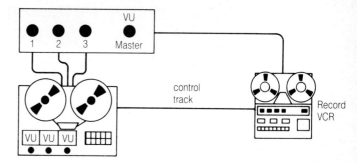

Figure 15.2 Multi-Track Sound Mixing
Sound mixing can also be done using a multi-track sound recorder. Each different type of sound is recorded on a separate track in proper synchronization. These separate tracks (accompanied by a video control track) can then be mixed down to one or two tracks on the record videotape in proper synchronization with accompanying images.

the playback speed of the tape recorder when the film sound is transferred from audiotape to 8mm, 16mm, or 35mm magnetic recording film. This magnetic film can then be physically cut and spliced just like motion picture film. Audiotape that has a sync signal track, like videotape with a control track, cannot be physically cut because a playback machine uses the sync signal as a speed guide and it is almost impossible to maintain precise speeds when the sync signal is interrupted at splice points.

Magnetic Film Splicing

Magnetic film has no sync or control track and can therefore be physically spliced in conjunction with film images. Splicing allows an editor to combine sounds in sequential order and synchronize them with accompanying images. This can be accomplished through physical cutting of magnetic film. If synchronization is not crucial, it may be advantageous to edit sounds initially on conventional ¼-inch tape (to be discussed later in this chapter)

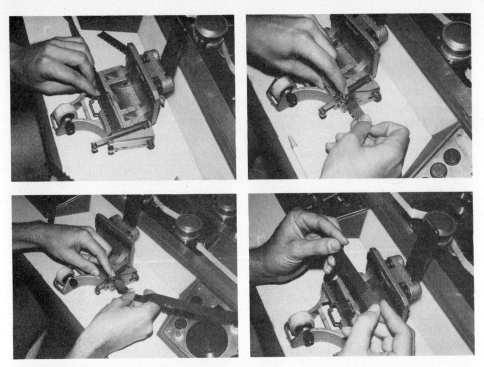

Film editing. From left: place magnetic film in the sprocket teeth of the splicer, make diagonal sound cuts for each of two sound takes to be joined, place both takes in the teeth of the splicer so that they abutt one another, make a diagonal sound splice, and then inspect the sound film splice.

since a common film format is not required. Any sounds that are to be synchronized with visual images during editing must first be dubbed to magnetic film.

Splicing magnetic film requires several pieces of equipment, including a splicing block and cutting blade, mylar splicing tape, and some means of locking pictures and sounds in synchronization, such as a gang synchronizer or a flatbed editor.

The first step in splicing magnetic film is locating the precise edit points on the two pieces of tape that are to be joined. These points are marked on the **base** (shiny) sides of the film. The magnetic film can then be placed in the splicing block so that the proper edit points line up with the diagonal splice edge of the cutting

block. Using a diagonal splice line minimizes the chance of creating a ''popping'' sound, when the splice passes over a playback head. A film splicing block normally has pegs on which the sprocket holes of the film are placed to ensure proper alignment for exact cutting and joining. There are basically two types of film splicers: those that use preperforated mylar tape laid horizontally across the splice and those that use unperforated tape laid vertically across the splice. In the latter case the sprocket holes are punched out as the tape is cut. Both types of tape splicers are available with diagonal splicing blocks for audio cutting and joining, allowing the two diagonally cut pieces of magnetic recording film to be held together with pegs in adjacent sprocket holes so that mylar tape can be applied to the base side to make a secure splice. The excess tape is cut off by a blade and the tape joint is smoothed out by rubbing across the top of the splice.

The splice should be inspected to see if the sprocket holes are clear and to make sure there are no gaps between the two pieces of audiotape. A tape splice can easily be redone by simply removing the mylar tape and putting the two pieces of audiotape back in the splicing block. Note that mylar splicing tape should never be placed on the oxide side (usually, but not always, the dull side) of the audiotape, where it will interfere with the playback of the recorded sound.

Magnetic film is synchronized with accompanying images by finding the precise frames where the sound of the clapstick is heard on the sound track and seen on the image track for each shot. Once synchronized, magnetic film can be edited frame for frame with the accompanying images. Prerecorded sound effects can be added at the precise points where they mirror the visual action. A crescendo or musical beat can be aligned with a specific action or cutline through physical splicing. To maintain synchronization between the sound and picture once it has been achieved, an editor must add or subtract the same number of frames in both the picture and the sound tracks when any change is required.

Separate magnetic film tracks are sometimes **slugged** or interspersed with **clear leader**, which is completely transparent film with no oxide coating. Using clear leader between recorded sounds is less expensive than using magnetic film, and it also clearly identifies where recorded audio occurs on the roll. Slugging with clear leader simultaneously on *all* edited sound tracks prevents any continuation of ambient noise or ''room tone'' and

results in patches of completely silent or dead audio. Thus clear leader should only be used with tracks that will eventually be mixed with others.

Mixing Magnetic Film

Synchronizing sounds with film images requires that the sounds be transferred to magnetic film of the same format as the recorded film images. When the sounds and images are in a common format, they can be spliced in complete synchronization. After several different sound tracks, such as separate music, dialogue, and sound effects tracks, have each been independently synchronized with the edited film images, they can be mixed together onto a single **master sound track.**

Each separate synchronized sound track is played back on its own magnetic film playback unit or **dubber** (as shown in Figure 15.3). Dubbers can be synchronized by means of a physical or electronic interlock between drive mechanisms or motors. The dubbers and the magnetic

Figure 15.3 Multiple-Source Film Sound Mixing

In film, multi-track mixing is done using separate magnetic film dubbers, each assigned to a single sound track or type of sound, such as speech, sound effects, or music. The dubbers are played back in synchronization with accompanying film images so that the separate sound tracks can be mixed together through an audio console and then recorded on a magnetic film recorder.

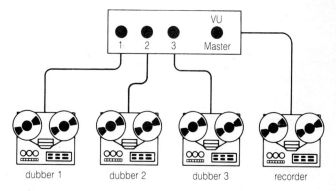

film recorder that will be used to record the master sound track must be driven at exactly the same speed. Each separate dubber can then be fed to a different fader at an audio console or mixer so that they can all be combined. The output signal of the audio console is fed to a single magnetic film recorder.

A synchronous film sound mix is often accompanied by a synchronous playback of the filmed images using an interlocked projector, which is connected to the same electrical signal as the sound playback and record machines. Mixing magnetic film provides precise synchronization between sound tracks as well as between all sounds and the film images.

EDITING AND MIXING AUDIOTAPE

When synchronization between sounds and images is not crucial, it is often convenient to edit and mix sounds in an audiotape format, such as ¼-inch audiotape. Audiotape editing can then be done using physical splicing techniques. A variety of

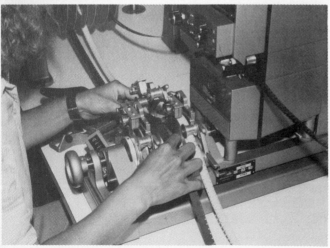

Top left: A transferring and dubbing studio for 16mm film and sound mixing. Bottom left: Editing the A and B sound rolls on a Moviola Jr. film editing machine. The picture runs through the viewer on the right. Below: Sixteen millimeter magnetic film recorder (top) and dubbers (bottom).

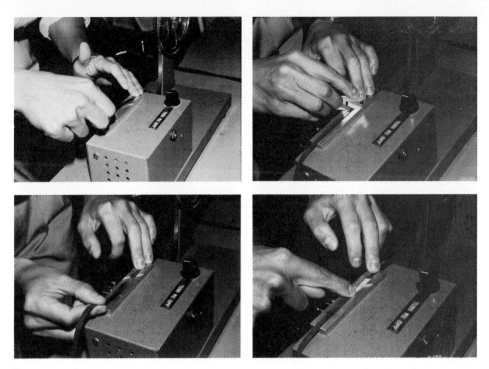

Splicing ¼-inch audiotape. From left: place the tape in the splicing block, cut the tape at the splice points diagonally with a single edge razor blade, place the two pieces to be spliced together in the splicing block, and finally put audio splicing tape over splice, remove, and inspect.

different audiotape formats can be used for nonsynchronous sound mixing. The resulting mix can be dubbed to the same format as the visual images.

Splicing Audiotape

Splicing ¼-inch audiotape requires several pieces of equipment, including a splicing block, a single-edge razor blade, a grease pencil, a set of rewinds with a playback head, an amplifier, and a speaker. Sometimes ¼-inch tape is edited while it is played back on a ¼-inch tape recorder with a built-in splicer. The best procedure for editing ¼-inch tape is to find the edit point on one piece of tape by running it over the playback head. This point

is then marked on the base side (usually the shiny side) of the audiotape with a grease pencil. The tape is then placed securely and flatly in the splicing block with the precise edit point over the diagonal cutline indentation on the block. The tape is severed with a single stroke of a sharp razor blade. The audiotape is then advanced and the second edit point is marked.

The second cut is made in the same manner as the first. After the excess tape has been removed from the splicing block, the two pieces of tape can be butted together and joined by placing a piece of adhesive ¼-inch splicing tape on the base side of the audiotape. The spliced tape should be removed from the splicing block and played back at normal speed to ensure that a correct splice has been made. If a pop is heard while the splice passes over the playback head, the splice should be inspected to see if the two pieces of tape are slightly separated. If they are, the splicing tape can be removed and the splice reattached in the splicing block. If there is no gap between the two pieces of tape, two other possible sources of the "popping" sound should be investigated. First, the pop could be caused by a magnetized razor blade. It is possible for a steel blade to become magnetized and alter a recording. If a magnetized razor blade is responsible, cut off the affected portion of the tape and demagnetize or throw the razor blade away. A second common cause of popping is the improper selection of an edit point on one or both tapes. Cutting in the middle of a sound or failing to eliminate a prior or subsequent sound at the edit point can create a perceptible pop at the splice point. In this case the audiotape may have to be recut so that the pop is eliminated.

When audiotape will be spliced it is best to maintain as high a tape-to-head speed as possible during initial recording. For music the best editing speed is 15 inches per second, but for voice a tape-to-head speed of 7½ inches per second is usually sufficient to separate most words. It is never advisable to use speeds below 7½ inches per second, since this will make it difficult to separate sounds or produce high quality recordings.

One advantage of editing of ¼-inch audiotape prior to transferring onto magnetic film or videotape is that this format is quite inexpensive. Sound effects, music, and narration, can often be edited very efficiently in the ¼-inch tape format prior to transferring them to magnetic film or videotape. When synchronization between images and sounds is necessary, sounds must be transferred to magnetic film or videotape so that they can be edited in conjunction with their corresponding visual images.

Mixing Nonsynchronous Audiotape Sounds

When precise synchronization between sounds or between sounds and images is not crucial, an editor has tremendous flexibility in terms of selecting playback devices. Sounds can be played back on many different machines, such as a ¼-inch reel-to-reel, a cartridge, a cassette tape recorder, or even a record player, without the necessity of dubbing them to a common format. (See Figure 15.4.) Each of these playback units can then be fed into an audio console or mixing board, where their individual volumes can be controlled as they are mixed together and sent out of the console to an audio recorder. A mix log sheet indicates when each playback machine should be started. Normally this involves prerolling the playback source in advance of the point where it will be blended into the master sound mix. Different machines are often started at different times. Combining sounds in this way eliminates the added step of dubbing sounds to a common format, such as magnetic film or videotape. When synchronization is not crucial and the production budget is too small to accommodate computerized editing, working in smaller audiotape formats can greatly increase the speed and efficiency of audio mixing.

Mixing with Multi-track Recorders

Multi-track recorders provide one means of maintaining synchronization between different sound sources that do not need to be synchronized with visual images. Most multi-track sound recording machines allow the sounds recorded on one track to be played at the exact original recording speed, while additional sounds are being recorded on a parallel track. For example, music might be prerecorded on one track. This music could be played back while a singer's voice is recorded on a parallel track. Using this technique several musicians and singers, for example, can each be recorded at different times and places. Multi-track recorders allow many different sound tracks to be combined, such as those for narration, music, and sound effects. Synchronization between the separate tracks is inherent in the tape since each track is recorded and played back on the

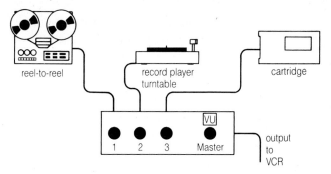

Figure 15.4 Mixing Nonsynchronous Sound
Sounds which do not have to synchronize precisely with video or film images can be mixed together using nonsynchronous audio playback machines, such as a ¼-inch reel-to-reel tape player, a record player turntable, and a cartridge player. The sound signal from each source is fed to an audio console, and the output of the console can be fed to a VCR or a magnetic film recorder so that it can eventually be combined with video or film images.

An Otari Model MTR-10 four channel (or track) mastering/production recorder.

tape parallel with the others. Narration can be recorded while the sound effects and music are played back, for example. When each of the different tracks has been properly recorded, they can all be mixed onto a single track. It is important to note that multi-track recorders can also be used to maintain synchronization between sounds and images when a sync signal or control track is laid down on one of the tracks. To initially synchronize sounds with visual images, they are usually edited and mixed in the same format as the accompanying visual images.

Summary

Sound editing can be approached from the aesthetic perspectives of functionalism, realism, and formativism. Functionalist sound editing focuses on the delivery of clear and distinct messages. Mistakes are removed, different types of sound are properly blended, and the order of audio presentation is logical and easy to understand. Realist sound editing preserves continuity in space and time. There are no apparent gaps or breaks in audio action. Sound and image combinations are usually synchronous, on-screen, and parallel in meaning. Formativist sound editing develops sound as an independent aesthetic element. Vivid sound impressions and abstract audio qualities are highlighted. Sound and image combinations are often asynchronous and off-screen.

Sound mixing is a process of blending together simultaneous sounds or sound tracks. This includes such transition devices as fades, cross-fades, and segues. Blending together different types of sounds, such as speech, sound effects, and music, demands smooth and precise operation of the faders on an audio console or mixer. It also requires careful preparation of a mix log, which specifies different audio levels and transitions from one sound track to another.

Specific principles of editing and mixing apply to different types of sound, such as speech, sound effects, and music. When editing speech sounds an editor must be sensitive to the speaker's performance level, intonation, and accuracy. Mistakes and pauses must be eliminated. An editor who is editing synchronous sounds and images may have to make editing decisions on the basis of the least objectionable way to combine these sounds and images. Sometimes cutaways must be inserted into the visuals to hide audio or visual problems. Through a technique known as looping speech sounds can be added to and perfectly synchronized with preedited prerecorded visual images. Voice-over interviews and narration are often edited prior to the selection of illustrative visuals.

There are three basic kinds of sound effects: library effects, spot effects, and actuality effects. Library effects are prerecorded on phonograph records and audiotapes. Spot effects are specially recorded in the sound studio, and actuality effects are recorded in the field. Synchronous sound effects must be immediately dubbed to magnetic film or videotape, so that they can be edited in conjunction with corresponding visual images. Spot effects are sometimes recorded in the sound studio in synchronization with specific visual images after the visuals have already been edited.

Sound effects that function primarily as background sounds are often mixed at sound levels well below primary speech or music sounds. Sometimes it is necessary to raise the level of sound effects during a mix so that they can be used to stimulate startlingly vivid sound impressions.

Music can be analyzed and used as a basis for editing visual images. In this case, the two are synchronized by editing the images to the music. Actions within the visual frame and cuts from one shot to another are frequently synchronized with the beat or rhythm of the music. Music can be synchronized to preedited visual images by composing the music specifically for these images. The music is then performed while the images are simultaneously projected on a screen or monitor for the conductor or musicians.

When mixing music and speech sounds, it is essential that the speech be audible and intelligible. Music that overlaps speech is normally faded down to a lower volume level. The music can be placed at a consistently low level or it can be faded down and under speech and faded back up to its full value during longer gaps in the recorded speech. When music is presented by itself without other sounds, it is normally recorded at its full value. Mixing music through fade-ins, cross-fades, and segues requires a smooth and consistent operation of faders or pots on an audio console, but loud sounds are sometimes "popped on" for emphasis and punctuation.

Videotape audio can be spliced electronically by using a basic editing unit. Various sounds can be inserted into one of the audio tracks of a videotape. Most editing units provide for audio-only, video-only, and audio-plus-video insert editing. Originally recorded synchronous sound and images are edited simultaneously, using a basic editing unit. Synchronous or nonsynchronous sound inserts can be added using the audio-only insert mode.

The advent of computer technology has stimulated the use of more complex sound tracks and multiple sound track editing techniques in video. Videotape sound mixing requires several audio channels on the Source videotape or several Source VCRs running simultaneously, which are computer controlled. An edited audio track on videotape is sometimes dubbed to a multitrack audio recorder so that it can be combined with other sounds before the combined master mix is transferred back to the original videotape. If synchronization is crucial the control track from the videotape must be dubbed to the audiotape as well.

Synchronous lip-sync dialogue for film is normally recorded during production using an audiotape recorder, which records both the sounds and a Pilotone track. The sound track is then dubbed to magnetic film so that it can be edited synchronously with the image. Exactly the same number of magnetic film frames will be obtained during the dubbing process as there are corresponding visual frames. During synchronous film audio dubbing, the sync signal is eliminated. Clapstick sound and corresponding images are recorded at the beginning of each shot, so that the separate sound and image tracks can be properly synchronized with each other during editing. Magnetic film can be physically spliced in conjunction with visual images and thus synchronization between them is maintained.

Synchronous film sound mixing requires several interlocked magnetic film Source machines, called dubbers. Several audio tracks can then be combined through an audio console or mixer into a single master sound mix on a magnetic film recorder.

Audiotape can be physically spliced in several different formats. Nonsynchronous splicing can be done with ¼-inch audiotape. The tape is cut diagonally with a razor blade and spliced together with mylar tape. The mylar tape should be placed only on the base side of the audiotape, so that it does not interfere with the audio recording and playback.

Nonsynchronous audio mixing can be done using a variety of audio formats, such as cassettes, cartridges, reel-to-reels, and even turntables. Each different source is played back and sounds are blended together through an audio console or mixer.

Multi-track sound recorders allow several different tracks to be recorded in synchronization with each other. A background music track can be recorded and then played back as an accompaniment to a singer whose voice is recorded independently on a separate track. In this way several different types of sounds can be combined on a single reel of audiotape in synchronization with each other. When precise synchronization between sounds and images is required, the audio must be immediately dubbed to a specific film or videotape format so that it can be edited in conjunction with the visual images.

Additional Readings

Alten, Stanley. *Audio in Media.* Belmont, CA: Wadsworth Publishing Co., 1980.

Mantell, Harold, ed. *The Complete Guide to the Creation and Use of Sound Effects for Films, T.V. and Dramatic Productions.* Princeton, NJ: Films for the Humanities, Inc., 1978.

Nisbett, Alec. *The Technique of the Sound Studio for Radio, Television, and Film.* New York: Hastings House, 1974.

Roberts, Kenneth H., and Win Sharples, Jr. *A Primer for Film-Making.* New York: Bobbs-Merrill, 1971.

Yoakam, Richard D., and Cremer, Charles F. *ENG: Television News and the New Technology.* New York: Random House, 1985.

Exercises

1. Using a shooting script as your guide, prepare a mix log for combining all of the various sound elements which will be used in postproduction editing. While precise volume control settings cannot be known until actual materials are prepared for a mix, virtually all other factors can be anticipated in advance. Try to compose separate and continuous sound tracks or channels on paper for each different type of sound, such as synchronous dialogue, narration, sound effects or background sound, and music. Indicate where one piece of music will cross-fade or segue to another, requiring separate tracks or channels, or where several different sound effects or background sounds must be combined. A mix log will graphically depict the depth and texture of sound by indicating when several types of sounds or sound tracks coexist, such as narration, sound effects, and music. Indicate which type of sound will be dominant if they will not all be of equal intensity. Determine the series of stages sound-track preparation must go through, if some types of sound must be ''pre-mixed'' prior to the final master mix.

2. Replace synchronous dialogue and sound effects (sound originally recorded with corresponding visuals) with looped dialogue and library or spot effects. Use the insert mode of videotape editing or physically splice the new sounds into the existing film sound track. Compare the edited sound track to the original for sound clarity and consistency.

3. Edit a voice-over narration track, music, or series of nonsynchronous sound effects using ¼-inch audiotape. Use a tape recorded at a speed of 7½ inches per second or faster for editing. Mark the base side of the tape with a china marker or grease pencil at the precise points where edits should be made. Try to make the edits as smooth and indistinguishable as possible. Be careful to maintain consistency in terms of pace and timing in the delivery of narration. Find similar phrases of music on which to make an instantaneous transition from one piece of music to another. Pay careful attention to any discrepancy in terms of audio levels and background sounds when editing together speech, sound effects, or music recorded outside the studio.

CHAPTER 16

Distribution and Exhibition

In most business operations, production is analogous to manufacturing, distribution to wholesaling, and exhibition to retailing. A distributor acts as a middle-man or intermediary between the people who produce something and those who consume it. Exhibiting film and video productions is similar to running a retail store from which individual consumers buy things.

In both television and film, distribution and exhibition are aspects of postproduction, but producers consider them during preproduction as well. The selection of a specific production format or technology and the preparation of a budget must mesh with the anticipated distribution and exhibition technology and outlets. The initial planning for a feature film, for example, may have to consider virtually every distribution and exhibition channel, from major theatrical distribution, to network television, videotape, laser disc, videodisc, cable television, syndication to local stations, nontheatrical distribution to college campuses, and public television. Even a corporate or institutional ''within-house'' production is designed with specific types of exhibition in mind. The final product may be sent out as videocassette copies or presented live on various television monitors on the company premises.

In chapter 2, ''Producing and Production Management,'' we saw that specific programs must be targeted for specific audiences. In this chapter we will see how a television or film producer attempts to reach that target audience by selecting the best distribution and exhibition channel(s). Specific projects are tailored for specific forms of presentation in the media, such as cable television or theatrical film, as well as for specific target audiences. A consideration of the technology and economics of distribution and exhibi-

tion follows logically from the concern for the audience begun in our study of preproduction. Selecting the best channels requires an understanding of media technology and economics.

TECHNOLOGY OF DISTRIBUTION AND EXHIBITION

Broadcasting

Television broadcasters send video and audio signals to home receivers through the airwaves. Local television broadcasters use a limited number of available channels in a restricted broadcast signal range to reach viewers. There are basically two different types of broadcast signals; very high frequency (VHF) and ultra high frequency (UHF). While VHF signals are usually stronger and travel farther than UHF signals, neither can be received with much clarity more than 100 miles away from the transmitter tower.

Television signals use up more area of the electromagnetic spectrum than do radio signals since they carry both video and audio information: about 6 megahertz (six million hertz) compared to 10 kilohertz (ten thousand hertz) for AM (amplitude modulation) radio signals and 200 kilohertz for FM (frequency modulation) radio signals. There are far fewer available television channels than radio channels. Television audio information is broadcast as an FM signal, while video information uses a high frequency AM signal. There are more UHF channels available (70 channels from 14 to 83, although the UHF channels above 70 are being phased out and are no longer assigned by the FCC in most locations) than VHF channels (12 channels from 2 to 13).

Broadcast television signals come from a variety of sources. A station can generate a live signal from the studio, or from a remote location in the field, as during a local news broadcast. A prerecorded signal can be played on a videotape playback machine, telecine or film chain, or a direct feed can come from the network, via satellite or telephone line to the station. Whatever its source, an RF (radio frequency) signal is impressed upon a carrier wave so that it can be amplified and transmitted through the airwaves to home receivers. An RF signal interweaves the audio and video information and is then decoded by a television receiver. Usually the stronger the wattage of the carrier wave is, the stronger the signal, and the better the television reception will be. The image quality of broadcast television is limited by the fact that a television station's **channel space** is restricted to a bandwidth of about 6 megahertz. This bandwidth restriction permits only about 350 lines of resolution (more lines of resolution mean better images) in video signals sent to home receivers. By way of comparison, a projected 35mm film image can have 1000 to 1200 lines of resolution.

A home receiver has two different tuners, one for VHF signals and another for UHF signals. When a specific channel is selected on a tuner, the carrier wave and television signal from a specific station are picked up by the antenna and then the video and audio signals are decoded. A color receiver separates the chrominance channel (red, green, and blue color information) from the luminance channel (black-and-white brightness information). Broadcast television signals are subject to interference from atmospheric conditions, other signals such as CB radios, and poor antenna placements, but they currently reach a larger nationwide

A local remote news broadcast, from which the station can generate a live signal.

viewing audience in the United States than any other means of television distribution.

Some local television stations are **affiliated** with television networks, such as ABC, NBC, and CBS; others, which are mainly in major metropolitan areas, are **owned and operated (O&O)** by these networks (the number of O&Os being limited by FCC rules), while still others are **independent** or nonaffiliated. PBS (Public Broadcasting Service) has member stations in local areas.

Top: Telstar, the first communications satellite. Bottom: The technicians at the control board are shown viewing monitors at the General Post Office Television sending station at Goonhilly Downs in Cornwall, England. This British telecast to the United States was made via the Telstar satellite on July 11, 1962. This picture was made from a CBS monitor in New York.

Satellite, Cable, and Closed-Circuit Television

Satellites are relay stations that orbit the globe and make possible instantaneous communication over vast distances. U.S. satellites are positioned in space so that they maintain a constant position and altitude with respect to land masses on the earth. Soviet satellites do maintain constant positions in space, yet their ground transmitters and receivers must be regularly repositioned. Henceforth, all references to satellites will be to U.S. systems. A satellite's antenna receives signals from the earth's surface and then relays them back to the earth. A satellite transmission, like a standard microwave signal used for ''live'' remote ENG transmissions, requires a direct uninterrupted, line-of-sight path between the transmitter and the receiver. But receiver dishes across a wide area on the earth's surface are capable of receiving satellite signals if they are properly positioned. A satellite transmitter or tracking station on the earth is aimed at the satellite's receiving antenna, to which it sends a signal. A transmitter on the satellite relays this signal to a wide area of possible satellite dishes on the ground.

Satellites can be used for transmitting live television signals from overseas as well as for coast-to-coast transmission of news and sporting events. Satellites are also used for transmitting cable television programming across the country to various local cable television operators, who distribute the programming along cable wires to individual homes. Some enterprising private citizens and businesses bypass local cable operators by purchasing their own satellite receiving dishes which are at least ten feet in diameter in order to receive strong, high quality signals. A decoder is needed for a few services, such as HBO, which scramble their signals and a dish must be capable of being precisely rotated and positioned to receive signals from several different satellites.

Cable television distributes television signals from a satellite dish to private homes via coaxial cable. (See Figure 16.1 for a diagram of cable television.) **Coaxial cable** consists of metal wires encased in plastic and/or metal insulators. The insulation makes it possible to send signals over wide areas with minimal interference and loss of signal. Nonetheless, the signal does decrease in strength as it spreads out from main trunk lines. Amplifiers are strategically located in a community to maintain a relatively constant signal strength as the signal passes along subtrunk lines and "drops" which carry the signal to individual homes. Some cable lines can be directly connected to a television receiver antenna jack, while others require an intermediate decoder and tuner box. The most sophisticated **cable systems** allow for two-way or **interactive communication** between the individual subscriber and the cable operator. Two-way communication can be used for opinion polling and obtaining viewer feedback. In addition to television signals, a cable system can be used to transmit information, such data for home computers, and to serve as a monitoring function for public and private utility companies.

A **closed-circuit television system** interconnects various recording, transmitting, and receiving devices within a single building or building complex. It can be used to send information from a central

Satellite receiving dishes enable home viewers to enjoy a wide variety of programs as well as greatly improved reception.

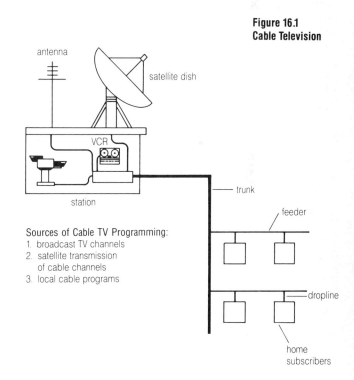

**Figure 16.1
Cable Television**

Sources of Cable TV Programming:
1. broadcast TV channels
2. satellite transmission of cable channels
3. local cable programs

A Sony High Definition (HDTV) Video System.

location to television monitors in various locations or to relay information from one room to another, such as the transmission of a surgical operation from the operating room of a hospital to a classroom in the medical school. Closed-circuit television systems are frequently used in government or educational institutions and businesses, as well as for arrival-departure displays at airports. The signals are carried to various parts of the building by coaxial cable.

High-Definition Television

Some closed-circuit television systems are capable of carrying signals of much wider bandwidth than conventional broadcast signals. **High-definition television (HDTV)** can produce a high-resolution wide screen video image, which rivals that of film. Work is currently under way to develop satellite transmission systems for high-definition television images. It is likely that high-definition television images will be used for public exhibition of feature films in this decade. When high quality large screen projection devices are available, HDTV reception could be virtually equivalent in image quality to standard 35mm film projection, but special cameras and receivers will be required.

Videotapes, Videodiscs, and Laser Discs

A relatively new and widely expanding market for film and video material is that of consumer videotapes, videodiscs, and laser discs. Feature films, video albums, and educational or informational programs can be purchased or rented for home or office use. The most commonly used home and office videotape formats are 8mm and ½-inch Beta and VHS. An 8mm videocassette is slightly larger than an audio cassette and has a recording capacity of 120 minutes. Beta and VHS are noncompatible ½-inch videotape formats. Experts generally agree that Beta looks better but VHS has greater storage capacity. VHS outsells Beta by about 2:1 in the home VCR market. Both formats use ½-inch videotape encased in a cassette, and the videocassette recorders use helical or slant-track scanning of the tape. At slow, low-quality playback and recording speeds, a single VHS cassette can record or play back up to eight hours of programming (although six hours is more common). Faster recording speeds mean better quality images and sounds. Video cassettes that record about thirty or sixty minutes of video material at high speed generally have thicker, more durable tape than 120-minute cassettes and are better suited for production purposes. Some professional ½-inch equipment (Recam and Betacam, as discussed in chapter 8) uses a very high recording speed, which is not compatible with conventional consumer VHS and Beta equipment. High speed ½-inch video images are of very high broadcast quality.

Discs come in two basic formats, laser discs and videodiscs, the latter of which is also known generically as a **CED system**. A single videotape can run for several hours but a disc is normally limited to about forty-five minutes to one hour per side. Discs are permanent recordings. Like phonograph records, they cannot be erased and rerecorded.

The **CED videodisc** is very similar to a phonograph record. A pressing is made in plastic from a master recording, which can then be played back on a turntable with a special stylus. There is physical contact between the stylus and the videodisc, as there is with a phonograph record. The

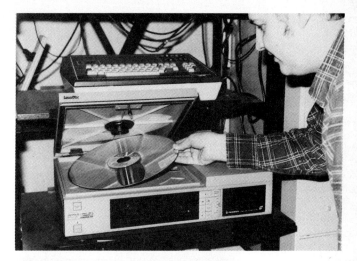

Top: An example of a laser disc system. The disc is placed on a turntable and is limited to about forty-five minutes to an hour of play time for each side. Bottom: A close-up of a laser disc, which is more resistant to damage from handling than a regular phonograph record or a CED videodisc.

variations in the grooves that are tracked by the stylus contain video as well as audio information. To store additional visual information there are more grooves on a CED disc than on a conventional phonograph record.

Laser discs do not rely on any physical contact between a stylus and a disc. Instead, a narrow beam of laser light tracks across a rotating metal disc, which is encased in transparent plastic. The laser light passes through small holes in the metal disc to produce video images and two separate stereophonic sound tracks. The plastic casing protects the metal disc. Because there is no physical contact with a stylus, there is virtually no deterioration of the disc with repeated use, as there is with stylus tracking. Laser disc technology is currently used by audiophiles in the form of compact disc (CD) players and records.

Unlike videotape, videodisc and laser disc systems cannot be used for home recording purposes. However, they can reproduce high quality video images and sounds and a permanent, wear-resistant recording. The ability to add video images to a high quality musical recording suggests that this medium may eventually become standard for the recording industry's music videos. Many audio recordings are already marketed in disc form. Discs are a viable medium for industry and educational uses where a fixed recording resistant to wear from repeated use is desirable. Videodisc technology is not as viable for home use, where the flexibility afforded home users by videotape, such as the ability to recycle recordings and record broadcasting and cable programming, makes a playback-only system less desirable. In the future home ownership of both a disc player and a VCR may be just as common as owning a record player *and* a cassette deck is today.

Electronic Projection

Electronic projection of large-screen video images is undergoing constant technological improvement and change. While there are obvious projection limitations inherent in broadcast images as noted earlier, the use of closed-circuit systems and the development of wide-screen high-definition television (HDTV) and digital recording is significantly improving the prospects for large-screen electronic projection. Standard television screens are currently made as large as twenty-six inches in diameter. Most electronic projection systems project three separate colored light beams, for the red, green, and blue components of the signal, onto an enlarged screen which is usually several feet wide and high. These types of projection systems are commonly used in bars, nightclubs, and video-game arcades, as well as for video projection in homes and institutional settings.

Larger-screen projection systems have been developed for electronic projection in commercial theaters. These electronic projection systems are often used for the live presentation of boxing matches and other exclusive events. The video transmission from the event itself can be carried across telephone lines or satellite relays as scrambled signals, which can then be picked up exclusively by designated theaters. This system of delivery may be used for electronic distribution of theatrical films across the country, once high-definition television transmissions and large-screen projection systems are perfected. Interactive cable may also make it possible to view these events in the home by selecting single programs via cable television.

Film Projection

While electronic means of projection are constantly improving, film projection maintains a high standard, which large-screen electronic projection attempts to duplicate. A basic film projection system consists of an intermittent film transport, a bright light source, and a highly reflectant screen. The film runs intermittently within the picture aperture or gate area while light passes through each individual frame to illuminate images on a screen. The film movement changes to a smooth, continuous motion over the sound head.

Film sound is recorded either optically or magnetically along the edge of the film, and is picked up by a sound head on the projector. The sound is then amplified and sent to a speaker. The most sophisticated feature film sound tracks have six magnetic sound tracks running along the edges of 70mm film prints, and these separate sounds are channeled to different speakers in the film theater so that the spectator is surrounded by multitrack, stereophonic sound. **Dolby** and other noise reduction systems are frequently used with magnetic film projection systems. A **noise reduction system** such as Dolby or DBX reduces noise and increases the range of sound frequencies (particularly high frequency sound reproduction) by selectively increasing the volume or strength of high frequency sounds during recording and then selectively reducing this strong signal to a normal level during playback.

Different films require slightly different aspect ratios or aperture dimensions in the projector gate. Wide-screen films, such as Panavision and CinemaScope, for example, require special film apertures, anamorphic lenses, and wider screens. These aspect ratios often exceed 2:1, that is, the image is more than twice as wide as it is high. **Cinerama** uses three separate projectors simultaneously to achieve a wide-screen effect. Theatrical 35mm projection uses an **academy aperture** of 1.85:1, while standard 16mm is 1.33:1, as is standard 35mm film shot for television commercials, since this latter ratio corresponds to that of a standard television screen, 4:3 or 1.33:1.

Projectors use a variety of different light sources. The brightest lamps are quartz lamps, HMI lamps, and carbon arc lamps. These light sources are capable of projecting images across wide open areas at drive-ins and large, major "hard-top"

A film projector synchronized to magnetic film recorder and dudders. Notice the separate synchronous motor and belt drive on the right.

theaters. Carbon arc lamps require special ventilation, because they produce noxious fumes, which could quickly asphyxiate the projectionist in a small projection booth. Most multicinemas today use tabletop projectors that run an entire two-hour film without requiring reel changes. These long-run projectors are semiautomatic, but projectionists constantly monitor them during actual operation to prevent damage to the film and to ensure a high-quality image. A single projectionist can monitor several projectors if the images are sent to a group of video monitors. Each projector has a built-in video camera and all the video outputs are sent to the projection booth where they can be viewed simultaneously by a single projectionist.

:::::::::::::::::::::::

ECONOMICS OF DISTRIBUTION AND EXHIBITION

:::::::::::::::::::::::

It is imperative that producers have a basic understanding of the potential markets for a television program or film. Projects that are initiated without any consideration for or knowledge of the economics of distribution and exhibition will rarely if ever reach their target audience. There are many different commercial and noncommercial distribution and exhibition channels, including network syndicated local, cable, and public television programming; consumer products such as videotapes, videodiscs, and laser discs; theatrical and nontheatrical film; and within-house production. Each distribution/exhibition channel has different needs, requirements, and economic structures.

Commerical Network Television

Commercial network television programming in the U.S. is produced for or by three primary networks: ABC, CBS, and NBC. News, sports, and most daytime programming is done by the networks themselves. Most prime-time evening entertainment programming is produced by a limited number of independent producers and production companies. Network television programming executives rarely take chances on unproven talent. They depend to a great extent on prior success as a guarantee of future success. Executive producers, such as Norman Lear (''All in the Family,'' ''Archie's Place,'' ''The Jeffersons'') and Aaron Spelling (''The Love Boat''), have had repeated commercial success, and are in a much better negotiating position with the networks than neophyte producers. Although the networks sometimes take a chance on unproven talent, there is usually some compensating factor, such as a presold property which was popular in another media or a major star who is willing to play a lead role. To be considered, a producer must put together an extremely attractive package that guarantees some measure of success in terms of attracting a sizeable audience.

The economics of commercial television revolves around the selling of audiences to advertisers. Entertainment programming is an indirect product. It provides revenues to the network or the station only when it attracts a large audience with the right demographic characteristics. The network or local station sells commercial time to advertisers on the basis of the size of the audience it is able to attract. Some advertisers believe that the most desirable audience in terms of demographics is women from eighteen to thirty-four years of age, since they do the bulk of the buying of commercial products at retail stores. Of course, other demographic groups are also sought for specific products and services, and programming is rarely aimed at just one demographic group.

A successful program is one that obtains a relatively high rating and audience share. The **rating** suggests the percentage of all 80 million-plus television households that are tuned to a specific program. Ratings translate into profit and loss figures since advertisers are charged for commercial air time on a cost-per-1000 viewers basis. The **share** refers to the percentage of television households actually watching TV at a specific time, called HUT (Households Using Television), that are tuned to a specific program. All the shares would add up to 100 percent. Ratings and shares of television programs are determined by organizations such as A. C. Nielsen and Arbitron, which collect data about what viewers watch by means of diaries kept by viewers or meters attached to home sets. Generally a network program that garners around a 30 percent share is doing quite well. Good ratings can vary from above 10 in daytime to over 20 in prime time. Shows that consistently fail to achieve these ratings or shares are likely to be canceled in midseason or by the next season. There are, of course, many factors that can affect a show's ratings. Scheduling is a crucial factor. Some time slots and days of the week are simply better than others in terms of ratings. Audience flow is another important factor. The popularity of the shows that precede and follow a specific program directly affects its share and ratings, because audiences often stay tuned to the same channel for a long period of time.

From the independent producer's standpoint, the survival of a show for at least five seasons is crucial to financial success. The amount of money that independent producers are given by the network to produce pilots and series episodes rarely covers the complete cost of production. This strategy is known as deficit financing. The producer usually signs a contract at the proposal or initial pilot script stage, granting a network exclusive rights to the series for at least five years. The contract specifies the year by year increase in network payments for each of the years that a series survives. After five years a sufficient number of episodes have usually been produced for the series to go into syndication. Syndicated programming, often called "stripping," is marketed to local stations for morning, early afternoon, or early evening broadcast, five days of the week. Independent producers make money from syndication, but they rarely make any revenues from network showings of series. Networks are forbidden by law to directly syndicate their old shows, despite the fact that they would like a share of syndication revenues. Producers take substantial risks in terms of program development, which only pays off if the program goes into syndication. The probability of a show lasting long enough to go into syndication is actually quite low, but the success of a single show can pay for many disasters.

Commercial Syndicated and Local Television

Syndicated programming generally bypasses the major commercial networks. Syndicated programs are broadcast by network-affiliated local television stations during times of the day when there is no network programming, such as late afternoon and early evening. Independent local television stations show syndicated programming during any time slot, including prime time: 8:00 PM to 11:00 PM EST. Affiliates may also broadcast syndicated programming during prime time. Each network pays its affiliated stations a fee for broadcasting network programming, although affiliates in very sparsely populated areas may actually receive no fee other than the free use of the programs as a means to attract or draw viewers for the local commercials that are run during "local station breaks" between shows. An affiliate can, of course, reject the network programming and substitute syndicated or its own local programming. The program "Nicholas Nickleby," for example, was syndicated by Mobil Oil Company to many network affiliates and was shown during prime time. Of couse, an affiliated local station that continually rejects its network's programming risks losing its affiliate status. Because of limited television channel space, local affiliates are themselves usually in a strong bargaining position with the networks, however. Affiliates and independents have sometimes banded together to partially finance their own entertainment programming, such as the prime-time miniseries "The Bastard," which was then syndicated to all supporting stations.

While entertainment programming usually comes to a local station through a network or through an independent syndicator, local news, sports, and public service and information programming is usually produced by the station itself. Local news is one of the most competitive and profitable areas of local TV programming. It is important in terms of both the audience it draws to the local news program itself and the audience drawn to the syndicated programming that surrounds the news. During these non-network time slots, local stations sell commercial time to advertisers who pay relatively high cost-per-thousand prices for commercial time, especially in the top fifty local television markets.

Obviously, the economic conditions of commercial broadcast television make it quite difficult for a small, unproven independent film or television producer to sell a single entertainment or informational program to commercial television stations. Television stations are interested in buying or showing a continuous supply of programming, such as a series or even a miniseries, rather than isolated or individual programs. Local stations will often show independently produced documentaries of local or regional interest during slow or weak time slots, such as Sunday morning or Saturday afternoon, but they will rarely pay much if anything for this type of programming. An independent producer would do better to find a corporate or individual sponsor for a single program and then guarantee that sponsor a credit line and a certain amount of exposure during slow or off-hours of commercial broadcasting rather than to try marketing a speculative program to television stations after it has been produced.

Commercial Cable Television

Similar kinds of marketing problems plague an independent producer who hopes to market a single program to cable television. Cable operators are more interested in filling time slots on a regular basis than in buying isolated programs. Nonetheless there is greater marketing potential for small, independently produced programming through cable television than through commercial broadcasting. The larger number of cable television channels ensures wider access and a greater ability to **narrowcast**, or target a small, relatively specialized audience. The economic structure of cable television is quite different from that of commercial broadcasting. The cable operator sells specific channels or packages of channels to individual consumers or subscribers, and the program producer and/or supplier often receives a percentage of the subscription fee or commercial advertising revenues. Some channels are allocated to locally produced programs and provide community access. They are usually available free of charge to anyone who wants to show something of community interest. Producers can advertise their own programs by publicizing a specific program topic and show time and date in print media. Unlike commercial broadcasters, a cable operator will often accept smaller format, lower quality video recordings, such as material on ½-inch videotape that is not of "broadcast quality." Broadcasters, of course, usually demand 1-inch or 2-inch videotapes and 16mm or 35mm films of high quality that meet or exceed NAB (National Association of Broadcasters) standards. Some cable television programming, such as that produced by Turner Broadcasting ("superstation" WTBS, Atlanta and Cable News Network, CNN, a cable program service), depends to a significant extent on commercial advertising for its revenues and must meet broadcast standards. Other program channels, such as various movie channels, distribute and sometimes produce expensive entertainment programs and are almost totally dependent on percentages of subscription charges for their revenue.

It is possible to initiate the production and marketing of some cable programs for far less money than is required for commercial broadcasting. Many cable producers are nonunion, and thus can save substantial production costs by paying lower salaries to their personnel. Cable distributors and suppliers have to sell their programming to local cable operators, invest in satellite transmission services, and assume the cost of program advertising. In return they demand a portion of subscription receipts. It is possible to produce isolated programs on an independent basis for specific cable channels such as Turner's WTBS or to produce cable programming speculatively for Arts and Entertainment or other cable distributors with greater hope of finding a potential buyer than is the case with commercial broadcasting.

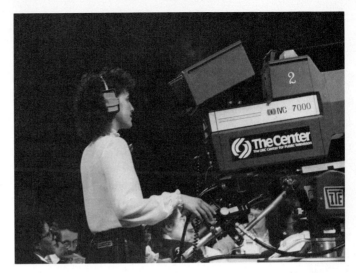

Several colleges and universities own and operate their own public broadcasting stations. Shown here is the University of North Carolina Center for Public Television facility.

Public Television

Public television is a noncommercial broadcasting distribution and exhibition channel. In the United States it is partially supported by the Corporation for Public Broadcasting, which was set up by an act of Congress in 1967 that also authorized funds for its operation. The CPB created the current network of public broadcasting stations. There are basically four types of public broadcasting stations: those owned and operated by colleges and universities such as stations at the Universities of Houston, Wisconsin, and North Carolina; those owned and operated by school systems such as that in Cincinnati (only 7 percent); those owned and operated by municipal (state) authorities, such as those in Georgia, New Jersey, and Iowa; and those developed and operated by nonprofit corporations, such as stations in Boston, New York, and Chicago.

Public broadcasting is often threatened by inadequate financial support. Federal budget allocations to the CPB are in constant jeopardy. The pursuit of large audiences through popular programming often attracts major corporate sponsors; however, such sponsorship is sometimes criticized on the basis that it gives these corporations power over noncommercial as well as commercial broadcasting. Some critics charge that on-the-air credits are tantamount to advertising and should not be permitted in noncommercial broadcasting.

Public television stations frequently raise money through funding drives. The money they collect is used to fund local productions, purchase national PBS programming (which they have a hand in selecting), and defray operating costs. PBS is responsive to member stations who are involved in determining which programs will be nationally distributed. This relationship is quite different from that between commercial networks and affiliates, although the extent to which public stations should be controlled by the national network as opposed to local management is an often hotly debated issue.

Public television programming comes from a variety of sources. Some of the programming is at least partially funded by the Corporation for Public Broadcasting and corporate sponsors at the national level and is then distributed through PBS to its member stations. PBS member stations produce much of the programming which is distributed through PBS to other stations. The largest producers of this type of national PBS programming are PBS member stations in Boston, Pittsburgh, Columbia, South Carolina, New York, Washington, Chicago, and Los Angeles. Member stations usually produce a series of programs on a specific topic rather than

single, isolated programs, however. Some programming comes from foreign producers, most notably the BBC (British Broadcasting Corporation). Individual stations themselves often produce a certain amount of local or regional public-interest programming, much of which never receives national distribution.

At the local or state level, it is sometimes possible for an independent producer to air an individual program on a PBS station or state system. Such programs are often independently funded by other sources, although partial funding can come from a PBS station in return for broadcast rights, usually specifying a specific number of airings over a two- or three-year period. The quality standards of PBS are similar to those of commercial broadcast television. The subject matter and format of PBS programming can be quite different from commercial broadcast programming, although PBS stations have become increasingly concerned about attracting large audiences, which help to generate public financial support. The length of a ''half-hour'' PBS program is currently twenty-seven minutes and forty-five seconds, compared to about twenty-two minutes for most programs intended for commercial television stations and cable channels.

Commercial Spots and Public Service Announcements

Commercial spots are short (often fifteen or thirty-second) television messages that attempt to sell commercial products and services to consumers. The production of network television commercials and ''national spot sales'' is largely controlled by major advertising agencies, such as J. Walter Thompson, Leo Burnett, N. W. Ayer, and McCann-Erickson, who contract with production specialists on a bidding basis. The advertising agency usually develops the basic storyline for a commercial in consultation with the client whose product, name, and/or services are being promoted. The advertising agency also develops a storyboard of hand-drawn images to visualize the spot. The director's job is to capture this idea on 35mm film or 1-inch videotape. Some creative innovation and play with the basic scrip idea is allowed a talented director, but the work of production companies is primarily that of technical and aesthetic execution, rather than of developing creative, original ideas. The production budget for a network commercial is often extremely high, given the relatively short duration of the final product. It is not unusual to spend from ¼ to ½ a million dollars for a single thirty-second network-level spot. The production company must be technically perfect in its execution of the commercial. Sometimes as much as 90,000 feet of 35mm film is shot to produce just 45 feet of final product for a beverage commercial, for example. Major advertisers often contract with a separate individual or company for different aspects of production and postproduction on a commercial, rather than allowing any single production company complete control. Many of the most talented creative producers of network-level commercials work on a freelance basis or have their own production companies.

Local television commercials are often made by a television station or a small production company. Television stations often sell local commercial time to businesses in their area, and then offer to produce the commercial themselves. Small independent production companies sometimes produce the entire commercial for a client, from script to screen. The budgets

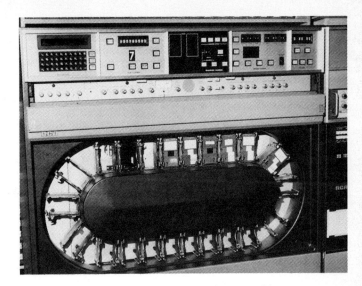

An automatic 2-inch videotape cartridge machine for commercials.

for locally produced television commercials are quite low compared to network-level commercials. Some are produced on videotape or 16mm film for a few thousand dollars. Only rarely is 35mm film used for the production of local commercials. In the largest local television markets, the production of commercials is handled by major advertising agencies. "National spot sales" place network-quality spots that are not part of the network schedule on smaller-market TV stations. The costs of commercial production represent but a small fraction of the total advertising budget for the promotion of a product, name, or service. Television time costs are usually much higher than production costs, and many other media besides television, such as magazines, newspapers, and radio, may be involved in a particular advertising campaign.

Public service announcements, or PSAs, are the least expensive type of "commercial." They are usually shown free of charge in the public interest to help promote public service agencies and nonprofit organizations. While PSAs must meet broadcast standards in terms of technical quality, they are often produced in the most economical format possible, such as ¾-inch videotape and 16mm film. PSAs offer an excellent opportunity for neophyte producers to become involved in a serious production, allowing them an opportunity to perfect their technical competence and to experiment with new techniques.

Videotape, Videodisc, and Laser Disc Markets

A relatively new and expanding market for film and video productions includes consumer-product videotapes and institutional videodiscs. These products are

A videotape rental store. The increase in VCR ownership has caused a great demand for many popular movies, sometimes exhausting a supply and frustrating a VCR owner, especially on the weekend!

rented and sold to individual consumers as well as to business, government, and educational institutions. Feature films, popular music with accompanying video images, and informational and educational materials can be marketed in this manner. The individual consumer or institution buys a tape or disc and shows it on their own player and monitor. Most entertainment programs currently being sold as commercial products were initially produced for distribution to commercial theaters, network television, or cable television. As more consumers possess their own players more programming will be designed for initial sale to consumers, just like records or books in retail stores.

Rental and sale of videotapes is a rapidly-expanding market for entertainment programming. In fact, 1985 was the first year that videotape sales of Hollywood products equaled domestic feature-film distribution receipts from theaters. The rental and sale of videocassettes is an area that can be easily exploited by smaller producers because many videotape rental and sales outlets are operated as small businesses and distribution is not as tightly controlled as is the theatrical outlet for feature films. Advertising expenses can be substantial, however, and these must be born by the producer who wants to sell videotapes to rental outlets and individual consumers. Most Hollywood films, such as *Ghostbusters* (1984) and *Beverly Hills Cop* (1985), have already had a great deal of publicity and generated much public interest prior to their availability as videocassettes. The former film sold 400,000 videocassette copies at $80 and the latter 1.4 million copies at $30 in 1985. (See Figure 16.2.)

The production of programming for small-screen exhibition raises a number of aesthetic problems as well. Composition

Figure 16.2
Big Rental Films of
1985 (U.S.–Canada
Market Only)

Title	Director-Producer-Distributor	Total Rentals
BACK TO THE FUTURE (R. Zemeckis; B. Gale/N. Canton/S. Spielberg/F. Marshall/K. Kennedy; Universal; July)		$ 94,000,000
RAMBO: FIRST BLOOD PART II (G.P. Cosmatos; B. Fietshans/A. Vajna/M. Kassar; Tri-Star; May)		80,000,000
ROCKY IV (S. Stallone; R. Chartoff/I. Winkler/UA; MGM/UA; November)		65,000,000
BEVERLY HILLS COP (continuing 1985 run)		50,000,000
COCOON (R. Howard; R. Zanuck/D. Brown/L.F. Zanuck; Fox; June)		40,000,000
THE GOONIES (R. Donner; R. Donner/H. Bernhard/S. Spielberg/F. Marshall/K. Kennedy; Warners; June)		29,900,000
WITNESS (P. Weir; E.S. Feldman; Par; February)		28,000,000
POLICE ACADEMY 2—THEIR FIRST ASSIGNMENT (J. Paris; P. Maslansky; Warners; March)		27,300,000
NATIONAL LAMPOON'S EUROPEAN VACATION (A. Heckerling; M. Simmons; Warners; July)		25,600,000
A VIEW TO A KILL (J. Glen; A.R. Broccoli/M.G. Wilson; MGM/UA; May)		25,200,000
FLETCH (M. Ritchie; A. Greisman/P. Douglas; Universal; May)		23,923,119
SPIES LIKE US (J. Landis; B. Grazer/G. Folsey Jr.; Warners; December)		23,000,000
PALE RIDER (C. Eastwood; Warners; June)		20,800,000
THE JEWEL OF THE NILE (L. Teague; M. Douglas; Fox; December)		20,000,000
MASK (P. Bogdanovich; M. Starger; Universal; March)		19,869,872
BREWSTER'S MILLIONS (W. Hill; L. Gordon/J. Silver; Universal; May)		19,383,925
PEE-WEE'S BIG ADVENTURE (T. Burton; R. Shapiro/R.G. Abramson; Warners; August)		18,100,000
E.T. THE EXTRA-TERRESTRIAL (reissue; July)		17,983,815
MAD MAX BEYOND THUNDERDOME (G. Miller/G. Ogilvie; G. Miller; Warners; July)		17,900,000
JAGGED EDGE (R. Marquand; M. Ransohoff; Col; October)		17,500,000
THE BREAKFAST CLUB (J. Hughes; N. Tanen/J. Hughes/A&M; Universal; February)		17,254,081
COMMANDO (M.L. Lester; J. Silver; Fox; October)		17,000,000
SILVERADO (L. Kasdan; Col; July)		16,582,358
ST. ELMO'S FIRE (J. Schumacher; L. Shuler; Col; June)		16,343,197

within the frame in a small-screen format must keep key information in the essential area of a TV receiver. Important details cannot be presented on the fringes of the screen as in a wide-screen feature film production designed primarily for theatrical release. Close-ups are used much more frequently for small-screen productions and wide vistas and panoramic shots are kept to a minimum. The pacing of entertainment programming intended for television and videocassette distribution is often faster and more action packed to hold the audience's attention. Programming designed specifically for the home videocassette market differs in many important respects from programming designed primarily for theatrical distribution.

At present the biggest users of disc technology are corporations, who create and distribute their own discs as corporate communications and information. Training materials and other informational programming can be produced internally by a media department or assigned to an independent producer. Initial recordings and editing are not done on disc. One inch videotapes or 35mm or 16mm films are made and then duplicated on disc, creating a master pressing or copy from which individual disc copies are made. Because the cost of this master runs quite high ($10,000 or more) it is only economical to use this technology when a large number of copies are needed. The high information capacity, relative permanence, and durability of discs make them an ideal information storage and retrieval medium. The low cost of producing numerous copies once the master disc is made makes the disc an excellent means of distributing promotional materials to salespeople or consumers in retail stores throughout the country.

In terms of direct sales to consumers, the main advantage offered by the sale of a product (rather than the sale of a seat in a theater or time on commercial television) and the relatively low cost of making multiple video copies, is that films and videotapes can be made for and marketed to specialized demographic groups. **Distribution channels** are not constrained by limited channels of access, as they are in the case of network television and commercial film theaters, where a product must be marketed to a mass, heterogenous audience. Individual copies can be manufactured and sold to smaller groups of consumers, just as popular rock, country, soul, and classical music can be marketed by the recording industry to smaller groups of people. Individual discs and videotapes can sell for anything from about $10 to $100, depending on the size of the market and the cost of production. As the consumer market expands, independent producers will proliferate and videotape and disc production may become as decentralized as production in the record industry.

Theatrical Film

Power in the feature film industry is concentrated primarily in distribution. **Major distributors** such as Paramount, Warner Bros., MGM, United Artists, Columbia, Universal, and 20th-Century Fox, receive the bulk of the distribution receipts from feature films. They negotiate with **exhibition chains**, such as National General, and independent theaters for a **split** of exhibition receipts. One of the most common splits for a major film is a **90/10 split**, which gives 90 percent of the admission receipts to the distributor and 10 percent to the exhibitor, above and beyond the latter's fixed operating costs for a specified period of time, such as several weeks. The distributor's percentage decreases gradually over time as the exhibitor's percentage increases. Exhibitors compete with each other for specific films by **bidding** a specific split and exhibition duration. About 50 percent of the major U.S. distributors' total theatrical receipts come from foreign distribution. Distributors also negotiate with television networks, cable television movie channels, and consumer videotape retailers. In 1985 Hollywood's domestic *film* income split up about as follows: theaters = $1.5 billion, videocassette sales = $1.5 billion, cable = $700 million, and broadcast television = $500 million.

An average Hollywood-produced feature film today costs over $10 million to produce. The distributor spends about 30 percent more than these production costs for advertising, release prints, and other distribution costs. It is virtually impossible to acquire financial backing for even an average budgeted feature film without a major distributor's endorsement. That endorsement usually requires the involvement of previously proven talent, such as well-known stars and directors, in a dramatic production. The distributor then either puts up the money for a production or provides some sort of guarantee to banks, which then finance the cost of production with a loan.

Only rarely are independently produced feature films that do not have initial major distributor endorsement later picked up by major distributors. But major motion pictures are being produced by people such as Dino DeLaurentis in right-to-work states, especially in the South, to lower production costs by avoiding unions and obtaining considerable state and local cooperation. Low-budget feature films are largely distributed by independent distributors, who do not have as much bargaining power with the largest theater chains and independent theaters as the majors. Of course, a producer can always distribute

his or her own film either by negotiating directly with theaters for a split, which is rarely done, or by renting a theater, doing some local advertising, and then receiving any and all gate receipts, a technique known as "**four-walling**."

Producers negotiate with distributors for a percentage of the distribution receipts. A producer can demand a certain percentage of either the **gross receipts** or the **net receipts** (after the distributor has subtracted certain "fixed" costs), or sell the film outright to the distributor. Obviously a producer who is able to negotiate a percentage of the gross receipts is in a strong bargaining position. The producer must consider a number of factors before deciding on a specific plan, such as the true earning potential of the film, the length of time before real receipts will be received during which interest on loans

Commercial tie-ins, such as the *Raider's of the Lost Ark* board game shown here, are another way successful movies make additional profits.

must be paid, the reliability of distributor accounting, and the hidden costs of production and distribution. An increasingly important area of negotiations is **ancillary rights** and **commercial "tie-ins,"** such as toys and T-shirts. Receipts from markets in addition to commercial theaters, such as network and cable television, must be considered. Musical records, books, posters, dolls, toys, clothing, and games that are off-shoots of a successful film, such as *E.T.*, can make huge profits. Sometimes an especially popular movie star will demand either a large initial payment of several million dollars, or a percentage of the gross distribution receipts. The involvement of major stars directly affects not only the production budget, but the producer's negotiations with the distributor and the banks.

The producer and financial backers of a feature film understand that film production is an extremely risky business. Few feature films earn a substantial profit, and most of those that do either are produced on an extremely tight budget for somewhat more smaller domestic and foreign markets, such as Earl Owensby's action-adventures, or are extremely high-budget films heavily promoted by major distributors. In both of these cases, the successful commercial producer understands the target audience and designs a film and budget that are realistic in terms of audience expectations, preferences, and size.

Nontheatrical Film

The term **nontheatrical film** refers to films that are shown in places other than commercial film theaters. Nontheatrical films are shown by colleges and universities, other educational institutions, civic groups, and other organizations. They are not always *exhibited* for profit, but often as a cultural or informational service. While nontheatrical exhibition is usually a nonprofit undertaking, nontheatrical *distribution* is largely a commercial business. Feature films, for example, are rented to various groups, institutions, and individuals in 16mm film formats for public showing. Renting these works for public showing is often far more expensive than purchasing a home videotape or disc copy, but videotapes and discs, which can be rented or purchased in retail stores, are strictly intended for individual, home use. Higher royalties are demanded for public showings of these films when they are rented from commercial, nontheatrical distributors.

Nontheatrical distribution is not limited to feature films. Individual film and video artists, documentary producers, and producers of other short informational and educational materials often have their work distributed by a nontheatrical distributor. Nontheatrical distributors who make a profit pass on a certain percentage of their gross receipts to producers. Other distributors are cooperatively organized by independent producers and artists themselves. The New York Filmmaker's Cooperative, for example, passes on a greater share of distribution receipts to individual artists, and keeps only a small percentage of rentals or sales for its own operating costs. Many commercial nontheatrical distributors, such as Pyramid Films, distribute successful short films. Many of the short subjects they distribute have previously won major awards, such as Academy Awards or major festival awards. One of the best means for beginning producers and directors to find good distributors for short works is to win awards at major festivals and contests. A nontheatrical distributor will often offer winners of major awards the opportunity to use the distributor's promotional and advertising services for a major percentage of the distribution receipts or offer an outright payment for exclusive distribution rights. These short films are then distributed individually to nonprofit institutions, as packages of shorts to cable television services, such as HBO (Home Box Office), and to colleges and universities. Nontheatrical distributors actively seek projects that have rather specialized audiences or limited markets, since they do not always have to distribute these works through mass media channels such as commercial broadcasting or commercial film theaters.

Corporate and Institutional Within-House Production

The overwhelming majority of production in the U.S. is done by corporations and institutions within house. This is one of the largest and fastest growing areas of possible employment in production. According to Department of Labor statistics, roughly 193,000 people in this country make their living in broadcast television, while 235,000 people make their living in non-broadcast television most of which consists of corporate and institutional production done within house. In the early 1980s the largest growth in sales of video equipment came from the industrial/business/institutional market, not in the broadcast market.

Within-house production by corporations, government agencies, and educational institutions constitutes a special type of distribution and exhibition channel. Much corporate video production is designed to train and motivate employees, to communicate with employees scattered all over the country or around the world, or to communicate with customers and clients. Different kinds of information can be presented in a more entertaining fashion than might be the case with a brochure or other publication. Sales representatives can be trained in the latest techniques and strategies for selling products. Corporate productions often demonstrate these techniques through dramatizations. Some corporations use videotape facilities to record executive speeches and sales meetings, so that corporate information can be widely disseminated. Specific products are often advertised and demonstrated in automobile showrooms or department stores using videotapes produced within house.

Hospitals and educational institutions often produce programs that are helpful to patients and students. Health-care information is often disseminated via closed-circuit television or by a mobile VCR unit that can be moved from room to room. Special diets, medications, and surgical procedures that a patient is about to undergo can be clarified and explained better and more efficiently on videotape than in person. One of the fastest growing areas of educational ''publishing'' is the production of instructional videotapes and computer interactive videotapes and videodiscs. Videotapes can help students learn an incredible range of tasks at their own individual rate, using a student-controlled VCR or interactive video unit, which consists of a computer and a VCR or videodisc player controlled by the computer. The viewer's response can be recorded on a touch pad that controls the operation of the computer and the rate at which new information or questions are presented.

A computer interactive system is a sophisticated teaching tool. Pictorial and textual information can be presented to and accessed by a student or trainee. A VCR can be combined with a personal computer to allow for various forms of viewer interaction, such as answering questions or requesting various options, while viewing pictorial and textual materials. Interactive video is a rapidly expanding area in corporate and institutional training and instruction.

A within-house production unit has varying degrees and types of accountability. The production unit may be directly accountable to management in a corporation in terms of its production budgets and production management. Government agencies and educational units are usually accountable to governmental or academic administrators. Since the programming that is produced is usually aimed at an internal audience or a specialized audience outside the institution, the means of assessing program success are sometimes quite informal, although sophisticated research into program effectiveness is often done by major corporations. Policy is sometimes controlled by a few individuals. There is usually a specific message to tell, and communication usually takes place in one-way direction down the hierarchy, although programming ideas sometimes originate from employee, patient, or student suggestions.

Most within-house production units produce videotapes that can be played at a time and place that is convenient for the recipient of the information. The within-house producer often has all of the facilities needed to produce a completed product and internally distribute and exhibit it. Medical schools, telephone companies, and public utilities, as well as government agencies, may have completely outfitted video production units with state-of-the-art equipment, such as 1-inch helical or 2-inch quad videotape recording and editing equipment, as well as high quality video cameras, lighting, and sound equipment. Small companies and agencies may only have a single ½-inch camera, a VCR with a monitor, and no sophisticated production or editing facilities. Individual project production costs are often kept low by having producers, directors, and technical support people on staff who can serve a variety of functions. Personnel who work in corporate or institutional production often have to be more flexible and have a broader range of skills than those who work in a particular broadcast television position. The staff for a within-house production unit is generally quite small. New personnel may be expected to work with slides, audiotape, and film on occasion, as well as videotape.

Production costs are usually kept to a minimum by using the most economical medium to communicate a specific message, but sometimes it may be necessary to use film (despite additional out-of-house expenses) when difficult location recording conditions such as high heat and humidity, will be encountered; when a soft, glamorous look is desired, as for a demonstration videotape for a new model automobile; or even when special effects or animation techniques such as pixillation are needed to add viewer interest or capture something that could not be recorded as live action. Sometimes film is used when it provides the best means of reaching the target audience, as when a school system has only film projectors or when a project must be shown to a large group and large-screen video projection is not a viable option. If motion is not essential, a slide and tape show may be a more economical and effective means of presenting the material. Technical information and statistics might be communicated more effectively and inexpensively by writing and illustrating a brochure or a pamphlet. Regardless of the specific medium that is eventually selected, basic writing and production skills are essential qualifications for anyone pursuing a career in the rapidly-expanding area of corporate and institutional within-house production.

Summary

The final stage of postproduction is known as distribution and exhibition. In television and film, exhibitors function somewhat like retail stores by selling or showing film and television products to audiences. Commercial broadcasting, public and cable television, videotape, videodisc, laser disc, and theatrical and nontheatrical film each represent different distribution and exhibition channels and different means of reaching target audiences. The selection of one of these channels affects the use of various television

and film production, postproduction, and distribution/exhibition technologies and formats.

Distribution and exhibition can be divided into two general areas: technology and economics. Distribution and exhibition channels can be differentiated on the basis of the specific technology they use. (See Figure 16.3.) Media producers need to be familiar with the technology used by different distribution and exhibition channels, so that they can tailor the production to specific technological requirements. They also need to be acquainted with the financial basis or economic structures by which each different channel functions. A producer must understand the financial exigencies of any potential distributor and funding source so that a realistic budget and estimate of market potential can be made.

Broadcasting refers to the transmission of television and radio signals through the air waves. A television signal is impressed upon a powerful carrier wave and sent from a transmitter tower to an individual receiver's antenna. The receiver separates the television signal from its carrier wave, and then decodes the separate luminance and chrominance aspects of the video signal. There are a limited number of channels available for television broadcasters. Broadcast television signals also have a limited range.

Satellites are relay stations that orbit the globe and allow television signals to be transmitted across wide distances, even around the world. Cable television distributes video transmissions, often received via satellite dish, to individual homes by way of coaxial cables. Amplifiers are needed at regular intervals to maintain a consistently strong signal throughout all of

Figure 16.3
Videotape and Film Formats for Distribution/Exhibition Markets

Production Formats

Videotape

A. 8mm
B. 1/2-inch Beta and VHS
C. 1/2-inch Betacam and Recam
D. 3/4-inch U-matic
E. 1-inch Helical
F. 2-inch Quadruplex
G. High Definition Television

Film

H. Super 8mm
I. 16mm
J. Super 16mm
K. 35mm Academy Aperture
L. 35mm Anamorphic
M. 35mm Standard
N. 65mm

Distribution/Exhibition Formats

Videotape

O. 8mm
P. 1/2-inch Beta and VHS
Q. 1/2-inch Betacam and Recam
R. 3/4-inch U-matic
S. 1-inch Helical
T. 2-inch Quadruplex
U. High Definition Television

Film

V. Super 8mm
W. 16mm
X. 35mm Academy Aperture
Y. 35mm Anamorphic
Z. 70mm

Laser Disc

Common Format Scenarios for Different Markets

1. Commercial Network Television Entertainment: E-S; M-S
2. Commercial Network Television News: D-R; D-S; C-Q; C-S
3. Commercial Local Television Entertainment: E-S; C-Q; C-S
4. Commercial Local Television News: D-R; C-Q
5. Commercial Syndicated Entertainment: E-S; M-S; M-T; M-W
6. Commercial Cable Programming Suppliers: E-S; K-S; K-T; L-S; L-T; N-S; N-T
7. Commercial Cable Operators News and Public Affairs: D-R; C-Q
8. Network Level Commercials and Public Service Announcements: M-S; M-T; E-S; E-Q; M-Q
9. Local Commercials and Public Service Announcements: D-R; E-S; D-S; C-Q; E-Q
10. Corporate and Institutional Television: D-P; E-P; B-P; D-R; D-S; E-S
11. Videotape Rentals and Sales: K-P; L-P; N-P; E-P; C-P; J-P; K-O; L-O; N-O; E-O; C-O; J-O
12. Theatrical Film Projection: K-X; L-X; N-X; N-Z; K-Z; J-X; L-Y; E-X; G-U (experimental)
13. Nontheatrical Film Projection: I-W; H-V
14. Interactive, Educational Video: D-S-Laserdisc; E-S-Laserdisc; C-S Laserdisc

A complex array of choices in terms of production and distribution formats confronts every producer. What is the best combination of production and distribution/exhibition formats to meet or exceed the needs and expectations of the target audience without going over budget? This chart presents a number of paths that have been successfully followed by video and film producers to match specific production and distribution/ exhibition formats at various levels and within various categories of production. Several paths or combinations of formats are presented for each different market. For example, market #1 for commercial network television entertainment, has several suggested format combinations, such as 1-inch helical videotape (E) for production combined with 1-inch helical videotape (S) for distribution/exhibition, as well as 35mm standard film (M) for production combined with 2-inch quadruplex videotape (T) for distribution/exhibition. The former is often used for situation comedies, while the latter is a common format path for action dramas. The latter path from M to T offers certain advantages for outdoor location recording, is somewhat more expensive, requires a film-to-videotape transfer, and produces an image quality that meets the expectations of network programmers and target audiences for a specific type of programming.

the trunk, subtrunk, and drop lines in a community. Individual subscribers either have a decoder box or a direct cable connection to their television set. Closed-circuit television systems interconnect various cameras, VTRs, and monitors within a single building or complex of buildings, using coaxial cable.

High-definition television (HDTV) provides a wide-screen television image that rivals the clarity, sharpness, and detail of 35mm film (about 1200 lines of resolution). HD television offers the prospect of providing high quality television images, which will someday be used by large screen electronic projection systems in commercial theaters and private homes.

Videotapes, CED videodiscs, and laser discs can be played on home and office players. There are three popular videotape formats, 8mm, Beta, and VHS, the latter of which are incompatible 1/2-inch videotape systems. The videodisc, a CED system, uses a stylus to scan a plastic phonograph-like pressing. The laser disc system, on the other hand, uses laser light projected at holes in a metal disc encased in clear plastic, rather than any physical contact with a stylus, and therefore the disc does not deteriorate with repeated use.

There are many electronic projection systems available. Some simply magnify a standard picture tube image, while others project three separately colored images at a distant screen, one each for red, green, and blue.

Film projectors move a continuous reel of film past a light source. An intermittent movement is used at the picture gate or aperture. When the shutter is closed, the film advances, and when the shutter is open, a single frame is projected on the screen. A standard film projector runs at a speed of twenty-four frames per second. The film runs intermittently through an aperture gate and continuously over a sound head. Different projectors are needed for different film formats, and a variety of light sources can be used to project images across wide distances.

From the standpoint of economics, television and film distribution and exhibition channels include: network, syndicated, local, cable, and public television programming; consumer products, such as videotapes, videodiscs, and laser discs; theatrical and nontheatrical film; and in-house productions.

Commercial network television sells audiences to advertisers. Programming is useful to the extent that it draws a large audience with specific demographic characteristics, such as women from eighteen to thirty-four years of age, to commercials aired during a broadcast. Scheduling is a key factor in the success of a program, as is the ability of a series to survive at least five seasons so that it can go into syndication.

Local television stations also sell audiences to advertisers. Network affiliate stations are paid a fee to carry network programming, but local stations, especially in the largest regional markets, make a considerable amount of money from selling commercial time for local and syndicated programming. Syndicated programming consists of reruns of old network series, movies, and other nonnetwork programming. Local stations rent this material from syndicators, who pay a portion of their distribution receipts to producers. Local stations also produce much of their own programming for news, sports, and public affairs. From an economic standpoint, a local news program is an important part of a local station's operations in terms of garnering an audience on which it can base its cost-per-thousand charges to advertisers. It is quite risky for an independent to speculatively produce programming for network or local television broadcasters.

Cable television offers a somewhat better potential market for independent, small scale productions. However, most cable operators are interested in filling time with continuing series, rather than with isolated individual programs. Cable suppliers either purchase or produce their own programming. Suppliers then try to sell commercial time to advertisers and/or receive a percentage of the subscription fee charged individual subscribers by the cable operator. Unlike network television producers, most cable producers and production personnel do not belong to unions, and production costs are often somewhat lower.

Public television is partially supported by the Corporation for Public Broadcasting and contributions from corporations, foundations, endowments, and individuals. PBS programming is produced largely by member stations, although some programming is purchased from foreign producers, such as the BBC. Member stations produce their own regional programming as well as programming of national interest that is distributed through PBS. Stations obtain funding from telethons, as well as government and private foundation grants. Individual stations pay for programming distributed by PBS. PBS stations rarely seek independently produced programming on a single program basis, although they sometimes broadcast individual programs of regional interest, if they meet broadcast standards in terms of technical, aesthetic, and ethical quality.

Commercials are brief messages used on commercial television to sell products, names, and services to consumers. At the national and major local market levels, they are usually produced on 35mm film by production specialists for advertising agencies. At the local level they are produced by local stations themselves and by small independent producers, usually on 1-inch or ¾-inch videotape or 16mm film. Public service announcements (PSAs) are noncommercial messages broadcast free of charge.

Videotapes, videodiscs, and laser discs are marketed to individual customers. They are also used for corporate communications. While it is relatively expensive to produce a master disc from which copies can be made, it is relatively inexpensive to make individual discs. Discs and videotapes can be designed for and marketed to relatively small demographic groups.

Economic power in the theatrical feature film industry resides in the major distributors, such as Paramount, Warner Bros., MGM, United Artists, Columbia, Universal, and 20th Century-Fox. An average feature film distributed by the majors costs above $10 million. About 30 percent more is spent on advertising and distribution costs. The major producers financially back the films they agree to distribute. Independent distributors rarely reach the same number or type of theaters as major distributors.

Nontheatrical film refers to the distribution and exhibition of films in places other than commercial theaters. Commercial nontheatrical distributors rent films to colleges, universities, and other institutions. Noncommercial nontheatrical distributors are sometimes cooperatively organized by filmmakers themselves or by educational institutions and foundations. Nontheatrical distribution provides a means for producers of short subject films and videotapes to reach an audience and receive a return on their production investment.

Within-house production refers to the production of programming by an organization for itself. Within-house production units exist in industry, government, and education, and collectively they represent the largest producer of video programming in the U.S. A production unit usually maintains a sufficient staff and supply of equipment to produce a videotape or film completely within house. Within-house production units use the most economical and efficient medium to communicate with employees, patients, students, and other groups. In some cases videotape or film will be used, but in others a slide and tape show or a brochure will suffice.

Additional Readings

Barnouw, Erik. *The Sponsor*. New York: Oxford University Press, 1978.

Becker, Samuel L. *Discovering Mass Communication*. 2nd edition. Glenview, IL: Scott, Foresman and Company, 1987.

Bluem, A. William, and Jason Squire, eds. *The Movie Business*. New York: Hastings House, 1972.

Eastman, Susan Tyler, Sydney W. Head, and Lewis Klein, eds. *Broadcast/Cable Programming: Strategies and Practices*. Belmont, CA: Wadsworth, 1985.

Gayeski, Diane M. *Corporate & Instructional Video: Design & Production*. Englewood Cliffs, NJ: Prentice-Hall, 1983.

Gitlin, Todd. *Inside Prime Time*. New York: Pantheon Books, 1984.

Hurst, Walter E., and William Storm Hale. *Motion Picture Distribution*. Hollywood: Seven Arts Press, Inc., 1975.

Jowett, Garth, and James M. Linton. *Movies as Mass Communication*. Beverly Hills: Sage Publications, 1980.

Kindem, Gorham, ed. *The American Movie Industry: The Business of Motion Pictures*. Carbondale, IL: Southern Illinois University Press, 1982.

Klein, Walter J. *The Sponsored Film*. New York: Hastings House, 1976.

Lees, David, and Stan Berkowitz. *The Movie Business*. New York: Vintage, 1978.

Owen, Bruce M., Jack H. Beebe, and Willard G. Manning. *Television Economics*. Lexington, MA: Lexington Books, 1974.

Shanks, Bob. *The Cool Fire: How to Make It in Television*. New York: Vintage, 1977.

Williams, Richard L. *Television Production: a vocational approach*. 2nd ed. Sandy, Utah: Vision Publications, 1981.

Exercises

1. Make a list of all the potential distribution and exhibition outlets for a specific production project. Then prioritize this list by arranging the potential distribution/exhibition outlets in a hierarchy from most to least important in terms of the funding source's or your own expectations and potential returns on production investments. Determine the ideal production, editing, and distribution medium (film or videotape) and format(s) (16mm, 1/2-inch VHS, and so on) for the most important outlet(s). Calculate the cost of producing a film or videotape using this (or these) format(s). Determine if the potential financial investments and returns from the outlets justify these expenses. If not, determine which medium and format(s) will work most effectively within the desired distribution/exhibition channels without exceeding potential investments and returns.

2. Consider your potential employment in a particular field of media production, such as corporate, public, or commercial television. What will you need to

obtain an entry-level position in this field? In what production capacity do you hope to be employed? Investigate the future employment potential of the field within which you hope to work. Is employment expanding or contracting? How many people are currently working in this field? Talk to someone who is currently working in this area and find out what it is like. Also talk to a personnel officer or director to find out exactly what he or she is looking for and what specific skills are needed. Request a copy of a résumé or vita from a previously successful applicant for such a position. Study this résumé carefully and compare it to your own. Outline a series of production projects and experiences that will help prepare you for this position and demonstrate your ability to perform a particular or wide range of tasks. Finally, when it comes time to actually seek employment, be persistent. Maintain periodic contact with potential employers, such as contacting them in person once a month for several months. When a job becomes available, it pays to be fresh in an employer's mind.

Glossary

A and B rolls Separate rolls of film or tape that are set up to be run simultaneously and mixed or printed onto a single tape or film.

Aberrations Disruptions of or imperfections in light transmission of a lens.

Above-the-line The portion of a production budget allocated to creative aspects of production, including the salaries of the producer, director, writer, and talent.

Academy aperture The size of the frame mask in 35mm cameras and projector (1.85:1) as standardized by the Academy of Motion Picture Arts and Sciences.

Academy leader A strip of film containing a sequential series of numbers indicating the exact number of seconds remaining before the beginning of a prerolled film.

Acceptable focus The adjustment of a lens so that the important objects are clear and sharp.

Acoustic echo chamber A recording studio baffled off in such a way that the sound reflection and reverberation delay can be controlled.

Actuality effects Sound effects recorded for a specific television program or film outside the sound studio.

Actual sound Sound that is presumed to come from some actual source either on-screen or just off-screen.

Actual time The time elapsed in a television program or film.

Adaptation A relatively faithful translation of a play or piece of literature into a film or television program.

Additive color The process of adding together red, green, and blue lights to reproduce other colors in the visible spectrum.

Advertising penetration An index of the number of people who have heard about a film, which is assumed to be related to the amount of advertis-

ing devoted to a specific film or television program.

Aerial image A technique for combining images by projecting them into a device that combines an animation stand with an optical printer. It is often used to record color titles on color film.

Affiliate A television station that is associated with a national television network.

Alligator clip A light-mounting device consisting of a spring-held clamp that somewhat resembles the jaws of an alligator.

Ambient noise Noise that is normally found in a particular location, which is usually preserved in an audio track.

Amortization Depreciation of the value of equipment and facilities over time for tax purposes.

Amplification An electronic increase in the intensity of sound.

Analog An electrical signal that represents a virtual one-for-one copy of sound or light waves.

Anamorphic Optically squeezed wide-screen film images, which require special lenses for recording and projection.

Ancillary rights The legal rights to sell a variety of commercial items that are somehow related to a television program or film.

Angle of acceptance The angle at which a lens gathers light in front of the camera.

Animation The creation of apparent motion from still-frame images recorded in succession on film or videotape.

Animation stand A table for recording still artwork and images for animation. It has lights, a camera platform that can be raised and lowered, and a rostrum on which artwork can be placed and moved.

Answer print The first test print made from the conformed film A and B rolls.

Antenna A device that improves the ability of a

television set to pick up broadcast television signals.

Aperture The open area through which light passes in a camera or projector; it determines the size or dimensions of the visual frame.

Arc Movement of a camera in a semi-circular pattern.

Art director In film production, the person who supervises the overall production design, including sets, props, costumes, settings, and even actual locations.

ASA *See* Exposure index.

Aspect ratio The ratio of the frame width to its height in a camera or projector.

Assemble editing The process of adding consecutive shots with their control tracks to a master tape.

Assistant director In video production, the person who relays the director's commands from the control booth to the studio floor and who keeps accurate account of the time. In film production, the person who helps the production manager break down the script during preproduction and helps the director keep the talent and crew happy during production.

Asynchronous sound Sound that does not match its actual or presumed on-screen source.

Atmospheric effects Environmental special effects, such as fog.

Audio console An audio board through which sounds are channeled, amplified, and mixed during production or postproduction.

Audio cue sheet *See* Mix log sheet.

Audio engineer In video production, the person who supervises the setup of microphones and other recording equipment and monitors the audio console during production.

Audio recordist *See* Mixer.

Audiotape Magnetic particles attached to a flexible support base, which are capable of storing an electrical audio signal.

Audition A function setting for a pot or fader on an audio console which is designed for listening without sending the signal outside the console.

Authority interviews Interviews with recognized experts, focusing information rather than personalities.

Automatic chroma key window tracking Maintaining the constant perspective shape of the image inside a chroma key window as the window itself is altered in size on a switcher by using a digital video manipulator.

Automatic gain control (AGC) A device that maintains a constant audio or video signal level on a videotape or audiotape recorder.

Axis of action Imaginary line formed by the direction of performer movement or by connecting stationary subjects. So long as the camera does not cross this line, screen directionality will be maintained.

Background light Light used to illuminate the set or background.

Back light Light coming from behind the subject and outlining it with a halo effect, helping to separate the subject from the background.

Backtime To prepare a prerecorded sound or music track so that it will end at a specified time.

Balanced microphone lines Mike cables consisting of two well-insulated conductors and a ground wire that inhibit cable noise.

Ball joint The part of a camera mount that can be adjusted in the cradle to level a camera.

Barn doors Black metal flaps that can be attached to a lighting instrument as a light shaping device.

Barney A soft sound insulator placed over a film camera for synchronous sound recording.

Base The shiny side of a piece of tape or film, which has no magnetic or chemical coating.

Based on Indicates an adaptation that is less faithful to the original literary source than a standard adaptation.

Base light level The minimum amount of light required to achieve a recording.

Base makeup Makeup that hides blemishes and creates a consistent overall facial color.

Below-the-line The portion of a production budget allocated to the technical aspects of production, including the salaries of the crew as well as equipment and material costs.

Beta One of two standard 1/2-inch helical-scan videotape recording formats.

Bias signal A very high frequency sound used during magnetic recording to erase a tape or improve the quality of an analog recording.

Bidirectional Responsive to sound from two opposite directions.

Binary code A series of on's and off's or 1's and

0's, which can digitally represent a wide range of values in coded form.

Black The darkest portion of the gray scale; a video source which provides sync signals but no picture.

Black-and-white An image that has brightness values only, that is, only blacks, shades of gray, and white, with no hues or colors.

Black-box radiator A theoretical standard for measuring the color temperature of different light sources.

Black crush A technique for recording animation-like images in real time by reducing the contrast range of a television screen so that movements of a black card are invisible.

Blimp A hard-shell sound insulator placed over a film camera for synchronous sound recording.

Blocking Working out talent and camera positions for a production.

Blooming A halo effect or added brightness around bright lights on some video camera pickup tubes.

Bloop (n) An audible tone recorded simultaneously with a flash of light for purposes of synchronizing images and sounds during editing. (v) To remove specific sounds from an audio track.

Blow up To increase film format by transferring it in an optical printer.

Blue-screen process A film process similar to video chroma key in which live action is shot against a blue screen and the blue screen is later filled in with a second live-action image.

Boom microphones Microphones that can be attached to an overhead stand or boom.

Box office returns The amount of money paid to theaters for tickets purchased by movie goers for specific films.

Breakdown sheets A listing of the facilities, material, equipment, and personnel needs for production at a specific setting called for in the script, which is filled out during a script breakdown.

Brightness The intensity of light.

Brightness contrast Visible differences between different colors or different objects in terms of brightness, regardless of hue or saturation.

Broad A rectangularly shaped lighting instrument used as a floodlight.

Broadcasting The sending of television and radio signals by attaching them to a carrier wave of elec-tromagnetic energy, which radiates in all directions.

Budget An itemized list of actual or estimated production costs.

Burn-in Image retention by the camera pickup tube, caused by an excessively bright subject, extreme contrast, or by photographing a static scene for an extended period of time. Also called ''lag.''

Bus A group of buttons on a switcher devoted to different image sources. Each bus is allocated to a different function, such as program, preview, or special effects.

Bufferfly diffuser A large nylon diffusion screen often used on location to soften sunlight, when it is placed overhead between the sun and the subject to be recorded.

Cable release A device that allows a film camera to be operated from a distance. It is often used for exposing still frames.

Cable sync A cable connection between the film camera and a synchronous sound recorder used for double-system recording.

Cable television A means of distributing television signals to receivers by using coaxial cables.

Cameo Lighting technique in which foreground subjects are lit in front of a completely black background, such as a cyclorama.

Camera blocking Organizing and plotting the movement of cameras prior to actual recording in such a way that movements and placements of cameras mesh with the movements and placements of performers. *See also* Performer blocking.

Camera chain A complete video camera unit consisting of five parts: a camera, a power supply, sync generator, a camera control unit, and an encoder.

Camera control unit A bank of controls that allows a video engineer to shade a video camera.

Camera operator The person who operates the camera and controls the actual camera placement, movement, framing, and focus.

Capacitor An electrical device that can store an electrical charge and alter the flow of electricity by changing the voltage of the electrical current passing through it.

Capstan A rotating metal cylinder used to drive tape through a recording or playback device.

Carbon arc light Intense, high color temperature light emitted by electrically burning carbon rods.

Cardioid   A microphone whose responsiveness to sound forms a heart-shaped pickup pattern.

Carpenters' elevation   A frontal and/or side view of a set drawn to exact scale, used as a guide in set construction.

Cartridge   A self-contained continuous loop of audiotape.

Cassette   A self-contained set of audiotape reels and audiotape.

Cassette recorder   A device that can record and/or play back sounds on cassette audiotapes.

Catharsis   An element in a tragedy that functions as an emotional learning process of the central character, characterized by a cleansing or purification of the emotions for the audience, which vicariously participates in this learning process.

Cathode ray tube (CRT)   A television picture tube.

C-clamp   An attachment device shaped like a C, which can be used to secure lighting instruments to a pipe grid or to connect flats and other set pieces.

CED system   The generic name for videodiscs.

Cel animation   Animating drawings made on individual acetate sheets.

Celebrity interviews   Interviews with well-known people focusing on emotional disclosure and personalities.

Cels   Individual sheets of clear acetate on which images can be drawn or painted, with precise perforation for placement on the rostrum of an animation stand.

Cement splicer   A device with a cutting blade and pressure plate for welding two pieces of film together with cement.

Central character   The most prominent figure or person in a story, who is often the primary source of audience interest and identification.

Changing bag   A light-tight black cloth or plastic bag used to load or unload camera magazines with film wound on cores.

Channel   (1) A separate audio signal. (2) A separate broadcast television signal.

Channel space   The amount of space in the broadcasting band allocated for broadcast television channels.

Character   A person or figure who acts and is acted upon in a story.

Character generator (CG)   An electronic device that creates letters on a television screen for titles and other graphic purposes.

Chroma   *See* Saturation.

Chroma key   Method of electronically inserting the image from one video source into the picture from another video source by selectively replacing the "key color" with another image.

Chroma key window   A monochrome board placed on the set into which a picture can be inserted by the switcher using chroma key during recording.

Chromatic aberration   Visual distortion occurring when different color wavelength bands bend at different angles and intersect at different points behind a lens.

Chrominance   The color component of a television signal.

Chronology   The temporal sequence of events in a story.

Cinema verité   Literally "cinema truth," a style of documentary filmmaking in which the camera runs continuously while recording unstaged events, resulting in relatively long, uninterrupted shots in the final film. It can be distinguished from American "direct cinema," which presumes a certain amount of objectivity or discounting of the effect of the camera upon the participants and less involvement of the people being recorded in the decision-making process of film making.

Cinerama   A wide-screen film process which used three cameras and three projectors placed side by side.

Clamps   Locks placed on the end of a rewind spindle on a film editing bench to hold the film reels tight on the rewind.

Clapstick   A hinged arm on a board used to make a highly visible and audible reference point at the beginning of a synchronous sound film shot or recording.

Clear leader   Film that has no magnetic coating or emulsion and is thus completely transparent base material.

Climax   The decisive point in a drama, where the central conflict becomes so intense that it must be resolved, the central crisis in a drama.

Clock time (1) Actual time of day on the studio clock. (2) The reference code often used for SMPTE time code recordings.

Closed circuit The sending of television signals through a self-contained system of electrical wires.

Closed shops Businesses or industries that require all employees to be members of a union or guild.

Close shot (CS) or Close-up (CU) While the terms close shot and close-up are sometimes used synonymously, a close-up technically refers to the isolation of elements in the shot, and normally indicates the head and shoulders of a subject. Both types of shots can be used for emphasis or to achieve a degree of intimacy or involvement. A very close camera position is sometimes called an **Extreme close-up (ECU)**.

Closure (1) Camera frame composition that inhibits continuity between on-screen and off-screen space. (2) The degree to which a story ending unambiguously resolves a problem, conflict, or plot.

CMX A type of computerized on-line videotape editing system developed by Consolidated Film Industries and Memorex.

Collapsible floor stand A portable light stand that collapses for storage and transport.

Color analyzer A closed-circuit color video system used to determine the best color and density for printing each scene of a motion picture.

Color bars A reference chart of color bands and black-and-white blocks that is used to adjust video equipment and is often placed at the head of a videotape recording.

Color commentator A narrator for a sports program who provides interesting background information and analysis of the game.

Color contrast Visible differences between adjacent colors in terms of hue and saturation.

Color film A film with three layers of color filters, which produce the various colors of the visible spectrum in combination with each other by the subtractive process.

Color harmony Colors that create a pleasing impression when used or presented together.

Color temperature The proportion of different wavelengths of light inherent in a white light source, based on heating a perfect light emitter to specific degrees Kelvin.

Color timing The art of setting the best color and density for the printing of each shot in a film.

Comedy A type of drama characterized by a less serious attitude toward life and an acceptance of its absurdities and incongruities.

Comet-tailing Lingering afterimage of a bright reflecting object moving by the camera in some video pickup tubes.

Commentative sound Sound that has no visible source and which seems to comment on the visual action.

Commercials Brief messages that advertise products, company names, and services.

Commercial tie-ins Commercial products sold in conjunction with a film or television program.

Compatibility That both color and black-and-white television sets receive the same signal; black-and-white sets ignore some encoded information, such as the chrominance portion of the signal.

Complementary colors Colors that, when mixed together, result in gray; such colors fall opposite each other on the color wheel.

Complications Interesting problems or obstacles that alter a basic dramatic conflict or inhibit a character's pursuit of a particular goal.

Composite print A single film containing both a picture and sound track.

Composite signal A complete video signal including sync pulse.

Composition The aesthetics of structuring images within a camera frame.

Compound lenses Lenses that have more than one piece of glass and usually combine several concave and convex lenses.

Compression ratio The rate at which sound compression occurs.

Computer-assisted film animation The use of a computer to control the movements of an animation stand.

Computer-assisted videotape editing The use of a properly programmed computer to edit videotapes automatically.

Computer control unit The central processor of a computer-assisted editing unit.

Computer graphics Pictorial images and illustrations designed by using a computer to alter the color and design of images within a video frame.

Concave Shape of a lens that bends light rays away from the center of the lens, causing them to diverge from each other.

Concealed lavalier microphone A lavalier microphone that can be concealed underneath the clothing of a performer.

Condenser microphone A microphone with an electrostatic element, called a capacitor or electret, which is placed between two charged plates: a diaphragm and a fixed back plate. A condenser mike requires a preamplifier and additional electrical current.

Conflict A point of contention, disagreement, or competition in a story.

Conformer A person who specializes in splicing A and B rolls of originally recorded film so that they match the edited workprint.

Conforming In film postproduction, the cutting and splicing of the originally recorded film so that it conforms exactly to the edited workprint.

Constant-speed motor An electric motor that runs at a constant speed which cannot be changed or controlled.

Contact printer A film printing device in which the original film is placed in direct emulsion-to-emulsion contact with the copy or print being made of it.

Contingency fund Ten or twenty percent added to the overall production budget in case of costly delays and production problems.

Continuity editing Editing of images and sounds that preserves a smooth flow from shot-to-shot so that actions which begin in one shot are completed in the next, without any apparent gaps in time or space.

Continuity person *See* Script supervisor.

Contrapuntal sound Sound that is presented simultaneously with visual images but is unrelated or contradictory in terms of meaning or emotional effect.

Contrast range The range of gray tones from white to black that a video or film recording process is capable of reproducing.

Contrast ratios The ratios between the different types of light and different reflectances of objects on the set, which each affect overall contrast in a scene.

Control track A sync signal used to ensure synchronization between the sweeping of the camera pickup tube and the sweeping of the television monitor or receiver, which is recorded with the video and audio signals on videotape.

Control track code A time code reference for videotape frames that relies on the control track.

Convertible cameras Video cameras designed for both studio and remote use.

Convex Shape of a lens that bends light towards the center of the lens so that the light rays converge or intersect at a specific point, beyond which the image is inverted.

Cookie *See* Cucalorus.

Copy stand A flat table with lights that illuminate artwork for an overhead camera.

Cores Plastic wheels on which film can be rolled; unexposed film placed on cores must be protected from light and loaded into a camera in darkness.

Cosmetic makeup Facial and hand makeup designed to hide imperfections and accentuate a performer's better features.

Costume designer The person who designs and supervises the making of clothing for the talent.

Countdown leader A strip of film or tape with a sequential series of numbers indicating the exact number of seconds remaining before the start of a film or videotape.

Counterpoint The simultaneous presentation of two separate melodies.

Crab dolly A four-wheeled camera support on which an operator can also sit and pedestal the camera.

Cradle The dish on the top of a tripod into which the ball joint of a fluid head or camera mount is placed.

Crane A relatively large camera mount consisting of a long counterweighted arm on a four-wheeled dolly.

Crawl Device using a large drum, or paper roll, which moves credits or other graphic material horizontally or vertically past the camera.

Credits Lists of the names of people who have contributed in some way to a production.

Credit sequence The opening or closing titles of a videotape or film which list the names of the people and organizations which have contributed in some way to the production.

Crisis An intensification of the central conflict in a drama, usually involving a threat to someone or something.

Cross fade   Transition in which one sound source is faded out while another is faded over it.

Crosstalk   Interface between two tracks recorded on the same tape.

Crystal oscillators   Small bits of quartz that oscillate and can be used to provide an accurate speed reference for a film camera or synchronous sound recorder, used for double-system recording without a cable.

Crystal sync   Separate crystal oscillators in the film camera and the synchronous sound recorder which drive them each extremely accurately so that double-system synchronous sound can be obtained without a cable connection between them.

Cucalorus   A metal or cardboard light-shaping device, which creates a pattern of light when placed inside an ellipsoidal instrument or between other lighting instruments and a background on which the pattern is projected.

Cut   To move directly from one shot or scene to another without any other transition device. Sometimes called a "straight cut."

Cutaways   Close-ups of actions and objects that can be inserted during postproduction editing to cover jumps in the actions or mismatched action from shot-to-shot.

Cutsound   Instruction to close a fader or pot abruptly.

Cycles per second (CPS)   The number of vibrations or successive waves of sound passing a specific point each second.

Cyclorama   A monochromatic background that creates the illusion of limitless space with no horizon or wall edge.

Dailies   Workprint copies of original recordings produced on a daily basis.

Daylight spool   A metal or plastic reel covering the edges of a roll of film so that it can be loaded into a camera in daylight.

Decibel (dB)   A unit of sound intensity.

Defocus   Placing one image out of focus and gradually bringing a replacement image into focus is known as a defocus transition device. It is sometimes used in place of wipes, fades, and dissolves.

Demographics   The characteristics of a television or film audience in terms of age, sex, etc.

Depth   The illusion of three-dimensionality in pictorial composition.

Depth of field   The range of distances in front of the lens which are in acceptable focus at the focal plane.

Depth-of-field charts   Table indicating the range of distances in front of different lenses within which objects will appear to be in acceptable focus at different lens settings.

Desk microphone   A microphone and stand designed to be placed on a desk or table.

Developer   The chemical solution which brings out the latent image on photographic film.

Developing   The process of making permanent images out of film exposures to light by placing the exposed film in chemical solutions.

Diaphragm   (1) The adjustable opening which varies the aperture size of a lens. (2) The element in a microphone which vibrates according to the pressure waves in the air created by the sound source.

Dichroic   A mirror or filter that transmits or reflects some wavelengths while absorbing others.

Diffraction   Spreading or scattering of light that often occurs around the blades of the iris in a lens.

Diffuser   Translucent material that breaks up and scatters light to soften it.

Digital   An electrical signal encoding sound and/or light values into a series of on's and off's, 0's and 1's called a binary code.

Digital video manipulator (DVM)   A special video effects device that uses digital techniques to alter visual images.

Dimmer board   An electrical control center for lighting that alters the voltage to different circuits in a patch board and thus changes the light intensity of instruments in those circuits, which also affects their color temperature.

DIN   A German or European standard rating of film sensitivity to light.

Director   The person in charge of actual production, who works with both the talent and crew. The director must be able to visualize the script, transforming abstract words into concrete images and sounds.

Director of photography (DP)   In film production, the person who determines the lighting and camera setup and placement or the cinematography.

Direct Cinema   *See* Cinema verité.

Direct-voice (DV)   Sync dialogue or narrations,

from a visible source; the opposite of a voice-over narration.

Disc frame storage An electronic device that stores single frames of visual information, such as titles and tables, in digital form so that they can be accessed immediately for live programming or used as single frames of animation.

Dissolve A simultaneous fade out and fade in. One scene or shot fades out at the same time that another scene or shot fades in to replace it. For a very short duration the two shots or scenes are superimposed over one another.

Distortion (1) Changes in magnification that occur in different parts of the image projected by a simple convex lens. (2) Undesired disruption of a sound signal, usually caused by overmodulation.

Distribution channels The means by which videotapes and films are disseminated to television stations, film theaters, various groups and individuals.

Distributors Companies and organizations that rent films to exhibitors or theater owners.

Docudrama A type of historical drama on television in which relatively recent historical events are treated in a semi-factual manner.

Documentary A nonfiction film or videotape that explores a topic in more depth than a news story.

Documentary structure The basic organizational elements in nonfiction television programs and films and the means by which specific elements are selected and ordered.

Dolly A camera platform or support on wheels.

Dolly shot A shot in which the camera moves towards or away from the subject while secured to a movable platform on wheels.

Double perf Film with sprocket holes or perforations on both sides or edges.

Double-system recording Recording synchronous sounds on a tape recorder that is separated from the film camera that is recording the corresponding images.

Drama A sequence of actions or events that tell a story.

Dramatic structure A combination of various elements, such as expositions, complications, crises, climaxes, etc., that affect the pace at which actions unfold and the emotional response of the audience to a drama.

Dress rehearsal The final rehearsal or dry run of a dramatic production with costumes and dressed sets prior to actual recording.

Drive mechanism The means by which a flexible tape or film is run through a recording or playback device.

Dual-redundancy microphones Two microphones clipped together so that if one of them fails, it can be turned off and the other turned on.

Dub A direct copy of a recording on the same format.

Dubbers Magnetic film playback machines.

Dubbing Copying sounds or video images from one tape without changing the tape format.

Dupe negative A negative copy of an interpositive which is used to make multiple prints of a negative original film.

Dyna lens A fluid-filled lens used to reduce vibrations for helicopter or airplane camera shots.

Dynamic ranges The range of sound intensities or loudnesses.

Dynamic microphone A microphone in which a moving coil attached to a diaphram, which vibrates with sound waves, is suspended between two magnetic poles.

Edge numbers Consecutive reference numbers printed on the edge of a piece of film.

Edit cue A cue that activates a video edit at a specific point on the videotape.

Edited master The final product of on-line editing of videotape.

Editing control unit An electronic device that controls the editing manipulations of videotape recordings.

Editing tempo The pacing or speed of visual images and sounds induced in the editing process.

Editor The person who determines the length, duration, and sequence of different shots and sound segments during postproduction by physically cutting film or electronically editing videotape.

Effects Visual sources which are being used for special effects on a switcher, usually placed on two different buses.

EFP mobile unit A portable van containing equipment for video recording action at remote locations.

Electret A permanently charged element or capacitor in a condenser microphone.

Electronic field production (EFP) Single-camera video production taking place at remote locations outside the studio.

Electronic news gathering (ENG) The use of video equipment to record news stories and information outside the television studio.

Electronic projection Large-screen television image projection systems.

Electronic synchronization Inducing a common speed in different machines or portions of machines by means of a common electrical distributor connected to independent motors or independent crystal oscillators.

Ellipsoidal A lighting instrument with a mirror reflector in the shape of an ellipse, which produces intense, harsh spot lighting.

Emulsion The dull side of a piece of film, containing the light-sensitive particles or the recorded images.

Encoded chroma key A form of chroma key that can use virtually any video image source.

ENG mobile unit A portable newsgathering van containing equipment for recording news events on videotape or microwaving them back to the studio.

Enlargement *See* Blowup.

Epic® A type of on-line computerized videotape editing system.

Epic drama A type of drama rooted in twentieth century critical thought about social, political, and economic problems, which offers an alternative dramatic approach to the individualism and emotional identification inherent in classical Western tragedy and drama since Aristotle.

Equalization The control or alteration of transmitted sound frequencies so that certain frequencies are amplified more than others.

Equalizer A signal-processing device that selectively increases or decreases the intensity of specific sound frequencies.

Erase head A device on a recording machine that is used to align all metal particles prior to recording and in so doing erase any previously recorded signals.

Essential area The area of the full frame within which crucial information should fall so as to be certain that it will not be cut off by a television receiver or film projector.

Establishing shot (ES) A shot in which the camera is generally located at a sufficient distance from

human subjects to record their actions in the context of their surroundings thus firmly establishing place and time.

Exhibition chains Collections of film theaters in different areas of the country.

Exhibitors Film theaters and theater owners.

Exposition A structural element in a drama where by characters are introduced or settings presented, providing background information and setting a specific mood.

Exposure The presentation of film to light.

Exposure index (EI) A rating of the sensitivity of a specific film stock to light.

Exposure latitude *See* Contrast range.

Extended scene A marking on a film workprint to indicate that a particular shop or scene extends beyond the point were actual workprint is present.

Fade A gradual increase or reduction and elimination of audio or visuals. The picture of a television program or film can **fade in** from blackness to picture or **fade out** from picture to blackness.

Fade in audio Instruction to raise the sound intensity gradually to an audible level and its proper volume setting.

Fade out audio Instruction to lower the sound intensity gradually to an inaudible level.

Fader A sliding knob which can be pushed up or down the scale to increase or decrease the sound level.

Fader bar A device for increasing or decreasing the intensity of a video signal on a switcher.

Fast forward A machine operational setting for rapidly advancing a tape or film.

Fast motion Recording images at a slower speed than normal playback speed.

Federal Communications Commission (FCC) The federal organization that monitors and oversees practices in the communications industry, including those in television and film.

Federal Trade Commission (FTC) The federal organization that monitors and oversees trade practices in many industries, including television and film advertising and industrial market structures and competition.

Feed The part of a recording device that supplies tape or film.

Feedback A continuous sound loop from a microphone through an audio console speaker which is picked up by the microphone, creating a loud squeal. Feedback can also occur with recording/playback units that form a continuous loop.

Fiction   The product of a writer's imagination as opposed to a depiction or presentation of actual occurrences.

Fidelity   The recording accuracy of video or film sounds and images.

Field   A complete scan of all even or all odd scan lines of a camera pickup tube or television picture tube.

Field curvature   Distortion caused when the image projected by a simple convex lens falls on a curved, rather than a flat, plane or image surface.

Field guide   A transparent sheet that indicates the proper field and spacing for letters and artwork on an animation stand.

Field of view   The exact spatial dimensions of the framed image in front of the camera.

Fill light   Softened, lower intensity light used to fill in the shadows created by key light and reduce contrast.

Film   Light-sensitive material that is run through a camera to record visual images. More generally, film refers to the whole process of recording, distributing, and viewing visual images produced by photochemical and mechanical, e.g., nonelectronic, means.

Film animation   Single-frame exposures of film images which create artificial motion when projected at normal speed.

Film camera   A light-proof mechanism within which film is exposed to light.

Film chain   *See* Telecine.

Film editing bench   A table used for mechanical splicing of film.

Film projection   The presentation of a film image on a screen by passing light through it in a film projector which is focused by a lens on the screen so that it can be viewed.

Film projector   A device that can play back a completed film and project it on a screen while amplifying the accompanying recorded sound track.

Film sensitivity   The amount of light required to produce a latent response in a film stock.

Film stock   A particular type of film in terms of format, sensitivity, process, graininess, etc.

Film-style   The use of a single video camera to

record a videotape in segments, as opposed to using multiple-camera production techniques.

Film-to-video transfer   Copying a film on videotape through a telecine or flying spot scanner.

Film viewer   A device that projects a film image during the editing process, such as a Moviescope.

Filter   A signal processing device that can be used to cut off all the sound frequencies above or below a specific frequency or to "notch out" specific frequencies of sound.

Fine grain   A film stock with particles that are invisible after development and projection.

Fishpole   A hand-held microphone boom.

Fixing   Placing the film in a chemical solution that permanently "sets" the developed image as part of the developing process.

Fixer   The chemical solution used in film developing to set the image, making the film no longer sensitive to light.

Flag   An opaque sheet of metal or cardboard that is separate from a lighting instrument but used to shape the light and prevent light from falling on certain areas.

Flat animation   Animating two-dimensional images, such as drawings and illustrations.

Flatbed   A horizontal film editing machine.

Flats   Relatively lightweight flat rectangular boards that can be lashed together to create a temporary wall in a studio.

Flicker fusion   The illusion of continuous light transmission from rapidly flashing or flickering lights and images. *See* Persistence of vision.

Floodlights   Lighting instruments without lenses which have reflectors and diffusers to spread and soften the light they emit.

Floor manager (FM)   The person who acts as the director's representative on the studio floor, relaying commands to the talent and crew during live or multiple-camera video production.

Floor plan   A scale drawing of the studio used in planning scenery design and construction, lighting, and camera and performer blocking.

Floor stands   Three-legged poles that can be raised and lowered, to which lighting instruments can be attached.

Fluid head   A camera mount filled with fluid which can help an operator create smooth camera pans and tilts.

Fluorescent light   Light produced by gases in a

fluorescent lamp, which lacks certain color wave-length bands.

Flutter An undesired fluctuation in sound pitch.

FM transmitter microphone Microphones connected to small FM radio transmitters, whose signals can be picked up across wide distances without requiring microphone cables.

Focal length The distance from the optical center of a lens to its focal point.

Focal plane The place behind a convex lens where the light rays form an inverted image in proper focus.

Focal point The place behind a convex lens at which the light rays intersect.

Focus distance The distance of the subject from the focal plane of a camera.

Focus ring The ring on the barrel of a lens that allows the focus to be changed.

Footage and frame counter A device that indicates the elapsed film length and duration in feet and frames.

Footcandle A basic unit of light intensity.

Formativism The aesthetic principle that film and video artists should completely control the structure or form and therefore the meaning of sounds and images.

Formats The standard widths of audiotape, videotape, and film.

Form follows function The aesthetic principle that a film or video artist must match particular forms to particular functions.

Formula *See* Genre.

Foundation makeup *See* Base makeup.

Four walling A means by which an independent film producer can distribute and exhibit his or her own film, namely by renting out a theater for a fixed fee.

Frame A complete video or film image, which occurs thirty times every second in NTSC standard television and twenty-four times every second in film, except for slow or fast motion.

Freely adapted Indicates a very loose adaptation that used the original literary work as merely a springboard for a videotape or film.

Freeze frame Holding the same frame on the screen so that motion is completely stopped.

Frequency distortion An unequal reproduction or elimination of some frequencies.

Fresnel A type of lens which bends light so that it travels in a confined area in parallel from a spot-light.

F-stop Unit of light transmission for a lens, mathematically calculated from its physical characteristics.

Full aperture area The full field of view in the aperture of a film camera.

Full-page script A script organized around scenes, in which both the visual and audio information appear in the same paragraphs.

Fully scaled floor plan A translation of the preliminary drawings or sketches of the set into the actual dimensions on gridded paper drawn to scale, usually providing an overhead view.

Full shot (FS) Sometimes used synonymously with the term establishing shot, a shot which orients the audience to subjects and settings by viewing them from a distance.

Functional lighting Lighting designed to create even or balanced brightness on the set so that every space is clearly and brightly lit and the lighting in general conforms to the functional utility of sets and actions.

Functional sets Sets designed for specific purposes, such as news, talk, game, and musical variety shows.

Gaffer In film production, the person who actually sets up or hangs the lights. This individual is sometimes called an electrician or engineer.

Gaffer's tape Extremely strong gray-colored tape used for securing lights and light mounting devices, among other things.

Gain control *See* Pot or Fader.

Galvanometer A device that converts fluctuation in the electrical current of a sound signal into fluctuations in a light which exposes film to make an optical sound track.

Gang synchronizer Several wheels or hubs with sprocket teeth that hold different pieces of film in exact registration frame for frame as they are advanced.

Gate The area of a film camera or projector where the film is exposed to light.

Gels Flexible sheets of transparent colored plastic, which can be used to create colored light or alter the color temperature of a light source.

Genre A particular type or category of films and television programs, such as musicals or westerns.

Giraffe A microphone boom attached to a three-wheeled dolly, which cannot be telescoped while recording is taking place.

Graininess The degree to which grains or crystals of silver halide are visible in a film stock after development and projection.

Grainy A film stock that has highly visible particles after development and projection.

Graphic design The organization and simplification of visual material and written titles and information for a television program or film.

Graphic set piece A three-dimensional structure, such as a weather map, placed on the set for illustration purposes.

Gray scale A sequential series of gray tones from white to mid-gray to black, which can be used to determine reflectance contrast and adjust television cameras or when recorded on film help to determine the contrast inherent in a particular film stock.

Grip A person who performs a variety of tasks during film production, including helping to set up cameras, lighting equipment, and sets, except in union productions where responsibilities are restricted primarily to camera setup and control.

Gross distributor rental receipts The total amount of money paid to motion picture distributors by theater owners for the rental of specific films.

Guillotine splicer A film tape splicer that uses unperforated tape, which it cuts off and perforates in a downward punch of its handle.

Halo effect *See* Blooming.

Hand-held cards Illustrations that a performer holds up to a camera during the recording of a scene.

Hand props Set furnishings that are handled by the performers.

Hanging microphone A microphone suspended from a ceiling or grid.

Hard light Direct light that creates harsh shadows.

Harmonic distortion Distortion of the primary signal by harmonics of the primary signal, usually caused by overmodulation.

Harmonics Sounds that are exactly one or more octaves above or below a specific sound frequency.

Harmony The combined effect of playing several consonant tones simultaneously.

Head leaders The beginning leaders placed on rolls of film for editing and projection purposes.

Headroom The space above the head of a person within a camera frame.

Helical scan A type of videotape recording in which the videotape is wrapped around a drum within which recording heads rotate, creating a slanted track on the tape.

Hertz (Hz) The number of vibrations or successive waves of sound passing a specific point each second.

High-angle shot A shot in which the camera is placed high above the subject, tending to reduce its size and importance.

High-definition television (HDTV) High-resolution television signals, which can produce wide screen images that are roughly comparable to film images in terms of overall sharpness and detail (lines of resolution).

High hat A camera mount for extremely low camera placements.

High impedance A type of electrical signal put out by some nonprofessional microphones and playback machines.

High-key lighting A lighting aesthetic characterized by a brightly lit low contrast scene created by equal intensities of key and fill light and a relatively low key-to-fill ratio.

Historical drama A recreation of historical events, actions, and people in fictional form.

Historical time *See* Story time.

Hitchhiker A spider on wheels.

HMI light The high-intensity, high color temperature light produced by energy-efficient HMI lamps.

Hook A dramatic device that grabs the audience's attention and secures their involvement in a story.

Horizontal blanking In television signal transmission, the period of time that an electron beam of a signal is shut off while the scan line is changed.

Horizontal sync A television signal that controls the horizontal scanning and blanking of the pickup tube and the picture tube.

Hot splicer Another name for a cement splicer that welds two pieces of film together with cement.

Hue A specific wavelength band of light, such as red, green, or blue.

Hypercardioid An extremely directional microphone pickup pattern.

I and Q signals *See* Chrominance.

Illustrations Stationary visual images such as charts and still photographs, which depict or illustrate concepts and ideas.

Image depth The perception of a range of distances within the image of a frame.

Image orthicon (I-O) A large black-and-white video camera pickup tube.

Image perspective The apparent depth of the image and the spatial positioning of objects.

Image tonality The overall appearance of the image in terms of its apparent contrast and color.

Impedance A measurement of electrical resistance.

In-camera editing Shooting a succession of shots on film or videotape so that they do not have to be edited in postproduction.

Incandescent bulb The standard light bulb used in household lamps, consisting of a tungsten filament in a glass-enclosed vacuum.

Incidental characters Minor, background figures in a story who often add texture, interest, and depth.

Incident light Direct light as opposed to indirect or reflected light.

Incident reading A light meter reading of the intensity of the light falling on the subject.

Independent A producer, distributor, exhibitor, or station that is not affiliated with a network or major national corporation.

In-line picture tube A color television picture tube that consists of lines rather than dots of color light-emitting phosphors, with the electron guns in parallel positions.

Insert A recording of specific actions in a scene, which can be inserted into a master shot. A technique used in single-camera production.

Insert key A removal of the portion of the background image where a foreground image, such as a title, will be inserted.

Insert mode A videotape editing function by which one piece of prerecorded video material can be inserted into another recording.

Instructional programs Educational videotapes and films designed to inform the public about new programs and policies in government, industry, or education, or simply as teaching aids for students or employees.

Intercutting A relatively rapid alternation between two or more different shots.

Internegative A copy of the A and B film rolls onto a single negative film which can be used for making multiple positive film prints.

Interpolation An animation technique in computer graphics, which allows the animator to compose the first and last frames of an action sequence so the computer can generate the images in between.

Interpositive (IP) An intermediate positive copy of the A and B film rolls which is made in order to produce multiple copies from original negative film.

Iris A variable aperture in a lens.

ISO *See* Exposure index.

Isolated camera A camera that feeds its own videotape machine as well as being used in the multiple-camera video mix, to provide additional editing footage.

Jingles Music and lyrics used in commercials, emphasizing melodies and phrases which are quickly associated with specific products.

Joy stick A lever on a video switcher which allows the operator to select a specific placement of a wipe, key, or other special effect.

Jump cuts Cuts across actions that do not match in terms of temporal or spatial continuity.

Key Replacement of a portion of one image by another.

Keying and chroma key Techniques for replacing certain parts of a video image that can be replaced with another image. Titles and graphics can be inserted into an image by keying. A new background can be inserted into a specifically colored area of the image using chroma key.

Key light The brightest light on a set, which creates shadows and provides modeling and texture.

Key-to-back ratio The ratio between the key light and the back light intensities, which indicates the amount of separation effected through back lighting.

Key-to-fill ratio The ratio of key plus fill light to fill light alone.

Kicker A separation light placed directly opposite the key light on the set to create side and back light.

Kill To turn off a light, sound, or video feed.

Kinescope A film recording of a live television program.

Laboratory color timer In film postproduction, the person who sets the printing light intensity and color for the best image quality of each shot in the final film.

Lab report *See* Camera report.

Laser disc A type of video recording in which a laser beam is used to scan minute holes in a metal disc encased in plastic.

Lavalier microphone A microphone designed to be suspended from a speaker's neck or attached to clothing on his or her chest.

Lead story The most important news story of the day, which is usually placed at the beginning of a news program.

Legal release A statement releasing a producer from future legal action, such as for slander or libel, which is signed by people appearing in a television program or film who are not professional performers.

Leitmotifs Musical themes associated with specific characters.

Lens A curved piece of glass which focuses light on a recording surface in a camera or projects an image in proper focus on a screen.

Lens coating Substance placed on the surfaces of a lens to reduce the reflection of light entering the lens and therefore increase light transmission.

Lens hood A device for shading a camera lens from direct sunlight.

Lens perspective The way in which a lens presents the spatial relations between objects it records or transmits.

Leveling Adjusting the horizontal axis of a camera frame in a mounting device so that it conforms to the horizon.

Library effects Sound effects catalogued and accessible in prerecorded form in a collection.

Light Electromagnetic energy which stimulates receptors in our eyes.

Lighting contrast ratio *See* Key-to-fill ratio.

Lighting director In video production, the person who designs and supervises the lighting setup.

Lighting instrument The housing within which a light source or lamp is enclosed.

Lighting plot An outline of a lighting setup on gridded paper which represents the studio floor space in reduced scale, providing an overhead view of the lighting setup and the set.

Light meter A device that measures light intensity by converting light energy into electrical signals whose strength can be measured.

Light pencil A stylus that allows a graphic artist to draw directly on a television screen.

Light reading The use of a light meter to determine the correct exposure of film or the light levels on a set or location.

Line levels The higher electrical signal strength of playback units as compared to most microphones.

Lip sync dubbing Replacing synchronous film sounds recorded on location with speech recorded in a sound studio which corresponds to the performer's lip movements.

Live on tape The use of multiple video cameras while recording continuous images on videotape during production.

Location production Film production work performed outside the studio.

Long shot (LS) A shot that provides a full frame (head-to-toe) view of the subject. It may or may not establish the setting, but it provides a view that includes all major action.

Looping The process of lip sync dubbing.

Loudness The human perception of sound intensity, determined by the amplitude of a sound pressure wave.

Loudness distortion Sound signal disruption caused by overmodulation.

Low-angle shot A shot in which the camera is placed closer to the floor than normal camera height. This angle tends to exaggerate the size and importance of the subject.

Low-impedance A type of electrical signal put out by most professional microphones and some playback equipment.

Low-key lighting A lighting aesthetic characterized by pools of light and harsh shadow areas created by minimal fill light on the set and a relatively high key-to-fill ratio.

Luminaire *See* Lighting instrument.

Luminance The brightness component of a television signal.

Magnetically striped film Film with magnetic tape along one edge for use in single-system (sound-on-film) recording.

Major distributors The largest feature film distributors, who receive the bulk of the distribution receipts from the rental of feature films, such as Warner Bros., MGM, United Artists, 20th Century-Fox, and Universal.

Master The final product of the audio recording and mixing process: the completed audiotape.

Master control The room to which all video and audio outputs of various production studios are fed for distribution and broadcast or recording.

Master program bus The selector switch for visual sources which are to be sent out of the switcher to a transmitter or videotape recorder.

Master shot A recording of as much of the action in a scene as possible in a single shot or camera take. Often used in single-camera production.

Master sound mix The final product of a sound mix on audio or videotape.

Master tape The tape to which other material will be added during videotape editing.

Matte Used in motion pictures to black out an area in one image and place another image into the blackened area. Matting is frequently used for special optical effects.

Matte keying Similar to insert keying except that it allows the portion of the background scene which is removed to be replaced with another visual source, such as one from another camera.

Matte shots Combinations of different images in the same film frame.

Mechanical interlock A physical connection between different machines or portions of machines that causes them to run at the same speed when driven by the same motor.

Medium shot (MS) A shot that provides approximately a three quarter (knee-to-head) view of the subject. The extreme distances within this type of shot are sometimes referred to as a **medium long shot (MLS)** and a **medium close-up (MCU)**.

Melody A series of musical notes or tones that create a structured unit or order.

Metamorphosis An animation technique in which one figure is gradually transformed into another figure which has an entirely different shape.

Metronome A device used by musicians to provide a regular beat or rhythm.

Microphone boom A long pole to which a microphone can be attached so that it can be placed just outside the camera frame.

Microphone cables Insulated wires that carry electrical sound signals from microphones to recorders.

Microphones Transducers that convert sound waves into fluctuations of electrical current.

Microwave A high-frequency signal used to transmit television signals by line of sight across relatively short distances.

Mike levels The lower electrical signal strength of microphones as compared to the line levels of playback and some signal processing equipment.

Mil A unit of measure of tape thickness (.001 inch).

Miniature A three-dimensional replica of a set or prop which is sufficiently realistic to be used as a substitute for a full-size construction during production.

Mirrored shutter A mirror coating on the front of a shutter that intermittently deflects all the light to a reflex viewfinder as the film is advanced in the camera.

Mirror shots (1) The use of two mirrors to make a large periscope that can be used for overhead video camera shots. (2) The removal of a portion of a mirror so that a background scene can be combined with a scene reflected in the mirror.

Mix To combine several sound tracks.

Mix bus A pair of buses with a fader bar control to permit the production of fades, dissolves, and supers.

Mixer An audio console; also, the person who controls sound levels and effects during audio mixing. In film production, the person who supervises the setup and operation of microphones and audio recording equipment.

Mix log sheet A list of all volume changes and transitions for a sound mix, which is organized sequentially for each of several sound tracks.

Model A three-dimensional replica of a set or building which is made prior to actual construction of the set.

Modeling Highlighting the appearance of a textured surface through the use of shadows.

Modulation Adjustment of sound intensity or loudness.

Modulometer *See* Peak program meter.

Moiré effect A distracting vibration of visual images caused by the interaction of narrow stripes in the design of the material being recorded.

Monitor (v.) To listen to a sound track or tracks in an audio console through a speaker in the studio. (n.) A closed-circuit television set, which does not necessarily have the ability to decode broadcast signals.

Monaural *See* Mono.

Mono or Monophonic Single-channel audio signal as opposed to stereo.

Motif Imagery which is repeatedly used in an artistic work to add depth and symbolism.

Moviola Jr. A mechanical film editing machine used to drive and view a film on a film editing bench.

Multiplane animation Walt Disney type of animation used in classic films, such as *Peter Pan*, in which several glass plates at different distances from the camera are recorded simultaneously to create depth.

Multiple-camera production The use of several video or film cameras to record the same actions simultaneously from several different viewpoints.

Multiple microphone interference *See* Phasing problems.

Multi-track A type of audiotape recording in which several separate tracks are recorded on the same audiotape.

Munsell color wheel A three-dimensional color wheel, which categorizes different color samples on the basis of brightness, hue, and saturation.

Music libraries Collections of musical recordings, usually by lesser known performers and artists, that require minimal royalty payment for use in a television program or film.

Mystery A type of drama in which the audience is aware of a threatening atmosphere rather than the specific object to be feared. Unlike suspense, the source of the threat is not known, but withheld until later.

Narrate To tell a story or provide a commentary on events.

Narration A verbal commentary on the events taking place within a fiction or nonfiction videotape or film.

Narrative A story that is told or narrated by someone.

Narrative structure The basic elements of a story from the standpoint of time and point of view, such as historical story time, actual film or television time, and omniscient versus first person narration.

Narrowcast A term often applied to cable television, signifying that it targets programs to more narrowly defined groups of people in comparison to broadcasting.

Naturalistic lighting Lighting that appears to come from known or presumed actual sources in a setting or location.

Natural wipe Cutting from one shot to another when a black object fills the frame at the end of the first shot and the beginning of the next so that the cut becomes virtually invisible.

Needle drop fees One means by which royalty payments for music library selections are made by charging a fixed fee each time a phonograph needle is dropped onto a particular recording; that is, each time it is played.

Negative A type of film that produces negative images when it is developed.

Negative image An image in which the brightnesses and darknesses of the original are reversed, making blacks white and whites black or reversing colors, turning them into their complements. In video this is accomplished by simply reversing the electrical polarity of the television signal. In film a negative film copy of a positive film image can be made photographically.

Negative/positive process A means of producing projectable film images in two steps by first exposing and developing negative film and then printing that negative film to make a positive film.

Net distributor rentals The amount of money a distributor receives from theater rentals of films minus the distributor's own costs.

Network A national distributor and producer of television programming, which usually has affiliated broadcasting stations in local areas.

Nielsen ratings Television audience information researched by the A. C. Nielsen Company, which consists of **ratings**, **shares**, and **demographics.**

Noise Unwanted sound.

Noise reduction The elimination or diminishing of equipment and/or tape noise by means of signal-processing devices.

Nonfiction Depiction, description, or presentation of actual, or unstaged, events.

Nonreflex A camera that has a separate viewfinder, as opposed to one that allows the operator to look directly through the objective lens.

Nontheatrical films Films that are not produced for or shown in commercial theaters.

Normal lens A lens that presents an image perspective which seems to approximate that of normal monocular (single-eye) human vision.

NTSC The American television standard system of 525 scanning lines and 30 frames per second.

Objective lens The lens on a camera that is used to record images.

Off-camera microphones Microphones that are invisible to viewers because they are either placed off-screen or hidden on-screen.

Off-screen sound A sound coming from off-camera sources in the same general location or setting as on-screen sounds.

Off-set graphics Graphic images that are not actually a part of the set.

Omnidirectional Responsive to sound from all directions.

Omniscient point of view In literature, a narrative written in the third as opposed to the first person, and in television and film, a story told from a relatively objective perspective or camera viewpoint.

On-camera microphones Microphones that are visible to viewers in the video or film frame.

180-degree axis of action rule A means of camera placement which ensures continuity and consistency in the placement and movement of objects from shot-to-shot.

On-screen sound A sound emanating from a source that is visible within the frame.

On-set graphics Graphic images recorded by cameras as part of the set during production.

Opaque black leader Film leader that is opaque to light, which is often used immediately before a film begins or during film conforming to prevent double exposure of an answer print when A and B rolls are printed.

Open mike Instruction to switch on the fader or pot for a specific mike or raise it to its proper level.

Optical printer A device consisting essentially of a film projector pointed at a film camera, which can be used to create special optical effects.

Optical sound Sound recorded optically on the edge of a film, where variations in intensity are recorded as variations in density or the width of film exposure.

Oscilloscope *See* Waveform monitor.

Outline sketch An outline of a figure or shape made with a pencil by tracing an image or roughly sketching an original image.

Out-takes Recorded shots that are discarded entirely and do not appear in the final edited version of a film.

Over budget A production that has exceeded the budgetary limitations specified in the production budget.

Overexposure Excessive exposure of the film to light, such that the quality of the image is affected and usually washed out or too bright.

Overhead shot A shot in which the camera is placed directly overhead, creating a unique perspective on the action. This can also be accomplished by a set of periscope mirrors, or mounting the camera on an airplane or a helicopter.

Overmodulation Adjusting the sound intensity so high that it exceeds the limits of the electrical system and creates distortion.

Over schedule A production that has exceeded the time limitations specified in the production schedule.

Over-the-shoulder shot A shot in which the camera is placed behind and to the side of a subject, so that the shoulder of that subject appears in the foreground and the face or body of another in the background. This type of shot tends to establish a specific subject's physical point of view on the action.

Owned and operated (O&O) A television station in a major metropolitan area that is owned and operated by a national television network.

Pace A subjective impression of the speed of sounds or visuals.

Package A marketable combination of production elements, such as well-known, previously successful talent and creative production staff.

Packaging Highlighting the most marketable or notable elements in a proposal for prospective sponsors and funding sources.

Painters' elevation A fully scaled frontal and/or side view of a set or prop showing its color values and designs.

PAL A European television standard system of 625 scanning lines and 25 frames per second.

Pan A horizontal pivoting of the camera.

Pan shot A shot in which the camera is rotated on a tripod or panning device.

Parabolic microphone A directional microphone consisting of a large dish, which collects distant sounds and is often used to record sounds of sporting events from the sidelines.

Parallax The discrepancy between the framed image in an objective lens and the image in a separate viewfinder in a nonreflex camera.

Parallel sound Sounds that complement or have virtually the same meaning or emotional effect as the visual images with which they are presented.

Patch board An electrical distribution center for lighting consisting of a variety of electrical circuits for different instruments.

Patch panel Connections between various sound outputs and inputs that can be rearranged so that signals can be diverted to other units or one unit substituted for another.

Pause A mode or function on a videotape recorder that holds the tape in position for single-frame scanning.

Peak program meter (PPM) A European standard device for measuring sound intensity or loudness, which reflects actual sound peaks rather than average sound peaks.

Pedestal dolly A camera support on wheels that allows a camera to be moved directly up and down on a pedestal.

Pedestal shot A direct vertical movement of the camera.

Pencil test An animation test of simple drawings prior to the creation of more elaborate and detailed drawings so that problems in motion, etc., can be detected early.

Perambulator A large microphone boom that provides maximum flexibility and control over the movement and placement of a microphone in a studio situation.

Perforations *See* Sprocket holes.

Performer Anyone who appears in front of a television camera.

Performer blocking Organizing and plotting the movements of performers on the set prior to actual recording.

Persistence of vision The illusion of continuous light transmission from rapidly flashing or flickering lights and images caused by the temporary lag in the eye's retention of images, so that one image is fused with another. This perceptual phenomenon does not explain the illusion of apparent motion in video and film. *See* Phi phenomenon and Flicker fusion.

Perspective The illusion of spatial distance in two-dimensional visual media.

Phasing problems The cancellation of certain frequencies, caused by placing microphones too close together when they are picking up the same sounds.

Phi phenomenon The illusion of apparent motion from rapidly flashing stationary lights and objects.

Photoelectric cell The transducer in a light meter which converts light energy into electricity.

Photofloods Lamps with self-contained reflectors that do not require lighting instruments.

Photographic enlargements Still photographs blown up in size so that they can be hung as parts of the set and used as illustrations.

Photographic film A light-sensitive material, consisting of silver halide particles attached to a flexible support base, that yields visual images after proper exposure to light and chemical development.

Phosphors Light-emitting optoelectronic semiconductors in a television picture tube.

Pickup pattern The area or space surrounding a microphone within which the sensitivity to sound is the greatest.

Pickup tube A device that converts light entering a video camera through the lens into electrical signals.

Pilotone A particular type of sync signal used in some synchronous sound film audio recorders.

Pipe grid A series of parallel pipes hung from a studio ceiling to which lighting instruments can be attached with C-clamps.

Pistol grip A hand-held camera mount.

Pitch The perception of or human response to difference in sound frequency.

Pixillation Animating still images of live-action objects by changing their positions from shot to shot.

Plastic animation Animating three-dimensional objects.

Plates The platters on a flatbed film editing machine that feed and take up film.

Playback head A magnetic device capable of transforming magnetic changes on a prerecorded tape into electrical signals.

Playback mode A machine operational setting for viewing or listening to a prerecorded signal.

Plot Actions or events occurring over time.

Plumbicon A type of color video camera pickup tube, a registered trademark of N. V. Phillips.

Point of attack The beginning of a drama, which usually generates interest and excitement.

Point of view The perspective or subjective viewpoint from which a story is told.

Point-of-view shot (POV shot) A shot in which the camera is placed in the approximate position of a specific character. It is often preceded by a shot of a character looking in a particular direction and followed by a shot of that same character's reaction to what has been seen. The latter shot is sometimes also called a **reaction shot**.

Polarizer filter A glass that reduces glare when properly adjusted over a camera lens and/or lights on an animation or copy stand.

Portable lighting kit A self-contained lighting unit for field production consisting of open quartz lights, stands, extension cords, and some accessories.

Positive A type of film image that reproduces the brightnesses of the original scene when it is developed.

Postproduction The final stage of the production process, during which recorded images and sounds are edited and the videotape or film completed.

Pot Short for potentiometer, a knob that can be rotated to increase or decrease the sound level.

Power pack Batteries used to power a piece of recording equipment.

Preamplifier A device that can boost a weak electrical signal to a usable level; often placed inside a recording device, such as a condenser microphone.

Preperforated splicing tape Film splicing tape that already has holes punched in it which conform to the holes in the film, for use in some types of tape splicers.

Preproduction The preparatory stages of production planning prior to actual recording of sounds and images.

Prerecorded black video signal A signal placed on a videotape that is to serve as the master tape for video insert editing, which has a consistent control track throughout.

Prerolling Rewinding a piece of prerecorded material ahead of the point where the playback will actually begin or an edit will be made, so that it will be fully up to speed when it is transmitted or recorded.

Pressure plate The surface inside a film camera that keeps the film flat in the gate at the aperture.

Preview To view an image source without sending it out of a video switcher.

Primary color pigments The basic colors used in painting, namely red, blue, and yellow, which can be mixed together in various proportions to produce virtually all colors.

Principal characters Friends and foils of the central character(s).

Print through One layer of recorded tape bleeding through so that it interferes with another layer.

Print-through edge numbers Edge numbers from the original film that have been printed through to the workprint by using an edge light on the printer.

Printing The process of making a copy of a film by passing light through it onto a second, unexposed piece of film, which is then developed.

Prism block A piece of glass in a color video camera that bends or refracts each color wavelength band to a different pickup tube.

Producer The person responsible for overall production management from project initiation to eventual completion, whose primary duties include project funding, budgeting, and scheduling.

Production The stage of production during which production materials and equipment are set up and sounds and images are actually recorded.

Production design The coordination of scenic design with other artistic aspects of production, such as lighting.

Production designer The name given to the few Hollywood art directors who have control over the entire production design of a motion picture.

Production manager In feature-film production, the person who breaks down the script into its component parts for budgeting and scheduling and who supervises the allocation and use of studio facilities.

Production strategy An organizational framework for channeling creative production energies consisting of three steps: defining project goals; assessing the potential audience; and researching the topic.

Professional sound studio   An audio recording, dubbing, transferring, and mixing facility that specializes in providing these production services for radio, television, music recording, and film industries.

Program   (1) A function setting for a pot or fader on an audio console that sends the signal out of the console. (2) A function for sending a specific visual source out of a switcher to be transmitted or recorded.

Properties   *See* Props.

Prop microphone   A microphone concealed inside or behind a prop on the set.

Proposal   The first step in initiating a television or film project, which provides basic information about who, what, how, where, and why for potential funding sources.

Props   Functional set furnishings that play a part in a television program or film.

Prosthetic makeup   Makeup and devices designed to transform the appearance of a performer's face or body through temporary "plastic surgery."

Proximity effect   Poor quality audio transmission caused by having the microphone too close to the sound source.

Pulldown claw   The square pin that grabs each sprocket hole of film in the gate to advance a single picture frame at the aperture.

Punch-out lettering   Lettering for titles produced by a mechanical punch, such as Kroy lettering.

Punch tape   A paper punch record of videotape edit decisions for a computer or for printing commands in film printing.

Pure text   Titles presented by themselves without visual accompaniment.

Pure tone   A single sound frequency.

Quadruplex (Quad)   A type of videotape recording in which the tape is contacted by vertically rotating heads in a transverse scanning direction; normally uses 2-inch videotape.

Quartz light   A tungsten light source consisting of a tungsten filament, a quartz housing, and halogen gas.

Rating   The percentage of *all* television households, that is, of all households with a television set regardless of whether that set is on or off at a particular time, that are tuned to a specific program.

Reaction shot   A close-up of a character's reactions to events.

Realism   (1) The aesthetic principle that film and television artists should preserve the perceptual continuity of space and time by following specific conventions or (2) a preservation of the underlying forces of social reality in a dramatic production.

Realist lighting   Lighting that conforms to the audience's conventional expectations of how a scene should appear in "real" life, such as consistently maintaining the directional placement of the main source of light in a scene.

Realistic sets   Sets designed to represent a specific or general type of place with which an audience is presumed to have some familiarity, usually filled with "naturalistic" details.

Rear projection   The projection of a slide or film on a screen behind the performers on the set.

Receiver   A television set capable of decoding a broadcast television signal.

Reception pattern   *See* Pickup pattern.

Recording head   A magnetic device that transforms electrical signals into changes in a magnetic field so that sounds and pictures can be recorded on tape.

Record mode   A machine operational setting for recording pictures and/or sounds.

Recycling   An animation technique for repeatedly using the same movements of hands and feet, etc.

Reduction   A transfer of a film to a smaller format on an optical printer.

Reel-to-reel recorder   A device that can record and/or play back sounds on a reel of tape.

Reference white   A white card or large white object in the frame that can be used for white balance or the proper color adjustment of a video camera.

Reflectance-contrast ratio   The ratio of the light intensity of the brightest reflecting object to the dullest or darkest reflecting object in the shot or scene.

Reflected light   Light that has been bounced or reflected from objects, as opposed to direct or incident light.

Reflected reading A light meter reading of the intensity of the light reflected by the subject and/or background.

Reflector A flat surface that light can be bounced off to create indirect light on a set or location.

Reflex A type of camera that allows the operator to look directly through the objective lens.

Refraction index The ratio of the speed of light in air to the speed of light in another medium.

Registration The steadiness of the film image in the gate or aperture.

Registration pin A device on some film cameras that holds the film steady while it is being exposed to light at the aperture.

Release prints Final copies of film with sound track that are distributed and exhibited.

Remote production Video production work performed outside the studio, usually involving a direct (microwave) link to the studio or TV station.

Remote survey A complete report of the facilities available and the equipment needed for a remote production at a specific site.

Remote van A large video production semi-trailer containing a virtual studio on wheels for high-level coverage of news, sports, and entertainment events.

Research The process of investigating and uncovering sources of information about a prospective video or film topic or audience.

Residuals Payment made to performers and talent for repeat uses of commercial products in which they appear.

Resolution (1) Overcoming the central conflict in a drama and fulfilling the goals and motivations that have stimulated the dramatic action. (2) Image clarity defined in terms of the number of distinct lines that can be visually reproduced in the frame.

Response curve A graph of the sensitivity of a microphone to different sound frequencies.

Reverberation The delay between direct and indirect sounds, the latter of which are reflected off surfaces in an enclosed area.

Reverberation unit A signal processing device that can create sound reverberation or echo.

Reversal process A means of producing projectable film images in a single step by using a type of film stock and development process that produces positive images from a single exposure and development.

Reverse-angle shot A shot in which the camera faces in exactly the opposite direction from the previous shot.

Rewinds Rotating spindles on a film editing bench used to advance or rewind the film.

RF microphone A wireless microphone.

RGB (Red, Green, Blue) Chroma key that is designed for use with video camera images only.

Rhythm The beat or tempo of music, which affects the perception of pace or speed.

Ribbon microphone A microphone containing a corrugated strip of foil, called a ribbon, suspended in a magnetic field, which responds to the velocity or speed of a sound wave.

Right-to-work laws State statutes prohibiting unions from enforcing closed shops or requiring union membership of all employees.

Risers Hollow rectangular boxes which can be placed on the floor of a studio to raise a portion of a set.

Rostrum A movable table on which artwork is placed on an animation stand for precise framing and movement from one still frame to the next.

Rotoscoping An animation technique in which the action is first filmed in live action and then the individual frames of live action are projected and outlines drawn as individual cels for subsequent single-frame recording.

Rough cutting Initial selection and ordering of shots and scenes during film editing.

Rough sketch A preliminary drawing of sets, props, or costumes, which usually provides a frontal view.

Royalty fees Money paid to composers, authors, and performers, etc., for the use of copyrighted materials.

Rub-on lettering Individual letters that can be transferred to virtually any flat surface to make titles by rubbing the plastic sheet to which they are initially adhered.

Rundown sheet A very basic outline of a television program, which simply indicates the time at which specific segments will occur.

Running time Actual program length or duration of a videotape, live television program, or film.

SAG Screen Actors Guild

Saticon A type of color television video pickup tube, a registered trademark of Hitachi.

Satellites Communications relay stations that orbit the earth and transmit television signals across wide distances.

Saturation The purity of a color hue, that is, the amount of grayness the color contains.

Scale The apparent size of objects within the frame.

Scan line A horizontal line of phosphors in a television receiver or optoelectronic semiconductors in a pickup tube.

Scanning area The full field of view picked up by the video camera pickup tube.

Scenic artists Craftsmen who compose detailed sketches, drawings, and set layouts.

Scenic design Overall artistic control and coordination of sets, props, costumes, and makeup.

Scenic designer In video production, the person who supervises the overall production design, including props and costumes.

Scoop A lighting instrument with an open bowl reflector that produces soft floodlight.

Score Music composed for a specific film or videotape.

Scouting report A complete report of the facilities available and the equipment needed for a location production at a specific site.

Screen A nondiffusion scrim.

Screen directionality The left-to-right movement and placement of objects in successive two-dimensional images or shots.

Scrim A piece of wire mesh that can be secured to a lighting instrument to decrease the light intensity and/or diffuse the light.

Script A written outline of a videotape, live television program, or film, which functions as a production guide.

Script breakdown Reorganizing the script in terms of specific settings so that production can be scheduled and an accurate estimate of the budget made in terms of equipment and personnel needs at each setting and each scheduled day of shooting.

Script continuity The dictates of the script in terms of temporal and spatial details that must be maintained during production.

Script outline A semi-scripted format in which only a portion of a videotape or live television program is fully scripted, such as the opening and closing segments if other elements are to be ad-libbed.

Script supervisor The person who maintains continuity in performer actions and prop placements from shot-to-shot and ensures that every scene in the script has been recorded.

Scriptwriting The process of creating a written outline for a videotape, live television program, or film.

Search A function on a videotape recorder that allows a specific point on the videotape to be found by moving the tape very slowly.

Search-and-cue function A machine operational setting that allows a playback machine to search for specific cues on a prerecorded tape.

SECAM A French television standard system.

Segue (seg′wā) The immediate replacement of one sound source with another.

Selective focus Utilizing depth of field to direct the viewer's attention to certain areas of the scene by varying those elements in and out of focus.

Self-blimped A film camera that is completely sound insulated for synchronous sound recording.

Sel sync An internal means of synchronization within an audiotape, which can be used to record consecutive sound tracks in synchronization with each other.

Semi-scripted A partial as opposed to a complete description or outline of a videotape, live television program, or film.

Separation light A general lighting term that includes back lights and kickers, which both help to separate foreground subjects and backgrounds.

Servo capstan A capstan with an accurate motor that varies the speed of the playback to maintain proper synchronization between a video recorder and playback machine.

Set designer In large-scale productions, the person who does the actual drawing of set floor plans and elevations and layouts and supervises the construction of sets.

Set furnishings Furniture and props that fill out a set.

Settings Specific exterior and interior places and locations specified in a script.

Shading Adjusting the brightness level, light sensitivity, and color of a video camera.

Shadow mask A series of windows or aperture deflectors inside a television picture tube which prevent electrons from each gun from striking the wrong color light-emitting phosphors.

Share The percentage of television households, called HUT (Households Using Television), with the set *on* at a specific time that are actually watching a specific program.

Sharpness A rating of the edge clarity and focus of images reproduced in video or film production.

Shock-mounted microphone A microphone designed to minimize all vibrations and noise except those inherent in sound waves.

Shooting ratio The ratio of material recorded during production to that which is actually used in the final edited version.

Shooting script The final version of a script with shot notations, which serves as an actual production guide.

Shotgun microphone A long, narrow highly directional microphone. *See also* Hypercardioid, Ultracardioid, and Unidirectional.

Shot lists Individual lists of specific camera shots for each camera operator.

Shoulder harness A body brace used as a camera mount.

Shutter An opaque device in a film camera that rapidly opens and closes to expose the film to light.

Shutters Metal slides inside an ellipsoidal lighting instrument which function like barn doors.

Signal level The signal strength of the electrical current from recording and playback equipment.

Signal processing Manipulation of the electrical sound signal.

Signal-to-noise ratio The ratio of desired to undesired sound, the latter of which usually comes from equipment or tape noise.

Single-camera production The use of a single video or film camera to record a videtape or film in segments.

Single perf Film with sprocket holes on only one side or edge.

Single-system recording Recording a synchronous sound track within the camera on the same roll of film as the pictures.

Skylight Indirect sunlight which has a higher color temperature than direct sunlight.

Slant track *See* Helical scan.

Slate *See* Clapstick.

Slating Placing a common reference point for separate but synchronous film images and sounds, as well as an identification of the recorded material, at the beginning of a shot.

Slides Still photographic transparencies which can be projected.

Sliding track An overhead light grid to which lighting instruments are attached so that they slide into position along the track.

Slo-mo disc recorder A video recorder that records live-action images on a rotating disc so that they can be played back in slow motion, such as for game analysis in a sports broadcast.

Slow motion Recording images at a faster speed than the normal playback speed.

Smearing *See* Comet-tailing.

SMPTE time code A reference code for individual videotape frames standardized by the Society of Motion Picture and Television Engineers.

Soft cut A very rapid dissolve.

Soft light Indirect, diffused light that minimizes shadows.

Softlights Floodlights that use a bank of lamps and/or diffusers to create very soft light.

Soft wipe A slight superimposition at the point two images intersect during a wipe from one to the other.

Solarization A technique that drains the normal color from a visual image and replaces it with artificially controlled colors.

Sound amplitude The intensity and height of a sound pressure wave.

Sound effects Sounds that are matched to their supposed visual sources during postproduction editing.

Sound fidelity The accuracy or illusion of reality inherent in a sound recording.

Sound frequency The rapidity with which air molecules move back and forth in direct relation to the vibrations of the sound source.

Sound intensity The amplitude of a sound wave, which is perceived as a specific loudness level.

Sound-on-film (SOF) *See* Single-system recording.

Sound perspective An enhanced perception of distance achieved through the use of different volume levels for near and far sounds.

Sound pressure wave The compression and expansion of air molecules in response to the vibrations of a sound source.

Sound test A test setting of the sound level prior to actual recording.

SOUND UP AND UNDER Instruction to cut the

sound in at its proper level and then fade it down to a lower level, where it is still audible but less prominent.

Sound velocity   The speed of a sound pressure wave.

Source music   Music that comes from a source within the actual scene portrayed on screen.

Spacers   Small wheels used to fill the gaps between take-up reels on a film editing bench so that their spacing matches the spacing of the individual hubs or wheels in a gang synchronizer.

Spatial distortion   An aural imbalance during stereophonic playback or recording which results from a faulty positioning of the sound source.

Special effects generator (SEG)   Electronic device usually installed in the video switcher, which is used to produce wipes, split screens, and inserts.

Speed of action   The speed of the movement of objects within the frame.

Spider   An adjustable device into which the spurs of a tripod are placed on a flat, hard surface.

Splicing   Physically cutting and cementing magnetic tape or film while editing.

Split   An agreed-upon division of box office receipts between exhibitors and film distributors.

Split-beam   A reflex viewing system in which mirrors between the lens and the viewfinder eyepiece continuously deflect about 18 percent to 20 percent of the light.

Split-page script   A script that has the visual specifications on the left side of the page and the corresponding audio specifications on the right side.

Split screen or shared screen   A special video effect in which one image occupies a portion of the frame and another image occupies the remaining portion is known as shared screen. When the frame is split in half between two images, it is called split screen.

Spot effects   Specific sound effects created expressly for a videotape, live television program, or film in a sound studio.

Spotlights   Lighting instruments with lenses that sharply focus the light they emit, producing intense, harsh lighting.

Spot reading   A light-meter reading of the intensity of the light reflected by the subject in a very narrow area as determined by the angle of acceptance of the spot meter.

Sprocket holes   The perforations in a piece of film which allow it to be advanced or drive through a camera or projector.

Sprocket teeth   Metal teeth which drive a piece of film through a camera, projector, or editing device by engaging the sprocket holes.

Spun glass   A flexible light diffuser made out of fiberglass.

Spurs   Points on the end of a tripod, which can be stuck into soft ground.

Spreader   *See* Spider.

Squashing and stretching   Animation techniques that exaggerate and caricature motions by accentuating the initial and ending movements of an action, such as running or jumping, to make them seem more active.

Stage manager   The person who supervise the use of studio space, such as the setup and breaking down of sets and props on the studio floor. *See* Floor manager.

Stand microphone   A microphone designed to be secured to a mike stand, which can be raised or lowered to conform to the height of the speaker.

Steadicam®   A servostabilizer camera mount attached to the operator's body to minimize camera vibrations when the operator moves with the camera.

Stereophonic sound   Separation of sounds coming from the right and the left during recording and playback which preserves the directionality of sound sources.

Stingers   Short phrases of music, usually characterized by a rapidly descending scale or series of notes, used as punctuation devices.

Storyboard   A series of sequential drawings or still photographs representing the different shots for a commercial or a longer film or television program.

Story time   The supposed historical time of events presented in a television program or film.

Strip lights   A series of lights connected in a straight line.

Studio   A controlled, indoor production environment designed expressly for video or film recording.

Studio production   The recording of video or film images inside a controlled production environment.

Stylized lighting   Lighting that is intended to

achieve a special kind of emotional effect or abstract design through nonnaturalistic patterns of light.

Stylized sets   Abstract, imaginative settings that reflect an artistic style or give external form to an interior state of mind, such as a specific character's subjective state of mind.

Subjective point of view   A story told from the perspective of a specific character or participant in the action.

Subjective shot   A presentation of images supposedly dreamed, imagined, recollected, or perceived in an abnormal state of mind by a character or participant in a videotape or film.

Subtitles   Titles placed in the bottom third of the video or film frame that clarify the image or present the spoken dialogue in written form.

Subtractive color   The process of using color-absorbing filters to subtract specific wavelengths of light from a white light source and produce the various colors of the visible spectrum.

Suggested by   *See* Freely adapted.

Sunlight   Natural light from burning gases on the sun's surface which emit light that strikes the earth.

Supercardioid   A highly directional microphone pickup pattern.

Superimposition   Two images occupying the entire frame at the same time. Normally one image is dominant and another recessive during a superimposition so as not to cause visual confusion. The more detailed the images, the less clear and visually pleasing the superimposition is likely to be.

Swish pan   A rapid turning of the camera on the tripod axis, causing blurring of the image, that can be used as a transition device between scenes.

Switcher   A video editing device that controls which picture and sound sources are transmitted or recorded. It can be used during multiple-camera production or during postproduction.

Symmetry   The degree to which composition within a camera frame is balanced.

Sync generator   An electronic device which produces various synchronizing signals necessary for the operation of the video recording system.

Sync head   An additional recording head on a synchronous sound recorder, used for recording the sync signal.

Synchronous sound recorder   A device capable of recording sounds in synchronization with the images recorded by a film camera.

Synchronous sounds   Sounds that match their on-screen sources.

Sync signal   A regular sine wave of electrical current, which can be used as a speed reference for sound and picture synchronization.

Syndicated programming   Commerical television programs and films that are distributed directly to local television stations, bypassing the major television networks.

Takes   Individual shots of a single action. There may be several takes of the same shot in single-camera production, from which one will be selected for use in the final edited version.

Takeup   The part of a recording device that collects the tape or film.

Talent   Anyone who appears on camera or before the microphone.

Talk-back system   An intercom system in a television studio, used for communication between the creative staff in the control room and the crew on the studio floor.

Tally light   A light on the top of a video camera which informs the talent and crew which of several cameras has been selected for recording or transmission at a particular time.

Tape splicer   A device with a cutting blade and guide for combining different pieces of film with transparent tape.

Technical director (TD)   In video production, the person who operates the switcher, a multiple-camera editing device, at the commands of the director during production.

Telecine   A device that converts film into television signals by projecting the film images into a video camera.

Telephoto   Long focal-length lenses.

Television   The electronic transmission and reception of visual images of moving and stationary objects, usually with accompanying sound.

Television quotient (TV-Q)   A popularity index of television performers, which is sometimes used to ensure success and aid casting decisions.

Temporal continuity   A continuous flow of events without any apparent gaps in time.

Texture   The roughness or smoothness of a surface.

Theatrical films Films produced for or shown in commercial theaters.

Theme (1) A central concept, idea, or symbolic meaning in a story. (2) A repeated melody in a symphony or other long musical composition.

Three- or four-point lighting A basic lighting technique that helps create an illusion of three-dimensionality by separating the subject from the background, using key, fill, and separation light.

Three shot A camera setup in which three subjects appear in the same frame.

Three-to-one rule To avoid phasing problems, two or more microphones used simultaneously should be placed at least three times as far apart as their subject-to-mike distances.

Through the lens (TTL) A type of light meter that measures the amount of light actually coming through the lens of a camera.

Tilt A vertical pivoting of a camera.

Tilt shot A camera shot accomplished by moving the camera up and down on a swivel or tilting device.

Timbre *See* Tonality.

Time-base corrector (TBC) A device that stabilizes pictures from videotape recorders.

Time code A series of digits that provides an exact reference for each frame on a videotape.

Titles Lettering recorded within the visual frame that identifies the visual image or adds additional text to the videotape, live television program, or film.

Title sequence *See* Credit sequence.

Tonality The particular quality or unique characteristics of a musical instrument or voice.

Topic research The process of gathering accurate information about a prospective videotape's program or film's subject matter.

Track A separate tape path.

Trucking shot A shot in which the camera moves from side to side on a wheeled dolly.

Tragedy A type of drama that has a serious tone and often focuses on the misfortunes and problems of life.

Transducer A device for converting one form of energy into another form of energy, such as a microphone.

Transfer A copy of a recording in which the format is changed.

Transferring Copying sounds or video images from one tape to a tape of a different format.

Transition devices Various means of changing from one shot to another to suggest changes of time and/or place.

Transverse track *See* Quadruplex.

Traveling matte A film matte that moves across the image to create special effects.

Treatment A narrative summary of a video or film project written in short story form with minimal dialogue.

Triangle *See* Spider.

Trims Portions of shots used in a final edited version of a film that are rejected or discarded.

Tripod A three-legged camera mounting device.

T-stop Unit of light transmission for a lens based on actual tests of light transmission.

Tungsten filament A wire in a lamp, made out of tungsten metal, which emits light when electricity is passed through it.

Tyler mount A helicopter or airplane camera mount that reduces vibrations.

Two-shot A camera shot including two subjects.

Ultracardioid The most directional (narrowest) microphone pickup pattern available, sometimes called a shotgun microphone.

Ultraviolet light Invisible light that has a shorter wavelength than visible light but can nonetheless affect film and is present in outdoor shadow areas.

U-Matic A standard 3/4-inch videotape format.

Unbalanced microphone line A mike cable consisting of a single conductor that is less well insulated than a balanced line and thus more susceptible to cable noise.

Unidirectional Responsive to sound from only one direction.

Union and guild contracts Agreements regarding salaries, working conditions, etc., made between various craft, trade, and talent unions or guilds and television and film producers.

Unscaled layout A bird's-eye view of the studio and set giving a rough approximation of the materials that must be constructed.

Upright A vertically arranged film editing machine.

Variable speed motor An electric drive motor whose speed can be varied and controlled.

Vertical blanking The period of time that the television electron beam is shut off, while the beam jumps from the bottom of one field or frame to the top of another.

Vertical sync A portion of a television signal that controls the rate of vertical scanning and blanking.

VHS One of two standard 1/2-inch helical-scan videotape recording formats.

Video The visual portion of a television signal.

Videocassette A self-contained set of reels with videotape.

Videocassette recorder (VCR) A machine that can record television signals on cassettes of videotape.

Video engineer In video production, the person who adjusts or shades the cameras for optimal recording and monitors the videotape recording equipment.

Video meters Meters on a videotape recorder that indicate the strength of the video portion of the television signal.

Video noise Static or unwanted light in a video image.

Video synthesizer A device that allows an artist to manipulate the analog signal of a video image so that colors and shapes can be creatively altered for special effect.

Videotape Relatively wide magnetic tape used to record both the video and the audio portions of television signals.

Videotape editing unit An electronic editing system consisting of a playback VTR or VCR, a recorder, and an editing control unit.

Videotape recorder (VTR) A machine that can record television signals on reels of videotape.

Video-to-film transfer Copying a videotape on film; also called kinescoping.

Vidicon A small black-and-white video camera pickup tube.

Viewfinder An eyepiece or screen through which a camera operator sees the images being recorded.

Visualization The creative process of transforming a script into a sequence of visual images and sounds.

Visual style The particular approach taken by a director to the visual presentation of events in a videotape, live television program, or film, including the selection of specific camera placements, movements, and types of shots.

Voice-over (VO) Speech sounds that are not synchronized to visual images. A performer may be narrating the action or tying together elements of a story, documentary, or news segment.

Voice-over narration Narration by a person who is not visible on the screen.

Volume unit (VU) meter A device that indicates sound intensity by measuring the flow of electrical energy caused by the effect of sound waves on a microphone.

Waveform monitor An electronic device which visualizes the television signal so that a video engineer can properly set the brightness levels, etc., or camera shading.

Wavelength The distance between the crests or valleys of each successive wave of energy in light or sound.

White balance The proper balance of the red, green, and blue components of a television signal which together create white lights.

Wide angle A lens with a relatively short focal length and wide field of view.

Wild sounds Sounds that are not recorded at the same time as the visuals.

Wind noise Unwanted sound caused by air blowing over the pickup elements of a microphone.

Wind screen A plastic foam covering placed over a microphone to inhibit wind noise.

Wipe A transition device in which one image is literally wiped off the screen by another. *See also* Natural wipe.

Within-house A production unit that creates programming for the organization or institution of which it is a part.

Work print A copy of the originally recorded film or videotape used for initial postproduction editing.

XLR connector The standard type of three-pronged plug used to connect balanced microphone cables.

Yellow-ink edge numbers Edge numbers printed

by a laboratory on the film as opposed to edge numbers placed there by the film manufacturer.

Y signal *See* Luminance.

Zero start The beginning point of SMPTE time code on a videotape recording.

Zoom-in A gradual increase of the focal length of a zoom lens.

Zoom lens A variable focal-length lens that maintains constant focus when the focal length is changed.

Zoom shot A shot that is made by changing the focal length of a variable focal-length lens in mid-shot.

The Moving Image

Production Principles and Practices

Acknowledgments

Position of photographs is shown in abbreviated form as follows: top (t), bottom (b), center (c), left (l), right (r). Unless specified below, all photos are courtesy of the author.

Cover photo: Geoffrey Gove/The Image Bank

Chapter 1: 8, Neg. No. 16227 (Photo by Abbe Breuil and Dr. Hugo Obermaier) Courtesy Department Library Services, American Museum of Natural History; 10, Museum of Modern Art/Film Stills Archive. By permission of MGM/UA Entertainment Co.; 11(l), Alec Duncan/Taurus Photos; 14, Museum of Modern Art/Film Stills Archive; 18, Oscar & Associates, Inc.

Part 1: 30, John Weinstein for Scott, Foresman, Courtesy of WLS-TV

Chapter 3: 57, Danuta Otfinowski; 58, Courtesy of Professor William H. Hardy; 60, Courtesy of Garner Simmons. From page 16 of his copyrighted screenplay TIE-BREAKER; 63, © Lucasfilm Ltd. (LFL) 1980. All rights reserved. Courtesy of Lucasfilm Ltd.; 69, Museum of Modern Art/Film Stills Archive. © RKO Radio Pictures

Chapter 4: 78, Courtesy Zipporah Films, Inc., Cambridge, MA; 79, Photo by Ethan Russell, Courtesy of Maysles Films, Inc.; 85, Courtesy WTVD in Durham, North Carolina. A Capital Cities/ABC owned and operated station; 87, © Allan S. Adler/Photoreporters

Part 2: 98, John Weinstein for Scott, Foresman, Courtesy of WLS-TV

Chapter 5: 104, 105, Courtesy of Paul Nickell; 106(t), From Jean-Luc Godard's 1960 film, BREATHLESS; 113, Joseph Burstyn Film Enterprises, Inc.; 129, © Ebet Roberts

Chapter 6: 135, Alan Carey/The Image Works; 138, Courtesy of Neil Beard; 139, Telex Communications, Inc.; 141(tr), Courtesy Ampex Corporation; 143, Courtesy of JVC COMPANY OF AMERICA; 148, Courtesy of Neil Beard

Chapter 7: 158(t), Courtesy Cinema Products Corporation; 164, Martin Kobler; 168, Courtesy Zenith Radio Corporation; 169(l), Courtesy Sony Corporation of America; 169(tr), Courtesy of JVC COMPANY OF AMERICA; 169(br), Courtesy RCA Corporation; 170(tr), (tl), Courtesy of Sharp Electronics Corporation; 170(b), Courtesy RCA Corporation; 172(tl), Courtesy Cinema Products Corporation; 172(b), Courtesy Canon U.S.A., Inc.; 173, 174, Courtesy Arriflex Corporation

Chapter 8: 187, Reprinted with permission of A.S.C. Press "Electronic Production Techniques"; 188(r), Courtesy of Ampex Corporation; 189(br), Reprinted from POPULAR SCIENCE with permission © 1985 Times Mirror Magazines, Inc.; 190(tl), Courtesy of JVC COMPANY OF AMERICA; Color plate I: Courtesy Anheuser-Busch, Inc.; Color plate II(b): Courtesy Munsell Color, 2441 North Culvert Street, Baltimore, MD 21218; Color plate III(t): Fritz Goro, LIFE Magazine © 1944 Time Inc.; 196, Reprinted courtesy of Eastman Kodak Company

Chapter 9: 202, Rick Kopstein/Monkmeyer Press Photo Service; 206, Courtesy New Yorker Films; 209, Courtesy of Chad McArver; 213(t), Courtesy of Strand Century Inc.; 213(tl), (b), Courtesy Colortran, Inc.; 214(tr), Lowel-Light Manufacturing, Inc.; 214(c), Mole-Richardson Co., Hollywood, U.S.A.; 214(b), Lowel-Light Manufacturing, Inc.; 215(tl), Courtesy Cine 60 Inc.; 215(tr), Mole-Richardson Co., Hollywood, U.S.A.; 215(c), Courtesy Colortran, Inc.; 216(t), 217(c), Lowel-Light Manufacturing, Inc.

Chapter 10: 234(bl), Telex Communications, Inc.; 244(t), Courtesy Otari Corporation, Belmont, CA; 252, Nagra Magnetic Recorders, Inc.; 253, Courtesy New York University Photo Bureau

Chapter 11: 261, Cheryl Woike-Kucharzak; 263, Courtesy of Janus Films; 264, Museum of Modern Art/Film Stills Archive; 265, Artkino Pictures, Inc.; 266, Museum of Modern Art/Film Stills Archive; 271, Scott, Foresman photo; 273, From PHOTOGRAPHIC Magazine, August 1974. Reprinted by permission of Petersen Publishing Co.; 275, © Lucasfilm Ltd. (LFL) 1983. All rights reserved. Courtesy of Lucasfilm Ltd.

Chapter 12: 293, Courtesy of Kimberly Otto; 295, Reprinted courtesy of Eastman Kodak Company; 297, Courtesy of David Hayner; 298, Reprinted courtesy of Eastman Kodak Company; 300(tl), (tr), Courtesy Oxberry, Division of Richmark Camera Service; 302(t), Courtesy Sony Corporation of America

Chapter 13: 312, Courtesy RCA Corporation; 316, Courtesy Susan L. Massengale, Producer/Director The University of North Carolina Center for Public Television; 318, Courtesy of Ampex Corporation; 319(tl), Courtesy Sony Corporation of America; 319(tr), Courtesy RCA Corporation; 319(b), Courtesy Cine 60 Inc.; 324(b), Courtesy Ikegami Electronics (U.S.A.) Inc.; 326, Courtesy Jefferson-Pilot Teleproductions; 327(b), Courtesy RCA Corporation

Part 3: 330, John Weinstein for Scott, Foresman, Courtesy of WLS-TV

Chapter 14: 346(b), 347, Courtesy of Ampex Corporation; 354(b), Courtesy KLM Associates, Inc. and AVIM, the Hague, the Netherlands; 356, Courtesy RCA Corporation; 357, Association of Cinema Laboratories

Chapter 15: 371, Courtesy RCA Corporation; 381, Courtesy Otari Corporation, Belmont, CA

Chapter 16: 387, Scott, Foresman photo; 388(t), NASA; 388(b), UPI; 389, Steve Harbison/TIME Magazine; 390, Courtesy Sony Corporation of America; 397, Courtesy of The University of North Carolina Center for Public Television; 403, © Lucasfilm Ltd. (LFL) 1984. All rights reserved. Courtesy of Lucasfilm Ltd.; 406, Courtesy Actronics Inc.

Index

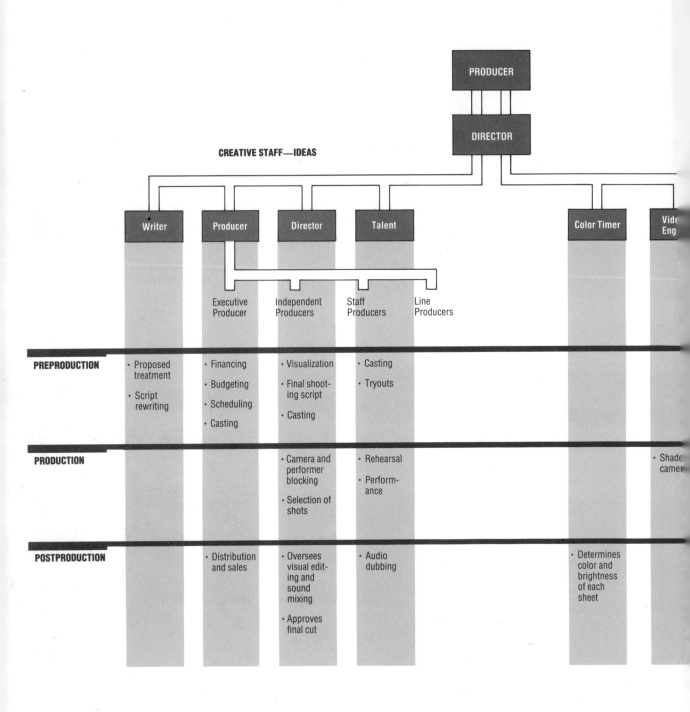

PRODUCER

DIRECTOR

CREATIVE STAFF—IDEAS

Writer | Producer | Director | Talent | Color Timer | Video Eng

Executive Producer | Independent Producers | Staff Producers | Line Producers

	Writer	Producer	Director	Talent	Color Timer	Video Eng
PREPRODUCTION	· Proposed treatment · Script rewriting	· Financing · Budgeting · Scheduling · Casting	· Visualization · Final shooting script · Casting	· Casting · Tryouts		
PRODUCTION			· Camera and performer blocking · Selection of shots	· Rehearsal · Performance		· Shade camera
POSTPRODUCTION		· Distribution and sales	· Oversees visual editing and sound mixing · Approves final cut	· Audio dubbing	· Determines color and brightness of each sheet	